Contributions to Finance and Accounting

The book series 'Contributions to Finance and Accounting' features the latest research from research areas like financial management, investment, capital markets, financial institutions, FinTech and financial innovation, accounting methods and standards, reporting, and corporate governance, among others. Books published in this series are primarily monographs and edited volumes that present new research results, both theoretical and empirical, on a clearly defined topic. All books are published in print and digital formats and disseminated globally. This book series is indexed in Scopus.

Yoshihiro Tokuga • Masaki Yoneyama
Editors

Controversies Over Accounting for Goodwill

Springer

Editors
Yoshihiro Tokuga
Kyoto University of Advanced Science
Kyoto, Japan

Masaki Yoneyama
The University of Tokyo
Tokyo, Japan

ISSN 2730-6038 ISSN 2730-6046 (electronic)
Contributions to Finance and Accounting
ISBN 978-981-92-0155-6 ISBN 978-981-92-0156-3 (eBook)
https://doi.org/10.1007/978-981-92-0156-3

This work was supported by the Kyoto University, University of Tokyo, and the Kyoto University of Advanced Science.

This Springer imprint is published by the registered company Springer Nature Singapore Pte Ltd.
The registered company address is: 152 Beach Road, #21-01/04 Gateway East, Singapore 189721, Singapore

Preface

Why do prolonged, technically sophisticated deliberations among accounting specialists fail to produce definitive resolutions? This question arose repeatedly during nearly a decade of discussions within the International Accounting Standards Board (IASB) and the Accounting Standards Advisory Forum (ASAF) on goodwill were repeatedly identified as problematic and subjected to extensive debate, and although numerous reform proposals were advanced, the deliberations ultimately led—at least superficially— to a reaffirmation of the existing impairment-only framework, accompanied by an increased emphasis on disclosure.

Our research group on goodwill accounting, composed of the same five members throughout, engaged in a similar process of sustained inquiry for nearly 8 years, beginning in 2018. During this period, we held 88 meetings (33 conducted online), for a cumulative total of approximately 351 hours of discussions. The fact that a considerable number of these meetings had to be conducted online reflected the constraints imposed by the COVID-19 pandemic, which limited in-person interaction for nearly 2 years. Although the length of these discussions may partly have reflected limitations in our analytical reach, it was due in large part to the inherently complex nature of goodwill accounting, in which theoretical, practical, and regulatory considerations are deeply intertwined and resist straightforward resolution. In addition to these discussions, our work involved an unprecedented large-scale investigation in Japan into the accounting values and beliefs held by key stakeholders—financial statement preparers, users, and auditors—as well as university faculty responsible for accounting education.

Despite the intensity and duration of our discussions, we did not arrive at a definitive alternative capable of replacing the approach maintained by the IASB and ASAF. This observation reinforces the view that the goodwill issue embodies structural characteristics that make resolution difficult within contemporary accounting standard-setting. Accordingly, this book aims not to advocate a superior solution or merely to document empirical findings, but to examine why sustained deliberation among specialists repeatedly leads to non-convergence.

Although three of the authors have been directly involved in Japan's accounting standard-setting, this book does not seek to advocate any particular accounting treatment for goodwill. Rather, we aim to examine the issue from as neutral and objective a perspective as possible.

The dynamics observed in the IASB and ASAF discussions—in which new proposals were repeatedly introduced, yet none ultimately displaced the prevailing framework—highlight the role of diverse perspectives among jurisdictions participating in global standard-setting. Although differences in economic interests among preparers, users, and auditors are widely acknowledged, this book emphasizes that divergences in accounting values, beliefs, institutional environments, and perceptions of economic facts also play a crucial role in sustaining disagreement. We consider this perspective to represent one of the book's key contributions to the existing literature.

Japan's institutional environment, in which the International Financial Reporting Standards (IFRS) and domestic standards coexist as optional alternatives, offers a distinctive setting for examining the issues surrounding the amortization versus non-amortization of goodwill. Building on this context, this book investigates the accounting values and beliefs of preparers, users, and auditors in Japan (Chaps. 5 and 6) and explores whether these differences may be linked to accounting education at universities and the structure of the national CPA examination (Chap. 8).

We anticipate that future work will continue to extend and refine the insights developed herein, contributing to a deeper understanding of the structural challenges inherent in goodwill accounting and accounting standard-setting more broadly. Extending similar analyses to other jurisdictions would also provide an opportunity to examine the extent to which the hypotheses developed in this study hold beyond the Japanese institutional context.

Kyoto, Japan Yoshihiro Tokuga

Acknowledgments

This book has benefited from the support, encouragement, and cooperation of many individuals and organizations. The questionnaire surveys and interviews conducted with preparers, users (particularly analysts), auditors, and accounting academics would not have been possible without their generous assistance. The positions and affiliations mentioned below are those held at the time of their contribution.

We first wish to acknowledge those who provided essential guidance and cooperation in the design and implementation of the surveys and interviews. The late Atsushi Kogasaka, former chairman of the Accounting Standards Board of Japan (ASBJ), offered invaluable advice from the questionnaire design stage through the interpretation of the results, agreed to be interviewed for this study, and kindly introduced us to members of the Autorité des Normes Comptables (ANC), including Patrick de Cambourg, then its president, while also helping to arrange our initial meetings in France. We respectfully dedicate this book to his memory. We are also grateful to Toshitake Inoue, then deputy director-general of the Financial Services Agency, who provided helpful advice on the questionnaire from the perspective of accounting regulation in Japan and generously agreed to be interviewed for this study.

We sincerely appreciate the assistance of Akira Suzuki of Keidanren, whose efforts to encourage Keidanren member companies to cooperate with our survey were instrumental in making the survey possible. We also thank the numerous listed companies that cooperated in the survey and interviews, including The Dai-ichi Life Insurance Company, Limited, Nippon Steel Corporation, Sumitomo Corporation, Sumitomo Mitsui Banking Corporation, Takeda Pharmaceutical Company Limited, and NTT DOCOMO, INC.

Our appreciation extends to the Japanese Institute of Certified Public Accountants and to Masahiko Tezuka, then its chairperson, for endorsing this initiative and facilitating participation by audit firms. We are grateful to major and mid-tier audit firms in Japan for their cooperation, including Ernst & Young ShinNihon LLC, Deloitte Touche Tohmatsu LLC, KPMG AZSA LLC, PwC Aarata LLC, Grant Thornton Taiyo LLC, Crowe Toyo & Co. Audit Corporation, GYOSEI & CO, BDO Sanyu & Co., PKF Hibiki Audit Corporation, and PwC Kyoto.

We also acknowledge the Japan Analysts Association for its substantial support. Yasuhiro Maehara, then chairperson of the Association, and Makoto Kaimasu, then managing director, provided particularly valuable insights and assistance. We are equally grateful to the many analysts who shared their perspectives through interviews, including Keiko Mizuguchi, Yoshiko Sato, Goro Kumagai, Masayuki Kubota, Toshinori Ito, Joji Iguchi, Kouei Otaki, Jun Goto, Naoki Hirai, and Natsumu Tsujino.

We further thank members of the Japan Accounting Association (JAA) who responded to our survey on accounting education.

We are deeply indebted to Professor Alan Burlaud, Professor Emeritus at the Institut national des techniques économiques et comptables of CNAM, who arranged several interviews in France, accompanied us during those interviews, generously agreed to be interviewed himself, and kindly reviewed the manuscript at the draft stage. We are equally grateful to the members of the Autorité des Normes Comptables—including Patrick de Cambourg, then its President—who, despite their demanding schedules, generously gave their time for lengthy interviews. Their insights provided an important impetus for our focus on international differences in accounting values.

Many colleagues provided opportunities for us to present this research and offered valuable comments. Among them, we gratefully acknowledge Professor Shyam Sunder, Professor Emeritus at Yale University, and Professor Takashi Obinata of the University of Tokyo for their thoughtful guidance and feedback.

We are profoundly indebted to Professor Tsunehiro Tsumori, Professor Emeritus at Kyushu University, whose lifelong mentorship has quietly shaped our intellectual paths and whose unwavering devotion to scholarship remains a source of enduring inspiration. We also express our deepest gratitude to Professor Shizuki Saito, Professor Emeritus at the University of Tokyo, whose thoughtful guidance has influenced both our academic development and our understanding of Japan's accounting institutions.

On a personal note, we express our heartfelt gratitude to the families of all five authors for their enduring support throughout this research.

Funding

This research was supported by Grants-in-Aid for Scientific Research from the Japan Society for the Promotion of Science (JSPS), including Grant-in-Aid for Scientific Research (B) (Principal Investigator: Yoshihiro Tokuga, 2017–2020, No. 17H02581), Grant-in-Aid for Scientific Research (B) (Principal Investigator: Yuko Asami, 2016–2023, No. 16KT0092), Grant-in-Aid for Scientific Research (B) (Principal Investigator: Masaki Yoneyama, 2022–2025, Nos. 22H00896 and 23K22167), Grant-in-Aid for Scientific Research (C) (Principal Investigator: Yoshihiro Tokuga, 2025–2027, No. 25K05416), Grant-in-Aid for Scientific Research (C) (Principal Investigator: Toshitake Miyauchi, 2020–2025, No.

20K02055), and Grant-in-Aid for Scientific Research (C) (Principal Investigator: Tomoaki Yamashita, 2020–2022, No. 20K13641).

Additional support was provided by the Center for Advanced Research in Finance (CARF) at the University of Tokyo (Masaki Yoneyama, 2018–2026), the Mizuho Securities Endowed Chair at the Kyoto University Graduate School of Management (Yoshihiro Tokuga, 2020–2026), Kyoto University of Advanced Science research funding (2025), and research support from the Japan Accounting Association (Yuko Asami, 2020–2022).

Yoshihiro Tokuga
Masaki Yoneyama
Kyoto and Tokyo, February 2026

Contents

1 **Research Objectives and Structure of This Book** 1
Yoshihiro Tokuga

2 **Goodwill Accounting Deliberations at the International Accounting Standards Board and Accounting Standards Advisory Forum** 19
Yoshihiro Tokuga and Tomoaki Yamashita

3 **Theoretical Issues** 45
Yuko Asami

4 **Empirical Issues** 133
Toshtiake Miyauchi

5 **Questionnaire Survey of Preparers, Users, and Auditors** 175
Yoshihiro Tokuga, Toshitake Miyauchi, Tomoaki Yamashita, Yuko Asami, and Masaki Yoneyama

6 **Perception of Preparers, Users, and Auditors–Follow-Up Interviews** 325
Masaki Yoneyama, Yoshihiro Tokuga, Yuko Asami, Toshitake Miyauchi, and Tomoaki Yamashita

7 **Empirical Studies on the 'Too Little, Too Late' Issue** 375
Toshitake Miyauchi and Tomoaki Yamashita

8 **Accounting Perspective and Accounting Education** 421
Toshitake Miyauchi, Yuko Asami, Yoshihiro Tokuga, Masaki Yoneyama, and Yamashita Tomoaki

9 **Concluding Remarks and Future Issues**......................... 455
Masaki Yoneyama

Editors and Authors

About the Editors

Yoshihiro Tokuga He received his PhD in Economics from Kyoto University. He was Professor at Kyushu University before joining Kyoto University, where he served as Dean of the Graduate School of Management and as Vice President. He is currently Professor of Accounting and Vice President at Kyoto University of Advanced Science (KUAS). He was also a visiting scholar at the University of Washington from 1990 to 1992 and a guest scholar at the Institute for Monetary and Economic Studies, Bank of Japan (IMES) from 2009 to 2011.

His research focuses on international and financial accounting. He has published widely in these fields and has authored and edited several influential books. He has received multiple distinctions from the Japan Accounting Association (JAA), including the Best Paper Award, the Best Book Award, Honorary Membership, and the Outstanding Contributor Award from the Japanese Association for International Accounting Studies (JAIAS). He has served as President of JAA and the Asian Academic Accounting Association (AAAA), and as Vice President of the International Association for Accounting Education and Research (IAAER).

His public service includes appointments as Chairperson of the Financial Services Agency's Business Accounting Council (BAC) and as a board member of the Certified Public Accountants and Auditing Oversight Board (CPAAOB) and the Accounting Standards Board of Japan (ASBJ).

Masaki Yoneyama He received his PhD in Economics from the University of Tokyo. Prior to joining the University of Tokyo, he served as Professor at the Faculty of Economics, Gakushuin University, and the Graduate School of Accountancy, Waseda University. He has been Professor at the Graduate School of Economics, the University of Tokyo, since 2012.

From 2001 to 2002, he served as a visiting researcher at the Mitsui Life Financial Research Center in Ann Arbor, University of Michigan. His primary research area is financial accounting, with a particular emphasis on accounting standard-setting. He has published extensively in this field and has authored and edited several influential books. He has received academic awards from both the Japan Accounting Association (JAA) and the Japanese Association for International Accounting Studies (JAIAS). He currently serves as President of JAIAS and has held public appointments as a member of the Financial Services Agency's Business Accounting Council (BAC) and of the Accounting Standards Board of Japan (ASBJ). His major book-length works include *Accounting for Impairment* (sole-authored), *An Analysis of the Consistency of Accounting Standards* (sole-authored), and *Release from Investment Risk* (co-authored with Kenichi AKIBA and Yuko ASAMI).

About the Authors

Yuko Asami She received her PhD from the University of Tokyo and is currently a professor at Nagoya University. Previously, she served as Professor at Gakushuin University, where she held the positions of Chair of the Graduate School of Management and Vice President. She has held visiting appointments at the University of Cambridge, the London School of Economics and Political Science, and the Open University.

Her research focuses on international and financial accounting. She has received academic honors, including the 67th Nikkei Prize for Excellent Books in Economic Science, the Best Paper Award from the American Institute of Higher Education, and the Selected Paper Award from the CFA Digest. She currently serves as Councilor of Japan Accounting Association.

Her public service includes appointments as a board member of CPAAOB; Auditor of Ibaraki University; Deputy Chair of the Evaluation Council of Tokyo Regional Taxation Bureau; Deputy Chair of the Evaluation Committee of Organization for SME and Regional Innovation in the Ministry of Finance; and a board member of the Corporate Accounting Standards Advisory Council of Financial Accounting Standards Foundation. She has also served as an examiner for the Certified Public Accountant, Certified Tax Accountant, and Real Estate Appraiser examinations.

Toshitake Miyauchi He received his PhD from Kyoto University. He has been affiliated with Otemon Gakuin University since 2011, initially as Lecturer, and is currently Professor of Accounting and Vice President of the University.

His primary research areas are financial accounting and finance, with a particular focus on the financial effects of M&A. One of his major publications is "Political Participation in Global Accounting Standard-Setting: Content Analysis of Comment Letters for the Establishment of the Accounting Standards Advisory Forum (ASAF)," published in the *Journal of Accounting & Organizational Change.*

He also held public appointments, including as an examiner for a Real Estate Appraisal examination.

Tomoaki Yamashita He received his PhD from Kyoto University. He joined the Department of Business Administration, Faculty of Economics, at Fukui Prefectural University as an assistant professor in 2015 and is currently associate professor at the same institution.

His primary research interests include accounting conservatism and the real effects of financial reporting. His major work has been published in *the Asia-Pacific Journal of Accounting & Economics* and the *Journal of International Accounting Research.*

Chapter 1
Research Objectives and Structure of This Book

Yoshihiro Tokuga

1.1 Introduction

The nature of "goodwill acquired in a business combination" (hereinafter, "goodwill") and its subsequent accounting treatment have been subjects of debate for over 140 years.[1] To date, there has been no established interpretation of goodwill consistent with the currently accepted fundamental accounting concepts, nor has a compromise for accounting for goodwill been reached to resolve practical conflicts.

The Financial Accounting Standards Board (hereafter, FASB) in the U.S. prohibited the systematic amortization of goodwill in 2001, and the International Accounting Standards Board (hereafter, IASB) followed suit in 2004, mandating an impairment-only approach. However, debates over whether to reinstate the systematic amortization of goodwill have persisted, both within individual jurisdictions and internationally. The IASB formally adopted "Goodwill and Impairment" as an agenda item in Oct. 2015. Including the Post-implementation Review of IFRS 3 (hereafter, PiR 3), which began at the July 2013 meeting, the Committee held 42 meetings over more than 9 years—until the IASB's tentative decision in 2022 not to reintroduce systematic amortization of goodwill. While that decision closed one major avenue of reform, the broader project continued, with the focus shifting toward targeted improvements to impairment testing and enhanced disclosures, later reflected in subsequent standard-setting steps. However, this conclusion was

[1] For example, see Bithell (1882). Courtis (1983) cites Bithell (1882) as the first paper to address accounting for goodwill.

Y. Tokuga (✉)
Faculty of Economics and Business Administration, Department of Business Administration, Kyoto University of Advanced Science, Kyoto, Japan
e-mail: tokuga.yoshihiro.6m@kyoto-u.ac.jp

Y. Tokuga, M. Yoneyama (eds.), *Controversies Over Accounting for Goodwill*, Contributions to Finance and Accounting,
https://doi.org/10.1007/978-981-92-0156-3_1

reached not because the various issues surrounding goodwill accounting had been resolved, but rather because they had not. Numerous theoretical, conceptual, and practical challenges remain unresolved, and discussions have continued in various jurisdictions worldwide beyond 2022.

The motivation for this study stems from a desire to understand why an accounting standard-setting body composed of accounting experts, despite expending such an enormous amount of time and effort, could not reach a clear conclusion or consensus, and was ultimately forced to settle for the status quo in the form of "suspending the discussion."

1.2 Brief Historical Background

This study addresses the debate surrounding goodwill accounting (Impairment-only vs. Amortization with Impairment). This historical section has two objectives. The first is to examine the theoretical/conceptual issues surrounding the accounting for goodwill, specifically the aspects that have been resolved and those that remain unresolved. If these theoretical/conceptual problems have already been resolved or settled, or if it is clear they are unsolvable, then the IASB and ASAF would not have needed to devote significant time to examining them. Learning from history can help avoid repeating the same debates. Another objective is to learn, from a historical perspective, about the problems and consequences that emerged when theoretical/conceptual solutions differed from practical solutions.

Considering these objectives, focusing solely on the debates that emerged after the FASB and IASB prohibited goodwill amortization risks obscuring the true context and causal relationships of the issues and losing sight of their deeper roots. However, excessively broadening the historical scope risks blurring the focus.[2] Therefore, this study rewinds history to a certain extent, focusing particularly on the debate surrounding the "pooling of interests method" (hereafter "Pooling method") vs. the "Purchase method," which developed closely tied to the "Amortization with Impairment" versus "Impairment-only" controversy.

---

[2] While this section only traces back to the 1960s debate surrounding the "Purchase method vs. Pooling method," delving further into history reveals the potential for serious problems with the purchase method (Some of these concerns are recognized as the issue of accumulating goodwill today).

Courtis (1983, pp. 3–4) notes that during the corporate consolidation period from the early twentieth century to the 1920s, the practice of recognizing massive goodwill to justify the purchase price paid by the acquiring company beyond the company's tangible capital became rampant. This led to capital watering. See also Briloff (1972), Chap. 3.

The key point is that, despite the difficulty in measuring goodwill value at the time, it was used as a tool to support stock valuations. If impairment is not properly implemented and goodwill that does not hold its recorded value continues to accumulate, it could lead to the same capital watering problem that occurred from the early twentieth century to the 1920s.

1.2.1 Pooling Method Versus Purchase Method

Accounting for business combinations was developed in the U.S. After various twists and turns, it settled into accounting standards that permitted only the purchase method (referred to as the acquisition method by the IASB) and prohibited goodwill amortization, as outlined in SFAS 141 (FASB 2004a) and 142 (FASB 2004b) (see Table 1.1).

The pooling and purchase methods were both in use as early as the 1920s[3] (Wyatt 1963, p. 19; Hughes 1982, p. 24). One characteristic of the pooling method, namely the concept of carrying forward the earned surplus of merging companies, had been accepted by the early 1930s (Montgomery 1934). Moreover, the pooling method became popular from the mid-1940s onward (Rayburn and Powers 1991, pp. 158–160),[4] with one reason for gaining such support being that it corrected the

Table 1.1 Accounting standards for business combinations in the U.S.

Publication period	Accounting standard setter	Accounting standard	Title
Dec. 1944	CAP	ARB 24	*Accounting for Intangible Assets*
Sep. 1950		ARB 40	*Business Combinations*
June 1953		ARB 43	*Restatement and Revision of Accounting Research Bulletins*
Jan. 1957		ARB 48	*Business Combinations*
Jan. 1963		ARS 5	*A Critical Study of Business Combinations*
Oct. 1965	APB	APBO 6	*Status of Accounting Research Bulletins*
Dec. 1966		APBO 10	*Omnibus Opinion -1966-*
Jan. 1968		ARS 10	*Accounting for Goodwill*
Aug. 1970		APBO 16	*Business Combinations*
Aug. 1970		APBO 17	*Intangible Assets*
Oct. 1975	FASB	SFAS 10	*Extension of 'Grandfather' Provisions for Business Combinations*
Sep. 1980		SFAS 38	*Accounting for preacquisition contingencies of purchased enterprises*
June 2001		SFAS 141	*Business Combinations*
June 2001		SFAS 142	*Goodwill and Other Intangible Assets*

[3] Wyatt (1963, p. 19) states, "while the term 'pooling of interests' probably did not evolve until later, the two principal accounting characteristics of the 'pooling' accounting treatment were recognized as early as the 1920s."

[4] According to Andrew Barr, then the SEC's Chief Accountant, the term "pooling of interests" was first used in the 1945 CAP report, and it was formally recognized as an accounting standard in ARB 40, published in 1950 (Barr 1959).

The 1940s coincided with growing support for and the establishment of historical cost accounting. The pooling method aligned with historical cost accounting principles because it involved taking over and com-bining the acquired company's assets and liabilities at their book values.

abuse of the purchase method (earnings management through non-recognition of goodwill and arbitrary amortization) (Chatov 1975, p. 213). The purchase method proved particularly problematic in stock-for-stock mergers. The acquiring company issued shares commensurate with the desired amount and capitalized on the exchanged shares at their measured consideration (fair value). However, under the purchase method, these shares were often recorded at values exceeding the fair value of the acquired company's assets (Chatov 1975, pp. 210–214). This constituted an overstatement of assets and an inflation of capital. In the 1940s, the Securities and Exchange Commission (SEC) took issue with the purchase method's contribution to asset overstatement, specifically its revaluation process. Asset revaluation became a major problem during periods of high inflation, such as the 1940s. The SEC initially concluded that the pooling method was appropriate and that asset revaluation should not be performed (Barr 1959, p. 7).

By contrast, the pooling method promoted conglomerate mergers. In the U.S., during the 1960s, Section 7 of the Clayton Act, an antitrust law, regulated only horizontal and vertical mergers, and conglomerate mergers were permitted until 1967[5] (Chatov 1975). Donald F. Turner, then the U.S. Assistant Attorney General for Antitrust also stated that conglomerate mergers cannot be controlled under Section 7 of the Clayton Act because they do not lead to monopolies (Turner 1965, pp. 1330–1350). The 1960s securities market valued companies demonstrating continuous earnings growth, with the price-earnings ratio (PER) functioning as an effective stock valuation metric. Expectations for capital returns from "growth stocks" created the relationship with the PER. Within this context, the pooling method created the illusion of "earnings growth stocks," driving numerous companies toward conglomerate mergers.[6] In addition, conglomerate mergers came under

[5] The reason conglomerate mergers subsided was not that the next Antitrust Division Chief, Richard W. MacLaren, formally stated the Justice Department's position in 1967 that Section 7 of the Clayton Act applied to conglomerate mergers, but rather because the recession cooled speculative fervor (Chatov 1975).

[6] To summarize the specific incentives for firms to prefer pooling-over-purchase methods, the relative advantages of pooling over purchase methods can be categorized into those related to contracts and those related to capital markets.

Contract-related advantages are as follows: Incentives to use the pooling method include the ability to conceal the acquisition premium paid to the target company during M&A (Robinson and Shane 1990; Aboody et al. 2000) and the potential for increased executive compensation in firms with performance-based compensation systems (Aboody et al. 2000). Empirical research has focused on these contractual relationships. Multiple empirical studies have shown that these factors motivated the adoption of the pooling method. Furthermore, as the use of the pooling method became restricted during the conglomerate merger movement, companies became willing to incur the costs necessary to satisfy the increasingly restrictive conditions for its use.

Regarding capital market, managers executing conglomerate mergers used the pooling method for accounting purposes to achieve apparent earnings growth. The acquiring company recorded the acquired company's undervalued book assets at the merger price. If these assets were subsequently sold at a price higher than their book value (market value), the difference could be recognized as profit. Additionally, they could generate capital gains by acquiring undervalued assets from companies with conservative accounting policies and selling them during periods of inflation. Furthermore, by adding the retained earnings of both companies and subtracting the combined

scrutiny because conglomerates shifted toward generating profits through mergers rather than through production activities. Once firms stopped pursuing continuous mergers, their growth halted (Burch 1969).

Regulations targeting the pooling method were developed because the said act had contributed to conglomerate mergers. In 1968, the Federal Trade Commission (FTC) accepted a request to investigate conglomerate merger issues. Senate hearings were held in 1969, and in August of that year, the FTC submitted an investigative report to the Senate Subcommittee on Trusts and Antitrust. This report criticized the Pooling Act and its tax advantages, recommending its elimination (FTC 1969).

However, opposition to pooling regulations came from many quarters. Accounting Research Study 5 (Wyatt's 1963), which advocated eliminating the pooling method, was not accepted as the American Institute of Certified Public Accountants' (AICPA) official position and did not become an Accounting Principles Board (APB) Opinion (nor did it become Generally Accepted Accounting Principles (GAAP)). Furthermore, during the Exposure Draft (ED) stage of APB Opinions 16(AICPA 1970a) and 17(AICPA 1970b), the criterion for a relatively small size difference was initially set at 3 to 1. However, owing to a large volume of opposition letters organized by the Financial Executive Institute, a compromise was reached to accept a ratio of 9 to 1. Ultimately, this size test was removed from APB Opinions 16 and 17 (Zeff 1972). Although significant conditions were watered down due to business pressure, APB Opinions 16 and 17 imposed detailed requirements[7] for applying the pooling method. Theoretically, the pooling method is not incorrect as an accounting approach for equal mergers or parent-subsidiary mergers. However, the complex application conditions[8] for the pooling method—which should have been designed to select the accounting method based on the economic substance of continuing equity ownership, as required by the U.S. APB—instead led to substantive discretionary actions by companies preferring the pooling method, targeting those very conditions. Managers who perceived the benefits of adopting the pooling

number of shares outstanding from the total shares of both companies, they artificially increased the merged company's "earnings per share" growth (Chatov 1975, pp. 207–208). According to Chatov (1975), expectations of capital returns for "growth stocks" created the PER relationship, leading to the creation of "growth stocks" using the pooling method and driving numerous companies toward conglomerate mergers (Chatov 1975).

[7] APB Opinion 16 required the application of the pooling method to mergers satisfying all three conditions: (1) attributes of the combining companies, (2) manner of combining interests, and (3) absence of planned transactions (AICPA 1970, para. 45).

Twelve specific conditions were formulated to concretize these three criteria, but these conditions were complex and open to interpretation. M. Sutton, the SEC's Chief Accountant, stated that "his staff spends nearly 40% of [their total work] time interpreting the complex pooling-of-interests criteria" (Beresford 2001; Zeff 2002). He further noted, "The economic effects reported in financial statements are not actually based on economic substance; they are based on whether specific criteria were met—that is, whether the transaction was structured in a particular way" (Sutton 2005). For details on these conditions, see AICPA 1970a, paras. 46–48.

[8] See note 5.

method acted as the pooling and purchase methods were optional, irrespective of the economic substance of the business combination.

Subsequently, criticism from regulatory bodies, such as the SEC, regarding the abuse of the pooling method intensified (Turner 1999). In 2001, the FASB issued SFAS 141 (FASB 2001a) and 142, prohibiting the use of the pooling method in the U.S. and eliminating goodwill amortization, mandating impairment testing as the sole accounting treatment. The historical background leading to the prohibition of the pooling method demonstrates that even accounting methods considered theoretically/conceptually sound can, owing to the standard-setting process and its practical distortions, fail to be used as intended by the original accounting standards from a practical benefits perspective. This could trigger societal problems. This divergence between theoretical/conceptual solutions and practical solutions suggests that, given the current assumption that the purchase method is the sole accounting approach for M&A transactions, debating the merits of goodwill amortization is inherently limited; at the very least, it highlights the difficulty of resolving the issue purely from a theoretical/conceptual standpoint.

1.2.2 Background of Goodwill Non-amortization

The FASB initially proposed eliminating the pooling method and requiring all business combinations to be accounted for using the purchase method, mandating the amortization of all acquired goodwill (FASB 1999). However, this proposal was rejected due to strong opposition from companies and legislators (U.S. House of Representatives 2000; U.S. Senate 2000).

Ramanna (2008, pp. 255–260) stated the following: "The FASB subsequently modified its original proposal. While continuing to eliminate the pooling method and mandate the purchase method, it proposed 'goodwill impairment' based on unverifiable fair value estimates of the residual value of acquired goodwill, replacing amortization....I confirmed that the board members who opposed FASB's proposal to eliminate the pooling method were linked through political contributions to companies opposing that proposal (i.e., supporters of the pooling method). It was also found that these pooling advocates were among those who proposed the 'revised' impairment rules now incorporated into SFAS 142".[9] Simply, the group that supported the pooling method (i.e., the group that opposed the ban on the

[9] Skinner (2008) criticizes Ramanna (2008) for basing the rationale for firms' desire for non-amortization and impairment-only conditions of goodwill on the unverifiability (manipulability) of goodwill impairment tests. According to Skinner (2008), the reason is to avoid recognizing amortization expenses. However, Skinner (2008, p. 282) highly values Ramanna's point that "provides evidence on how firms use contributions from their political action committees (PACs) to members of Congress as a means of lobbying for these firms' preferred positions in the accounting standard-setting process." He supported a political compromise in which the FASB maintained its proposal to eliminate the pooling method while conceding not to amortize goodwill.

pooling method) demanded that the impairment-only method be required to prevent amortization of goodwill under the purchase method when the pooling method was banned, and further supported reducing the stringency of impairment requirements.

Amortization carries the risk of the amortization period being determined arbitrarily for management purposes. Conversely, applying the impairment-only strategy without amortization may result in the recognition of impairment losses that are "too little, too late," leading to the recording of fictitious assets on the balance sheet, potentially inflating capital. The SEC viewed the abuse of the pooling method in conglomerate mergers as a more serious problem than arbitrary goodwill amortization. Therefore, the compromise reached between the business community and FASB addresses these issues. However, this capital inflation could cause serious problems.

1.3 Structure of This Book

The current section describes the structure of this book (See Fig. 1.1). Below, we outline each chapter, starting with Chap. 2, which together with Chap. 1, provides the foundation for the analyses in Chaps. 3 and beyond. This chapter examines the IASB/ASAF deliberations on goodwill accounting from PiR 3 through the IASB's

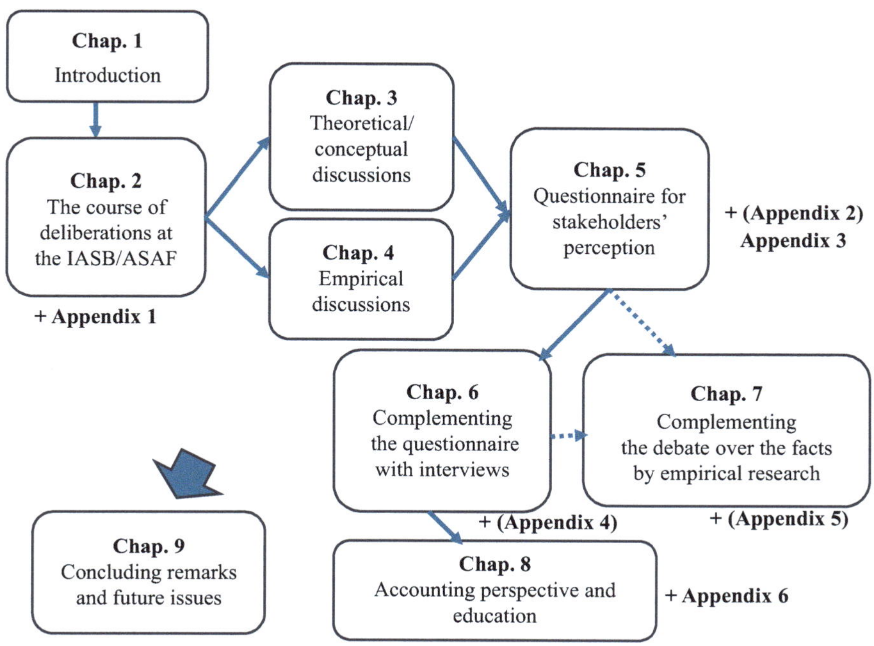

Fig. 1.1 Structure of the book

2022 decision not to reintroduce systematic amortization and considers subsequent developments that culminated in the 2024 Exposure Draft. The chapter shows that the debate did not proceed merely as a contest between amortization and impairment-only. Rather, the central difficulty arose from the tension between attempts to clarify the nature and definition of goodwill and the asset concept in the conceptual framework, com-pounded by practical operability, judgmental costs, and institutional constraints. As these constraints became salient, deliberations gradually shifted from a measurement-centric orientation to a disclosure-centric orientation 1.1.

Subsequently, we review prior theoretical and conceptual studies on the amortization and non-amortization of goodwill and conduct our theoretical analysis. Since such research has not been widely covered in major academic journals in recent years, we have included a historical literature review in Chap. 3. The primary objective of the theoretical consideration is to determine whether the issue of whether to amortize goodwill has been resolved from a theoretical and conceptual perspective. If the theoretical and conceptual issues surrounding the accounting for goodwill have already been resolved, then discussions within the IASB and ASAF would lose much of their significance and time should be devoted solely to resolving practical problems. Based on the results of the theoretical analysis presented in this chapter, it is impossible to determine, either theoretically or conceptually, whether goodwill should be amortized. Specifically, amortizing goodwill to zero excludes the portion of excess earnings from realized earnings, resulting in an understatement of earnings. However, accounting for acquired goodwill without amortization also creates the fundamental problem of overstating equity, as goodwill value is recognized in equity upon realization.[10] Therefore, regardless of whether goodwill is amortized, as long as goodwill is recorded as a contra-account to shareholders' equity rather than in other comprehensive income (OCI), the fundamental problem of distinguishing between equity and profit remains. Thus, answering the question surrounding whether goodwill should be amortized requires a return to the fundamental dimension of business combination accounting (pooling vs. purchase method) and engaging in theoretical and conceptual debate. However, in practice, considering the adverse effects of past abuses of the pooling method, such a return may prove difficult.

Next, Chap. 4 surveys past empirical research on the amortization, non-amortization, and impairment treatment of goodwill. Given the numerous empirical studies on goodwill, this review focuses exclusively on the empirical research published in highly ranked peer-reviewed academic journals.[11] This chapter's primary objective is to identify the "recognized facts" within the academic community's

[10] See, for example, Fukui and Saito (2025).

[11] Using journal databases, including EBSCO Host and ScienceDirect, we conducted a search using "Goodwill" as the keyword. Setting the period from January 2000 to December 2022, we collected empirical research literature classified as archival research. To ensure research quality, the scope of target journals was limited to those ranked within the top 100 in the SCImago Journal Rank for "Accounting" and that publish empirical studies in the financial accounting field. Consequently, this study examines 103 papers from 31 journals. For details, refer to Chap. 4.

factual understanding regarding managers' accounting reporting behavior concerning accounting for goodwill and its economic consequences—specifically, research findings based on statistical verification methods—as distinct from the practitioner's perspective in discussions surrounding the facts of goodwill. Through a review of prior research, this study attempted to synthesize empirical findings on how management's financial reporting behavior regarding goodwill changed, and what economic consequences the accounting information on goodwill produced, following the shift in goodwill accounting from a "Amortization with Impairment" to an "Impairment-only" approach. According to the results, while some studies have reported that goodwill and goodwill impairment losses now provide useful information for investment decisions, many studies point out the following:

1. The remaining goodwill balance and goodwill impairment losses provide information useful for investment decisions.
2. There are management delays in recognizing goodwill impairment losses.
3. Management exercises discretion regarding discount rates and projected cash flow growth rates to avoid recording impairment losses.
4. Various incentives and determinants (e.g., firm characteristics and execution capabilities) influence management's recognition of goodwill impairment.
5. In purchase price allocation, management may exercise discretion in determining how much of the consideration transferred in M&A transactions is allocated to goodwill.
6. Delaying the recognition of goodwill impairment reduces its usefulness in investment decision-making.
7. The non-application of goodwill amortization weakens the contractual role of accounting.
8. Excess earning power in companies generally reverts to the level of the cost of capital within five to 10 years, even when considering post-acquisition management efforts (i.e., even when accounting for the additional portion of self-generated goodwill after M&A).

A comparison between the review of these empirical studies and the discussions of stakeholders with an interest in accounting standards (Chaps. 2, 5, and 6) reveals that these stakeholders do not necessarily accept the "recognized facts" derived through academic methods as "facts." Therefore, Appendix 1 examines why practitioners (or those outside academia) do not recognize the same statistical facts identified in empirical research.[12]

Here, we note that the following point should be kept in mind. Even identical facts or phenomena may be perceived differently depending on the theories, values, and experiences held by the perceiving entity.[13] While academic empirical research

---

[12] Consequently, we must ask what values and beliefs stakeholders hold regarding accounting for goodwill, and what factual recognition they have of it. This task is undertaken in Chaps. 4 and 5.

[13] The idea that observation is not an objective phenomenon unaffected by theory, but rather that the observer's theories and background knowledge alter how things are seen and interpreted, is called the theory-ladenness of observation. This perspective is shared not only by relativists but also by

captures broad averages, preparers, users, and auditors perceive facts within their own unique experiential contexts (different from the averages). Differences in educational background and specific practical experience shape those contexts and, in turn, may lead to variations in the "recognized facts" among practitioners. This may be one reason discussions among accounting standard-setters regarding goodwill amortization remain unresolved.

A large-scale questionnaire survey was conducted to understand the views of financial statement preparers, users, and auditors in Japan regarding the accounting for goodwill and underlying accounting values that form the basis for their judgments. Specifically, this survey targeted three groups: financial statement preparers, users (analysts), and auditors (affiliated with major audit firms). We received 447 responses from preparers, 130 from users, and 620 from auditors.

The questionnaires revealed that the amortization with impairment method received the highest level of support in all three groups: financial statement preparers (73.4%), users (62.3%), and auditors (89.5%) (see Chap. 5 for details). However, statistically significant differences in support rates were observed among these three groups. Furthermore, common grounds for both support and opposition were observed across all three groups. Furthermore, while users showed the highest proportion of support for amortization, the proportion opposing it was also high, indicating divided responses. This differs significantly from statements in publications by international accounting standard-setters and Certified Financial Analyst (afterwards, CFA) research reports suggesting that many users reject the "amortization with impairment approach." Therefore, we conducted two types of interviews. The first targeted users, preparers, and auditors, focusing on identifying factors determining similarities and differences in responses. The second targeted users only, aiming to identify reasons for the split in user responses and why their responses differed from those of users in other jurisdictions. The results suggest that the causes might lie in accounting education at Japanese universities and professional education for certified public accountants and analysts.[14]

Moreover, how do perceptions of facts gathered from practitioners through questionnaires and interviews differ from facts derived from academic empirical research? To clarify this aspect, we conducted empirical research on the "too little, too late problem" to supplement Chap. 5. The "too little, too late problem" is a key

positivist philosophers of science. As the subject matter becomes more complex and specialized, these differences in perception become more pronounced. For the theory-laden nature of perception, see Hanson (1969) and Kuhn (1962).

Furthermore, according to Schemata theory in cognitive and social psychology, people interpret and understand new information using "schemata"—knowledge frameworks formed based on past experiences. Consequently, differing past experiences lead to differing perceptions of the same object. For Schemata theory, see Bartlett (1932) and Rumelhart (1980).

[14] Meanwhile, the views of users supporting the "impairment-only approach" expressed by representatives from many jurisdictions at IASB and ASAF meetings are not necessarily reflected in the findings of the CFA Institute (2021) survey (20% supported the current "impairment-only approach (status quo)," while 38% supported maintaining the current approach while addressing issues through disclosure).

point frequently discussed at IASB and ASAF meetings, forming the core of debates over the merits of the impairment-only approach. Interviews revealed that many analysts had already recognized goodwill impairment losses prior to the announcements (consistent with findings from Peters (2021); hereafter, CFA Survey). Many users may perceive the recognition of goodwill value declines as "too little, too late." Therefore, we conducted empirical analysis using, as our sample, data[15] from Japanese companies that announced goodwill impairment losses. Long-term cumulative abnormal returns declined even before the goodwill impairment announcement, suggesting that, on average, market participants may have anticipated the impairment. However, results from short-term event studies around the announcement also indicate that the announcement contained information. These results suggest that stakeholders perceive the facts regarding goodwill impairment losses differently. Accounting standard-setters and stakeholders tend to view many issues in a dualistic manner, and regarding goodwill, they primarily advance one of the following arguments: "Goodwill impairment losses are anticipated prior to announcement and therefore do not contain value relevant information," or "The occurrence of goodwill impairment is unexpected and thus contains value relevant information." However, our analysis suggests that, while market participants can predict the occurrence of goodwill impairment to some extent, they cannot fully predict its specifics. Therefore, the announcement can still provide market participants with new value-related information.

According to the interviews conducted with prepares, users, and auditors, based on responses to questionnaires, it is presumed that these differences stem from the influence of accounting education at universities and other educational institutions; the subsequent impact of professional education; and, in the case of auditors, the influence of the national examination.[16] A survey conducted among members of the Japan Accounting Association[17] revealed that accounting education at Japanese universities emphasizes the traditional flow concept of accounting, focusing on the income statement.

Furthermore, this study focused on the essay-type questions of the Certified Public Accountant examination.[18] Moreover, investigated whether the questions posed from 2009 to 2018 were related to an income statement-centered accounting perspective. It was found that many of the questions were indeed related to this

---

[15] The sample of IFRS-adopting firms was small, and no statistically significant results were obtained; therefore, caution is required in interpreting the results.

[16] Appendix 6 in Chap. 8 examines trends in the national CPA examination, specifically focusing on whether it emphasizes the income statement or the balance sheet.

[17] The survey respondents are as described above.

[18] To become a Certified Public Accountant (CPA) in Japan, one must pass both the multiple-choice and essay sections of the National CPA Examination, followed by "completing practical training units and passing the final examination." Additionally, a minimum of 3 years of practical experience is required, regardless of whether it is gained before or after passing the examinations. For details, refer to the "About the Certified Public Accountant Examination" section on the Japanese Institute of Certified Public Accountants website (https://jicpa.or.jp/cpainfo/applicant/examination/)

accounting perspective. Japanese auditors not only learn revenue and expense views at university but also further study the importance of this accounting concept in preparing for the national exam. It is presumed that, after taking up the position of a certified public accountant, the said auditors tend to make judgments from this accounting perspective. These results indicate that, to understand the controversy surrounding accounting for goodwill, factors such as accounting education, which have not received sufficient attention until now, must be considered.

1.4 Uniqueness and Advantage of Our Study

We discuss the unique aspects of this book and its advantages over other similar studies.

1.4.1 Unique Organization of the Controversies

This study not only analyzes IASB published materials, but also thoroughly investigates statements made by accounting standard setters from various jurisdictions at ASAF meetings. These statements are categorized and organized into theoretical, conceptual, and practical views.

Theoretical/conceptual issues may arise at multiple levels, ranging from those that can be resolved at the level of specific accounting treatments to more fundamental problems that require changes to basic concepts. Under a given conceptual framework, the more fundamental the required change, the more serious the implications for consistency with other concepts and accounting treatments become. Similarly, practical issues also cover a wide range of concerns, including technical difficulties, cost-benefit imbalances, and convenience. However, the significance of these issues may differ depending on the interests of the parties affected by the establishment, amendment, and abolition of accounting standards, such as financial statement preparers, users, and auditors. Moreover, when the accounting treatment theoretically or conceptually required differs from the treatment sought as a result of practical interest adjustments, resolving the issue necessarily involves a political question of which should be given priority.

Furthermore, the causes of these conflicting opinions can be divided not only into those stemming from such interests, but also into those stemming from differences in accounting values, beliefs, and experiences, and those stemming from differences in the recognition of related facts. In other words, there exists a wide range of conflicting opinions, arising from various causes. The fact that these statements are discussed in IASB/ASAF meetings without clear organization makes resolving the issue difficult.

1.4.2 An Unprecedented Large-Scale Questionnaire Survey

We conducted an unprecedented large-scale survey in Japan, targeting financial statement preparers (Keidanren member companies and non-member companies listed on the Tokyo Stock Exchange First Section; respondents: 447/2718 companies, response rate: 16.4%), users (currently practicing analysts belonging to the Japan Securities Analysts Association, 130/673 individuals, response rate: 19.3%), and auditors (partners at the Big Four and five other major audit firms, 620/1961 individuals, response rate: 31.6%). This survey clarifies aspects of their accounting values, beliefs, and factual perceptions. Furthermore, we conducted a large-scale survey of the content of accounting education at universities, targeting Japanese accounting scholars (members of the Japan Accounting Association who teach accounting courses (279/1698, 16.4% response rate)).

The opinions expressed by stakeholders in the setting of accounting standards are influenced not only by their interests in the matter but also by their accounting values, beliefs, experiences, and the resulting perceptions of facts. Differences in these accounting values and perceptions of facts may arise from their educational backgrounds and professional experience. Therefore, we investigated whether preparers, users, and auditors held differing accounting values and perceptions of facts; confirmed the nature of these differences; and subsequently analyzed their causes. Furthermore, because some causes could not be clearly identified through the questionnaire alone, we conducted interviews focused on specific issues to supplement the findings.

1.4.3 Japan's Institutional Environment

The institutional environment surrounding this research in Japan holds advantages compared with jurisdictions that have fully adopted IFRS.[19] Alternatively, the U.S. institutional environment limits the application of IFRS to foreign companies in the U.S. market. Limiting the scope to large, listed companies, neither full-adoption jurisdictions nor the U.S. have companies that amortize goodwill; they operate under an impairment-only framework. Therefore, within the same business environment, it is impossible to compare companies that amortize goodwill with those that do not. By contrast, in Japan, IFRS and domestic GAAP coexist and compete on an optional basis. This allows for the assumption of a common business

[19] "Incommensurability" is a term coined by Thomas Kuhn to describe a state in which mutual understanding or comparison between groups holding different theories or values is impossible because there is no common yardstick or standard; see Kuhn (1962).

Table 1.2 Accounting for goodwill in the world

	Domestic firms	Foreign firms	Accounting for goodwill
Full- adoption jurisdictions	IFRS	IFRS	Impairment-only
U.S.	U.S.-GAAP	U.S.-GAAP or IFRS	Impairment-only
Japan	J-GAAP, IFRS, U.S.-GAAP, or JMIS[a]	J-GAAP, IFRS, U.S.-GAAP, or JMIS	Amortization with Impairment, or Impairment-only

In Table 1.2, jurisdictions referred to as "Full-adoption" either accept IFRS directly with identical content or endorse IFRS one standard at a time, allowing amendments but including those that are substantially equivalent. Additionally, although not covered here, jurisdictions such as China and India are converging toward IFRS but have not yet adopted it. The environment we are addressing here involves the coexistence of companies that amortize goodwill and those that do not, under similar business conditions. For example, companies listed on Germany's regulated market (börslich regulierter Markt) and unlisted companies can choose between the Handelsgesetzbuch (HGB), which mandates goodwill amortization, and the HGB and International Financial Reporting Standards (IFRS) which only requires impairment. Thus, the regulatory framework could be considered analogous to the situation for Japanese listed companies. However, companies listed on Germany's EU-regulated market (Regulierter Markt) are required to prepare consolidated financial statements under IFRS and separate financial statements under HGB. Consequently, it is not possible to observe the coexistence of "goodwill amortization" and "non-amortization" in Germany's major capital market.

environment, meaning that Japanese companies adopting IFRS can be compared with those adopting domestic standards (Table 1.2)[20].

Furthermore, in Japan, preparers of financial statements choose between IFRS and domestic GAAP, based on their understanding of both standards and their company's circumstances. Analysts who analyze these financial statements and auditors who conduct audits are also well-versed in both sets of standards. Consequently, it can be assumed that both the questionnaire and the interview respondents fully understood the survey questions, thereby ensuring the quality of the questionnaire survey.

[20] Although the EU has fully adopted IFRS, a closer look reveals a slightly more complex situation. For example, in Germany, non-listed companies must report the planned amortization of good will over its economic useful life in both individual and consolidated financial statements. However, forconsolidated financial statements of non-listed companies, IFRS may be voluntarily applied. Consequently, for non-listed companies, there are simultaneously consolidated financial statementsthat amortize goodwill and those that do not. However, listed companies are required toapply IFRS to their consolidated financial statements. Therefore, it is not possible to comparelisted companies that amortize goodwill with those that do not.

1.5 Summary and Challenges

This chapter began by presenting our research question: "Why did the debate over the subsequent accounting treatment of purchased goodwill shift toward disclosure-oriented responses, leaving the measurement problem unresolved?" Put differently, our objective is to clarify why the debate did not converge on a conceptually definitive resolution and what underlying factors sustained the impasse.

A natural question underlying this research is why prolonged deliberations among accounting specialists within the IASB and ASAF—spanning nearly a decade—failed to produce a definitive resolution or even a stable convergence of views. Given the technical expertise and extensive due process involved, one might expect such debates to culminate in conceptual clarification or policy agreement. However, the persistence of disagreement suggests that the difficulty does not arise solely from technical measurement issues. Rather, it points to the possibility that certain accounting problems—particularly those involving goodwill—are structurally resistant to resolution within contemporary standard-setting. Differences across jurisdictions in accounting values, institutional environments, perceptions of economic facts, and normative views about the role of financial reporting create tensions that cannot be eliminated through technical refinement alone. From this perspective, the absence of convergence is not merely a temporary failure. However, it may reflect an inherent characteristic of accounting standard-setting itself, where conceptual, practical, and institutional dimensions interact in ways that make definitive resolution elusive. This perspective motivates the subsequent empirical investigation in later chapters, which explores whether such divergences are observable in stakeholders' views and how Japan's institutional and educational context may shape distinctive interpretations of goodwill accounting.

While theoretical and conceptual solutions are indispensable in accounting standard setting to maintain overall consistency, the history of the pooling vs. purchase method debate clearly shows that when the direction of theoretical/conceptual solutions diverges from that of practical/political solutions, the former often retreats. Moreover, the issue of goodwill amortization is not a simple problem that can be solved by reintroducing the pooling method. History shows that, if the pooling method were reintroduced, larger practical problems may resurface.

To address the aforementioned research question, we first examined whether the issue of goodwill amortization has been resolved theoretically/conceptually, before subsequently investigating how past empirical studies have captured facts concerning goodwill. However, because financial statement preparers, users, and auditors—who wield significant influence over accounting standard-setting—do not necessarily share the same perceptions of the facts as researchers, we conducted questionnaire surveys and interviews to determine the accounting values and beliefs they hold and how they perceive the facts surrounding goodwill. We also conducted empirical research on the resulting differences in opinion regarding these facts (the "too little, too late" issue). Furthermore, similarly, these investigations revealed that the content of accounting education may be contributing to the differing views among stakeholders. We surveyed the content of accounting education at Japanese universities using a questionnaire. Given the relatively high proportion of auditors supporting the systematic amortization of goodwill, we conducted an additional analysis of the national examination content to examine its influence. The details and conclusions of the issues mentioned above are clarified in the subsequent chapters.

Statement on AI Usage: During the preparation of this manuscript, the author used AI-assisted tools such as DeepL and ChatGPT to improve the English expression and clarity of the manuscript. The author thoroughly reviewed and approved the final version and takes full responsibility for the content.

References

Aboody, David, Ron Kasznik and Michael Williams (2000), "Purchase versus Pooling in Stock-for-Stock Acquisitions: Why Do Firms Care?," *Journal of Accounting and Economics*, Vol. 29, No. 3, pp. 261–286.

AICPA (1970a), *Business Combinations,* APB Opinion No. 16.

AICPA (1970b), *Intangible Assets*, APB Opinion No. 17.

Barr, A (1959), "Accounting Aspects of Business Combination," *Accounting Review*, Vol. 34, No. 2, pp. 175–181.

Bartlett, Frederic C. (1932), Remembering*: A Study in Experimental and Social Psychology*, Cambridge University Press.

Beresford, D. R. (2001), Congress Looks at Accounting for Business Combinations, *Accounting Horizons,* Vol. 15, No. 1, pp. 73–86.

Bithell, R. A. (1882), *Accounting House Dictionary*, George Routledge & Sons.

Briloff, A. J. (1972), Unaccountable *Accounting*, HarperCollins.

Burch, G. (1969), "The Merger Movement Rides High," *Fortune,* 79, February, pp. 78–82.

Chatov, R. (1975), *Corporate financial reporting: public or private control*, Free Press.

Courtis, J. K. (1983), "Business goodwill: Conceptual clarification via accounting, legal and etymological perspectives," *Accounting Historians Journal,* Vol. 10, No. 2, pp. 1–38.

Federal Trade Commission (1969), *Economic Report on Corporate Mergers*, Staff Report to the Federal Trade Commission and Subcommittee on Antitrust and Monopoly, U.S. Senate, Ninety-First Congress.

Fukui, Yoshitaka, and Shizuki Saito. (2025), "Economically Consistent Recognition of Goodwill and Its Amortization". Working Paper. Available at: https://doi.org/10.2139/ssrn.5114458

Hanson, Norwood (1969), *Patterns of discovery: An inquiry into the conceptual foundations of science*, Cambridge University Press.

Hughes, Hugh P. (1982). *Goodwill in Accounting: A History of the Issues and Problems,* Georgia State University. Jenkins, E. L. (May 4, 2000), *Testimony of Edmund L. Jenkins Chairman, Financial Accounting Standards Board,* the Subcommittee on Finance and Hazardous Materials of the Committee on Commerce.

Kuhn, Thomas S. (1962), *The structure of scientific revolutions*, University of Chicago Press.

Peters, Sandra J. (2021), *Goodwill: Investor Perspectives – Improve Disclosures, Rather Than Revert to Amortization,* CFA Institute.

Ramanna, K. (2008), "The implications of unverifiable fair-value accounting: Evidence from the political economy of goodwill accounting," *Journal of Accounting and Economics*, Vol. 45, pp. 253–281.

Rayburn, Frank R. and Ollie S. Powers (1991), A History of Pooling of Interests Accounting For Business Combinations in the United States, *The Accounting Historians Journal*, Vol. 18, No. 2, pp. 155–192.
Robinson, J. R and P. B. Shane (1990), "Acquisition Accounting Method and Bid Premia for Target Firms," *The Accounting Review*, Vol. 65, No. 1, pp. 25–48.
Rumelhart, David E. (1980), "Schemata: The Building Blocks of Cognition". In: Spiro, R., Bruce, B. and Brewer, W., Eds., Theoretical Issues in Reading Comprehension, Erlbaum Associates, pp. 33–58.
Skinner, Dougla J. (2008), Discussion of "The Implications of Unverifiable Fair-Value Accounting: Evidence from the Political Economy of Goodwill Accounting," *Journal of Accounting and Economics*, Vol. 45, Nos. 2–3, pp. 282–288.
Sutton, M. (2005), *SEC Historical Society Interview with Mike Sutton Conducted by Gary Previts at Case Western Reserve University in Cleveland,* SEC Historical Society.
Turner, Donald F. (1965), "Conglomerate Mergers and Section 7 of the Clayton Act," *Harvard Law Review*, Vol. 78, No. 7, pp. 1313–1395
Turner, L. E. (February 10, 1999), *Speech by SEC Staff: Initiatives for Improving the Quality Of Financial Reporting, to the New York Society of Security Analysts, Inc. New York, N.Y.*, U.S. Securities and Exchange Commission.
Wyatt, A. R. (1963), *A Critical Study of Accounting for Business Combinations*, Accounting Research Study No. 5, American Institute of Certified Public Accountants.
Zeff, S.A. (2002), "Political" Lobbying on Proposed Standards: A Challenge to the IASB, *Accounting Horizons* Vol. 16, No. 1, pp. 43–54.

Chapter 2
Goodwill Accounting Deliberations at the International Accounting Standards Board and Accounting Standards Advisory Forum

Yoshihiro Tokuga and Tomoaki Yamashita

2.1 Purpose and Organization of This Chapter

This chapter examines discussions on goodwill accounting within IASB and ASAF to explain why this issue remains unresolved. Emphasis is placed on ASAF discussions, which provide a platform for accounting standard setters from various jurisdictions.[1]

ASAF functions as a forum for examining issues on which the IASB seeks advice, with participation from major jurisdictions or groups of jurisdictions. This forum facilitates communication and discussion of relevant issues, opinions regarding proposed approaches, and the status of stakeholder interests.

From a methodological perspective, ASAF discussions offer a complementary lens through which the dynamics of IASB standard-setting can be examined.

Following the Post-implementation Review of IFRS 3 (PiR 3), the IASB/ASAF began a prolonged reconsideration of goodwill accounting. This process included the publication of a Discussion Paper (DP, IASB (2020)), which presented the

[1]ASAF differs from the IASB in that its members consist of accounting standard-setters from jurisdictions worldwide, reflecting diverse institutional and environmental backgrounds. This structure allows differences in accounting values and beliefs across jurisdictions, as well as practical observations of preparers, users, and auditors, to be articulated and shared in the standard-setting process (see Table 2.1).

Y. Tokuga (✉)
Faculty of Economics and Business Administration, Department of Business Administration, Kyoto University of Advanced Science, Kyoto, Japan
e-mail: tokuga.yoshihiro.6m@kyoto-u.ac.jp

T. Yamashita
Faculty of Economics, Department of Business Administration, Fukui Prefectural University, Fukui, Japan

Y. Tokuga, M. Yoneyama (eds.), *Controversies Over Accounting for Goodwill*, Contributions to Finance and Accounting,
https://doi.org/10.1007/978-981-92-0156-3_2

Table 2.1 ASAF membership (illustrative: Mar. 2025)

Region	Members
Africa	Pan African Federation of Accountants (PAFA)
Americas	Canadian Accounting Standards Board (AcSB) Financial Accounting Standards Board, USA (FASB) Group of Latin American Accounting Standard Setters (GLASS)
Asia-Oceania (including two at large)	Accounting Regulatory Department, Ministry of Finance, China (ARD) Accounting Standards Board of Japan (ASBJ) Australian Accounting Standards Board (AASB) and external reporting board, New Zealand (XRB), referred together as AASB/XRB Saudi Organization for Chartered and Professional Accountants (SOCPA) Asian-Oceanian Standard-Setters Group (AOSSG)
Europe (including two at large)	Accounting Standards Committee of Germany (ASCG) Autorité des Normes Comptables, France (ANC) Organismo Italiano di Contabilita, Italy (OIC) UK Endorsement Board (UKEB) EFRAG

Source: Accounting Standards Advisory Forum, meeting (24–25 Mar. 2025), summarized by IASB

IASB's preliminary views on potential reforms, extensive consultations, further deliberations, and ultimately an Exposure Draft (ED, IASB (2024)).

In 2022, after evaluating feedback on the DP, the IASB tentatively decided not to reintroduce systematic amortization of goodwill. However, the broader project continued—focusing on targeted improvements to the impairment test and enhanced disclosure requirements—and subsequently culminated in the 2024 Exposure Draft.

Against this background, this chapter argues that the persistence of the goodwill accounting problem within the IASB cannot be solely attributed to technical disagreements over measurement methods. Instead, the central difficulty arises from the unresolved tension between the definition of goodwill and its alignment with the asset concept in the Conceptual Framework. By focusing on this conceptual dimension, the chapter aims to clarify why repeated reform attempts have failed to yield a definitive resolution.

Despite over 9 years of deliberations within the IASB and ASAF—more than a decade if the period up to the publication of the Exposure Draft is included—the outcome seems, at least superficially, to resemble the pre-deliberation position (impairment-only with no major changes). This chapter does not interpret this outcome as evidence of the IASB's rigid commitment to the impairment-only approach. Instead, it examines whether the result reflects an extensive process of experimentation and reconsideration, during which various alternatives were explored but ultimately set aside. The following sections analyze this process of trial and error to clarify why the debates over goodwill accounting did not converge on a definitive solution.

Broadly speaking, the analysis shows that during this period, the IASB gradually shifted from a measurement-centric to a disclosure-centric approach, emphasizing user orientation. To clarify this transformation, the chapter organizes the IASB/

ASAF discussions into three interrelated dimensions: (1) theoretical and conceptual issues, (2) practical application issues, and (3) institutional and standard-setting constraints. Based on this analytical framework, the chapter examines why discussions on goodwill accounting failed to converge on a definitive resolution.

Drawing on this framework, Sect. 2.2.1 examines the Post-implementation Review of IFRS 3, *Business Combinations* (PiR 3), identifying the conceptual and practical challenges revealed through the review. Sect. 2.2.2 addresses the efforts to simplify impairment testing in response to concerns regarding complexity and cost, focusing primarily on practical application issues. Sect. 2.2.3 analyzes discussions regarding the nature of goodwill, highlighting key theoretical and conceptual issues. Sect. 2.2.4 reviews alternative measurement approaches proposed to supplement or replace the impairment-only model, underscoring theoretical and institutional dimensions. Sect. 2.2.5 elucidates the IASB's gradual shift from a measurement-centric to a disclosure-centric approach—a transition shaped by both practical constraints and institutional considerations. Finally, Sect. 2.3 evaluates the overall outcomes of the IASB/ASAF deliberations from the perspective of these three interrelated dimensions.

2.2 Evolution of IASB/ASAF Deliberations

2.2.1 Post-implementation Review of IFRS 3 Business Combinations

PiR 3 conducted by IASB since October 2011 (IASB July 2013), concluded with the publication of the report and feedback statement *Post-implementation Review of IFRS 3 Business Combinations* in June 2015 (IASB 2015). The PiR assessed whether IFRS 3 was achieving its intended objectives and whether the information provided by the Standard was useful to users of financial statements. While the review concluded that IFRS 3 largely met its original objectives, it identified goodwill accounting as an area requiring further study. These findings formally triggered the IASB's Goodwill and Impairment project, which became one of the longest-running PiR standard-setting initiatives.

In particular, the PiR highlighted two project streams related to goodwill. The first concerned the effectiveness and complexity of the impairment-only approach to accounting for goodwill, particularly the cost and subjectivity involved in applying the impairment test. The second addressed the broader issue of subsequent accounting for goodwill, evaluating whether the impairment-only approach reflects the consumption or decline of goodwill over time, or whether alternative measurement approaches should be considered to address concerns about the "too little, too late" recognition of impairment losses.

These two aspects framed the IASB's subsequent Goodwill and Impairment project. The IASB examined whether the impairment-only approach could be improved through simplifications or modifications to address concerns about complexity, cost, and delayed recognition of impairments. It also considered whether more fundamental changes to subsequent accounting for goodwill were necessary, including the possible reintroduction of amortization or the adoption of alternative measurement models.

An essential feature of the PiR process was the extensive outreach conducted with stakeholders, the results of which are summarized in the IASB's *Feedback Statement on the Implementation of IFRS 3* (IASB 2015). Notably, the IASB analyzed investor feedback separately from that of other respondents, such as preparers, auditors, and regulators. This distinction reveals that the controversy surrounding goodwill accounting was not merely technical; it reflected fundamentally different perspectives on the role of accounting information and the objectives of financial reporting.

Feedback from investors showed divided views on the impairment-only approach. Some preferred reintroducing systematic amortization of goodwill, arguing that goodwill acquired in a business combination is, over time, supported and replaced by internally generated goodwill. They contended that estimating the useful life of goodwill is feasible and comparable to estimating the useful lives of other intangible assets, and that goodwill represents a paid-for investment that should ultimately affect profit or loss. From this perspective, amortization was seen as a means of reducing volatility in reported earnings relative to an impairment-only model and easing pressures associated with identifying and separately recognizing intangible assets (IASB (2015), pp. 21–22).

Conversely, other investors supported the impairment-only approach. These respondents emphasized that impairment testing provides valuable information by linking the price paid in an acquisition to the assets acquired, thereby facilitating assessments of returns on invested capital. They viewed impairment losses as critical for evaluating management stewardship and verifying whether acquisitions are performing as expected. This divergence among investors indicates that even within the user community, there was no consensus on whether goodwill should be treated primarily as an asset subject to valuation-based testing or as an investment whose cost should be systematically allocated over time (IASB (2015), pp. 21–22).

In contrast, feedback from preparers and other non-investor participants focused on operational challenges associated with the impairment-only approach. Common concerns included difficulties in determining appropriate pre-tax discount rates for value-in-use calculations; limitations of the value-in-use model, such as restrictions on including expansion capital expenditures in cash flow projections; and reliance on the most recent approved budgets, which may significantly diverge from the business plans underlying the original acquisition. Respondents also noted the lag between economic impairment and its recognition in financial statements, the high costs of performing annual impairment tests without impairment indicators, and the substantial subjectivity involved in key assumptions. Additional issues included the allocation of goodwill to cash-generating units and the need to reallocate goodwill after restructurings, both seen as complex and judgment-intensive (IASB (2015), pp. 21–22).

Taken together, the outreach results documented in the PiR 3 revealed that the goodwill accounting debate involved multiple, intersecting fault lines, including differences between investors and preparers, divergences within the investor community, and tensions between conceptual preferences and practical constraints. Importantly, these differences anticipated issues that would later dominate the IASB/ASAF deliberations, such as debates over income statement versus balance sheet orientations, allocation-based versus valuation-based models, and the balance between recognition and measurement versus disclosure.

Accordingly, the PiR 3 did not resolve the goodwill accounting issue but served as the foundation for a prolonged and multifaceted standard-setting process. By identifying goodwill as a persistent problem area and documenting diverse, sometimes conflicting stakeholder views, the PiR laid the groundwork for the subsequent 9-year deliberative process by the IASB and ASAF. The following sections examine how these concerns were addressed through efforts to simplify impairment testing, explore the nature of goodwill, evaluate alternative measurement approaches, and reconsider the role of disclosure in addressing the informational challenges associated with goodwill accounting.

2.2.2 *Simplification of Impairment Testing*

PiR 3 identified two main concerns regarding the impairment-only model: operational complexity and high costs of impairment testing, and the tendency for impairment losses to be recognized "too little, too late," partly due to multiple shielding effects—namely, the existence of unrecognized headroom at the acquisition date and the subsequent generation of internally created goodwill that is not recognized on the balance sheet.[2] The resulting interaction between recognized goodwill and unrecognized economic value within the reporting unit is often described as a "two-layer structure.

In response, IASB/ASAF deliberations focused on three areas: (1) simplifying or improving the impairment-only model, (2) developing alternative measurement approaches to replace the impairment-only model, and (3) addressing deficiencies primarily through enhanced disclosure.

PiR 3 criticized impairment testing, highlighting that IFRS 3 requires an acquiring entity to compare the carrying amount of goodwill with its recoverable amount within the related cash-generating unit (CGU). An impairment loss is recognized if

[2] Two types of shielding effects are considered. The first shielding effect refers to the presence of unrecognized headroom that already existed in the acquirer at the acquisition date, which can mask subsequent declines in the value of recognized goodwill when impairment tests are performed. The second shielding effect refers to the creation of internally generated goodwill after the acquisition, which is not recognized on the balance sheet and may further offset declines in the carrying amount of recognized goodwill. Measurement approaches addressing both or either of these shielding effects were proposed.

the recoverable amount is lower than the carrying amount, defined as the higher of value in use and fair value less costs of disposal. The complexity of this procedure and the high costs of estimating value in use, fair value, and disposal costs were deemed problematic. Concerns were also raised regarding management discretion influencing the choice of recoverable amounts.

In response, the IASB considered proposals to simplify the impairment test, including replacing the dual measurement criteria with a single measurement criterion (the "single-method") and substituting the mandatory annual impairment test with an indicator-based approach that requires impairment testing only when an impairment indicator exists (See Table 2.2). However, the single-method was not adopted because it would likely increase subjective judgment in selecting the measurement basis. Additionally, the existing measurement criteria serve different economic circumstances; thus, consolidating them into a single criterion could reduce the quality of information for users. Furthermore, entities would still need to perform calculations under both criteria before selecting one, limiting expected cost savings (See Table 2.2). The indicator-based approach was also rejected on the grounds that it would reduce the usefulness of impairment information.

These limitations of impairment test simplification led the IASB and ASAF to shift the focus from how to test goodwill for impairment to fundamental questions about the nature of goodwill itself. Since simplification could not address the delayed recognition problem without increasing subjectivity concerns, attention turned to whether the problem stemmed from the assumption of what goodwill represents.

Table 2.2 Simplification of impairment test

Proposed solutions	Explanation of the solution	Main proposer	Adopted or not adopted	Reason for adoption/ rejection
Single method	Single method is replacing the "higher of value in use and fair value less costs of disposal" with a single measurement basis, one of them.	IASB	Not adopted	Each measure captures different economic perspectives, and adopting only one would reduce the decision usefulness of impairment testing without delivering meaningful cost reductions.
Indicator-based (impairment test) approach	An approach that eliminates the mandatory quantitative impairment test conducted each fiscal period (annual impairment test) and instead performs a quantitative impairment test only when impairment indicators are present.	IASB	Not adopted	Users (investors and analysts) strongly expressed concern that "the timing of goodwill impairment would be entirely left to management's discretion." This also raised issues regarding auditability, and the IASB could not accept the systemic risk of "diminished reliability of financial reporting."

2.2.3 Nature of Goodwill

Several reasons may explain why discussions on goodwill accounting failed to converge, but a primary cause was the inability to define goodwill clearly. In philosophical and epistemological terms, a conceptual definition concerns what an object is understood to be. In contrast, an operational definition specifies how it is identified or measured within a given system. These definitions coexist in the IASB/ASAF discussions on goodwill.

One approach seeks to define goodwill arising from a business combination, termed the conceptual definition of real-world goodwill. The other defines accounting goodwill (the residual amount or difference) resulting from the recognition and measurement of real-world goodwill, known as the operational definition.

The IASB/ASAF addressed the shortcomings of the impairment-only approach—particularly the "too little, too late" issue—while prioritizing the discussion on the nature of goodwill. Since impairment-only falls under valuation-based models within the measurement approach, examining alternatives to impairment-only or improving impairment-only itself necessitates prior discussion of the nature of goodwill. The valuation approach addresses "how to measure," but requires clarity on "what to measure" as a prerequisite. This necessitates a conceptual definition of real-world goodwill. However, as the exploration of real-world goodwill progressed, inconsistencies with the asset concept in the Conceptual Framework (IASB 2018) became evident, as several proposed elements of goodwill do not meet the definition of an economic resource under that framework.

During the period under consideration, the primary conceptual definitions proposed for goodwill at ASAF meetings are summarized in Table 2.3.[3] These definitions can be further subdivided based on the real-world elements they refer to: future benefits (e.g., Expected future economic benefits, Future excess earnings/economic rents, Synergies from business combinations); intangible assets (e.g., Unrecognized intangible assets, Intangibles that cannot be separately identified); items of questionable economic value (e.g., overpayment/overpricing, Acquisition premium/Control premium); and mixed/intermediate definitions (e.g., Residual business value).[4]

These proposals highlight that the goodwill recorded across jurisdictions worldwide comprises diverse elements. It may include definitions indicating economic

---

[3] Table 2.3 summarizes proposals about what goodwill is; Table 2.4 summarizes proposals about how goodwill is operationally derived under acquisition accounting. These definitions were proposed by various jurisdictions during ASAF meetings and are neither exclusive nor independent. Consequently, the content indicated by some definitions may overlap.

[4] While it is a real-world business value, the term "Residual" also indicates it is the result of a subtraction operation. In other words, it could be considered an operational/conceptual definition.

Table 2.3 Conceptual definitions

Conceptual definitions (in the real world)	Meeting year and month
Expected future economic benefits[a]	Dec. 2015; July 2017
Conceptual definitions (in the real world)	Meeting year and month
Future excess earnings (economic rents, benefits in excess of normal returns)[b]	Dec. 2013; June 2014; June 2015. Dec. 2015
Synergies arising from the business combination (a bundle of expected synergies, going concern synergies)	Dec. 2014; Mar. 2016; July 2017. June 2019
Residual business value[c]	July 2016; Dec. 2016
Unrecognized intangible assets	Dec. 2015
Intangibles that cannot be separately identified	Dec. 2015
Overpayment (overpricing)[d]	Dec. 2015; July 2017
Acquisition premium[e]	Dec. 2015; July 2017
Control premium[f]	Dec. 2015; July 2017

[a]Here, unlike in the Conceptual Framework, the inclusion of "expected" reflects an emphasis on anticipated economic benefits and uncertainty, rather than a purely abstract asset definition

[b]Future excess earnings result from economic rents

[c]This definition occupies an intermediate position between conceptual and operational definitions

[d]Overpayment arises from intentional or unintentional overpricing

[e]An acquisition premium refers to the excess of the consideration transferred over the fair value of the acquiree's identifiable net assets at the acquisition date. Elements often argued to be included in goodwill

[f]A control premium is the additional amount paid by an acquirer to obtain control over an entity, reflecting the value of control-related benefits such as decision-making authority and access to future synergies

value, such as future excess profits or synergies, as well as items like overpayment and acquisition premium,[5] which do not necessarily hold economic value.

Conceptually, no observable constraint bounds the proportion of "noises (non-asset components)"[6] embedded in goodwill. In purely logical terms, this proportion could range from none to the entirety of the reported goodwill. However, because this composition is unobservable, the precise proportion cannot be empirically estimated. The average mixture ratio would likely vary by jurisdiction, industry,

[5]The term "acquisition premium" is a definition encompassing various elements, as is "control premium." For example, a control premium represents the additional consideration paid by the acquiring company to achieve 100% ownership of the target company, but it does not necessarily possess economic value in and of itself. That is, part of it may include overpayments resulting from management's personal motives or the competitive acquisition process. On the other hand, to the extent that full ownership through 100% control brings future economic benefits by clarifying the chain of command and accelerating decision-making, a portion of the control premium can be interpreted as having economic value.

[6]Noises, such as overpayments, do not translate into future cash flows; however, arguably, if impairment testing functions adequately, it should naturally be recognized as an impairment loss. That is, impairment testing was expected to function as a mechanism for resolving definitional issues.

management optimism, and the competitive landscape of individual M&A deals. Therefore, the degree of this mixture varies across M&A transactions.

Conversely, the definition of an asset in the IASB's Conceptual Framework (IASB 2018) states:

> An asset is a present economic resource controlled by the entity as a result of past events. (IASB (2018), 4.3)

> An economic resource is a right that has the potential to produce economic benefits. (IASB (2018), 4.14)

According to the Conceptual Framework's definition of an asset, "non-asset components," such as overpayments, are clearly excluded. Based on this definition, goodwill includes both asset and non-asset elements,[7] with the proportion of each remaining unknown. This creates a tension between the conceptual definition of goodwill[8] and the Conceptual Framework.

The FASB (1976) Discussion Memorandum, though an early document, remains among the few authoritative standard-setting texts that explicitly distinguish between definitions reflecting economic reality ("real-world definitions") and those structured around their financial representation (FASB [1976], A-1). The former approach was ultimately adopted (FASB 1976, Appendix A). Later conceptual frameworks, including the IASB (2018), emphasize the notion of economic resources and faithful representation; nevertheless, they do not explicitly articulate the issue in terms of the real-world versus representational definition dichotomy advanced in FASB (1976).

On the other hand, as shown in Table 2.4, numerous operational definitions have been proposed at the ASAF meetings. Terms such as "Residual," "Accounting construct," and "Record of past investment decisions" are presented as differences or balances arising from acquisition accounting mechanics. In other words, they assume goodwill is a single asset (single-asset approach) and aim to define its substance based on the accounting procedures' process and outcome.

Such definitions are also found in the current IFRS 3 (IASB (2008)). The definition of goodwill in IFRS 3 (IASB (2008)) states:

---

[7] The definition of assets in APB Statement No. 4 (AICPA (1970), para. 132) has the following structure: assets consist of economic resources and non-economic resources (i.e., non-assets = the second sentence). "Assets — economic resources of an enterprise that are recognized and measured in conformity with generally accepted accounting principles. Assets also include certain deferred charges that are not resources but that are recognized and measured in conformity with generally accepted accounting principles." This structure is conceptually similar to the asset definition in APB Statement No. 4, which was widely criticized by academics and practitioners in the United States.

[8] As shown in Table 2.3, conceptual discussions on the nature of goodwill within the IASB/ASAF were largely confined to the period between 2015 and 2017. A continued exploration of the conceptual definition of goodwill would have inevitably led to a reconsideration of the asset definition in the Conceptual Framework. In this context, the IASB/ASAF appear to have chosen to retain the existing operational definition of goodwill under IFRS 3, thereby avoiding broader conceptual revisions.

Table 2.4 Operational definition

Operational definitions	Meeting year and month
Residual (residual amount/ Calculated difference/Calculated residual)	July 2016, July 2017, Sep. 2017, Mar. 2018, Dec. 2018, Nov. 2019, Apr. 2020
Accounting construct	July 2017
Plug figure (balancing item)[a]	July 2017
Fair value of identifiable net assets[b]	July 2016, July 2017
By-product of the acquisition accounting model[c]	July 2017
Not a directly observable asset (assumption-based asset[d])	July 2016, July 2017
Record of past investment decisions	Dec. 2020, Mar. 2022

[a]"Plug figure" is not an official ASAF term. It was used descriptively, primarily from a user perspective, in the 2016–2017 ASAF discussions to characterize goodwill as having limited informational usefulness

[b]The explanation of goodwill as a residual measured with reference to the fair value of identifiable net assets originates in IFRS 3 (Appendix A, B63)

[c]The explanation that goodwill is a by-product conveys the idea that goodwill does not represent a distinct economic asset in itself, but rather comes into being as a result of applying the acquisition accounting model

[d]The term "assumption-based" indicates that goodwill, as an asset that is not directly observable, relies heavily on management assumptions, particularly in impairment testing

> Goodwill is an asset representing the future economic benefits arising from other assets acquired in a business combination that are not individually identified and separately recognized (IASB (2008), Appendix A (Defined terms)).

This definition indicates that goodwill is a single asset (under the single-asset approach) and that it represents future economic benefits rather than the benefits themselves. While mindful of the Conceptual Framework in its phrasing, this remains an operational definition.

Goodwill may contain "noise," and its precise composition is unclear. Examining it further would increase the tension with the Conceptual Framework. Therefore, the IASB/ASAF retained the definition of goodwill as per IFRS 3, using terminology from the Conceptual Framework's definition of an asset to establish an operational definition, thereby halting further debate over whether it constitutes an asset.

2.2.4 Measurement Approaches

One key issue identified in PiR 3 was that the impairment-only approach led to impairment losses being recognized "too little, too late." In response, the IASB considered whether to improve the impairment-only model or develop alternative measurement approaches. A central factor identified was the shielding effect, where unrecognized economic value delays goodwill impairment recognition.

Before examining individual measurement approaches, it is essential to clarify the relationship between the definition and measurement of goodwill. Although the IASB/ASAF retained an operational definition of goodwill, there was broad recognition that, in the real world, goodwill is a composite of heterogeneous elements. If measurement were to align with this understanding, the Discernible Elements Approach[9] proposed by EFRAG would be a natural candidate. This approach does not prescribe specific measurement techniques; instead, it links goodwill's nature to measurement by applying appropriate methods to each identifiable element.

However, the Discernible Elements Approach was not adopted. Decomposing goodwill into elements was considered technically challenging, highly subjective, and costly to implement. Additionally, some components—such as overpayment—were inconsistent with the asset definition in the Conceptual Framework (IASB 2018). Continued reliance on a conceptual definition of goodwill would have led to fundamental tensions with the asset concept. In contrast, the operational definition in IFRS 3 treats goodwill as a single asset without reopening these foundational issues. Consequently, the single-asset approach was adopted. Table 2.5 summarizes how considerations regarding the nature of goodwill influenced the choice of measurement approaches.

Table 2.5 The relationship between the nature of goodwill and its measurement methods

Proposed solutions	Explanation of the solution	Main proposer	Adopted or not adopted	Reason for adoption/ rejection
Discernible elements approach	Goodwill is treated as comprising multiple separately identifiable elements. Each element would be assigned an appropriate measurement method.	EFRAG	Not adopted	Goodwill cannot be reliably disaggregated (technical difficulties, considerable room for subjective judgment). Measuring each element individually is costly.
Single-asset approach	Goodwill is treated as a single unit of account, without disaggregation into separately identifiable elements.	IASB	Not adopted	Consistency with IFRS 3's acquisition accounting mechanics; operational feasibility; avoidance of redefining assets/ revisiting the Conceptual Framework.

[9] The Discernible elements approach indicates that goodwill consists of diverse elements, each requiring an appropriate measurement method, but it does not specify particular measurement methods. The Discernible Element Approach was proposed as a model that assesses impairment at the level of internal, identifiable value components to overcome the limitations of current impairment tests that treat goodwill as a simple residual. Therefore, it is compatible with valuation-based models.

Against this background, the measurement approaches discussed at IASB/ASAF meetings (Tables 2.6 and 2.7) can be classified into allocation-based and valuation-based models. Allocation-based models do not require a precise conceptual definition of goodwill; once recognized as a residual, goodwill may be allocated as a cost over time regardless of its underlying economic composition. Valuation-based models, however, attempt to measure goodwill directly, necessitating a more precise articulation of what goodwill represents. Thus, the question "What is goodwill?" becomes significantly more consequential under valuation-based models. This distinction parallels the broader conflict between the income statement and balance sheet approaches to financial reporting.

Table 2.6 Allocation-based approaches

	Proposed solutions	Explanation of the solution	Main proposer	Adopted or not adopted	Reason for adoption or rejection
Allocation	Systematic amortization	Amortization refers to applying depreciation methods such as the straight-line method, declining balance method, or accelerated depreciation method to goodwill.	ASBJ	Not adopted	⑤ ⑥ ⑦ ⑪
	Consumption based allocation approach (CBAA)	It treats acquired goodwill as a source of future excess earnings and allocates its carrying amount over time on the premise that its economic benefits are gradually consumed. While it relies on valuation inputs, such as discounted cash flow estimates, these inputs are used to inform the allocation pattern rather than to remeasure goodwill. (ASBJ/EFRAG/OIC (2014), ASAF (2018))	EFRAG	Not adopted	① ② ④ ⑤ ⑩
Recognition based approach	Direct write-off approaches	Direct write-off approaches immediately eliminate goodwill through recognition in profit or loss, equity, or other comprehensive income.	IASB	Not adopted	⑨

Table 2.7 Valuation-based models

	Proposed solutions	Explanation of the solution	Main proposer	Adopted or not adopted	Reason for adoption or rejection
Valuation	Impairment-only approach	Goodwill is the intangible asset recognized at the acquisition date when the consideration transferred, including non-controlling interest and previously held equity interests, exceeds the net identifiable assets acquired and liabilities assumed. (IASB (2008, 2018): IFRS 3)	IASB	Retained	① ② ③ ④ ⑦
	Headroom approach	The headroom approach involves identifying the headroom (recoverable amount-carrying amount) of the cash-generating unit (CGU) in each impairment test period. If a decrease in the recoverable amount occurs, this approach allocates the decrease first to the acquired goodwill. This approach is intended to address both the first and second shielding effects.	IASB	Not adopted	① ② ④ ⑤ ⑧
	Goodwill accretion approach	Under the goodwill accretion approach, accretion is applied only notionally for the purpose of impairment testing and does not result in an increase in the recognized carrying amount of goodwill. Accretion is therefore an analytical adjustment rather than a recognition or remeasurement of goodwill on the balance sheet.	EFRAG	Not adopted	① ② ③ ④ ⑥ ⑧
	PH approach	The pre-acquisition headroom (PH) approach conceptually adjusts impairment testing by isolating the portion of headroom that existed prior to the business combination, with the aim of preventing internally generated headroom from shielding acquired goodwill from impairment. It represents an analytical extension of the headroom approach, highlighting rather than remedying its conceptual and practical limitations.	IASB	Not adopted	① ② ③ ④ ⑤ ⑧

One allocation-based model considered was systematic amortization.[10] PiR 3 proposed amortization combined with impairment as an alternative to the impairment-only model, and the IASB/ASAF devoted considerable attention to this option. Systematic amortization was favored for its simplicity, low implementation cost, and its ability to convey management's intended investment recovery period through the amortization schedule. Nevertheless, it was not adopted, primarily because amortization does not reflect changes in the economic value of goodwill, rendering both amortization expense and the amortized carrying amount of goodwill of limited informational value, and because determining useful life allows substantial management discretion.[11]

In contrast, the consumption-based allocation approach seeks to allocate goodwill based on the pattern of consumption of underlying economic benefits, typically expressed in terms of expected excess earnings. While motivated by allocation, this approach fundamentally differs from systematic amortization in that it requires valuation techniques to estimate the timing and magnitude of economic consumption. It occupies an intermediate position between pure allocation-based models and valuation-based models. Although conceptually attractive, it was not adopted due to its reliance on forward-looking estimates, measurement uncertainty, and high implementation costs.

Within valuation-based models, the impairment-only approach serves as the benchmark. To address its shortcomings, several modifications were examined. One was the pre-acquisition headroom (PH) approach, discussed in the March and April 2016 IASB Board meetings. Under this approach, pre-acquisition headroom—defined as the excess of a unit's recoverable amount over its carrying amount at the acquisition date using pre-acquisition assumptions—is incorporated into the impairment test. This seeks to eliminate shielding present at the time of acquisition (the first shielding effect).

However, the PH approach does not address the headroom generated after acquisition. To overcome this limitation, the IASB later explored the headroom approach, which reallocates part of the decline in the value of a cash-generating unit containing goodwill to acquired goodwill, rather than allowing unrecognized headroom to absorb losses first. While the headroom approach reduces shielding, it does not eliminate it entirely and may be viewed as a continuous and general

[10] Among the measurement approaches discussed within the IASB/ASAF, systematic amortization may be regarded as the only approach that can be characterized as a purely allocation-based model. Under systematic amortization, goodwill is treated operationally as an investment whose cost is allocated over a predetermined recovery period, regardless of its underlying economic composition. By contrast, the consumption-based allocation model is likewise motivated by allocation—specifically, by the desire to rationalize expense recognition over time—but it requires valuation techniques to estimate the pattern of consumption of excess earnings. It may therefore be more appropriately characterized as a valuation-based allocation model.

[11] Other reasons cited for non-adoption include concerns that amortization could discourage M&A activity by adversely affecting reported performance or solvency, as well as the potential weakening of the signaling role of impairment losses.

extension of the PH approach, addressing post-acquisition headroom (the second shielding effect).

Another valuation-based proposal was the goodwill accretion approach, advanced by EFRAG in 2017. This approach conceptualizes acquired goodwill as the present value of future excess earnings and applies notional accretion for impairment testing. Although praised for addressing the "too little, too late" problem, accretion does not increase the recognized carrying amount of goodwill and has been criticized for allowing goodwill to increase in value without new transactions, thereby creating tension with the asset definition in the Conceptual Framework. Additionally, it was seen as technically complex, costly, and prone to managerial discretion.

Direct write-off approaches—whether through profit or loss, equity, or other comprehensive income—were also discussed. These methods immediately eliminate goodwill, resolving the timing problem mechanically. However, they were rejected due to concerns about the loss of decision-useful information and issues of stewardship and accountability.

Overall, none of the proposed measurement approaches—allocation-based or valuation-based—were adopted. As summarized in Tables 2.6 and 2.7, the primary reasons related to practicability constraints include technical difficulty, complexity, cost, and limited incremental information benefits. These constraints are relative and context-dependent, but in the case of goodwill accounting, they proved decisive.

Consequently, the IASB/ASAF concluded that the "too little, too late" problem could not be resolved satisfactorily through measurement reform alone. This realization marked a turning point in the project, leading to a shift from a measurement-centric to a disclosure-centric strategy, which is examined in the next section.

2.2.5 *From Measurement-Centric Approach to Disclosure-Centric Approach*

As highlighted in the Post-implementation Review of IFRS 3 (PiR 3), the impairment-only approach has been criticized for recognizing impairment losses "too little, too late."

The IASB's response to this problem in goodwill accounting indicates a shift from a measurement-centric to a disclosure-centric approach. The IASB and ASAF explored various alternative measurement models, including allocation-based approaches, valuation-based models, and modifications to the impairment-only model. However, none were adopted due to concerns about practicability, including technical difficulty, complexity, cost, and management discretion.

This outcome reflects a broader judgment that further refinement of recognition and measurement would not necessarily enhance the usefulness of financial information and could increase complexity and subjectivity. Consequently, the IASB shifted its focus to disclosure as the primary means of addressing the informational deficiencies associated with goodwill impairment.

Evidence of this shift can be found in the trajectory of the Goodwill and Impairment project itself.[12] Early stages emphasized improving impairment testing mechanics, while later discussions focused on enhanced disclosures as a more feasible response to users' information needs. Ultimately, the IASB concluded that the limitations of goodwill measurement could not be addressed satisfactorily through changes in recognition and measurement alone; therefore, disclosure should play a more prominent role in communicating information about acquisitions and subsequent performance.

Importantly, this movement toward a disclosure-centric approach is not unique to goodwill accounting; it aligns with a broader evolution in the IASB's Conceptual Framework.[13] The Conceptual Framework (IASB 2018) no longer views disclosure as merely supplementary to recognition and measurement. It characterizes

[12] The shift toward a disclosure-centric approach is clearly observable in the transition from the Discussion Paper (IASB 2020) to the Exposure Draft (IASB 2024) in the Goodwill and Impairment project.

In the Discussion Paper, the IASB's preliminary views proposed extensive disclosures based on information monitored by the chief operating decision maker (CODM), including acquisition objectives, performance metrics used to assess whether those objectives were being met, and changes in such metrics over time. The Discussion Paper also proposed expanding the disclosure objectives of IFRS 3 to include information enabling investors to understand both the benefits expected at the acquisition date and the extent to which those benefits were subsequently realized.

In contrast, the Exposure Draft refines and institutionalizes these proposals by narrowing their scope and increasing their operability. In particular, the Exposure Draft focuses on strategically significant business combinations identified through a threshold approach, shifts the emphasis from CODM-based monitoring to information reviewed by key management personnel, and introduces structured exemptions from disclosure where providing certain information could seriously prejudice the achievement of the acquisition's objectives.

This evolution should not be interpreted as a retreat from the disclosure-centric orientation articulated in the Discussion Paper. Rather, it reflects a process of institutional refinement, through which exploratory disclosure ideas were transformed into a disclosure regime capable of functioning as an enforceable accounting standard.

[13] The role of disclosure in financial reporting differs markedly between the IASC's Conceptual Framework (1989) and the IASB's Conceptual Framework (2018).

Under the IASC Framework, financial reporting was centered on recognized elements of the financial statements. Disclosure, primarily through notes, was treated as "explanatory material" accompanying the balance sheet and income statement (IASC 1989, para. 7), and the usefulness of financial statements was framed largely in terms of information about financial position and performance (IASC (1989), para. 12).

By contrast, the IASB's Conceptual Framework explicitly integrates disclosure into the structure of general purpose financial reporting. The Framework recognizes that information useful to users is conveyed through both recognized amounts and disclosures, and emphasizes that disclosure provides descriptions and explanations "necessary for users to understand the information in [the] statements" (IASB (2018), para. 7.2). Moreover, the Framework acknowledges that recognition and measurement may fail to provide relevant or faithfully representative information in cases of high uncertainty, in which case disclosure plays a substantive role in communicating information to users (IASB (2018), para. 2.39).

general-purpose financial reports as a combination of recognized amounts and disclosures that collectively provide useful information to users.

The Framework acknowledges that recognition and measurement may not always provide sufficiently relevant or faithful information, especially when uncertainty is high, measurement is costly, or measurement is subjective. In such cases, disclosure plays a critical role in explaining the nature of recognized items, the assumptions used, and the uncertainties involved (IASB 2018). Thus, disclosure is positioned as an integral component of financial reporting, rather than a secondary explanatory device.

From this perspective, the IASB's increased reliance on disclosure in the goodwill project reflects the broader principles in the Conceptual Framework, not an ad hoc retreat from measurement reform. This shift indicates an institutional judgment that, when measurement reaches its practical limits, disclosure may better serve the objective of providing decision-useful information.

Although recent developments—most notably the IASB's 2024 Exposure Draft on Business Combinations: Disclosures, Goodwill and Impairment (IASB (2024)[14]—have further elaborated disclosure requirements related to business combinations and goodwill, these reforms remain focused on information provision rather than revisiting the underlying measurement model.

2.3 Concluding Remarks-Overall Outcomes of IASB/ASAF's 9-Year Deliberative Process-

After nearly a decade of deliberation, the outcomes of the IASB/ASAF discussions are striking. Efforts to refine the conceptual definition of goodwill ultimately returned to the operational definition in IFRS 3, while the exploration of alternative measurement approaches did not displace the impairment-only model. Thus, the long-running debate concluded with a reaffirmation of IFRS 3's original architecture.

As discussed in Sects. 2.2.2 through 2.2.5, the deliberations revealed persistent practical difficulties in impairment testing, conceptual ambiguities surrounding the nature of goodwill, and increasing reliance on disclosure-based solutions. However, this outcome does not reflect a lack of analytical effort or technical capability from IASB or ASAF members. Instead, it stems from two broader conditions: the IASB's gradual shift toward a more disclosure-oriented view of financial reporting and the inherently complex nature of goodwill, which involves theoretical, practical, and institutional dimensions. These conditions indicate that the encountered difficulties were structural and not easily resolved by any single set of measurement or definitional refinements.

[14] See IASB (2024), Business Combinations—Disclosures, Goodwill and Impairment, Exposure Draft. The ED proposes enhanced disclosures focusing, inter alia, on management objectives for business combinations, subsequent performance of acquisitions, and information intended to help users assess whether acquisitions have met their objectives.

Building on this analysis, this concluding section synthesizes the reasons why the IASB/ASAF deliberations ultimately reaffirmed IFRS 3's original architecture.

Furthermore, this debate has highlighted several fundamental trade-offs in standard-setting that extend beyond the specific issue of goodwill accounting.

A key point is that the IASB/ASAF discussions on goodwill accounting did not unfold along a single analytical dimension but arose across three interrelated dimensions: (1) theoretical and conceptual issues, (2) practical application problems,[15] and (3) concerns regarding standard-setting judgments.[16] The first dimension includes questions about the definition of goodwill, consistency among definition, recognition, and measurement, alignment with the conceptual framework, and conflicting views on the nature of accounting. The second dimension includes practical concerns raised by preparers, auditors, and users, such as complexity, difficulty in understanding, technical implementation challenges, cost-benefit considerations, and the substantial negative impact on reported profits and capital from adopting the accounting treatment.[17] The third dimension reflects the IASB's normative judgments as the standard-setter, including whether revising a specific standard is worthwhile (justifying the standard-setting cost) or whether a proposed approach enhances information usefulness. The latter judgement reflects the user's perspective and emphasizes the IASB's commitment to user orientation as a core value.

A significant outcome of these discussions was the shared recognition that pursuing goodwill intensively creates greater tension with the Conceptual Framework's definition of assets. Additionally, as efforts to refine the measurement model increase, its practicality decreases, while reliance on management discretion grows. This does not necessarily enhance the usefulness of the information to users, representing a clear trade-off between conceptual refinement and practical convenience.

The positions observed across jurisdictions can be analytically organized into two ideal-type patterns rather than strictly defined blocks. The first pattern—represented most clearly in the IASB's recent deliberations—supports a conceptual definition of goodwill, adopts a valuation-based measurement model, favors the balance sheet

---

[15] In this chapter, the term *practical issues* refer primarily to concerns raised by stakeholders in accounting standard-setting, in particular financial statement preparers, users, and auditors.

[16] This dimension reflects expressions of the IASB's own accounting-related values and normative beliefs. For example, the degree to which subjectivity in measurement is considered acceptable is heavily influenced by the standard setter's judgment. Similar judgments may, of course, also be made by other stakeholders, so the boundary between these perspectives is not always clear-cut. Nevertheless, for analytical purposes, this chapter distinguishes among three dimensions of issues.

[17] Moreover, concerns about the economic consequences of alternative accounting treatments have also played an important role in the debates. For example, investor organizations such as the CFA Institute have argued that reintroducing mandatory amortization could have substantial negative effects on reported earnings and equity, potentially affecting capital market outcomes. However, the CFA Institute's argument holds true only when goodwill, despite possessing economic value, is fully amortized to zero. In such cases, capital is understated. Yet, the significant economic and social impact of overstating capital when goodwill lacking economic value remains on the balance sheet is well demonstrated by U.S. history.

approach for accounting value, prioritizes user orientation, and leans toward a disclosure-centric approach. The second pattern—most explicitly articulated in statements by the Accounting Standard Borad of Japan (ASBJ)—adopts an operational definition, supports an allocation-based measurement model, favors the income statement approach, maintains a more neutral stance regarding the relationship between users and preparers, and emphasizes that disclosure alone cannot resolve measurement issues. Other jurisdictions exhibit variations across specific issues rather than consistently aligning with one pattern.

The debates illuminate deeper, structurally complex issues inherent to financial accounting, not just goodwill. These include the relationship between the Conceptual Framework and individual standards, the roles of recognition and measurement versus disclosure, competing conceptions of accounting, tensions between theoretical coherence and practical feasibility, and differences between proposals from national standard setters and the normative orientation of the IASB.

Against this broader backdrop, this chapter makes three key contributions to the literature on goodwill and standard-setting. First, it reinterprets the apparent policy "return" to the impairment-only approach not as regulatory inertia, but as the outcome of a prolonged experimentation process restricted by conceptual, practical, and institutional factors. Second, it identifies and theorizes the gradual transition in the IASB's deliberations from a measurement-centric to a disclosure-centric orientation, suggesting a broader transformation in the financial reporting architecture. Third, it demonstrates how the normative commitments and institutional positioning of standard setters delimit the scope of conceptual reform in financial accounting.

The following two chapters progress beyond the institutional deliberations examined here and address goodwill as an object of academic inquiry. Chapter 3 develops a theoretical model to examine whether goodwill should be amortized or impaired under the Purchase Method, abstracting from the practical constraints identified in this chapter. Chapter 4 surveys prior empirical research to assess the empirical evidence concerning goodwill. Furthermore, the cross-jurisdictional differences identified in this chapter may reflect deeper institutional and value-based divergences among stakeholders, a theme that will be further explored in Chap. 5.

Appendix 1

Tomoaki Yamashita

The Goal of This Appendix

This chapter examined discussions on the subsequent accounting for goodwill within the IASB and the ASAF from PiR3 to the IASB's 2022 decision. Later chapters of this book (Chaps. 3 and 4) additionally reviews theoretical and empirical research on goodwill, summarizing previous findings and identifying issues inherent in this area of study. However, they do not address how the academic research discussed may influence accounting standard setting, despite this being relevant to both researchers and practitioners. This Appendix examines the relationship between accounting standard setting and academic research for readers interested in this topic. First, we briefly present the efforts of accounting standard-setting bodies, particularly the IASB, and the related discussions among accounting researchers, considering the recent trend toward evidence-based policymaking.[18] Next, we discuss how academic research may contribute to standard setting and the potential problems that may arise during this process.

Evidence-Based Policymaking and Accounting Standards Setting

In recent years, evidence-based policymaking has become widely recognized in fields such as public and healthcare policy, and this approach has also influenced accounting standards setting. The IASB has increasingly emphasized the use of "evidence" in its standard-setting process, moving toward "evidence-based standard-setting" (Teixeira 2014, p. 5). For example, the IASB and the International Sustainability Standards Board (ISSB) state on their website that they actively use "evidence" in standard setting. The website also notes, "[they] use evidence to support their standard-setting decisions."[19] Regarding the benefits, they state, "Evidence-supported decision-making gives the IASB and the ISSB confidence that they are making appropriate decisions."[20]

The IASB's move toward evidence-based standard setting reflects increasing pressure on accounting standard setters and regulators to adopt evidence-based approaches, as evidence-based policymaking has expanded in related fields (see Leuz 2018, p. 583). The IASB refers to "evidence" as findings from academic research and, as a result, expects accounting researchers to provide academic evidence that can improve accounting standards setting. The IASB has also undertaken several initiatives to collect evidence relevant to accounting standards setting. The post-implementation review (PiR) conducted by the IASB after new accounting standards are implemented serves as an example of such an initiative.[21] The IASB identifies academic research as a source of information considered when deciding

---

[18] The definition of evidence-based policymaking differs among researchers. For example, Leuz (2018, p. 582) defines "evidence-based policymaking as a rigorous attempt to base policy decisions (e.g. new regulation) on scientific and empirical evidence, including impact studies, cost–benefit analyses, programme evaluation, and academic research in general."

[19] https://www.ifrs.org/academics/#evidence-based-standard-setting (Accessed: June 25, 2025)

[20] https://www.ifrs.org/academics/#evidence-based-standard-setting (Accessed: June 25, 2025)

[21] The FASB also conducts PIR. Therefore, the scope for academic research to contribute to accounting standards setting is not necessarily limited to the IASB's standard-setting process.

to initiate a PiR.[22] Furthermore, during the PIR process, the IASB reviews relevant academic research in both the initial stage of identifying issues for investigation and the subsequent stage of evaluating the information and comments collected.[23] This indicates that the standard setter values academic insights as "evidence" useful for decision-making in the standard-setting process.

The standard-setter has also engaged with academic researchers through additional initiatives. For example, a section of its website is dedicated to posting research papers on relevant topics.[24] Research conferences, such as the IASB Research Forum, are organized to facilitate participation by academic researchers, standard-setters, and practitioners. A review of the IASB Research Forum 2024 presentations shows numerous sessions and discussions on key issues, including intangible assets and R&D expenses. At this forum, Professors Stephen Penman and Hyung Il Oh presented "A proposal for goodwill accounting" (Oh and Penman 2025), which addressed post-acquisition accounting for goodwill, the subject of this book. The presentation was followed by a discussion involving both academic researchers and standard-setter representatives.[25,26]

The IASB has also collaborated with academic journals.[27] At the time of writing, a special issue resulting from a partnership between the IASB and the European Accounting Review, the journal of the European Accounting Association, is planned.[28] Additionally, while still in the call-for-papers stage, at the time of writing, submissions are being invited for peer-reviewed pre-registration research proposals on intangible assets, hedge accounting, and other topics on the IASB's work plan.[29] According to the IASB, such initiatives are expected to provide "an opportunity for accounting researchers to engage directly with standard-setters and contribute meaningfully to IFRS Accounting Standards."[30] These efforts demonstrate the IASB's expanded collaboration with academia as part of its approach to gathering "evidence" to inform accounting standards setting.[31]

---

[22] https://www.ifrs.org/projects/post-implementation-reviews/ (Accessed June 25, 2025)

[23] https://www.ifrs.org/projects/post-implementation-reviews/ (Accessed June 25, 2025)

[24] https://www.ifrs.org/academics/#contact-us-and-paper-submission (Accessed: June 25, 2025)

[25] https://www.ifrs.org/news-and-events/events/2024/november/iasb-research-forum-2024/. (Accessed June 25, 2025)

[26] One of the contributors of this book, Yuko Asami, participated in the IASB Research Forum 2017 and presented her research titled "Profit or loss in the IASB Conceptual Framework," which was co-authored with Professor Carien Van Mourik. https://www.ifrs.org/news-and-events/events/2017/november/iasb-research-forum-2017/ (Accessed: July 18, 2025)

[27] IFRS - Resources for academics (Accessed: June 26, 2025)

[28] https://www.ifrs.org/news-and-events/news/2025/06/ear-iasb-launch-special-issue-registered-reports/ (Accessed: June 25, 2025)

[29] https://www.ifrs.org/content/dam/ifrs/news/2025/ear-iasb-call-registered-reports.pdf (Accessed: June 26, 2025)

[30] https://www.ifrs.org/news-and-events/news/2025/06/ear-iasb-launch-special-issue-registered-reports/ (Accessed June 26, 2025)

[31] Such collaboration between accounting standard setters and academia is not unique to the IASB. Campbell and Evans (2024) provide examples of mutual exchanges between standard set-

Evidence-Based Policymaking and Accounting Researchers

In response to the shift toward evidence-based policymaking and standards setting, accounting researchers have increasingly participated in the accounting standards setting process.[32] The academic community has long debated the potential contributions of research to standards setting. Schipper (1994, p. 63) notes that empirical accounting research using archival data is inherently descriptive and explanatory, and therefore does not directly address the normative questions posed by standards setting bodies. However, Schipper (1994, pp. 67–68) also argues that the facts and theoretical predictions produced by accounting research can help identify issues that should be considered when applying concepts such as assets and liabilities to economic events and transactions. Furthermore, Schipper (1994, pp. 69–70) observes that, despite the limitations and challenges of research contributions to standard setting, accounting researchers can use their expertise to provide consulting services for field tests conducted by standard setters.

Recently, many arguments have suggested that accounting researchers not only can contribute to accounting standards setting but should actively participate. One reason is that accounting researchers, along with accounting standard setters and regulators, have responded to the increasing emphasis on evidence-based policymaking and standards setting.[33] For example, Leuz (2018) notes that numerous accounting studies examine the effects of new or revised accounting standards and disclosure regulations, and these studies are highly relevant to policy and regulatory debates. Leuz (2018, p. 585) states, "There is no question in my mind that accounting and financial markets research can contribute valuable insights to standard setters and policymakers." Support is increasing among current accounting scholars for the view that researchers should address conceptual and normative issues relevant to standard setters (e.g., Rajgopal 2021; Fülbier and Sellhorn 2023), which contrasts with the traditional position represented by Schipper (1994). Some researchers suggest that, to address research topics with societal effect, accounting researchers should draw ideas from standard-setters' agendas and engage directly with them (e.g., Garcia Osma et al. 2023, pp. 21–22).

Although these arguments exist, several accounting researchers have expressed concerns that academic research has not yet had sufficient influence on

---

ters and regulators, such as the FASB and SEC, and accounting researchers. Garcia Osma et al. (2023) discuss collaboration between the American Accounting Association (AAA) and the American Institute of Certified Public Accountants (AICPA), while Clor-Proell et al. (2025) note collaboration between the Accounting Review and the PCAOB. These initiatives offer potential channels for academic research to affect the accounting standards setting process, either directly or indirectly.

[32] This section does not offer a comprehensive review of all prior research on the contribution of academic research to accounting standards setting; rather, it presents several representative discussions.

[33] Furthermore, this movement is likely affected by advances in policy evaluation concepts and methodologies in economics and econometrics (see Leuz 2018, p. 587).

accounting standards setting as expected (e.g., Dichev 2020; Garcia Osma et al. 2023; Whittington 2024). For example, Dichev (2020) notes that accounting researchers are less involved in standards setting and accounting practice than those in related fields such as economics, and that research intended to contribute to accounting standards setting is not highly valued in academic journals. He notes that "[s]tandard setters have trouble finding value in the academic literature, and the decisions on standards are rarely driven by research findings" (Dichev 2020, p. 247). Rajgopal (2021, p. 5436) and others have made similar observations. These critiques highlight the ongoing issue of accounting researchers' incentives: while they pursue topics favored by higher-ranked academic journals, they often avoid practical issues, including normative problems related to accounting standards setting (e.g., Singleton-Green 2010; Basu 2012; Rajgopal 2021; Fülbier and Sellhorn 2023).

To address this issue, accounting researchers have discussed potential solutions. One approach is the increasing focus on collaboration between standard-setters and regulators, and academic journals and professional associations, as advocated by some accounting researchers (Garcia Osma et al. 2023, p. 20; Clor-Proell et al. 2025, p. 10). For academic research to be effectively used in the accounting standards setting process, its content must be relevant to the problems faced by accounting standard setters and understandable to them (Schipper 1994). To support this, new initiatives have been proposed, including special issues in journals and new formats, such as handbooks or monographs, to present research findings in ways that are useful to accounting standard setters and practitioners (Clor-Proell et al. 2025, p. 11; Schrand 2019, pp. 14–15).[34]

Some Concerns Regarding the Interaction Between Accounting Research and Accounting Standards Setting

Both accounting standard setters and researchers have expressed positive views on using academic research findings to advance evidence-based standards setting. Although academic research has been argued to contribute to accounting standards setting, historical developments indicate that its findings and insights have rarely been effectively used in the standards setting process. Signs of change are emerging because of the efforts of both standard setters and scholars. However, identifying the challenges in using academic research for accounting standards setting is useful for examining the role academic research has played (or has failed to play as expected) in discussions on the subsequent accounting treatment of goodwill.

---

[34] These issues are closely related to the discussion of accounting standard-setting bodies' efforts, particularly the IASB, to use academic research. Consequently, the recent collaboration between these bodies and academia reflects a two-way approach.

First, as previously discussed, for academic research to inform accounting standards setting, its content must be understandable to standards setting bodies such as the IASB and to stakeholders in the standards setting process (Leisenring and Johnson 1994, p. 77; Schipper 1994, p. 68). However, much research published in academic journals, whether empirical or analytical, uses advanced statistical or econometric techniques and mathematically constructed models, which may make it difficult for standards setting bodies and their members to understand (Leisenring and Johnson 1994, pp. 75–76; Singleton-Green 2010, p. 158).[35]

Even when research relevant to accounting standards setting bodies exists, different studies often produce varying observations and conclusions (Singleton-Green 2010, p. 133, p. 135). From an academic perspective, this is not considered negative because accounting issues are often complex, and, particularly when research is still developing, it is academically valuable to examine a problem from multiple perspectives using different approaches. However, when results for a single issue are inconsistent, accounting standards setting bodies may find it challenging to interpret the findings and determine how to use them in the standards setting process (i.e., what normative conclusions can be drawn). In these cases, there is a risk that accounting standards setting bodies and stakeholders may, intentionally or unintentionally, engage in the "cherry-picking" problem by referencing only empirical results that support their own beliefs (Teixeira 2014, p. 9; Leuz 2018, p. 595, p. 597).[36,37]

In recent years, the reproducibility of academic research has emerged as a significant concern for the reliability of research results (Leuz 2018; Hail and Lang 2020; Clor-Proell et al. 2025). Additionally, scholars have increasingly noted that empirical research in accounting journals is predominantly biased toward "hypothesis-testing" studies, while "descriptive" studies—essential for accounting standard setters and regulators—have been largely overlooked (Clor-Proell et al.

---

[35] Moreover, identifying and demonstrating causal relationships between a standard and its consequences remains challenging, regardless of the rigor of statistical or econometric methods used. Even when such methods produce research results with high internal validity regarding a phenomenon's causal relationship, this does not ensure external validity or applicability to other contexts (see Leuz 2018, pp. 589–591).

[36] Leuz (2018, p. 595) contends that this is why evidence-based policymaking is necessary. Evidence-based policymaking requires the use of more rigorous and systematic evidence, rather than selective evidence. However, without effective mechanisms to support evidence-based policymaking, the issue of cherry-picking may continue in the situations described. Some researchers do not currently view this issue as particularly significant. For instance, a European researcher interviewed by Garcia Osma et al. (2023, p. 19) stated: "I think standard setters largely ignored what researchers did and if they used it they just cherry-picked the research that corroborate on the use ··· In the last ten years I think it has changed again in a more positive way for accounting research, I have the impression now, specially IASB but EFRAG also ··· as now they are very active."

[37] Leuz (2018, p. 595) notes that concerns about cherry-picking in policy decisions necessitate evidence-based policymaking. Additionally, there is concern that a problem similar to the "market for excuses" issue identified in classical normative accounting theories (Watts and Zimmerman 1979) could also occur in empirical research.

2025; Rajgopal 2021; Schrand 2019; Gow 2025; Gow et al. 2016). Moreover, even when both accounting standard setters and researchers share interest in certain questions, research may be constrained by data limitations (Amel-Zadeh et al. 2023; Schipper 1994; Leuz 2018). Although efforts to address these challenges are ongoing, they cannot be resolved quickly. In the short term, these factors may limit the contribution of academic research to accounting standards setting.

Statement on AI Usage During the preparation of this manuscript, the authors used AI-assisted tools such as DeepL and ChatGPT to improve the English expression and clarity of the manuscript. The authors thoroughly reviewed and approved the final version and take full responsibility for the content.

References

Amel-Zadeh, A., M. Glaum, and T. Sellhorn. (2023). Empirical goodwill research: Insights, issues, and implications for standard setting and future research. *European Accounting Review* 32(2): 415–446.

American Institute of Certified Public Accountants. (1970) The Accounting Principles Board (APB) Statement No. 4, *Basic Concepts and Accounting Principles Underlying Financial Statements of Business Enterprises*, AICPA.

Basu, S. (2012). How can accounting researchers become more innovative? *Accounting Horizons* 26(4): 851–870

Campbell, J. L., and M. E. Evans. (2024). Practice-informed accounting research: The role of macroeconomic events and changes in financial reporting and disclosure. *Foundations and Trends® in Accounting* 18(4): 268–355.

Clor-Proell, S., O. Even-Tov, C. M. C. Lee, and S. Rajgopal. (2025). Bridging the gap between academic and practice in accounting. *Accounting Horizons* 39(1): 1–14.

Dichev, I. D. (2020). Fifty years of capital markets research in accounting: Achievements so far and opportunities ahead. *China Journal of Accounting Research* 13(3): 237–249.

Financial Accounting Standards Board (1976). Discussion Memorandum, *Conceptual Framework for Financial Accounting and Reporting: Elements of Financial Statements and Their Measurement*, FA Foundation.

Fülbier, R. U., and T. Sellhorn. (2023). Understanding and improving the language of business: How accounting and corporate reporting research can better serve business and society. *Journal of Business Economics* 93: 1089–1124.

Garcia Osma, B., A. Mora, and J. Pierk. (2023). Dissemination of accounting research. *European Accounting Review* 32(5): 1053–1083.

Gow, I. D. (2025). The elephant in the room: p-hacking and accounting research. *Accounting, Economics, and Law: A convivium* 15(1): 81–98.

Gow, I. D., D. F. Larcker, and P. C. Reiss. (2016). Causal inference in accounting research. *Journal of Accounting Research* 54(2): 477–523.

Hail, L., M. Lang, and C. Leuz. (2020). Reproducibility in accounting research: Views of the research community. *Journal of Accounting Research* 58(2): 519–543.

International Accounting Standards Board (IASB). (2018). *Conceptual Framework for Financial Reporting*, IASB Foundation.

IASB. (2008). *IFRS 3 Business Combinations*, Appendix A, definition of goodwill, IASB Foundation.

IASB. (December 2013, September 2014, March 2015, December 2015, July 2016, July 2017, September 2017, April 2018, July 2018, October 2018, December 2018, April 2020, October 2020, June 2021, July 2021, March 2022), *IASB Staff Papers for Accounting Standards Advisory Forum Meetings*, IASB.

IASB (2015). *Report and Feedback Statement: Post-implementation Review of IFRS 3*, Business Combinations, IASB Foundation.
IASB (2020). Discussion Paper, Business Combinations—Disclosures, Goodwill and Impairment, IASB Foundation.
IASB (2024). Exposure Draft, Business Combinations—Disclosures, Goodwill and Impairment, IASB Foundation.
IASC (1989). *Framework for the Preparation and Presentation of Financial Statements*, IASC Foundation.
Leisenring, J. J., and L. T. Johnson. (1994). Accounting research: On the relevance of research to practice. *Accounting Horizons* 8(4): 74–79.
Leuz, C. (2018). Evidence-based policymaking: promise, challenges and opportunities for accounting and financial markets research. *Accounting and Business Research* 48(5): 582–608.
Oh, H. I., and Penman, S. H. (2025). A Proposal for Goodwill Accounting. *Abacus 61*(4): 833–856.
Rajgopal, S. (2021). Integrating practice into accounting research. *Management Science* 67(9): 5430–5454.
Schipper, K. (1994). Academic accounting research and the standard setting process. *Accounting Horizons* 8(4): 61–73.
Schrand, C. M. (2019). Impediments to relevant research: The journal review and publication process. *Accounting Horizons* 33(2): 11–16.
Singleton-Green, B. (2010). The communication gap: Why doesn't accounting research make a greater contribution to debates on accounting policy? *Accounting in Europe* 7(2): 129–145.
Teixeira, A. (2014). The International Accounting Standards Board and evidence-informed standard-setting. *Accounting in Europe* 11(1): 5–12.
Watts, R. L., and J. L. Zimmerman. (1979). The demand for and supply of accounting theories: The market for excuses. *The Accounting Review* 54(2): 273–305.
Whittington, G. (2024). Reflections on the past, present and future of the academic/professional interface in accounting. *Accounting and Business Research* 54(7): 811–820.

Chapter 3
Theoretical Issues

Yuko Asami

3.1 Purpose and Organization of this Chapter

The controversy surrounding the accounting treatment of goodwill can be traced at least as far back as 1882. Over the following 140 years, a wide range of debates has developed. As early as the 1970s, Lee (1971, p. 318) noted that "over the last eighty years or so, goodwill has been the subject of a controversial debate which has failed to produce a consensus of opinion regarding its accounting treatment." Chapters 1 and 2 of this book showed that various views coexist regarding accounting methods for goodwill and that opinions on accounting standards differ significantly depending on the standard-setting body.

Building on the findings from Chaps. 1 and 2, this chapter provides a theoretical examination of goodwill accounting treatments. It first traces the origin of the definition of goodwill to a 1571 court case and reviews how the definition has evolved up to the present. Based on this foundation, it then provides an overview of accounting standards related to the treatment of goodwill in the United States, the United Kingdom, the European Union, and Japan, focusing on the period beginning in 1917. This chapter also examines debates over the appropriateness of different accounting treatments, including amortization, non-amortization, impairment, and immediate write-off against equity. The period under review spans approximately 120 years, from the 1880s, when discussions on goodwill accounting first emerged, to around 2000, when non-amortization and impairment treatments were introduced under the Statement of Financial Accounting Standards (SFAS) 141/142 and IFRS 3.

This chapter is a revised version of the discussion papers (Asami et al. 2022; Asami 2025, 2026).

Y. Asami (✉)
Graduate School of Economics, Nagoya University, Aichi, Japan
e-mail: asami.yuko.j3@f.mail.nagoya-u.ac.jp

Y. Tokuga, M. Yoneyama (eds.), *Controversies Over Accounting for Goodwill*,
Contributions to Finance and Accounting,
https://doi.org/10.1007/978-981-92-0156-3_3

This chapter then considers whether internally generated goodwill should be recognized. It first outlines arguments supporting the recognition of internally generated goodwill as an asset and then analyzes opposing views, dividing them into two levels: recognition and measurement, and the objectives of financial reporting. Drawing on these discussions, the relationship between purchased goodwill and internally generated goodwill is examined within the framework of Edwards and Bell (1961). This chapter presents the process by which subjective goodwill (internally generated goodwill), representing an ex ante expectation of excess earnings, is subsequently verified by ex post facts and gradually reflected in periodic profits.

After examining the process of goodwill transformation proposed by Edwards and Bell (1961), this chapter organizes discussions on the appropriate accounting treatment of goodwill based on prior studies of purchased goodwill in business combination accounting. Previous research has identified suitable accounting treatments for goodwill and the related issues arising from them. Building on these findings, this chapter advances the following argument. The purchase method involving amortization of goodwill poses a fundamental problem of understating profits, since amortization expenses exclude from realized profit the portion corresponding to excess earnings. Conversely, the acquisition method without amortization presents a fundamental problem of overstating equity, as the value of goodwill is reflected twice in net assets—once upon initial recognition and again upon its realization. The purpose of this chapter is to provide a theoretical conclusion on whether purchased goodwill recognized under the purchase method should be amortized.

3.2 Previous Normative Research

3.2.1 Definition and Accounting Standards for Goodwill

3.2.1.1 Definition of Goodwill

The term "goodwill" has been used in a commercial context since at least 1571. In the 1571 case *Wills and Inventories.* (Surtees 1835, p. 352), the court stated: "I gyue to John Stephen … my whole interest and good will of my Quarrell." The definition of goodwill is said to have been first formally established in the 1810 case *Crutwell v. Lye* (17 Ves. 335; 1 Rose. 123), in which Judge Lord Eldon held that "The goodwill which had been the subject of sale was nothing more than the probability that the old customers will resort to the old place" (17 Ves. 347). This judgment later gained authoritative status. Until the late nineteenth century, the treatment of goodwill was effectively determined by law and case law (Ding et al. 2008, p. 728), which had already been established through numerous cases.

This legal perspective continued to exert significant influence even after discussions on the accounting treatment of goodwill began in the 1880s. Bithell (1882, p. 142), considered by Courtis (1983, p. 2) as the first article discussing the nature of goodwill, defined it as the advantage connected with an established business of good repute, stating that a well-established business presents an expectation of profits to anyone entering it and is worth paying for. Lisle (1900), who was frequently cited at the time (Esquerrē 1913, p. 21; Wildman, 1914, pp. 142–146), stated that goodwill is the monetary value placed on the connection and reputation of a mercantile or manufacturing concern, and that it discounts the value of the turn-over of a business in consequence of the probabilities of the old customers continuing (Lisle, 1900, p. 134).

Around 1910, the discussion shifted from a legal to an economic perspective, and the definition of goodwill began to be interpreted in a commercial context. This expansion reflected changes in the business environment, transforming the concept of goodwill from one understood in terms of individual companies to one applicable to large-scale enterprises (Yang 1927, pp. 90–93).

Leake (1914, p. 81) subsequently defined goodwill as the present value of future excess profits.[1] That is, the privilege granted by the seller of a business to the purchaser to trade as the recognized successor; the possession of a ready-formed "connection" of customers, considered an element of the saleable value of a business in addition to the value of the plant, stock-in-trade, book debts, and other assets. Goodwill, in its commercial sense, is the present value of the right to receive expected future super-profits, where "super-profits" refers to the amount by which future revenue, increase, or advantage is expected to exceed any and all expenditures incurred in its production.

This definition, provided by Leake (1914), has been widely adopted. For instance, the American Institute of Accountants (AIA) (1931, p. 67) stated that goodwill, in its commercial sense, is the present value of the right to receive expected future super-profits, with "super-profits" meaning the amount by which future revenue, increase, or advantage is expected to exceed all economic expenditures incurred in its production, plus a normal profit.

Similarly, Paton and Littleton (1940, p. 92) explained that recognizable costs of goodwill or other general intangibles arise primarily when a going concern is acquired in its entirety. If an enterprise has superior earning power and such superiority cannot be accounted for by specific monopolistic grants, such as patents or franchises, the concern may be said to possess goodwill or general intangible value. If, under these conditions, there is an outright change of ownership, the amount paid by the buyer, on a cash or cash-equivalent basis, in excess of the total attributable to the tangible factors acquired constitutes a recognizable cost of goodwill.

According to Hendriksen (1970, pp. 432–433), from an accounting perspective, three major conceptions of goodwill frequently appear in the literature: (1) the valuation of intangible attitudes toward the firm; (2) the present discounted value of expected future profits in excess of a normal return on total investment, excluding goodwill; and (3) a master valuation account, defined as the excess of the value of

[1] In the literature review section, the terminology and expressions employed generally follow those of the original authors.

the business as a whole over the values assigned to its individual tangible and intangible net assets.

Of these, the third definition is presented by Catlett and Olson (1968, p. xv), who defined business goodwill value as the difference between the total value of an enterprise and the aggregate value of its separable resources and property rights, less liabilities. Similarly, Lee (1973, p. 177) defined goodwill as the portion of the purchase price paid by an acquiring company that represents profits over and above the purchase price of the acquired net tangible assets necessary to generate those profits. In other words, it is the difference between the value of the acquired entity as a whole and the sum of the separate values attributed to the acquired tangible net assets.

In addition, regarding the distinction between internally generated goodwill and purchased goodwill, Leake (1914, pp. 82, 85; 1921, p. 23) argued the following. Although the value of goodwill forms part of the present value of every profit-seeking undertaking expected to yield future super-profits, it assumes a recorded and visible form—and becomes a practical financial concern—only when the goodwill has been purchased, that is, transferred from one person to another for valuable consideration. Consequently, most existing goodwill value is likely unrecorded in financial books or accounts, and for this unrecorded portion, questions about its accounting treatment rarely arise. This is because, in most profit-seeking enterprises, whether private or public, goodwill has been created and developed through the ability and effort of the current owners. Keeping this in mind is important, as it materially contributes to a true understanding of the nature of goodwill—a value that extends far beyond the comparatively small portion recorded in financial books and accounts.

3.2.1.2 A Brief History of Accounting Standards for Goodwill

This section provides a brief overview of the history of accounting standards for the treatment of goodwill in the United States, the United Kingdom, the International Accounting Standards Committee (IASC)/International Accounting Standards Board (IASB), and the European Union. A detailed discussion of each accounting method will follow in later sections. The overview begins with the accounting standards for goodwill in the United States.

(1) The United States

The first accounting standard addressing the treatment of goodwill was a provision in *Uniform Accounting*, the initial accounting regulation in the United States, published by the AIA in 1917. The Balance Sheet format presented in this regulation suggested that the book value of goodwill should be shown as a deduction from "net worth," effectively advocating an immediate write-off against equity as the accounting treatment for goodwill (AIA 1917, p. 433).

In 1929, the AIA issued *Verification of Financial Statements*, a revision to *Uniform Accounting*. Notably, the Balance Sheet format prescribed in this document omitted any reference to intangible assets and goodwill, which can be interpreted as a withdrawal of the prior endorsement of the lump-sum write-off (AIA 1929, p. 353).

In 1944, the AIA issued Accounting Research Bulletin (ARB) No. 24: *Accounting for Intangible Assets*. Under this provision, intangible assets were categorized as either Type (a) or Type (b), with specific accounting treatments prescribed for each. The intangibles were broadly classified as follows: (a) those having a term of existence limited by law, regulation, agreement, or by their nature (such as patents, copyrights, leases, licenses, franchises for a fixed term, and goodwill for which there is evidence of limited duration); and (b) those having no such limited term of existence and for which, at the time of acquisition, there is no indication of a limited life (such as goodwill generally, going value, trade names, secret processes, subscription lists, perpetual franchises, and organization costs) (ARB 24, p. 195).

The cost of Type (a) intangibles should be amortized through systematic charges to the income statement over the period benefited, as in the case of other assets with a limited period of usefulness. The cost of Type (b) intangibles may be carried indefinitely unless and until it becomes reasonably evident that their term of existence has become limited or that they have become worthless. In the former case, the cost should be amortized by systematic charges to the income statement over the estimated remaining period of usefulness; alternatively, if such charges would result in distortion of the income statement, a partial write-down may be made by a charge to earned surplus, with the balance of the cost amortized over the remaining period of usefulness (ARB 24, p. 196).

Regarding the lump-sum write-off (immediate write-off against equity), the committee stated that, in the past, it had been accepted practice to eliminate Type (b) intangibles by writing them off against existing surplus, whether capital or earned, even though the value of the asset was unimpaired. Because this practice had long been established and widely approved, the committee did not feel warranted, at that time, in recommending the adoption of a rule prohibiting such treatment. The committee noted, however, that such dispositions should be discouraged, particularly when effected by charges to capital surplus (ARB 24, p. 197).

In 1945, the Securities and Exchange Commission (SEC) issued Accounting Series Release (ASR) No. 50, *The Propriety of Writing Down Goodwill by Means of Charges to Capital Surplus*. The SEC publicly stated that writing down goodwill through charges to capital surplus was contrary to sound accounting principles and it should instead be charged to income. The SEC explicitly rejected the use of capital surplus for this purpose.

In response, the AIA issued ARB 43: *Restatement and Revision of Accounting Research Bulletins* in 1953. ARB 43 stipulated that write-offs against shareholders' equity should not be made to earned surplus immediately after acquisition, nor should intangibles be charged against capital surplus (ARB 43, Chap. 5, para. 9). In other respects, ARB 43 largely mirrored ARB 24, maintaining the classification of intangible assets into Types (a) and (b) and prescribing corresponding accounting treatments. However, two notable differences became apparent.

First, systematic amortization[2] was explicitly placed at the company's discretion: when a corporation determines that a Type (b) intangible may not retain value throughout the life of the enterprise, it may amortize the cost of that intangible through systematic charges against income, even without present indications of limited existence or loss of value that would classify it as Type (a), and even if expenditures are made to maintain its value. Such amortization is at the company's discretion and is not considered obligatory (ARB 43, Chap. 5, para. 7). Second, ARB 43 provides more explicit guidance on retaining intangibles at cost compared to ARB 24. It states that if intangibles are not amortized systematically, they should be carried at cost until an event occurs indicating a loss or limitation in their useful life (ARB 43, Chap. 5, para. 9).

These provisions of ARB 43 were subject to criticism in Accounting Principles Board (APB) Opinion No. 17 (para. 9). That is, current accounting for goodwill is often criticized because alternative methods of accounting for costs are acceptable. Some companies amortize the cost of acquired intangible assets over a short, arbitrary period to reduce the asset balance as rapidly as practicable, while others retain the cost as an asset until evidence of impairment appears and then record a material reduction in a single period. Selecting an arbitrary amortization period is criticized because it may understate net income during the amortization period and overstate net income in subsequent periods. Conversely, retaining the cost as an asset is criticized because it may overstate net income before the loss of value is recognized and understate net income in the period of write-off.

The American Institute of Certified Public Accountants (AICPA) issued APB 16, *Business Combinations* and APB 17, *Intangible Assets*, in 1970. APB 17 required companies to record the cost of goodwill acquired in a business combination as an asset and to amortize it through systematic charges to income over the period estimated to be benefited; the amortization period was not to exceed 40 years (APB 17, para. 9). Write-offs against equity were prohibited: the cost of goodwill acquired in a business combination could not be written off in a lump sum to capital surplus or retained earnings, nor could it be reduced to a nominal amount at or immediately after acquisition (APB 17, para. 13). Following APB 17, its provisions remained in effect for 30 years, until 2001,[3] when the Financial Accounting Standards Board (FASB) issued SFAS No. 141, *Business Combinations,* and SFAS No. 142, *Goodwill and Other Intangible Assets.*

(2) The United Kingdom

In 1984, the Institute of Chartered Accountants in England and Wales issued Statement of Standard Accounting Practice (SSAP) No. 22, *Accounting for Goodwill.* This standard required that purchased goodwill should normally be

---

[2] Systematic amortization is regulated as follows: once it becomes reasonably evident that the term of existence of a Type (b) intangible has become limited, making it a Type (a) intangible, its cost should be amortized through systematic charges to the income statement over the estimated remaining useful life (ARB 43, Chap. 5, para. 6).

[3] For SFAS 141/142 and later, refer to Chap. 4. Johnson and Petrone (1998) discusses the goodwill recognized by ARB 43 and APB 17.

eliminated from the accounts by an immediate write-off against reserves, rather than as a charge to the profit and loss account.

It stipulated that, while companies should normally follow the preferred treatment of writing off goodwill immediately against reserves, they were also permitted to carry positive goodwill as an asset and to amortize it through the profit and loss account over its useful economic life (SSAP 22, para. 10). Purchased goodwill (other than negative goodwill) could be eliminated from the accounts by amortization through the profit and loss account, in arriving at profit or loss on ordinary activities, on a systematic basis over its useful economic life (amortization) (SSAP 22, para. 34). Purchased goodwill was not to be carried in the balance sheet of a company or group as a permanent item (SSAP 22, para. 31).

In 1997, the Accounting Standards Board (ASB) issued Financial Reporting Standard (FRS) No. 10, *Goodwill and Intangible Assets*. This standard required that positive purchased goodwill be capitalized and classified as an asset on the balance sheet, while internally generated goodwill should not be capitalized (FRS 10, paras. 7–8). Where goodwill and intangible assets were regarded as having limited useful economic lives, they were to be amortized on a systematic basis over those lives.[4] Where they were regarded as having indefinite useful economic lives, they were not to be amortized. There was a rebuttable presumption that the useful economic lives of purchased goodwill and intangible assets were limited to periods of 20 years or less (FRS 10, paras. 15–19).[5]

(3) IFRS

Regarding International Accounting Standards (IAS), the treatment of goodwill has followed a trend similar to that in the United Kingdom. In 1983, the IASC issued IAS No. 22: *Accounting for Business Combinations*. It required that an enterprise adopt one of the following policies for dealing with any difference between the cost of acquisition and the fair values of the net identifiable assets acquired: (a) recognition in income, or (b) immediate adjustment against shareholders' interests (IAS 22, para. 40). Where the policy in paragraph 40(a) is adopted, any excess of the cost of acquisition over the fair values of the net identifiable assets acquired should be recognized as an asset in the consolidated financial statements as goodwill arising on acquisition and amortized to income on a systematic basis over its useful life. If it is

[4] The method of amortization should be selected so as to reflect the expected pattern of consumption of the goodwill or intangible asset. The straight-line method should be used unless another method can be demonstrated to be more appropriate (FRS 10, para. 30).

[5] This presumption may be rebutted, and the useful economic life may be regarded as longer or as indefinite (FRS 10, para. 19). Companies legislation, however, requires goodwill that is treated as an asset to be amortized systematically over a finite period. Where a company's financial statements depart from this requirement, the departure must be justified as necessary to achieve the overriding purpose (FRS 10, para. 18). In addition, goodwill and intangible assets amortized over a finite period not exceeding 20 years from the date of acquisition should be reviewed for impairment (FRS 10, para. 34). Goodwill and intangible assets amortized over a period exceeding 20 years from the date of acquisition, or not amortized, should be reviewed for impairment at the end of each reporting period (FRS 10, para. 37). Also see FRS 11.

found at any time that goodwill arising on acquisition is not supported by future income, it should, to the extent necessary, be charged immediately to income (IAS 22, para. 41).

In 1993, IAS 22 was revised to require that acquired goodwill be recognized as an asset and amortized systematically, while the description of a write-off against equity was deleted. Under the revision, any excess of the cost of acquisition over the acquirer's interest in the fair value of the identifiable assets and liabilities acquired as at the date of the exchange transaction should be described as goodwill and recognized as an asset (IAS 22 rev. 1993, para. 40). Goodwill should be amortized by recognizing it as an expense over its useful life. In amortizing goodwill, the straight-line basis should be used unless another amortization method is more appropriate in the circumstances. The amortization period should not exceed 5 years unless a longer period, not exceeding 20 years from the date of acquisition, can be justified (IAS 22 rev. 1993, para. 42). Because goodwill represents future economic benefits from synergy or assets for which separate recognition is not possible, it is frequently difficult to estimate its useful life. The presumption in this Standard is that goodwill does not normally have a useful life in excess of 5 years (IAS 22 rev. 1993, para. 45).

When initially accounting for the acquisition, there may be circumstances in which goodwill on acquisition does not reflect future economic benefits that are expected to flow to the acquirer. In these circumstances, goodwill is written down and an expense recognized immediately. The unamortized balance of goodwill should be reviewed at each balance sheet date and, to the extent that it is no longer probable of being recovered from the expected future economic benefits, it should be recognized immediately as an expense (IAS 22 rev. 1993, paras. 46, 47). An impairment in the value of goodwill may be caused by factors such as unfavorable economic trends, changes in the competitive situation, and legal, statutory, or contractual proceedings. It may be evidenced by a reduction in the cash flows generated, or reasonably likely to be generated, by the acquiree's business. In these circumstances, the carrying amount of goodwill is written down and an expense recognized (IAS 22 rev. 1993, para. 48).

IAS 22 (rev. 1998) largely followed IAS 22 (rev. 1993) and continued to require systematic amortization. Goodwill arising on acquisition should be recognized as an asset (IAS 22 rev. 1998, para. 41) and amortized on a systematic basis over its useful life. There is a rebuttable presumption that the useful life of goodwill will not exceed 20 years from initial recognition (IAS 22 rev. 1998, para. 44). To determine whether goodwill is impaired, an enterprise should apply IAS 36, Impairment of Assets (IAS 22 rev. 1998, para. 55).

(4) The European Union

In 1978, the Fourth Directive 78/660/EEC, *The Annual Accounts of Certain Types of Companies*, stipulated that Article 34(1)(a), which requires formation expenses under assets to be written off within a maximum period of 5 years, shall apply to goodwill. Member States may, however, permit companies to write off goodwill systematically over a limited period exceeding 5 years, provided that this period does not exceed the useful economic life of the asset (Article 37 (2)).

In 1983, the Seventh Council Directive 83/349/EEC, *Consolidated Accounts,* stipulated that a positive consolidation difference shall be dealt with in accordance with the rules laid down in Directive 78/660/EEC for the item of goodwill. A Member State may permit a positive consolidation difference to be immediately and clearly deducted from reserves (Article 30).

In 2013, the Fourth Directive 78/660/EEC and the Seventh Council Directive 83/349/EEC were revised, and Directive 2013/34/EU of the European Parliament and of the Council, The Annual Financial Statements, Consolidated Financial Statements and Related Reports of Certain Types of Undertakings, was issued by the European Union. It provides that intangible assets shall be written off over the useful economic life of the intangible asset. In exceptional cases where the useful life of goodwill cannot be reliably estimated, such assets shall be written off within a maximum period set by the Member State. That maximum period shall not be shorter than 5 years and shall not exceed 10 years (Article 12, No. 11).

(5) Accounting Standards for Goodwill in Japan

1. Goodwill in Unconsolidated Financial Statements

In Japan, goodwill was first addressed in accounting standards in the *Standards for Financial Statements,* issued by the Temporary Industrial Rationalization Bureau's Financial Management Committee in 1934. These standards stipulated that the amortization of goodwill, known as "eigyo-ken" in Japanese, should be recognized in the classification of net profit or loss. In 1936, the *Standards for Assets Evaluation*, issued by the Finance Management Committee of the Temporary Industrial Rationalization Bureau, specified that intangible fixed assets should be recognized at cost only when acquired for consideration (para. 32) and amortized over the shortest possible period based on the estimated period of benefits to be derived (para. 34). Regarding amortization, the standards emphasized that caution should be exercised in valuation to avoid retaining assets that are essentially worthless (para. 3).

In 1949, the *Corporate Accounting Principles* were issued by the Economic Stabilization Headquarters Corporate Accounting System Investigation Committee.[6] These principles stipulated that goodwill (business rights) should be recognized as an intangible fixed asset at the amount of consideration paid, but only when acquired for consideration, and amortized using a specific method (Sec. 3, paras. 4(1)B, 5E). In 1974, the *Corporate Accounting Principles* were revised to require amortization in equal installments, or more, each period (Note 25).

Meanwhile, the Commercial Code was revised in 1962, establishing provisions regarding goodwill. Goodwill acquired through a paid transfer or merger was required to be amortized in equal installments, or more, each period within 5 years of acquisition (Article 285-7).

These provisions are considered to reflect the principle of conservatism due to the uncertainty inherent in goodwill (Yoshinaga and Iino 1974, p. 240). More

[6] *The Corporate Accounting Principles* have been issued by the Business Accounting Deliberation Council since their revision in 1954.

specifically, the draft by the Civil Affairs Bureau of the Ministry of Justice, Outline for Reform of the Commercial Code Concerning the Content of Corporate Accounting, explains the rationale as follows:

Because current law does not explicitly address the valuation of goodwill, interpretations vary. One holds that goodwill cannot be recognized as an asset; another allows recognition of its acquisition cost only when acquired for consideration and by succession; a third permits recognition as an asset regardless of how it was acquired. The stipulation that goodwill be recognized as an asset at its acquisition cost only when acquired for consideration reflects the difficulty of valuing internally generated or gratuitously acquired goodwill. Although goodwill has economic value, its reasonable valuation is generally difficult and carries a risk of arbitrary overstatement. Therefore, to protect creditors, goodwill must be amortized in equal annual installments, or more, over a period not exceeding 5 years[7] after acquisition.

Thus, in Japan, a provision for amortization was established in the Financial Statements Guideline of 1934, and the 1962 revision of the Commercial Code required amortization in equal installments, or more, within 5 years.[8] In 2003, the *Accounting Standard for Business Combinations* was issued by the Business Accounting Deliberation Council. It stipulated that systematic amortization of goodwill should be applied over a period not exceeding 20 years (Sec. 3, para. 2(4)), and that impairment losses should be recognized in accordance with the *Accounting Standard for Impairment of Fixed Assets* (Sec. 3, para. 3(4)). The rationale for systematic amortization and recognition of impairment losses, according to the standard, is as follows.

Systematic amortization allows the income resulting from a business combination to correspond with the amortization of the investment elimination difference, which forms part of the consideration. Since goodwill is part of the investment cost, systematically amortizing goodwill aligns with the principle that any excess recovered beyond the investment cost is recognized as profit for the company. Furthermore, as acquired goodwill may be replaced over time by internally generated goodwill, systematic amortization prevents the actual recognition of internally generated goodwill as an asset owing to the non-amortization of acquired goodwill (Sec. 3, para. 3(4)).

---

[7] The amortization period was limited to 5 years because this rule was established in accordance with the provision in current law regarding the amortization period for founding expenses (Ueda 1960, p. 6). Also see Civil Affairs Bureau of the Ministry of Justice (1960).

[8] Regarding the Commercial Code, a 1974 revision stipulated that commercial books should comply with generally accepted accounting principles (Article 32, para. 2). Since then, accounting standards, such as the *Corporate Accounting Principles,* have served as interpretative guidelines for the accounting provisions of the Commercial Code, as stated in the preamble to the *Corporate Accounting Principles*. In 2005, the Companies Act was enacted, separating certain provisions from the Commercial Code. The Act stipulated that company accounting must follow generally accepted accounting principles (Article 431). Consequently, company accounting has come to follow the provisions of accounting standards rather than those of the Companies Act (formerly the Commercial Code).

Given that the period over which goodwill exerts its effect and the pattern of its impairment cannot be reasonably predicted, continuously determining the impairment amount would be difficult and cumbersome. Systematically amortizing goodwill over a set period is therefore more reasonable than adopting a method that does not recognize impairment in a given fiscal year. Additionally, although certain portions of goodwill may not lose value, separating these portions in a reasonable way is generally difficult. Consequently, the entire amount of goodwill is amortized systematically, including portions that cannot be separated. The amortization period is based on current consolidated financial statement principles and is set at the period during which the effect of goodwill is expected to be recognized, which is within 20 years (Sec. 3, para. 3(4)).[9]

2. Goodwill in Consolidated Financial Statements

Up to this point, we have summarized the accounting treatment of goodwill arising from a merger in nonconsolidated financial statements. Next, we turn to the treatment of goodwill in consolidated financial statements. Regulations on consolidated financial statements were introduced in Japan in 1977. Regarding goodwill in consolidated financial statements, the *Accounting Standard for Consolidated Financial Statements*, issued by the Business Accounting Deliberation Council in 1975, stipulated that goodwill should be amortized in equal installments, or more, each period (sec. 4, para. 3, 2). Subsequently, the *Revised Accounting Standard for Consolidated Financial Statements* of 1997 established systematic amortization over a period not exceeding 20 years (sec. 4, para. 3, 2). The rationale for this is as follows.

Since the main component of the consolidation adjustment account is considered to be goodwill, the account should be amortized over the period during which its effects are realized, in order to appropriately reflect the actual status of the investment. However, in practice, particularly for long-term investments, estimating the period over which the effects will be realized is often difficult, creating a risk of an extended amortization period. Therefore, companies must establish a specific period based on the actual circumstances of the subsidiary to determine an appropriate amortization schedule. Under the *Revised Accounting Standard for Consolidated Financial Statements*, taking into account international developments, systematic amortization should, in principle, be conducted on a regular basis using the straight-line method or another reasonable method, within 20 years from the date of recognition (*Opinion Paper on the Amendment of the Regulations for Consolidated Financial Statements*, Part 2, Sec. 2, para. 6-2).

3. Goodwill Acquired in Business Combination

In 2008, the Accounting Standards Board of Japan (ASBJ) issued ASBJ Statement No. 21, *Accounting Standards for Business Combinations*, and ASBJ Statement No. 22, *Accounting Standards for Consolidated Financial Statements*, thereby establishing comprehensive accounting standards covering business combinations.

[9] The arguments presented here closely mirror those of Leake (1914, 1921). For further details, see the next section of this chapter.

Regarding the accounting treatment of goodwill, the provisions of the 2003 *Accounting Standards for Business Combinations* were fully adopted, applying systematic amortization over a period of 20 years or less, along with recognition of impairment losses.[10]

Since then, the accounting treatment of goodwill under Japanese domestic standards has not changed. However, in 2015, Japan's Modified International Standards (JMIS) No. 1[11] was issued by the ASBJ, stating that "deletions or modifications" shall be made to the requirements regarding the accounting for goodwill acquired in a business combination under IFRS 3, Business Combinations (JMIS 1, para. 4).

Under JMIS No. 1, the acquirer shall account for goodwill as follows: (a) After initial recognition, goodwill shall be carried at the amount recognized at the acquisition date, adjusted for any accumulated amortization and accumulated impairment losses. (b) Goodwill shall be amortized on a systematic basis, using the straight-line method or another reasonable method, over its useful life. The useful life of goodwill is the period during which it is expected to have an effect, which shall not exceed 20 years.[12] The amortization expense shall be recognized in profit or loss (JMIS 1, para. J-58A).

Opponents of non-amortization of goodwill argue that goodwill should be amortized, primarily for the following reasons (JMIS 1, para. 15):

(a) Goodwill represents the cost paid to acquire the assets and liabilities of the acquiree in a business combination. Since the acquirer's profit after the combination should be viewed as the excess recovered beyond the invested cost, goodwill should be amortized to appropriately recognize, in each period, the income and the corresponding cost of the investment.
(b) Assuming certain portions of goodwill reflect excess earning power, the value of such power typically diminishes owing to competitive forces. Non-amortization fails to account for this phenomenon.
(c) Although some argue that the useful life of acquired goodwill is generally unknown, an entity should typically be able to estimate it because an acquirer

[10] The accounting treatment of goodwill in consolidated financial statements shall follow ASBJ Statement No. 21, *Business Combinations* (ASBJ Statement No. 21, para. 24).

[11] "Japan's Modified International Standards (JMIS) is the Accounting Standards Comprising IFRSs and the ASBJ Modifications (ASBJ, 2015b, para.1). Under the Present Policy, the endorsement process is a mechanism of determining whether individual Standards and Interpretations (collectively referred to as 'Standards') issued by the International Accounting Standards Board ('IASB') are acceptable in Japan and, for certain Standards, making 'deletions or modifications' when considered necessary (ASBJ, 2015a. para.6). The process of endorsing IFRS is introduced in the "Interim Report: Opinion on the Application of International Financial Reporting Standards (IFRS) in Japan" published by the Business Accounting Deliberation Council in 2009.

[12] The ASBJ considered setting an upper limit for the useful life of goodwill because reliably estimating the period over which goodwill will have an effect is difficult, especially when that period is long. In determining the specific length of the upper limit, the ASBJ noted that a limit set too short could fail to reflect economic reality. Consequently, the ASBJ decided that the upper limit should be 20 years, with reference to the requirements in IAS 22 (1998) and existing Japanese accounting standards (JMIS 1, para. 19). Also see ASBJ et al. (2014).

decides to undertake the acquisition after diligent analysis of the acquiree. Furthermore, although the pattern of goodwill decline may be difficult to predict, systematically amortizing goodwill over a set period is more reasonable than adopting an approach that might fail to recognize value decreases in specific periods. The difficulty in estimating useful life or amortization patterns exists not only for goodwill but also for tangible fixed assets. Determining the useful life of a tangible fixed asset requires considering factors such as expected physical wear and technical obsolescence from changes or improvements in production. Similarly, choosing a depreciation method requires reflecting the pattern in which the asset's future economic benefits are expected to be consumed.

(d) Paragraph OB7 of the *Conceptual Framework for Financial Reporting* issued by the IASB states that general-purpose financial reports are not designed to show the value of a reporting entity. This implies that the recognition of internally generated goodwill is not relevant for general-purpose financial reporting. Although the view described in paragraph 13(b) opposes amortization on the grounds of inconsistency with accounting for internally generated goodwill, the accounting treatment of advertising costs and the subsequent measurement of goodwill acquired in a business combination are entirely separate issues.

(e) The impairment test for goodwill cannot be considered a substitute for amortization because the two serve different objectives: amortization focuses on the periodic allocation of costs, whereas the impairment test focuses on recoverable amounts. Moreover, recoverable amounts inevitably include the value of internally generated goodwill arising after the combination, meaning impairment tests may sometimes fail to reflect decreases in the value of acquired goodwill.

The ASBJ stated that, as a result of discussions at its Board meetings, it decided to make "deletions or modifications" to the Standards issued by the IASB to require the amortization of goodwill. This decision was based on the recognition that the IFRS approach of not amortizing goodwill differs fundamentally from the approach generally accepted in Japan, particularly with respect to its impact on the determination of profit or loss after a business combination (JMIS 1, para. 17) (Table 3.1).

3.2.2 Accounting Treatment for Goodwill

3.2.2.1 Literature Review Process

Our literature review process proceeded as follows. First, in Scopus, the search was conducted with "paper title" set to "goodwill" and "paper title, abstract, and keywords" set to "accounting" or "account." The publication year was limited to 2000 or earlier, the field was set to "business, management, and accounting" or "economics, econometrics, and finance," and the document type was restricted to "article, book chapter, or book." This search yielded 42 relevant documents. Next, in Web of

Table 3.1 Accounting standards for goodwill in Japan

Goodwill in non-consolidated financial statements				
Commercial Code, Companies Act		1962	Commercial Code of 1962	amortize in equal installments or more within 5 years
		1974	Commercial Code of 1974	(take into account fair accounting practices)
		2005	Companies Act of 2005	(comply with corporate accounting practices)
Accounting Standards	Temporary Industrial Rationalization Bureau Financial Management Committee	1934	Financial Statement Guideline	recognize goodwill as an asset
	Temporary Industrial Rationalization Bureau Financial Management Committee	1936	Standards related to financial evaluation	amortize and verify the value of goodwill
	Economic Stability Headquarters Corporate Accounting System Measures Investigation Committee	1949	Corporate Accounting Principles	amortize using a specific method
	Business Accounting Deliberation Council	1974	Revised Corporate Accounting Principles	amortize in equal installments or more
	Business Accounting Deliberation Council	2003	Accounting Standard for Business Combinations	systematic amortization within 20 years and impairment

Goodwill in consolidated financial statements				
Accounting Standards	Business Accounting Deliberation Council	1975	Accounting Standard for Consolidated Financial Statements	amortize in equal installments or more
	Business Accounting Deliberation Council	1997	Revised Accounting Standard for Consolidated Financial Statements	systematic amortization within 20 years

Goodwill in Business Combinations				
Accounting Standards	Accounting Standards Board of Japan	2008	Accounting Standard (ASBJ Statement) No. 21, Business Combinations	systematic amortization within 20 years and impairment
	Accounting Standards Board of Japan	2008	Accounting Standard (ASBJ Statement) No. 22, Consolidated Financial Statements.	(subject to ASBJ statement No. 22)
	Accounting Standards Board of Japan	2015	Japan's Modified International Standards (JMIS) No.1, Accounting for Goodwill.	systematic amortization within 20 years and impairment

Science, we searched with "title" set to "goodwill," "all fields" set to "accounting," and the publication year limited to 2000 or earlier, while excluding "book review" and "editorial material" from the document type. This search returned 32 documents. The year 2000 or earlier was targeted to capture discussions formed around the introduction of goodwill impairment under IAS 3, SFAS 141, and 142.

From the documents retrieved using these criteria, we excluded those that did not discuss the accounting treatment of goodwill, such as case studies, calculation examples, and empirical research papers. In addition, seven documents appearing in both Scopus and Web of Science were removed, resulting in 26 documents for this study. Furthermore, Scopus documents prior to 1970 and Web of Science documents prior to 1922 were excluded, as both databases lacked sufficient search functionality for earlier literature. Therefore, we also included the references cited in the 26 selected documents. For literature published after 2000, empirical research papers were excluded, and only a portion of the remaining documents was considered. In the following sections, we organize the views of various theorists on goodwill accounting chronologically, beginning in the 1880s when the debate first emerged.

3.2.2.2 Classification of Accounting Treatment

According to APB 17, *Intangible Assets*, issued by the AICPA in 1970, the literature on business combinations and goodwill identifies at least four possible accounting treatments for goodwill and similar intangible assets (APB 17, para. 17):

(a) Retain the cost as an asset indefinitely unless a reduction in its value becomes evident.
(b) Retain the cost as an asset but permit amortization as an operating expense over an arbitrary period.
(c) Retain the cost as an asset but require amortization as an operating expense over its estimated limited life or over an arbitrary but specified and minimum period.
(d) Deduct the cost from stockholders' equity at the date acquired.

Regarding the accounting treatment for goodwill, FASB (1976) provides the following classification (FASB 1976, paras. 162, 195):

1. Recognize as an asset:
   (a) Maintain without amortization unless a decline in the value of goodwill becomes evident.
   (b) Amortize by charges to income.
   (c) Amortize by charges to stockholders' equity.
2. Recognize as an immediate charge to income.
3. Recognize as a reduction of stockholders' equity.

In this chapter, while generally following the classification of APB 17, reference is also made to the FASB (1976) approach, which emphasizes the distinction between capitalization and immediate write-off against equity. Based on these frameworks, the classifications are organized as follows. For category c under APB 17, which includes both accelerated amortization and immediate expensing, this study adopts a classification that does not distinguish between the two, in line with APB 17, even though FASB (1976) treats immediate expensing as a separate category. For the purpose of reviewing previous research, systematic amortization, accelerated amortization, and immediate expensing are collectively categorized as "amortization," since they share the common feature of being recognized as expenses, and are further subdivided within that category.

1. Retain the cost as an asset ("non-amortization")
2. Amortize by charges to income ("amortization")
3. Deduct the cost from stockholders' equity at the date acquired ("immediate write-off against equity")

Based on this classification, (1), (2), and (3) are referred to as "non-amortization," "amortization," and "immediate write-off against equity," respectively. Category (3) is also addressed in ARB 24 and APB 17, para. 13, presented as follows: "write off against any existing surplus, capital, or earned" (ARB 24, p. 197), and "write off as a lump sum to capital surplus or to retained earnings at or immediately after acquisition" (APB 17, para. 13).

In the following sections, we organize our examination of each accounting method for goodwill, covering the period from the 1880s, when the debate over goodwill accounting first emerged, to around the year 2000. The analysis proceeds in chronological order, beginning with the earliest established accounting treatments. The order of establishment is amortization, followed by the equity deduction method, and then non-amortization. Accordingly, the discussion for each period follows this sequence. The classification of historical periods is based on Ding et al. (2008) and Hughes (1982).

3.2.3 Amortization

3.2.3.1 Developments in the 1880s

The author generally regarded as the first to discuss the nature of goodwill in accounting is Bithell in 1882[13] (Courtis 1983, p. 2). Following that, numerous discussions on the accounting treatment of goodwill appeared. During this period, roughly 1880 to 1900, the dominant view was that goodwill was not a true asset and should be expensed immediately, or at least rapidly. A large number of accountants

[13] In Bithell (1882), referencing cases such as *Crutwell v Lye*, goodwill is described as the advantage of an existing business with a good reputation that has value, for which consideration is paid, based on the expected profits that can be obtained by entering into the business (Bithell 1882, p. 142). Andrews (1981) identifies the issues relating to goodwill by time period partitioned.

were in favor of immediately or rapidly writing off goodwill against profits (Ding et al. 2008, p. 728). The arguments of these early scholars are summarized below. Harris (1884) is regarded as the first to discuss goodwill accounting comprehensively (Hughes 1982, p. 24).

He argued that the most sound and satisfactory method of determining the value of goodwill is to base the purchase price on the principle of a short annuity. He noted that this method is not always practicable, but where it can be applied, it is far preferable to any other approach. The amount of the annuity and the period over which it should extend would vary with circumstances. In a commercial business, the tendency would likely be to ask for a comparatively large sum, payable over a comparatively short period. In a professional business, the period would probably be extended. Three and 7 years, respectively, would be about fair periods for the two types of business. In both cases, however, the payment should be a proportion of the profits actually accrued to the purchaser. This ensures that, once the proportion of profits and the repayment period are agreed, the vendor receives precisely the value of what was sold, while the purchaser pays a fair price for the acquisition. In Harris's example, the premises were leased, and in the books of the retail business, a goodwill account was opened. The debit balance was written off annually by transfers from the Profit and Loss Account, sufficient to extinguish the item by the termination of the lease (Harris 1884, p. 10). In other words, Harris (1884) considered the short annuity method the most appropriate approach to valuing goodwill and noted that, in leasing businesses, amortization was carried out annually. This indicates that Harris (1884) accepted the regular amortization of goodwill.

In response, More (1891) strongly advocated early amortization and is regarded as the first to examine goodwill valuation in detail (Carsberg 1966, pp. 2–4; Hughes 1982, p. 26). He argued that when the consideration is a cash payment, there is a significant risk of treating the payment as a permanent capital investment rather than as an advance by capital to be recovered from revenue at the earliest possible date. Goodwill, particularly marketable goodwill, can disappear at any time; therefore, it is highly imprudent for a company to allow a large sum to remain on its balance sheet as goodwill unless a reserve exists to absorb potential losses should profits fall to ordinary trade levels, causing the goodwill to vanish (More 1891, p. 286).

Similarly, Matheson (1884) argued: Where the item of goodwill appears, or where it is known that the purchase price was considerably increased because the business was a going concern or earning a high rate of profit, the goodwill should be specifically written down; otherwise, shareholders may consider that they have the full value of the goodwill and the reserve as well. The stability of goodwill depends on a variety of circumstances that cannot be assured. A change of management or vicissitudes of trade beyond the proprietors' control are examples (Matheson 1884, p. 42).

If the undertaking has been purchased as a going concern and a specific sum paid for goodwill, similar considerations arise. There are also cases where goodwill constitutes such a real and significant asset that it would be incorrect to cancel it in the capital accounts. This occurs, for example, when the name, trade-mark, or brand of a manufacturer has been so long or widely established as to ensure a regular and profitable flow of business (Matheson 1884, pp. 23–24).

If there is goodwill, the undertaking evidently possesses a certain live value that it would not have as a mere aggregation of buildings and plant. The special value derived from this factor will naturally vary. Better prices may be obtainable than in other, less well-known undertakings, or during slow periods, the factory may remain fairly well employed while others are idle. However, because the permanence of such favorable conditions depends on many future and uncertain contingencies, their capitalized value must be calculated conservatively. Goodwill, whether paid for directly or not, generally represents substantial past expenditure in establishing the business. Even if proprietors have prudently written this off, since it is not represented by material assets, it may still legitimately be charged to new entrants who are to benefit from it (Matheson 1884, pp. 68–69).[14]

Furthermore, Guthrie (1898) also argued that early amortization is desirable. That is, no goodwill is eternal. Its value may fluctuate over time, but in the long run, according to human experience, nothing lasts forever (Guthrie 1898, p. 428). Some provision, however small, should be made for its eventual extinction, whether its estimated life—an estimate that is almost always entirely arbitrary—is 10 years or a hundred. The number of years' purchase paid for the goodwill is seldom a reliable guide. For example, in the case of goodwill purchased at 5 years' purchase, it could not be extinguished within the next 5 years, as that would deprive the capitalist or shareholder of all income for that period from a property acquired for the benefit of a much longer term. The judgment then arises as to what ratio the period of redemption should bear to the period of the purchase. Guthrie could not answer this definitively and opted to leave this element of charge to the judgment of the proprietor or company management. The closest approximation Guthrie could suggest was to set aside annually, as a charge against revenue, a sum equal to half the amount of the year's purchase of the goodwill as originally paid, so far as the excess profits would allow (Guthrie 1898, p. 429).

Similarly, the view that early amortization is desirable was widely held, as reflected in Bourne (1888), Roby (1892), and others. Bourne (1888) argued that a successful business could comfortably amortize the amount and that doing so was prudent, given the uncertainty of future events (Bourne 1888, p. 604). Roby (1892, p. 293) emphasized the variability of goodwill value, noting that accidental factors could enhance its value and that the purchase of goodwill often carried significant uncertainty: "Probably your conclusion will be that the purchase of goodwill is like the purchase of a lottery ticket. You may win the prize, but more likely you will draw a blank" (Roby 1892, p. 293).

[14] Where such goodwill has been maintained through advertising or other active measures, its value must not be assessed without also considering the expenditure required to maintain it (Matheson 1884, p. 70). This implies that internally generated goodwill should be recognized as an asset.

Additionally, Densham (1898) argued that early amortization is preferable, as described below.[15] Goodwill is an intangible and unreliable asset. It is often initially over-valued, being assessed on total profits rather than after deducting interest on capital. No asset is more uncertain in valuation than the goodwill of a business. Its value depends so heavily on trade contingencies that it can never safely be regarded as permanent; even substantial goodwill may disappear entirely within a few months. In the event of liquidation, goodwill becomes worthless, potentially resulting in only, for example, ten shillings in the pound being paid to the proprietors. It is prudent, therefore, to reduce the value of an asset that may prove worthless on realization and which, in the event of liquidation, is almost certain not to yield its recorded value (Densham 1898, p. 570).

3.2.3.2 Developments During 1900–1929

As outlined above, when discussions on the accounting treatment of goodwill began in earnest in the 1890s, many believed that goodwill was not permanent and should be amortized promptly. In the 1900s, the Companies Act (1900) in the United Kingdom required that the amount paid for goodwill be disclosed in the prospectus at the time of share issuance. This created a need to clarify methods for valuing goodwill, leading to extensive debate on goodwill accounting (Dicksee and Tillyard 1906, pp. vi, 29). Around the turn of the twentieth century, immediate expensing or accelerated amortization against the year's profits fell increasingly out of favor, while a more static approach, involving charging goodwill to equity, gained popularity (Ding et al. 2008, p. 731; Garcia et al. 2018).

Early writers on goodwill focused on partnership and proprietorship forms of business rather than corporations, considering in detail the legal implications arising from the sale and transfer of such firms. One reason for this focus may have been the sale of professional practices, which was more common in England than in the United States. In both countries, corporations were not yet as economically significant as they would later become. Attention shifted to corporate issues around the turn of the century, when large trusts came to dominate the economic landscape (Hughes 1982, p. 24). In the United States, a major issue concerned the treatment of capital without inflating or diluting it by recording goodwill as an asset on the balance sheet to address capital shortages. This practice was frequently employed during mergers of large companies, and considerable debate arose regarding the difference between goodwill recorded in this way and actual goodwill (Wildman 1914, p. 146).

Amid these developments, debate persisted over the desirability of capitalizing and amortizing so-called original goodwill. By the 1900s, arguments favoring systematic amortization over early amortization began to emerge. This approach

[15] Furthermore, Knight (1908, p. 197) argued that goodwill has an uncertain value and considered the best approach to be the disposal of such an account through a charge to amortization, with writing off encouraged.

involves recording goodwill at its acquisition cost and amortizing it regularly over its useful life or over the period of revenue generation used to calculate its present value. The first to propose this method in the 1900s was Hatfield (1909), who stated the following.

This doctrine of the permanence of goodwill appears inconsistent with the theory of valuing it as the purchase of a temporary, terminating annuity (Hatfield 1909, p. 116). The most satisfactory approach is generally to write off goodwill in proportion to the number of years. In any case, it remains an uncertain asset, and amortization—though not legally required—is justified on the grounds of conservatism. Where it is clear that the goodwill has been over-valued and is not worth its book value, the best method of adjustment, as advocated by Dicksee, is to offset the decline in value by a reduction of capital rather than by a charge against profits (Hatfield 1909, p. 117).

In this respect, Hatfield supported the systematic amortization of goodwill based on a conservative approach. This differs from the argument for systematic amortization in cost accounting, which became established after 1930. He further argued that impairment of goodwill should be recognized as a deduction from capital rather than as an expense when its value declines, contrasting with cost accounting principles, which treat costs as expenses.

Responding to this, Leake (1914, 1921) provided a different justification for amortization, which contributed to the widespread acceptance of amortization. He defined goodwill as the present value of future super-profits, where super-profit represents the amount by which revenue, increase in value, or other advantage received exceed all economic expenditures incidental to its production (Leake 1914, p. 81; Leake 1921, p. 19). Accordingly, goodwill should be amortized over time.[16] The reasons are as follows.

First, regarding the permanence of goodwill, it is clear that, owing to the operation of economic laws, super-profit can never exist permanently. One principal reason for the temporary nature of super-profit is competition. Commercial competition is universal and constantly seeks to capture any super-profit wherever it arises. Whenever an undertaking earns super-profits, it tends to attract imitators, which reduces earnings and ultimately levels them to a rate of profit not exceeding the normal return on invested capital, considering the nature of the risk. Another reason why super-profit is inherently temporary is that demand for any commodity or service may at any time decline or cease, owing to changing conditions, including new inventions. On these commonly accepted economic grounds, super-profit cannot be treated as perpetual; it is essentially an annuity over an unknown but limited period, and therefore the value of goodwill is not permanent (Leake 1914, pp. 83–84; 1921, p. 26). Evidently, commercial super-profit cannot persist indefinitely (Leake 1921, p. 81).

---

[16] Leake (1921, pp. 82–89) proposed that the amortization amount should not be treated as an expense but allocated to profits after dividend distribution, and that amortization should not be required when profits after dividends are low.

Even if the value of the now existing goodwill is not less than the value of the goodwill which existed at the date of purchase, it is still necessary to write off the cost of the earlier goodwill gradually, because part of that cost has expired. There is no question that part of the cost has expired; the only issue is determining the proportion that has expired. It can be safely stated that capital outlay on the purchase of goodwill inevitably expires year by year, whether the profits of an undertaking are increasing or decreasing (Leake 1921, p. 77). A common objection to writing off goodwill is that the goodwill of a prosperous undertaking earning large surplus profits is worth no less now than it was when purchased 10 or 20 years ago. The response is that the present goodwill is not the same goodwill that was purchased 10 or 20 years ago (Leake 1921, p. 78).

In this regard, Leake (1914, 1921) identified two points as the basis for systematic amortization of goodwill. First, the value of goodwill is not permanent and will eventually disappear. Second, current goodwill differs from the goodwill acquired at the time of purchase, and the goodwill acquired at the time of purchase will diminish over time.[17]

Similar to Leake (1914, 1921), Yang (1927) also argued that systematic amortization is preferable. When purchasing tangible assets such as machinery and equipment, we typically estimate their useful life in advance and allocate the purchase price over this period to compare cost and efficiency, thereby assessing the advisability of the purchase. For intangible assets, following the same procedure is reasonable. The purchaser estimates the number of years during which superior earnings are expected to accrue. In the absence of definite evidence to the contrary, the purchaser's judgment at the time of appraisal must be deemed correct and should be applied consistently throughout the succeeding periods. It is generally true that, in any individual case, it is almost impossible to analyze precisely the factors affecting earnings from one period to another. As a practical suggestion, no serious error is likely to result if the purchaser's basis of amortization is applied consistently (Yang 1927, pp. 196–197).

Regardless of how the superior earning capacity was created by the former proprietor, the purchaser of such earnings has incurred a cost or made an investment to enjoy the associated privileges. In other words, what constitutes profits to the vendor represents a pecuniary sacrifice to the purchaser—a condition that must be met to secure the profit-generating capacity created by the vendor. In accounting, expense or cost is a monetary concept, and the fact that the payment may relate to the opportunity to realize excess earnings does not justify a different treatment. Payments for intangible properties often include expenses that would have been necessary had the purchaser developed the present earnings independently (Yang 1927, p. 208).

In this regard, Yang (1927) argued that intangible assets should be subject to systematic amortization in the same way as fixed assets. Although estimating useful

[17] The arguments put forward by Leake for systematic amortization closely parallel those set out in ASBJ Statement No. 21, Business Combinations, issued in 2008 by the ASBJ (para. 105), as noted above.

lives involves uncertainty, this applies equally to both intangible and fixed assets, and applying the same procedures as for amortization should not create practical problems. Furthermore, he asserted that the consideration for intangible assets represents purely historical cost, and the fact that expenses or costs are monetary concepts reflecting expenditures for the opportunity to realize excess profits does not justify a different treatment.

Similarly, Stockwell (1912, p. 111) maintained that goodwill acquired in a purchase should be amortized annually until the book balance is fully eliminated. Roth (1929, p. 104) added that conservative business policy requires goodwill to be written off in proportion to the super-profits for which payment has been made in advance. Under this treatment, purchased goodwill is regarded as a prepayment to be gradually charged off—either as a business expense, analogous to amortization, or as a charge against the net profits or surplus account, similar to a true dividend payment.[18]

3.2.3.3 Developments During the 1930s–1970s

In the 1930s, conservative attitudes that developed during the Depression coincided with a discernible shift in accounting focus from determining net worth to measuring periodic net income. As a result, only amounts actually paid for an asset in the purchase of a going concern were accepted for accounting for goodwill, and the cost basis for goodwill became firmly established (Hughes 1982, p. 201). Regarding historical cost accounting, Scott and O'Brien (2012, p. 3) noted that one accounting practice of the 1920s—appraisal valuation—was criticized for overstating capital assets, the values of which collapsed in 1929. A major lesson from the Great Depression was that asset values are fleeting, leading to a strengthening of historical cost accounting based on completed transactions.

Between 1940 and 1970, three main developments occurred in the United States: the doctrine and practice of writing off goodwill declined, dynamic approaches gained prominence, and some resistance persisted to doctrines that excluded goodwill from profit calculations. The decline in the traditional doctrine is particularly evident from around 1945 to 1970. Paton, the leading accounting author of the time, supported dynamic approaches and opposed goodwill write-off. His opponents were generally minor authors, often practitioners, such as Catlett and Olson (1968) and Spacek (1969) (Ding et al. 2008, p. 735). First, we summarize the arguments of Paton, Littleton, Walker, and others who advocated for systematic amortization. Next, we summarize the arguments of Catlett, Olson, Spacek, and others who opposed systematic amortization.

[18] Canning (1929, pp. 43–44) observed that, characteristically, these accounts are written off over relatively short periods. This occurs despite the fact that the conditions prompting the original outlay may still be ongoing. In other words, accountants tend to exclude items that do not represent separable sets of services yet to be received, while carefully identifying all separable sets of future services that can be reliably valued.

3.2.3.3.1 Arguments on Accounting Standards for Systematic Amortization in the U.S.

As noted above, following the Great Depression of 1929, systematic amortization became established alongside historical cost accounting. From the 1940s onward, systematic amortization methods, such as those proposed by Paton and Littleton (1940) and Paton (1941), gained broad support. Accounting standards reflected this trend as well. ARB 24, issued by the AIA in 1944, stipulated that in the event that it becomes reasonably evident that the term of existence of intangibles has become limited, the cost should be amortized by systematic charges in the income statement over the estimated remaining period of usefulness (ARB 24, p. 196).[19]

APB 17, issued in 1970, provided the rationale for prescribing systematic amortization as the primary method for accounting for goodwill. It noted that all assets represented by deferred costs are essentially alike in historical-cost based accounting. They result from expenditures or owners' contributions and are expected to increase revenue or reduce costs to be incurred in future periods. Associating deferred costs with the revenue or period to which they are expected to relate is a basic problem in historical-cost based accounting both in measuring periodic income and in accounting for assets. The basic accounting treatment does not depend on whether the asset is a building, a piece of equipment, or whether it is tangible or intangible. The cost of goodwill is therefore essentially the same as the cost of land, building, or equipment under historical-cost based accounting. Deducting the cost of an asset from stockholders' equity at the date incurred does not match costs with revenue (APB 17, para. 21).

Accounting for the cost of a long-lived asset after acquisition normally depends on its estimated life. The cost of assets with perpetual existence is carried forward as an asset without amortization, and the cost of assets with finite lives is amortized by systematic charges to income. Goodwill and similar intangible assets do not clearly fit either classification: their lives are neither infinite nor specifically limited but are indeterminate. Thus, although the principles underlying present practice conform to the principles of accounting for similar types of assets, their applications have led to alternative treatments. Amortizing the cost of goodwill and similar intangible asset on arbitrary bases in the absence of evidence of limited lives or decreased value may recognize expenses and decreases of assets prematurely, but delaying amortization of the cost until a loss is evident may recognize the decreases after the fact (APB 17, para. 22).[20]

[19] As noted above, ARB 43, issued by the AIA in 1953, also provided guidance on the application of systematic amortization for goodwill.

[20] One solution to this dilemma is to establish minimum and maximum amortization periods. This accounting follows from the observation that few, if any, intangible assets last forever, although some may seem to last almost indefinitely. Allocating the cost of goodwill with an indeterminate life over time is necessary because the value almost inevitably becomes zero at some future date. Since the date at which the value becomes zero is indeterminate, the end of the useful life must necessarily be set arbitrarily at some point or within some range of time for accounting purposes (APB 17, para. 23).

The value of intangible assets at any one date eventually disappears and that the recorded costs of intangible assets should be amortized by systematic charges to income over the periods estimated to be benefited. The period of amortization of intangible assets should be determined from the pertinent factors (APB 17, para. 27). The period of amortization should not exceed 40 years (APB 17, para. 29). APB 17 is notable in that its justification for capitalizing purchased goodwill as an asset is based on its consistency with the treatment of other assets under historical-cost accounting. This differs from the arguments for the equity method cited by Catlett and Olson (1968, ARS 10) and others, which focus on aligning the accounting treatment of purchased goodwill with that of internally generated goodwill.

3.2.3.3.2 Support for Systematic Amortization

Paton and Littleton (1940) are representative proponents of systematic amortization during this period. They argued that the cost of goodwill included in the purchase price of a going concern is essentially the discounted value of the estimated excess earning power: the amount of net income anticipated in excess of the income sufficient to provide the tangible resources involved with a normal rate of return. Thus, purchased goodwill represents an advance recognition of a debit for a portion of income that is expected to materialize later. It follows that the amount expended for goodwill should be absorbed by revenue charges during the period implicit in the computation on which the price paid was based, so that the income not paid for in advance may be measured (Paton and Littleton 1940, p. 92).

This conclusion is supported by the fact that there is ample evidence in available business histories showing that extraordinary earning power cannot be expected to persist indefinitely. An investment in anticipated excess earnings should be construed as a temporary investment, recoverable within a period of a few years. Even if a superior level of income persists beyond the period anticipated, the amortization of the cost of goodwill in terms of the original computation is generally justified on the ground that there is no way of demonstrating that the later earning power is due to factors and conditions present when the business was acquired. It is just as easy, and perhaps more reasonable, to assume that the success achieved beyond that originally predicted is due to new developments in no way represented by the cost of the goodwill (Paton and Littleton 1940, p. 93).

The fact that it is not considered feasible to accumulate as a deferred charge costs presumably assignable to future revenues is hardly adequate justification for failing to write off a cost that is presumably expiring (Paton 1941, p. 409). Accounting should treat the periodic charge as a revenue deduction, except in situations in which interpretation as a loss is clearly called for (Paton 1941, p. 410). Some claim that, since the existence of intangibles depends upon earning power, the cost or value of goodwill may be maintained on the books undisturbed so long as the level of income does not fall below that implicit in the original purchase or valuation. This position is objectionable in that it is inconsistent with the assumptions ordinarily made in determining the intangible value. If the amount of goodwill as acquired is conceived as the present worth of a terminable series of special incomes, it would seem to follow that the asset should be written off against revenues through the period in which such incomes are expected to be realized (Paton 1941, p. 435).

In this regard, Paton and Littleton (1940) and Paton (1941) present the following arguments in favor of amortizing goodwill. First, goodwill is regarded as excess earning power. Second, excess earning power is considered temporary. Third, the amount of goodwill should be expensed over the period on which its valuation was based, in correspondence with the actual earnings generated after the acquisition. Regarding the second point, when excess profit-generating capacity appears to persist, one should distinguish between acquired goodwill and internally generated goodwill arising after the business combination, because the continued excess profitability may result from factors other than the business combination itself.

Similar to the arguments advanced by Paton and others, Walker (1938, 1953) also examined the case for systematic amortization in detail. He described the amortization of goodwill as the cost of a fixed intangible asset in the form of a charge to operations. That is, the first stage of such cost is that of a fixed intangible asset; the second stage is that of a cost of operation. It is therefore suggested that when purchased goodwill is written off, "Amortization Expense" should appear as an operating expense on the profit-and-loss statement for that period (Walker 1938, p. 181).

Walker further argued that the cost of purchased goodwill should be written off or amortized on a systematic basis, without regard to the profitability of the enterprise during a given year or even a period of years. At the time that goodwill is brought into the accounts, a decision should be made as to the length of the period over which annual charges are to be made to operations. The method or plan of amortization can be as scientific or objective as any plan for charging depreciation on fixed tangible assets (Walker 1953, pp. 212–213). He maintained that when purchased goodwill is amortized according to a systematic plan, a charge to current operations is the only type of charge consistent with the definition and meaning of goodwill and the functions of accounting. The cost of the goodwill represents a cost of securing income in the same sense that the costs of machinery and rent are costs of securing income. The annual amortization charge should be matched with the income for the year in the same manner as other costs of current operations (Walker 1953, p. 215).

In support of the systematic amortization of purchased goodwill, several points can be summarized. First, in accordance with the primary function of accounting to match costs and incomes, the cost of purchased goodwill should be amortized as a means of matching the cost of securing the income against the income actually received. All purchases are made for the purpose of an income return greater than the outlay, or as an aid to that goal. The cost of these purchases is matched with that part of the income stream to which each cost is applicable. The matching is not in terms of the changed value of each asset. The basis for the most confusion on the question of amortizing goodwill can be traced to the word "value." Although accounting is not a process of valuation, writers continue to reach conclusions regarding the treatment of goodwill on the assumption that its present value has changed or has not changed. Depreciation charges are not made in an attempt to show present value, but as a means of allocating the cost of the asset over the period of its estimated usefulness. Goodwill amortization charges are of the same nature. The fact that the value of the building or the goodwill has increased during the year is beside the point (Walker 1953, pp. 213–214).

Critics have argued that no scientific method exists for amortizing goodwill, since accurately determining the extent to which goodwill exists or has diminished is impossible. It is readily admitted that the purchase price of goodwill is based on an estimate of the value of future expectations. However, the same is true for buildings, advertising, equipment, and all other purchased items. Likewise, practically all cost and income matching items are based on estimates. Any difference is one of degree, not of kind. Certainly, goodwill does not exist in perpetuity. Owing to the operation of economic forces, excess earnings can never exist permanently. Purchased goodwill expires, sometimes very quickly. Management must always make expenditures to maintain or increase goodwill. The cost of purchased goodwill that expires and the expenditures subsequently made to maintain goodwill must ultimately be matched against income. Similarly, the original cost of a building and current repair and maintenance costs are matched against income over a period of years (Walker 1953, p. 214).

The argument for systematic amortization presented by Walker (1938, 1953) is similar to that of Paton and Littleton (1940). His position may be summarized as follows. The amount paid for acquired goodwill is a cost of obtaining income in the same sense that machinery and rent are costs of obtaining income, and its amortization should be matched with income for the year in the same way as other operating expenses. Systematic amortization of goodwill can be as reasonable as the depreciation of tangible fixed assets. Depreciation is not intended to indicate present value but to allocate the cost of an asset over its estimated useful life, and the amortization of goodwill is of the same nature.

Wyatt (1963, ARS 5) likewise argued in favor of systematic amortization. A business combination, which is essentially an exchange transaction between independent parties, should be accounted for in a manner similar to other exchange transactions. Any excess of the fair value of assets acquired over their book value should be accounted for as follows (Wyatt 1963, pp. 105–106):

(a) Any portion of the excess attributable to tangible assets or specific intangibles should be so allocated and amortized over the appropriate period of useful life.
(b) Any portion attributable to goodwill that appears to have limited value should be amortized over the period of expected limited life.
(c) Any portion attributable to goodwill that does not appear to have a limited life should be carried forward to future periods until evidence indicates that the value is impaired.

Summarizing these conclusions on the proper treatment of the excess of the fair value of consideration given over the book value of assets acquired: (1) any portion attributable to tangible assets or specific intangibles other than goodwill should be amortized over the appropriate period of useful life; (2) any portion attributable to goodwill that appears to have limited value should be amortized over the period of expected limited life; and (3) any portion attributable to goodwill that does not appear to have a limited life should be carried forward to future periods until evidence indicates that the value is impaired (Wyatt 1963, p. 98).

Further support for systematic amortization has been provided by other authors. In particular, Emery (1951, pp. 565–566) argued that, as a matter of theory, purchased goodwill should be written off systematically even when intangible value continues to exist at a level at least equal to that present at the time of purchase. The purchaser pays for the super-profits expected to arise from the intangible value associated with the business at the time of acquisition. However, these super-profits cannot be expected to persist unless new intangible value is created to replace that originally acquired.

Furthermore, Nelson (1953) argued as follows. Momentum Theory holds that a buyer acquires a promotional "push" rather than an annuity in the form of a series of excess earnings, and this "push" diminishes over time like momentum. The assumption that such an asset may exist in perpetuity is highly questionable. Therefore, the investment should be charged against income over the estimated life of the momentum, that is, the period during which it contributes its benefit (Nelson 1953, pp. 491–492). If the investment in purchased goodwill were carried on the books without amortization even after the momentum had dissipated, and if the buyer had created new momentum to replace it, the recorded amount would no longer represent the purchased momentum. Instead, it would represent self-developed goodwill (Nelson 1953, p. 493). The money spent on goodwill is no different from money spent on plant and equipment, and the representation of purchased assets on the balance sheet should reflect this fact (Nelson 1953, p. 492).

Similarly, Meigs and Johnson (1962, p. 424) argued that the cost of goodwill generally represents the price paid to obtain excess profits for a limited period, typically 4 or 5 years from the date of purchase. Accordingly, the goodwill account should be written off against earnings during those same years. This treatment aligns with the general principle of matching costs with revenues. They noted that current accounting practice increasingly treats goodwill in a manner consistent with other tangible and intangible fixed assets, by writing off the cost over the years during which benefits are expected. If a company that has purchased goodwill subsequently experiences operating losses, the goodwill may appropriately be written off immediately. Companies justify carrying intangible assets on the balance sheet only when sound reason exists to expect benefits from them in future periods.

Hylton (1964, p. 30) made a similar point. The accounting convention of matching costs with related revenues requires that only those costs associated with generating the revenue of the period be recognized in the income statement. Increases in the value of tangible assets represent a cost of acquiring earning power, and the same is true of the amount paid for goodwill. Determining the appropriate period for writing off purchased goodwill is difficult owing to the intangible and highly variable nature of goodwill. However, a relatively short amortization period is considered prudent. Ideally, purchased goodwill should be written off over the years during which it contributes to increased earnings.

3.2.3.3.3 Critiques of Systematic Amortization

During this period, many commentators supported systematic amortization, but several also raised arguments critical of the practice (Ding et al. 2008, p. 735).

Catlett and Olson (1968) argued that the charge for amortization of goodwill resulting from one alternative method of accounting for goodwill should be eliminated from the income statement. Amortization can neither be reasonably related to the revenue of a period nor reasonably associated in any other manner with specific time periods (Catlett and Olson 1968, p. 91). In their view, the amortization of purchased goodwill in the determination of earnings does not represent the cost of a resource consumed to produce those earnings. Goodwill is a result of earnings or of the expectations of earnings; amortization of goodwill has an improper circular effect because it may affect the values those earnings are intended to measure (Catlett and Olson 1968, p. 112).

Spacek (1964, p. 39) similarly criticized systematic amortization. He argued that the amortization of goodwill against income is improper. Income statements should show earnings from operations, undistorted by items that are unrelated to operations, such as charges for the amortization of goodwill. The public then forms an opinion, which is constantly changing, as to what future earnings are likely to be. Viewed in this light, charges to the income statement for the cost of earning power result in a statement that is misleading and likely to confuse unsophisticated users.

Similarly, Burton (1970, p. 88) also argued against amortization.[21] He maintained that goodwill is fundamentally different from other assets reported on the financial statements because it is based on future earning power rather than being the source of it. Therefore, it should not be treated as an operating asset of the acquiring firm, and amortizing it through the income statement is inappropriate. The basic matching model of accounting assumes that costs are incurred in order to produce revenues and should be matched against those revenues to determine income. However, stockholder-purchased goodwill does not affect the firm's revenue stream; revenues are generated by the operation of the purchased assets. Amortizing goodwill as a charge against earnings would therefore distort operating reality and obscure the economic results of the firm's activities.

Burton proposed that goodwill should be presented in a separate section of the balance sheet as "Cost of Future Earning Power Acquired in Business Combination," with a corresponding new stockholders' equity account titled "Equity Representing Future Earning Power Acquired in Business Combinations." The amounts in the asset and equity accounts would then be gradually reduced over a period of years, preferably based on a percentage of the earnings of the acquired entity (Burton 1970, p. 89).

Eiteman (1971, pp. 48–49) also argued against amortization, noting that the cost of goodwill has an indeterminate life and provides no sound basis for calculating expense for any single period or longer. The cost of goodwill represents a payment

---

[21] This proposal is also attributed to Burton in FASB (1976, paras. 181–183, 208–209).

for the outcome of earnings, or the expectation of them, and this cost is not consumed in the production of those earnings. Furthermore, significant expenditures are often made after acquisition, such as for advertising, to maintain or enhance the value of the investment as an income-producing factor and to preserve or increase excess earnings. Accordingly, the original cost of unidentifiable intangibles should not be amortized against revenue or written off as an extraordinary item unless and until a permanent impairment in earning power occurs.

3.2.3.4 Developments Since the 1980s

3.2.3.4.1 Arguments on Accounting Standards for Systematic Amortization in the U.K. and IASC

As discussed in the previous section, the concept of systematic amortization had become widespread in the United States by the 1970s and was made mandatory under accounting standards. In line with this development, even in the United Kingdom, where the write-off against equity approach had long been applied, the practice became mandatory under SSAP 22, which came into effect in 1984.

Subsequently, FRS 10, which came into force in 1997, prohibited the equity method and required systematic amortization. The rationale for systematic amortization is as follows. Goodwill arising on an acquisition is neither an asset like other assets nor an immediate loss in value. Rather, it forms the bridge between the cost of an investment, shown as an asset in the acquirer's financial statements, and the values attributed to the acquired assets and liabilities in the consolidated financial statements. Although purchased goodwill is not itself an asset, its inclusion among the assets of the reporting entity, rather than as a deduction from shareholders' equity, recognizes that goodwill is part of a larger asset—the investment—for which management remains accountable (FRS 10, Summary b).

Reflecting this view of goodwill as a bridge between the value of an acquired business in the entity's own financial statements and the values of its net identifiable assets in the consolidated financial statements, the useful economic life of purchased goodwill is defined as the period over which the value of the acquired business is expected to exceed the values of its identifiable assets and liabilities. Accounting standards create a rebuttable presumption that the useful economic lives of purchased goodwill and intangible assets are limited and do not exceed 20 years from the acquisition date. Where goodwill and intangible assets are regarded as having limited useful economic lives, they should be amortized over those lives. Where goodwill and intangible assets are regarded as having indefinite useful economic lives, they should not be amortized (FRS 10, Summary f–h).

In this regard, the rationale behind FRS 10 requiring the recognition of purchased goodwill as an asset and its systematic amortization is that goodwill is viewed as a bridge between the value of the acquiree and the value of its net identifiable assets. Goodwill with these characteristics is subject to management accountability as part of the broader investment. Therefore, although goodwill is not an asset in itself, it is included in the assets of the reporting entity rather than deducted from shareholders' equity. Moreover, where a useful life can be identified, purchased goodwill must be amortized over that period.

FRS 10 recognizes the asset value of purchased goodwill from the perspective of management responsibility, but this position directly conflicts with the argument put forward by Catlett and Olson, Spacek, and others that goodwill reduces the assets for which management is responsible. Furthermore, the rationale for systematic amortization presented in FRS 10 differs from the idea of matching the allocation of historical cost with revenue, as described by Paton and Littleton (1940).

Developments within the IASC during the same period were similar to those in the United Kingdom. Specifically, IAS 22, issued in 1983, accepted systematic amortization and explained its reasoning as follows. Those who recognize goodwill arising on acquisition as an asset in the consolidated financial statements believe that it represents a payment made in anticipation of future income and that it is appropriate to treat it as an asset to be amortized to income on a systematic basis over its useful life (IAS 22, para. 20).

Subsequent revisions to IAS 22 in 1993 and 1998 required systematic amortization as the primary method of accounting. The rationale was that goodwill arising on acquisition represents a payment made by the acquirer in anticipation of future economic benefits. The future economic benefits may result from synergy between the identifiable assets acquired or from assets which, individually, do not qualify for recognition in the financial statements but for which the acquirer is prepared to make a payment in the acquisition. With the passage of time, goodwill diminishes, reflecting its reduced capacity to contribute to the future income of the enterprise. Therefore, it is appropriate that goodwill is amortized and charged as an expense on a systematic basis over its useful life (IAS 22, rev. 1993, paras. 41, 43).

Similarly, the 1998 revision of IAS 22 stated that goodwill arising on acquisition represents a payment made by the acquirer in anticipation of future economic benefits. The future economic benefits may result from synergy between the identifiable assets acquired or from assets which, individually, do not qualify for recognition in the financial statements but for which the acquirer is prepared to make a payment in the acquisition. Goodwill should be amortized on a systematic basis over its useful life. The amortization period should reflect the best estimate of the period during which future economic benefits are expected to flow to the enterprise (IAS 22, rev. 1998, paras. 41, 42, 44).

3.2.3.4.2 Support for Systematic Amortization

During the 1980s and 1990s, systematic amortization gradually gained acceptance in accounting standards not only in the United States but also in the United Kingdom and under IAS. Positive arguments supporting systematic amortization during this period include those presented by Grinyer et al. (1990).[22] They assumed that the most fundamental, and therefore primary, purpose of accounts is the monitoring and motivation of management, and its arguments are developed within an "accountability" context (Grinyer et al. 1990, p. 225). The objective of accountability implies that purchased goodwill should be charged against profits under a matching approach to profit measurement. It requires that all sums paid by management to generate future cash inflows are, at some point, charged to that account, which is desirable when using financial statements to assess managers' financial performance (Grinyer et al. 1990, p. 231).

Given the accountability role of financial reporting, management should be required to expense, through the profit and loss account, all outlays incurred to generate additional revenues over time. Acquired goodwill is, by definition, such an outlay. The matching convention requires that this cost be allocated according to the pattern of inflows it generates. On this basis, the primary stewardship purpose of financial statements is best served by capitalizing and amortizing goodwill (Grinyer et al. 1990, p. 111).

In addition, Glautier and Underdown (1997, p. 172) argued in favor of systematic amortization as follows. Goodwill should be shown as an asset and treated like other fixed assets. Therefore, it should be capitalized and written off over a period of years, a treatment commonly found in the United States. Proponents of this view argued that an expense is incurred in acquiring the benefit of future earnings. As the benefits associated with goodwill are realized and the enhanced earnings actually materialize, they should be matched with the costs associated with the goodwill that gave rise to them. If costs are not matched in this way, profits will be overstated.

Similarly, Bryer (1995) presented the following argument. In late nineteenth-century Britain, leading authorities widely accepted that "goodwill" represented the purchase of sufficient expected "surplus profits" to persuade business owners to relinquish their net assets and control. This expenditure should be capitalized and amortized against those surplus profits as they are realized (Bryer 1995, p. 283). If the surplus profits of one company are purchased by another entity, this expenditure is necessary to gain control of its production process. To report the rate of return on the purchaser's capital, the cost of the surplus profits must be included as part of its productive capital, with a portion of this expenditure charged against the surplus profits as they are earned (Bryer 1995, p. 288).

---

[22] Brown (1995) presented the interest method as a theoretical benchmark and used it to illustrate the pattern of expected future benefits implicitly assumed by the main amortization methods observed in practice: the straight-line method and the inverse sum-of-the-years'-digits (ISOYD) method. Also see Black and Zyla (2018), Bloom (2008) and Weirich and Turner (1995).

3.2.3.4.3 Critiques of Amortization

Relatively few commentators expressed negative views on systematic amortization. Of these commentators, Ma and Hopkins (1988, 1992) argued that purchased goodwill is calculated by subtracting the fair value of the acquired company's net assets from the purchase price, which reflects the future prospects of the entity after the acquisition. Because this calculation compares two different concepts, the resulting difference cannot be given a meaningful economic interpretation (Ma and Hopkins 1988, pp. 81–82).

When no meaningful economic interpretation can be assigned to goodwill on acquisition—that is, when it does not represent the present value of a defined stream of benefits—systematic amortization becomes difficult to justify (Ma and Hopkins 1988, p. 83). Purchased goodwill is often not identifiable with a specific source of future benefits, and this lack of an identifiable source results in largely arbitrary, and sometimes conflicting, judgments about amortization within the matching process (Ma and Hopkins 1992, p. 114).

Several arguments oppose not only systematic amortization but also the earliest forms of amortization. For example, Heckler (1997, p. 18) argued that amortization should not be applied for purely discretionary purposes by management. The lack of guidance creates potential inconsistencies between financial statement preparers, resulting in confusion for users of financial information.

Similarly, Reed et al. (2000, pp. 87, 90) argued that the creative accounting practice of expensing the excess purchase price as identifiable in-process research and development (IPR&D), rather than capitalizing it as goodwill, affects future periods. Because companies do not amortize goodwill to offset future revenues from the benefits of IPR&D, this practice reduces the comparability of financial statements across companies and industries.

3.2.4 Non-Amortization

3.2.4.1 Developments in the Late Nineteenth–Early Twentieth Centuries

The accounting treatment of goodwill as an asset retained at cost, without amortization or deduction from capital, is not a concept introduced by IFRS 3 or FAS 141/142 in the 2000s. Rather, it was proposed as early as the late 1880s, when the debate over the accounting treatment of goodwill first began. For example, Densham (1898) stated the following regarding non-amortization: "The amount at which goodwill is stated in the Balance Sheet is never supposed to represent either its maximum or its minimum value; no one who thought of purchasing a business would be influenced by the amount at which the goodwill was stated in the accounts; in short, the account is absolutely meaningless except as an indication of what the goodwill may have cost in the first instance. Inasmuch, therefore, as nobody can be deceived by its retention, there is no practical necessity for the amount of the Goodwill Account to be written down" (Densham 1898, p. 570).

Other scholars of this period also expressed positive views on non-amortization. Dawson (1908, p. 226) argued that the primary purpose of accounts is to provide a true statement not only of the company's financial position but also of its trading for the current period. This latter objective is naturally obscured if extraneous profits or losses are allowed to affect the profit and loss account. Even if it is considered desirable to write off goodwill gradually, the proper method is undoubtedly not by means of a charge to the profit and loss account. Any amount credited to the goodwill account must be a sum set aside from profits and is not a charge against profits.[23]

Similarly, Browne (1902, p. 1342) stated that the elimination of goodwill is clearly not possible through the capital account of a company, as the subscribed capital cannot be increased or decreased except by methods prescribed in the Companies Acts. Therefore, goodwill can only be dealt with out of profits. Browne expressed the view that, since goodwill is an asset distinctly paid for by shareholders and represented in their capital on the opposite side of the balance sheet, profits should not be charged for its reduction or extinction. He further noted that the very possibility of applying current profits to reduce or extinguish goodwill, as it stands in the books, is one of the strongest proofs of its value.[24]

In the 1910s, while the write-off against equity became widespread in practice, the accounting treatment of non-amortization increasingly came to be strongly advocated as the sound approach. Montgomery (1912) stated: "This asset is in a class by itself. The question of depreciation certainly cannot be applied to it as to other items. If earnings decline for any reason, the value of goodwill declines correspondingly, because by its very nature its value depends on earnings of a certain amount being maintained. Goodwill, however, always appears, or should appear, on the balance sheet as a separate item, and well-established practice permits it to appear at cost, irrespective of fluctuations which affect its value. In fact, its actual value changes from day to day, and there would be so much uncertainty in any attempt to adjust its book value that, by common consent, it is left alone, except in cases where earnings are unusually large and it is considered advisable to write it off. As goodwill does not suffer wear and tear, does not become obsolescent, and is not used up in the operation of the business, depreciation, as such, cannot be charged against it. When it is written off, a secret reserve may be created, so that no criticism can be sustained where it is permitted to stand at cost" (Montgomery, 1912, p. 131).

[23] In Dawson (1898) and the first edition of Dawson (1908), references to goodwill (Dawson 1898, pp. 190–192) are limited to introducing case law and discussions by other commentators, such as Dicksee, and do not include any arguments regarding accounting treatment, such as non-amortization.

[24] Similarly, Dawson (1901, p. 50) argued that goodwill does not amortize but rather improves with age, provided that profits are maintained. He suggested that the best course of action is to keep goodwill in the Balance Sheet at cost and to gradually set aside a special reserve from profits until the reserve equals the cost of the goodwill.

Similarly, Dickinson (1913) argued that goodwill represents the value of the trade name, business connections, and organization of the undertaking. If the business's earnings remain at or above the level anticipated at the date of purchase, no amortization of value or need for a provision arises. On the other hand, if serious amortization occurs, profits are likely so reduced that making such a provision is impracticable. Goodwill is, in fact, a fixed asset whose value is to some extent dependent on the profits earned, with its fluctuations resulting from, rather than causing, profits. Unlike wasting or partially wasting assets, it should not be taken into account in determining profits. Goodwill can reasonably be treated as part of the permanent invested capital of the business, which may be maintained at its original value as long as the business remains a going concern (Dickinson 1913, pp. 79–80).

Esquerrē (1913, 1914) also supported non-amortization: "If a concern has paid a large sum to acquire the goodwill of another, and has not only retained it but even increased it, there is no apparent reason why so-called conservatism should demand writing off the asset, to the detriment of the very profits which its purchase gave the right to expect" (Esquerrē 1913, p. 25; 1914, p. 248). He later added: "There is no reason why it [goodwill] should be amortized, depreciated, written down, or otherwise deprived of its vitality and meaning" (Esquerrē 1927, p. 191).

Similarly, Kester (1918, pp. 337–338) expressed his opinion in favor of non-amortization. That is, since the essence of goodwill is its ability to earn excess profits, its value must naturally fluctuate over time with the earnings of the business. The effect of periodic write-offs, so long as any value remains in goodwill, is to create a secret reserve, which is justified on the ground of conservatism. The practice is not reprehensible, though it is usually to be discouraged.

The weight of authority holds that all purposes are best served by allowing goodwill to remain on the books at cost. There is usually no logical basis for writing it off. When profits are large, goodwill is a very real asset, and writing it off then is not logically consistent. When profits are small and goodwill has declined, it would hardly be logical to write off any portion less than its decreased value, yet profits at such times are rarely sufficient to permit such treatment. Since the asset does not depreciate but only fluctuates in value, and since it is neither prudent nor consistently possible to record these changes in the books, the best course for all purposes appears to be retaining goodwill in the accounts at its cost (Kester 1918, p. 338).

Similarly, Couchman (1924) presented arguments in favor of non-amortization that are virtually identical to those of Kester (1918). That is, it would evidently not be desirable to write down goodwill if doing so would create a deficit or prevent the payment of ordinary dividends to stockholders. If the earnings of an organization are sufficient only to meet regular demands for reserves and dividends, that condition casts doubt upon the value of the goodwill and might justify a reduction of the asset. However, in such circumstances, there would be no excess profits, and a reduction in asset value would involve an impairment of capital. On the other hand, if earnings exceed dividend demands sufficiently to create an amount that could offset a reduction of goodwill, that fact itself implies that the value of the goodwill is justified and there is no reason for reducing it. In brief, if you can write it down, you need not; if you cannot, you should (Couchman 1924, p. 138).

In addition, similar arguments are found in Bentley (1911), Owens (1923), and others. The balance of this account represents an intangible fixed asset, which should remain unchanged. If a business purchases the goodwill of another business, the charge is clearly legitimate and should be carried as a permanent asset, not subject to amortization or write-off (Bentley 1911, p. 157). Since the goodwill amount in the balance sheet is not intended to represent either the maximum or minimum value of the concern, its retention in the accounts does not mislead anyone. Therefore, writing it off is unnecessary. Retaining goodwill in the accounts at its purchase price seems reasonable. Ordinarily, the only argument in favor of amortizing goodwill is conservatism (Owens 1923, p. 295).

3.2.4.2 Developments Since the 1930s

3.2.4.2.1 Support for Non-Amortization

By the early 1900s, accounting authorities generally agreed that properly recorded goodwill need not—and should not—be written off the books (Walker 1953, p. 211). Reflecting this view, accounting standards such as ARB 24, issued in 1944, and ARB 43, issued in 1953, also accepted the non-amortization treatment. In this period, Walker (1953, p. 211) presented arguments supporting non-amortization from three perspectives.

First, it is overconservative to write goodwill off the books when it has not amortized in value below the purchase price. Writing off goodwill in such cases creates a secret reserve, and recognizing this reserve is considered unorthodox accounting. Goodwill suffers no actual decline in value as long as the earning capacity of the enterprise is maintained.

Second, when goodwill has actually amortized, it is not necessary to record that amortization in the operating accounts. The extent to which goodwill exists is best reflected in the profit-and-loss record. Its value fluctuates according to the expected future earning potential of the enterprise. It is permissible to write goodwill off the books when it is declining in value or has lost its value, but amortization is not required.

Third, it is impossible to determine accurately the extent of goodwill amortization. This fact has been accepted by some accountants as a major reason why it should not be included in the accounts unless purchased. The owner of a business cannot make an impartial estimate of the extent to which goodwill has amortized. Consequently, since appreciation of goodwill is not recognized in the accounts, neither should amortization be charged.

These debates are reflected in later discussions. For instance, Staub (1945, p. 5) argued that there is no fundamental reason for, or scientific method of, writing off or amortizing the cost of intangibles whose value continues. Requiring compulsory amortization of intangibles, the value of which is being maintained or even enhanced, seems to depart from the "going concern" concept of financial statements and represents an attempt to provide for losses that may occur upon termination or liquidation of an enterprise in the future.

Similarly, May (1943, 1957) contended that if the cost of all intangible values is written off even when earning capacity is unimpaired, if all permanent declines in the earning capacity of any tangible fixed property are reflected in write-downs, and if no appreciation for any reason is allowed to be recorded, the distortion will increase (May 1943, p. 155). The conclusion indicated by this discussion is that writing off intangibles is permissible but not mandatory. In the past, accountants favored it solely on grounds of conservatism. Some regarded intangible assets as unreal and favored writing them off for that reason; but once the view is accepted that value depends on expectations for the future, the proposal is either invalid or applies almost equally to tangible assets. Experience shows that intangibles are often more enduring than tangible values (May 1943, pp. 158–159).

The corporation might be required to present in its balance sheet a statement of amortizable capital assets, which could include intangibles with a clearly limited period of usefulness. However, changes in the value of other intangible assets should neither be required nor permitted to be included in the determination of business income. The corporation might be allowed to present, in addition, a statement of other intangible assets, but changes in the value of these should also neither be required nor permitted to be included in the determination of business income (May 1957, p. 36).[25]

In addition, rather than advocating outright non-amortization, Gynther (1969) proposed that the value of goodwill be evaluated periodically, with any increase in value recognized as an ideal accounting treatment. Goodwill must at least be maintained as long as the earning power of the entity is unimpaired. Amortization should be considered only when and if earning power diminishes. Periodic recognition, revaluation, appreciation, and amortization of goodwill are necessary to present the most relevant financial-position information for external decision makers. The valuation and revaluation of goodwill should be carried out using a method that considers the capitalization of the entity's profits, the net present values of some assets, approximations of the net present values of other assets, and management's knowledge of business conditions (Gynther 1969, p. 253). Amortization should occur only when there are indications of limited existence, and a write-down should be made only when there is evidence of loss of value. A general license to amortize and write off goodwill over arbitrary periods does not constitute responsible accounting (Gynther 1969, pp. 251–252).

As noted above, APB 17 requires systematic amortization, while arguments in favor of non-amortization emphasize that goodwill is not consumed or used to produce earnings in the same manner as tangible property rights. Therefore, net income

[25] According to Simon (1956, p. 277), legal decisions are generally consistent with accounting principles and ideas regarding goodwill.

should not be reduced by amortization of goodwill. All methods of amortizing goodwill are criticized as arbitrary because the life of goodwill is indefinite and an estimated period of existence is not measurable. The basis for proposing that the cost of goodwill be retained as an asset until a loss in value becomes evident is that the cost incurred for acquired goodwill should be accounted for as an asset at the date acquired and in later periods. The cost should not be reduced as long as the value of the asset is at least equal to that cost (APB 17, paras. 18–19).

Eiteman (1971, pp. 47–48) and others argued in favor of non-amortization, noting that goodwill represents a cost incurred in good faith by competent individuals at the time of business acquisitions. Goodwill and related intangibles are valid capital assets of economic significance to the typical business enterprise; generally, they are intrinsically attached to business operations and constitute a valuable part of the economic worth of a going concern. Purchased goodwill is not a finite-lived asset like a building, equipment, or patent; it is an investment by the acquiring enterprise in a set of intangible resources of the selling company that are inherently elusive. As an investment asset, it should be carried at an unamortized amount in the balance sheet as long as there is no evidence of impairment or limitation of its existence. Recurring appraisal of the intangible asset should be the primary requirement for proper accountability.

3.2.4.2.2 Critiques of Non-Amortization

Several arguments have been presented against non-amortization. For example, Grinyer et al. (1990) and Grinyer and Russell (1992) argued that non-amortization is inevitably based on a "valuation" conceptual model, which is incompatible with the matching approach—the method considered most appropriate for achieving accountability; that is, monitoring and motivating management (Grinyer et al. 1990, p. 231). The transactions-based matching approach does not require the valuation of goodwill or any other assets in the sense of establishing their worth (Grinyer and Russell 1992, p. 109).

IAS 22, issued in 1983, also expressed a negative view of non-amortization. It noted that the view is sometimes held that goodwill arising on an acquisition may be retained as an asset as long as it is regarded as having economic value. This view, however, ignores the fact that with the passage of time the goodwill of a business derives increasingly from the efforts of the continuing business rather than from the amount expended by the buyer at the date of acquisition (IAS 22, para. 22).

Similarly, Saito (2021, p. 104) presented a critique of non-amortization. Among the arguments against non-amortization, the most representative is that goodwill does not generally decline in value, or at least that part of it does not. However, denying that goodwill generally declines is inconsistent with the market equilibrium process. In this process, the value of goodwill—arising from the deviation of the total value of identifiable assets from the firm's equilibrium value—disappears as the firm approaches equilibrium. In the real world, where market tendencies toward equilibrium coexist with shocks that prevent it, goodwill is constantly created and destroyed. When the expectation of excess profits embodied in goodwill becomes realized, goodwill decreases accordingly. When a portion does not decline even without additional investment, analysts require a clear criterion to separate and measure that portion.[26]

Most arguments denying the decline in goodwill value appear to lack a sound rationale, often relying on analogies with the replacement amortization method. These arguments suggest that a company's investments and business activities maintain the value of goodwill and that management is continuously working to create it. The replacement method treats expenses incurred for partial replacements as current expenses rather than amortization, thus preserving the book value of assets whose value is maintained. However, goodwill includes not only the acquired portion but also internally generated goodwill that exceeds the acquired amount. All expenditures related to a company's investments or operations that create value constitute internally generated goodwill, while acquired goodwill does not increase. Value amortization affects both acquired and internally generated goodwill. Therefore, even if the amortization of each component is offset by the creation of a corresponding amount, resulting in the overall value of goodwill being maintained, this does not necessarily mean that the value of acquired goodwill is preserved. In other words, amortizing acquired goodwill while imputing replacement amortization for internally generated goodwill does not result in double counting of expenses. The analogy of replacement amortization cannot be applied when the acquired portion cannot be separated from the internally generated portion (Saito 2021, p. 105).

Other arguments against amortizing goodwill include the difficulty of reasonably estimating its useful life. However, this challenge is no different from estimating the economic useful life of tangible assets, and amortization based on prior estimates is not unique to goodwill. Some argue that goodwill amortization expenses lack informational value, since analysts often add them back to profits when assessing corporate value. The rationale for adding back non-cash amortization expenses is likely that corporate value depends on expected cash flows rather than accounting profits. In that case, using free cash flow after deducting investment expenditures would be inconsistent. Assuming a steady state where an amount equivalent to amortization is reinvested, profit figures excluding amortization could arguably provide greater informational value (Saito 2021, p. 106).

In this context, while many discussions support adopting the purchase method to avoid underreporting profits by not amortizing goodwill, these discussions generally deny the amortization of goodwill. Such claims are considered erroneous because they are incompatible with the market equilibrium process. Similarly, the argument that corporate investments and operations maintain goodwill and that managers continually strive to create it relies on replacement cost analogies that do

[26] "Equilibrium goodwill," an economic asset that is not traded on the market—or cannot be traded because its rights cannot be clearly defined—is continually reproduced as long as a company continues its business activities. This internally generated goodwill can be considered the essence of corporate activity (Saito and Fukui 2022b, p. 44).

not apply to goodwill, which includes both internally generated and acquired components.

In other words, while all expenditures made after a business combination for investments or operations generate internally created goodwill, impairment affects both acquired and internally generated goodwill. Consequently, even if the impairment of acquired goodwill is offset by the creation of internally generated goodwill, leaving the overall value of goodwill unchanged, this does not necessarily mean that the value of acquired goodwill is preserved. Therefore, for goodwill that comprises both acquired and internally generated components, the replacement amortization analogy cannot be applied.

Arguments against amortizing goodwill also include the difficulty of estimating useful lives and the common practice of adding back amortization expenses when evaluating a company. Regarding the first point, the challenge of estimating useful life is not unique to goodwill but also applies to tangible assets. As for the second point, given the central role of free cash flow in corporate valuation, the practice of adding back amortization expenses when assessing corporate value can itself be questioned.

3.2.5 Write-off Against Equity

3.2.5.1 Developments from the 1900s to the 1920s

As discussed, in the 1880s, when debates on the accounting treatment of goodwill began, early amortization was broadly supported. However, since Dicksee (1897) introduced the concept of writing off goodwill against equity, this method became widely accepted. According to Ding et al. (2008, p. 731), during this period, a weakened static approach—charging goodwill to equity—gained popularity. The decline of immediate expensing or accelerated amortization is evident from practice. The prevailing solution was to eliminate goodwill by charging it to equity, a method that combined the basic static approach, which treats goodwill as not an asset, with the ability to distribute dividends based on current profits.

From the early 1900s onward, writing off goodwill against equity became a broadly accepted accounting treatment in both the United Kingdom and the United States. In the United Kingdom, this approach remained standard until the late 1980s (Ding et al. 2008, p. 732). In the United States, the method of directly debiting goodwill to capital surplus and recording it at a nominal value of $1 was widely used until it was prohibited by SEC ARS No. 50 in 1945.

3.2.5.1.1 Derivation of the Write-off Against Equity

The write-off against equity finds its origins in *Wilmer v. McNamara* (1895) (Densham 1898, p. 570; Hatfield 1909, p. 116). In his judgment, Stirling, J., stated: "It is necessary, however, to consider whether the amortization in goodwill and leaseholds is to be treated as loss of 'fixed' capital or of 'floating' or 'circulating' capital, and on this point I am of the opinion that it is to be treated as a loss of 'fixed' capital" (1895, 2 Ch. 245).

The English courts in *Wilmer v. McNamara* held that even when goodwill has actually declined in value, charging the reduction against profits is not necessary. This decision was grounded in the view that goodwill constitutes "fixed" capital, following the principle established in an earlier ruling that a decline in the value of fixed capital (or permanent assets) need not be reflected in profit calculations (Hatfield 1909, p. 116). As Dicksee and Stevens (1897, p. 16) explained, "There can be no question whatever but that goodwill is a fixed asset, and not a floating asset; that is to say, it comes under the category of something which has to be acquired by an undertaking in order to enable it to carry on its business." This provided legal authority for the view that fluctuations in goodwill value do not affect profits.

The perspective established in the 1895 Wilmer v. McNamara case had a significant influence on subsequent accounting treatments of goodwill. For example, Dicksee and Stevens (1897) built upon this reasoning in his arguments regarding goodwill accounting as follows.

With regard to the sole trader or private firm, it seems unnecessary to lay down any definite rules, as the accounts are their own. The amount of goodwill should not be written off from profits, as it has no connection with profits in the sense of being of a wasting nature. The proper method appears to be to debit the Capital Account and credit the Goodwill Account with the full amount of goodwill at the earliest possible stage. Turning to the consideration of goodwill in relation to a company's accounts, two points arise. First, everything said regarding the undesirability of retaining the cost price as a permanent asset applies here. On the other hand, when the value of goodwill has been paid for out of capital, it is practically impossible to write it off except from profits, which is incorrect (Dicksee and Stevens 1897, p. 21).

The expediency of writing it off by reducing the company's capital is generally disregarded. First, the cost of doing so would be substantial and unlikely to be willingly incurred. Second, it is uncertain whether any judge would sanction a reduction of capital on such grounds, as the court typically requires evidence that the capital has been lost. As already stated, it would be incorrect to write down the amount of goodwill from profits. Doing so is considered fundamentally wrong, as it creates a reserve fund, or in other words, a secret reserve. The only alternatives are for a company to maintain its goodwill at the original cost or not to pay for goodwill out of capital. The most common method of acquiring goodwill without using capital is through the creation of founders' shares (Dicksee and Stevens 1897, pp. 22–23).

In this regard, Dicksee (1897) and Dicksee and Stevens (1897) stated that for private firms, maintaining goodwill as a permanent asset at historical cost is inappropriate, and charging it to profits is also unsuitable; therefore, deducting it immediately from capital is preferable. However, in corporate accounting, deducting goodwill from capital is not feasible, and amortizing it through profits is also undesirable. Consequently, proposals recommended either not amortizing goodwill or funding it from sources other than capital. Although the latter approach is preferable, Dicksee himself expressed doubts about its practicality, and some aspects of his proposed accounting treatment remained unclear. According to Ding et al. (2008, pp. 731–732), Dicksee (1897) and Dicksee and Stevens (1897) were unable to offer an optimal solution.

Later, Dicksee and Tillyard (1906, pp. 83, 92) argued that purchased goodwill should be deducted from capital reserves. That is, it would be incorrect to write down the amount of goodwill from profits. Although many of the soundest undertakings follow this practice, upon reflection it is considered fundamentally wrong, as the process effectively creates a reserve fund without stating it as such—in other words, a secret reserve. There does not appear to be any valid reason why, when a company takes over a business from a date earlier than that on which it is entitled to commence business and the profits are apportioned accordingly, the portion of profits carried to a special Capital Reserve Account should not be used to write down the goodwill. Indeed, this would seem to be the most desirable course of action.[27]

3.2.5.1.2 Support for the Write-off Against Equity

In this era, most proponents expressed positive views on writing off goodwill against equity. For example, Nox (in Guthrie 1898, p. 430) argued that the sooner an item of goodwill could safely be removed from the credit side of the balance sheet, the better it would be for the concern. Although times might be prosperous when the change was made, bad times could arise, perhaps due to competition—a fresh kind of article might push out the old one—and if the concern experienced such adverse conditions, the goodwill could become of little or no value, often leading to liquidation in some form or another.

Similarly, Smith (1904, p. 48) argued that goodwill was a very indefinite asset. The amount for which it could be sold depended on many factors, including past profits, prospects, the personal influence of certain officials, and popular opinion. The value of goodwill in a trading business was most frequently, though not always, based on net profits for several years—usually from one and a half to four—and, as a saleable asset, it fluctuated accordingly. Even when admitting that its value had

[27] According to Ding et al. (2008, pp. 731–732), although Dicksee (1897) was unable to find an optimal solution, subsequent scholars—citing Tillyard's description in Dicksee and Tillyard (1920)—have stated that acquired goodwill should be amortized directly to reserves. However, several points in this claim appear to be incorrect. First, the idea was actually presented in Dicksee and Tillyard (1906), not in the 1920 edition. Furthermore, the statement was made by Dicksee himself, not by Tillyard. Dicksee and Tillyard (1906, p. vii) clearly indicates that the first seven chapters, which discuss legal perspectives, were written by Tillyard, whereas Chap. 10, which contains the description in question, was written by Dicksee in the latter part of their book.

fallen, business owners relied on the fixed capital principle, as they had an undoubted right to do.

Finney (1923, Chap. 41, p. 12) also noted that many concerns, realizing that the goodwill account had been so misused as to be meaningless, proceeded to write it off against Surplus. If profits had continued or increased, the goodwill value had not diminished; writing it off would create a secret reserve, understating net worth and accumulated profits, which could prejudice the interests of stockholders wishing to sell their holdings. If profits had diminished to the point that the goodwill, once of real value and paid for, no longer existed, writing off the account would reduce the surplus still further.

The first accounting standards in the United States, *Uniform Accounting*, issued in 1917, also recommended the equity method. A memorandum entitled *Uniform Accounting*, published by the AIA and accepted by the Federal Trade Commission and Federal Reserve Board, stated that goodwill should be shown as a deduction from net worth (AIA 1917, p. 433). According to Ding et al. (2008, p. 732), while this treatment was only compulsory for financial statements prepared for loan purposes, it nonetheless reflects the prevailing mindset at the time.

3.2.5.2 Developments from the 1930s to the 1960s

Until the 1930s, opinion and practice diverged markedly on whether to write off goodwill and, if so, which method to use. A considerable number of prominent companies recorded goodwill at a nominal value of $1 (Sanders et al. 1938, p. 68). Widespread distrust of goodwill, combined with the knowledge that it had often been used to capitalize inflated expectations of future earnings, created an almost universal sense that the balance sheet appeared stronger without it (Sanders et al. 1938, p. 14).[28] In response to this situation, as noted above, following the Great Depression, systematic amortization became widely accepted in the United States with the rise of historical cost accounting, while the practice of writing off goodwill against equity gradually declined.[29]

In the United States, items related to intangible assets in the capital section, as described in the 1917 Uniform Accounting, were removed in the Verification of Financial Statements issued in 1929 (AIA 1929, p. 353). The proposed balance

[28] Goodwill, like other assets, should be shown at its bona fide cost to the owner. Attributing to goodwill an excessive value, whether based on the par value of stock issued or otherwise, is not sound accounting. If goodwill is no longer valuable or its value has been clearly impaired, it should be written down. The resulting charge should be made against capital or surplus, not against income (Sanders et al. 1938, pp. 68–69).

[29] Even at that time, a few proponents supported the equity method. For example, Sherwood and Culey (1939, pp. 205–206) argued that goodwill is generally considered to represent the value of the excess earning capacity of a property over and above a fair rate of return for the industry or line of endeavor concerned. Its value is the difference between the total amount paid for an enterprise and the aggregate value of the assets received, considered individually.

sheet form made no mention of intangible assets. Presumably, goodwill would have been classified under "Other fixed assets" or "Other assets" (Hughes 1982, p. 57).

In 1944, ARB 24 was issued, expressing a restrictive view regarding the equity method. The committee recognized that, in the past, it had been accepted practice to eliminate Type (b) intangibles by writing them off against any existing surplus, whether capital or earned, even when the value of the asset was unimpaired. Since the practice had been long established and widely approved, the committee did not feel justified in recommending, at that time, adoption of a rule prohibiting such disposition. The committee did, however, believe that such dispositions should be discouraged, especially if proposed to be effected by charges to capital surplus (ARB 24, p. 197).

In 1945, the SEC issued ASR No. 50, which prohibited the deduction of goodwill from capital surplus.[30] ASR 50 stated that the SEC's Chief Accountant had expressed an opinion on the propriety of writing down or written off goodwill by means of charges to capital surplus. Inquiry had been made as to whether, in a financial statement required to be filed with the Commission, goodwill could be written down or written off by means of charges to capital surplus. The proposed charge to capital surplus was deemed contrary to sound accounting principles. It was clear that if the goodwill here involved were, or became, worthless, it would be necessary to write it off (ASR 50).

Preferably, such a write-down should be accomplished through timely charges to income, but under no circumstances would it be permissible, under sound accounting principles, to charge the loss to capital surplus. The proposed procedure would, in effect, evade charges to income or earned surplus, resulting in an overstatement of income and earned surplus and an understatement of capital. This practice would allow a corporation to circumvent charges that should be made against income or earned surplus by recognizing them in advance as a charge against capital surplus, which, in the SEC's view, is inconsistent with the fundamental principle that a distinction should be maintained between capital and income (ASR 50).

Regarding these criticisms of write-offs against equity, Walker (1953, p. 213) noted that, in the past, accountants often sanctioned the writing off of goodwill as a single charge or as soon as earnings or surplus permitted, because goodwill—under a worthwhile accounting concept—either never existed or was not obtained through a bona fide purchase. This policy remains sound in cases where goodwill was brought into the accounts without justifiable reason, but it is unsound with respect to the writing off of bona fide purchased goodwill.

---

[30] Regarding the write-down of goodwill, the opinion of the courts appeared to be that it is a matter of internal corporate administration, to be governed by the judgment of the directors (Preinreich 1936, p. 329). Also see Frank (1948).

3.2.5.3 Developments Since the 1970s

3.2.5.3.1 Support for the Write-off Against Equity

Discussion Regarding the Pooling of Interests Method

Until the 1950s, at least in the United States, goodwill could be removed from the books only through charges to current income. Of the two main approaches—permanent retention and amortization to current income—amortization was generally preferred. The issue of goodwill's subsequent treatment became more complex with the introduction of the pooling of interests concept in 1950. The importance of this method grew roughly in proportion to the elimination of lump-sum write-offs as an acceptable treatment for goodwill. The pooling method could be applied in ways that produced accounts approximating the results of a goodwill write-off. Consequently, the treatment of goodwill became intertwined with the broader problem of accounting for business combinations. When the issue was resolved in 1970, the debate had been waged on two fronts: mandatory amortization of goodwill and the elimination of the pooling alternative (Hughes 1982, p. 202).

From the 1960s to the 1970s, alongside discussions on the pooling method, some scholars advocated for write-offs against equity. For instance, Spacek argued that capitalizing goodwill under acquisition accounting is not appropriate, since stockholders' equity in a balance sheet should not include amounts assigned to earning power in excess of the producing assets; this excess merely reflects the public's opinion of a company's earnings potential. The clear distinction of responsibility between the presenter of information and the maker of market-value judgments is fundamental to a fair presentation of financial statements. Amortization of goodwill against income is improper. Income statements should report earnings from operations, undistorted by items unrelated to operations, such as charges for the amortization of goodwill (Spacek 1964, p. 39). Goodwill, representing the cost of the portion of earning power acquired through a purchase, should be accounted for as a reduction of the corporation's equity value, not as a reduction of operating results on which the market evaluates the enterprise as a whole (Spacek 1964, p. 40; 1969, pp. 301–302).

In this way, Spacek (1964, 1969) advocated for a write-off against equity. He argued that goodwill acquired through purchase reflects only investors' opinions of a company's potential profits and should not be recorded as part of shareholders' equity. This can be considered a pioneering view in relation to the discussions of Chambers (1966) and Catlett and Olson (1968), which addressed the issue of separability. From the perspective of emphasizing a strict separation of responsibilities between the presenter of financial information and the preparer of market-value judgments, the rationale for the write-off against equity aligns with that of Chambers (1966) and Catlett and Olson (1968). At the same time, when viewed from the perspective of financial reporting objectives, the distinction from the current approach—which prohibits the recording of self-created goodwill—remains a relevant issue for further examination.[31]

Similarly, Chambers addressed these points in detail. The question arises whether goodwill is an asset of a firm. First, the goodwill of a firm is not severable from that firm. The capacity to earn the rate of return that a firm, in fact, earns subsists in its collection of assets and liabilities and the advantages that flow from them as they are arranged among themselves and in relation to the market; it does not subsist in any separable thing. As the property of severability was stipulated as a defining characteristic of assets, goodwill does not, therefore, rank as an asset. This definition arose from the necessity of considering the capacity of an entity to adapt itself to changes in its state and its environment. Goodwill subsists in a certain collection and arrangement of assets and liabilities; it cannot be sold separately from that collection for adaptive purposes (Chambers 1966, p. 238).

Second, in ascertaining financial position, we have stipulated that the assets and liabilities are to be measured. But the goodwill of a going concern is the subject of evaluation, not of measurement. A going concern has, by definition, some future as such; and it is only with reference to the future that it has any goodwill. If the evaluation of the constituents did not exceed the current cash equivalent of the firm's capital, they would prefer the return of their investment. But clearly, this value can only be calculated anticipatively. The value of goodwill may be obtained by estimating the excess of the present value of expected future income over the "normal" return on the investment in tangible assets. Such a valuation is not the same in kind as measurements and cannot, therefore, be added to measurements in any statement of financial position. Third, inasmuch as the assessment of opportunities rests with constituents, it is their affair to choose their own capitalization rates and time horizons, disregarding any valuation of goodwill interpolated in the financial statements (Chambers 1966, pp. 239, 240).

Finally, the goodwill of a going concern runs to the constituents, not to the firm. It is they who put valuations on expected superior returns. It is they who have the right to dispose of going concerns or of their interests in them. To regard goodwill as an asset of a going concern is to confuse two entities—the constituents as persons and the firm as an instrument. If the constituents accept an offer for a going concern in excess of the current cash equivalent of its capital, the difference is simply a gain to them. That cash has been paid may be recognized in the record, but its effect is in no way to increase the adaptability of the firm, and the indicated treatment of it is to reduce the amount of the residual equity from the price paid to the current cash equivalent of the new firm's component assets less its liabilities. We conclude, therefore, that goodwill is not an asset of a firm. It is not the function of accounting

[31] Hendriksen (1970, p. 437) also criticized both amortization and non-amortization treatments of goodwill. He argued that, after the date of acquisition, there is little evidence that the continued presentation of goodwill as an asset provides useful information to investors or other users of financial statements. Furthermore, amortizing goodwill to income using arbitrary procedures appears of doubtful validity owing to the problems of homogeneity and interactions. Also see Hendriksen (1965).

to determine the going value of a firm as a whole; this function rests with constituents and potential constituents—those who are in the market for investments in going concerns (Chambers 1966, p. 241).

Accounting Research Study (ARS) No. 10, *Accounting for Goodwill*, by Catlett and Olson also argued in favor of the write-off against equity. They maintained that goodwill is not a resource or property right that is consumed or utilized in the production of earnings. Rather, it is a result of earnings, or of the expectations of them, as appraised by investors. Goodwill exists only as part of the value of a business as a whole and has no existence or life separate from the business (Catlett and Olson 1968, p. 107). Accordingly, amounts paid for goodwill in a business combination represent disbursements of a portion of a company's resources in anticipation of future earnings. The disbursement of resources reduces the stockholders' equity in a company's separable resources and property rights by a corresponding amount, and accounting for purchased goodwill as a reduction in stockholders' equity evidences that fact (Catlett and Olson 1968, p. 90).

Thus, the amount assigned to purchased goodwill represents a disbursement of existing resources, or of proceeds of stock issued to effect the business combination, in anticipation of future earnings. The expenditure should be accounted for as a reduction of stockholders' equity. The accounting can be achieved by one of two methods: (a) an immediate direct write-off to capital surplus or retained earnings (the preferred method), or (b) showing a deduction from stockholders' equity in the balance sheet for several periods, followed by a later write-off to capital surplus or retained earnings. The recommended treatment of purchased goodwill results in balance sheet and income statement reporting for purchased goodwill that is consistent in principle with existing practices of accounting for internally developed or non-purchased goodwill—practices which Catlett and Olson considered proper (Catlett and Olson 1968, p. 106).

Prevailing practices of accounting for goodwill purchased in a business combination and for non-purchased (internally developed) goodwill were completely different. The difference in accounting was not supported by differences in the nature of the two types of goodwill, since the characteristics that distinguish goodwill from other assets apply to purchased goodwill as well as to non-purchased goodwill (Catlett and Olson 1968, pp. 110, 111).

In this context, Catlett and Olson (1968, ARS 10) advocated for a write-off against equity, arguing that it ensures consistency with the accounting treatment of internally generated goodwill and reflects the inseparable nature of goodwill.[32] This approach is almost identical to that of SSAP 22 in the United Kingdom, which also requires the equity method as the primary method of accounting. Notably, the currently applicable IAS 38 does not recognize internally generated goodwill on the grounds of separability.

[32] Along with Wyatt (1963, ARS 5), it was commissioned by the APB to address criticisms of the expanding use of the pooling method, and both studies concluded that the method should not be widely adopted.

Regarding the consistency of accounting for internally generated goodwill, Solomons (1989) argued as follows. For examples of how present methods produce inconsistencies within a single accounting period, in the sense that they do not always make like things look alike, consider the methods of accounting for goodwill and for the amortization of buildings. When one business acquires another, part of the purchase price will usually be attributable to goodwill. The goodwill of the acquired company may then appear in the balance sheet of the combined business, while the non-purchased goodwill of the acquiror—which may be much more valuable—may not (Solomons 1989, p. 36). Most assets are acquired by purchase and are initially recorded at cost. But it is not the cost that qualifies the item to be treated as an asset. What qualifies it is the probable future economic benefit that is expected to flow from it. The same would be true if the item were acquired at no cost (Solomons 1989, p. 21).

The accounting treatment of goodwill must depend on the answers to two questions. Is it an asset? And if it is, should the same criteria for recognition apply to it as apply to other assets? Present practice answers the first question affirmatively, and the second question by according it recognition only when it is bought and sold. Non-purchased goodwill, therefore, should not be recognized, in accordance with present practice; and SSAP 22 rightly favors "the immediate write-off of purchased goodwill ... against reserves ... in order to achieve consistency of treatment with non-purchased goodwill ..." (para. 7). It is regrettable that the standard permits an alternative treatment of carrying purchased goodwill and amortizing it through the profit and loss account over its useful economic life, for this needlessly sacrifices the comparability of financial statements (Solomons, 1989, pp. 68–69).

Similarly, Arnold (1992, p. 42) noted the following. It is desirable that consistency of treatment between internal and purchased goodwill be achieved if possible—and, where appropriate, between goodwill and other intangibles—not least to preclude manipulation of classifications—but this may not be essential and needs to be examined on its merits. As far as possible, there should be consistency of treatment between companies in the same circumstances. But given the nature of the uncertainties involved, it may often be legitimate for different companies to form different judgments about the nature of particular circumstances.[33]

Accounting Standards in the United Kingdom and IAS

In the 1960s, a debate in the United States over the purchase and pooling methods refocused attention on the write-off against equity method of accounting for goodwill. Meanwhile, in the United Kingdom, the write-off against equity had been widely adopted as a standard accounting practice since the early 1900s. In SSAP 22, published in 1984, the write-off against equity was also required, with the following rationale provided.

---

[33] As noted above, SSAP 22 states that there is no difference in character between purchased and non-purchased goodwill (SSAP 22, para. 5), also in ED 30; *Accounting for goodwill* by ASC in 1982. Chitty (1997), ICAEW (1997) and Kirkham and Arnold (1992) discuss the emerging issues around these periods.

There is no difference in character between purchased goodwill and non-purchased goodwill. However, the value of purchased goodwill, although arising from a subjective valuation of the business, is established as a fact at a particular point in time by a market transaction; this is not true of non-purchased goodwill (SSAP 22, para. 5). The standard requires that purchased goodwill should normally be eliminated from accounts by immediate write-off. The principal reason for this is that immediate write-off of purchased goodwill is consistent with the accepted practice of not including non-purchased goodwill in accounts. Thus, if purchased goodwill is treated as an asset while non-purchased goodwill is not, a balance sheet does not present the total goodwill of a company (or group); it reflects only the purchased goodwill of the acquired business(es) at the date of acquisition, to the extent that it has not been written off (SSAP 22, para. 6).

The standard requires that the immediate write-off of purchased goodwill should be made against reserves, not as a charge in the profit and loss account. This is because (a) purchased goodwill is written off as a matter of accounting policy, that is, in order to achieve consistency of treatment with non-purchased goodwill, rather than because it has suffered a permanent diminution in value, and (b) the write-off is not related to the results of the year in which the acquisition was made (SSAP 22, para. 7).

Similarly, IAS 22, which was issued at the same time as SSAP 22, required the write-off against equity and provided the following explanation for this treatment. Others believe that any difference between the cost of acquisition and the fair values of the net identifiable assets acquired should be adjusted against shareholders' interests in the period of acquisition. They argue that goodwill is not an independently realizable asset, that it has an indeterminate life for which any amortization program is arbitrary, and that, as self-generated goodwill is not recognized, it is inappropriate to recognize goodwill arising on acquisition (IAS 22, para. 23).

3.2.5.3.2 Critiques of the Write-off Against Equity

In the United States, the write-off against equity was prohibited by ASR 50, issued by the SEC in 1945, and was subsequently prohibited by ARS 43 in 1953 and APB 17 in 1970. Similarly, in the United Kingdom, the write-off against equity gradually fell out of favor and had few supporters by the late 1980s (Arnold, 1992).

According to APB 17, issued in 1970, the following arguments are presented against the write-off against equity. The basis for proposing that the cost of goodwill be deducted from stockholders' equity at the date acquired is that the nature of goodwill differs from other assets and warrants special accounting treatment. Since goodwill attaches only to a business as a whole and its value fluctuates widely for innumerable reasons, estimates of either its term of existence or current value are unreliable for purposes of income determination (APB 17, para. 20). The cost of goodwill is therefore essentially the same as the cost of land, buildings, or equipment under historical-cost-based accounting. Deducting the cost of an asset from stockholders' equity at the date incurred does not match costs with revenue (APB 17, para. 21).

Proponents against the write-off against equity, such as Grinyer et al. (1990, pp. 225–231), argued as follows. They assumed that the most fundamental, and therefore primary, purpose of accounts is the monitoring and motivation of management, and such arguments are developed within an accountability context. The objective of accountability requires that purchased goodwill be charged against profits under a matching approach to profit measurement. Immediate write-off to reserves is unacceptable for the primary purpose assumed above. The validity of arguments for immediate write-off to reserves seems to be related to a balance-sheet approach derived from concepts within the "valuation" school of thought and is not appropriate to an earnings-oriented, matching-based approach to financial reporting.

Similarly, Nobes (1992, p. 148) expressed a negative view of the write-off against equity. The most obvious problem was the "hole in the balance sheet," which frequently occurred in groups where the net assets of the group were lower than the net assets of the parent. Its counter-intuitive nature might suggest, even to sophisticated non-accountants, that something was wrong with conventional accounting measurements. In some cases, the hole was visible in the form of a negative reserve. A more extreme form of this problem was the creation of negative net assets for a group when very large goodwill items were written off. This is again counter-intuitive and leads to bizarre profitability and gearing calculations.

Furthermore, Bryer (1995, p. 295) expressed a negative view of the write-off against equity. Writing off purchased goodwill against capital reserves would simply compound that blunder. It would not make two otherwise identical companies comparable—one with purchased goodwill and the other with internal goodwill. While it would make their reported profits and capital equal, it would mean that the capital of the former company would be understated and its subsequent profits overstated. These two companies are clearly not comparable, and therefore their reported capital and profits should not be equal. One has purchased profits with capital, the other has earned them.

Similarly, Miller (1973 pp. 290–291; 1995, p. 5) noted the following. Under this treatment, purchased goodwill is treated consistently with internally generated goodwill in the balance sheet (no asset shown) but treated inconsistently in the profit and loss statement (no expense for purchased goodwill, while the amounts spent in building up the goodwill of existing businesses are expensed). This inconsistency causes incomparability in reported results. In addition, immediate write-off of goodwill reduces accountability and distorts rate-of-return measures.

Other critics have also expressed negative views on the equity method. For example, Welsch et al. (1976, p. 593) argued that because analysts often viewed intangibles as of questionable asset value and because of over-conservatism, accounting practice in the past tended to encourage their arbitrary write-down to a nominal amount. Contemporary accounting principles and practice do not support the arbitrary write-down because it misstates net income and financial position.

Similarly, Brunovs and Kirsch (1991, pp. 155–157) emphasized that the difference between the write-off against equity and systematic amortization reflects a conceptual division regarding the underlying question of what goodwill represents. According to the write-off against equity, costs and expenses that may in all other circumstances be charged against revenue in the income statement could be charged directly against reserves.

Davis (1992, p. 78) argued that because a company's intangible resources often separate it from the competition, it seems incomprehensible to remove from the balance sheet an item that results from an arm's-length transaction and must have some future value; otherwise, the acquiring company would be discarding valuable resources. In addition, Beier (1993, p. 154) highlighted the troubling issue of supporting the notion that an acquirer at an acquisition date should charge shareholders' equity, even though there is no evidence that an asset has been impaired.

In addition, FRS 10, issued in 1997, expressed a negative view of the write-off against equity, outlining five main arguments (FRS 10, Appendix 3, para. 4). First, immediate elimination of goodwill gives the impression that the acquirer's net worth has been depleted or even eliminated. Second, the problem of equity depletion has encouraged companies to reduce amounts attributed to purchased goodwill by separately valuing brands and similar intangible assets at the date of purchase. Given that such intangible assets are very similar in nature to goodwill and the allocation of value between the two can be subjective, it is widely considered inappropriate for goodwill to be accounted for differently.

Third, management is not held accountable for the amount it has invested in goodwill: this investment is not taken into account when measuring the assets on which a return must be earned, and there is no requirement to disclose a loss if the value of the goodwill is not maintained. Fourth, although there is consistency in the balance sheet treatment of purchased and internally generated goodwill, there is no consistency in the profit and loss account treatment: the costs attributable to building up internally generated goodwill are offset against profits in the profit and loss account, whereas the costs of acquired goodwill are not charged against profits in this way unless the acquired business is sold. Fifth, this inconsistency serves to make companies that grow by acquisition appear more profitable than those that grow organically.

Similarly, the *Issues Related to Accounting Standards for Business Combinations*, issued by the Business Accounting Deliberation Council (BADC) of Japan in 2001, presented an argument against the immediate write-off against equity. It noted that, while some countries previously deducted from paid-in capital (contributed capital) or retained earnings, few supported this approach. The prevailing view was that all investment consideration in a business combination should be treated as an expense and fully expensed in the accounting period in which it is incurred. Given the basic framework of financial reporting, which allocates investment expenditures to expenses to measure annual performance, immediate write-off against equity is difficult to justify (BADC 2001, p. 19).

Up to this point, the rationale for the write-off against equity has often been cited as achieving consistency in accounting treatment between internally generated and acquired goodwill. Indeed, under the immediate write-off method, acquired goodwill is not recognized as an asset, which appears consistent with the treatment of internally generated goodwill, also not recognized as an asset. However, this consistency is limited to the narrow scope of asset recognition and does not extend to other aspects of financial reporting.

When the write-off against equity is applied, acquired goodwill is simply deducted from equity, resulting in a corresponding reduction in the amount of expenses recognized. In contrast, internally generated goodwill is recognized as an expense equal to its value, whereas acquired goodwill subject to the write-off against equity is not recognized as an expense in the same way. Consequently, the amount of acquired goodwill is deducted from equity, and the corresponding amount is effectively added to income.

In conclusion, the write-off against equity represents an accounting treatment that creates inconsistency in the classification of capital and profit between internally generated goodwill and acquired goodwill. This inconsistency in classifying capital and income is a far more significant issue than the limited inconsistency regarding asset recognition in the treatment of capitalizing and expensing. Therefore, the equity method cannot be considered a reasonable accounting treatment with a sound theoretical basis, as it distorts the consistency in the classification of capital and income between acquired and internally generated goodwill.

3.2.6 Brief Summary

The debate over the accounting treatment of goodwill began with Bithell (1882) and has continued to the present day. This section summarizes various views on goodwill accounting from 1882 to around 2000, when non-amortization and impairment accounting were established by IFAS 3 and FASB 141/142. Goodwill accounting treatments are classified into amortization, non-amortization, and write-off against equity, following APB 17 and FASB (1976).

In the 1880s, when debates on goodwill accounting began, the preferred method was early amortization. Goodwill was considered an asset representing future profits, which were inherently uncertain. From a conservative perspective, amortizing goodwill as soon as possible was therefore desirable. By 1900, with the establishment of provisions regarding goodwill in the Companies Act in the United Kingdom, debates over valuation methods for goodwill intensified.

In this context, the write-off against equity was based on British case law, including *Wilmer v. McNamara* (1895), Dicksee (1897), and Dicksee and Tillyard (1906). The issue of goodwill arising from capital inflation and dilution, which became prominent during the merger movement of large corporations around 1910, further reinforced the write-off against equity as a widely used practice in both the United Kingdom and the United States. Around the same time, proponents began to argue for non-amortization as a preferable treatment, emphasizing the perpetual nature of goodwill. This argument persisted, with discussions of non-amortization largely focusing on whether goodwill was perpetual.

Around 1920, Leake (1914, 1921) and Yang (1927) argued that systematic amortization was the preferred treatment. Their main arguments were that the value of goodwill is not permanent but diminishes over time, and that the current value of goodwill differs from the purchase price paid at acquisition, with the latter declining over time.

Following the Great Depression of 1929, conservative tendencies strengthened, and recognizing goodwill at cost became the established practice. Paton and Littleton (1940) and others argued in favor of systematic amortization from the perspective of aligning historical cost allocation with revenue. Goodwill was viewed as excess profitability, expected to eventually disappear. Therefore, some argued that goodwill should be recognized as an expense over the period it generates revenue. Even if excess profitability persisted, this was attributed to factors arising after the business combination, distinguishing between goodwill acquired at acquisition and internally generated goodwill arising afterward.

In the 1960s, when the accounting treatment of goodwill in conjunction with the pooling method was debated, Catlett and Olson (1968, ARS 10) and Chambers (1966) argued in favor of the write-off against equity, citing consistency with the treatment of internally generated goodwill and management responsibility. However, from the 1950s to the 1990s, most proponents criticized the write-off against equity for various reasons, including inconsistencies with the treatment of acquired goodwill and other cancellable assets, conflicts with historical cost accounting, and distortion of the distinction between capital and earnings.

Under accounting standards in the United States, the first standard, Uniform Accounting, issued in 1917, recommended the write-off against equity. References to the write-off against equity were later removed in the Verification of Financial Statements issued in 1929. ARB 24, issued in 1944, permitted both systematic amortization and non-amortization and passively allowed the write-off against equity. In 1945, ASR 50, issued by the SEC, prohibited the write-off against equity on the grounds that it distorted the distinction between capital and other components. Subsequently, ARB 43, issued in 1953, prohibited the write-off against equity and established systematic amortization as the preferred method. APB 17, issued in 1970, also required systematic amortization, which remained the prescribed treatment for goodwill until the issuance of SFAS 141/142 in 2001.

In the United Kingdom, where the write-off against equity had been widely used until the 1980s, SSAP 22, issued in 1984, stipulated the write-off against equity as the primary method while also permitting systematic amortization. Similarly, IAS 22, issued in 1983, allowed both the write-off against equity and systematic amortization. However, numerous criticisms of the write-off against equity emerged, and to align with international trends, it was prohibited and systematic amortization mandated in the revised IAS 22 in 1993 and 1998, as well as in FRS 10, issued as a UK standard in 1997. The IASB subsequently issued IFRS 3 in 2004, establishing accounting treatment for non-amortization and impairment.

The previous debates on goodwill accounting largely focused on whether goodwill amortization should be treated as an expense or as capital. As the SEC noted in 1945, this reflected a concern with the distinction between capital and earnings. In contrast, accounting treatments introduced since 2000—such as amortization, non-amortization, and impairment—assume that the cost of goodwill is expensed, with the debate focusing solely on the timing of expense recognition. In other words, in the current debate over the accounting treatment of goodwill in the post-2000 era, the distinction between capital and income is largely ignored, and the discussion focuses entirely on when goodwill costs should be recognized as expenses.

3.3 Theoretical Consideration on Accounting for Goodwill

3.3.1 Controversies Surrounding Internally Generated Goodwill

This book examines issues related to the accounting treatment of goodwill. Debates have arisen not only over acquired goodwill but also over internally generated goodwill. Because other chapters primarily address acquired goodwill, this section focuses on the debates concerning internally generated goodwill.

Since the 1880s, discussions on the accounting treatment of internally generated goodwill have generally opposed recognizing it as an asset. Dicksee, a leading proponent of this view, argued that only acquired goodwill should be recognized on the balance sheet (Dicksee 1897, p. 45), and that the amount recognized should be limited to the actual consideration paid for it (Dicksee and Tillyard 1906, p. 79). Similarly, Hatfield (1909, pp. 107, 110) stated that the value of customer relationships developed by a company, even if they could be sold for a high price, should not be recorded on the balance sheet, and that goodwill should only be recognized when it is purchased. Leake (1914, pp. 82, 85; 1921, pp. 2, 19) took an even more explicit position, asserting that only acquired goodwill obtained through an exchange involving payment to another entity may be recognized as an asset, and that recognition of goodwill created within the company is not permitted.

Accounting standards did not serve as a basis for recognizing internally generated goodwill as an asset. ARB 24, the first comprehensive accounting standard addressing goodwill, issued in 1944, stipulated that the initial carrying value of all types of intangible assets should be recorded at cost, in accordance with the generally accepted accounting principle that assets are stated at cost when acquired (ARB 24, pp. 195–196).[34] A similar provision was included in ARB 43, issued in 1953 (ARB 43, para. 4).[35]

---

[34] The cost may be defined generally as the price paid or the consideration given to acquire the asset in question (ARB 24, p. 197).

[35] However, it does not address the problems of accounting for intangibles developed in the regular course of business through research, experimentation, advertising, or other activities (ARB 43, para. 1).

APB 17, issued in 1970, explicitly stated that internally generated goodwill should not be recorded as an asset. Specifically, the Board concluded that a company should recognize as assets the costs of intangible assets acquired from others, including goodwill acquired in a business combination (APB 17, para. 9). Because the costs of developing other intangible assets are usually recorded as expenses when incurred (APB 17, para. 11), the Board concludes that a company should record as assets the cost of intangible assets acquired from other enterprises or individuals. Costs of developing, maintaining, or restoring intangible assets that are not specifically identifiable, have indeterminate lives, or are inherent in a continuing business and related to an enterprise as a whole—such as goodwill—should be deducted from income when incurred (APB 17, para. 24). As described below, the requirement not to recognize internally generated goodwill as an asset is also clearly reflected in current U.S. GAAP and IFRS.

From the beginning of the debate on the accounting treatment of goodwill to the present, the predominant view has opposed recognizing internally generated goodwill as an asset. However, several arguments in favor of its recognition have also been presented. The following sections summarize the arguments on both sides of this issue. As is explained in detail later, this discussion proceeds from the widely accepted view that the purpose of financial reporting is to support investor decision-making.[36] In the next section, we first examine the arguments advanced in support of the recognition of internally generated goodwill as an asset. We then summarize the arguments of those who oppose such recognition, clarifying the basis for their position.

3.3.1.1 Support for Recognizing Internally Generated Goodwill as an Asset

The argument for recognizing internally generated goodwill as an asset was advanced by Scott and O'Brien. In their discussion of the concept of current value, they state the following: Two main current value alternatives to historical cost for assets and liabilities are value in use, such as the discounted present value of future cash flows, and fair value, also called exit price or opportunity cost, the hypothetical amount that would be received or paid should the firm dispose of the asset or liability. When no distinction is necessary, valuations that depart from historical cost are referred to as current values (Scott and O'Brien 2012, p. 4).

[36] As noted earlier, even in the early period when debates on the accounting treatment of goodwill first emerged, the predominant view opposed recognizing internally generated goodwill as an asset. The arguments against recognition were grounded in the principle that items recorded in financial statements should be limited to those for which the expenditure can be objectively verified, a view supported by the rationale of conservative accounting practices (for details, see Asami 2012). In this respect, this perspective differs markedly from the current understanding that the purpose of financial reporting is to provide information useful for investor decision-making.

In practice, recording current values on the balance sheet will increase decision usefulness only if the firm prepares reliable and unbiased estimates of the current values of its assets and liabilities. If balance sheet values are unreliable, this contributes to firm-specific risk. If values are biased, investors must correct for the bias in their projections of future abnormal earnings. However, assuming reasonably reliable and unbiased valuations, using current value accounting increases the decision usefulness of the financial statements, since a greater proportion of firm value can simply be read from the balance sheet. This is particularly true for investors who may not be fully rational, who may benefit from reading the effects of current value changes directly from the financial statements (Scott and O'Brien 2012, p. 223).

Clean surplus theory has had a major impact on financial accounting theory and research. By demonstrating that firm value can be expressed equally well in terms of financial accounting variables as in terms of dividends or cash flows, it has led to increased research attention to earnings prediction. Much of this research explores how current financial statement information can improve this prediction. Better earnings prediction enables better estimates of unrecorded goodwill, leading to better predictions of firm value and hence better investment decisions. Arguably, the theory also supports a valuation approach to accounting, since more current values reported on the balance sheet mean a lower proportion of firm value is included in unrecorded goodwill, hence less potential for investor mistakes in estimating this complex component of firm value (Scott and O'Brien 2012, p. 231).

From this perspective, measuring balance sheet items at current value—representing either the discounted present value of future cash flows or fair value—effectively records unrecognized or internally generated goodwill. The more items measured at current value, the greater the amount of internally generated goodwill recorded on the balance sheet, and the smaller the portion of unrecognized internally generated goodwill relative to firm value. As a result, the forecast of firm value improves, leading to better decision-making by investors. In other words, this view suggests that recognizing internally generated goodwill as an asset enhances the usefulness of financial statements for investment decisions.

This view, similar to that of Scott and O'Brien (2012), was already developed by Gynther, Lee, and others around the 1970s. Gynther (1969, p. 253) stated: "The most relevant financial-position information for external people in their decisions to buy, hold, or sell shares is the present value of the total expected net cash flows of an entity as assessed by skilled management and comprising the values of all assets, including the human and other intangible assets. The valuation and periodic revaluation of goodwill would have to be carried out via a method involving the capitalization of the entity's profits, the net present values of some assets, approximations of the net present values of the other assets, management's knowledge."

Here, the argument is that since managers' estimates of the present value of future cash flows provide useful information for investors, the value of goodwill should be reflected in the financial statements, and internally generated goodwill should be recognized as an asset. Similarly, Lee (1971) presented the following discussion:

There is no major difference between purchased and created goodwill, except that the former is bought as part of a purchase consideration, whilst the latter is developed from within the business; however, it is purchased in the sense that money and other resources are expended to create and maintain it (Lee 1971, p. 321). Business continually incurs expenditure to maintain, replace, and augment existing goodwill. Basically, therefore, there is little to distinguish purchased and created goodwill. But, because traditional accounting does not recognize the latter aspect of goodwill, there is a danger of disclosing a figure in the balance sheet that is not representative of the nature or the valuation of the resources it is intended to describe (Lee 1971, p. 324).

Lee further argued that the most valuable information for this type of investment appraisal is that which describes future business activity, including information regarding the financial rewards to be anticipated from it. It is submitted that future business performance is most relevant and useful in this respect, not past activity. It is therefore suggested that, in the first instance, quoted companies should publish cash transaction forecasts (Lee 1971, p. 325). A present value of anticipated cash flows can be calculated, thereby acknowledging the existence of all the resources of the company contributing to its overall financial success or failure, including those resources represented by the term goodwill. In this way, there would be no need to separately account for goodwill, or indeed any of the other so-called business assets. They would be recognized and accounted for in a manner that reflects the fundamental interrelationship of all business resources in a going concern—their contribution to the total business cash flow. There would therefore be no artificial distinction between purchased and created goodwill (Lee 1971, p. 326).

Proponents of recognizing internally generated goodwill as an asset argue that managers' estimates of the present value of future cash flows provide useful information for investors' decision-making. Accordingly, the value of goodwill should be reflected in the financial statements, and internally generated goodwill should be recognized as an asset. Doing so enhances investors' ability to predict firm value, which in turn supports better investment decisions. In other words, this perspective holds that recognizing internally generated goodwill contributes directly to investor decision-making.

3.3.1.2 Critiques of Recognizing Internally Generated Goodwill as an Asset

In contrast to the positive view described above, critics argue against recognizing internally generated goodwill as an asset. These negative views can be broadly divided into two categories.

The first perspective treats the recognition of internally generated goodwill as an issue of recognition or measurement. Proponents of this view argue that recording internally generated goodwill as an asset on the balance sheet is undesirable owing to concerns about recognition criteria and the reliability and certainty of measurement.

The second perspective frames the issue in terms of purpose. From this standpoint, recognizing internally generated goodwill as an asset is inconsistent with the primary objective of financial accounting, which is to provide information useful for investment decision-making. This perspective emphasizes the distinct roles of investors, who evaluate corporate value, and companies, which provide information to support that evaluation. The following sections summarize the debates from each of these two perspectives.

3.3.1.2.1 Argument on Perspective of Recognition and Measurement

This section examines the debate on the appropriateness of recognizing internally generated goodwill as an asset from the perspective of recognition and measurement. Solomons provided the following argument. Assets are defined as resources or rights incontestably controlled by an entity at the accounting date that are expected to yield it future economic benefits (Solomons 1989, p. 20). Assets need not be tangible. Rights, by their nature intangible, are expressly included in the definition. Goodwill, which is neither separable nor tangible, is nevertheless something that purchasers are willing to pay for over and above what they pay for other assets, and that is the best evidence that someone expects to reap future benefits from it. It is usually possible to identify a number of component parts of what passes as goodwill, such as the benefits of location, a customer list, brand names, superior managers, a smoothly functioning organization, a creative research staff, and so on (Solomons 1989, p. 21).

According to Solomons, an item should be recognized in financial statements if it satisfies the following recognition criteria (Solomons 1989, p. 43): (a) it conforms to the definition of an asset, a liability, or one of the sub-elements[37] derived therefrom; (b) its magnitude, as specified by the accounting model being used, can be measured and verified with reasonable certainty; and (c) the magnitude so determined is material in amount.

Goodwill does indeed conform to the definition of an asset, as noted earlier. It is the second criterion for recognition—namely, that it should be measurable and verifiable with reasonable certainty—that presents problems. Even when a business is bought and sold, the value attributed to goodwill is usually simply the difference between the total amount paid by the buyer and the aggregate of the amounts assigned to the separable assets. The goodwill is not created by the sale; it is merely made visible. Its value will not be the same for all prospective buyers. The market for going concerns is imperfect, and one buyer may see opportunities to profit from the acquisition that are not available to others. Any amount attributed to goodwill is

[37] The essential building blocks of financial statements are an entity's assets and liabilities, from which all sub-elements presented in the statements are derived. Issues related to the recognition of revenues and expenses, gains and losses, are fundamentally issues of recognizing changes in assets and liabilities (Solomons 1989, p. 43). In this way, Solomons (1989) clearly demonstrates support for the assets–liabilities view.

unique to the valuer and to the specific point in time at which it is measured, and it is valid only at that time and under the circumstances then prevailing (SSAP 22, para. 2). Determining the value of goodwill where it is not the subject of a purchase-and-sale transaction, and in the presence of a highly imperfect market, is too subjective to yield a reliable measure for recognition. Non-purchased goodwill, therefore, should not be recognized, in accordance with present practice (Solomons 1989, pp. 68–69).

The discussions presented in Solomons (1989) have been directly incorporated into IAS 38. The standard states that the recognition of an item as an intangible asset requires an entity to demonstrate that the item meets (a) the definition of an intangible asset and (b) the recognition criteria (IAS 38, para. 18). The definition of an asset is a resource (a) controlled by an entity as a result of past events, and (b) from which future economic benefits are expected to flow to the entity,[38] and the definition of an intangible asset is an identifiable non-monetary asset without physical substance (IAS 38, para. 8). An intangible asset shall be recognized if, and only if, (a) it is probable that the expected future economic benefits attributable to the asset will flow to the entity, and (b) the cost of the asset can be measured reliably (IAS 38, para. 21).

Internally generated goodwill shall not be recognized as an asset. In some cases, expenditure is incurred to generate future economic benefits, but it does not result in the creation of an intangible asset that meets the recognition criteria in this standard. Such expenditure is often described as contributing to internally generated goodwill. Internally generated goodwill is not recognized as an asset because it is not an identifiable resource controlled by the entity and cannot be measured reliably at cost (IAS 38, paras. 48–50).

The rationale for prohibiting the recognition of internally generated goodwill under IAS 38 is that, while it is expected to generate future economic benefits, it does not constitute an identifiable asset controlled by the entity that can be measured reliably at its cost.[39] In other words, internally generated goodwill fails to meet both the definition of an intangible asset and the recognition criteria, which forms the basis for its non-recognition. Specifically, internally generated goodwill does not meet the definition of an intangible asset because it is not identifiable. While it satisfies criterion (a) of the recognition criteria—indicating a high likelihood of obtaining economic benefits—it fails to satisfy criterion (b), which requires reliable measurement. Notably, IAS 38 does not debate whether internally generated goodwill meets the definition of an "asset."

Under IFRS, the non-recognition of internally generated goodwill is governed solely by IAS 38 and is not explicitly addressed in the *Conceptual Framework for*

[38] The definition of an asset in this Standard was not revised following the revision of the definition of an asset in the *Conceptual Framework for Financial Reporting* issued in 2018 (IAS 38, para. 8, footnote 1).

[39] The debate over excluding internally generated goodwill from recognition as an asset and its measurement is similar under U.S. standards (SFAC 5, para. 63; SFAS 141, paras. 3j, 3k, A19; SFAS 142, paras. 9–10; ASC Topic 350).

Financial Reporting (IASB CF). However, the two are considered consistent. The IASB CF states that items that do not meet the recognition criteria, such as reliability of measurement, are not recognized in financial statements. Since internally generated goodwill does not meet these criteria, it is not recognized as an asset. Thus, the provisions of IAS 38 align with the guidance in the IASB CF.

Regarding the identifiability requirement in the definition of intangible assets under IAS 38, Barker et al. (2021) emphasized separability as the key factor for determining whether an asset is identifiable. They explained that internally generated goodwill cannot be recognized because it fails to meet the separability criterion. Additionally, they highlight uncertainty as a second reason, addressing the recognition of internally generated goodwill in terms of measurement reliability, which is one of the recognition criteria under IAS 38. Thus, according to Barker et al. (2021), the exclusion of internally generated goodwill from recognition is based on two factors: separability, which relates to identifiability, and uncertainty, which concerns the reliability of measurement.[40]

3.3.1.2.2 Argument on the Perspective of Financial Reporting Objectives

Next, we examine the argument that internally generated goodwill should not be recognized as an asset from the perspective of financial reporting objectives. Catlett and Olson argued as follows: Financial statements should provide information that investors can use in appraising the value of a business enterprise—in deciding on prices at which its stock should be traded. Regardless of how investors use that information or how significantly it influences their opinions, the essence of the role financial statements play in investor decision-making is to provide information regarding the value of the separable resources and property rights (principally on the cost basis) of a business. Investors appraise the potential earning power of a business and determine the value of the entire business, including its goodwill. Capitalizing the value of a company's internally developed—non-purchased—goodwill and amortizing it against earnings thus appears to conflict directly with financial statement objectives today (Catlett and Olson 1968, p. 69).

---

[40] Barker et al. (2021, p. 612) criticized the expensing of expenditures incurred to generate internally generated goodwill as follows. In current accounting practice, investments in internally generated intangibles are recognized as expenses in the income statement. This clearly results in a mismatch with revenues. Stocks and the flows from those stocks are not distinguished; they are commingled. Accordingly, valuation based on earnings from investment is frustrated. The problems are rooted in the special accounting for intangibles required by IFRS. There are inconsistencies between the accounting for tangible and intangible assets that have no clear basis. The general principles apply to the accounting for any investment in an asset intended to generate future cash flows. Separability and uncertainty reflect the attributes of an asset. Tangibility, per se, is unlikely to be an attribute useful in developing accounting requirements; indeed, it is a distraction. It creates inconsistencies in practice while also diverting attention from the separability and uncertainty criteria that are relevant to all assets (Barker et al. 2021, p. 626).

Under existing accounting practices, ordinarily neither the cost nor the value of non-purchased goodwill is reported in the balance sheet to be amortized to future income. Current practices are appropriate and should not be changed because expenditures that create goodwill cannot be identified with the particular values they may generate, and any capitalization and amortization of costs would be based on arbitrary or hypothetical assumptions and therefore could not form the basis for a meaningful measure of assets or of charges to income. Recognition of the value of non-purchased goodwill in the financial statements would suggest the untenable position that the continually changing composite opinion of investors regarding the prospective earning power of a business should be capitalized by the business and amortized as a reduction of the earnings being evaluated. Such a procedure would introduce investor opinions of values into the financial statements, which are designed to furnish information that investors use in arriving at their opinions (Catlett and Olson 1968, p. 111). The role of accounting is to provide information that the investor can use in arriving at their opinion of the value of a business; accounting does not determine that value (Catlett and Olson 1968, p. 107).

From this perspective, distinguishing the roles of investors and managers is important. Since the objective of financial reporting is to provide useful information for investors' decision-making,[41] it follows that recognizing internally generated goodwill as an asset is not appropriate.

Similarly, Chambers (1966, p. 241) argued as follows: It is the constituents who assign valuations to expected superior returns. It is not the function of accounting to determine the going value of a firm as a whole; this function rests with constituents and potential constituents—those who are in the market for investments in going concerns. In this regard, the roles of managers and investors are different, and the evaluation of firm value is not the role of managers but rather the role of the current and future constituents of the firm. It is the role of the members themselves to select discount rates, estimation periods, and evaluate investment opportunities. Therefore, the value of goodwill should not be evaluated and disclosed by managers, but rather by the constituents.

Furthermore, the AICPA (1994), known as the Jenkins Report, and Spacek (1964) stated the following: While users would welcome improvements in disclosure about the identity, source, and life of a company's purchased or internally

---

[41] Before the concept that financial reporting should provide useful information for investors' decision-making was established, conservative and objective measurement was considered the primary objective of financial reporting. Even under this earlier objective, however, internally generated goodwill would not be recognized as an asset. Walker (1938, pp. 253–254) stated the following: The actual cost of assets is the only one capable of accurate determination, and the accountant has taken the more conservative point of view. To set up the present estimated value of the earning power of a business is inconsistent with the generally accepted function of accounting. The balance sheet shows only those valuable resources of an enterprise that are, by their nature, fairly clearly identifiable and measurable, and that have been acquired through expenditure or are clearly expected to be realized in the course of the enterprise as a going concern. The creation of goodwill normally requires expenditure, but the amount of that expenditure that actually created the goodwill is not calculable. Also see Kripke (1961) and Zanoni (2009).

generated intangible assets, they generally oppose recognizing internally generated intangible assets in financial statements. In general, users do not expect management to provide forecasted financial statements. They are concerned about the reliability of the information and believe that forecasting financial performance is a function of financial analysis rather than business reporting (AICPA 1994, p. 14). The sharp distinction of responsibility between the presenter of the information and the maker of market-value opinion is at the very essence of a fair presentation of financial statements (Spacek 1964, p. 39).

In this context, investors favor enhanced disclosure regarding self-created intangible assets but generally oppose recognizing such assets on the balance sheet. They do not expect management to produce projected financial statements that treat internally generated goodwill as an asset. Performance forecasting is viewed as the domain of investors' financial analysis rather than financial reporting. Therefore, from the perspective of financial reporting as a tool for informing investors' decision-making, the recognition of internally generated goodwill as an asset is rejected.

Additionally, the *Discussion Paper on the Conceptual Framework for Financial Reporting* issued by the ASBJ in 2006, explicitly excludes the recognition of internally generated goodwill. From the perspective of the purpose of financial reporting, internally generated goodwill is excluded from the scope of financial reporting (ASBJ 2006, Chap. 3, para. 17, note 14). The entity responsible for predicting corporate performance and evaluating corporate value is the investor, and investment decisions are made at the investor's own risk (ASBJ 2006, Chap. 1, para. 2). The purpose of financial reporting is to measure and disclose investment positions and their results as part of disclosure that assists investors' decision-making, and the role of financial statements is to disclose financial conditions in a manner that assists investors in predicting corporate performance and evaluating corporate value (ASBJ 2006, Chap. 1, Preface, para. 2). The responsibility that management bears in fulfilling this role is fundamentally to disclose facts (ASBJ 2006, Chap. 1, paras. 8, 18).

In this regard, investors use disclosed information as inputs for their own forecasting models. Management's responsibility is to provide the input information that contributes to corporate value assessment, not to provide its own forecasts on behalf of investors. If management were to predict and disclose corporate value themselves, it could be interpreted as the issuer of securities asserting the value of those securities. This would contradict the spirit of the Financial Instruments and Exchange Act, which seeks to safeguard the functions of the capital market, and would hinder management's ability to take responsibility for such judgments. In other words, internally generated goodwill is not considered a "fact" and therefore does not align with the role of financial statements derived from the purpose of financial reporting.

A similar view is presented by Saito (2019, pp. 115–116), who emphasized that accounting information based on corporate performance disclosure represents factual information used by investors to form uncertain future forecasts. Disclosure of expectations is limited to estimates of facts up to the present. The formation of expectations regarding future corporate performance and the evaluation of corporate value based on those expectations are the responsibility of investors, not of management. Consequently, recognizing internally generated goodwill as an asset by management does not align with the purpose of financial reporting.

In contrast, the IASB Conceptual Framework (CF) does not explicitly prohibit the recognition of internally generated goodwill as an asset. The CF contains no description of internally generated goodwill or goodwill in general. According to IASB CF (BC4.33), the Board concluded that referencing a specific asset, such as goodwill, in the CF was not appropriate. As a result, goodwill is not mentioned in the IASB CF.

However, while not explicitly stated, recognizing internally generated goodwill as an asset appears to be contrary to the objective of financial reporting. The IASB CF states that the objective of general-purpose financial reporting is to provide financial information about the reporting entity that is useful to existing and potential investors, lenders, and other creditors in making decisions related to providing resources to the entity (IASB CF, para. 1.2). General-purpose financial reports are not designed to show the value of a reporting entity, but they provide information to help existing and potential investors, lenders, and other creditors estimate the value of the reporting entity (IASB CF, para. 1.7). Financial statements are not required to recognize the value of the entity in the statement of financial position or to recognize all assets and liabilities; Chap. 5 discusses recognition criteria for assets and liabilities (IASB CF, BC. 2.44).

During the formulation of the IASB CF, issued in 2018, several discussions addressed internally generated goodwill. The Discussion Paper *A Review of the Conceptual Framework for Financial Reporting* (2013) argued that goodwill meets the definition of an asset. This conclusion applies equally to internally generated goodwill and to acquired goodwill. However, the IASB concluded that recognizing internally generated goodwill is unnecessary to meet the objective of financial statements. Financial statements are not designed to show the value of a reporting entity. Measuring internally generated goodwill would require an estimate of the value of the reporting entity. Consequently, recognizing internally generated goodwill does not provide relevant information (IASB 2013, para. 4.9).

In response, the Exposure Draft *Conceptual Framework for Financial Reporting*, issued in 2015, stated that, because the recognition of internally generated goodwill would require a valuation of the entity as a whole, its recognition is unnecessary to meet the objective of financial reporting. Although the IASB continues to believe this statement is valid, the Exposure Draft does not include this case as an indicator that recognition might not result in relevant information. The IASB agrees with respondents who argued that such an indicator is not useful because it applies only to internally generated goodwill. However, the IASB concluded that the difficulty in assessing whether an asset exists separately from the business as a whole—that is, whether there is an asset distinct from goodwill—is a factor that could indicate that recognition of the asset would not provide relevant information (IASB 2015, BC5.35).

In this regard, although the IASB had held the view that internally generated goodwill should not be recognized as an asset from the perspective of the objective of financial reporting, the 2015 Exposure Draft and the 2018 IASB CF, from the perspectives of the separability and purpose-suitability of goodwill, did not include language in the main text explicitly prohibiting the recognition of internally generated goodwill as an asset on the basis of the objective of financial reporting. The 2018 IASB CF does not mention internally generated goodwill, nor does it include any discussion of goodwill in general.

However, the IASB CF appears to adopt the position that recognizing internally generated goodwill as an asset is not permitted from the perspective of the purpose of financial reporting. Specifically, it states that the purpose of financial reporting is to provide financial information about the reporting entity that is useful for decision-making by investors and others, and that financial statements are not designed to demonstrate the value of the reporting entity but rather to provide information necessary to estimate that value. In particular, the CF explicitly notes that the statement of financial position does not require the recognition of enterprise value, does not require the recognition of all assets and liabilities, and that separate recognition criteria apply to the recognition of assets.

Therefore, we can reasonably conclude that, under the IASB CF, internally generated goodwill representing the value of the reporting entity is not permitted from the perspective of the objectives of financial reporting and the roles required of financial statements. On the other hand, the CF also states that separate recognition criteria apply to assets, leaving the level at which internally generated goodwill is excluded unclear. In this regard, the IASB CF does not necessarily contradict the view that recognition of internally generated goodwill as an asset is excluded from the perspective of purpose, but it does not rely solely on that perspective and does not conflict with the view based on recognition and measurement. This allows it to form a theoretical structure that is consistent with both perspectives. In the individual accounting standard IAS 38, the recognition of internally generated goodwill is excluded from the perspective of recognition and measurement, meaning that the rationale for excluding internally generated goodwill differs between the CF and the individual accounting standard.

3.3.2 Subjective Value and Subjective Goodwill

3.3.2.1 Characteristics of Subjective Goodwill

According to the American Accounting Association (AAA) (1977, pp. 5–6), the concept of subjective goodwill was first comprehensively presented by Edwards and Bell (1961), and debates based on deductive theories, distinct from the so-called classical model, subsequently developed. In this context, concepts such as the subjective value and subjective profit of a firm, as well as realizable profit and managerial profit, are introduced under the influence of neoclassical economic theory, independent of the constraints of historical cost.[42] Edwards and Bell defined goodwill and subjective goodwill as follows: goodwill reflects expected earning power arising from factors such as monopoly power or efficiency, while subjective goodwill refers to the portion by which subjective value exceeds the total market value of individual assets (Edwards and Bell 1961, p. 37).

Subjective value is defined as the expected value of dividends from an asset, discounted at the target rate of interest. It represents the estimated value of the expected dividend stream from an individual asset or investment proposal and indicates the value of a specific combination of assets as a means of generating profits for a company. If a company seeks to maximize profits, it will select the asset portfolio with the highest subjective value—that is, the highest subjective goodwill. The subjective value of the chosen asset portfolio should exceed the sum of the market values of the individual assets; otherwise, selling the assets would be the preferred option (Edwards and Bell 1961, pp. 34–37). In this regard, the subjective goodwill defined by Edwards and Bell (1961) is the portion by which subjective value exceeds the market value (market price) of the asset, aligning with the concept of internally generated goodwill.[43]

In contrast, objective goodwill is defined as the amount by which the market value of a company as a whole exceeds the market value of its assets; it represents the market value of goodwill (Edwards and Bell 1961, p. 37). It is not uncommon for a company to be sold as a single entity at a price exceeding the sum of the market values of its individual assets. This implies that investors also consider the company as a source of dividends and value the dividend stream as exceeding the market values of the individual assets (Edwards and Bell 1961, pp. 31, 37). According to Edwards and Bell (1961), objective goodwill is the amount by which the market value of the entire company exceeds the sum of the fair values of its individual assets. Therefore, objective goodwill corresponds to what is commonly referred to as purchased or acquired goodwill in the accounting treatment of business combinations.

Objective goodwill is observable through market prices, as it reflects the amount by which a company's market value exceeds the total market value of its individual assets. Consequently, it can be captured in accounting figures through fair value accounting. In contrast, subjective goodwill represents the portion of subjective value that exceeds the market prices of individual assets. Because subjective value is not observable through market prices, it cannot be captured through fair value accounting. Essentially, only objective goodwill can be recorded using fair value or market value accounting, whereas subjective goodwill cannot.

[42] The description in this section is based on Asami et al. (2022).

[43] Value in use is the subjective expected value of the reporting entity, encompassing both the market price at the measurement date and any intangible goodwill exceeding it. It is therefore used when estimating the overall value of the company, including intangible assets not recognized on the balance sheet, rather than the value of individual assets. When an asset is measured at a value in use that exceeds its historical cost, internally generated goodwill would be recognized (ASBJ 2006, Chap. 3, para. 21).

This distinction aligns with Nissim and Penman (2008, p. 24), who noted that the first of the five primary principles regarding situations in which fair value accounting is meaningful states that fair value accounting is meaningful for reporting to shareholders only when shareholder value is determined solely by market price exposure That is, the first of the five primary principles regarding the circumstances under which fair value accounting is meaningful states that fair value accounting is meaningful as a report to shareholders only when shareholder value is determined solely by exposure to market prices.

Thus, when shareholder value is determined solely by market prices, shareholder value and market price are identical, and no subjective goodwill exists. This principle can therefore be restated as follows: fair value accounting is meaningful for reporting to shareholders only when subjective goodwill does not exist.

3.3.2.2 Relationship Between Subjective and Objective Goodwill

As discussed above, Edwards and Bell (1961) addressed subjective and objective goodwill as follows. Subjective goodwill is defined as the excess of subjective value over the total market value of individual assets. Objective goodwill, on the other hand, is the excess of the market value of a firm as a whole over the market value of its assets. Regarding the relationship between subjective and objective goodwill, Edwards and Bell noted three points. First, subjective goodwill must exceed objective goodwill; otherwise, ownership of the firm would change hands. Second, subjective goodwill must be positive; otherwise, the firm would go out of business. Third, given available resources, a firm should select the plan whose subjective value is greatest (Edwards and Bell 1961, p. 37).

Concerning the first point, because the difference between a company's market value and the sum of the market values of its individual assets is considered objective goodwill, stating that subjective goodwill must exceed this implies the following: subjective goodwill is not the difference between the subjective value of the entire company and its market value, but rather the difference between the subjective value of the entire company and the market value of its individual assets. This also implies that the subjective value of the entire company exceeds its market value.[44] The fact that the subjective value of the entire company exceeds its market value—that is, that subjective goodwill exceeds objective goodwill—arises because, otherwise, shareholders, as the owners of the company, would sell their investment in the market to recover its value, resulting in a change of ownership.

In this context, Edwards and Bell (1961) defined subjective goodwill as the difference between the subjective value of the company and its market value, while

[44] Depending on whether subjective goodwill is defined as the difference between the company's overall subjective value and its market value, or as the difference between the company's overall subjective value and the market value of its individual assets, its magnitude differs by the amount of objective goodwill—that is, the difference between the company's market value and the market value of its individual assets.

objective goodwill is defined as the difference between the market value of the company and the market value of its individual assets. Essentially, subjective goodwill can be expressed as the sum of the difference between the firm's subjective value and its market value and the amount of objective goodwill. Subjective goodwill is included in subjective value, whereas objective goodwill is not—it is only included in market value. The objective goodwill included in market value represents the portion of the company's total market value, when considering multiple assets as a whole, that exceeds the sum of the market values of individual assets. This arises only when evaluating the total assets rather than individual assets.

The amount of subjective goodwill varies depending on whose subjective value is used. Subjective goodwill measured based on investors' evaluations of the company should differ from that measured based on management's evaluations. Consequently, at least two types of subjective goodwill exist. The first type is measured as the difference between the subjective value of the company as assessed by investors and the market value of individual assets. The second type is measured as the difference between the subjective value of the company as assessed by management and the market value of individual assets. Notably, the discussion in Edwards and Bell (1961) on the conversion process of subjective goodwill pertains to the latter type—subjective goodwill based on management's assessment—not the type based on investors' assessment.

3.3.3 Subjectivity and Objectivity in the Concept of Income

3.3.3.1 Subjective Profit

The most widely accepted concept of income is Hicks' concept of economic income (Edwards and Bell 1961, p. 24; Barker and Penman 2019, p. 341), and it is generally accepted as a benchmark for evaluating accounting profits.[45] According to Hicks, a man's income is defined as the maximum value he can consume during a week while still expecting to be as well off at the end of the week as he was at the beginning. The practical purpose of income is to serve as a guide for prudent conduct; it is fairly clear that this is the central meaning. However, businessmen and economists alike are usually content to employ one or another of a series of approximations to this central meaning (Hicks 1946, p. 172).

The first approximation, Income No. 1, is defined as the maximum amount that can be spent during a period while maintaining the capital value of prospective receipts in money terms. The second, Income No. 2, is defined as the maximum amount an individual can spend in a week while still expecting to be able to spend the same amount in each ensuing week. The third, Income No. 3, is defined as the

[45] Hicks' income theory is influenced by Fisher's income theory, as reflected in Lindahl and the Stockholm School, and continues the tradition of Hayek's income theory (for details, see Fukui 2012, p. 19; Asami 2021, Chap. 3, Sec. 2).

maximum amount of money an individual can spend in a week while still expecting to spend the same amount in real terms in each ensuing week (Hicks 1946, pp. 173–176).[46]

Among Hicks' concepts of economic income, Edwards and Bell (1961) focus particularly on Income No. 1 and discuss it in relation to changes in the values of net assets (Bromwich et al. 2010, p. 353).[47] In Edwards and Bell (1961), several concepts of profit are proposed,[48] with subjective profit presented as the starting point. Subjective profit is defined as the amount a firm could pay in dividends without depleting its subjective value. The expected subjective profit of the firm in any period can be defined as interest at the target rate on the subjective value of the firm's assets at the beginning of the period. The characteristics of subjective profit are as follows: first, it is subjective in nature; second, it permits the maintenance of subjective value; and third, it allows for the conversion of subjective value into market value (Edwards and Bell 1961, pp. 40, 42).

Investment performance can be evaluated by assessing how much of the expected profit was actually realized. This is done by comparing actual events during a period with prior expectations. By evaluating the gap between expectations and outcomes, managers can take corrective actions if results are unfavorable or revise future expectations and modify the business plan accordingly. In this way, expected profits and actual profits are linked. Expectations at a given point in time should be revised based on changes in conditions resulting from events that have occurred up to that point, and such revisions are a key function of managers in going concerns. Regular profit measurement should aid managers in making these revisions by clearly identifying the difference between actual and expected profits (Edwards and Bell 1961, pp. 33, 38–39).

Similarly, to evaluate the subjective profit expected at the beginning of a period, measuring the actual profit retrospectively and comparing it with the expected profit is necessary. Comparing ex post subjective profit at the end of the period with ex ante subjective profit at the beginning allows assessment of how much wealthier management feels at the end of the period relative to the beginning. However, if ex post profit is intended to inform management decision-making by revealing errors in expectations, comparing ex post subjective profit with ex ante subjective profit has a significant limitation. This is because subjective profits calculated using end-of-period values are based on end-of-period expectations, which have already been

---

[46] Regarding Income No. 1, Hicks (1946, p. 173) clearly noted that it is far from being a good approximation to the central concept in all circumstances. However, a misperception has persisted in academia and among accounting standard setters that comprehensive income represents the superior concept of income. This view is based on the rationale that comprehensive income approximates Hicks' Income No. 1 in terms of economic income, at least since the 1990s (Asami 2021, Chap. 1). As is evident from the recent description by the FASB (2020), this misperception continues to persist (Asami 2022, p. 3).

[47] Parker et al. (1986) also discussed an income concept tied to changes in net asset value, focusing on Hicks' income theory and specifically on Income No. 1 (Bromwich et al. 2010, p. 353).

[48] Edwards and Bell (1961, p. 42) argued that viewing profit as a reward for the ability to make decisions that exceed the average is reasonable.

revised from beginning-of-period expectations. Even if one identifies the difference between subjective values based on beginning-of-period expectations and those based on revised end-of-period expectations, this comparison does not provide a useful retrospective evaluation of subjective values based on beginning-of-period expectations (Edwards and Bell 1961, pp. 42–44).

In this regard, Edwards and Bell (1961) noted that, to evaluate at the end of a period how much of the profit expected at the outset was actually realized, objectively measuring the profit is necessary.[49] This is because subjective profit is inherently subjective, and end-of-period subjective profit does not capture the actual facts of the past. Subjective profits at the end of the period are therefore not useful for evaluating the subjective profits expected at the beginning of the period, which are based on prior expectations. Comparing the expectations at the beginning of the period with the facts at the end allows revision of future expectations and formation of new subjective values based on these revisions. This process explicitly reflects the basic concept of profit measurement in corporate accounting: verifying expectations against actual outcomes.

3.3.3.2 Realizable Profit

As discussed above, subjective profit is inherently subjective, and therefore the subjective profit at the end of a period cannot be used to evaluate the subjective profit at the beginning of the period, which is based on ex ante expectations. This is because subjective profit at the end of the period does not reflect ex post facts. To address this, Edwards and Bell (1961) introduced the concept of realizable profit, a measure of income that captures ex post facts to assess ex ante expectations.[50]

Expected realizable profit is defined as the amount of dividend a firm could plan to pay at the end of a period without reducing the market value of its assets (Edwards and Bell 1961, p. 45).[51] Realizable profit has three principal characteristics. First, it is objective in nature. Second, it provides an accurate measure of changes in the market value of the firm. Third, its use in determining dividend payments allows any excess of subjective value over market value to be converted into market value that can be distributed as dividends over the life of the plan (Edwards and Bell 1961, pp. 47, 48).

Realizable profit is defined as the amount that can be paid while maintaining the market value of assets, since market value reflects objective circumstances. The

[49] Edwards and Bell (1961, pp. 1–2) argued the following regarding the difference between accounting and economics: while accounting focuses on the past, economics focuses on the future. Economics concerns future events and decisions, whereas accounting primarily deals with descriptions of past events. However, this difference in perspective does not serve to separate accounting from economics; rather, it highlights the important relationship between the two.

[50] As a conceptual bridge between economic income and accounting profit, Alexander (1950), for example, proposed the concept of variable income.

[51] The change in market value, when appropriately defined, is far more than an approximation; it represents the ideal concept of short-run profit itself (Edwards and Bell 1961, p. 25).

concept of profit used for ex post verification must be useful for guiding new decisions by measuring, accurately and realistically, the extent to which past decisions were correct or incorrect. The correctness or incorrectness of decisions is ultimately verified in the market, so the ex post profit concept should capture changes in market value. Subjective value reflects subjective circumstances, whereas market value represents objective facts. In theory, market value can be measured objectively and does not depend on management's subjective estimates. If the difference between the subjective profit expected at the beginning of the period and the actual outcomes, and the difference between that and the subjective profit expected at the end of the period, can be clearly distinguished, this represents an effective step toward objective evaluation (Edwards and Bell 1961, pp. 24, 44).

However, realizable profit is merely an ideal concept of profit from a short-term perspective, whereas the ideal concept of profit from a long-term perspective is considered to be business profit.[52] In realizable profit, the achievable standard is applied to both the production and time aspects to measure profit. In contrast, in business profit, the realization standard is applied to the production aspect, while the achievable standard is applied to the time aspect. Under this approach, purchase value is used for asset valuation, which is treated as the market price at that point in time. In essence, all assets are recorded at current cost, and gains from production are not recognized until they are sold. By following this procedure, operating profit can be measured as the difference between current selling prices and current costs (Edwards and Bell 1961, pp. 25, 88–90).

Regarding the concept of business profit, Edwards and Bell examined market value according to market type and time series, dividing it into 18 categories, including historical cost, current cost, machine cost, and current selling price. Based on this analysis, they demonstrated that capital gains arising from holding activities can be distinguished from operating profits generated through operational activities (Edwards and Bell 1961, pp. 75–77). From a long-term perspective, business profit is therefore considered the ideal profit concept, rather than realizable profit.

Categorizing and analyzing market value in this manner allows the proposal of results that clearly distinguish gains from holding activities and gains from operating activities, and defines business profit as a concept separate from realizable profit. However, the purpose of this section is to examine how subjectively expected value or goodwill is transformed into ex post facts, rather than to discuss current cost accounting or the measurement of operating profit. With respect to capturing profit at the point when ex ante expectations are converted into market value, realizable profit and business profit are similar. Therefore, business profit will not be explicitly addressed in the remainder of this chapter.

Realizable profit is an objective profit measured based on events that actually occurred during the current period. It is regarded as a useful profit concept for ex post confirmation of whether the decisions made at the beginning of the period,

[52] Business profit is described as a profit concept that does not conflict with generally accepted accounting standards any more than realizable profit does (Edwards and Bell 1961, p. 88).

based on expectations at that time, were correct. In other words, it evaluates whether ex ante expectations were accurate using the ex post fact of market value. Here, market value plays a central role, as it is used to capture profit as an ex post fact.

In this respect, realizable profit and accounting profit share a common feature in that both aim to capture ex post facts to verify ex ante expectations. In accounting profit, cash is treated as an ex post fact, while market prices are treated as ex post facts only in the case of financial investments, where cash and market prices are considered to be consistent.[53] In the concept of realizable profit, market prices are treated as ex post facts, and therefore the interpretation of what constitutes an ex post fact and how it is realized differs between realizable profit and accounting profit. However, the fundamental idea of evaluating ex ante expectations based on ex post facts is common to both. At a more abstract conceptual level, where expectations are confirmed by subsequent outcomes,[54] the concepts of realizable profit and accounting profit can be regarded as equivalent.

3.3.3.3 Conversion of Subjective Goodwill

Up to this point, based on the discussion in Edwards and Bell (1961), we have distinguished between subjective rent and objective goodwill, and clarified the concepts of subjective profit (subjective income) and realizable profit (objective income). Subjective value, that is, the portion of value that exceeds market value, is assessed by comparing it with the ex post fact represented by market value, thereby determining whether the initial expectation was correct. Whether profit maximization has been achieved is ultimately justified by the objective fact of market value.

The relationship between realizable profit and subjective profit can be understood in terms of the expected conversion of goodwill into market value. The accomplishment of profit maximization reflects a continuous effort to have subjective goodwill validated by the market, that is, to convert subjective goodwill into some form of market value. The test of success, and thus the logical criterion for evaluating business decisions, is the extent to which the realized increases in market value approximate the increases originally anticipated. The conversion of subjective goodwill into market value as the plan develops constitutes an element of realizable profit because a market value now exists that did not exist previously, indicating that the market judges the firm to be better off to that extent (Edwards and Bell 1961, p. 48).[55]

---

[53] Regarding the interpretation of ex post facts, Alexander (1950) used the concept of variable income to propose confirming ex ante windfalls related to future cash flows by means of the actual cash flows realized ex post.

[54] This concept corresponds to the notion of "release from risk of investment" in the ASBJ Conceptual Framework in Japan.

[55] In Edwards and Bell (1961), objective goodwill is assumed to be zero in their analysis of the conversion process of subjective goodwill. However, even if objective goodwill is positive, the conclusion does not change, because objective goodwill is already included within subjective goodwill.

In this regard, Edwards and Bell (1961) viewed the conversion of ex ante expected subjective goodwill into ex post facts as a conversion into market value (market price). The portion of subjective goodwill included in subjective value is recognized as realizable profit in each period as it is converted into market value. This process of converting subjective goodwill is illustrated in (Fig. 3.1) below.[56]

Regarding this conversion of subjective goodwill, Saito (2010, pp. 217–218) provided a similar explanation (Fig. 3.2). The process by which the results of an investment are realized as cash flow is also the process by which the initial goodwill value disappears as expectations are realized. Once the facts are confirmed, the expectations themselves no longer remain. The value of goodwill, which represents the capitalization of ex ante expectations, either materializes as ex post profits or disappears without materializing. Thus, realized profit includes the portion of goodwill that has materialized and become an objective fact. If goodwill represents the expectation of excess profits, then realized excess profits, together with normal profits corresponding to the cost of capital, constitute the components of profit. The criterion for realization is simply the confirmation of this "fact" through cash flows.

Next, we move to a more generalized model. As shown in (Fig. 3.1) and elsewhere, Edwards and Bell (1961) explained the conversion process of subjective goodwill primarily through numerical examples, and their model is not necessarily fully generalized. Following Asami (2021), we therefore use a more generalized model rather than numerical examples to illustrate how the subjective goodwill that managers aim to maximize as subjective value is transformed into reality, that is, the conversion process of subjective goodwill.[57] First, the subjective goodwill (internally generated goodwill) G_t at time t is defined as the difference between the capital value V_t and the market price P_t at that time, expressed as:

$$G_t = V_t - P_t$$

Where;

V_t: subjective value of assets at time t

$$V_t = \sum_{i=t+1}^{n} \frac{C_i}{(1+r)^{i-t}}$$

C_t: cash flows to be realized from assets at time t
r: discount rate
P_t: market price of the asset at time t
B_t: book value of the asset at time t
n: remaining economic life

---

[56] Note that the analysis presented in (Fig. 3.1) assumes that dividend payments are equal to realizable profit.

[57] The following description is based on Chap. 6 of Asami (2021).

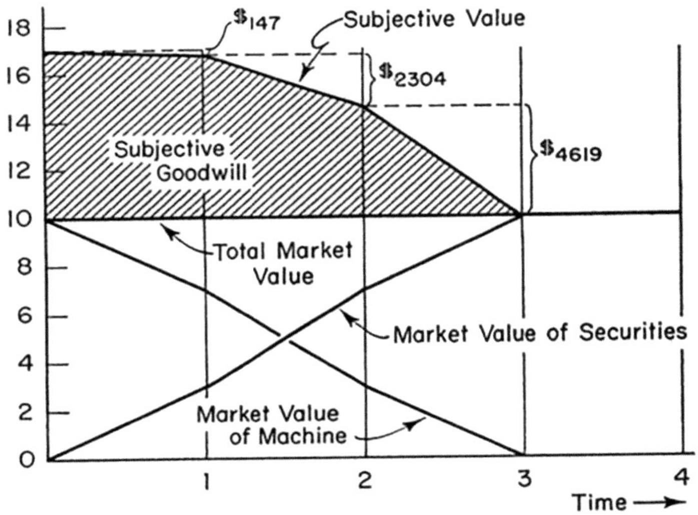

Fig. 3.1 Conversion of subjective goodwill (Edwards and Bell 1961, p. 50)

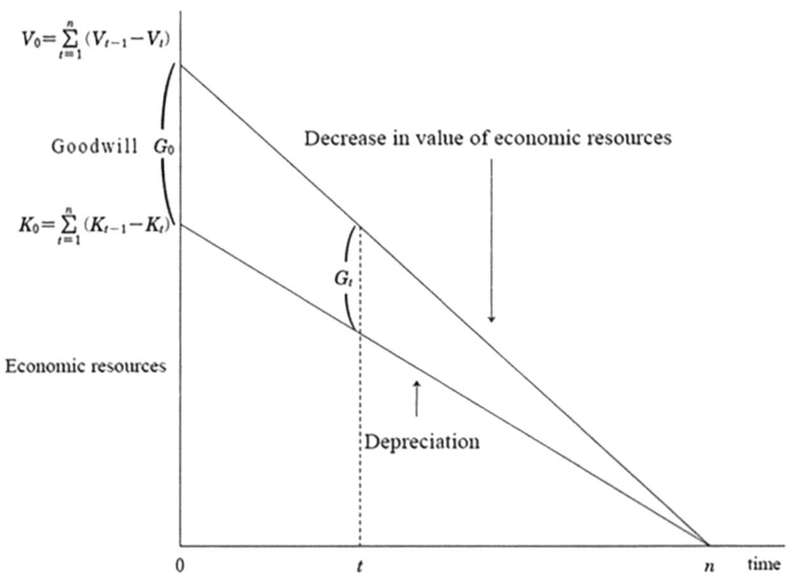

Fig. 3.2 Capital decrease and depreciation (Saito 2010, p. 218)

According to the definitions of subjective profit and realizable profit presented by Edwards and Bell (1961), subjective profit Y_t and realizable profit I_t for a given period can be expressed as follows:

$$\begin{aligned}\text{Subjective Profit } Y_t &= (C_t + V_t) - V_{t-1}\\ &= C_t - (V_{t-1} - V_t)\\ &= C_t - \{(G_{t-1} + P_{t-1}) - (G_t + P_t)\}\\ &= C_t - \{(G_{t-1} - G_t) + (P_{t-1} - P_t)\}\end{aligned}$$

$$\begin{aligned}\text{Realizable Profit } I_t &= (C_t + P_t) - P_{t-1}\\ &= C_t - (P_{t-1} - P_t)\end{aligned}$$

$$\begin{aligned}\text{Realizable Profit } I_t - \text{Subjective Profit } Y_t &= \{C_t - (P_{t-1} - P_t)\} - \{C_t - (V_{t-1} - V_t)\}\\ &= (V_{t-1} - P_{t-1}) - (V_t - P_t)\\ &= G_{t-1} - G_t\end{aligned}$$

This shows that the difference between realizable profit and subjective profit is equal to the change in subjective goodwill ($G_{t-1} - G_t$). By combining the change in subjective goodwill with subjective profit, realizable profit can be calculated. In essence, the relationship between the two profits is: realizable profit = subjective profit + change in subjective goodwill, or $I_t = Y_t + (G_{t-1} - G_t)$.

In terms of subjective profit, the cash flow C_t realized at time t is reduced by both the change in subjective goodwill ($G_{t-1} - G_t$) from t−1 to t and the change in the fair value of assets ($P_{t-1} - P_t$) over the same period. Therefore, subjective profit does not include changes in subjective goodwill, and this holds for any given period. By contrast, realizable profit includes the full amount of the conversion in subjective goodwill. Regarding accounting profit, the portion of subjective goodwill included in accounting profit for a given period is calculated as: $(G_{t-1} - G_t) - \{(B_{t-1} - P_{t-1}) - (B_t - P_t)\}$. The relationships between subjective profit and subjective goodwill, and between realizable profit and subjective goodwill, are illustrated in Figs. 3.3 and 3.4, respectively.

In this regard, subjective goodwill gradually converts into facts over time. Differences in what is considered a fact lead to differences in the amounts of subjective goodwill included in realizable profit and accounting profit. In realizable profit, the full amount of conversion in subjective goodwill is included, whereas in accounting profit, only a portion is recognized. This constitutes the key difference between the two. However, as noted earlier, both approaches share the underlying principle of confirming expectations with facts. Accounting profit, like realizable profit, recognizes as profit the portion of subjective goodwill that has been converted into facts, and this mechanism is applied to profit recognition during the reporting period. Conceptually, accounting profit can therefore be regarded as the sum of subjective profit and the conversion portion of goodwill.

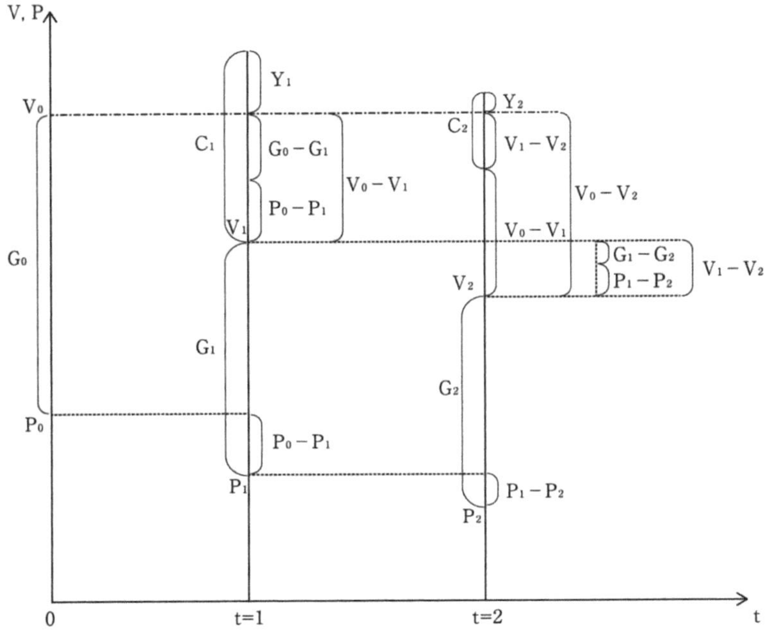

Fig. 3.3 Subjective profit and subjective goodwill (Asami 2021, p. 144)

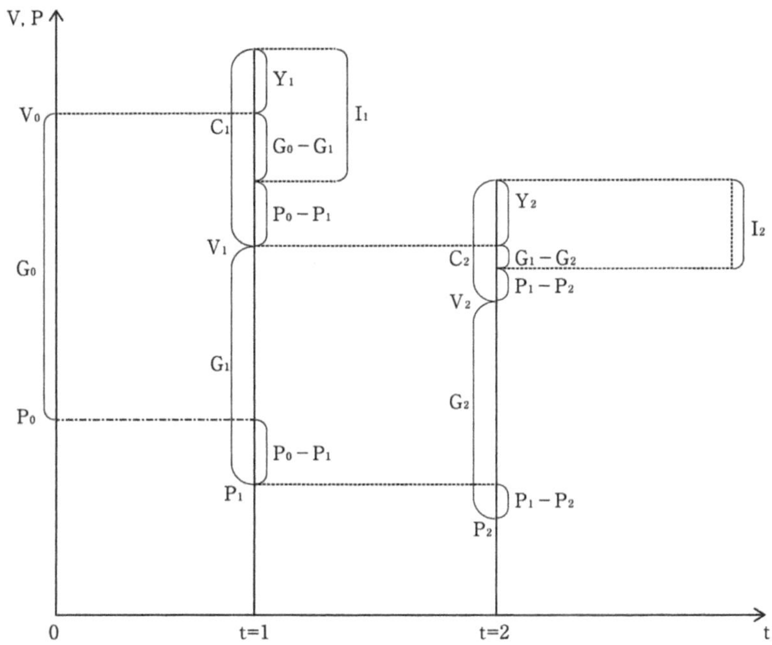

Fig. 3.4 Realizable profit and subjective goodwill (Asami 2021, p. 145)

Up to this point, we have examined the process by which subjective goodwill is converted into facts and recognized as either realizable profit or accounting profit for each period. Although the definition of "fact" differs between the two approaches, subjective goodwill clearly possesses the characteristics of profit or income and is never considered an element of capital that must be maintained. Building on the discussions in this section, the next section addresses the treatment of subjective and objective goodwill in financial accounting.

3.3.4 Accounting for Goodwill in Business Combinations

3.3.4.1 Purchased Goodwill in Business Combinations

As noted in the previous section, goodwill, which represents excess profits, should be recognized as profit or income rather than as a component of equity to be maintained. Both subjective goodwill (internally generated goodwill), represented by the difference between subjective value and the market value of individual assets, and objective goodwill (purchased goodwill), represented by the difference between the market value of the company as a whole and the market value of its individual assets, are treated the same in this respect.

In business combinations, current accounting standards require the use of the purchase method (acquisition method), resulting in objective goodwill being recognized on the balance sheet as purchased goodwill. Consequently, the same intangible assets may be recognized on the balance sheet in some cases but not in others. While objective goodwill, which is part of subjective goodwill, is recognized as an asset, subjective goodwill exceeding objective goodwill is not. Moreover, subjective goodwill arising from changes in subjective value after the business combination is also not recognized as an asset.

Regarding purchased goodwill recognized in connection with the transfer of assets and liabilities resulting from such business combinations, Saito and Fukui examined this from on-balance and off-balance perspectives. Specifically, for internally generated goodwill included in the consideration for a business combination, the portion transferred to the assets or liabilities assumed at the time of acquisition is recognized as purchased goodwill on the balance sheet of the acquiring company. Only the portion of internally generated goodwill acquired through payment of consideration is recognized as an asset. Internally generated goodwill essentially represents an expectation of future benefits, and the principle that these expectations are recognized as accounting income once realized remains consistent. Therefore, whether it remains off-balance or is partially transferred on-balance, the total amount should be the same when considered over the entire period (Saito and Fukui 2022a, pp. 87–88).

Under the purchase method, the corresponding account for goodwill is treated as equity and is not transferred to income even when the value of goodwill is realized. If the realized amount of goodwill were transferred to income, it would offset the amortization expense of goodwill recognized as an asset, and the realized excess profits would be included in each period's income. However, under the purchase method, where the corresponding account for goodwill is treated as equity and goodwill is amortized, realized excess profits are offset by goodwill amortization and excluded from accounting income. Essentially, when the purchase method is applied in a business combination, the income from the acquired company does not include the realized portion of the excess profits expected from the acquisition (Saito and Fukui 2022a, p. 88).

If goodwill is not amortized, this deficiency is partially resolved. However, because the equity in the corresponding account remains unchanged, even if goodwill declines in value, net assets are effectively recorded twice: once at the creation of goodwill and again upon its realization. Neither the method of acquiring purchased goodwill through amortization nor the method of acquiring it without amortization fully aligns the total income and equity of the acquiring company with those of the acquired company as if the merger had not occurred. Recognizing purchased goodwill and reflecting it in equity while ignoring its eventual realization as income—leaving it fixed as equity—is logically flawed (Saito and Fukui 2022a, pp. 90, 92).

As long as the corresponding account for goodwill in the purchase method is treated as equity, future excess profits will not be transferred to income even after they are realized. Consequently, under the purchase method with amortization, the portion of excess profits is excluded from realized profits, whereas under the purchase method without amortization, excess profits are reflected in net assets both when expected and when realized (Saito and Fukui 2022a, p. 94). In this respect, under the purchase method, where the corresponding account for purchased goodwill in a business combination is treated as equity, income is understated when goodwill is amortized, while equity is overstated when goodwill is not amortized. Therefore, problems arguably arise regardless of whether amortization is applied.

3.3.4.2 Appropriate Accounting Treatment for Purchased Goodwill

From the perspective of accounting income, which approximates economic income, the gross return on assets—including the cost of equity—defined as economic income must be at least equal to the accounting income recognized on a full-year aggregate basis. The economic asset value and shareholders' equity must ultimately be equal. If a merger is neutral in terms of economic income, the accounting income and equity of the acquiring company at the time of the merger must equal the total accounting income and equity of the acquiring and acquired companies if the merger had not occurred (Saito and Fukui 2022a, pp. 90, 91). Internally generated goodwill arising from expectations regarding future performance is recognized as income upon realization, and whether recorded on-balance or off-balance, both approaches yield consistent results on a full-year aggregate basis. Based on this understanding, the following two methods are proposed as the appropriate accounting treatment for purchased goodwill in a business combination (Saito and Fukui 2022a, pp. 87, 88):

1. Recognize the expected value as an asset, and when realized, deduct the amount from net assets, which is the correspondent account, and transfer it to income.
2. When transferring investment accounts to assets and liabilities, offset the amount equivalent to the acquired company's internally generated goodwill included therein against net assets and eliminate it initially.

Method (1), under the acquisition method, recognizes a portion of internally generated goodwill as purchased goodwill and records it on the balance sheet as an asset, while the corresponding amount is recorded in other comprehensive income as part of net assets. After the fiscal year in which goodwill is recognized, the portion of expected goodwill that has been realized is transferred to income. Essentially, this method treats purchased goodwill as an asset, the corresponding account as other comprehensive income, and then recycles the amount to income as it is realized in subsequent fiscal years. However, this method assumes the acquired company continues as a going concern and treats the corresponding account for the purchased goodwill as accumulated other comprehensive income. As a result, it may be inconsistent with the conceptual basis of the current accounting standards for the purchase method (Saito and Fukui 2022a, pp. 88, 92).

Under Method (2), goodwill is not recognized as an asset, and no amortization expense is recorded. As a result, the portion of realized excess profit is recognized directly as income. Within Method (2), the pooling of interests approach determines the amount of net assets by valuing each individual asset and liability of the acquired company at its book value.[58] This method treats the internally generated goodwill of the acquired company, recognized on the balance sheet through the acquisition of shares, as removed from the balance sheet. The portion of the acquired shares corresponding to identifiable assets and liabilities is included in net assets, while the excess, representing goodwill, is treated as a claim on future earnings and offset against equity. However, Method (2) would not be permitted under current accounting standards because it assumes the continuity of the acquired company (Saito and Fukui 2022a, pp. 88–90).

Accordingly, if either of the following approaches is used—(1) recognizing purchased goodwill as an asset under the purchase method, with the corresponding account treated as other comprehensive income and subsequently recycled to income as the goodwill is realized, or (2) eliminating purchased goodwill by offsetting it against equity from the outset using the pooling of interests method—accounting income and equity, as well as economic income and asset values, would be identical whether or not a business combination occurs. However, both methods conflict with the purchase method's underlying assumption that the continuity of the acquiree is disrupted and are therefore inconsistent with current accounting standards. Method (1) assumes continuity by treating the corresponding account as part

[58] In addition, company law and other regulations allow a method in which the individual assets and liabilities to be transferred are revalued at fair value rather than at the book value of the acquired company, with the difference between the revalued amount and the book value adjusted in capital (Saito and Fukui 2022a, p. 89).

of accumulated income, such as other comprehensive income, while Method (2) also assumes continuity in connection with the transfer of assets and liabilities (Saito and Fukui 2022a, pp. 88, 94).

In this regard, the purchase method that amortizes goodwill has the problem of understating income, because the portion of excess profits is excluded from realized income through the recognition of goodwill amortization expense.[59] On the other hand, the purchase method that does not amortize goodwill avoids understating income. However, goodwill is recognized twice in net assets—once at the initial recognition of goodwill and again upon its realization—resulting in an overstatement of equity. In essence, whether goodwill is amortized or not, both approaches present issues regarding the classification of equity and income. This arises because shareholders' equity is recorded as the corresponding account for goodwill. As long as the corresponding account for purchased goodwill remains equity, realized excess profits will not be transferred to income.

To address this issue, the corresponding account for purchased goodwill could be recognized as other comprehensive income. Even when a portion of off-balance internally generated goodwill is brought on-balance as purchased goodwill in a business combination, the corresponding account should be other comprehensive income, recorded as accumulated income. Then, when the anticipated excess profits are realized, transferring them to income would prevent both overstatement of equity and understatement of income. Essentially, applying the purchase method in which purchased goodwill is recognized as an asset, with the corresponding account recorded in other comprehensive income and recycled to income as realized, resolves the difficulty in distinguishing between equity and income.

However, these treatments conflict with the assumption underlying the purchase method, which considers the acquiree's discontinuity. Recognizing expected value as an asset and transferring realized amounts from net assets to income assumes the continuity of the acquired entity. Similarly, eliminating the portion of internally generated goodwill included in purchased goodwill by offsetting it against net assets when replacing investment accounts with assets and liabilities also assumes continuity. In essence, while the accounting treatments described above could resolve the question of whether goodwill should be amortized, they rely on the continuity of the acquired entity, which is inconsistent with the purchase method's assumption of the acquiree's discontinuity. Therefore, they are incompatible with the purchase method's assumption of discontinuity and do not conform to current accounting standards.

[59] Even if amortization is not applied, recognizing impairment over the entire investment period ultimately produces the same problem—understatement of income. Therefore, it is more accurate to classify based on whether expenses are recognized rather than on whether amortization is applied. Depending on the treatment—"amortization and/or impairment" versus "non-amortization and non-impairment"—the former results in understated income, while the latter results in overstated equity. In essence, recognizing purchased goodwill through amortization and/or impairment leads to income understatement, whereas not amortizing or impairing purchased goodwill, and thus not recognizing it, leads to equity overstatement. Also see Fukui and Saito 2022a, b; Saito 2017.

3.4 Summary and Remaining Issues

This chapter examined the origins of the definition of goodwill, tracing it back to the 1571 judicial precedent, and described how the definition has evolved to the present day. It then discussed the accounting standards for goodwill in the United States, the United Kingdom, the European Union, and Japan. This chapter also reviewed the debate on the accounting treatment of goodwill over approximately 120 years, from the 1880s—when discussions on goodwill accounting began—up to around 2000, when non-amortization and impairment treatments were introduced under SFAS 141/142 and IFRS 3.

In the earliest debates concerning goodwill accounting in the 1880s, the characterization of goodwill as an asset was contested, and early amortization was considered the preferable accounting treatment. With the establishment of company law provisions and the advocacy of Dicksee (1897) for write-offs against equity, this approach became widely adopted in both the United States and the United Kingdom around 1900. Following the Great Depression of 1929, a conservative trend emerged alongside the establishment of historical cost accounting. After the SEC prohibited the equity method in 1945 to distinguish equity from income, its use declined in the United States, while systematic amortization based on the allocation of historical cost, as proposed by Paton and Littleton (1940), gained widespread acceptance.

Discussions on writing off against equity resurfaced in the 1960s alongside debates on the pooling of interests method, but support for systematic amortization remained dominant. From the 1980s onward, write-offs against equity were prohibited in both the United Kingdom and under IAS, and systematic amortization was required. Throughout its more than 120-year history, the primary focus of debate was the distinction between equity and income. In contrast, in the contemporary period since around 2000, debates have centered on amortization, non-amortization, and impairment. In this context, goodwill is universally treated as an asset to be recognized as an expense, and the main issue concerns the allocation of those expenses.

This chapter then examined the appropriateness of recognizing internally generated goodwill. It first discussed the debate supporting the recognition of internally generated goodwill as an asset. The argument in favor is that information about internally generated goodwill, based on management's future cash flow projections, is useful for investors' decision-making and therefore should be recognized as an asset. However, this view has not been widely accepted. From the 1880s, when debates on goodwill accounting began, to the present, the negative view on recognizing internally generated goodwill as an asset has predominated. This perspective can be categorized into two types.

The first holds that, at the level of recognition and measurement, internally generated goodwill should not be recognized as an asset. The reasoning is that it does not meet recognition criteria because its cost cannot be objectively measured and its identifiability is insufficient. The second holds that, at the level of the objective of financial reporting, internally generated goodwill should not be recognized as an asset. Under this view, the objective of financial reporting is to provide useful information for investors' decision-making. Investors evaluate the value of the firm at their discretion, while management provides information to assist in that evaluation. Therefore, internally generated goodwill expected by management should not be recognized as an asset. While the Japanese CF explicitly prohibits the recognition of internally generated goodwill from this perspective, the IASB CF remains ambiguous regarding which perspective it adopts.

Building on this debate, this chapter then examined the relationship between subjective and objective goodwill based on Edwards and Bell (1961) and clarified the connection to types of goodwill considered in accounting standard-setting, such as purchased goodwill and internally generated goodwill. The discussion was systematized to describe the process by which subjective goodwill—internally generated goodwill representing expected future excess returns—is confirmed by ex post facts and converted into profit each period. A partial component of subjective goodwill, initially an ex ante expectation, gradually becomes ex post fact over time. This process illustrates how that amount is subsequently recognized as realizable profit or accounting income in each period. While subjective profit includes expected amounts, realizable profit or accounting income does not recognize them until they are confirmed by ex post facts.

We examined the conversion process of goodwill, discussed that goodwill is a component of income, and, drawing on prior research regarding the treatment of purchased goodwill in business combination accounting, organized the debate on its appropriate accounting treatment. Previous studies have proposed appropriate accounting treatments for purchased goodwill. One approach recognizes the expected value as an asset and, when realized, deducts the corresponding amount from net assets and transfers it to income. The other approach offsets the amount equivalent to the acquired company's internally generated goodwill against net assets and eliminates it initially when transferring investment accounts to assets and liabilities. However, both methods have been criticized as incompatible with the conceptual basis of the purchase method, which assumes discontinuity of the acquired entity, and therefore are not fully consistent with current accounting standards.

Based on these considerations, this section clarifies the following points. The purchase method that amortizes goodwill inherently faces the problem of understated income, because the expense recognized for goodwill excludes the amount equivalent to excess profits from realized income. Conversely, the purchase method that does not amortize goodwill faces the problem of overstated equity, as goodwill is recognized twice in net assets—once at initial recognition and again upon realization. Regardless of whether goodwill is amortized, as long as it is recognized with shareholders' equity rather than other comprehensive income as the corresponding account, the fundamental distinction between equity and income remains unresolved. Under the purchase method, purchased goodwill is recorded with shareholders' equity and the method does not assume the continuity of the acquired entity;

therefore, it is theoretically impossible to reach a definitive conclusion regarding whether purchased goodwill should be amortized.

Statement on AI Usage: During the preparation of this manuscript, the author used AI-assisted tools such as DeepL and Gemini to improve the English expression and clarity of the manuscript. The author thoroughly reviewed and approved the final version and takes full responsibility for the content.

References

Accounting Standards Board (ASB), 1997, Financial Reporting Standard No.10 (FRS10), *Goodwill and Intangible Assets*, ASB.

Accounting Standards Board (ASB), 1998, Financial Reporting Standard No.11 (FRS11), *Impairment of Fixed Assets and Goodwill*, ASB.

Accounting Standards Board of Japan (ASBJ), 2006, The Discussion Paper, *Conceptual Framework of Financial Accounting*, ASBJ.

Accounting Standards Board of Japan (ASBJ), 2008a, Accounting Standard (ASBJ Statement) No. 21, *Business Combinations*, ASBJ.

Accounting Standards Board of Japan (ASBJ), 2008b, Accounting Standard (ASBJ Statement) No. 22, *Consolidated Financial Statements*, ASBJ.

Accounting Standards Board of Japan (ASBJ), 2015a, *Foreword to 'Japan's Modified International Standards (JMIS): Accounting Standards Comprising IFRSs and the ASBJ Modifications,'* ASBJ.

Accounting Standards Board of Japan (ASBJ), 2015b, Japan's Modified International Standards (JMIS): Accounting Standards Comprising IFRSs and the ASBJ Modifications, *Applications of 'Japan's Modified International Standards,'* ASBJ.

Accounting Standards Board of Japan (ASBJ), 2015c, Japan's Modified International Standards (JMIS): Accounting Standards Comprising IFRSs and the ASBJ Modifications, ASBJ Modification on Accounting Standard No.1, *Accounting for Goodwill*, ASBJ.

Accounting Standards Board of Japan (ASBJ), European Financial Reporting Advisory Group and Organismo Italiano di Contabilita (Italian Standard Setter, OIC), 2014, *Should Goodwill Still Not Be Amortised?*, ASBJ, EFRAG, OIC.

Accounting Standards Committee (ASC), 1982, Statement of Standard Accounting Practice, Exposure Draft ED30, *Accounting for goodwill*, ASC.

Accounting Standards Committee (ASC), 1984, Statement of Standard Accounting Practice No.22 (SSAP22), *Accounting for Goodwill*, ASC.

Alexander, S., 1950, 'Income measurement in a Dynamic Economy,' in *Five Monographs on Business Income,* American Institute of Accountants, Study Group on Business Income, AIA.

American Accounting Association (AAA), Committee on Concepts and Standards for External Financial Reports, 1977, *Statement of Accounting Theory and Theory Acceptance*, AAA.

American Institute of Accountants (AIA), 1917, 'Uniform Accounting,' *The Journal of Accountancy*, Vol.23, No.6, pp. 401–433, AIA.

American Institute of Accountants (AIA), 1929, 'Verification of Financial Statement,' *The Journal of Accountancy*, Vol. 47, No, 5, pp. 321–354, AIA.

American Institute of Accountants (AIA), 1931, Preliminary Report of a Special Committee on Terminology, *Accounting Terminology*, AIA.

American Institute of Accountants (AIA), Committee on Accounting Procedure (CAP), 1944, Accounting Research Bulletin No. 24, *Accounting for Intangible Assets*, AIA.

American Institute of Accountants (AIA), Committee on Accounting Procedure (CAP), 1953, Accounting Research Bulletin No. 43, *Restatement and Revision of Accounting Research Bulletins*, AIA.

American Institute of Certified Public Accountants (AICPA), Accounting Principles Board (APB), 1970a, Opinions of Accounting Principles Board No. 16, *Business Combinations*, AICPA.
American Institute of Certified Public Accountants (AICPA), Accounting Principles Board (APB), 1970b, Opinions of Accounting Principles Board No. 17, *Intangible Assets*, AICPA.
American Institute of Certified Public Accountants (AICPA), Special Committee on Financial Reporting, 1994, *Improving Business Reporting - a Customer Focus: Meeting the Information Needs of Investors and Creditors; Jenkins Report*, AICPA.
Andrews, W. T., 1981, 'Evolution of APB Opinion No.17 Accounting for Intangible Assets; a Study of the U.S. Position on Accounting for Goodwill,' *Accounting Historians Journal*, Vol.8, No.1, pp. 37–49.
Arnold, J., 1992, *Goodwill and Other Intangibles*, The Institute of Chartered Accountants.
Asami (Katsuo) Y., 2012, 'Chap. 4, Jikososetsunoren no Ninshiki – 1900nen zengo no Giron wo Chushin tosite – (Recognition of Internally Generated Goodwill – Discussion around 1900 –),' in Obinata, T., *Kaikeikijunnkenkyu no Genten (Fundamental Essence of Research on Accounting Standards)*, Chuo-Keizaisha, Tokyo, Japan, pp. 59–76, in Japanese.
Asami, Y., 2021, *Kaikeirieki no Kisogainen (Fundamental Concept of Accounting Income)*, in Japanese, Chuo-Keizaisha, Tokyo, Japan.
Asami, Y., 2022, 'IASB Gainen Framework to Kinhon Zaimusyohyo Project niokeru Riekigainen (Income Concept of IASB's Conceptual Framework and Fundamental Financial Reporting Project),' *Kaikei (The Accounting)*, Vol.201, No.6, pp. 1–12, in Japanese.
Asami, Y., 2025, 'Accounting Treatment for Goodwill,' *Discussion Paper*, No.E25-7, Economic Research Center, Graduate School of Economics, Nagoya University, in Japanese.
Asami, Y., 2026, 'Recognition of Internally Generated Goodwill,' *Discussion Paper*, No.E26-1, Economic Research Center, Graduate School of Economics, Nagoya University, in Japanese.
Asami, Y., T. Miyauchi, T. Yamashita, M. Yoneyama, 2022, 'Kigyoketsugo ni okeru Noren no Kaikeishori – Jisshobunseki oyobi Chosahyo Chosa (Accounting Treatment of Goodwill in Business Combination – Empirical Research and Questionnaire Survey),' *Discussion Paper*, Research Institute of Economics and Management, Gakushuin University, No.22-1, in Japanese.
Barker, R. and S. Penman, 2019, 'Moving the Conceptual Framework Forward: Accounting for Uncertainty,' *Contemporary Accounting Research,* Vol.37, No.1, pp. 322–357.
Barker, R., A. Lennard, S. Penman and A. Teixeira, 2021, 'Accounting for Intangible Assets: Suggested Solutions,' *Accounting and Business Research*, Vol.52, No.6, pp. 601–630.
Beier, R. J., 1993, 'SEC Addresses Goodwill Write-Offs in Supermarkets General; What Will the FASB Do?, *Journal of Corporate Accounting and Finance*, Vol.5, No.2, pp. 153–159.
Bentley, H. C., 1911, *The Science of Accounts*, The Ronald Press Company, New York, US.
Bithell, R., 1882, *A Counting-House Dictionary*, George Routledge and Sons, New York, US.
Black E. L. and M. L. Zyla, 2018, *Accounting for Goodwill and Other Intangible Assets*, John Wiley & Sons, Inc., New Jersey, US.
Bloom M., 2008, *Double Accounting for Goodwill*, Routledge, New York, US.
Bourne, J. H., 1888, 'Goodwill,' *The Accountant*, Vol.14, No.720, pp. 604–605.
Bromwich, M., R. Macve and S. Sunder, 2010, 'Hicksian Income in the Conceptual Framework,' *A Journal of Accounting, Finance and Business Studies*, Vol.46, No.3, pp. 348–376.
Browne, E. A., 1902, 'Goodwill: Its Ascertainment and Treatment in Accounts,' *The Accountant*, Vol.28, No.1439, pp. 1339–1344.
Brown, P., 1995, 'A Note on the Inverse (Reverse) Sum-of-the-Years'-Digits Method and Other Ways to Amortise Goodwill,' *Australian Accounting Review*, Vol.5, No.9, pp. 17–21.
Brunovs, R. and R.J. Kirsch, 1991, 'Goodwill Accounting in Selected Countries and the Harmonization of International Accounting Standards,' *Abacus*, Vol. 27, No.2, pp. 135–161.
Bryer, R. A., 1995, 'A Political Economy of SSAP22: Accounting for Goodwill,' *British Accounting Review*, Vol.27, pp. 283–310.
Burton, J. C., 1970, *Accounting for Business Combinations; A Practical and Empirical Commet*, Financial Executives Research Foundation, New York, US.

Business Accounting Deliberation Council (BADC), 1974, *Shusei Kigyo Kaikei Gensoku (Revised Corporate Accounting Principles)*, in Japanese, BADC.
Business Accounting Deliberation Council (BADC), 1975, *Renketsu Zaimusyohyo Gensoku (Accounting Standard for Consolidated Financial Statements)*, in Japanese, BADC.
Business Accounting Deliberation Council (BADC), 1997, *Kaitei Renketsu Zaimusyohyo Gensoku (Revised Accounting Standard for Consolidated Financial Statements)*, in Japanese, BADC.
Business Accounting Deliberation Council (BADC), 1997, *Renketsu Zaimushohyoseido no Minaoshi ni Kansuru Ikensho (Opinion Paper on the Amendment of the Regulations for Consolidated Financial Statements), in Japanese*, BADC.
Business Accounting Deliberation Council (BADC), 2001, *Kigyokaikei ni kakaru Kaikeishorikijun ni Kansuru Rontenseiri (Issues Related to Accounting Standards for Business Combinations*, in Japanese, BADC.
Business Accounting Deliberation Council (BADC), 2002, *Koteishisan no Genson ni kakaru Kaikeikijun (Accounting Standard for Impairment of Fixed Assets)*, in Japanese, BADC.
Business Accounting Deliberation Council (BADC), 2003, *Kigyoketsugo ni Kakaru Kaikeikijun (Accounting Standard for Business Combinations)*, in Japanese, BADC.
Business Accounting Deliberation Council (BADC), 2009, *Wagakuni ni okeru Kokusaikaikeikijun no Toriatsukai ni Kansuru Ikensho (Chukan Hokoku) (Interim Report; Opinion on the Application of International Financial Reporting Standards in Japan)*, in Japanese, BADC.
Canning, J. B., 1929, *The Economics of Accountancy*, The Ronald Press Company, New York, US.
Carsberg, B. V, 1966, 'Contribution of Leake, P. D. to Theory of Goodwill Valuation,' *Journal of Accounting Research*, Vol.4, No.1, pp. 1–15.
Catlett, G.R. and N. Olson, 1968, Accounting Research Study No.10, *Accounting for Goodwill*, AICPA.
Chambers, R. J., 1966, *Accounting, Evaluation and Economic Behavior*, Prentice-Hall Inc., New Jersey, US.
Chitty, D.,1997, 'Goodwill and Intangibles,' in the Institute of Chartered Accountants in England and Wales, *Financial Reporting Today- Current and Emerging Issues*, 1998 ed., Gloucester House, Milton Keynes, UK.
Civil Affairs Bureau of the Ministry of Justice, 1960, *Kabushikikaisha no Keisan no Naiyo ni kansuru Shohokaiseiyoko (Outline for Reform of the Commercial Code Concerning the Content of Corporate Accounting)*, in Japanese, Civil Affairs Bureau of the Ministry of Justice.
Cooper, J. 2007. 'Debating Accounting Principles and Policies: The Case of Goodwill, 1880–1921,' *Accounting, Business & Financial History*, Vol.17, No.2, pp. 241–264.
Couchman C. B., 1924, *The Balance – Sheet; Its Preparation, Content and Interpretation*, Oxford Print, Massachusetts, US.
Council of the European Communities, 1978, Fourth Council Directive, *The Treaty on Annual Accounts of Certain Types of Companies*, Council of the European Communities.
Council of the European Communities, 1983, Seventh Council Law Directive, *The Treaty on consolidated accounts*, Council of the European Communities.
European Parliament and the Council, 2013, Directive 2013/34/EU, *The Annual Financial Statements, Consolidated Financial Statements and Related Reports of Certain Types of Undertakings*, European Parliament.
Courtis, J.D. 1983, 'Business Goodwill: Conceptual Clarification via Accounting, Legal and Etymological Perspectives,' *The Accounting Historians Journal*, Vol.10, No. 2. pp. 1–38.
Davis, M., 1992, 'Goodwill Accounting - Time for an Overhaul,' *The Journal of Accountancy*, Vol.173, No.6, pp. 75–82.
Dawson, S. S., 1898, Accountant's Compendium, 1st ed, Gee & Co., London, UK.
Dawson, W. J., 1901, 'Goodwill,' *The Accountant*, January 12, pp. 49–50.
Dawson, S. S., 1908, *Accountant's Compendium*, 3rd ed, Gee & Co., London, UK.
Densham F. W., 1898, 'Depreciation of Assets and Goodwill of Limited Companies,' *The Accountant*, May 28, pp. 567–571.

Dicksee, L. R, 1897, 'Goodwill and its treatment in accounts,' *The Accountant*, January 9, pp. 40–48.
Dicksee, L. R. and T. M. Stevens, 1897, *Goodwill and Its Treatment in Accounts*, Gee & Co., London, UK.
Dicksee, L. R. and F. Tillyard, 1906, *Goodwill and Its Treatment in Accounts*, 3rd ed., Gee & Co., London, UK.
Dickinson, A. L., 1913, Accounting Practice and Procedure, Ronald Press Co., New York, US.
Ding, Y., J. Richard and H. Stolowy, 2008, 'Towards an Understanding of the Phases of Goodwill Accounting in Four Western Capitalist Countries: From Stakeholder Model to Shareholder Model,' *Accounting, Organizations and Society*, Vol.33, No.7/8, pp. 718–755.
Edwards, E. O. and P. W. Bell, 1961, *The Theory and Measurement of Business Income*, University of California Press, California, US.
Eiteman, D. S., 1971, 'Critical Problems in Accounting for Goodwill,' *The Journal of Accountancy*, Vol.131, No.3, pp. 46–50.
Emery, K. G., 1951, 'Should Goodwill Be Written Off?' *The Accounting Review*, Vol.26, No.4, pp. 560–567.
Esquerrē, P., 1913, 'Goodwill, Patents, Trade-Marks, Copyrights and Franchises,' *The Journal of Accountancy*, Vol.15, No.1, pp. 21–34.
Esquerrē, P., 1914, *The Applied Theory of Accounts*, The Ronald Press Company, New York, US.
Esquerrē, P., 1927, *Accounting*, The Ronald Press Company, New York, US.
Financial Accounting Standards Board (FASB), 1976, Discussion Memorandum, *An Analysis of Issues related to Accounting for Business Combinations and Purchased Intangibles*, FASB.
Financial Accounting Standards Board (FASB), 2001a, Statement of Financial Accountings Standards No.141, *Business Combinations*, FASB.
Financial Accounting Standards Board (FASB), 2001b, Statement of Financial Accountings Standards No.142, *Goodwill and Other Intangible Assets*, FASB.
Financial Accounting Standards Board (FASB), 2020, Exposure Draft, *Proposed Statement of Financial Accounting Concepts, Concept Statement No.8*, FASB.
Finney, H. A., 1923, *Principles of Accounting*, Vo.2, Prentice-Hall, Inc. New York, US.
Fukui, Y., 2012, 'Hayek- Hicks Shotoku Gainen to Gakumon toshiteno Kaikei no Kanosei (Income Concept of Hayek-Hicks and Possibility of Accounting as Academic Studies)', in Obinata, T., *Kaikeikijun Kenkyu no Genten (Fundamental Essence of Research on Accounting Standards)*, Chuo-Keizaisha, Tokyo, Japan, pp. 17–39, in Japanese.
Fukui, Y. and S. Saito, 2022a, 'Nature of Goodwill in Competitive Markets,' *Working Paper*, https://ssrn.com/abstract=5114467.
Fukui, Y. and S. Saito, 2022b, 'Economically Consistent Recognition of Goodwill and Its Amortization.' *Working Paper*, https://ssrn.com/abstract=5114458.
Frank, V. H., 1948, *Company Accounts -the law and practice-*, Sweet & Maxwell Limited, London, UK.
Garcia, C., Y. Katsuo (Asami), and C. van Mourik, 2018, 'Goodwill Accounting Standards in the United Kingdom, the United States, France, and Japan,' *Accounting History*, Vol.23, No.3, pp. 314–337.
Glautier, M. W. E. and B. Underdown, 1997, *Accounting Theory and Practice*, 6th ed. Pitman Publishing, London, UK.
Grinyer, J. R. and A. Russell, 1992, 'Goodwill —An Example of Puzzle-Solving in Accounting — a Comment,' *Abacus*, Vol. 28, No.1, pp. 107–112.
Grinyer, J. R., A. Russell and M. Walker, 1990, 'The Rationale for Accounting for Goodwill,' *British Accounting Review*, Vol.22, No.3, pp. 223–235.
Guthrie, E., 1898, 'Goodwill,' *The Accountant*, Vol.24, pp. 425–431.
Gynther, R. S., 1969, 'Some "Conceptualizing" on Goodwill,' *The Accounting Review*, Vol.44, No.2, pp. 247–255.
Harris, W., 1884, 'Goodwill,' *The Accountant*, Vol.10, No.487, pp. 8–11.

Hatfield, H. R., 1909, *Modern Accounting: Its Principles and Some of Its Problems*, D. Appleton and Company, New York, US.
Heckler, B. L., 1997, 'Accounting for Goodwill in an Age of Mergers,' *Journal of Corporate Accounting and Finance*, Vol.8, No.3, pp. 13–24.
Hendriksen, E. S., 1965, *Accounting Theory*, Richard D. Irwin, Inc, Illinois, US.
Hendriksen, E. S., 1970, *Accounting Theory*, revised ed., Richard D. Irwin, Inc, Illinois, US.
Hicks, J. R., 1946, *Value and Capital -An Inquiry into Some Fundamental Principles of Economic Theory*, 2nd ed., The Clarendon Press, Oxford, UK.
Hughes, H. P., 1982, *Goodwill in Accounting: A History of the Issues and Problems*, Research Monograph No.80, the College of Business Administration, Georgia State University, Georgia, US.
Hylton, D. P.,1964, 'The treatment of goodwill (letters to the editor),' *The Journal of Accountancy*, Vol.117, No.4, p. 30.
Institute of Chartered Accountants in England and Wales (ICAEW), 1984, Statement of Standard Accounting Practice (SSAP) No.22, *Accounting for Goodwill*, ICAEW.
Institute of Chartered Accountants in England and Wales (ICAEW), 1997, *Financial Reporting Today -Current and Emerging Issues the 1998 Edition*, Gloucestor House, London, UK.
International Accounting Standards Board (IASB), 2004, International Financial Reporting Standard 3, *Business Combinations*, IASB.
International Accounting Standards Board (IASB), 2004, International Accounting Standards No.38, *Intangible Assets*, IASB.
International Accounting Standards Board (IASB), 2013, Discussion Paper, *A Review of the Conceptual Framework for Financial Reporting*, IASB.
International Accounting Standards Board (IASB), 2015, Exposure Draft, *Conceptual Framework for Financial Reporting*, IASB.
International Accounting Standards Board (IASB), 2018, *Conceptual Framework for Financial Reporting*, IASB.
International Accounting Standards Committee (IASC), 1983, International Accounting Standards No.22, *Accounting for Business Combinations* (Revised in 1993, 1998), IASC.
International Accounting Standards Committee (IASC), 1998, International Accounting Standards No.36, *Impairment of Assets*, IASC.
Johnson T. and K. R. Petrone, 1998, 'Is Goodwill an Asset?' *Accounting Horizons*, Vo.12, No.9, pp. 293–303.
Keizai Antei Honbu Kigyo Kaikei Seido Taisaku Chosakai (Economic Stability Headquarters Corporate Accounting System Measures Investigation Committee), 1949, *Kigyo Kaikei Gensoku (Corporate Accounting Principles),* in Japanese, Economic Stability Headquarters Corporate Accounting System Measures Investigation Committee.
Kester, R. B., 1918, *Accounting Theory and Practice*, Vol.2, The Ronald Press Company, New York, US.
Kirkham, L. and J. Arnold, 1992, 'Goodwill Accounting in the UK: A Fresh Approach to an Old Problem,' *European Accounting Review*, Vol.1, No.2, pp. 421–425.
Knight, A., 1908, 'Depreciation and other reserves,' *The Journal of Accountancy*, Vol.5, No.3, pp. 189–200.
Kripke, H., 1961, 'A Good Look at Goodwill in Corporate Acquisitions,' *The Banking Law Journal*, Vol.78, pp. 1028–1040.
Leake, P. D., 1914, 'Goodwill: Its Nature and How to Value It,' *The Accountant*, Vol.50, No.2041, pp. 81–90.
Leake, P. D., 1921, *Commercial Goodwill; Its History, Value, and Treatment in Accounts*, Sir Isaac Pitman & Sons Ltd., London, UK.
Lisle, G., 1900, *Accounting in Theory and Practice*, William Green & Sons, Edinburgh, UK.
Lee, T. A, 1971, 'Goodwill An Examples of Will-o'-the-Wisp Accounting,' Accounting and Business Research, vol.1, No.4, pp. 318–328.

Lee, T. A, 1973, 'Accounting for Goodwill: An Empirical Study of Company Practices in the United Kingdom 1962 to 1971,' Accounting and Business Research, vol.3, No.11, pp. 175–196.
Ma, R. and R. Hopkins, 1988, 'Goodwill — An Example of Puzzle-Solving in Accounting,' *Abacus*, Vol.24, No.1, pp. 75–85.
Ma, R. and R. Hopkins, 1992, 'Goodwill — An Example of Puzzle-Solving in Accounting — a Reply,' *Abacus*, Vol.28, No.1, pp. 113–115.
Matheson, E. 1884, *The Depreciation of Factories and their Valuation*, E. & F. N. Spon, London UK.
May, G. O., 1943, *Financial Accounting; A Distillation of Experience*, The Macmillan Company, New York, US.
May, G. O., 1957, 'Business Combinations; An Alternative View,' *The Journal of Accountancy*, Vol. 3, No. 4, pp. 33–36.
Meigs, W. B. and C. E. Johnson, 1962, *Accounting*, McGraw-Hill, New York, US.
Miller, M. C., 1973, 'Goodwill -an Aggregation Issue,' *The Accounting Review*, Vol.48, No.2, pp. 280–291.
Miller, M. C., 1995, 'Goodwill Discontent: The Meshing of Australian and International Accounting Policy,' *Australian Accounting Review*, Vol.5, No.9, pp. 3–16.
Montgomery, R. H., 1912, *Auditing Theory and Practice*, The Ronald Press Company, New York, US.
More, F., 1891, 'Goodwill,' *The Accountant*, Vol. XVII, No.853, pp. 282–286.
Nelson, R. H., 1953, 'the Momentum Theory of Goodwill,' *The Accounting Review*, Vol.28, No. 4, pp. 491–499.
Nissim, D. and S. Penman, 2008, 'Principles for the Application of Fair Value Accounting,' Columbia Business School, *White Paper*, No.2, Center for Excellence in Accounting and Security Analysis, Colombia Business School.
Nobes, C., 1992, 'Political History of Goodwill in the U.K.: An Illustration of Critical Standard Setting,' *ABACUS*, Vol.28, No.2, pp. 142–167.
Owens, R. N., 1923, 'Goodwill in the Accounts,' *University Journal of Business*, Vol.1, No. 3, pp. 282–299.
Parker, R. H., G. C. Harcourt and G. Whittington (eds), 1986, *Readings in the Concept and Measurement of Income*, 2nd ed., Philip Allan, London, UK.
Paton, W. A. and A. C. Littleton, 1940, *An Introduction to Corporate Accounting Standards*, AAA.
Paton, W. A., 1941, *Advanced Accounting*, The Macmillan Company, New York, US.
Preinreich, G., 1936, 'The Law of Goodwill,' *The Accounting Review*, Vol.11, No.4, pp. 317–329.
Reed, R. O., J. Elsea and M.S. Lilly, 2000, 'Accounting for Excess Purchase Price: Goodwill or Expense? Instructional Issues,' *Journal of Education for Business*, Vol.76, No.2, pp. 87–92.
Rinji Sangyo Gorikyoku Zaimu Kanri Iinkai (Temporary Industrial Rationalization Bureau Financial Management Committee), 1934, *Zaimusyohyo Junsoku (Financial Statement Guideline)*, in Japanese, Temporary Industrial Rationalization Bureau Financial Management Committee.
Rinji Sangyo Gorikyoku Zaimu Kanri Iinkai (Temporary Industrial Rationalization Bureau Financial Management Committee), 1936, *Zaisanhyoka ni kansufu Kijun (Standard for Assets Evaluation)*, in Japanese, Temporary Industrial Rationalization Bureau Financial Management Committee.
Roby, A. G., 1892, 'Goodwill,' *The Accountant*, Vol.18, pp. 288–293.
Roth, L., 1929, 'Accounting for Goodwill,' *The Journal of Accountancy*, Vol.48, No.2, pp. 102–104.
Saito, S., 2010, *Kigyo Kaikei to Disclosure (Corporate Accounting and Disclosure)*, in Japanese, The University of Tokyo Press, Tokyo, Japan.
Saito, S., 2017, 'Noren no Shokyaku to Genson -Kigyoketsugokaikeikijun no Meiso- (Amortization and Impairment of Goodwill -Straying of Accounting Standards for Business Combination)', *Kigyo-Kaikei (Accounting)*, Vol.69, No.1, pp.13–19, in Japanese.
Saito, S., 2019, Kaikei Kijun no Kenkyu (Study on Accounting Standards), revised ed., in Japanese, Chuo-Keizaisha, Tokyo, Japan.

Saito, S., 2021, 'Noren no On-Balance to Off-Balance (On-Balance and Off-Balance of Goodwill)', *Kaikei (The Accounting)*, Vol. 199, No.5, pp. 98–111, in Japanese.

Saito, S. and Y. Fukui, 2022a, 'Noren no Kaikeininshiki to Keizaibunseki (Accounting Recognition of Goodwill and Economic Analysis) (1)', *Kaikei (Accounting)*, Vol. 201, No.3, pp. 85–96, in Japanese.

Saito, S. and Y. Fukui, 2022b, 'Noren no Kaikeininshiki to Keizaibunseki (Accounting Recognition of Goodwill and Economic Analysis) (2)', *Kaikei (Accounting)*, Vol. 201, No.4, pp. 39–50, in Japanese.

Sanders, T. H., H. R. Hatfield and U. Moore, 1938, *A Statement of Accounting Principles*, American Institute of Accountants.

Scott W. and P. O'Brien, 2012, *Financial Accounting Theory*, 8th ed., Pearson Canada Inc., Ontario, Canada.

Securities and Exchange Commission (SEC), 1945, Accounting Series Release No.50, *The Propriety of Writing Down Goodwill by Means of Charges to Capital Surplus*, SEC.

Sherwood, J. F. and R. T. Culey, 1939, *Auditing Theory and Procedure*, South-Western Publishing Company, Ohio, US.

Simon, S. I., 1956, 'Court-Decisions Concerning Goodwill,' *The Accounting Review*, Vol.31, No.2, pp. 272–277.

Smith S. G., 1904, 'Depreciation of Assets and Goodwill of Limited Companies,' *The Accountant*, January 9, p. 44–52.

Solomons, D., 1989, *Guidelines for Financial Reporting Standards*, Institute of Chartered Accountants in England and Wales and the Accounting Standards Committee.

Spacek, L.P., 1964, 'The Treatment of Goodwill in the Corporate Balance Sheet,' *The Journal of Accountancy*, Vol. 117, No.2, pp. 35–40.

Spacek, L.P., 1969, *A Search for Fairness in Financial Reporting to the Public*, Arthur Andersen & Co, Chicago, US.

Staub, W. A., 1945, 'Chap. 8; Intangible Assets,' in *Contemporary Accounting: a refresher course for public accountants*, edited by T. W. Leland, American Institute of Accountants.

Stockwell, H. G., 1912, *Net Worth and the Balance Sheet*, The Ronald Press Company, New York, US.

Surtees, 1835, Oxford English Dictionary, Surtees Society, Oxford, UK.

Ueda, A., 1960, 'Kaisetsu Kabushikikaisya no Keisan no Naiyo nikansuru Shoho Kaisei Yokoshian (Explanatory Notes, Draft Outline for the Amendment of the Commercial Code Concerning the Content of Corporate Accounting),' *Junkan Shoji Homu Kenkyu*, No.190, pp. 3–10, in Japanese.

Walker, G. T., 1938, 'Non purchased Goodwill,' *The Accounting Review*, Vol.13, No.3, pp. 253–259.

Walker, G. T., 1953, 'Why Purchased Goodwill Should be Amortized on a Systematic Basis,' *The Journal of Accountancy*, Vol.95, No.2, pp. 210–216.

Weirich, T.R. and L. E. Turner, 1995, 'FAS 121 and APBIT: How to Handle Goodwill when Accounting for the Impairment of Long-Lived Assets,' *Journal of Corporate Accounting and Finance*, Vol.7, No.1, pp. 55–63.

Welsch, G. A., Zlatkovich, C. T. and White, J. A, 1976, *Intermediate Accounting*, 4th ed., Richard D. Irwin, Inc., Illinois US.

Wildman, J. R., 1914, *Principles of Accounting*, William G. Hewitt Press, New York, US.

Wyatt, A.R., 1963, Accounting Research Study No. 5, *A Critical Study of Accounting for Business Combinations*, AICPA.

Yang, J. M. 1927, *Goodwill and Other Intangibles*, The Ronald Press Company, New York, US.

Yoshinaga, E., and T. Iino, 1974, *Kaisha no Keisan (The Accounting of Companies)*, Vol.1, in Japanese, Shojihomukenkyukai, Tokyo, Japan.

Zanoni, A. B., 2009, *Accounting for Goodwill*, Routledge, New York, US.

Chapter 4
Empirical Issues

Toshtiake Miyauchi

4.1 Purpose and Organization of this Chapter

A debate over the accounting treatment of acquired goodwill, which is recognized as an asset following M&A transactions, has been ongoing. While some accounting standards, such as the International Financial Reporting Standards (IFRS) and U.S. GAAP, require "Impairment-only", other standards, such as Japanese GAAP and national standards prior to IFRS adoption, require "Systematic amortization with impairment".

As the number of countries and firms adopting the "Impairment-only" approach (Hereafter, TIOA) has increased, concerns have been raised that goodwill impairments are not recognized in a timely manner or that impairment losses are quantitatively insufficient. This phenomenon is often referred to as the "too little, too late" issue. In response, extensive discussions have emerged regarding the appropriateness of current goodwill impairment testing practices, including proposals for revising impairment testing procedures and reintroducing the systematic amortization of goodwill (EFRAG, ASBJ and OIC 2014; EFRAG 2016; EFRAG 2017; FASB 2019; ASBJ and HKICPA 2020; ISAB 2020).

This study reviews empirical studies on the accounting treatment of positive goodwill, focusing on managerial behavior and the economic consequences of the

This chapter is based on the journal paper Miyauchi (2021) with significant additions.

T. Miyauchi (✉)
Faculty of Management, Otemon Gakuin University, Osaka, Japan
e-mail: tomiyauc@otemon.ac.jp

Y. Tokuga, M. Yoneyama (eds.), *Controversies Over Accounting for Goodwill*, Contributions to Finance and Accounting,
https://doi.org/10.1007/978-981-92-0156-3_4

two accounting standards: "Impairment-only" and "Systematic amortization with impairment." The goal is to summarize the current findings on these issues.[1]

A keyword search for "Goodwill and Accounting" was conducted across journal databases (Scopus, Web of Science) to gather empirical studies classified as archival research, covering the period from January 2000 to December 2022. To ensure the quality of the findings, the selection was limited to empirical studies published in financial accounting journals ranked within the top 100 in the "Accounting" category according to the Scimago Journal Rank.[2] Journals on management accounting, auditing, accounting history, accounting education, and finance were excluded.

Furthermore, Japanese peer-reviewed journals such as *Kaikei Progress* (published by the Japan Accounting Association) and *Bulletin of Japanese Association for International Accounting Studies* were considered to include empirical findings from Japanese firms. Table 4.1 lists the selected journals and the relevant articles identified.

Before this review, Miyauchi (2020) conducted a "stocktaking" of empirical studies on goodwill accounting treatment in ten journals, including the top five international peer-reviewed journals and five leading empirical accounting journals. Miyauchi's study aimed to identify changes in "research themes" and "research methods," which differs from the focus of this study. However, Miyauchi (2020) found that empirical studies primarily addressed themes such as the "timeliness of goodwill impairment recognition" and its "impact on investment decision-making support." This review follows those same themes in its overview. Additionally, while Miyauchi (2020) examined ten journals, this study expands the scope to include findings from 31 journals.

To explore whether goodwill diminishes over time, this study reviews literature on the "time-series evolution of firms' excess profitability" (commonly known as profit mean reversion) in Sect. 4.2. As studies on the time-series behavior of profits extend beyond accounting journals, this review includes references to research books in addition to the journals listed in Table 4.1.

The remainder of this paper is structured as follows. Section 4.2 provides an overview of studies on the time-series evolution of firms' excess profitability to assess the possibility that goodwill deteriorates over time. Section 4.3 discusses research on managerial accounting discretion regarding goodwill impairment recognition. Subsequently, Sect. 4.4 analyzes studies examining whether goodwill and its impairment loss support investment decision-making and the impact of goodwill on contractual support functions. Further, Sect. 4.5 reviews findings from other research areas and summarizes insights from empirical studies on goodwill accounting treatment while highlighting remaining issues. Finally, Sect. 4.6 concludes this chapter.

---

[1] Cultural and business practices, the frequency of M&A transactions, and the components considered goodwill vary across countries and jurisdictions. Therefore, this review seeks to organize empirical findings while considering these differences and drawing conclusions.

[2] The selection of target journals was based on the Scimago Journal Rank, available at https://www.scimagojr.com/journalrank.php?category=1402 accessed August 24, 2020.

Table 4.1 Name of journal and number of articles reviewed

Title of academic Journal	Number of relevant papers
Journal of Accounting Research	3
Journal of Accounting and Economics	0
The Accounting Review	7
Review of Accounting Studies	6
Contemporary Accounting Research	4
Accounting Horizons	2
Journal of Accounting and Public Policy	4
British Accounting Review	2
Journal of Accounting Literature	0
European Accounting Review	7
Accounting Forum	0
Journal of Business Finance and Accounting	5
Accounting and Business Research	2
Journal of Accounting, Auditing and Finance	6
Review of Quantitative Finance and Accounting	6
Journal of Contemporary Accounting and Economics	7
Journal of International Financial Management and Accounting	2
International Journal of Accounting	3
Abacus	1
Accounting and Finance	6
Journal of International Accounting, Auditing and Taxation	5
Journal of Financial Research	0
Journal of International Accounting Research	2
Advances in Accounting	5
Accounting in Europe	2
Journal of Applied Accounting Research	3
Asian Review of Accounting	1
International Journal of Finance and Economics	0
Review of Accounting and Finance	4
Kaikei Progress	1
Bulletin of Japanese Association for International Accounting Studies	1
Total	97

4.2 Research on Mean Reversion of Excess Profits

The core components of goodwill include the acquired firm's excess profitability and the synergy between the acquiring and acquired firms, often referred to as "core goodwill." Understanding whether a firm's excess profitability persists indefinitely or diminishes over time is crucial for determining the appropriate accounting treatment of goodwill. This section provides an overview of studies analyzing the time-series evolution of firms' excess profitability, addressing the key question of whether goodwill amortizes as an asset.

The economic hypothesis behind these studies is that highly profitable industries attract new entrants, increasing competition and leading to a decline in excess profitability over time. Additionally, capital flows from unproductive industries to more profitable ones (including business closures and market exits), causing industries with low excess profitability to experience an upward trend in profitability.

First, studies on the evolution of overall profitability, rather than excess profitability, include those of Fama and French (2000) and Palepu et al. (2000). Fama and French (2000) estimated the rate of mean reversion in profitability using data from U.S. firms over a 33-year period (1964–1996). They analyzed how well profitability in period t explains that in period $t + 1$ and found that return on assets (ROA) tends to revert to the mean, with an estimated mean reversion rate of approximately 38% per year.

Palepu et al. (2000) studied U.S. firms from 1979 to 1998 by ranking them into five portfolios based on their first-year return on equity (ROE) and tracking the subsequent evolution of ROE. They found that the ROE of the first-quintile portfolio declined from an initial 27% to 17% after 3 years and further to 14% after 10 years. Conversely, the ROE of the fifth-quintile portfolio increased from −33% to +13% over 10 years. These results suggest that, under competitive equilibrium, ROE tends to revert to a level approximating the cost of equity capital.

Next, studies on the evolution of excess profitability, rather than overall profitability, are reviewed. Nissim and Penman (2001) examined a sample of approximately 65,000 U.S. firms from 1963 to 1999, categorizing them into decile portfolios based on their residual operating income rate. Subsequently, they tracked the evolution of this profitability measure over time. Their findings showed that the first-decile portfolio, which had the highest profitability, maintained its high residual operating income rate. However, for the remaining portfolios (from the second to the tenth decile), residual profitability exhibited mean reversion within approximately 5 years.

Dickinson and Sommers (2012) used the Return on Net Operating Assets (RNOA) of firms as a proxy for efforts to prevent a decline in firm value. They categorized firms into five decile portfolios based on their RNOA levels and analyzed the time-series trends of these portfolios using 65,220 U.S. firm-year observations from 1972 to 2003.

Their findings revealed that for portfolios in the second to fifth deciles, RNOA reverted to around 10%. Conversely, the first-decile portfolio experienced a decline from 30% to just above 15%, although it remained at a higher level than the other four deciles. When adjusting for capital costs to calculate residual RNOA, all five portfolios exhibited mean reversion to a level between 2% and slightly above 5% within 5 years.

Healy et al. (2014) investigated whether the tendency of ROA to revert to the mean varies based on country-specific factors, such as the intensity of competition in financial, capital, and labor markets. Their analysis of 48,465 firms across 49 countries from 1997 to 2008 revealed that ROA generally reverts to the mean within 5–10 years. Countries with intense competition in financial and capital markets experienced faster mean reversion.

Studies on Japanese firms include those of Obinata (2013), Muramiya (2010), and Sakurai (2010). Obinata (2013) created 10 quantile portfolios based on excess profitability (exceeding the industry average) using operating income, net income, and other metrics, analyzing variations over the next 10 years. The results showed that profitability levels decreased by 60–80% within 5 years for the top three portfolios with high excess profitability.

Additionally, regarding the accounting treatment of acquired goodwill, Obinata (2013) argued that even if systematic amortization is chosen, an amortization period of up to 20 years may be excessively long.

Muramiya (2010) conducted an analysis similar to that of Nissim and Penman (2001) using a sample of Japanese firms from 1977 to 1997. The study constructed 10 decile portfolios and analyzed their evolution over 9 years. The results indicated that residual profits for portfolios from the second to tenth deciles reverted to the mean (close to zero) within 5–9 years. Conversely, residual profits for the first-decile portfolio remained at a higher level compared to the other portfolios.

Sakurai (2010) focused on analyzing the persistence of residual profits using a sample of 11,841 Japanese firms from March 2000 to March 2007. The study found that the persistence coefficient for residual profits was 0.3729—if the residual profit level in a given period is set at 1, it adjusts to a level of 0.0072 over 5 years (0.3729 raised to the power of 5).

To summarize the findings from this section, while the case that the profitability of the first decile portfolio tends to remain high have been observed, ROE and excess profitability generally experience mean reversion over about 5 years, even when accounting for the subsequent managerial efforts during the observation period.[3] This empirical fact provides a foundation for discussions on how to account for goodwill—whether through impairment treatment, systematic amortization, or a combination of both—and how to represent the value of goodwill as an asset.

4.3 Research on Whether the Recognition of Impairment Is Delayed, and Accompanying Discretionary Actions

4.3.1 Background of Accounting Standards for Goodwill and Academic Warnings

In the U.S., SFAS No. 142, "Goodwill and Other Intangible Assets," became effective for fiscal years beginning after December 15, 2001. This standard eliminated the systematic amortization of goodwill and introduced an annual impairment test,

[3] Research also suggests that the value of goodwill may decline over time. Bugeja and Gallery (2006) analyzed 475 Australian firms from 1995 to 1999 to examine the relationship between stock price and goodwill. They categorized goodwill into three groups: "recently acquired goodwill," "goodwill acquired in the previous year," and "goodwill acquired earlier." The results showed a significant positive correlation between stock price and goodwill acquired in the past 2 years but no significant correlation between stock price and older goodwill. This indicates that the market may not recognize older goodwill as an asset.

aligning with SFAS No. 121 (later replaced by SFAS No. 144), which required impairment testing. In the European Union (EU), from January 1, 2005, consolidated financial statements had to be prepared under IFRS, with IFRS 3—Business Combinations applied alongside IAS 36, which governs impairment. Consequently, the annual impairment test became mandatory.

Countries that adopted IFRS as their national accounting standard also shifted from previous national approaches to the annual impairment testing method for goodwill. In Japan, IFRS became available for voluntary adoption starting with fiscal years ending on March 31, 2010. The standard requiring only the annual impairment test is often referred to as TIOA.

TIOA assumes that an informed insider, with access to privileged internal information, estimates the value of goodwill through the annual impairment test. If a decline in future cash flows is expected, the manager should reduce the goodwill valuation and record an impairment loss. However, Watts (2003) argued that managers may exercise discretion in deciding when to recognize an impairment loss, potentially leading to opportunistic behavior. Along with findings from empirical studies, academic discussions have raised concerns about this risk.

The following section reviews studies addressing questions such as "Is goodwill impairment recognized in a timely manner?" "What incentives influence impairment recognition?" and "How does the attitude toward disclosing goodwill impairment information vary?"

4.3.2 Research on the Timeliness of Goodwill Impairment Recognition

Research on the timeliness of goodwill impairment recognition explores whether firms with significant amounts of goodwill recognize impairment when signs of impairment, such as a decline in stock price, are first observed or if they delay recognition until later periods. Studies on the transition to TIOA and the timeliness of impairment recognition include those of Beatty and Weber (2006), Zang (2008), and Lapointe-Antunes et al. (2009). Beatty and Weber (2006) examined the incentives influencing managers in recognizing goodwill impairment, particularly during the first application of SFAS No. 142. Their study analyzed a sample of 176 U.S. firms with goodwill on their books at the end of the fiscal year 2001 when SFAS No. 142 was first implemented. The findings indicated that firms facing various contractual provisions delayed recognizing impairment. The timing of impairment recognition was influenced by covenants, executive compensation, long executive tenure, and delisting criteria.

However, firms with high stock price volatility and large earnings response coefficients were more likely to recognize impairment losses promptly, as they could treat the loss as a one-time expense owing to changes in accounting standards. Additionally, a deterioration in the book-to-market ratio of total assets increased the likelihood of recognizing impairment. The study revealed a tendency to recognize impairment during the transition to SFAS No. 142, although recognition could also be delayed owing to the factors mentioned above.

Zang (2008) analyzed 969 U.S. firms that recognized impairment losses between March 2001 and June 2003. The findings were as follows. First, even when stock prices had fallen (based on cumulative abnormal returns (CAR)), or ROA had declined 1–4 years before transitioning to SFAS No. 142, firms did not always recognize goodwill impairment. Second, firms with high leverage often recorded only minimal impairment losses to avoid breaching financial covenants. Third, when manager turnover occurred, newly appointed managers were more likely to recognize goodwill impairment as part of a "big bath" accounting strategy.

Henning and Shaw (2004) noted that goodwill impairment recognition was timely before the transition to TIOA. Their study examined 1576 U.S. firms that made acquisitions between 1990 and 1994 and subsequently recognized impairment losses by 2001. The study found that firms recognized goodwill impairment when cumulative stock returns had significantly declined since the acquisition and when a considerable amount of time had passed since the goodwill was initially recorded.

Chen et al. (2008) examined the transition to SFAS No. 142 and found that goodwill impairment losses were recognized more promptly under the new standard. Similarly, Lapointe-Antunes et al. (2009) studied 341 Canadian firms to assess the timeliness of goodwill impairment recognition during the transition to new accounting standards. Their findings revealed a significant negative correlation between goodwill impairment losses and stock prices—impairment information was effectively conveyed to investors. Moreover, when firms with potential impairment indicators based on the book-to-market ratio recognized impairment losses, the market responded positively, confirming the timeliness of the recognition.

Beatty and Weber (2006), Zang (2008), Chen et al. (2008), and Lapointe-Antunes et al. (2009) focused on the incentives influencing recognition in the initial year of the transition to TIOA. Ramanna and Watts (2012) extended the analysis beyond the first year of SFAS No. 142 adoption. Their study examined whether firms that did not recognize goodwill impairment, despite signs of it, signaled private information about future cash flow improvement or whether incentives prevented impairment recognition.

The analysis found that proxy variables representing private information signaling, such as share buybacks and insider purchases, did not explain the decision to delay impairment recognition, suggesting that managers were not disclosing private information about future cash flow improvements. However, financial covenants, executive compensation, and executive tenure significantly explained the decision to delay recognition—managers were postponing impairment recognition for their benefit.

André et al. (2016) analyzed a sample of 35,000 firm-year observations from the EU and the U.S. between 2006 and 2015. They found that during the 2008–2009 financial crisis, U.S. firms recorded 63% of their goodwill as impaired in 2008 and 40% in 2009. Conversely, only 6% of European firms recognized impairment in 2008 and 7% in 2009, suggesting that U.S. firms engaged in more timely goodwill impairment recognition.

Studies comparing the periods before and after the adoption of TIOA (SFAS No. 142) include that of Kim et al. (2013), who analyzed 11,034 U.S. firm-year observations from 1995 to 2006. They found that after transitioning to SFAS No. 142, firms recognized losses more quickly, becoming more conservative. However, focusing solely on firms that recorded goodwill, the study revealed that loss recognition was delayed for these firms.

Li and Sloan (2017) examined whether the timeliness of goodwill impairment recognition differed before and after the adoption of SFAS No. 142 and whether the market appropriately valued goodwill. By dividing the sample into two periods—1996–2000 (systematic amortization with impairment) and 2004–2011 (impairment only)—they found that goodwill impairment recognition was slower after the adoption of SFAS No. 142 and that the market tended to overvalue excessive goodwill.

Dinh et al. (2018) analyzed changes in firms' accounting reporting on goodwill impairment recognition and the amortization of intangible assets under Australian GAAP and IFRS for a sample of 802 Australian firms from 2000 to 2010. Their findings revealed that under IFRS, from 2005 onward, a greater amount of goodwill impairment loss was recognized, particularly during the 2008–2009 financial crisis. This suggests that managers recorded impairment losses that accurately reflected the underlying economic reality.

Research on Japan has focused on cases that do not compare the periods before and after the transition to TIOA. As the voluntary adoption of IFRS has been allowed for fiscal years ending in March 2010 and beyond, some firms apply the Japanese standard, which requires "Systematic amortization with impairment," while others voluntarily adopt IFRS, which requires only an annual impairment test. Shimamoto and Takeda (2020) studied this situation and found that firms voluntarily adopting IFRS tend to delay loss recognition compared to those using the Japanese standard.

The following section discusses studies examining how a firm's reporting incentives affect the triggers for impairment recognition. Additionally, some analyses consider the impact of "national factors" (external factors) on managerial behavior.[4] Even when the same accounting rules based on TIOA are applied, differences in legal systems (customary law vs. codified law), the strength of auditing (i.e., adherence to accounting standards), and the liquidity of capital markets can influence the economic consequences of IFRS 3 and SFAS No. 142, as well as managerial behavior.

Ayres et al. (2019a) investigated whether the presence of sell-side analysts—who forecast firm performance—encourages the recognition of goodwill impairment. Their sample included 33,854 U.S. firm-year observations from 2004 to 2015. The analysis found that firms experiencing potential impairment and covered by numerous analysts, as well as those facing potential impairment accompanied by a downgrade in recommendations, were more likely to recognize goodwill impairment

[4] For changes in research methods in empirical studies on goodwill, see Miyauchi (2020).

promptly. This indicates that pre- and post-monitoring by analysts are effective in encouraging timely recognition.

Albersmann and Quick (2020) examined the impact of audit characteristics on the timeliness of impairment recognition. Their sample included 2119 German firm-year observations from 2006 to 2013. The results showed that in Germany, goodwill impairment recognition is often delayed by at least 1–2 years. However, when the auditing corpration is one of the Big Four, recognition timeliness improves. Nevertheless, if the auditor receives relatively high non-audit fees from the client or has a long tenure with them, impairment recognition tends to be delayed.

Glaum et al. (2018) explored whether the timeliness of goodwill impairment recognition is influenced by the strength of legal and institutional enforcement. They analyzed a sample of 9468 firms from IFRS-adopting countries and jurisdictions between 2005 and 2011. The study focused on the relationship between the "activation of the goodwill impairment switch" and "signs of impairment," specifically whether stock prices were falling in the previous period (t-1); nonetheless, impairment was not recognized in the current period (t). Such a situation would suggest that impairment recognition was delayed.

The analysis found that in countries with weak enforcement, (1) impairment recognition tended to be delayed, as it was significantly correlated with stock price declines in the current period and those in the previous period, and (2) executive compensation contracts with a large performance-based component were associated with delayed recognition of impairment. Conversely, no such results were observed in countries with strict enforcement. The study also suggested that in countries with weak enforcement, institutional investors played a complementary role in improving the timeliness of recognition.

Contrarily, André et al. (2015) investigated whether asymmetry in firms' recognition of gains and losses (particularly the delayed recognition of losses) improved before and after the adoption of IFRS, focusing on the accounting treatment of goodwill impairment. The sample included 13,711 firm-year observations from 16 EU countries between 2000 and 2010.

Their findings indicated the following: (1) in countries with strong enforcement, the adoption of IFRS reduced the asymmetry in recognition of gains and losses; (2) after transitioning to IFRS, the accounting treatment of goodwill impairment helped reduce this asymmetry by ensuring the timely recognition of impairment. The study concluded that the "impairment without amortization" approach was more effective in incorporating bad news promptly compared to the "Systematic amortization with impairment" approach.

To summarize the research findings, studies indicating a delay in goodwill impairment recognition following the transition to accounting standards based on TIOA include those of Beatty and Weber (2006), Zang (2008), Ramanna and Watts (2012), Kim et al. (2013), Li and Sloan (2017), and Shimamoto and Takeda (2020). Conversely, Chen et al. (2008), Lapointe-Antunes et al. (2009), André et al. (2016), and Dinh et al. (2018) found the timeliness of goodwill impairment recognition. There are relatively many studies pointing out delays in impairment recognition. Furthermore, external factors—analysts monitoring firm performance, auditor characteristics, and the enforcement system in the country or jurisdiction—significantly influence a firm's recognition of impairment.

4.3.3 Incentives Determining Goodwill Impairment Recognition

In this section, we review studies that explore the incentives behind the decision to recognize or avoid goodwill impairment rather than analyzing the timeliness of impairment recognition.

Gros and Koch (2019) examined "expected impairment," which stems from economic factors and leaves little room for managerial discretion. They estimated expected impairment based on stock price changes and economic indicators such as ROA and GDP. They defined "unexpected impairment" as the difference between reported impairment losses and expected impairment. They investigated whether this discrepancy—subject to managerial discretion—reveals private information about managers or is used opportunistically. Their sample included 4200 firm-year observations from European firms between 2007 and 2013. The analysis showed that goodwill impairment is often recorded opportunistically, especially when a firm's earnings fall short of analysts' expectations, leading to a "negative unexpected impairment" that reduces the expected impairment. However, opportunistic behavior decreases when a firm has an experienced board of directors or operates in a country with strong enforcement. This suggests that managerial discretion may drive the decision to record goodwill impairment losses. The study raised the question of what factors act as incentives.

Sun (2016) analyzed 30,426 firm-year observations of U.S. firms from 2002 to 2011 and tested the hypothesis that competent managers seeking to maximize shareholder value would avoid recognizing goodwill impairment. The study found a significant negative correlation between indicators of managerial competence and the likelihood and amount of goodwill impairment. This result held even when executive tenure was considered.

Chung and Hribar (2021) reported that overconfident managers are less likely to recognize goodwill impairments in any quarter and tend to delay impairment recognition.

Hamberg et al. (2011) studied Swedish firms to identify factors influencing goodwill impairment triggers. They regarded financial covenants, market attention (stock trading volume), performance-based executive compensation, and CEO tenure as potential determinants. Their findings revealed that only CEO tenure—particularly whether the CEO had held the position for at least 5 years or served as chairperson—significantly influenced the decision to recognize goodwill impairment.

AbuGhazaleh et al. (2011) examined managerial discretion in impairment recognition following the mandatory adoption of IFRS 3 in the UK. Their findings showed that recent management changes, income smoothing motives, and big bath accounting impact goodwill impairment loss amounts. Nevertheless, in firms with strong governance mechanisms, managers are more likely to recognize impairment losses in a way that reflects the firm's economic reality rather than for opportunistic reasons.

Majid (2015) investigated whether the concentration of ownership by the largest external shareholder affects goodwill impairment loss reporting incentives in Malaysia under IFRS 3. The study used a sample of 1911 firm-year observations from 2006 to 2010 and found that goodwill impairment losses were often recognized when pre-impairment earnings were high or for big bath accounting purposes. Nonetheless, as the ownership stake of the largest external shareholder increased, stronger monitoring by shareholders reduced the likelihood of recognizing impairment losses for big bath purposes.

Kabir and Rahman (2016) analyzed 1783 Australian firms from 2007 to 2014 to examine the impact of corporate governance on managerial discretion in goodwill impairment under IFRS. Their study first showed that goodwill impairment is influenced by economic factors such as revenue growth rates, cash flow growth rates, earnings before impairment losses, industry-median ROA, prior-year asset write-downs, and GDP growth rates. Additionally, they found that the strength of corporate governance—measured by board independence (ratio of outside directors), audit committee independence (ratio of outside members), Big Four audit involvement, audit committee expertise (whether a certified accountant is present), audit committee meeting frequency, and CEO-Chairman separation—affects which economic factors remain significant in explaining goodwill impairment recognition. However, the study revealed that even with strong governance, certain factors influenced impairment recognition: (1) goodwill impairment is not recognized if pre-impairment earnings are negative; (2) impairment is recognized when management is in its first year of tenure to engage in big bath accounting.

Research has also identified external factors. Han et al. (2020), against the background that the amount of goodwill recognized in China quadrupled between 2007 and 2016, examined how managers engage in earnings management regarding the recognition of goodwill impairment losses under analyst coverage (i.e., under analyst pressure). The sample comprised 3618 Chinese firms applying IFRS 3 or Chinese Accounting Standard No. 8—Asset Impairment (CAS 8) from 2007 to 2016.

Their results showed that: (1) firms covered by a larger number of analysts tend to delay the recognition of goodwill impairment and (2) more optimistic analyst forecasts (i.e., higher forecasted earnings) also lead firms to postpone impairment recognition. These findings suggest that, during the transition to the TIOA regime, managers are exposed to pressure to meet analyst earnings forecasts and may engage in income-increasing earnings management.

In addition to the incentives and external factors discussed in Sect. 4.3.2—analysis presence, auditing attributes, and institutional enforcement— firm-specific attributes, such as ownership structure and the strength of corporate governance can influence the timing of goodwill impairment recognition.

4.3.4 *Managerial Discretion Associated with Goodwill Impairment Recognition*

In addition to studies examining the timeliness and determinants of goodwill impairment recognition, some research highlights how managers engage in discretionary actions when triggering goodwill impairment recognition.

Avallone and Quagli (2015) found that managers manipulate key variables, such as the "long-term growth rate," which is multiplied by future cash flows, and the "discount rate" (weighted average cost of capital), used in impairment tests. They showed that the divergence between the rates chosen by managers and those estimable from available external data significantly explains the reduction in goodwill impairment loss amounts.

Filip et al. (2015) revealed that managers engage in discretionary behaviors to justify not recognizing goodwill impairment to auditors and analysts. These behaviors include inflating current period cash flow, which serves as the basis for their "business plans." As the credibility of future cash flow projections depends on the current period's cash flow, managers may reduce R&D expenses, cut production volumes, or conduct inventory clearance sales to present a more favorable cash flow.

Filip et al. (2020) investigate whether managers manipulate goodwill impairment test outcomes by choosing the discount rates and future cash flow forecasts used in fair value measurements. They also analyzed how the strength of national enforcement affects such opportunistic behavior. The sample comprises firms from 36 IFRS-adopting countries from 2007 to 2014 and includes 1958 firm-year observations suspected of goodwill impairment (3916 firm-year observations, including control firms).

The results indicated that: (1) firms in countries with stronger enforcement use higher discount rates (making impairment more likely); however, (2) among firms suspected of impairment in strong-enforcement countries, managers upwardly revise future cash flow forecasts compared with control firms. These findings imply that managers prefer to manipulate future cash flow forecasts, which are difficult for outsiders to verify, rather than discount rates, which can be benchmarked against observable market information.

Duh et al. (2009) studied whether the reversal of losses through fixed asset impairment recognition (big bath) serves as an opportunity for earnings management and how such behavior is linked to managerial incentives. Using a sample of 55 Taiwanese firms from 2005 to 2007, they found that the larger the impairment loss recognized, the greater the subsequent earnings reversal, helping managers avoid reporting two consecutive periods of declining profits. Firms with higher debt ratios were more likely to engage in such earnings management to avoid breaching financial covenants, although strong corporate governance mechanisms restrained this behavior.

Cready et al. (2012) examined whether the recognition of extraordinary losses, including goodwill impairment, functions as a "period-shifting mechanism" (big bath), transferring future expenses to the current period. Their analysis of 9234

U.S. firms from 2002 to 2009 found that among extraordinary losses, "restructuring costs" had the strongest relationship with future profit growth, followed by asset impairment losses. However, goodwill impairment losses showed little to no relationship with future profit growth or cash flow increases.

This result arises from the fact that recognizing goodwill impairment and reducing the book value of goodwill do not provide the same amortization cost-saving effect that existed before SFAS No. 142. Nevertheless, Duh et al. (2009) focused on fixed assets generally, while Cready et al. (2012) specifically analyzed goodwill.

Research also examines discretionary behavior during the initial recognition of goodwill. Under IFRS, U.S. GAAP, and even Japanese standards (since 2010), the portion of the acquisition price that exceeds the book value of the target firm's net assets is referred to as the "purchase price." This amount must be allocated between "intangible assets" (such as patents, brands, and customer lists) and "goodwill" through purchase price allocation (Hereafter, PPA). While intangible assets are subject to amortization, goodwill undergoes an annual impairment test. Managers have discretion over whether to recognize impairment.

Key studies on managerial discretion in PPA include those of Shalev et al. (2013) and Zhang and Zhang (2017). Shalev et al. (2013) analyzed a sample of 320 U.S. firms from 2001 to 2008 (after the implementation of SFAS No. 142). They found that if executive compensation contracts were based on profits, managers tended to allocate a larger portion of the purchase price to goodwill, which does not require amortization and is subject to discretionary impairment recognition rather than to intangible assets that require amortization.

Zhang and Zhang (2017) studied 173 U.S. firms from 1996 to 2007, spanning the pre- and post-SFAS No. 142 periods. They found that older managers and those with longer tenures were more likely to allocate a larger portion of the acquisition price to goodwill. They also observed that before SFAS No. 142, when goodwill was subject to amortization, such over-allocation was not evident.

Lynch et al. (2019) focused on the tax implications of PPA. If more of the purchase price is allocated to goodwill, no amortization expense is incurred, which boosts reported earnings but reduces tax savings. Conversely, if more is allocated to intangible assets, amortization expense is incurred, reducing reported earnings but providing tax benefits. Analyzing 993 U.S. firms from 1995 to 2011, they demonstrated a trade-off between reported earnings and tax-saving effects, highlighting how managerial incentives can influence the allocation to goodwill in PPA.

Bugeja and Loyeung (2015) examined the allocation ratio to goodwill in PPA after a successful M&A using a sample of Australian firms. They found that 42% of the acquired firms reported "zero goodwill." Moreover, they revealed that when the acquired firm's CEO compensation is based on accounting figures, managers tend to allocate a higher portion of the purchase price to goodwill in the PPA, engaging in opportunistic behavior. This occurs particularly in three situations: when the acquired firm has a high debt ratio, the acquisition premium is high, or the acquisition consideration is paid in cash.

Frii and Hamberg (2021) analyze 1112 M&A transactions involving firms listed on the Stockholm Stock Exchange during the period from 2005 to 2013, and examine whether managerial discretion in allocating the purchase price to goodwill in PPA is shaped by firms' institutional and governance environments.

Frii and Hamberg (2021) argued that: (a) while share ownership is widely dispersed in Anglo-Saxon countries, the average ownership stake of the largest shareholder in Sweden is 31.9% (compared with 13.0% in the U.S., 17.3% in the U.K., and a global average of 31.5%), implying that the presence of a dominant shareholder may constrain managers' opportunistic behavior; and (b) whereas approximately 80% of U.S. firms allow CEO duality (i.e., CEOs also serving as board chair), such duality is prohibited in Sweden, suggesting that profit-based managerial compensation contracts are less likely to create incentives for managers to opportunistically allocate acquisition prices to goodwill which is not subject to amortization.

Their empirical results showed that: (1) in environments with dominant shareholders, the proportion of the purchase price allocated to goodwill in PPA is not associated with the level of CEOs' performance-based compensation; (2) firms with stronger family ownership allocate a larger proportion of the acquisition price to goodwill; and (3) when firms pay acquisition premiums that are substantially higher than those in comparable M&A transactions, a larger share of the purchase price is allocated to goodwill in PPA.

Thus, research has increasingly highlighted how managers avoid recognizing goodwill impairment by manipulating discount rates and engaging in other discretionary behaviors during impairment tests, as well as their accounting discretion in the initial recognition of goodwill in PPA.

4.3.5 Disclosures About Goodwill Impairment

In addition to studies examining whether managers recognize goodwill impairment losses, some research focuses on the extent of information disclosure related to goodwill impairment tests and the firm's approach to these disclosures.

Mazzi et al. (2017) analyzed a sample of 831 firms from 16 European countries between 2008 and 2011. They found that the median disclosure score—an indicator of compliance with mandatory goodwill impairment disclosures, measured using over 50 checklist items—was high, at 83.3%. The median score increased over the years, from 78.6% in 2008 to 83.3% in 2011.

Devalle et al. (2016) studied 189 Italian firms from 2010 and found that firms recognizing impairments of intangible assets (including goodwill) under IFRS exhibited significantly higher disclosure scores.

Glaum et al. (2013) explored whether "firm-specific factors" and "country-specific factors" affect compliance with mandatory disclosures under IFRS 3 and IAS 36. Using a sample of 357 firms from 17 EU countries from 2005, they found that among firm-specific factors, the size of goodwill relative to total assets, auditor characteristics (e.g., Big Four auditors), the presence of an audit committee, and whether the firm issued equity or bonds in 2005 and 2006 contributed to higher compliance. Regarding country-specific factors, while cultural factors tended to reduce compliance, the strength of enforcement (measured by the LaPorta indicator) and the size of the country's capital market helped enhance compliance.

Chen et al. (2019) conducted a study on the relationship between auditors' roles and disclosures in goodwill impairment testing, considering auditors as a factor in the enforcement of the system. As external parties cannot easily verify managers' subjective judgments in goodwill impairment testing, this area is particularly vulnerable. Therefore, auditors bear responsibility for ensuring that disclosures do not mislead investors and must verify the measurement basis underlying impairment losses.

Analyzing a sample of 3492 U.S. firms from 2004 to 2014, Chen et al. (2019) found that disclosure improvement was positively correlated with audit fees, reflecting the auditors' efforts to mitigate reputational damage and litigation risks. However, the study also noted that this relationship weakened when significant information asymmetry existed between the firm and investors or when investor scrutiny was high, as even with reduced auditor effort, litigation risk remains inherently low.

In addition to studies examining the relationship between disclosures related to goodwill impairment losses and "firm-specific factors" and "country-specific factors," some research investigates how a firm's lifecycle affects impairment disclosures. Kabir et al. (2020) classified 1807 Australian firms from 2007 to 2012 into lifecycle stages[5] (entry, growth, restructuring, and decline) based on the cash flow patterns described by Dickinson (2011).

The results indicated that firms in the "restructuring" stage exhibit an insignificant positive correlation with impairment disclosure indicators, with relatively small absolute regression coefficients. Conversely, firms in the "decline" phase show a significant positive correlation with impairment disclosure indicators, with larger absolute regression coefficients, suggesting a tendency to reduce impairment disclosures. This implies that firms in the "restructuring" stage are more proactive in information disclosure than those in the "decline" stage.

Under TIOA, despite criticism that impairment recognition—which directly affects the accounting figures embedded in many contractual provisions—is not timely, studies have found that compliance with disclosures (i.e., the rationale behind impairment recognition or non-recognition and the validity of reported amounts) is generally high.[6] Additionally, beyond "firm-specific factors" and "country-specific factors," "firm lifecycle" has emerged as a new determinant influencing the level of disclosures.

[5] Four of the five lifecycle stages were used, excluding "Maturity."

[6] Contrarily, Shalev (2009) noted that when future performance, based on ROA and stock returns, is strong, the acquired firm takes a proactive approach to disclosures about business combinations. However, when the goodwill amount is large (indicating a potential overpayment) or when an excessive portion is allocated to goodwill in the PPA, the firm becomes less transparent.

4.4 Research on Economic Consequences

4.4.1 *Event Studies*

The previous section highlighted findings suggesting that managers, who control the timing of goodwill impairment recognition, may engage in opportunistic behavior motivated by various incentives. Conversely, other studies indicate that impairment is recognized promptly—impairment loss information can signal relevant insights depending on managerial discretion. This section reviews studies on whether "goodwill impairment loss" and "goodwill balance," which involve managerial discretion, provide valuable information for investment decision-making.

This section discusses findings from event studies examining stock price changes before and after the announcement of goodwill impairment.

Jarva (2014) analyzed 280 firms that reported goodwill impairment losses between 2002 and 2006. By calculating long-term stock returns (from 9 months before the fiscal year-end to 3 months after), the study found no significant correlation between stock returns and goodwill impairment losses. This suggests that recognizing goodwill impairment does not lead to abnormally high future stock returns.

Hamberg et al. (2011) conducted an event study on Swedish firms under IFRS 3, classifying them into "goodwill-reporting firms" (which ceased amortization, inflating profits) and "non-goodwill-reporting firms." They found that the first group experienced significant positive abnormal returns, indicating the possibility of market misdirection.

Acknowledging that a firm's stock price often drops before it officially recognizes goodwill impairment, some event studies distinguish between "expected" and "unexpected" impairment losses. These studies assess the information value of unexpected impairment losses, controlling for delays in recognition.

Zang (2008) investigated stock market reactions to the impairment of goodwill and other intangible assets following the adoption of SFAS No. 142, which eliminated goodwill amortization. Analyzing a sample of 1764 U.S. firms that recognized impairment losses between March 2001 and June 2003, the study found that CAR in the (−1, +1) window were near zero.

It also found the following: (1) no correlation existed between CAR and inflated earnings that excluded goodwill amortization expenses,[7] (2) a significant positive correlation with CAR appeared when earnings surprises occurred relative to I/B/E/S analyst forecasts, and (3) unexpected goodwill impairment losses were positively correlated with stock price declines, especially for firms with higher leverage.

Bens et al. (2011) used a method comparing a firm's stock market capitalization with the book value of shareholders' equity (before goodwill impairment deduction) to estimate the expected goodwill impairment loss from the difference when

[7] The amount of amortization of goodwill is calculated based on the goodwill recorded prior to the adoption of SFAS No. 142 and information on accounting policies.

stock market capitalization falls below the book value. For firms with multiple business segments, the study allocated stock market capitalization and book value of shareholders' equity to each segment and calculated the unexpected goodwill impairment loss for each. The findings showed that unexpected goodwill impairment loss had a significantly negative impact on stock price, although this explanatory power diminished after the transition to SFAS No. 142.

Li et al. (2011) conducted an event study to determine whether goodwill impairment signals managers' private information about future cash flows or if the potential for impairment is already reflected in stock prices, making the disclosure uninformative. The study divided the period from 1996 to 2006 into three segments based on the adoption of SFAS No. 142: "Pre-adoption (477 firms)," "Transition (253 firms)," and "Post-adoption (854 firms)." The results showed that while stock prices reacted negatively to unexpected goodwill impairments, the informational value was smaller in the post-adoption period. The study also highlighted that before SFAS No. 142, managers had an incentive to recognize goodwill impairments, as it reduced the amortization of goodwill.

Hayn and Hughes (2006) took a different approach, focusing on impairment before TIOA. They developed a "goodwill impairment prediction model" using a sample of U.S. firms from 1988 to 1998. Their study found that when firms with low expectations of goodwill impairment recorded an impairment loss, it had a significant negative impact on stock price changes.

Paugam et al. (2015) conducted an event study on 308 U.S. firms from 2002 to 2011, controlling for over-allocation of goodwill during PPA. As goodwill amounts may include over-allocated portions by managers, they categorized goodwill into "expected goodwill" and "unexpected goodwill" (the over-allocated portion). The study found that stock prices reacted significantly negatively to unexpected goodwill—the market does not view over-allocated goodwill as an asset.

In the field of investment decision-making support, some studies consider the degree of enforcement of laws and regulations as "country-specific factors" and examine how the stock market reacts to the disclosure of goodwill amounts and impairment losses.

Knauer and Wöhrmann (2016) conducted an event study to explore whether the usefulness of the information contained in goodwill impairment losses varies based on the degree of enforcement of laws and regulations. Their sample included 564 firms in the U.S. and 20 EU countries from 2005 to 2009 that adopted IFRS 3. The results showed that in countries with statutory law (as opposed to common law), unexpected goodwill impairment losses had a significant negative impact on stock prices. This suggests that in common law countries, strong enforcement prevents delays in recognizing goodwill impairments, while in statutory law countries, weaker enforcement leads to delayed recognition of unexpected impairments, causing a market reaction.

In the field of event studies on goodwill impairment losses, several studies aim to control for factors such as delays in impairment recognition, over-allocation of goodwill in PPA, and the degree of enforcement of laws and regulations. These studies also seek to extract insights across different countries and jurisdictions.

Many studies have pointed out that unexpected goodwill impairment losses often contain information that negatively affects stock prices. However, as Li et al. (2011) noted, after the adoption of SFAS No. 142, the amount of unexpected impairment losses became relatively smaller owing to delayed recognition, and their information value also decreased.

Nevertheless, the interpretation of unexpected impairments is not uniform. Li et al. (2011) viewed them as the result of managers disclosing information, while Knauer and Wöhrmann (2016) interpreted them as the outcome of opportunistic behavior by managers who delayed recognition in the past and were later forced to recognize impairments.

4.4.2 Value Relevance Studies

This section reviews studies examining whether accounting figures for goodwill and impairment losses explain stock price levels or stock returns.

Some studies report that the transition to TIOA accounting standards improved the value relevance of goodwill and goodwill impairment losses. For example, Lapointe-Antunes et al. (2009) analyzed a sample of 345 Canadian firms from January 2004 and found a significant negative correlation between goodwill impairment losses and stock prices. They also observed that when firms with signs of impairment recognize impairment losses, the market responds positively—such recognition is valued by investors.

Goodwin et al. (2008) analyzed 1065 Australian firms from January 2006 and found that among the reconciliation table items between Australian GAAP and IFRS, goodwill adjustment items increased value relevance. Gjerde et al. (2008) examined 145 Norwegian firms after the IFRS transition and noted that goodwill had higher value relevance as an asset compared to when it was amortized. Horton and Serafeim (2010) found that when the UK first adopted IFRS, goodwill impairment information disclosed in the reconciliation statements with domestic standards had significant negative explanatory power for stock prices. Oliveira et al. (2010) used a sample of 354 Portuguese firms post-IFRS transition and showed that goodwill had value relevance under Portuguese accounting standards, but its relevance increased after IFRS adoption.

Cordazzo and Rossi (2020) analyzed the value relevance of intangible assets in Italian firms from 2000 to 2015. They found that under Italian GAAP, goodwill, intellectual property, other rights, and startup costs had value relevance, while R&D expenditures did not. After the IFRS transition, in firms with a high concentration of intangible assets, the value relevance of intellectual property, other rights, and R&D expenditures declined, whereas that of goodwill and other intangible assets improved.

Burge and Wen (2021) focused on the argument advanced by proponents of "Impairment-only" approach that managers may use their expanded discretion to convey private information, thereby reducing information asymmetry, and

examined whether the value relevance of goodwill has improved following the transition to TIOA. Their sample of U.S. listed firms from 1988 to 2017 comprised 22,577 firm-year observations (4830 firms) in the pre-SFAS 142 period and 33,425 firm-year observations (4591 firms) in the post-SFAS 142 period.

They employed an empirical model that detects changes in explanatory power when goodwill (and changes in goodwill) is added as an independent variable to a baseline model that includes stock price levels (or stock returns) as the dependent variable, and tangible fixed assets (and their changes), other assets (and their changes), and earnings (and their changes) as independent variables. This framework allowed them to test whether the inclusion of goodwill (and changes in goodwill) improves value relevance from the perspectives of incremental and relative information content and whether such information content differs between the pre- and post-SFAS 142 periods.

The results showed that: (1) in both the stock price level model and the stock return model, the inclusion of goodwill (and changes in goodwill) increases value relevance over the entire sample period; (2) the explanatory power of goodwill for stock prices is higher in the post-SFAS 142 period (whereas the explanatory power of tangible fixed assets and other assets declines after the adoption of SFAS 142); and (3) changes in goodwill are not significantly associated with stock prices in the pre-SFAS 142 period, but exhibit a significantly positive association in the post-SFAS 142 period (i.e., goodwill impairments are associated with negative stock returns).

However, several studies reported that the transition to TIOA accounting standards led to a decline in the value relevance of goodwill and goodwill impairment losses. Lopez et al. (2020) found that after adopting SFAS No. 142, the frequency of recording extraordinary loss items increased, but the recorded amounts became smaller. Consequently, their incorporation into stock prices, reflecting expectations of future performance, also deteriorated. They concluded that while extraordinary losses had previously provided useful information for stock price formation, their usefulness diminished following the accounting reform.

Ji and Lu (2014) analyzed a sample of 6650 Australian firm-year observations from 2001 to 2009. They found that, although goodwill exhibited value relevance throughout the entire period, after the adoption of IFRS, earnings quality improved, while the value relevance of intangible assets, including goodwill, declined. Hamberg and Beisland (2014) examined a sample of Swedish firms from 2001 to 2010 and revealed that before the IFRS transition, impairment losses had explanatory power for stock returns (whereas amortization expenses did not). However, after the transition, impairment losses lost their explanatory power.

Empirical evidence from Japan, where voluntary IFRS adoption is permitted, also exists. Noguchi (2022) examined whether the "Systematic amortization with impairment" approach or "Impairment-only" approach provides more value-relevant accounting information (i.e., goodwill impairment information), using a sample of 509 Japanese GAAP firms and 509 matched IFRS-adopting firms from 2010 to 2020.

Noguchi (2022) tested three hypotheses. First, goodwill amortization expenses recognized under the amortization approach are positively associated with capital market valuations. Larger amortization expenses reflect shorter expected recovery periods and are interpreted as signaling stronger managerial confidence in investment recovery.

Second, goodwill impairment losses recognized under the systematic amortization approach are more negatively associated with capital market valuations than those recognized under "Impairment-only" approach because, under TIOA, impairment recognition tends to be delayed, and therefore informational value of impairment losses is weaker.

Third, the initial amount of goodwill recognized under the systematic amortization approach is more positively associated with capital market valuations at the time of recognition than goodwill recognized under "Impairment-only" approach because goodwill may be overstated under TIOA.

The empirical results supported the first and second hypotheses, indicating that goodwill amortization expenses and goodwill impairment losses reported by Japanese GAAP firms (under the systematic amortization approach) provide more useful information for stock price formation than goodwill impairment losses reported by IFRS firms (under TIOA).

While some studies have documented an increase in the value relevance of goodwill following the transition to TIOA, others have argued that managers engage in opportunistic reporting, and impairment recognition is not timely, thereby reducing value relevance. Against these ambivalent findings, Chatterjee et al. (2022) argued that assuming the presence of certain incentives and analyzing the types of contracts that induce such accounting behavior by firms is more consistent.

Chatterjee et al. (2022) focused on debt contracts. Specifically, they argued that: (a) at the time of contract initiation, both lenders and borrowers have discretion in choosing financial covenants, either tangible net worth (TNW), which excludes goodwill, or total net worth (NW), which includes goodwill; and (b) lenders have access to firms' internal information, enabling them to infer managerial incentives and potentially mitigate managers' opportunistic behavior regarding the timing of impairment recognition.

Their sample comprised firms that entered into private debt contracts and adopted either NW or TNW covenants (firms adopting both were excluded), comprising 1799 firm-year observations for the pre-SFAS 142 period (1987–2001) and 1395 firm-year observations for the post-SFAS 142 period (2002–2017).

Comparing the value relevance before and after the adoption of SFAS 142 revealed the following: (1) after the transition to TIOA, the value relevance of goodwill improves for firms using NW covenants that include goodwill (whereas no such improvement is observed for firms using TNW covenants that exclude goodwill); (2) goodwill impairment recognition is more timely for firms using NW covenants than for those using TNW covenants; and (3) violations of financial covenants occur more frequently under NW covenants than under TNW covenants.

These results suggest that including goodwill in financial covenants may discipline managerial behavior. It is also noteworthy that the number of firms adopting NW covenants that include goodwill declines after the transition to TIOA, which is consistent with Frankel et al.'s (2008) findings, which are discussed later.

Sahut et al. (2011) conducted an analysis using a multi-country sample of 1885 European listed firms from 2002 to 2007. They examined changes in value relevance by splitting the data into the overall sample and country-specific subsamples. Their results showed that regarding stock price levels, the value relevance of goodwill was higher under local GAAP than under IFRS (local GAAP > IFRS), while for other intangible assets, it was lower under local GAAP than under IFRS (local GAAP < IFRS). For stock returns, the change in goodwill was more value-relevant under local GAAP than under IFRS (local GAAP > IFRS), while the change in other intangible assets was less value-relevant under local GAAP than under IFRS (local GAAP < IFRS). They concluded that the usefulness of goodwill and its changes under IFRS had deteriorated.

Aharony et al. (2010) focused on whether the value relevance of the information in the "goodwill balance" under IFRS or local GAAP varied based on the strength of law and regulation enforcement. Their sample included 2298 firms from 14 EU countries from 2005, when IFRS was made mandatory. The results revealed that, in countries with strong enforcement, the goodwill balance under IFRS had greater explanatory power for stock prices compared to countries with weak enforcement. Conversely, in countries with weak enforcement, the incremental information content of goodwill was higher than in countries with strong enforcement.

Alshehabi et al. (2021) examined whether cross-country differences in legal institutions, culture, and religion affect the value relevance of goodwill impairment losses using a sample of 18,143 firm-year observations from 21 IFRS-adopting countries over the period from 2005 to 2018. They employed a regression model in which market capitalization is used as the dependent variable, and the book value of equity, earnings, goodwill, and interaction terms between goodwill impairment losses and social factors are included as independent variables.

Their results showed that: (1) the value relevance of goodwill impairment losses reported by firms in countries with higher institutional quality—characterized by stronger investor protection, more effective legal enforcement, and more developed stock markets—is substantially higher than that in countries with lower institutional quality; (2) firms in countries belonging to cultural Group A (e.g., high individualism, low power distance, and low uncertainty avoidance) report goodwill impairment losses with higher value relevance than firms in cultural Group B (e.g., low individualism, high power distance, and high uncertainty avoidance); and (3) in countries with strong religious norms, goodwill impairment losses exhibit no value relevance. These findings suggest the need for further research to explore the role of law and regulation enforcement as a country-specific institutional factor.

4.4.3 Analysts' Forecasts

Some studies explore how recognizing goodwill impairment impacts analysts' forecasts, which shape firm performance estimates and influence capital market expectations. Li et al. (2011) analyzed data from 521 firms issuing analysts' profit forecasts. They examined forecasts from the quarter before goodwill impairment was disclosed and checked whether analysts revised their forecasts within 30 days after the disclosure. The results showed that 93% of the firms (485 out of 521) experienced statistically significant downward revisions. The effect was notably stronger during the "transition" and "post-adoption" periods of SFAS No. 142 compared to the "pre-adoption" period.

Jarva (2014) highlighted that recognizing goodwill impairment is closely linked to forecast errors in future performance. He analyzed the accuracy of analysts' earnings forecasts in the post-SFAS No. 142 period but found no significant correlation with goodwill impairment losses. Although Jarva (2014) concluded that analysts' forecast accuracy was not poor and that the market was efficient, goodwill impairment losses may not offer useful information for revising expectations.

Chen et al. (2015) studied a sample of U.S. firms from 2003 to 2007, covering 2828 quarter observations. They found that recognizing goodwill impairment losses reduced analysts' forecast errors but increased the variance of forecasts. This indicates that while impairment losses provide useful information, their reliability may be low.

Zang (2008) distinguished between "expected" and "unexpected" goodwill impairments. The study found that unexpected impairments were strongly negatively correlated with analysts' forecasts, suggesting that such impairments led analysts to revise their predictions.

Chalmers et al. (2012) analyzed 3328 Australian firms from 1993 to 2007 and found that under IFRS, goodwill information reduced forecast errors and the variance of forecasts. Additionally, the post-2005 impairment-only period provided more useful information for analysts compared to the pre-2005 amortization period.

Conversely, Li and Sloan (2017) suggested that analysts revising their forecasts after a goodwill impairment loss could indicate that they might not be correctly assessing overvalued goodwill, which has actually declined.

Some studies have focused on how the transparency of disclosures related to goodwill impairment tests affects the dispersion of analysts' forecasts. Andreicovici et al. (2020) examined whether a more transparent disclosure of goodwill impairment tests conveys more useful information to sell-side analysts (i.e., how it affects analysts' interpretations in research reports). Their sample comprised 154 European firms from 2006 to 2014. In this study, disagreement among analysts was defined as "information uncertainty," while disagreement between analysts and managers was defined as "information asymmetry." Additionally, 25 disclosure items were coded from footnotes on goodwill impairment to construct an index of "disclosure transparency."

The results showed that higher levels of disclosure transparency are significantly and negatively associated with both disagreement measures (i.e., they reduce disagreements). Specifically, (1) greater transparency regarding discount rates for future cash flows significantly reduces disagreement among analysts, as well as between analysts and managers, since discount rates can be benchmarked against external market information such as government bond yields; and (2) greater transparency regarding future cash flows reduces disagreement only among analysts, as cash flow forecasts are complex and difficult for outsiders to verify, resulting in weaker effects.

4.4.4 Capital Costs

This section reviews studies examining the impact of goodwill impairment loss announcements on firm's capital costs. Jarva (2014) analyzed 280 firms that recorded goodwill impairment losses between 2002 and 2006 and investigated their effect on capital costs. The results showed that recognizing goodwill impairment did not affect future capital costs, as the regression coefficient was insignificantly positive.

Conversely, Kimbro and Xu (2016) studied the impact of SFAS No. 142—before and after its adoption—on stock return volatility. They found that volatility was higher in the "pre-adoption" period (when goodwill was subject to either systematic amortization or amortization with impairment) and lower in the "post-adoption" period (when only goodwill impairment was applied). Additionally, during the post-adoption period, the goodwill balance showed significantly negative explanatory power on volatility, suggesting that it helps reduce stock return volatility. Although the study did not directly examine capital costs, reduced stock return volatility could lead to lower capital costs.

Mazzi et al. (2017) investigated whether increasing the level of disclosure regarding a firm's goodwill impairment would lower forecast risks for external parties and, in turn, reduce capital costs. Using a sample of firms from 16 European countries, they found that firms with high compliance with IFRS 3 and IAS 36 and a proactive approach to disclosures tend to have lower capital costs (a significant negative correlation between compliance and capital cost was detected). Based on whether the book-to-market ratio of total assets was worsening, the sample was divided into two groups: "firms showing signs of impairment with a high disclosure score" and "firms not showing signs of impairment with a high disclosure score." The study revealed that goodwill impairment disclosures only lowered capital costs for the first group.

In summary, the impact of accounting information—specifically goodwill impairment losses—on capital costs varies across studies. While Jarva (2014) and Kimbro and Xu (2016) showed no clear effect, Mazzi et al. (2017) found that increased disclosure of goodwill impairment losses leads to lower capital costs.

4.4.5 Impact on Contract Assistance

Information asymmetry exists between shareholders (principals) and managers (agents), as shareholders cannot continuously observe managers' actions. This creates the potential for managers to engage in behavior that may harm shareholders' interests (moral hazard). To address this, incorporating accounting figures into contractual provisions can help mitigate the issue. This section reviews studies examining whether information related to goodwill and its impairment loss following the transition to TIOA accounting standards has been used to inform or influence contracts.

Darrough et al. (2014) analyzed whether compensation committees in public firms consider goodwill impairment losses after SFAS No. 142 an effective tool for evaluating managers' performance. Using a sample of 3543 U.S. firms from 2002 to 2009, the study found that firms with larger goodwill impairment losses tended to offer lower executive compensation, suggesting that goodwill impairment information is used in determining executive pay.

Detzen and Zülch (2012) found that with the transition to TIOA accounting standards, the proportion of short-term cash compensation in executive pay packages increased. Executive compensation typically includes short-term cash-based rewards and long-term stock-based incentives, such as stock grants and options. For managers under short-term compensation schemes, whose pay increases with firm profits,[8] goodwill that does not incur amortization expenses (i.e., goodwill subject only to annual impairment testing) benefits the firm's profit figures. Moreover, as goodwill may eventually be impaired, long-term incentives appear less attractive to managers.

Detzen and Zülch (2012) analyzed a sample of 123 European firms from January 2005 to December 2008 to examine the relationship between goodwill and executive compensation following M&A under IFRS. The results revealed a significantly positive correlation between the percentage of cash-based (short-term) compensation and recognized goodwill. In other words, as cash-based compensation increased, the amount of recognized goodwill also grew.[9] In light of the changing composition of executive compensation, Detzen and Zülch (2012) suggested that to mitigate the risk of future goodwill impairment losses, an upper limit should be set on the proportion of cash-based payments in executive compensation. They also noted that the decline in long-term, stock-price-based compensation could foster conflicts of interest between shareholders and managers.

Saito (2018) analyzed 11,236 firm-year observations of U.S. firms from 1993 to 2003 to examine the relationship between goodwill, restructuring-related nonrecurring items (such as profit and loss from discontinued operations and extraordinary items), and stock-based executive compensation. Profit and loss from

---

[8] Krolick (2005) indicated that, in the pre-SFAS No. 142 period, compensation and nomination committees of firms that actively invest in intangible assets and have many unrecognized intangible assets tend to avoid using rate-of-return-type indicators, such as ROA and ROE, which incorporate balance sheet figures as performance measures. This is because unrecognized intangible assets provide advantages for managers. Instead, these committees are more likely to use income statement-based indicators, such as profit, as performance measures.

[9] This finding aligns with the results of Shalev et al. (2013), which indicated that when executive compensation is based on accounting figures, a larger portion of the PPA is assigned to non-amortization goodwill rather than amortizable intangible assets.

discontinued operations, arising from decisions such as business withdrawals or sales, serve as signals that contribute to future performance forecast revisions and adjustments to the appropriate balance sheet book value. Extraordinary profit and loss items often reflect industry-level shocks. The study found the following. First, information from extraordinary items increased industry-specific goodwill, signaling future growth opportunities, while profit and loss from discontinued operations decreased goodwill. Second, the signaling of future growth opportunities through extraordinary items showed a significantly negative correlation with stock-based executive compensation, while profit and loss from discontinued operations exhibited a positive correlation. Recognizing that executive compensation is stock-based, the study suggested that extraordinary items and profit and loss from discontinued operations are value-relevant and contract-supportive, with goodwill acting as an intermediary.

Turning to debt contracts, Frankel et al. (2008) analyzed whether goodwill information effectively functions as an accounting item used in "net asset maintenance covenants"—a type of financial covenant in debt contracts. Using a sample of 4096 U.S. firms from 1992 to 2003, they distinguished between two types of covenants: those that incorporate goodwill amounts and "tangible assets maintenance covenants," which exclude goodwill. The analysis revealed that, from 1992 to 2003, firms with larger goodwill amounts tended to use "net asset maintenance covenants" that included goodwill rather than "tangible net asset maintenance covenants." However, from 2002 onward, the use of "tangible net asset maintenance covenants" increased. These results suggest that post-SFAS No. 142, goodwill no longer contains information effective for debt agreements.

These studies highlight the changes in executive compensation composition (short-term versus long-term) and the covenants used in financial contracts following the transition to the TIOA accounting standard.

4.5 Findings on Other Issues

4.5.1 Forecasting Ability of Goodwill for Future Performance

This section discusses empirical findings related to goodwill that do not fall under the themes covered in Sects. 4.3 and 4.4. One prominent topic is the examination of the correlation between the amount of goodwill or goodwill impairment loss disclosed by a firm and financial figures such as profit and cash flow in subsequent periods. These analyses seek to determine whether the reported amounts of goodwill and goodwill impairment loss can effectively forecast future performance.[10]

[10] As these studies do not involve the stock market, they have been classified separately from investment decision support functions (capital market research).

Lee (2011) found a significant positive correlation between goodwill information after the adoption of SFAS No. 142 and future cash flows, demonstrating its forecasting ability. Similarly, Jarva (2009) reported that goodwill impairment loss information showed a significant positive correlation with future cash flows 1–2 years ahead, indicating its forecasting potential. However, this ability disappears for firms that have recorded restructuring costs.

Conversely, Li et al. (2011) pointed out that goodwill impairment has a significantly negative effect on future performance, including revenue and operating profit growth rates, acting as a leading indicator of performance deterioration. Bostwick et al. (2016) also found that goodwill impairment loss information was negatively correlated with future cash flows, showing its ability to forecast declines in cash flow.

Lopez et al. (2020) examined whether the information in extraordinary loss items, including goodwill impairment, changed before and after the transition to SFAS No. 142. Their analysis of the overall sample did not confirm a decline in the relationship between extraordinary losses and future profit. However, when divided by the frequency of extraordinary loss recognition, they found that firms with higher frequencies of extraordinary loss recognition showed a weaker relationship with future profit, indicating weaker forecasting abilities.

Russell (2017) investigated whether the adoption of IFRS changed managers' incentives for recognizing intangible assets, using a sample of Australian firms from 1987 to 2012. The study found that after the transition to IFRS, firms issuing stock recognized more intangible assets. While the recognition of intangible assets with weak or no correlation to the firm's economic reality increased, goodwill remained strongly tied to the firm's economic fundamentals and could serve as a performance forecasting signal. Additionally, the study revealed that the impairment signal was stronger during the impairment period than during the amortization period.

Tahat et al. (2018) examined the relationship between a firm's intangible assets (goodwill and R&D) and its current and future performance (profit and stock price) using a sample of UK firms from 1995 to 2015. The study found that goodwill had a significant positive correlation with profit and stock price in the following year, indicating its role in forecasting future performance. Contrarily, while R&D showed a positive correlation with the following year's profit, it had a negative correlation with stock price.

Johnson et al. (2021) examined whether market participants are better able to understand the implications of goodwill and other intangible assets for firms' future earnings and cash flows following the adoption of SFAS 142. Their sample comprised 29,983 firm-year observations for U.S. firms over the period 1996–2007 (15,527 observations for 1996–2000 and 14,456 observations for 2003–2007).

Their results showed that: (1) the level of goodwill exhibits a significantly negative association with future earnings and future cash flows in the pre-adoption period, whereas in the post-adoption period, the association becomes insignificantly positive or negative, suggesting improved investor understanding; (2) changes in goodwill are significantly negatively associated with changes in future earnings and cash flows (i.e., decreases in goodwill due to impairment are followed by declines in future earnings and cash flows); and (3) although the explanatory power of other intangible assets for future performance does not change materially between the pre- and post-SFAS 142 periods, the predictive ability of goodwill and changes in goodwill (including impairment-related changes) improves after the adoption of SFAS 142.

In addition to studies directly examining goodwill's forecasting ability for future accounting profits and cash flows, some research explores the relationship between goodwill and indicators of "future investment opportunities." These studies investigate whether goodwill and its impairment reflect future growth opportunities.

Makrominas (2017) examined whether goodwill reflects future growth potential without specifically addressing accounting treatment after its acquisition. Using a sample of U.S. firms from 1976 to 2010, the study analyzed the relationship between intangible assets and a "growth option" measure, defined as the difference between stock market capitalization and the capitalized value of profits generated by assets. The results indicate a significant positive correlation between goodwill and the "growth option," suggesting that goodwill information is valuable for decision-making and loan assessments.

Conversely, Godfrey and Koh (2009) focused on the accounting treatment of goodwill after its acquisition. They analyzed a sample of 575 firm-year observations of U.S. firms from 2002 to 2004 after the adoption of SFAS No. 142. Their findings revealed a significant correlation between a decline in investment opportunities (measured through factor analysis) and goodwill impairment loss, suggesting that goodwill impairment reflects the deterioration of economic conditions.

Chalmers et al. (2011) examined the relationship between investment opportunities and goodwill expenses (including impairment, amortization, and forced write-downs) using a sample of 4310 Australian firm-year observations from 1999 to 2008. They found a significant negative relationship during the IFRS period (which requires an impairment test) but no significant relationship during the Australian GAAP period (which requires systematic amortization). The study concluded that goodwill expenses under the impairment test-only approach provide a better signal of investment opportunities than those under the systematic amortization and forced write-down approach.

These findings suggest that goodwill and goodwill impairment loss information likely offer insights that influence external stakeholders' expectations regarding a firm's future cash flow stream.

4.5.2 *Options for the Recognition of Goodwill Impairment and Disclosure of Initially Recognized Goodwill*

Prior to the recognition of goodwill impairment and disclosure of goodwill amounts, firms are allowed to apply certain accounting options; several studies have analyzed how the use of such options affects goodwill impairment recognition.

In September 2011, the FASB introduced an option to perform a qualitative assessment before conducting the goodwill impairment test, which had previously comprised a two-step quantitative test. Under the existing quantitative approach, in Step 1, firms compare the fair value of a reporting unit, including goodwill, with its carrying amount to determine whether the fair value is below the book value. In Step 2, if the fair value is below the carrying amount, firms must conduct additional testing to measure the amount of the goodwill impairment loss. With the introduction of the qualitative option, firms may first perform a qualitative assessment (on an optional basis), and if they conclude that the fair value of a reporting unit is likely to exceed (i.e., greater than 50%) its carrying amount, they will be exempt from performing the subsequent two-step quantitative impairment test.

Black et al. (2022) examined (1) the characteristics of firms that adopt the qualitative assessment option, (2) whether the incidence of impairment changes after the introduction of qualitative criteria, and (3) whether the use of the qualitative option reduces the timeliness of impairment recognition. Their sample comprised 636 U.S. firms that reported goodwill amounting to at least 1% of their total assets from December 15, 2009, to December 15, 2015, yielding 3816 firm-year observations.

Their results showed that: (1) among firms with low book-to-market ratios (i.e., high stock prices), small firm size, and a low frequency of past impairment losses, those with larger balances of goodwill and other intangible assets and a greater number of business segments—firms for which the expected costs of conducting quantitative impairment tests are relatively high—are more likely to adopt the qualitative option; (2) firms that apply the qualitative assessment exhibit slightly higher impairment rates than firms that do not disclose the use of the qualitative option, indicating that firms cannot avoid recognizing goodwill impairment simply by relying on the qualitative assessment; and (3) no evidence indicates that firms using the qualitative option postpone the recognition of impairment losses until the fourth quarter, suggesting that the qualitative option does not delay impairment recognition.

Owing to the inherent difficulty in measuring the fair value of goodwill and allocating the acquisition price to goodwill through purchase price allocation (PPA), IFRS 3 stipulates that, at initial recognition, firms must either recognize goodwill at a finalized amount or, if the accounting for a business combination has not been completed by the end of the reporting period, report a provisional amount (para. 45). Additionally, if new information becomes available during the measurement period (within 1 year), firms are required to retrospectively adjust provisional amounts and recognize additional assets or liabilities as necessary.

In other words, firms have discretion over whether to disclose finalized goodwill amounts or report provisional amounts by taking advantage of the measurement period. Moreover, goodwill recognized on a provisional basis is subject to ex post upward or downward adjustments at the end of the measurement period.

Roncagliolo and Avallone (2022) examined whether firms' use of the "provisional goodwill recognition option" is driven by managerial compensation incentives (i.e., opportunistic behavior) or signaling motives related to information asymmetry (i.e., informational behavior), or reflects the substantive difficulty of estimating the fair value of target firms in M&A transactions. Their sample comprised 110 large M&A deals completed by European firms between January 1,

2014, and December 31, 2015, each with a transaction value exceeding €500 million.

Their results showed that: (1) the hypothesis that firms do not use provisional goodwill recognition when the acquirer and the target operate in similar product markets (i.e., when both firms belong to the same industry and goodwill amounts are easier to finalize) is rejected; (2) firms are more likely to choose provisional goodwill recognition when the time lag between the acquisition date and the first financial reporting date is shorter; and (3) firms are more likely to use the provisional option when they are overvalued in the stock market and face higher litigation risk (e.g., in countries with stronger investor protection), suggesting that firms use the provisional option to more cautiously assess goodwill amounts.

4.5.3 Acquisition Price and Goodwill Impairment Probability

This section highlights findings suggesting that the amount of consideration paid in M&A transactions increases the likelihood of goodwill impairment. Gu and Lev (2011) analyzed a sample of 54,218 firm-year observations from U.S. firms acquired through M&A between 1990 and 2006. They found that managers of firms with overvalued stock were more likely to finance acquisitions by issuing new stock, often paying excessive acquisition prices that exceeded the expected synergies. This overpayment often led to goodwill impairment. The study also noted that this tendency was more pronounced in firms with weak corporate governance.[11]

Li et al. (2011) analyzed 313 U.S. firms from 1991 to 2005 that recorded impairments after an acquisition, investigating factors that trigger goodwill impairment owing to acquisition price overpayment. They found that (1) excess payment (the difference between the acquisition price and book value of the target firm), (2) premiums (the difference between the stock price paid to the target firm's shareholders and the stock price 4 weeks before the acquisition announcement), and (3) the presence of termination fee covenants[12] were all positively correlated with goodwill impairment. Based on these findings, they concluded that overpayment in M&A transactions contributes to the occurrence of goodwill impairment.

Olantem (2013) analyzed 929 U.S. firms from 1999 to 2007 and found that goodwill impairment loss was more likely when a higher proportion of the acquisition

---

[11] Henning et al. (2000) divided goodwill into four components: (1) the revaluation portion of the target firm's assets, (2) the fair value portion of the target firm alone, (3) the synergies between the acquiring and target firms, and (4) the residual overpayment portion of the acquisition price. They found that components (1, 2, 3) (core goodwill) showed a significant positive correlation with stock price, while component (4) showed a significant negative correlation.

[12] Termination fee covenants in M&A refer to contractual provisions that allow the target firm to cancel the previously agreed-upon acquisition agreement if a competing firm emerges as a potential acquirer. If the target firm determines that the proposal from the new acquirer is more beneficial, it must pay a predetermined amount to the original acquirer, as specified in the contract.

consideration was paid in stock, as opposed to cash, and when a larger portion of the total acquisition price was allocated to goodwill.

Some studies have indicated that acquisition premiums increase after transitioning to TIOA. Under TIOA, the absence of systematic goodwill amortization inflates operating income and makes it more difficult to evaluate M&A performance, thereby weakening managerial accountability. Consequently, managers may engage in more aggressive M&A investments.

Bartov et al. (2021) examined whether managers engage in more overbidding M&As after adopting TIOA (SFAS 142). Using 1734 completed U.S. M&A deals from 1992 to 2014 (729 before and 1005 after SFAS 142), excluding pooling-of-interests cases, they find that the dummy variable "after SFAS 142" is significantly positive in explaining "overbidding." Overbidding is defined as an excess of the acquisition price over the economically optimal bid derived from the valuation models. The study concluded that firms using the purchase method overbid more after adopting SFAS 142.

4.5.4 Labor Union Strength and the Likelihood of Goodwill Impairment

In addition to acquisition premiums, some studies have identified labor unions as a firm-level factor that affects goodwill impairment recognition. Kallousa et al. (2022) focused on the possibility that when labor unions in acquiring firms are strong, they may impede post-merger resource reallocation and lead to insufficient integration (i.e., the expected synergy effects fail to materialize).

Based on this argument, the authors examined the relationship between labor union strength and both the probability of recognizing goodwill impairment and the magnitude of goodwill impairment losses. Labor union strength was measured as the interaction between firm-level labor intensity and industry-level unionization rates. The sample comprised 7979 firm-year observations of U.S. firms from 2007 to 2016, including 973 firm-year observations with recognized goodwill impairment and 7006 firm-year observations without impairment. The results indicated that labor union strength has a significantly positive association with both the likelihood of recognizing goodwill impairment and the amount of impairment losses.

4.5.5 Goodwill and Auditors

Although this review does not focus on journals specializing in auditing, we would like to highlight the limited findings available, as financial accounting journals occasionally publish articles related to goodwill and auditing. Previous sections presented studies assuming a causal relationship of "audit → goodwill impairment," including research on the timeliness of audits and goodwill impairment recognition (Kabir and Rahman 2016; Albersmann and Quick 2020) and the level of disclosures related to audits and goodwill impairment (Chen et al. 2019). However, this section introduces findings from studies assuming the reverse causal relationship of "goodwill impairment → audit."

The decision regarding goodwill impairment can potentially affect audit risk and audit fees. Jarva (2014) observed that under SFAS No. 142, auditors must evaluate and audit the entire fair value of the reporting units when determining whether goodwill impairment recognition is appropriate. This process, requiring the evaluation and auditing of every accounting report, demands significant effort, particularly when auditing a firm that has recognized impairment. Jarva (2014) hypothesized that audit fees would increase consequently. Nevertheless, the analysis of U.S. firms from 2002 to 2005 showed that, under SFAS No. 142, while audit fees for firms recognizing goodwill impairment increased significantly, a similar upward trend was also observed in the control sample (firms not recognizing goodwill impairment). Thus, the results did not fully support the hypothesis.

Ayres et al. (2019b) used a model to estimate expected goodwill impairment loss applied in an event study and interpreted situations where potential goodwill impairment existed but was not recognized as a sign of disagreements between managers and auditors. An analysis of 21,664 U.S. firm-year observations from 2001 to 2014 revealed that (1) recognizing goodwill impairment increased the "probability of auditor dismissal," and (2) disagreements between managers and auditors also increased the "probability of auditor dismissal."

Carcello et al. (2020) focused on the breakdown of auditor fees and analyzed the impact of the ratio of audit fees to non-audit fees on goodwill impairment loss recognition. The sample included 2126 U.S. firm-year observations from 2005 to 2016. The results showed that, in cases where the expected goodwill impairment was large, firms that did not recognize impairment paid auditors higher non-audit fees in terms of monetary value and fee composition ratio.

These findings suggest that, in the context of potential goodwill impairment, the decision to recognize impairment can influence the continuation of the audit contract and the structure of audit fees.

Some studies have also documented that the transition to TIOA has led to an increase in audit effort. Ghosh and Xing (2021) argued that auditing goodwill involves: (a) Level 3 fair value measurements that require verification of estimation processes; (b) valuation at the reporting-unit level; and (c) negotiations with management to challenge potential biases in managerial estimates. Based on these considerations, they examined whether audit effort has increased following TIOA adoption. As a proxy for audit effort, they used abnormally high audit fees, defined as the portion of audit fees exceeding their predicted values.

Their sample comprised 32,198 U.S. firm-year observations from 2000 to 2015. This period can be broadly divided into three sub-periods: (1) 2000–2001, when firms applied systematic amortization with an impairment test; (2) 2003–2010, when firms conducted annual goodwill impairment tests using the two-step quantitative approach; and (3) 2011–2015, when the qualitative assessment option[13] was introduced.

The results showed that: (1) goodwill, goodwill impairment, Big 4 × goodwill, and Big 4 × goodwill impairment are all significantly positively associated with abnormally high audit fees, indicating that audit effort related to goodwill has increased following the transition to TIOA; (2) Big 4 auditors appear to provide more specialized audits; and (3) among the three sub-periods, audit effort is relatively higher in the period when only the two-step quantitative test was applied, compared with the other two periods.

4.5.6 M&A/Goodwill and Preferences for Accounting Standards

Before TIOA accounting standards, when an M&A occurred (assuming the Purchase Method), acquired goodwill was recognized, and many countries required systematic amortization. However, countries that transitioned to TIOA accounting standards no longer required firms to amortize acquired goodwill, although impairment testing was mandatory. Assuming that firms aim to avoid the burden of goodwill amortization, (a) firms that actively engage in M&As or hold goodwill might prefer TIOA accounting standards, and (b) TIOA accounting standards could encourage firms to engage in M&As, as they would not bear the goodwill amortization burden.

In Japan, where Japanese standards are generally applied, firms were given the option to voluntarily apply IFRS to consolidated financial statements starting in the fiscal year ending March 2010. This makes Japan an ideal research site to examine the research topics mentioned in (a) and (b).

Kim et al. (2019) investigated (a), focusing on the motivations of firms in Japan to voluntarily adopt IFRS. They analyzed Japanese firms from the fiscal year ending March 2010 to March 2018, examining changes in their characteristics before and after IFRS adoption. Their results revealed that firms with larger goodwill and R&D expenditures were more likely to adopt IFRS voluntarily.

Kashiwazaki et al. (2019) investigated (a) and (b) using a sample of 164 Japanese firms that had voluntarily adopted or were planning to adopt IFRS by 2017. In their examination of (a), they found a significant positive correlation between the frequency of M&A transactions, the magnitude of goodwill, and the voluntary adoption (or preference) for IFRS. Regarding (b), they analyzed changes in M&A frequency and goodwill before and after IFRS adoption, revealing that while the number of M&A transactions significantly increased after IFRS adoption, the scale

[13] When firms first conduct the qualitative assessment and find no indications of impairment, they are exempted from performing the subsequent two-step quantitative test.

of goodwill remained high before and after adoption, with no significant change observed.

Amano (2020) analyzed the relationship between intangible assets and voluntary IFRS adoption using a sample of Japanese firms. From 12,104 firm-year observations from 2010 to 2015, 40 IFRS adopters and 40 matched Japanese GAAP firms are divided into 20 firms with large intangible assets and 20 firms with small intangible assets. The results showed that: (1) firms with larger intangible assets are more likely to voluntarily adopt IFRS; and (2) after IFRS adoption, firms increase their intangible assets compared with non-adopters. This increase is attributed to the increase in the number and value of M&A transactions following IFRS adoption.

The issue of whether M&A and goodwill drive the preference for certain accounting standards or whether accounting standards promote M&A can only be empirically tested using Japan as a subject, given the differences between mandatory and voluntary adoption. Therefore, further research on this issue is necessary.

4.5.7 Alternative Goodwill Accounting Treatments

The discussion surrounding the accounting treatment of goodwill focuses on the current systems of "impairment only" and "Systematic amortization with impairment." However, empirical evidence also exists regarding the procedure of "immediate write off (equity)," which was used in the U.K.

In the U.K., before 1998, under SSAP No. 22, goodwill was offset against the surplus of capital, and its amount was disclosed in the notes. From 1998 to 2005, under FRS No. 10, the treatment of goodwill changed, requiring it to be recognized as an asset on the balance sheet. Firms were then given the option to either amortize goodwill over its useful life or perform an annual impairment test.

Jifri and Citron (2009) investigated how the market evaluated "goodwill disclosed in the notes" (from previous acquisitions) versus "goodwill recognized as an asset" (from 1998 onward) in 186 UK firms in 2002. Their findings revealed that "goodwill recognized as an asset" had a higher value relevance compared to "goodwill disclosed in the notes." This study provides valuable insights into the issue of "on-balance-sheet versus note disclosure" and the "value relevance of older goodwill."

4.5.8 Informational Value and Other Effects of Goodwill Amortization

Few studies among those reviewed specifically focus on the systematic amortization treatment of goodwill, but some findings highlight its positive aspects. Henning and Shaw (2003) identified signals within the amortization period of goodwill. They analyzed a sample of 1741 U.S. firms from 1990 to 1994, examining whether the choice of amortization period for acquired goodwill could forecast post-M&A profit levels. Their hypothesis was that managers confident in achieving synergies after the merger would opt for a more aggressive (shorter) amortization period.

The analysis found that factors such as the "expected growth in earnings per share (EPS) of the combined firm post-M&A" and the "average EPS growth rate of the acquiring firm in the three years before the merger" led to the selection of a shorter amortization period. Conversely, firms that chose a 40-year amortization period for goodwill experienced a decline in stock excess returns. In other words, opting for a shorter amortization period signaled the expectation of future profits. The study also noted that the abolition of goodwill amortization under SFAS No. 142, which allowed goodwill to be reported without amortization, resulted in the disappearance of this signaling effect.

Additionally, Li et al. (2011) pointed out that the systematic amortization of goodwill could incentivize managers to recognize goodwill impairment. Under the "Systematic amortization with impairment" system, recognizing goodwill impairment reduces future amortization burdens, incentivizing managers to acknowledge impairment. Furthermore, Shalev et al. (2013) and Zhang and Zhang (2017) highlighted that in the context of PPA, firms often over-allocate goodwill to avoid amortization requirements for intangible assets. Nonetheless, such incentives might be suppressed under the "Systematic amortization with impairment" approach.

4.6 Summary and Remaining Issues

This chapter reviewed empirical research on the accounting treatment of goodwill within the context of the ongoing debate on the topic. The review focused on key issues related to managerial behavior and the economic consequences of accounting standards, particularly those concerning "impairment only" and "Systematic amortization with impairment." The goal was to organize and summarize the findings reported to date.[14]

In Sect. 4.2, we reviewed research on the time-series progression of firms' profitability. The analysis showed that, except for a few highly profitable firms, excess profits generally revert to a level close to the capital cost within approximately 5 years, even after considering managerial efforts. This suggests that excess profitability does not persist indefinitely.

In Sect. 4.3, we examined whether managers under TIOA recognize goodwill impairment promptly. While findings were mixed, studies highlighting various

[14] The references Wong and Wong (2001, CAR) and Hirschey and Richardson (2002, JAPP) in Table 4.1 could not be included owing to issues related to the theme and their analysis period.

managerial incentives—executive compensation and financial covenants—that lead to untimely recognition were more prevalent than those supporting timely recognition. The relationship between managers' incentives and timeliness was significantly influenced by firm-specific factors (e.g., shareholder composition and corporate governance strength) and country-specific factors (e.g., regulatory enforcement, presence of auditors, and analysts). Additionally, discretionary behaviors such as excessive allocation to goodwill in PPA were observed in relation to goodwill impairment recognition.

In Sect. 4.4, we reviewed studies on the usefulness of goodwill and impairment loss information for investment decision-making. Event studies on "unexpected impairment," which accounts for delays in impairment recognition, generally indicated that such information is useful. Nevertheless, post-TIOA, some studies noted a diminished magnitude and explanatory power of impairment losses. Results on value relevance varied by country. Given the impact of firm- and country-specific factors, further research using multi-country samples is necessary to gain more comprehensive insights.

Moreover, we reviewed studies on the effectiveness of goodwill and impairment loss information in contract support. Changes in executive compensation contracts and financial covenants in debt contracts were observed. However, as the number of studies in this area is limited, more research is necessary to gather additional insights.

In Sect. 4.5, we explored additional topics, including studies on the usefulness of goodwill and impairment information for forecasting future performance and the impact of conflicts between auditors and managers. We also discussed how the systematic amortization of goodwill can signal future performance to the stock market and how combining amortization with impairment recognition incentivizes managers to recognize impairments.

Empirical studies under TIOA, based on samples from various countries, have produced mixed results. To better understand impairment timeliness, managers' opportunistic behavior, and capital market effects, further research considering country-specific factors and differences is necessary. Additionally, given the limited focus on the systematic amortization of goodwill, empirical studies using Japan as a sample—where firms following the Japanese standard of "Systematic amortization with impairment" coexist with those voluntarily adopting IFRS (TIOA)—could provide valuable insights for future discussions.

Empirical evidence on goodwill accounting has continued to accumulate since 2023, suggesting that the conclusions drawn in this chapter may evolve as ongoing research develops.

Chapter 2 showed that stakeholders express a wide range of views on various issues in the debate over setting accounting standards for goodwill. However, when stakeholders' perceptions of facts are compared with the empirical evidence presented in this chapter, several discrepancies can be identified. This suggests the need to clarify what kinds of facts are perceived and recognized by stakeholders who can influence accounting standard setting.

Statement on AI Usage During the preparation of this manuscript, the author used AI-assisted tools such as DeepL and ChatGPT to improve the English expression and clarity of the manuscript. The author thoroughly reviewed and approved the final version and takes full responsibility for the content.

References

In English

AbuGhazaleh, N. M., O. M. Al-Hares, and C. Roberts (2011) "Accounting Discretion in Goodwill Impairments: UK Evidence", *Journal of International Financial Management & Accounting*, Vol. 22, No. 3, pp. 165–204.

Aharony, J., R. Barniv, and H. Falk (2010), "The Impact of Mandatory IFRS Adoption on Equity Valuation of Accounting Numbers for Security Investors in the EU", *European Accounting Review*, Vol. 19, No. 3, pp. 535–578.

Albersmann, B. T. and R. Quick (2020) "The Impact of Audit Quality Indicators on the Timeliness of Goodwill Impairments: Evidence from the German Setting: The Impact of Audit Quality Indicators on the Timeliness of Goodwill Impairments", *Abacus,* Vol. 56, No. 1, pp. 66–103.

Alshehabi, A., G. Georgiou, and A. S. Ala (2021), "Country-specific drivers of the value relevance of goodwill impairment losses", *Journal of International Accounting, Auditing and Taxation*, Vol. 43, pp. 1–22.

Amano, Y. (2020), "Real Effects of Intangibles Capitalization—Empirical Evidence from Voluntary IFRS Adoption in Japan", *Journal of International Accounting Research*, Vol. 19, No. 3, pp. 19–36.

André, P., A. Filip. And L. Paugam (2015), "The Effect of Mandatory IFRS Adoption on Conditional Conservatism in Europe", *Journal of Business Finance and Accounting*, Vol. 42, No. 3, pp. 482–514.

André, P., A. Filip and L. Paugam (2016) "Examining the Patterns of Goodwill Impairments in Europe and the US", *Accounting in Europe*, Vol. 13, No. 3, pp. 329–352.

Andreicovici, I., A. Jeny, and D. Lui (2020), "Disclosure Transparency and Disagreement Among Economic Agents: The Case of Goodwill Impairment", *European Accounting Review*, vol. 29, No. 1, pp. 1–26.

Accounting Standards Board of Japan (ASBJ) and Hong Kong Institute of Certified Public Accountants (HKICPA) (2020) *Goodwill: Improvements to subsequent accounting and an update of the quantitative study*. Staff Research Paper.

Avallone, F., and A. Quagli (2015), "Insight into the Variables used to Manage the Goodwill Impairment Test under IAS 36", *Advances in Accounting*, Vol. 31, No. 1, pp. 107–114.

Ayres, D. R., J. L. Campbell, J. A. Chyz, and J. E. Shipman (2019a) "Do Financial Analysts Compel Firms to Make Accounting Decisions? Evidence from Goodwill Impairments", *Review of Accounting Studies*, Vol. 24, pp. 1214–1251.

Ayres, D. R., T. L. Neal, L. C. Reid, and J. E. Shipman (2019b), "Auditing Goodwill in the Post-Amortization Era: Challenges for Auditors", *Contemporary Accounting Research*, Vol. 36, No. 1, pp. 82–107.

Bartov, E, C.S. Agnes Cheng, and H. Wu (2021), "Overbidding in Mergers and Acquisitions: An Accounting Perspective", *The Accounting Review*, Vol. 96, No. 2, pp. 55–79.

Beatty, A. and J. Weber (2006) "Accounting Discretion in Fair Value Estimates: An Examination of SFAS 142 Goodwill Impairments", *Journal of Accounting Research*, Vol. 44, No. 2, pp. 257–288.

Bens, D. A., W. Heltzer, and B. Segal (2011), "The Information Content of Goodwill Impairments and SFAS 142", *Journal of Accounting, Auditing and Finance*, No. 26, Vol. 3, pp. 527–555.

Black, D. E., J. Krupa, and M. Minutti-Meza (2022), "The Optional Qualitative Assessment in Impairment Tests", *Journal of International Accounting Research*, Vol. 21, No. 2, pp. 1–30.

Bostwick, E. D., K. Krieger and S. L. Lambert (2016), "Relevance of Goodwill Impairments to Cash Flow Prediction and Forecasting", *Journal of Accounting, Auditing and Finance*, Vol. 31, No. 3, pp. 339–364.

Bugeja, M., and N. Gallery (2006) "Is Older Goodwill Value Relevant?", *Accounting and Finance*, Vol. 46, No. 4, pp. 519–535.

Bugeja, M. and A. Loyeung (2015) "What Drives the Allocation of the Purchase Price to Goodwill?", *Journal of Contemporary Accounting & Economics*, Vol. 11, No. 3, pp. 245–261.

Burge, M. and H. Wen (2021), "The relative and incremental value relevance of goodwill before and after SFAS No. 142", *Journal of Accounting and Public Policy*, Vol. 40, No. 6, pp. 1–21.

Carcello, J. V., T. Neal, L. C. Reid, and J. E. Shipman (2020) "Auditor Independence and Fair Value Accounting: An Examination of Nonaudit Fees and Goodwill Impairments" *Contemporary Accounting Research*, Vol. 37, No. 1, pp. 189–217.

Chalmers, K.G., J. M. Godfrey, and J.C. Webster (2011), "Does a Goodwill Impairment Regime Better Reflect the Underlying Economic Attributes of Goodwill?" *Accounting and Finance*, Vol. 51, No. 3, pp. 634–660.

Chalmers, K., G.Clinch, J. M. Godfrey, and Z. Wei (2012), "Intangible Assets, IFRS and Analysts' Earnings Forecasts", *Accounting and Finance*, Vol. 52, No. 3, pp. 691–721.

Chen, C., M. Kohlbeck, and T. Warfield (2008), "Timeliness of Impairment Recognition: Evidence from the Initial Adoption of SFAS 142", *Advances in Accounting*, Vol. 24, No. 1, pp. 72–81.

Chen, L. H., J. Krishnan and H. Sami (2015), "Goodwill Impairment Charges and Analyst Forecast Properties", *Accounting Horizons*, Vol. 29, No. 1, pp. 141–169.

Chen, V. Y. S., E. C. Keung, I. Lin (2019) "Disclosure of Fair Value Measurement in Goodwill Impairment Test and Audit Fees", *Journal of Contemporary Accounting and Economics*, Vol. 15, No. 3, Article: 100160.

Chatterjee, C., A. A. Shroff, and K. Sivaramakrishnan (2022), "Debt contracting and the goodwill debate", *Journal of Contemporary Accounting and Economics*, Vol. 18, No. 2, pp. 1–22.

Chung, B. H. and P. Hribar (2021), "CEO Overconfidence and the Timeliness of Goodwill Impairments", *The Accounting Review*, Vol. 96, No. 3, pp. 221–25.

Cordazzo, M. and P. Rossi (2020) "The Influence of IFRS Mandatory Adoption on Value Relevance of Intangible Assets in Italy", *Journal of Applied Accounting Research*, Vol. 21, No. 3, pp. 415–436.

Cready, W. M., T. J. Lopez, and C. A. Sisneros (2012), "Negative Special Items and Future Earnings: Expense Transfer or Real Improvements?", *The Accounting Review*, Vol. 87, No. 4, pp. 1165–1195.

Darrough, M. N., L. Guler, and P. Wang (2014), "Goodwill Impairment Losses and CEO Compensation", *Journal of Accounting, Auditing and Finance*, Vol. 29, No. 4, pp. 435–463.

Detzen, D. and H. Zülch (2012) "Executive Compensation and Goodwill Recognition under IFRS: Evidence from European Mergers", *Journal of International Accounting, Auditing and Taxation*, Vol. 21, No. 2, pp. 106–126.

Devalle, A., F. Rizzato, and D. Busso (2016), "Disclosure Indexes and Compliance with Mandatory Disclosure -The Case of Intangible Assets in the Italian Market", *Advances in Accounting*, Vol. 35, pp. 8–25.

Dickinson, V. (2011) Cash Flow Patterns as a Proxy for Firm Life Cycle. *The Accounting Review*, Vol. 86, No. 6, pp. 1969–1994.

Dickinson, V. and G. A. Sommers (2012), "Which Competitive Efforts Lead to Future Abnormal Economic Rents? using accounting rations to assess competitive advantage", *Journal of Business Finance and Accounting*, Vol. 39, No. 3–4, pp. 360–398.

Dinh, T., H. Kang, R. D. Morris, and W. Schultze (2018) "Evolution of Intangible Asset Accounting: Evidence from Australia", *Journal of International Financial Management and Accounting*, Vol. 29, No. 3, pp. 247–279.

Duh, R., W. Lee, C. Lin (2009) "Reversing an Impairment Loss and Earnings Management: The Role of Corporate Governance", *The International Journal of Accounting*, Vol. 44, No. 2, pp. 113–137.
European Financial Reporting Advisory Group (EFRAG), Accounting Standards Board of Japan (ASBJ), and Organismo Italiano di Contabilità (OIC) (2014), "Should Goodwill Still Not Be Amortised?: Accounting and Disclosure for Goodwill", EFRAG Discussion Paper July 2014.
EFRAG (2016), "What Do We Really Know About Goodwill and Impairment?: A Quantitative Study", EFRAG Discussion Paper September 2016.
EFRAG (2017), "Goodwill Impairment test: Can It Be Improved?" EFRAG Discussion Paper June 2017.
Fama, E. F. and K. R. French (2000), "Forecasting Profitability and Earnings", *The Journal of Business*, Vol. 73, No. 2, pp. 161–175.
FASB (2019) "Invitation to Comment-Identifiable Intangible Assets and Subsequent Accounting for Goodwill" (https://www.fasb.org/jsp/FASB/Document_C/DocumentPage&cid=1176172950529)
Filip, A., T. Jeanjean, and L. Paugam (2015), "Using Real Activities to Avoid Goodwill Impairment Losses: Evidence and Effect on Future Performance", *Journal of Business Finance and Accounting*, Vol. 42, No. 3, pp. 515–554.
Filip, A., G. J. Lobo, and L. Paugam (2020), "Managerial discretion to delay the recognition of goodwill impairment: The role of enforcement", *Journal of Business Finance & Accounting*, Vol. 48, No. 1–2, pp. 36–69.
Frankel, R., C. Seethamraju, and T. Zach (2008), "GAAP Goodwill and Debt Contracting Efficiency: Evidence from Net-worth Covenants", *Review of Accounting Studies*, Vol. 13, No. 1, pp. 87–118.
Frii, P. and M. Hamberg (2021), "What motives shape the initial accounting for goodwill under IFRS 3 in a setting dominated by controlling owners?", *Accounting in Europe*, Vol. 18, No. 2, pp. 218–248.
Ghosh, A. and C. Xing(2021), "Goodwill Impairment and Audit Effort", *Accounting Horizons*, Vol. 35, No. 4, pp. 83–103.
Gjerde, Ø., K. Knivsfl, and F. Sættem (2008), "The Value-Relevance of Adopting IFRS: Evidence from 145 NGAAP restatements", *Journal of International Accounting, Auditing and Taxation*, Vol. 17, No. 2. pp. 92–112.
Glaum, M., P. Schmidt, D. L. Street, and S. Vogel (2013), "Compliance with IFRS 3- and IAS 36-Required Disclosures across 17 European Countries: Company- and Country-level Determinants", *Accounting and Business Research*, Vol. 43, No. 3, pp. 163–204.
Glaum, M., W. R. Landsman, and S. Wyrwa (2018), "Goodwill Impairment: The Effects of Public Enforcement and Monitoring by Institutional Investors", *The Accounting Review*, Vol. 93, No. 6, pp. 149–180.
Godfrey, J. M.and P. Koh (2009) "Goodwill Impairment as a Reflection of Investment Opportunities", *Accounting and Finance*, Vol. 49, No,1, pp. 117–140.
Goodwin, J., K. Ahmed, and R. Heaney (2008) "The Effects of International Financial Reporting Standards on the Accounts and Accounting Quality of Australian Firms: A Retrospective Study", *Journal of Contemporary Accounting & Economics*, Vol. 4, No. 2, pp. 89–119.
Gros, M. and S. Koch (2019) "Discretionary Goodwill Impairment Losses in Europe", *Journal of Applied Accounting Research*, Vol. 21, No. 1, pp. 106–124.
Gu, F. and B. Lev (2011), "Overpriced Shares, Ill-Advised Acquisitions, and Goodwill Impairment", *The Accounting Review*, Vol. 86, No. 6, pp. 1995–2022.
Hamberg, M., M. Paananen, and J. Novak (2011), "The Adoption of IFRS 3: The Effects of Managerial Discretion and Stock Market Reactions", *European Accounting Review*, Vol. 20, No. 2, pp. 263–288.
Hamberg, M. and L. Beisland (2014) "Changes in the Value Relevance of Goodwill Accounting following the Adoption of IFRS 3", *Journal of International Accounting, Auditing and Taxation*, Vol. 23, No. 2, pp. 59–73.

Han, H., J. J. Tang, and Q. Tang (2020), "Goodwill Impairment, Securities Analysts, and Information Transparency", *European Accounting Review*, Volume 30, No. 4, pp. 767–799
Hayn, C., and P. J. Hughes (2006), "Leading Indicators of Goodwill Impairment", *Journal of Accounting, Auditing and Finance*, Vol. 21, No. 3, pp. 223–265.
Healy, P., G. Serafeim, S. Srinivasan, and G. Yu (2014), "Market Competition, Earnings Management, and Persistence in Accounting Profitability around the World", *Review of Accounting Studies*, Vol. 19, No. 4, pp. 1281–1308.
Henning, S. L., B. L. Lewis, and W. H. Shaw (2000) "Valuation of the Components of Purchased Goodwill" *Journal of Accounting Research*, Vol. 38, No. 2, pp. 375–386.
Henning, S. L., and W. H. Shaw (2003) "Is the Selection of the Amortization Period for Goodwill a Strategic Choice?", *Review of Quantitative Finance and Accounting*, Vol. 20, No. 4, pp. 315–333.
Henning, S. L., and W. H. Shaw (2004) "The Amount and Timing of Goodwill Write-Offs and Revaluations: Evidence from U.S. and U.K. Firms", *Review of Quantitative Finance and Accounting*, Vol. 23, No. 2, pp. 99–121.
Horton, J. and G. Serafeim (2010) "Market Reaction to and Valuation of IFRS Reconciliation Adjustments: First Evidence from the UK", *Review of Accounting Studies*, Vol. 15, No. 4, pp. 725–751.
International Accounting Standards Board (IASB) (2020) "Business Combinations – Disclosure, Goodwill and Impairment" IFRS Standards Discussion Paper.
Jarva, H. (2009), "Do Firms Manage Fair Value Estimates? An Examination of SFAS 142 Goodwill Impairments", *Journal of Business Finance and Accounting*, Vol. 36, No. 9–10, pp. 1059–1086.
Jarva, H.(2014), "Economic Consequences of SFAS 142 Goodwill Write-offs", *Accounting and Finance,* Vol. 54, No. 1, pp. 211–235.
Johnson, P. M., T. J. Lopez, and T. L. Sorensen (2021) "Did SFAS 141/142 improve the market's understanding of net assets, goodwill, or other intangible assets?", *Review of Quantitative Finance and Accounting*, Vol. 56, No. 3, pp. 891–915.
Ji, X. and W. Lu (2014), "The Value Relevance and Reliability of Intangible Assets: Evidence from Australia Before and After Adopting IFRS", *Asian Review of Accounting*, Vol. 22, No. 3, pp. 182–216.
Jifri, K. A., and D. Citron (2009), "The Value-Relevance of Financial Statement Recognition versus Note Disclosure: Evidence from Goodwill Accounting", *European Accounting Review*, Vol. 18, No 1, pp. 123–140.
Kabir, H. and A. Rahman (2016) "The Role of Corporate Governance in Accounting Discretion under IFRS: Goodwill Impairment in Australia", *Journal of Contemporary Accounting & Economics*, Vol. 12, No. 3, pp. 290–308.
Kabir, H., L. Su, A. Rahman (2020) "Firm Life Cycle and the Disclosure of Estimates and Judgments in Goodwill Impairment Tests: Evidence from Australia" *Journal of Contemporary Accounting and Economics*, Vol. 16, No. 3, Article: 100207.
Kallousa, N. Y. Jang, B. Jung, and H. Warsame (2022), "Labor unions and post-acquisition integration capability: Evidence from goodwill impairment", *Journal of Business Finance & Accounting*, Vol. 50, No. 3–4, pp. 764–794.
Kashiwazaki, R., S. Sato, and F. Takeda (2019) "Does IFRS Adoption Accelerate M&A? The Consequences of Different Goodwill Accounting in Japan", *International Advances in Economic Research*, Vol. 25, pp. 399–415.
Kim, S., C. Lee, and S. W. Yoon (2013) "Goodwill Accounting and Asymmetric Timeliness of Earnings", *Review of Accounting and Finance*, Vol. 12, No. 2, pp. 112–129.
Kimbro, M. B., and D. Xu (2016), "The Accounting Treatment of Goodwill, Idiosyncratic Risk, and Market Pricing", *Journal of Accounting, Auditing and Finance*, Vol. 31, No. 3, pp. 367–387.
Knauer, T, and A. Wöhrmann (2016), "Market Reaction to Goodwill Impairments", *European Accounting Review*, Vol. 25, No. 3, pp. 421–449.

Krolick, D. L.(2005), "The Relevance of Financial Statement Information for Executive Performance Evaluation: Evidence from Choice of Bonus Plan Accounting Performance Measures", *The International Journal of Accounting,* Vol. 40, No. 2, pp. 115–132.

Lapointe-Antunes, P., D. Cormier, and M. Magnan (2009), "Value Relevance and Timeliness of Transitional Goodwill-Impairment Losses: Evidence from Canada", *The International Journal of Accounting*, Vol. 44, No. 1, pp. 56–78.

Lee, C. (2011), "The Effect of SFAS 142 on the Ability of Goodwill to Predict Future Cash Flows", *Journal of Accounting and Public Policy*, Vol. 30, No. 3, pp. 236–255.

Li, Z., P. K. Shroff, R. Venkataraman, and I. X. Zhang (2011) "Causes and Consequences of Goodwill Impairment Losses", *Review of Accounting Studies*, Vol. 16, No. 4, pp. 745–778.

Li, K. K., and R. G. Sloan (2017), "Has Goodwill Accounting Gone Bad?" *Review of Accounting Studies*, Vol. 22, No. 2, pp. 964–1003.

Lopez, T. J., C. A. Sisneros, and T. Sorensen (2020) "The Market Pricing of Negative Special Items through Time: an Unintended Consequence of Regulation Change?", *Review of Quantitative Finance and Accounting*, Vol. 54, pp. 753–777.

Lynch, D., M. Romney, B. Stomberg, and D. Wangerin (2019) "Trade-offs between Tax and Financial Reporting Benefits: Evidence from Purchase Price Allocation in Taxable Acquisitions" *Contemporary Accounting Research*, Vol. 36, No. 3, pp. 1223–1226.

Majid, J. A. (2015) "Reporting Incentives, Ownership Concentration by the Largest Outside Shareholder, and Reported Goodwill Impairment Losses", *Journal of Contemporary Accounting & Economics*, Vol. 11, No. 3, pp. 199–214.

Makrominas, M. (2017) "Recognized Intangibles and the Present Value of Growth Options", *Review of Quantitative Finance and Accounting*, Vol. 48, No. 2, pp. 311–329.

Mazzi, F., P. André, D. Dionysiou, and I. Tsalavoutas (2017) "Compliance with Goodwill-Related Mandatory Disclosure Requirements and the Cost of Equity Capital", *Accounting and Business Research*, Vol. 47, No. 3, pp. 268–312.

Nissim, D. and S. H. Penman (2001), "Ration Analysis and Equity Valuation", *Review of Accounting Studies*, Vol. 6, No. 1, pp. 109–154.

Olantem M. E. (2013), "Overpaid Acquisitions and Goodwill Impairment losses — Evidence from the US", *Advances in Accounting*, Vol. 29, No. 2, pp. 243–254.

Oliveira, L., L. L. Rodrigues, and R. Craig (2010), "Intangible Assets and Value Relevance: Evidence from Portuguese Stock Exchange", *The British Accounting Review*, Vol. 42, No. 4, pp. 241–252.

Palepu, K. G., P. M. Healy, and V. L. Bernard (2000) *Business Analysis & Valuation: Using Financial Statements (2nd ed)*, Boston, International Thomson Publishing Inc.

Paugam, L., P. Astolfi, and O. Ramond (2015), "Accounting for Business Combinations: Do Purchase Price Allocations Matter?", *Journal of Accounting and Public Policy*, Vol. 34, No. 4, pp. 362–391.

Ramanna, K., and R. L. Watts (2012), "Evidence on the Use of Unverifiable Estimates in Required Goodwill Impairment", *Review of Accounting Studies*, Vol. 17, No. 4, pp. 749–780.

Roncagliolo, E. and F. Avallone(2022), "Recognition of provisional goodwill: Real need or communication strategy?", *Journal of International Accounting, Auditing and Taxation*, Vol. 49, pp. 1–16.

Russell, M. (2017) "Management Incentives to Recognise Intangible Assets", *Accounting and Finance*, Vol. 57, No. 1, pp. 211–234.

Sahut, J., S. Boulerne and F. Teulon (2011), "Do IFRS Provide Better Information about Intangibles in Europe?", *Review of Accounting and Finance*, Vol. 10, No. 3, pp. 267–290.

Saito, Y. (2018), "The Effect of Nonrecurring Items on Goodwill and CEO Market-based Compensation", *Review of Accounting and Finance*, Vol. 17, No. 2, pp. 150–176.

Shalev, R. I. (2009) "The Information Content of Business Combination Disclosure Level", *The Accounting Review*, Vol. 84, No. 1, pp. 239–270.

Shalev, R., I. Zhang, Y. Zhang (2013), "CEO Compensation and Fair Value Accounting: Evidence from Purchase Price Allocation", *Journal of Accounting Research*, Vol. 51, No. 4, pp. 819–854.

Shimamoto, K. and F. Takeda (2020) "IFRS Adoption and Accounting Conservatism of Japanese Firms with Governance System Transition", *International Advances in Economic Research*, Vol. 26, pp. 161–173.

Sun, L. (2016), "Managerial Ability and Goodwill Impairment", *Advances in Accounting*, Vol. 32, pp. 42–51.

Tahat, Y. A., A. H. Ahmed, and M. M. Alhadab (2018) "The Impact of Intangibles on Firms' Financial and Market Performance: UK evidence", *Review of Quantitative Finance and Accounting*, Vol. 50, No. 4, pp. 1147–1168.

Watts, R. L. (2003), "Conservatism in Accounting, Part I: Explanations and Implications", *Accounting Horizon*, Vol. 17, No. 3, pp. 207–221.

Zang, Y. (2008) "Discretionary Behavior with Respect to the Adoption of SFAS no. 142 and the Behavior of Security Prices", *Review of Accounting and Finance*, Vol. 7, No. 1, pp. 38–68.

Zhang, I. X., and Y. Zhang (2017), "Accounting Discretion and Purchase Price Allocation after Acquisitions", *Journal of Accounting Auditing and Finance*, Vol. 32, No. 2, pp. 241–270.

In Japanese

Kim, J., T. Nakano, and H. Naruoka (2019), IFRS Nini Tekiyō Kigyō no Tokusei (Characteristics of Companies that Voluntarily Adopted the IFRS), *Accounting progress*, Vol. 20, pp. 78–94.

Miyauchi, T. (2020), "Noren no Kaikei Syori wo meguru Jisyō Kenkyu no Tanaoroshi to Tenbō" (A Review and Future Prospects of Empirical Research on Accounting for Goodwill), *Kokusai Kaikei Kenkyū Gakkai Nenpō 2019 (Bulletin of Japanese Association for International Accounting Studies 2019)*, No. 1–2, pp. 29–44.

Miyauchi, T. (2021), "Noren no Kaikei Syori ni kansuru Jisyō Kenkyu Rebyū" (Accounting for Goodwill: Literature Review of Empirical Studies), *Keizai Ronsō (The Economic Review - Kyoto University-)*, Vol. 195, No. 2, pp. 85–113.

Muramiya, K. (2010), "Zanyo Rieki Moderu wo Kousei Suru Zaimu Hiritsu no Tokusei Bunseki" (An Analysis of the Characteristics of Financial Ratios Comprising the Residual Income Model), in Sakurai, H. *Kigyō Kachi Hyouka no Jissyou Bunseki -Moderu to Kaikei Jyōhō no Yūyou Sei Kensyō (An Empirical Analysis of Firm Valuation: Valuation Model and the Usefulness of Accounting Information)*, pp. 230–269, Tokyo, CHOKEIZAI-SHA.

Noguchi, T. (2022), "Noren no Jigo Sokutei to Kachi Kanren Sei – Syoukyaku Apurouchi vs Genson nomi Apurouchi" (Subsequent Measurement of Goodwill and Value Relevance: The Amortization Approach vs. the Impairment-Only Approach), *Kokusai Kaikei Kenkyū Gakkai Nenpō 2022 (Bulletin of Japanese Association for International Accounting Studies 2022)*, No. 1, pp. 19–32.

Obinata, T. (2013) *Rieki Ritu no Jizoku Sei to Heikin Kaiki (Persistence and Mean Reversion of Profitability)*, Tokyo, CHOKEIZAI-SHA.

Sakurai, T. (2010), "Zanyo Rieki no Jizoku Sei to Kigyō Kachi Hyouka" (Persistence of Residual Income and Firm Valuation), in Sakurai, H. *Kigyō Kachi Hyouka no Jissyou Bunseki -Moderu to Kaikei Jyōhō no Yūyou Sei Kensyō (An Empirical Analysis of Firm Valuation: Valuation Model and the Usefulness of Accounting Information)*, pp. 270–315, Tokyo, CHOKEIZAI-SHA.

Chapter 5
Questionnaire Survey of Preparers, Users, and Auditors

Yoshihiro Tokuga, Toshitake Miyauchi, Tomoaki Yamashita, Yuko Asami, and Masaki Yoneyama

5.1 Purpose and Organization of This Chapter

There has been extensive debate, both in practice and academia, regarding the accounting treatment of goodwill.[1] Central to this debate is the disagreement over whether goodwill should be amortized systematically (in accordance with Japan's current approach), or whether it should only be subject to impairment without

This chapter originates from the integration and substantial revision of Tokuga et al. (2020) and Yamashita et al. (2021), incorporating selected sections from Tokuga et al. (2021).

[1] In principle, this study focuses exclusively on acquired (purchased) goodwill and does not address internally generated goodwill. It also assumes the presence of positive goodwill and excludes the treatment of negative goodwill, despite its importance in accounting.

Y. Tokuga (✉)
Faculty of Economics and Business Administration, Department of Business Administration, Kyoto University of Advanced Science, Kyoto, Japan
e-mail: tokuga.yoshihiro.6m@kyoto-u.ac.jp

T. Miyauchi
Faculty of Management, Otemon Gakuin University, Osaka, Japan

T. Yamashita
Faculty of Economics, Department of Business Administration, Fukui Prefectural University, Fukui, Japan

Y. Asami
Graduate School of Economics, Nagoya University, Aichi, Japan

M. Yoneyama
Graduate School of Economics, The University of Tokyo, Tokyo, Japan

Y. Tokuga, M. Yoneyama (eds.), *Controversies Over Accounting for Goodwill*, Contributions to Finance and Accounting,
https://doi.org/10.1007/978-981-92-0156-3_5

systematic amortization, a controversy that continues to generate global discussion.[2]

Under current standards, both U.S. Generally Accepted Accounting Principles (GAAP) and International Financial Reporting Standards (IFRS) require only impairment testing following the acquisition of goodwill and prohibit systematic amortization. In contrast, Japanese GAAP (J-GAAP) mandates both systematic amortization and impairment. Notably, the systematic amortization of goodwill is identified as a key departure from IFRS in Japan's Modified International Standards (JMIS), which represent Japan's adaptation of IFRS (Accounting Standards Board of Japan [ASBJ] 2015a, b). This highlights the emphasis placed on amortization in the Japanese context.[3]

The question of whether goodwill should be amortized systematically remains unresolved, reflecting deeper differences in the underlying perceptions supporting each approach. To examine these perceptions, we conducted a comprehensive survey targeting three key stakeholder groups: preparers of financial statements ("preparers"), users of financial statements ("users"), and Certified Public Accountants (CPAs) ("auditors"). The survey, titled "Survey on Accounting for Goodwill," aimed to clarify stakeholders' views on the appropriate accounting treatment of goodwill.[4]

Previous studies, such as those by the Japan Business Federation (JBF)[5] (Keidanren 2017)[6] and the ASBJ (2015c, 2017),[7] have explored preparers' attitudes toward goodwill accounting. While these surveys were pioneering, they had limited scope, involving only a small number of preparers and users (specifically, analysts). Moreover, despite their influence on standard-setting, auditors have not been

---

[2] In this study, accounting treatments requiring both systematic amortization of goodwill and impairment are referred to as "Systematic amortization with impairment." Treatments requiring only impairment without systematic amortization are referred to as "Impairment-only (non-amortization)" or "Impairment-only."

[3] The accounting treatment of goodwill represents a major difference between IFRS and JMIS.

[4] In the survey, preparers responded via a web form or, in some cases, through paper-based questionnaires. Users and auditors responded exclusively via a web form.

[5] The Japanese Business Federation (Keidanren) is a major economic organization in Japan. According to its website, Keidanren is "a comprehensive economic organization with a membership comprised of 1,574 representative companies of Japan, 106 nationwide industrial associations, and the regional economic organizations for all 47 prefectures (as of April 1, 2025). Its mission as a comprehensive economic organization is to draw upon the vitality of corporations, individuals, and local communities to support corporate activities which contribute to the sustainable development of the Japanese economy and improvement in the quality of life for the Japanese people." (URL: https://www.keidanren.or.jp/en/profile/pro001.html, Accessed: February 19, 2026)

[6] While this survey produced notable insights on the accounting treatment of goodwill, such as perspectives on systematic amortization and the conceptualization of goodwill as an asset, it did not analyze results by firm characteristics.

[7] Although not discussed in this paper, the ASBJ has published a second research report (ASBJ 2016). It has also issued a joint discussion paper titled *"Should goodwill still be amortised? Accounting and disclosure for goodwill"* (ASBJ et al. 2014), in collaboration with the European Financial Reporting Advisory Group (EFRAG) and the Italian accounting standard setter (OIC).

included in prior surveys. Their perspectives may significantly affect goodwill accounting, as their perceptions and decision-making frameworks, such as those involving audit risk, may differ from those of preparers and users.

To address these limitations, our study expands the scope by including a larger and more diverse group of preparers, users, and auditors. Furthermore, we incorporated survey items not found in previous studies to facilitate a more comprehensive academic analysis of goodwill accounting.

Section 5.2 reviews prior surveys, including those conducted by Keidanren and the ASBJ, which form the basis of our research. The section also reviews research conducted by the ASBJ, the Financial Accounting Standards Board (FASB), the staff of the ASBJ and the Hong Kong Institute of Certified Public Accountants (HKICPA), the Chartered Financial Analyst (CFA) Institute, and the International Organization of Securities Commissions (IOSCO). Section 5.3 presents our survey design and the results. Section 5.4 provides an additional analysis of comparing the responses from preparers, users, and auditors. Section 5.5 concludes this chapter.

5.2 Overview of Prior Surveys and the Positioning of Our Survey

Keidanren conducted a survey on the accounting treatment of goodwill following business combinations (Keidanren 2017; hereafter, the "Keidanren Survey"), which is particularly relevant to this study. To clarify the position of our survey, we begin by summarizing the Keidanren Survey. The ASBJ also conducted a related questionnaire survey (ASBJ 2015c), referred to as "ASBJ Survey 1," which addressed subsequent accounting treatment of goodwill. Unlike our survey and the Keidanren Survey, ASBJ Survey 1 did not address the question of whether systematic amortization is preferable. However, several questions in our survey were designed with reference to ASBJ Survey 1. In addition, the ASBJ published a summary of interviews with analysts (ASBJ 2017), referred to as "ASBJ Survey 2." We therefore present an overview of both ASBJ surveys and their relevance to our study.

Beyond these Japanese studies, we also consider international perspectives. Specifically, we review the Financial Accounting Standards Board (FASB)'s *Invitation to Comment—Identifiable Intangible Assets and Subsequent Accounting for Goodwill* (FASB 2019; hereafter, the "FASB Survey") and a joint study conducted by the staff of the ASBJ and the HKICPA regarding goodwill accounting (Staff of the ASBJ and Staff of the HKICPA 2020; hereafter, the "ASBJ and HKICPA Study"). We also introduce findings from the Chartered Financial Analyst (CFA) Institute's survey of investors on goodwill accounting (Peters 2021; hereafter, the "CFA Survey"), as well as findings from the International Organization of Securities Commissions' report (IOSCO 2023b; hereafter, the "IOSCO Report").

The remainder of this section summarizes the following studies in sequence: the Keidanren Survey, ASBJ Survey 1, ASBJ Survey 2, the FASB Survey, the ASBJ and HKICPA Study, the CFA Survey, and the IOSCO Report.

5.2.1 *Keidanren Survey*

The Keidanren Survey sought Japanese firms' views on the accounting treatment of goodwill, specifically comparing systematic amortization with non-amortization. The survey covered 58 companies applying J-GAAP, U.S. GAAP, or IFRS (including those planning to adopt IFRS), with 31 companies responding, a response rate of 53.4% (p. 2).

Although the specific survey questions were not disclosed, the results suggest that firms were asked about (1) their preferred accounting treatment ("amortization with impairment" or "impairment-only"), (2) the nature of goodwill, (3) reasons for supporting a particular treatment after a business combination, (4) current practices in estimating amortization periods, and (5) suggestions for improving impairment testing (p. 6).

According to the survey (p. 4), 94% of respondents favored "amortization with impairment" (p. 8), including firms using U.S. GAAP or IFRS, which do not currently require goodwill amortization.[8] The results also highlighted differing perceptions of goodwill as an asset between proponents of the two approaches and presented various arguments supporting each method (p. 7 and pp. 9–13).

This survey is significant in that it directly captures firms' opinions on goodwill accounting. Despite the limited sample size, it is noteworthy that firms subject to standards prohibiting amortization, such as IFRS and U.S. GAAP, expressed support for reintroducing systematic amortization.

However, the Keidanren Survey has limitations beyond sample size. The sample is biased toward certain industries, as it primarily targeted members of the Subcommittee on Corporate Accounting of the Financial and Capital Markets Committee of Keidanren. Among the 31 respondents, 15 were in manufacturing, 10 in finance, and 6 in other industries (p. 2). This concentration limits the generalizability of the findings.

Furthermore, the survey's results were presented qualitatively, without accompanying quantitative analysis. From both academic and policy perspectives, a detailed statistical examination of the characteristics of firms supporting each approach and the reasons for their positions would be valuable. Given these limitations, we conducted an independent survey that builds on the Keidanren findings.

[8] However, the findings of a survey conducted by the Keizai Doyukai (Japan Association of Corporate Executives) Regulatory and Competition Policy Committee in fiscal year 2022 among its members and startup executives reported that 153 out of 163 respondents (approximately 94%) supported either abolishing the systematic amortization of goodwill or making systematic amortization optional under J-GAAP (Keizai Doyukai 2023, URL: https://www.doyukai.or.jp/policyproposals/2023/230706.html, Accessed: February 20, 2026). This result differs from that of the Keidanren survey.

5.2.2 ASBJ Survey 1

We now summarize the relevant content of ASBJ Survey 1, which informed the design of our own survey. This survey did not assess support for or against goodwill amortization, but rather gathered factual information on current amortization practices and views on determining the amortization period in accounting standards.[9]

Questionnaires were sent to 56 large Japanese multinational firms, with 26 responses received (response rate: 46.4%). Among respondents, 15 were manufacturing firms (58%), five were financial firms (19%), and six represented other industries (23%) (p. 8, para. 18). Three respondents adopted IFRS, four used U.S. GAAP, and the remainder followed J-GAAP (p. 7, para. 17).

The main topics of the survey included (1) factors considered when estimating the goodwill amortization period, (2) the amortization method employed (including whether methods other than straight-line were used), (3) whether goodwill's residual value was estimated as other than zero, and (4) preferred regulatory approaches for setting amortization periods under a reinstated goodwill amortization requirement (pp. 24–26, Appendix-I). Items (1) and (4) overlap with the Keidanren Survey, while items (2) and (3) are unique to ASBJ Survey 1. Notably, the survey found that no respondents reported using amortization methods other than the straight-line method (p. 14, para. 30), and none reported estimating a residual value other than zero (p. 15, para. 31).

Regarding item (1), many firms indicated that their estimation of the amortization period was based on the duration over which the acquiree, on a stand-alone basis, is expected to generate higher future cash flows, the period over which synergies between acquirer and acquiree are expected to materialize, and the expected investment payback period (p. 10, para. 21(a), (b)). Reported amortization periods for major mergers were typically 20 years, 10 years, and 5 years, in that order (p. 12, Chart 2; p. 28, Table 2, Appendix II). By industry, most manufacturing firms reported amortization periods within 10 years, while many financial firms reported 20 years (pp. 12–13, paras. 24–27). Concerning item (4), most companies supported the use of a maximum amortization period, potentially subject to a "rebuttable presumption."[10] A majority favored setting the maximum at 20 years (pp. 15–16, para. 33).[11]

As with the Keidanren Survey, the ASBJ Survey 1 suffers from limited generalizability due to sample bias. The targeted firms were large multinationals with experience in large-scale mergers and acquisitions domestically and/or internationally,

[9]This study includes a review of disclosures by J-GAAP firms listed in the JPX Nikkei 400, and a limited academic review on the usefulness of goodwill amortization expenses. However, these topics are not discussed here.

[10]The "rebuttable presumption" refers to the assumption that a default amortization period must not be exceeded unless justified with a rebuttal.

[11]Although a direct comparison is not feasible, responses to the Keidanren Survey on amortization period limits tended to support maximum durations of 10 or 20 years.

making it difficult to extrapolate the findings to the broader corporate population in Japan. To address these limitations in our own study, we asked respondents about the factors influencing their determination of amortization periods and included a distinct question regarding how amortization periods should be prescribed in accounting standards.[12]

5.2.3 ASBJ Survey 2

The ASBJ Survey 2 is an interview-based study of 11 prominent Japanese analysts, including one credit analyst. It examines: (1) how analysts use financial information on business combinations disclosed in financial statements to assess firm valuation or creditworthiness; (2) which goodwill-related disclosures are most useful; and (3) which accounting treatment of goodwill (impairment only, systematic amortization with impairment, or direct write-off) is most appropriate (p. 10, para. 10). The survey also asked analysts to indicate their preferred approach to goodwill accounting after an acquisition: impairment only (non-amortization) or systematic amortization with impairment. This question is central to our own survey. Among equity analysts, regardless of their emphasis on cash flows or a combination of accounting earnings, net assets, and cash flows, opinions on goodwill amortization were divided. Some supported amortization, while others did not. The credit analyst favored goodwill amortization.

The use of goodwill-related accounting information by analysts is frequently referenced in international accounting standard-setting discussions (p. 7, para. 4), yet supporting evidence remains limited. The ASBJ Survey 2 contributes to this gap by investigating how analysts evaluate such information in security analysis and how they incorporate the assumption of potential goodwill impairment. The results reveal how both equity and credit analysts actually use goodwill-related disclosures, yielding valuable insights.

Although the ASBJ Survey 2 offers detailed qualitative responses from a small number of Japanese analysts, its scope is limited. The extent to which analysts support systematic goodwill amortization remains unclear.[13] As a result, generalizing the findings to the broader population of financial statement users is difficult. Furthermore, the study lacks quantitative analysis regarding the use of goodwill-related information in securities analysis. To address these limitations, our survey

---

[12] Only respondents who selected "Systematic amortization with impairment" as their preferred goodwill treatment following an acquisition were asked about the amortization period. This was deemed appropriate, as it allowed for targeted insights from supporters of systematic amortization.

[13] This point highlights the strengths and limitations of interview versus questionnaire-based research. While questionnaires facilitate generalization, they often fail to establish causal relationships between factors (Bloomfield et al. 2016; Suzuki 2016).

expanded the sample size and included both questions on the accounting treatment of goodwill and on its practical use in security analysis.

5.2.4 FASB Survey

The FASB conducted its study after our primary research was completed, seeking feedback on whether the current standards for subsequent goodwill accounting provide benefits that justify their costs for public firms. Specifically, the FASB released the "*Invitation to Comment—Identifiable Intangible Assets and Subsequent Accounting for Goodwill*," open for public comment from July 9 to October 7, 2019. A total of 101 comments were received from preparers, users, auditors, standard setters, academic institutions, and individuals.[14]

The study focused on four main concerns. The first was whether to change the subsequent accounting treatment of goodwill from the current impairment-only model to systematic amortization with impairment. The FASB sought stakeholder input on the following questions: (1) Do the benefits of the impairment-only model outweigh its costs?, (2) Is systematic amortization with impairment more cost-beneficial than impairment only?, (3) If amortization were reintroduced, what amortization period would be appropriate?, and (4) How might the impairment test be improved in terms of cost-effectiveness? (pp. 6–16).[15] The remaining concerns addressed the recognition of intangible assets in business combinations (pp. 16–21),[16] disclosure practices for goodwill and intangible assets (pp. 21–24), and comparability between public firms, private firms, and not-for-profit entities (pp. 24–26).[17]

In our research, we focused on two issues discussed in the FASB Survey: the conceptual meaning of goodwill and the desirable amortization period. We excluded the other topics from our survey.

---

[14] See "Comment Letter Summary on the Invitation to Comment, *Identifiable Intangible Assets and Subsequent Accounting for Goodwill*" (URL: https://storage.fasb.org/Public_Comment_Letter_Summary.pdf, Accessed: January 30, 2025). This section focuses only on concerns raised by the FASB Survey regarding goodwill accounting.

[15] To reduce the costs associated with the goodwill impairment test, the FASB simplified the test procedures through ASU 2011–08 (FASB 2011) and ASU 2017–04 (FASB 2017).

[16] Early communication of information could be enhanced by disclosing "changes in facts and circumstances that could lead to a future goodwill impairment loss" (p. 23), even though "the facts and circumstances resulting in a goodwill impairment loss" (p. 23) are already disclosed. The FASB requested comments on the benefits and costs of providing such additional disclosure (p. 23).

[17] For private firms and not-for-profit entities, goodwill amortization is optional. The FASB, therefore, solicited comments on the comparability of goodwill and intangible asset information between public and private/not-for-profit entities (pp. 24–26).

5.2.5 ASBJ and HKICPA Study

The joint study by the ASBJ and HKICPA includes a quantitative comparison of goodwill balances among U.S., European, Hong Kong, and Japanese firms (Part 1), followed by a conceptual discussion on three issues[18]: (i) the scope and measurement basis of acquired goodwill (Part 2), (ii) the case for reintroducing amortization alongside impairment (Part 3), and (iii) the amortization period and method (Part 4). The study concludes with separate viewpoints from the ASBJ and HKICPA staff.

5.2.5.1 Quantitative Survey (Part 1)

The quantitative research section analyzed trends in goodwill and impairment losses from 2014 to 2018 across firms listed in the S&P 500 (U.S.), S&P Europe 350 (Europe), Hang Seng Composite Index (Hong Kong), and Nikkei 225 (Japan). For Japan, the sample included firms in the Nikkei 225 that adopted IFRS in 2018; in some analyses, only firms applying IFRS throughout the period were included.[19] The results showed an overall increase in goodwill balances in all regions, with the trend in Japan being particularly pronounced. The study concluded that under the impairment-only model, the issue of "too little, too late" in recognizing impairment losses is likely to arise, due to the long time required to expense goodwill (pp. 17–18, para. 1.20).[20]

5.2.5.2 Scope and Measurement Basis for Acquired Goodwill (Part 2)

The study distinguished between internally generated and acquired goodwill, focusing only on the latter. It argued that the appropriate measurement basis for acquired goodwill is historical cost (acquisition cost), not current fair value (p. 21, para. 2.8).

5.2.5.3 Arguments for Reintroducing Amortization in Addition to Impairment (Part 3)

The study supported reintroducing amortization as part of the subsequent accounting for goodwill (pp. 32–33, para. 3.26; p. 34, para. 3.27). However, the ASBJ and HKICPA staff offered different rationales, and their perspectives were presented separately.

[18] "Goodwill" in this study refers specifically to acquired goodwill.

[19] See the ASBJ and HKICPA Study (p. 9, Note 2) for a Japanese sample.

[20] The time required to fully expense goodwill is calculated as the prior period's goodwill balance divided by the current period's goodwill expense (pp. 16–17, paras. 1.17–1.18).

The ASBJ staff identified three main areas of disagreement concerning the merits of goodwill amortization: (1) differing views on the scope of goodwill, (2) differing interpretations of its nature, and (3) differing perspectives on the appropriate accounting method to reflect that nature (pp. 22–23, para. 3.3). Their views on each issue are summarized as follows:

1. Scope of goodwill
   - (ASBJ Staff View) In light of the financial reporting objective (to present useful information to assist financial statement users in assessing the value of an entity, not to directly indicate the value of an entity), they distinguish between internally generated and acquired goodwill and limit their discussion to the latter (p. 23, paras. 3.5–3.6).
2. Nature of acquired goodwill
   - (ASBJ Staff View) The "going concern element" and the "synergies element," both of which are components of goodwill, are depletable elements, and (acquired) goodwill is an overall wasting asset (p. 25, para. 3.9; p. 29, para. 3.18).
3. Accounting treatments
   - (ASBJ Staff View) It is the amortization approach, rather than the impairment-only approach, that can depict that the acquired goodwill is a wasting asset (consumption of acquired goodwill) (pp. 31–32, para. 3.24).

Next, the HKICPA staff introduced the concept of "economic goodwill" (including acquired goodwill) as a higher-level category encompassing both acquired and internally generated goodwill, thereby organizing the goodwill concept more comprehensively. This concept did not appear in the ASBJ staff discussion and reflected a unique perspective of the HKICPA staff. Economic goodwill is defined as "the difference between the fair value of an entity and its identifiable net assets (book value) recogni[z]ed under prevailing accounting standards" (p. 35, para. 3.32). At acquisition, the values of acquired goodwill and economic goodwill coincide; however, these values diverge over time (p. 36, para. 3.38; p. 38, para. 3.44).

Like the ASBJ staff, the HKICPA staff argued that goodwill is a wasting asset (p. 38, para. 3.43; p. 39, Note 31). They maintained that reintroducing goodwill amortization is necessary to improve subsequent accounting for goodwill. Amortization reflects that acquired goodwill may no longer represent the value of the underlying acquired entity over time (p. 39, para. 3.48), aligns with accounting's role in showing the use of economic resources over time (p. 40, para. 3.49), and demonstrates that acquired goodwill has been consumed (p. 40, para. 3.51).[21] Additionally, the HKICPA staff expressed concern that under an impairment-only

[21] The HKICPA staff noted that amortizing acquired goodwill enhances comparability between firms growing through acquisitions and those growing organically, compared to a model that relies solely on impairment (p. 42, para. 3.56).

approach, accumulating goodwill balances might create adverse management incentives, such as avoiding impairment losses, engaging in big bath accounting, and overvaluing acquired goodwill (pp. 43–44, paras. 3.60–3.61). These concerns further support their preference for reintroducing amortization (p. 44, paras. 3.63–3.64).[22]

5.2.5.4 Amortization Period and Method (Part 4)

The ASBJ and HKICPA staff also presented their views on the amortization period and method. The ASBJ staff considered two approaches[23] to determining the amortization period for goodwill (p. 48, para. 4.8), supporting the first approach as it provides useful information to users (p. 49, para. 4.11). However, they proposed an upper limit of 10 years for the amortization period (p. 51, para. 4.15), based on relevant empirical studies (albeit indirect evidence).[24] They emphasized that this 10-year period should not create a rebuttable presumption, to facilitate international consensus (p. 51, para. 4.15).

The HKICPA staff maintained that the acquiring entity should determine the amortization period based on the expected duration of the business combination's effects (p. 52, para. 4.18). While agreeing that management judgment is essential, they opposed mandatory upper or lower limits on the amortization period. Nevertheless, they suggested a rebuttable presumption that amortization periods should not exceed a specific timeframe, such as 10 years, to prevent excessively long estimates (pp. 53–54, para. 4.22).

Regarding the amortization method, the HKICPA staff argued that management should apply judgment to select the pattern that best reflects expected acquisition benefits, rather than restricting amortization to the straight-line method. However, they recommended using the straight-line method when reliability concerns arise (p. 54, paras. 4.23–4.24).

5.2.6 CFA Survey

In addition to earlier surveys conducted in Japan, the CFA Institute administered an international survey in 2020 targeting its portfolio manager and analyst members regarding the accounting treatment of goodwill. Notably, this survey coincided with

---

[22] The HKICPA staff also observed that if acquired goodwill accumulates under an impairment-only regime and is later written down all at once due to adverse economic conditions, the result could exacerbate the business cycle (p. 43, para. 3.60(a)).

[23] The first approach is to "[r]equire management to estimate the amorti[z]ation period, taking into account the nature of" goodwill. The second approach is to require the accounting standard setter to "determine the amorti[z]aion period" (p. 48, para. 4.8).

[24] An alternative approach proposes a default amortization period of 10 years, consistent with the upper limits previously discussed, while allowing shorter periods in certain cases (p. 51, para. 4.17).

the timing of our own, and several topics overlapped. The CFA Institute randomly selected 23,800 CFA® charter holders and received 1607 responses, yielding a response rate of 7%.

Consistent with widespread opinion, the survey first asked respondents about their preferred direction for goodwill accounting (p. 26, Chart 1). Among them, 38% supported enhanced disclosure for both recognition and measurement of goodwill, while 20% favored improvements to the current impairment-only model.[25] Only 31% supported the reintroduction of amortization. Respondents were also asked about their perceptions of goodwill as an asset: 45% considered it a wasting asset, 29% disagreed, and 26% were neutral.

A majority of respondents (72% of 222 respondents) believed that firms fail to recognize goodwill impairment on time (p. 59, Chart 16B). However, fewer investors (52% of 193 respondents; p. 61, Chart 18B) believed that the market priced in impairment information before it was officially recognized. Despite concerns about timeliness, many respondents still viewed impairment as informative. For example, 73% of 179 respondents agreed that impairment signals unsuccessful acquisitions, and 80% of 192 respondents believed it helps hold management accountable for poor decisions (p. 63, Chart 20B; p. 64, Chart 21B).

The survey also explored views on goodwill amortization. A majority (61% of 386 respondents) indicated that amortization was inferior to impairment-only approach because it obscures differences between successful and unsuccessful acquisitions (p. 81, Chart 31B). Moreover, 63% of 383 respondents believed amortization distorts profitability metrics such as ROE and ROA (p. 82, Chart 32B). Interestingly, only 50% of 381 respondents considered amortization less useful for investment analysis (p. 83, Chart 33B). When asked about the potential advantages of amortization, 51% of 385 respondents agreed it was beneficial because it compensated for delayed impairment recognition (p. 84, Chart 34). However, fewer respondents viewed amortization as preferable due to administrative convenience (46% of 383 respondents, p. 85, Chart 35B) or its potential to better match revenues and expenses (38% of 383 respondents, p. 87, Chart 36).[26]

The survey also inquired about preferred amortization periods if amortization were reinstated.[27] Nearly half (49% of 364 respondents) supported a "cash flow-based amortization period," defined as the period over which acquisition-related cash flows are received (pp. 92–93, Chart 37). In contrast, fewer supported a fixed default period (22%) or a management-determined period within a defined range (26%). Only 3% favored an amortization period set entirely at management's discretion (p. 93, Chart 37).

---

[25] The interpretation was that 58% of respondents supported the current impairment-only approach. However, the CFA Survey also revealed that many respondents favoring improved disclosure believed such changes should precede, or be independent of, changes in goodwill accounting (pp. 29–30, Charts 3–4). Hence, this interpretation should be treated cautiously.

[26] Survey results varied by region (p. 86). For example, only 34% of U.S. respondents agreed with this view.

[27] While we do not detail all results here, the CFA Survey asked multiple questions concerning the need for improved disclosures in goodwill accounting and the areas requiring such improvements.

Before presenting these survey findings, the CFA Institute also analyzed empirical data on goodwill balances in the U.S. (2018) and internationally (2019, including the U.S.). They examined goodwill as a proportion of equity and total assets, concluding that goodwill balances are substantial, except in Asia and India. Based on this analysis, the CFA Institute urged accounting standard setters, including the FASB and the International Accounting Standards Board (IASB), to consider the economic implications of reintroducing amortization (p. 25). They emphasized that such decisions "must be contextualized with real data, not just accounting theory" (p. 25). Regardless of the merit of this argument, it is notable that the CFA Survey expressed significant concern about the broader economic consequences of reintroducing goodwill amortization.

5.2.7 *IOSCO Report*

The IOSCO Report provides recommendations concerning the accounting treatment of goodwill for issuers,[28] audit committees (or those charged with governance; TCWG),[29] external auditors, and standard setters. These recommendations were informed by a 2021 IOSCO survey of Committee 1 members and stakeholder feedback gathered during the consultation process.[30] The report responded to concerns about the delayed recognition of goodwill impairment ("too little, too late") and the appropriateness of future cash flow projections used in impairment testing, along with related disclosures (p. 3). Notably, the IOSCO Report predated the release of the IASB Exposure Draft (ED) (IASB 2024a, b).

According to survey results from 18 IOSCO Committee 1 members (IOSCO Report, Chap. 3), 83% expressed concern with the current accounting treatment of goodwill. Key issues raised regarding issuers included the excessive allocation of acquisition payments to goodwill and the failure to properly recognize or measure identifiable intangible assets (p. 9). Respondents also noted a lack of entity-specific disclosure on the components of goodwill (p. 9), concerns over the assumptions used in forecasting cash flows for impairment testing, and weaknesses in internal controls over the impairment process (p. 10). Additionally, inconsistencies were observed between these assumptions and management commentary (p. 10).

Regarding audit committees (or TCWG), some respondents identified limited access to information necessary to evaluate the appropriateness of impairment testing (p. 11). They called for improved interaction between audit committees (or

---

[28] Although we use the term "preparers" for those drafting financial statements, we use "issuers" here in line with terminology used in the IOSCO Report.

[29] When referring to audit committees, the IOSCO Report used the phrase "audit committees (or TCWG)." We adopt the same phrasing in this chapter.

[30] Survey findings are also summarized in IOSCO (2023a), which lists the questions posed to stakeholders. The results of this consultation are discussed in the IOSCO Report.

TCWG), management, and external auditors (pp. 11–12). Concerns about external auditors included insufficient challenge to management assumptions and inadequate evidence collection during impairment testing (p. 12). Respondents also cited a lack of disclosure about these assumptions and indicated that, in some cases, auditors failed to apply appropriate professional skepticism, relying instead on mechanical checks of IFRS-required disclosures (p. 13).

Similar concerns emerged in stakeholder consultation feedback (IOSCO Report, Chap. 3). Stakeholders provided perspectives on how issuers, audit committees, and external auditors could improve practices and offered feedback directed at the IASB. Notably, there were divergent views both between and within stakeholder groups.[31]

For instance, regarding the reliability of assumptions used in impairment testing, investor groups, external auditors, and regulators suggested that firms employ internal or independent external experts. In contrast, some issuers contended that expert involvement would not resolve the core issues (p. 18). While investor groups and regulators criticized current disclosure practices as inadequate, issuer respondents argued that expanded disclosure would not resolve the "too little, too late" issue and would impose disproportionate costs (p. 19). Feedback to the standard setter reflected similar divergence, with some investors believing that enhanced disclosure could prompt more timely impairment recognition, while others disagreed (p. 21). Stakeholders also offered specific suggestions for improving impairment testing, including expanded disclosure requirements (pp. 23–25). Nevertheless, some argued that significant improvements to the current impairment-only approach may be unfeasible and advocated for goodwill amortization as a more practical and effective solution to the timeliness issue (p. 25).

In sum, the IOSCO Report highlights stakeholder concerns regarding goodwill impairment testing and related disclosures. It presents a range of viewpoints, particularly those of investors, who generally support enhanced disclosure in the accounting for goodwill.

5.2.8 Content of This Survey Study

This survey shares some of the same issues explored in the Keidanren and ASBJ Surveys but is designed from an independent perspective. While several questions were developed with reference to the content and results of the Keidanren and ASBJ surveys,[32] we also included new questions not addressed in these earlier studies.[33]

[31] However, this survey did not quantitatively analyze stakeholder differences regarding the concerns identified.

[32] In designing the questionnaire, we also referred to the Suda et al. (2011a, b) survey.

[33] Note that there are differences in the methodology, question order, and wording, including variations in the content of the questions.

The following sections outline the key topics covered in our survey and introduce the specific questions posed.

1. *Which accounting treatment of goodwill is preferred by preparers, users, and auditors: "Impairment-only (non-amortization)" or "Systematic amortization with impairment"?*

Japanese market participants, including corporations, are generally believed to favor the systematic amortization with impairment (hereafter, "Systematic amortization with impairment") as the accounting treatment of acquired goodwill.[34] This preference is supported by the Keidanren Survey. However, the Keidanren Survey's limited scope restricts its ability to reflect broader preparer preferences. Similarly, ASBJ Survey 2, which relies on analyst interviews, provides only partial insights.[35,36] To address these limitations, our survey targets a broader range of respondents, including preparers, users, and auditors. Notably, auditors were not included in the Keidanren or ASBJ surveys.

The Keidanren Survey required respondents to choose between the impairment-only approach (hereafter, "Impairment-only") and "Systematic amortization with impairment." In contrast, we introduced an additional option to identify respondents who are open to either treatment, thereby clarifying the extent of active support for systematic amortization.

Our survey also asked respondents to explain their preference between "Systematic amortization with impairment" and "Impairment-only." While previous surveys touched on this issue, they did not quantify the reasons behind each preference. We aimed to fill this gap by offering a more detailed analysis.[37] In cases where respondents preferred systematic amortization, we further explored issues such as the determinants of the amortization period and appropriate regulatory guidance. Although ASBJ Survey 1 also addressed these questions, our results complement and extend prior findings.

2. *What kind of assets do preparers, users, and auditors consider acquired goodwill to be?*

A central objective of this study is to clarify how preparers, users, and auditors conceptualize acquired goodwill. The question of how goodwill should be accounted for depends largely on how its economic nature is understood.

---

[34] See ASBJ (2015c) for a discussion of the advantages and disadvantages of prohibiting systematic amortization of goodwill in Japan.

[35] ASBJ Survey 2 does not indicate the percentage of respondents who support or oppose goodwill amortization. Instead, it highlights the diversity of views and presents the rationale behind each.

[36] Although various studies using archival data (e.g., financial statements and stock prices) have examined the impact of prohibiting systematic amortization of goodwill on the usefulness of financial information (e.g., Li and Sloan 2017), they do not reveal the perspectives of key market participants, namely preparers. Clarifying these perspectives is a strength of our survey-based analysis.

[37] In this survey, we included "Either (is fine)" as a response option to accommodate respondents who are indifferent to the choice of treatment.

If goodwill reflects excess earning power, its value is expected to decline due to market competition. Research suggests that this erosion may occur rapidly (Obinata 2013; Li and Sloan 2017).[38] However, other perspectives argue that goodwill's value can be partially retained or may not necessarily diminish (Daigo 2007; ASBJ 2015a; IASB 2020, 2024b).[39]

To investigate this issue, our survey not only asked which accounting treatment respondents prefer but also how they conceptualize goodwill. Specifically, we explored whether they view goodwill as a semi-permanent, non-amortizable asset and what components they believe constitute goodwill. The questionnaire design drew on insights from the Keidanren Survey.

3. *How do users treat the amount of goodwill and goodwill amortization in their securities analysis?*

ASBJ Survey 2 conducted interviews with analysts to assess how they use information related to business combinations and its disclosure. Since understanding how analysts and other users incorporate goodwill-related data into security analysis is critical from both academic and policy perspectives, our survey included related questions. We asked users how they treat the amount of goodwill and goodwill amortization in their analyses, and whether they believe the post-amortization goodwill balance provides useful information.

4. *To what extent is goodwill difficult to audit, and does auditing goodwill increase the risk of litigation from shareholders, etc., and the risk of being pointed out in quality control reviews, etc.?*

This study also addresses audit-specific issues related to goodwill and audit quality. The accounting treatment of goodwill poses significant audit challenges due to the extensive scope for managerial discretion (Ayres et al. 2019; Carcello et al. 2020). To assess auditors' views, we asked how difficult they consider auditing goodwill relative to other assets. We also inquired whether they perceive an increased risk of litigation from shareholders and heightened scrutiny in quality control reviews by the Japanese Institute of Certified Public Accountants (JICPA) and monitoring by the Certified Public Accountants and Auditing Oversight Board (CPAAOB) of Japan.

5. *Is goodwill impairment recognized in a timely manner, and is the amount of impairment estimated appropriately?*

We posed the following question to auditors: "From an auditor's perspective, do you believe goodwill impairment is appropriately recognized?" This aimed to

[38] Li and Sloan (2017), citing the example of trademarks in note 2 (p. 968), point out that "while the future benefits represented by goodwill are very difficult to forecast, they may often be quite short-lived."

[39] Dickinson and Sommers (2012) suggest that firms' strategic actions to gain a competitive advantage contribute to sustaining their profitability.

determine whether impairment losses are recognized in a timely manner under both "Systematic amortization with impairment" (J-GAAP) and "Impairment-only" (U.S. GAAP/IFRS) approaches. A subsequent question addressed whether the estimated impairment losses were appropriate, excessive, or underestimated.

The issue of "too little, too late" recognition of impairment has been widely discussed in international accounting debate (IASB 2020; ASBJ and HKICPA Study). Scholars have noted that impairment accounting, given its discretionary nature, can be used for earnings management, including "big bath" accounting (Francis et al. 1996; Riedl 2004). To probe these concerns, we asked auditors about their perceptions of such risks and the factors that may contribute to inappropriate impairment recognition.

Additionally, we asked whether reporting net assets excluding goodwill on the balance sheet would motivate preparers to recognize impairments more promptly. This question is linked to a proposal by the IASB (2020) to disclose total equity excluding goodwill (IASB 2020, pp. 75–77, paras. 3.107–3.115; pp. 104–105, Appendix—Presenting total equity excluding goodwill).[40]

6. *How would preparers, users, and auditors evaluate possible accounting treatments of goodwill apart from the treatment allowed in the current accounting standards (optional use of "amortization" or "non-amortization" and theoretically possible alternative treatments)?*

In addition to the core questions, the survey asked respondents to evaluate potential accounting treatments of goodwill beyond those currently permitted under existing standards. Specifically, we explored two possible alternatives: (1) Allowing preparers to choose either "Systematic amortization with impairment" or "Impairment-only" for individual acquisitions, subject to disclosure of the rationale for their selection; and (2) Allowing non-amortization for goodwill that meets conditions set by the standard setter, while requiring systematic amortization for all other goodwill.

These options aim to introduce conditional or selective flexibility into goodwill accounting. The current policy debate primarily centers on the dichotomy between "Systematic amortization with impairment" and "Impairment-only." However, other methods, some historically applied or theoretically conceivable, have also been proposed (ASBJ et al. 2014). These include (1) retaining the historical cost of goodwill with no requirement for amortization or impairment; (2) applying systematic amortization without impairment testing; (3) revaluing goodwill at fair value on a continuous basis, with changes reflected in profit or loss; (4) Charging goodwill immediately to earnings[41]; and (5) Charging goodwill directly to equity (retained earnings).

[40] Note that as indicated in the ED published by the IASB in 2024, the IASB decided not to consider further "whether to require an entity to present on its statement of financial position an amount representing total equity excluding goodwill" (IASB 2024b, p. 5, para. BC16).

[41] ASBJ Survey 2 reports that some analysts support the immediate amortization of goodwill, noting that both systematic amortization and non-amortization present issues.

The survey asked whether respondents consider any of these five alternative treatments preferable to the two dominant methods currently under debate.

7. *Do additional disclosures and accounting treatments of goodwill affect corporate behaviors?*

The survey also investigated whether additional disclosure requirements or changes in accounting treatments of goodwill would influence corporate behavior. One question asked whether requiring the disclosure of net assets excluding goodwill would encourage more timely and appropriate recognition of goodwill impairments.[42] This proposal is intended to address the ongoing issue of delayed and insufficient recognition of goodwill impairment losses, often referred to as the "too little, too late" problem. The disclosure of net assets less goodwill functions as a hypothetical measure, simulating the effect of immediately writing off goodwill from the balance sheet. If impairment is not recognized despite the need for it, such disclosure would more accurately reflect the firm's financial condition. While this might incentivize more proactive impairment recognition, it could also lead to misinterpretation for firms whose goodwill represents genuine excess earning power.

Another question addressed whether the method of accounting for goodwill, specifically, the presence or absence of systematic amortization, affects corporate M&A behavior.[43,44] There is a growing body of empirical research examining the link between accounting standards, financial reporting quality, and firms' real investment decisions (Biddle and Hilary 2006; Biddle et al. 2009; Shroff 2017; Garcia Lara et al. 2016; Gao and Yu 2020; Nakano et al. 2015). These studies suggest that financial reporting quality and specific accounting treatments influence not only capital investment decisions but also acquisition activities.[45]

Francis and Martin (2010) find that timely loss recognition was associated with more profitable acquisitions. In contrast, Kravet (2014) suggests that such recognition might discourage firms from undertaking economically viable but risky acquisitions, thus potentially contributing to underinvestment. Cedergren et al. (2015) report that following the elimination of systematic amortization in the U.S., post-acquisition profitability declined and acquisition overpayment increased. Similarly, in the ASBJ Survey 2, analysts noted that systematic amortization of goodwill could influence managerial behavior in M&A transactions, both positively and negatively.[46]

---

[42] As noted in Note 40, the IASB decided not to require firms to present the amount of total equity excluding goodwill (IASB 2024b, p.5, para. BC16).

[43] The Keidanren Survey addressed related topics, particularly under the section "Decisions to Adopt IFRS and Accounting for Goodwill." It reports that many firms adopting IFRS considered the implications of de-amortizing goodwill at the time of adoption.

[44] This survey asked only whether the accounting treatment of goodwill affects M&A decision-making. Future research could explore the timing and mechanisms through which such accounting treatments influence M&A decisions.

[45] Research on "real effects" has recently gained academic attention (Roychowdhury et al. 2019; Shakespeare 2020). Relatedly, Amano (2020) notes that the voluntary adoption of IFRS may have influenced firms' investment behavior in intangible assets.

[46] ASBJ Survey 2 also reports that some analysts expressed similar concerns.

Table 5.1 Survey topics addressed in this survey

Topics	Preparers	Users	Auditors
Whether "Impairment-only" or "Systematic amortization with impairment" is desirable (or whether "Either" is acceptable) for accounting for goodwill	✓	✓	✓
When amortizing goodwill, what amortization period is desirable?	✓	✓	✓
What is the nature of goodwill as an asset?	✓	✓	✓
How is the amount of goodwill and amortization of goodwill used in the securities analysis?		✓	
To what extent is goodwill difficult to audit, and does the audit of goodwill increase the risk of litigation from shareholders and other parties and the risk of being pointed out in quality control reviews, etc.?			✓
Is goodwill impairment recognized in a timely manner and is the estimate of the amount appropriate?			✓
How are the possible accounting treatments of goodwill away from the current approaches (optional and conditional use of "amortization" and "non-amortization" and logically possible alternative treatments) evaluated?	✓	✓	✓
Does goodwill and related additional information (net assets less goodwill) enhance the timeliness of impairment recognition?	✓	✓	✓
Does the subsequent treatment of goodwill affect corporate investment behavior such as M&A?	✓	✓	✓

In light of these findings, it is important, both from academic and policy perspectives, to understand how goodwill accounting treatments affect managerial decision-making in mergers and acquisitions.

Table 5.1 summarizes the survey topics. It identifies which questions were common to all respondent groups (preparers, users, and auditors) and which were targeted to specific groups. Topics marked with ✓ were addressed in each respective survey.

5.3 Survey Design and Results

5.3.1 Survey Design

The survey was conducted via an online response form and questionnaire, targeting preparers, users (securities analysts), and auditors (CPAs).[47] First, we classified the preparers into two groups:

[47] In reviewing the questionnaire and web response form, we aimed to ensure comparability with prior surveys referenced in Sect. 5.1. We also conducted three pilot tests with practitioners to assess whether the questionnaire elicited the intended responses.

1. Keidanren[48] member firms (including both listed and non-listed firms).
2. Firms listed on the First Section of the Tokyo Stock Exchange (excluding those already included as Keidanren members), for which mailing addresses were obtained from Nikkei NEEDS.

For the first group, an email invitation was sent to Keidanren member firms, requesting responses via a web form. Valid responses totaled 263 out of 1379 (19.07%) for Keidanren-affiliated firms and 184 out of 1339 (13.74%) for non-Keidanren-affiliated firms. Overall, 447 out of 2718 firms (16.45%) provided valid responses.[49] Duplicate responses from the same company were excluded, as were responses that omitted answers to the primary survey question (Q1 below). However, incomplete responses were retained where possible for subsequent questions. Two responses were excluded due to internal inconsistencies between answers to Q1 and Q3. The survey period for preparers was from July 23 to October 20, 2018.

For users, the survey targeted practicing analysts affiliated with the Securities Analysts Association of Japan (SAAJ) and individuals registered with the Financial Accounting Standards Foundation as international accounting personnel. The focus was on those actively engaged in securities analysis utilizing accounting information. Among 673 individuals surveyed,[50] 130 valid responses were received, resulting in a 19.32% response rate. All user responses were submitted via a web form.

While much of the questionnaire mirrored that used for preparers, it included additional questions specific to users, such as the treatment of goodwill amortization in financial statement analysis. The survey period for users was from July 24 to October 20, 2018.

Auditors were surveyed from among the partners of four major audit firms and six second-tier audit firms, totaling 1961 partners (1680 from major [Big 4] audit firms and 281 from second-tier audit firms). Responses were collected via a web form. After excluding two responses due to inconsistencies, 620 valid responses remained, yielding a response rate of 31.62%. The survey was conducted in two phases: December 1, 2020, to January 10, 2021, and April 3 to April 30, 2021.

[48] As in the previous section, "Keidanren" refers to the Japan Business Federation (JBF).

[49] One questionnaire was returned as undeliverable.

[50] Mr. Makoto Kaimasu, Director of the SAAJ, distributed the questionnaire to analysts, requesting their cooperation. It was sent to: (1) members of the SAAJ Disclosure Study Group; (2) members of this group and its industry-specific subcommittees; and (3) respondents to the "Securities Analysts' Selection of Excellent Disclosure Companies" survey. Among the 26 registered international accounting personnel, four overlapped with active analysts and full-time managers and were excluded from this count.

5.3.2 *Responses from Preparers*

5.3.2.1 Characteristics of Respondents

When respondents provided their firm name and, where applicable, securities code, their responses were matched with financial data from Nikkei NEEDS. Data for the fiscal year ending between April 2017 and March 2018 were used. For firms lacking data in Nikkei NEEDS, relevant financial and other information was collected manually using Kaiji Net.[51] In cases where the most recent data were unavailable, missing data was recorded. For respondents who did not disclose their firm name or securities code, industry affiliation (based on the Tokyo Stock Exchange [TSE] classification), sales, total assets, net assets, goodwill, and adopted accounting standards were requested instead.[52]

Tables 5.2, 5.3, and 5.4 present the characteristics of the responding firms. Panel A of Table 5.2 shows the breakdown between Keidanren-affiliated and non-Keidanren-affiliated firms: 58.84% and 41.16%, respectively. Unlike previous surveys conducted solely among Keidanren-affiliated firms, this survey included non-affiliated firms to assess whether responses differed between the two groups. Panel B of Table 5.2 presents the industry distribution of respondents based on the TSE classification. Manufacturing firms (highlighted in the table) constituted approximately 39.64% of the sample (178 firms). Unlike prior studies that excluded financial institutions such as banks and securities firms, this survey included them. Panel C of Table 5.2 displays the breakdown of listed and unlisted firms, showing that approximately 89% of respondents were listed firms.

Tables 5.3, 5.4, and 5.5 present the distribution of respondent firm attributes. Table 5.3 shows the distribution by firm age. Table 5.4 provides distributions based on firm size. Panel A (Sales) indicates a concentration of both relatively small firms (with sales below 100 billion yen) and relatively large firms (with sales of 500 billion yen or more). Panels B (Total Assets) and C (Net Assets) display similar patterns, with a substantial representation of firms at both ends of the size spectrum. Panel D (Goodwill Balance) reports the distribution of goodwill recorded on firms' balance sheets. Approximately 44.07% of respondents either had not recorded any goodwill or were classified as unknown due to unavailable financial data. About 22.60% reported goodwill of less than 1 billion yen, while the remaining 33.33% recorded goodwill of 1 billion yen or more. Notably, only 10.51% reported goodwill balances of 50 billion yen or more. Table 5.5 presents the distribution by accounting standards adopted. A majority (87.92%) used

---

[51] Due to corporate reorganization within one company, we used data as of June 30, 2018, rather than data from April 2017 to March 2018.

[52] Respondents were asked to answer based on the most recent consolidated annual financial statements.

Table 5.2 Number of responses by group, industry classification, and listing status

Panel A: Number of responses by group

	Number of respondents	Percentage (%)
Keidanren-affiliated	263	58.84
Non-Keidanren-affiliated	184	41.16
Total	447	100.00

Panel B: Number of responses by industry classification

Industry	**Number of respondents**	%			
1. Fishery, Agriculture & Forestry	1	0.22	18. Precision equipment	8	1.79
2. Mining	0	0.00	19. Other Products	9	2.01
3. Construction	29	6.49	20. Electric Power and Gas	3	0.67
4. Foods	17	3.80	21. Land Transportation	6	1.34
5. Transportation & Equipment	6	1.34	22. Marine Transportation	4	0.89
6. Pulp and Paper	1	0.22	23. Air Transportation	1	0.22
7. Chemical	12	2.68	24. Warehousing & Harbor Transportation	2	0.45
8. Pharmaceutical	9	2.01	25. Information & Communication	42	9.40
9. Oil and Coal Products	27	6.04	26. Wholesale Trade	42	9.40
10. Rubber Products	4	0.89	27. Retail Trade	37	8.28
11. Glass and Ceramics Products	5	1.12	28. Banks	7	1.57
12. Iron and Steel	7	1.57	29. Securities and Commodities Futures	3	0.67
13. Nonferrous Metals	4	0.89	30. Insurance	4	0.89
14. Metal Products	7	1.57	31. Other Financing Business	6	1.34
15. Machinery	17	3.80	32. Real Estate	9	2.01
16. Electric Appliances	28	6.26	33. Services	41	9.17
17. Transportation Equipment	17	3.80	34. Unclassified	32	7.16
			Total	447	100.00

Panel C: Number of responses by listing status

	Number of respondents	Percentage (%)
Unlisted	48	10.74
Listed	399	89.26
Total	447	100.00

J-GAAP, which requires "Systematic amortization with impairment" for goodwill. The remaining 12.08% adopted either U.S. GAAP or IFRS, both of which require "Impairment-only."[53]

[53] Regarding accounting standards, we relied on respondents' answers where available. Otherwise, we referred to Nikkei NEEDS and Kaiji Net. If these sources lacked data, we collected information from company websites.

Table 5.3 Firm age

	Number of respondents	Percentage (%)
1. Less than 10 years	15	3.36
2. More than 10 years and less than 30 years	48	10.74
3. 30–50 years	56	12.53
4. More than 50 years and less than 70 years	109	24.38
5. More than 70 years and less than 100 years	121	27.07
6. More than 100 years	44	9.84
7. Unknown	54	12.08
Total	447	100.00

Notes: When no response was available, firm age was calculated only for firms whose founding year could be obtained from Nikkei NEEDS. For consistency, firm age was calculated as of October 31, 2018. Firms for which data could not be collected were classified as "Unknown."

Table 5.4 Distribution of the sample based on firm characteristics other than firm age

	Number of respondents	Percentage (%)
Panel A: Net sales		
1. Less than 100 billion yen	177	39.6
2. 100 billion yen or more, but less than 200 billion yen	54	12.08
3. 200 billion yen or more but less than 300 billion yen	35	7.83
4. 300 billion yen or more, but less than 400 billion yen	19	4.25
5. 400 billion yen or more but less than 500 billion yen	18	4.03
6. 500 billion yen or more	114	25.50
7. Unknown	30	6.71
Total	447	100.00
Panel B: Total assets		
1. Less than 100 billion yen	185	41.39
2. 100 billion yen or more, but less than 200 billion yen	47	10.51
3. 200 billion yen or more but less than 300 billion yen	28	6.26
4. 300 billion yen or more, but less than 400 billion yen	21	4.70
5. 400 billion yen or more but less than 500 billion yen	13	2.91
6. 500 billion yen or more	123	27.52
7. Unknown	30	6.71
Total	447	100.00
Panel C: Net assets		
1. Less than 50 billion yen	177	39.6
2. 50 billion yen or more but less than 100 billion yen	53	11.86
3. 100 billion yen or more but less than 150 billion yen	29	6.49
4. 150 billion yen or more, but less than 200 billion yen	21	4.70
5. 200 billion yen or more but less than 250 billion yen	18	4.03
6. 250 billion yen or more	119	26.62
7. Unknown	30	6.71
Total	447	100.00

(continued)

Table 5.4 (continued)

	Number of respondents	Percentage (%)
Panel D: Goodwill balance		
1. Unaccounted for/unknown	197	44.07
2. Less than 1 billion yen	101	22.6
3. 1 billion yen or more but less than 5 billion yen	50	11.19
4. 5 billion yen or more, but less than 10 billion yen	23	5.15
5. 10 billion yen or more but less than 50 billion yen	29	6.49
6. 50 billion yen or more	47	10.51
Total	447	100.00

Table 5.5 The distribution of accounting standards employed

	Number of respondents	Percentage (%)
J-GAAP	393	87.92
U.S. GAAP	10	2.24
IFRS	44	9.84
Total	447	100.00

Notes: For the respondents that did not answer their accounting standards, we judged the accounting standards employed based on data obtained from the Nikkei NEEDS or Kaiji Net.

5.3.2.2 Questions Regarding Accounting for Acquired Goodwill

5.3.2.2.1 Impairment-Only, Systematic Amortization with Impairment, or Either?

The first question, which is central to this study, asked respondents to indicate their preferred method of subsequent accounting for goodwill: "Systematic amortization with impairment," "Impairment-only," or "Either," to account for those firms without a strong preference.

> (Q1) If a uniform accounting method for goodwill is required, is "Impairment-only (non-amortization)" or "Systematic amortization with impairment" the more preferable accounting treatment of your company? (Options: "Impairment-only (non-amortization)," "Systematic amortization with impairment," and "Either")

Table 5.6 summarizes the survey responses regarding preferred accounting treatment of goodwill. The following key points emerge:

Table 5.6 Desirability of "Impairment-only (non-amortization)" versus "Systematic amortization with impairment"

	Entire sample		Firms that recognized goodwill	
	Number of respondents	Percentage (%)	Number of respondents	Percentage (%)
Impairment-only (non-amortization)	71	15.88	37	14.80
Systematic amortization with impairment	328	73.38	193	77.20
Either	48	10.74	20	8.00
Total	447	100.00	250	100.00

- "Systematic amortization with impairment" was the most preferred option, selected by 328 respondents (73.38%). This preference remained strong among firms that had recorded goodwill,[54] with 193 out of 250 respondents (77.20%) selecting this option.
- Although consistent with prior research, 71 respondents (15.88%) from the full sample, and 37 respondents (14.80%) from the subset of firms with recorded goodwill, preferred "Impairment-only" as the most desirable treatment.[55] A total of 48 respondents (10.74%) found "Either" approach acceptable. Among firms that recognized goodwill, 20 respondents (8.00%) indicated no strong preference between the two methods.

To examine whether the tendencies observed in Table 5.6 vary according to the characteristics of survey respondents, we categorized the sample based on three criteria: (1) whether the preparers were affiliated with Keidanren (Table 5.7), (2) whether they belonged to the manufacturing or non-manufacturing sector (Table 5.8), and (3) whether they employed J-GAAP or non-J-GAAP (U.S. GAAP and IFRS) (Table 5.9). For the first classification, we separated the subsample into Keidanren-affiliated and non-affiliated firms to assess the potential influence of endogenous characteristics, given that approximately 94% of preparers in a prior survey targeting only Keidanren-affiliated firms supported goodwill amortization. The second classification was designed to evaluate whether industry affiliation affects response patterns, as Japanese manufacturing firms are often described as favoring "organic growth" through the expansion of core operations, whereas non-manufacturing firms are more inclined toward "M&A growth." The objective is to determine whether these organizational attributes influence the selection of responses. The third classification was designed to analyze the relationship between accounting standards and responses

[54] Preparers classified as not recording goodwill include both those who did not record goodwill and those for whom the presence of a goodwill balance could not be confirmed. The same classification applies hereafter.

[55] As noted in the previous section, the Keidanren Survey found that approximately 94% of respondents supported amortization plus impairment, a treatment nearly equivalent to "Systematic amortization with impairment" in this study.

Table 5.7 Results of responses to Q1 by Keidanren affiliation

	Impairment-only (non-amortization)	Systematic amortization with impairment	Either	Total
Panel A: Entire sample (Upper row: Number of responses, Lower row: Percentage [%])				
Keidanren-affiliated	37	201	25	263
	14.07	76.43	9.51	100.00
Non-Keidanren-affiliated	34	127	23	184
	18.48	69.02	12.50	100.00
Total	71	328	48	447
	15.88	73.38	10.74	100.00
$\chi^2 = 3.0381$, p-value = 0.219				
Panel B: Only for firms that recorded goodwill (Upper row: Number of responses, Lower row: Percentage [%])				
Keidanren-affiliated	24	113	11	148
	16.22	76.35	7.43	100.00
Non-Keidanren-affiliated	13	80	9	102
	12.75	78.43	8.82	100.00
Total	37	193	20	250
	14.80	77.20	8.00	100.00
$\chi^2 = 0.6715$, p-value = 0.715				

Table 5.8 Results of responses to Q1 by industry sector

	Impairment-only (non-amortization)	Systematic amortization with impairment	Either	Total
Panel A: Entire sample (Upper row: Number of responses, Lower row: Percentage [%])				
Manufacturing	26	140	12	178
	14.61	78.65	6.74	100.00
Non-manufacturing	40	166	31	237
	16.88	70.04	13.08	100.00
Unknown	5	22	5	32
	15.63	68.75	15.63	100.00
Total	71	328	48	447
	15.88	73.38	10.74	100.00
$\chi^2 = 6.0289$, p-value = 0.197				
Panel B: Only for firms that recorded goodwill (Upper row: Number of responses, Lower row: Percentage [%])				
Manufacturing	16	88	8	112
	14.29	78.57	7.14	100.00
Non-manufacturing	21	104	12	137
	15.33	75.91	8.76	100.00
Unknown	0	1	0	1
	0.00	100.00	0.00	100.00
Total	37	193	20	250
	14.80	77.20	8.00	100.00
$\chi^2 = 0.5995$, p-value = 0.963 Fisher's exact = 0.888				

Table 5.9 Results of Q1 responses by accounting standard adopted

	Impairment-only (non-amortization)	Systematic amortization with impairment	Either	Total
Panel A: Entire sample (Upper row: Number of responses, Lower row: Percentage [%])				
J-GAAP	57	294	42	393
	14.50	74.81	10.69	100.00
Non-J-GAAP	14	34	6	54
	25.93	62.96	11.11	100.00
Total	71	328	48	447
	15.88	73.38	10.74	100.00
$\chi^2 = 4.8155$, p-value = 0.090				
Panel B: Only for firms that recorded goodwill (Upper row: Number of responses, Lower row: Percentage [%])				
J-GAAP	24	160	15	199
	12.06	80.40	7.54	100.00
Non-J-GAAP	13	33	5	51
	25.49	64.71	9.80	100.00
Total	37	193	20	250
	14.80	77.20	8.00	100.00
$\chi^2 = 6.5034$, p-value = 0.039				

to Q1. The χ^2 and p-values reported in Tables 5.7, 5.8, and 5.9 present the results of the independence tests. Where appropriate, Fisher's exact probability test was also conducted, with Fisher's exact p-values provided.[56]

We summarize the findings from Tables 5.7, 5.8, and 5.9 as follows:

- Both Keidanren-affiliated and non-affiliated respondents predominantly preferred "Systematic amortization with impairment." This preference remained consistent even when limiting the analysis to preparers that had recorded goodwill. A similar pattern was observed across both manufacturing and non-manufacturing sectors, where the majority also favored "Systematic amortization with impairment." The results of the independence tests yielded high p-values, suggesting that firm characteristics, such as Keidanren affiliation or industry sector, did not significantly influence whether respondents favored "Impairment-only" or "Systematic amortization with impairment."
- The respondents employing non-J-GAAP more frequently preferred "Impairment-only" compared to those employing J-GAAP. Conversely, a lower percentage of respondents employing non-J-GAAP preferred "Systematic amortization with impairment." The result of the independent test shows that for the entire sample (for firms recognizing goodwill), the null hypothesis of no association was also rejected at the 10% (5%) level.

[56] In Panel B of Table 5.8, we used the Fisher exact probability test rather than the standard χ^2 test of independence because "more than 25% of all cells" had "expected frequencies of five or less" (Jin 2016, p. 57; translated by the authors). The Fisher exact test is also used in subsequent analyses under similar conditions.

5.3.2.2.2 Additional Question for Respondents Who Indicated in Q1 That "Impairment-Only" Is More Desirable

Respondents who identified "Impairment-only" as the more desirable option in Q1 (excluding those who selected "Either") were asked to elaborate on their rationale and to answer several follow-up questions. The following section presents the content and results of these additional questions.

5.3.2.2.3 Reasons Why "Impairment-Only" Is More Desirable

(Q1-1) To what extent do you agree with the following reasons that "Impairment-only (non-amortization)" is more desirable? (Options: 1 = "Yes," 2 = "Somewhat yes," 3 = "Somewhat no," 4 = "No," 5 = "Unsure").

1. It is difficult to estimate the useful life and amortization pattern of the carrying amount of goodwill.
2. The value of goodwill is maintained by firm efforts after it is acquired.
3. Goodwill amortization expense and the carrying amount of goodwill after amortization are not useful for financial statement users.
4. If an appropriate impairment test is conducted, systematic amortization of goodwill is not needed.
5. The goodwill amortization expense amount decreases accounting earnings.
6. Amortization of goodwill can be a competitive disadvantage with rival firms that need not amortize the carrying amount of goodwill.
7. Amortizing goodwill weakens the signaling effect of goodwill impairment.

These seven reasons were derived from prior discussions and surveys. Respondents were asked to indicate the degree to which each reason applied to them. Table 5.10 reports the results.

The results presented in Table 5.10 are summarized as follows:

- Many respondents who answered "Yes" or "Somewhat yes" cited the following reasons: "It is difficult to estimate the useful life and amortization pattern of the carrying amount of goodwill" (Panel A); "The value of goodwill is maintained by firm efforts after it is acquired" (Panel B); and "If an appropriate impairment test is conducted, systematic amortization of goodwill is not needed" (Panel D).
- More than 50% of respondents answered "Yes" in both Panel A and Panel D. These results align with the IASB's position, suggesting that concerns reg-

Table 5.10 Reasons why "impairment-only" is more desirable

	Entire sample		Firms that recognized goodwill	
	Number of respondents	Percentage (%)	Number of respondents	Percentage (%)
Panel A: It is difficult to estimate the useful life and amortization pattern of the carrying amount of goodwill.				
1. Yes	36	51.43	20	55.56
2. Somewhat yes	24	34.29	11	30.56
3. Somewhat no	4	5.71	2	5.56
4. No	5	7.14	3	8.33
5. Unsure	1	1.43	0	0.00
Total	70	100.00	36	100.00
Panel B: The value of goodwill is maintained by firm efforts after it is acquired.				
1. Yes	27	38.57	15	41.67
2. Somewhat yes	31	44.29	17	47.22
3. Somewhat no	6	8.57	1	2.78
4. No	5	7.14	3	8.33
5. Unsure	1	1.43	0	0.00
Total	70	100.00	36	100.00
Panel C: Goodwill amortization expense and the carrying amount of goodwill after amortization are not useful for financial statement users.				
1. Yes	12	17.14	8	22.22
2. Somewhat yes	22	31.43	9	25.00
3. Somewhat no	12	17.14	7	19.44
4. No	17	24.29	9	25.00
5. Unsure	7	10.00	3	8.33
Total	70	100.00	36	100.00
Panel D: If an appropriate impairment test is conducted, systematic amortization of goodwill is not needed.				
1. Yes	37	52.86	21	58.33
2. Somewhat yes	25	35.71	11	30.56
3. Somewhat no	3	4.29	3	8.33
4. No	4	5.71	1	2.78
5. Unsure	1	1.43	0	0.00
Total	70	100.00	36	100.00
Panel E: The goodwill amortization expense amount decreases accounting earnings.				
1. Yes	16	23.19	10	27.78
2. Somewhat yes	24	34.78	10	27.78
3. Somewhat no	15	21.74	9	25.00
4. No	12	17.39	7	19.44
5. Unsure	2	2.90	0	0.00
Total	69	100.00	36	100.00

(continued)

Table 5.10 (continued)

	Entire sample		Firms that recognized goodwill	
	Number of respondents	Percentage (%)	Number of respondents	Percentage (%)
Panel F: Amortization of goodwill can be a competitive disadvantage with rival firms that need not amortize the carrying amount of goodwill.				
1. Yes	15	21.43	9	25.00
2. Somewhat yes	23	32.86	10	27.78
3. Somewhat no	18	25.71	9	25.00
4. No	11	15.71	7	19.44
5. Unsure	3	4.29	1	2.78
Total	70	100.00	36	100.00
Panel G: Amortizing goodwill weakens the signaling effect of goodwill impairment.				
1. Yes	8	11.43	5	13.89
2. Somewhat yes	26	37.14	14	38.89
3. Somewhat no	16	22.86	7	19.44
4. No	14	20.00	7	19.44
5. Unsure	6	8.57	3	8.33
Total	70	100.00	36	100.00

arding estimation uncertainty and the sufficiency of impairment testing underpin support for "Impairment-only" over "Systematic amortization with impairment."[57]

- Notably, over 80% of respondents and nearly 90% among those who recorded goodwill answered "Yes" or "Somewhat yes" in Panel B. This indicates that preferences for "Impairment-only" are influenced not only by practical challenges in estimating amortization inputs but also by how goodwill is conceptually understood. Specifically, many respondents view goodwill as an asset.
- Responses were divided in Panels C and E through G. However, in each case, the percentage of "Yes" or "Somewhat yes" responses exceeded that of "Somewhat no," "No," and "Unsure."
- Several important observations emerge from the divergence in these responses. First, even among respondents who prefer "Impairment-only," some believe that amortization expense and post-amortization goodwill balances are useful for financial statement users. Second, preparers held varied views regarding the signaling function of goodwill impairment losses (ASBJ Survey 1, p. 18, para. 36); although some respondents based their preferences on this rationale, many did not consider it a decisive factor. Third, while some preparers cited the income-

[57] Theoretically, amortization and impairment are not alternative treatments. However, the IASB has suggested that amortization serves as an alternative to impairment, as impairment is often viewed as "too little, too late," despite being the preferable method. Conversely, impairment can be viewed as an alternative to amortization (e.g., Li et al. 2011). For instance, frequent small impairment losses may yield similar effects to amortization in earnings calculations.

reducing effect of amortization as a reason for supporting "Impairment-only," this rationale was not universally endorsed. Importantly, these patterns remained consistent even when the analysis was limited to respondents whose firms had recognized goodwill.[58]

The survey also included an open-ended question asking respondents to provide any additional reasons for preferring "Impairment-only" over "Systematic amortization with impairment":

(Q1-2) If you have any reasons other than those listed in Q1-1 why you prefer "Impairment-only (non-amortization)," please indicate them in the space provided below.

A total of 12 responses were received. The additional reasons provided are summarized as follows:

- Impairment-only treatment facilitates M&A implementation.
- Impairment testing better reflects the success or failure of M&A activities.[59]
- Comparability is reduced when firms use different amortization periods and methods.
- The approach is more consistent with international accounting standards.
- It aligns with overseas subsidiaries that adopt IFRS.
- When divesting an acquired business, goodwill, including its acquisition cost, serves as a meaningful metric for evaluating the success of the sale.

5.3.2.2.4 Additional Question for Respondents Who Indicated in Q1 That "Systematic Amortization with Impairment" Is More Desirable

Reasons Why "Systematic Amortization with Impairment" Is More Desirable

Respondents who preferred "Systematic amortization with impairment" were also asked to explain their rationale.

[58] This finding is difficult to interpret, as the amount of goodwill recorded by Japanese firms is generally smaller than that recorded by firms in other countries (e.g., the U.S.). Furthermore, except for a few Japanese firms, goodwill amortization may not significantly affect accounting earnings. Psychological factors may also discourage respondents from identifying this point as a positive rationale in the survey.

[59] Some respondents noted that systematic amortization does not reflect business realities during periods of rapid change. They argued that annual impairment testing would promote healthier and more transparent management. Additionally, they preferred a system in which the recorded amount of goodwill is explained to investors through disclosures or other means, allowing investors to assess the goodwill, including how it is presented.

(Q1-3) To what extent do you agree with the following reasons that "Systematic amortization with impairment" is more desirable? (Options: 1 = "Yes," 2 = "Somewhat yes," 3 = "Somewhat no," 4 = "No," 5 = "Unsure").

1. Excess earnings power represented by goodwill gradually decreases due to market competition.
2. The carrying amount of goodwill should be allocated to the appropriate periods to match revenues and expenses.
3. It is impossible to distinguish between the diminished and maintained components of goodwill value.
4. It is consistent with the accounting treatment of other depreciable assets.
5. Amortization cannot be replaced by impairment.
6. It leads to prudent M&A decisions.
7. It reduces the cost of the goodwill impairment test.

The following table (Table 5.11) presents their responses and the corresponding results.

- In Panel A, 76.76% of the total sample and 78.65% of firms that recognized goodwill responded "Yes" or "Somewhat yes."
- In Panel B, 88.99% of the total sample and 92.71% of firms that recorded goodwill answered "Yes" or "Somewhat yes." This proportion exceeds that of Panel A. The emphasis on matching revenues and expenses[60] indicates that the return-on-investment perspective remains important for respondents.
- In Panel C, 63.30% of the total sample and 63.02% of firms that recorded goodwill answered "Yes" or "Somewhat yes."
- In Panel D, 70.46% of the total sample and 73.30% of firms that recorded goodwill answered "Yes" or "Somewhat yes."
- In Panel E, 57.80% of the total sample and 61.46% of firms that recorded goodwill answered "Yes" or "Somewhat yes." While some respondents acknowledged the unique role of amortization, which cannot be substituted by impairment alone, the level of agreement was lower compared to Panels B and D. It remains unclear whether these views were driven by theoretical or practical considerations, and a significant portion of respondents did not support this reasoning.
- In Panel F, 53.37% of the total sample and 60.73% of firms that recognized goodwill answered "Yes" or "Somewhat yes." While over half supported the view that systematic amortization encourages more careful M&A behavior, a notable number did not agree.

[60] This may reflect the influence of university or in-house (on-the-job) training aligned with corporate accounting principles in Japan.

Table 5.11 Reasons why "Systematic amortization with impairment" is more desirable

	Entire sample		Firms that recognized goodwill	
	Number of respondents	Percentage (%)	Number of respondents	Percentage (%)
Panel A: Excess earnings power represented by goodwill gradually decreases due to market competition.				
1. Yes	97	29.66	66	34.38
2. Somewhat yes	154	47.09	85	44.27
3. Somewhat no	36	11.01	18	9.38
4. No	26	7.95	13	6.77
5. Unsure	14	4.28	10	5.21
Total	327	100.00	192	100.00
Panel B: The carrying amount of goodwill should be allocated to the appropriate periods to match revenues and expenses.				
1. Yes	171	52.29	106	55.21
2. Somewhat yes	120	36.70	72	37.5
3. Somewhat no	18	5.50	6	3.13
4. No	14	4.28	6	3.13
5. Unsure	4	1.22	2	1.04
Total	327	100.00	192	100.00
Panel C: It is impossible to distinguish between the diminished and maintained components of goodwill value.				
1. Yes	50	15.29	32	16.67
2. Somewhat yes	157	48.01	89	46.35
3. Somewhat no	54	16.51	32	16.67
4. No	49	14.98	29	15.10
5. Unsure	17	5.20	10	5.21
Total	327	100.00	192	100.00
Panel D: It is consistent with the accounting treatment of other depreciable assets.				
1. Yes	69	21.23	48	25.13
2. Somewhat yes	160	49.23	92	48.17
3. Somewhat no	56	17.23	29	15.18
4. No	32	9.85	17	8.90
5. Unsure	8	2.46	5	2.62
Total	325	100.00	191	100.00
Panel E: Amortization cannot be replaced by impairment.				
1. Yes	53	16.21	30	15.63
2. Somewhat yes	136	41.59	88	45.83
3. Somewhat no	66	20.18	33	17.19
4. No	39	11.93	21	10.94
5. Unsure	33	10.09	20	10.42
Total	327	100.00	192	100.00

(continued)

Table 5.11 (continued)

	Entire sample		Firms that recognized goodwill	
	Number of respondents	Percentage (%)	Number of respondents	Percentage (%)
Panel F: It leads to prudent M&A decisions.				
1. Yes	61	18.71	42	21.99
2. Somewhat yes	113	34.66	74	38.74
3. Somewhat no	73	22.39	38	19.90
4. No	54	16.56	23	12.04
5. Unsure	25	7.67	14	7.33
Total	326	100.00	191	100.00
Panel G: It reduces the cost of the goodwill impairment test.				
1. Yes	58	17.79	31	16.23
2. Somewhat yes	109	33.44	66	34.55
3. Somewhat no	83	25.46	53	27.75
4. No	67	20.55	35	18.32
5. Unsure	9	2.76	6	3.14
Total	326	100.00	191	100.00

- In Panel G, 51.23% of the total sample and 50.79% of goodwill-recognizing firms responded "Yes" or "Somewhat yes," indicating only modest support for this argument.[61]

(Q1-4) If you have any other reasons why you think "Systematic amortization with impairment" is more desirable, other than those mentioned in Q1-3, please describe them below.

The survey also included the following open-ended question:

A total of 36 responses were received and are summarized as follows[62]:

- Impact on earnings available for dividend distribution
- Simplifies the re-measurement of goodwill
- Mitigates the risk of future impairment

[61] There are several possible explanations for the variation in responses. For instance, some groups stated that systematic amortization reduces the cost of impairment, while others disagreed or argued that, although amortization reduces impairment costs, this alone does not justify a combined "Systematic amortization with impairment" approach. In the open-ended responses, some groups acknowledged that without amortization, the monetary significance of goodwill would persist, requiring rigorous impairment testing at each financial statement closing, which would impose a practical burden. In contrast, groups supporting the "Impairment-only" approach argued that strict impairment testing is the only viable method to assess M&A success.

[62] In the following, some responses that merely supplemented answers to the previous question have been omitted.

- Reduces the discretion involved in impairment testing, including earnings management (e.g., "big bath" accounting)
- Aligns with the matching principle between revenues and expenses
- Concerns that non-amortization could result in the recognition of internally generated goodwill
- Reduces the practical burden of impairment testing
- Encourages a conservative approach to financial reporting
- Enhances financial transparency
- Doubts regarding the classification of goodwill as an asset
- Potential tax savings on certain projects
- Avoids negative impacts on medium- to long-term decision-making due to large impairment losses

The most frequently cited reason emphasized the importance of matching revenues and expenses.[63] Other responses highlighted accountability, such as how estimating the amortization period can facilitate more informed dialogue with investors and promote more prudent M&A decisions.[64] One notable comment questioned whether a balance sheet with a high goodwill ratio accurately reflects a firm's financial condition.

5.3.2.2.5 Factors Considered Important in Determining the Amortization Period of Goodwill

Respondents who favored the "Systematic amortization with impairment" approach were also asked to identify the factors they consider important when determining the amortization period for goodwill.

(Q1-5) To what extent do you think the following factors are important when preparers estimate the goodwill amortization period? For each factor, please choose one of the following options (Options: 1 = "Yes," 2 = "Somewhat yes," 3 = "Somewhat no," 4 = "No," 5 = "Unsure").

1. The investment-return period based on management's business plan
2. The period over which synergies are expected to be maintained
3. Periods over which an acquirer, on a stand-alone basis, is expected to maintain higher future cash flows
4. Useful lives of related tangible assets
5. Useful lives of related other intangible assets

[63] We sought to capture this viewpoint in the second rationale, "The carrying amount of goodwill should be allocated to the appropriate periods to match revenues and expenses" (Panel B of Table 5.11). However, in the open-ended responses, several participants reiterated the importance of "matching revenues with expenses and calculating the return on investment."

[64] This aligns with the contemporary perspective of positive accounting theory (Kothari et al. 2010).

Table 5.12 Important factors in determining amortization period

	Entire sample		Firms that recognized goodwill	
	Number of respondents	Percentage (%)	Number of respondents	Percentage (%)
Panel A: The investment-return period based on management's business plan.				
1. Yes	166	50.76	101	52.33
2. Somewhat yes	129	39.45	72	37.31
3. Somewhat no	22	6.73	13	6.74
4. No	8	2.45	5	2.59
5. Unsure	2	0.61	2	1.04
Total	327	100.00	193	100.00
Panel B: The period over which synergies are expected to be maintained.				
1. Yes	101	30.89	60	31.09
2. Somewhat yes	158	48.32	92	47.67
3. Somewhat no	42	12.84	24	12.44
4. No	17	5.20	9	4.66
5. Unsure	9	2.75	8	4.15
Total	327	100.00	193	100.00
Panel C: Periods over which an acquirer, on a stand-alone basis, is expected to maintain higher future cash flows.				
1. Yes	50	15.29	30	15.54
2. Somewhat yes	145	44.34	94	48.7
3. Somewhat no	85	25.99	47	24.35
4. No	33	10.09	16	8.29
5. Unsure	14	4.28	6	3.11
Total	327	100.00	193	100.00
Panel D: Useful lives of related tangible assets.				
1. Yes	14	4.28	9	4.66
2. Somewhat yes	64	19.57	39	20.21
3. Somewhat no	135	41.28	76	39.38
4. No	95	29.05	56	29.02
5. Unsure	19	5.81	13	6.74
Total	327	100.00	193	100.00
Panel E: Useful lives of related other intangible assets.				
1. Yes	17	5.21	12	6.22
2. Somewhat yes	90	27.52	59	30.57
3. Somewhat no	123	37.61	66	34.2
4. No	81	24.77	46	23.83
5. Unsure	16	4.89	10	5.18
Total	327	100.00	193	100.00

The results presented in Table 5.12 are summarized as follows:

- In Panel A, 90.21% of the total sample and 89.64% of firms recognizing goodwill responded "Yes" or "Somewhat yes," indicating the significance of this factor. Notably, 50.76% of the total sample and 52.33% of firms recognizing goodwill responded "Yes," identifying the payback period as the most important factor in goodwill-related investment decisions.

- In Panel B, 79.21% of the total sample and 78.76% of firms recording goodwill selected "Yes" or "Somewhat yes." In contrast, Panel C ("Periods over which the acquirer, on a stand-alone basis, is expected to maintain higher future cash flows") received affirmative responses from 59.63% of the total sample and 64.25% of firms recognizing goodwill.
- These findings suggest that respondents viewed the synergy-maintenance period (Panel B) as important; however, the responses for Panel A indicate even greater emphasis on the investment-return period. Additionally, the differences in response distributions between Panels A and B suggest a nuanced interpretation of the relevant time horizons.
- It is plausible that some respondents conceptually aligned with the synergy period in Panel B but selected Panel A due to the relative difficulty of forecasting the former. For instance, synergies may be anticipated over a 15-year period, while the investment plan assumes recovery within 10 years. Conversely, synergies may be projected over only 7 years, but the recovery plan may extend to 30 years, utilizing normal profits.
- It is also important to acknowledge potential variation in respondents' interpretations of the "investment-return period" in Panel A of Table 5.12. For example, in the case of a ¥10 billion investment in a firm valued at ¥8 billion, some respondents may interpret the return period as the recovery of the full ¥10 billion, while others may focus only on the ¥2 billion excess investment. The survey does not allow for the determination of which interpretation respondents applied, thus limiting the precision of the results.
- Regarding Panel D, 23.85% of the total sample and 24.87% of firms with goodwill responded "Yes" or "Somewhat yes." Panel E received slightly higher affirmative responses (32.72% of all firms and 36.79% of firms recording goodwill), though these figures remain lower than those for Panels A through C. These results suggest that tangible and intangible asset lives were considered less critical in determining the goodwill amortization period.

Following Q1–5, respondents were asked the following open-ended question:

(Q1-6) If you have any important factors when estimating the goodwill amortization period, other than those listed in Q1-5, please describe them below.

Ten responses were received. The key responses are summarized as follows:

- After establishing a maximum amortization period, multiple factors should be considered comprehensively, including industry characteristics and the firm's investment recovery approach.
- The projected future cash flow period at the time of acquisition should be incorporated.

- A uniform regulatory standard is desirable to reduce discretion.
- Consideration of the gap between the average employee age and retirement age in the acquired firm.
- The market's growth potential that gave rise to the goodwill.
- The expected duration of brand value persistence or growth.

Additional comments referenced factors already listed in Q1–5. For example, "useful lives of related tangible assets" and "useful lives of other intangible assets" were considered acceptable proxies if reasonably estimated. Several comments noted that the period over which goodwill is accumulated closely aligns with the expected synergy period. Others stated that the investment-return period is comparable to the expected duration of synergies. Some respondents emphasized that the most appropriate investment-return period is the one determined by the acquiring firm.

5.3.2.2.6 How Should the Provisions Regarding the Amortization Period of Goodwill Be Addressed?

The survey also sought input from respondents who supported "Systematic amortization with impairment" in Q1 regarding how the amortization period should be governed. Specifically, it asked whether firms should have full or partial discretion in determining the amortization period, or whether discretion should be eliminated in favor of a uniform period.

(Q1-7) Given that "Systematic amortization with impairment" is more desirable as the accounting approach for goodwill, how do you think a requirement determining the goodwill amortization period should be prescribed? Please choose an option you think is the most desirable for you.

(Options)

1. An upper limit should be set for the amortization period (e.g., the rule should be prescribed in the form "Be amortized within ... years").
2. A uniform amortization period should be set (e.g., the rule should be prescribed in the form "Be amortized in just ... years").
3. No provision about the amortization period should be set.

The results reported in Table 5.13 are summarized as follows:

- Over 70% of respondents in both the entire sample and the subset of firms that recorded goodwill selected "1. An upper limit should be set for the amortization period."
- Only 11% of respondents in the full sample and 10% in the subset of firms that recorded goodwill chose "2. A uniform amortization period should be set."

Table 5.13 Provision of the amortization period

	Entire sample		Firms that recognized goodwill	
	Number of respondents	Percentage (%)	Number of respondents	Percentage (%)
1. An upper limit should be set for the amortization period.	232	71.17	137	70.98
2. A uniform amortization period should be set.	36	11.04	20	10.36
3. No provision about the amortization period should be set.	58	17.79	36	18.65
Total	326	100.00	193	100.00

Table 5.14 Upper limit of the goodwill amortization period

	Entire sample		Firms that recognized goodwill	
	Number of respondents	Percentage (%)	Number of respondents	Percentage (%)
20 years	131	56.96	87	63.97
15 years	17	7.39	8	5.88
10 years	69	30.00	33	24.26
5 years	9	3.91	4	2.94
Other	4	1.74	4	2.94
Total	230	100.00	136	100.00

Although several respondents expressed support for a uniform amortization period, this option received the fewest selections.

- Approximately 18% of respondents in the full sample and 19% in the goodwill sample selected "3. No provision about the amortization period should be set."
- It is notable that most respondents preferred some provision on the amortization period, either an upper limit or a uniform duration, while fewer than 20% opposed any provision. This suggests that many preparers favor a balance between discretion and regulation, endorsing a framework that allows some flexibility but imposes limits. They appear to seek disciplined freedom and accountability within established rules, rather than complete discretion.

The following question was then posed to respondents who selected "1. An upper limit should be set for the amortization period":

> (Q1-8) How many years do you think should be chosen as the upper limit of the goodwill amortization period? Please choose one of the following options. If you choose "Other," please fill in the blank with any specific number of years.

Table 5.14 presents the following findings:

Table 5.15 A uniform amortization period

	Entire sample		Firms that recognized goodwill	
	Number of respondents	Percentage (%)	Number of respondents	Percentage (%)
20 years	5	13.89	4	20.00
15 years	1	2.78	1	5.00
10 years	15	41.67	9	45.00
5 years	14	38.89	5	25.00
Other	1	2.78	1	5.00
Total	36	100.00	20	100.00

- In the overall sample, the largest group (56.96%) preferred amortization within 20 years, consistent with the current J-GAAP system. The next largest group (30%) favored amortization within 10 years. This pattern persisted among firms that recorded goodwill, aligning with the ASBJ survey, which also showed a majority favoring a 20-year amortization. Respondents were likely influenced by the existing J-GAAP framework.
- Respondents who selected "Other" specified maximum amortization periods of 3, 25, 30, and 50 years.

Respondents who chose "2. A uniform amortization period should be set" were asked the following question:

> (Q1-9) How many years do you think a uniform amortization period should be? If you choose "Other", please fill in the blank with any specific number of years.

The results presented in Table 5.15 are summarized as follows:

- Among those favoring a uniform amortization period without managerial discretion, 5 and 10 years were the most common choices.
- Similarly, respondents selecting "Other" most frequently reported 5 or 10 years.[65]

Finally, respondents who chose either "1. An upper limit should be set" or "2. A uniform amortization period should be set" in Q1-7 were asked whether exceptions should be allowed:

> (Q1-10) Do you think the rebuttable presumption of a goodwill amortization period should be made? (Options: 1 = "Should be made," 2 = "Should not be made")

[65] Strictly speaking, the "Other" responses included cases where respondents selected "5 years" and then wrote "or 10 years" in the comment section. These were reclassified as "Other" during tabulation.

Table 5.16 Should the rebuttable presumption be made?

	Entire sample		Firms that recognized goodwill	
	Number of respondents	Percentage (%)	Number of respondents	Percentage (%)
1. Should be made	109	41.44	64	41.83
2. Should not be made	154	58.56	89	58.17
Total	263	100.00	153	100.00

Table 5.16 reports the following findings:

- Unexpectedly, more respondents answered "2. Should not be made" than "1. Should be made," indicating a strong preference against allowing exceptions, possibly to reduce discretionary decisions.
- However, this result may depend on the assumed length of the uniform amortization period. For instance, if the period is 5 years, respondents might favor exceptions, whereas if it is 10 or 20 years, they might oppose them. Therefore, this finding warrants cautious interpretation.

5.3.2.3 Characteristics of Goodwill as an Asset

This section presents the survey responses concerning the nature of goodwill as an asset. The second question (Q2) was stated as follows:

5.3.2.3.1 Is There a Semi-permanent, Non-amortizable Portion of Goodwill?

(Q2) Do you think there is a part of goodwill that preserves its value semi-permanently? Please select one answer from the options below.

(Options)
1. All or the majority of the value is preserved semi-permanently.
2. There is both a part that preserves its value semi-permanently and a part that does not.
3. There is no part that preserves its value semi-permanently.
4. Unsure.

The key findings in Table 5.17 are summarized as follows:

- The majority of responses (90%) selected either "2. There are both a part that preserves its value semi-permanently and a part that does not" or "3. There is no part that preserves its value semi-permanently," with each option receiving a similar number of responses.

Table 5.17 Characteristics of goodwill as an asset

	Entire sample		Firms that recognized goodwill	
	Number of respondents	Percentage (%)	Number of respondents	Percentage (%)
1. All or the majority of the value is preserved semi-permanently	5	1.13	4	1.61
2. There is both a part that preserves its value semi-permanently and a part that does not	190	42.89	111	44.58
3. There is no part that preserves its value semi-permanently	207	46.73	117	46.99
4. Unsure	41	9.26	17	6.83
Total	443	100.00	249	100.00

- As with Q1, responses to Q2 did not vary significantly based on the presence of goodwill, Keidanren affiliation (i.e., Keidanren-affiliated or non-affiliated), or industry type (manufacturing or non-manufacturing) (untabulated).
- Some respondents who chose options 1 or 2 may have equated goodwill with brand value. For instance, under J-GAAP, goodwill may encompass brands.[66] However, under IFRS, the difference between the acquisition price and the net market value of the acquired firm's assets is further allocated to identifiable intangible assets, such as brand value and customer lists. The remaining amount is then recorded as goodwill.

5.3.2.3.2 Components of Goodwill

The Respondents who selected "1. All or the majority of the value is preserved semi-permanently" or "2. There are both a part that preserves its value semi-permanently and a part that does not" in Q2 were asked two additional questions (Q2-1 and Q2-2),[67] aimed at exploring the underlying components of goodwill, an area that remains insufficiently understood.

[66] ASBJ Guidance No. 10, "6. Treatment of So-Called Brands" (ASBJ 2024, pp. 115–116, para. 370), states that brands can be classified as either product brands or corporate brands, and outlines the conditions for recognizing them as intangible assets. Therefore, under J-GAAP, identifying brands separately from goodwill in a business combination is not entirely precluded; rather, they are cases where brands can be recognized as distinct intangible assets.

[67] Only responses that included answers to all items in 1–6 were tabulated. Responses missing even a single item were excluded. Incorrect responses, such as answering Q2–1 despite selecting options 3 or 4 in Q2, were considered invalid. This issue did not arise in the web-based responses due to the guided question flow. However, such invalid responses appeared in the paper-based questionnaires.

(Q2-1) The following is a list of items that are considered components of goodwill. Please select one that applies to each of the following items. (Select one for each of the following, 1 = Amortized, 2 = Amortized to some extent, 3 = Not amortized much, 4 = Not amortized, 5 = Unsure, 6 = It is not a component of goodwill)

(Components addressed in this survey)
1. Brand
2. Sales know-how
3. Proprietary technology
4. Business model
5. Human resources
6. Site-specific conditions

The results reported in Table 5.18 are summarized as follows:

Table 5.18 Components of goodwill

	Entire sample		Firms that recognized goodwill	
	Number of respondents	Percentage (%)	Number of respondents	Percentage (%)
Panel A: Brand				
1. Amortized	8	4.1	5	4.35
2. Amortized to some extent	60	30.77	38	33.04
3. Not amortized much	84	43.08	48	41.74
4. Not amortized	28	14.36	15	13.04
5. Unsure	9	4.62	4	3.48
6. It is not a component of goodwill	6	3.08	5	4.35
Total	195	100.00	115	100.00
Panel B: Sales know-how				
1. Amortized	26	13.33	18	15.65
2. Amortized to some extent	98	50.26	55	47.83
3. Not amortized much	47	24.1	29	25.22
4. Not amortized	14	7.18	7	6.09
5. Unsure	2	1.03	1	0.87
6. It is not a component of goodwill	8	4.10	5	4.35
Total	195	100.00	115	100.00
Panel C: Proprietary technology				
1. Amortized	33	16.92	23	20.00

(continued)

Table 5.18 (continued)

	Entire sample		Firms that recognized goodwill	
	Number of respondents	Percentage (%)	Number of respondents	Percentage (%)
2. Amortized to some extent	103	52.82	59	51.30
3. Not amortized much	38	19.49	22	19.13
4. Not amortized	12	6.15	4	3.48
5. Unsure	5	2.56	3	2.61
6. It is not a component of goodwill	4	2.05	4	3.48
Total	195	100.00	115	100.00
Panel D: Business model				
1. Amortized	35	17.95	24	20.87
2. Amortized to some extent	103	52.82	61	53.04
3. Not amortized much	33	16.92	20	17.39
4. Not amortized	10	5.13	4	3.48
5. Unsure	6	3.08	2	1.74
6. It is not a component of goodwill	8	4.10	4	3.48
Total	195	100.00	115	100.00
Panel E: Human resources				
1. Amortized	34	17.44	22	19.13
2. Amortized to some extent	72	36.92	47	40.87
3. Not amortized much	40	20.51	24	20.87
4. Not amortized	16	8.21	8	6.96
5. Unsure	18	9.23	7	6.09
6. It is not a component of goodwill	15	7.69	7	6.09
Total	195	100.00	115	100.00
Panel F: Site-specific conditions				
1. Amortized	10	5.13	6	5.22
2. Amortized to some extent	46	23.59	32	27.83
3. Not amortized much	68	34.87	41	35.65
4. Not amortized	17	8.72	10	8.70
5. Unsure	21	10.77	7	6.09
6. It is not a component of goodwill	33	16.92	19	16.52
Total	195	100.00	115	100.00

- In Panels A (Brand) and F (Site-specific conditions),[68] the proportion of preparers responding "3. Not amortized much" or "4. Not amortized" exceeded those choosing "1. Amortized" or "2. Amortized to some extent." This trend held for both the overall sample and the subset of firms reporting goodwill.
- In contrast, for Panels B (Sales know-how), C (Proprietary technology), D (Business model), and E (Human resources), more respondents selected "1. Amortized" or "2. Amortized to some extent" than those who chose "3. Not amortized much" or "4. Not amortized." These results are consistent across the entire sample and the subgroup recognizing goodwill.

These findings suggest that respondents generally perceive brand power as enduring and resistant to amortization once established. Conversely, they view know-how, technology, and business models as more susceptible to value decline over time.

An open-ended follow-up (Q2-2) asked respondents to identify any additional components they considered part of goodwill beyond those listed in Q2-1:

(Q2-2) If there are any components considered to constitute goodwill, other than those listed in Q2-1, please write them below.

Twenty responses were received, which included the following examples:

- Clients and suppliers
- Rights (e.g., commercial area, patent rights)
- Contracts related to business
- Company policy and the know-how to implement it

The most frequently mentioned component was "customers/business partners" of the acquired firm. Several respondents also cited synergies with the acquiree.[69] Some emphasized that the elements in Q2-1 cannot be mechanically classified as either amortizable or non-amortizable, arguing that the assumption of inevitable value deterioration is flawed. Others noted that, depending on the industry, some of the elements listed in Q2-1 may be valued as identifiable intangible assets and therefore excluded from goodwill.

[68] Regarding location-based factors, the assumption is that these include sites with excess earning power, such as stores located near train stations or on busy streets, factories close to ports, or examples like Kyoto's pickles.

[69] Synergy was broadly related to the factors in the preceding question but was difficult to address explicitly. Some respondents mentioned that synergy constituted a goodwill component in another form.

5.3.2.4 Alternative Accounting Treatment of Goodwill (Part 1)

The survey asked respondents not only to choose between "Impairment-only" and "Systematic amortization with impairment" as the preferred accounting treatment of acquired goodwill, both permitted under J-GAAP and international standards (IFRS and U.S. GAAP), but also to indicate their preference when alternative treatments are considered.

(Q3) The following methods could be considered as accounting treatments after goodwill is acquired, instead of only recognizing either "Impairment-only (non-amortization)" or "Systematic amortization with impairment."

- A method that recognizes discretionary selection of "Impairment-only (non-amortization)" or "Systematic amortization with impairment"
- A method in which goodwill that meets certain conditions (e.g., it can be proved that goodwill does not amortize semi-permanently, etc.) for each acquisition deal is not amortized, and for any other conditions, it is amortized systematically.

Taking into account the above methods, please choose one accounting treatment option that is best suited for your firm.

(Options[70])

1. Impairment-only (non-amortization)
2. Systematic amortization with impairment
3. Discretionary selection of "Impairment-only (non-amortization)" or "Systematic amortization with impairment"
4. Goodwill that meets certain conditions for each acquisition deal is not amortized, and anything else is amortized systematically

Table 5.19 shows the following key findings:

- Regarding the accounting treatment of acquired goodwill, 58.60% of respondents in the total sample and 62.25% of respondents in the subset of firms that recorded goodwill selected "2. Systematic amortization with impairment," even considering the current system and the possibility of alternative treatments. Although this question did not allow for a direct comparison, as it lacked the "Either" option present in Q1, the proportion selecting "2. Systematic amortization with impairment" was lower than in Q1.
- The percentage of respondents choosing "1. Impairment-only (non-amortization)" was 11.31% for the entire sample and 10.84% for firms that recorded goodwill. This percentage was also lower than in Q1.[71]

---

[70] This question did not offer "Either" as a response option.

[71] Responses to this question likely reflect current practice ("Impairment-only" or "Systematic amortization with impairment").

Table 5.19 Preferable accounting treatment methods when other possibilities are considered

	Entire sample		Firms that recognized goodwill	
	Number of respondents	Percentage (%)	Number of respondents	Percentage (%)
1. Impairment-only (non-amortization)	50	11.31	27	10.84
2. Systematic amortization with impairment	259	58.60	155	62.25
3. Discretionary selection of "Impairment-only (non-amortization)" or "Systematic amortization with impairment"	67	15.16	34	13.65
4. Goodwill that meets certain conditions for each acquisition deal is not amortized, and anything else is amortized systematically	66	14.93	33	13.25
Total	442	100.00	249	100.00

- Among respondents, 15.16% of the entire sample and 13.65% of the firms that recorded goodwill preferred "3. Discretionary selection of 'Impairment-only (non-amortization)' or 'Systematic amortization with impairment'" over "4. Goodwill that meets certain conditions for each acquisition deal is not amortized, and anything else is amortized systematically."
- The predominance of "2. Systematic amortization with impairment" aligns with earlier survey results. When designing the questionnaire, we anticipated that preparers might favor a method allowing greater discretion, such as the optional response. However, the responses indicate that relatively few preferred this option. This result likely reflects users' preference for a clear rule, either "1. Impairment-only (non-amortization)" or "2. Systematic amortization with impairment," to enhance comparability and avoid accounting methods that differ significantly from current rules.

As in Q1, we examined whether responses differed between "Keidanren-affiliated" and "Non-Keidanren-affiliated" firms and between "Manufacturing" and "Non-manufacturing" firms.

- Table 5.20 shows that a higher percentage of Keidanren-affiliated firms selected "2. Systematic amortization with impairment," whereas more Non-Keidanren-affiliated firms favored "3. Discretionary selection of 'Impairment-only (non-amortization)' or 'Systematic amortization with impairment.'"
- Table 5.21 shows that, comparing manufacturing and non-manufacturing industries, a larger share of manufacturing respondents preferred "2. Systematic amortization with impairment." Conversely, a greater proportion of non-manufacturing

Table 5.20 Results for Q3 when categorized as Keidanren-affiliated/non-Keidanren-affiliated

	1	2	3	4	Total
Panel A: Entire sample (Upper row: Number of responses, Lower row: Percentage [%])					
Keidanren-affiliated	27	170	31	35	263
	10.27	64.64	11.79	13.31	100.00
Non-Keidanren-affiliated	23	89	36	31	179
	12.85	49.72	20.11	17.32	100.00
Total	50	259	67	66	442
	11.31	58.60	15.16	14.93	100.00
$\chi^2 = 10.6899$, p-value = 0.014					
Panel B: Firms that recorded goodwill (Upper row: Number of responses, Lower row: Percentage [%])					
Keidanren-affiliated	19	100	14	15	148
	12.84	67.57	9.46	10.14	100.00
Non-Keidanren-affiliated	8	55	20	18	101
	7.92	54.46	19.80	17.82	100.00
Total	27	155	34	33	249
	10.84	62.25	13.65	13.25	100.00
$\chi^2 = 10.3757$, p-value = 0.016					

Note: Options: 1 = "Impairment-only (non-amortization)"; 2 = "Systematic amortization with impairment"; 3 = "Discretionary selection of 'Impairment-only (non-amortization)' or 'Systematic amortization with impairment'"; and 4 = "Goodwill that meets certain conditions for each acquisition deal is not amortized, and anything else is amortized systematically."

respondents favored "3. Discretionary selection..." and "4. Goodwill that meets certain conditions for each acquisition deal is not amortized, and anything else is amortized systematically." Given that the manufacturing sector is dominated by tangible assets, whereas the non-manufacturing sector relies more heavily on intangible assets, respondents from non-manufacturing industries may view some intangible assets (e.g., brand value, as noted in this survey) as non-identifiable yet not necessarily subject to long-term amortization. They might also consider impairment-only treatment more appropriate in certain M&As.

5.3.2.5 Alternative Accounting Treatment of Goodwill (Part 2)

Thus far, our investigation has focused on two accounting methods: "Impairment-only" and "Systematic amortization with impairment." However, other plausible treatments, including those used historically, may exist. Therefore, we examined whether any alternative accounting treatments might be preferable to these two debated methods.[72]

The key results in Table 5.22 are summarized as follows:

[72] As with the interpretation of Q3, it is important to consider that responses to this question may reflect current practices rather than theoretical preferences.

Table 5.21 Results for Q3 when categorized as manufacturing/non-manufacturing

	1	2	3	4	Total
Panel A: Entire sample (Upper row: Number of responses, Lower row: Percentage [%])					
Manufacture	18	117	19	20	174
	10.34	67.24	10.92	11.49	100.00
Non-manufacturing	29	124	44	39	236
	12.29	52.54	18.64	16.53	100.00
Unknown	3	18	4	7	32
	9.38	56.25	12.5	21.88	100.00
Total	50	259	67	66	442
	11.31	58.60	15.16	14.93	100.00
$\chi^2 = 11.0890$, p-value = 0.086 Fisher's exact = 0.082					
Panel B: Firms that recorded goodwill (Upper row: Number of responses, Lower row: Percentage [%])					
Manufacture	11	78	12	11	112
	9.82	69.64	10.71	9.82	100.00
Non-manufacturing	16	77	21	22	136
	11.76	56.62	15.44	16.18	100.00
Unknown	0	0	1	0	1
	0	0	100.00	0	100.00
Total	27	155	34	33	249
	10.84	62.25	13.65	13.25	100.00
$\chi^2 = 11.136$, p-value = 0.085 Fisher's exact = 0.111					

Note: Options: 1 = "Impairment-only (non-amortization)"; 2 = "Systematic amortization with impairment"; 3 = "Discretionary selection of 'Impairment-only (non-amortization)' or 'Systematic amortization with impairment'"; and 4 = "Goodwill that meets certain conditions for each acquisition deal is not amortized, and anything else is amortized systematically."

(Q4) There are several accounting methods other than "Impairment-only (non-amortization)" and "Systematic amortization with impairment" that could theoretically be considered after acquiring goodwill. Please share your opinion on the following accounting treatment methods for acquired goodwill. (Options: 1 = "Desirable," 2 = "Somewhat desirable," 3 = "Somewhat undesirable," 4 = "Undesirable," and 5 = "Unsure")

1. No amortization and no impairment (acquisition cost as is)
2. Systematic amortization without impairment
3. Continual revaluation based on fair value (the difference in value is included in the profit and loss calculation)
4. Immediate charge to earnings
5. Immediate charge to equity

Table 5.22 Accounting treatments currently being discussed compared to potential alternatives

	Entire sample		Firms that recognized goodwill	
	Number of respondents	Percentage (%)	Number of respondents	Percentage (%)
Panel A: No amortization and no impairment (acquisition cost as is)				
1. Desirable	24	5.43	15	6.05
2. Somewhat desirable	21	4.75	10	4.03
3. Somewhat undesirable	123	27.83	62	25.00
4. Undesirable	255	57.69	154	62.10
5. Unsure	19	4.30	7	2.82
Total	442	100.00	248	100.00
Panel B: Systematic amortization without impairment				
1. Desirable	36	8.14	17	6.85
2. Somewhat desirable	119	26.92	60	24.19
3. Somewhat undesirable	149	33.71	93	37.50
4. Undesirable	119	26.92	71	28.63
5. Unsure	19	4.30	7	2.82
Total	442	100.00	248	100.00
Panel C: Continual revaluation based on fair value (the difference in value is included in the profit and loss calculation)				
1. Desirable	14	3.17	5	2.02
2. Somewhat desirable	70	15.84	40	16.13
3. Somewhat undesirable	145	32.81	71	28.63
4. Undesirable	178	40.27	118	47.58
5. Unsure	35	7.92	14	5.65
Total	442	100.00	248	100.00
Panel D: Immediate charge to earnings				
1. Desirable	11	2.49	5	2.02
2. Somewhat desirable	44	9.95	22	8.87
3. Somewhat undesirable	129	29.19	67	27.02
4. Undesirable	233	52.71	142	57.26
5. Unsure	25	5.66	12	4.84
Total	442	100.00	248	100.00
Panel E: Immediate charge to equity				
1. Desirable	14	3.17	6	2.42
2. Somewhat desirable	67	15.16	42	16.94
3. Somewhat undesirable	113	25.57	61	24.60
4. Undesirable	167	37.78	102	41.13
5. Unsure	81	18.33	37	14.92
Total	442	100.00	248	100.00

- The method receiving the highest percentage of "1. Desirable" or "2. Somewhat desirable" responses was "Systematic amortization without impairment" (Panel B): 35.07% of the entire sample and 31.05% of firms that recorded goodwill. Other methods received less than 20% support.

- Notably, many respondents rated "No amortization and no impairment (acquisition cost as is)" (Panel A) as "2. Somewhat undesirable" or "4. Undesirable": 85.52% for the entire sample and 87.10% for firms recording goodwill. Conversely, 60.63% of the entire sample and 66.13% of firms recording goodwill favored "Systematic amortization without impairment" (Panel B).
- The results for Panel B suggest that while some respondents preferred avoiding impairment and favor systematic expense allocation for assets such as goodwill, a larger portion regarded impairment as necessary.
- "Immediate charge to equity" (Panel E), previously used in the U.K., attracted more "1. Desirable" or "2. Somewhat desirable" responses than "Immediate charge to earnings" (Panel D).
- It is important to note that under Panel D's method, various stakeholders absorb the impairment loss, whereas under Panel E's method, shareholders alone bear this loss.

5.3.2.6 Impact of Disclosure and Accounting Treatment Related to Goodwill on Corporate Activities

The focus shifts from the accounting treatment of goodwill to the impact of goodwill-related disclosure, specifically the disclosure of net assets after deducting goodwill, on recognizing impairment losses and on corporate investment decisions such as mergers and acquisitions (M&A). The first question addressed preparers' views on whether disclosing net assets after deducting goodwill reduces reported equity, lowers the equity ratio, and, if goodwill's asset status is doubtful, might reveal excess debt.

5.3.2.6.1 Impact of Disclosure of Net Asset Amount After Deducting Goodwill

(Q5) Currently, there are concerns that goodwill impairment losses are not being recorded at the appropriate time.

Therefore, so that the recording of goodwill impairment losses is timelier, an idea has been proposed to request disclosure of the net asset amount after deducting goodwill (= net asset amount−goodwill balance). Do you think asking for disclosure of net assets after deducting goodwill will encourage more timely recording of goodwill impairment losses? Choose one answer that applies from the options below. (Options: 1 = "It will encourage more timely recording of impairment loss," 2 = "If anything, it would encourage more timely recording of impairment loss," 3 = "If anything, it would not encourage more timely recording of impairment loss," 4 = "It will not encourage more timely recording of impairment loss," 5 = "Unsure")

Table 5.23 Does disclosure of net assets after deducting goodwill impact the timing of impairment loss recognition?

	Entire sample		Firms that recognized goodwill	
	Number of respondents	Percentage (%)	Number of respondents	Percentage (%)
1. It will encourage more timely recording of impairment loss	17	3.82	9	3.61
2. If anything, it would encourage more timely recording of impairment loss	94	21.12	46	18.47
3. If anything, it would not encourage more timely recording of impairment loss	107	24.04	65	26.10
4. It will not encourage more timely recording of impairment loss	157	35.28	102	40.96
5. Unsure	70	15.73	27	10.84
Total	445	100.00	249	100.00

- Table 5.23 shows that only 24.94% of the entire sample and 22.09% of firms recognizing goodwill responded that such disclosure "1. It will encourage more timely recording of impairment loss" or "2. If anything, it would encourage more timely recording." A notable portion of respondents selected "5. Unsure."

5.3.2.6.2 Impact of Accounting Treatment of Goodwill on Mergers and Acquisitions

As introduced in Sect. 5.2, the influence of goodwill accounting on M&A decisions is a key issue in assessing the impact of accounting rules on corporate behavior. This survey specifically asked whether goodwill accounting affects M&A decision-making:

(Q6) Do you think the choice between systematic amortization and non-amortization of goodwill has an impact on your company's decisions regarding mergers and acquisitions (M&A)? Choose one answer that applies from the options below.

(Options)
1. It is highly likely to have an impact.
2. It is somewhat likely to have an impact.
3. It is somewhat unlikely to have an impact.
4. It is highly unlikely to have an impact.
5. Unsure.

Table 5.24 Impact of accounting treatment of goodwill on M&A decisions

	Entire sample		Firms that recognized goodwill	
	Number of respondents	Percentage (%)	Number of respondents	Percentage (%)
1. It is highly likely to have an impact	88	19.78	57	22.89
2. It is somewhat likely to have an impact	162	36.40	89	35.74
3. It is somewhat unlikely to have an impact	119	26.74	69	27.71
4. It is highly unlikely to have an impact	59	13.26	31	12.45
5. Unsure	17	3.82	3	1.20
Total	445	100.00	249	100.00

The key findings in Table 5.24 are summarized as follows:

- Only 19.78% of the entire sample and 22.89% of firms recognizing goodwill believed there was "1. It is highly likely to have an impact" on M&A decisions. Additionally, 36.40% of the total sample and 35.74% of firms recording goodwill selected "2. It is somewhat likely to have an impact."
- Conversely, 40.00% of the total sample and 40.16% of firms recording goodwill believed goodwill accounting was unlikely to affect M&A, selecting "3. It is somewhat unlikely to have an impact" or "4. It is highly unlikely to have an impact." These responses may reflect differing views on how accounting figures influence investment decisions within firms.

5.3.3 *Responses from Users*

5.3.3.1 Characteristics of Respondents

Before addressing the main questions regarding the accounting treatment of acquired goodwill, respondents were asked to provide background information, including their careers and positions. Tables 5.25, 5.26, and 5.27 summarize these characteristics. Table 5.25 presents the respondents' work experience as analysts. The mean and median years of experience were approximately 17 years, with the 25th percentile at 10.08 years. Table 5.26 shows the distribution of analyst positions: 60.00% of the 130 respondents were sell-side analysts, and 36.15% were buy-side analysts.[73] Table 5.27 indicates no significant bias in the distribution of industries for which respondents were responsible.[74]

[73] Respondents did not include credit analysts.

[74] The survey permitted multiple responses regarding the types of industries for which each respondent was responsible.

Table 5.25 Years of experience working as an analyst

	N	Mean	S.D.	Min	p25	p50	p75	Max
Years of experience	130	16.71	7.88	1.33	10.08	17	22	35.33

Table 5.26 Position as an analyst

	Number of responses	Percentage (%)
Sell-side analyst	78	60.00
Buy-side analyst	35	26.92
Buy-side and fund manager	12	9.23
Others (e.g., manager)	5	3.85
Total	130	100.00

Table 5.27 Distribution of industries covered by respondents

Industry	N	%	Industry	N	%
1. Fishery, Agriculture & Forestry	9	1.7	18. Precision Instruments	18	3.4
2. Mining	6	1.1	19. Other Products	17	3.2
3. Construction	17	3.2	20. Electric Power and Gas	12	2.2
4. Foods	14	2.6	21. Land Transportation	16	3.0
5. Transportation & Equipment	12	2.2	22. Marine Transportation	15	2.8
6. Pulp and Paper	10	1.9	23. Air Transportation	14	2.6
7. Chemical	26	4.9	24. Warehousing & Harbor Transportation	14	2.6
8. Pharmaceutical	19	3.5	25. Information & Communication	27	5.0
9. Oil and Coal Products	8	1.5	26. Wholesale Trade	16	3.0
10. Rubber Products	9	1.7	27. Retail Trade	21	3.9
11. Glass and Ceramics Products	16	3.0	28. Banks	13	2.4
12. Iron and Steel	16	3.0	29. Securities and Commodities Futures	12	2.2
13. Nonferrous Metals	17	3.2	30. Insurance	13	2.4
14. Metal Products	15	2.8	31. Other Financing Business	16	3.0
15. Machinery	21	3.9	32. Real Estate	16	3.0
16. Electric Appliances	35	6.5	33. Services	29	5.4
17. Transportation Equipment	17	3.2	Total	536	100.0

5.3.3.2 Questions Regarding Accounting for Acquired Goodwill

5.3.3.2.1 "Impairment-Only (Non-amortization)" and "Systematic Amortization with Impairment"

The most important question in this survey asked which accounting treatment users preferred: "Impairment-only" or "Systematic amortization with impairment." As with the preparer survey, the option "Either" was also included.

Table 5.28 Desirability of "Impairment-only" versus "Systematic amortization with impairment"

	Number of responses	Percentage (%)
Impairment-only (non-amortization)	26	20.00
Systematic amortization with impairment	81	62.31
Either	23	17.69
Total	130	100.00

(Q1) When a unified approach to the accounting treatment of acquired goodwill is required, which approach do you think would be better for yourself, "Impairment-only (non-amortization)" or "Systematic amortization with impairment"? (Options: "Impairment-only (non-amortization)," "Systematic amortization with impairment," and "Either")

- Table 5.28 shows that a majority of users (62.31%) preferred "Systematic amortization with impairment" over the other options. Compared to preparers, a smaller proportion of users supported "Systematic amortization with impairment," while support for "Impairment-only" and "Either" increased. Notably, however, more than 60% still favored systematic amortization. A limited minority also viewed "Impairment-only" or "Either" as the more desirable treatment.

5.3.3.2.2 Additional Question for Respondents Who Indicated in Q1 That "Impairment-Only (Non-amortization)" Is More Desirable

Respondents who selected either "Impairment-only" or "Systematic amortization with impairment" (excluding "Either") were asked additional questions. This section reports results from the 26 respondents who preferred "Impairment-only."

Reasons Why "Impairment-Only (Non-amortization)" Is More Desirable

(Q1-1) To what extent do you agree with the following reasons that "Impairment-only (non-amortization)" is more desirable? (Options: 1 = "Yes," 2 = "Somewhat yes," 3 = "Somewhat no," 4 = "No," 5 = "Unsure").

1. It is difficult to estimate the useful life and amortization pattern of the carrying amount of goodwill.
2. The value of goodwill is maintained by firm efforts after it is acquired.
3. Goodwill amortization expense and the carrying amount of goodwill after amortization are not useful for financial statement users.

4. If an appropriate impairment test is conducted, systematic amortization of goodwill is not needed.
5. It reduces comparability with firms that are not required to amortize goodwill.
6. Amortizing goodwill weakens the signaling effect of goodwill impairment.

The results presented in Table 5.29 are summarized as follows:

- In Panel A, 88.46% answered "Yes" or "Somewhat yes" to the statement, "It is difficult to estimate the useful life and amortization pattern of the carrying amount of goodwill." This rationale was strongly supported by both users and preparers, with 84.72% of the overall sample and 84.21% of firms recording goodwill giving similar responses.
- In Panel B, similarly, 88.46% answered "Yes" or "Somewhat yes" to the statement, "The value of goodwill is maintained by firm efforts after it is acquired."
- In Panel C, only 30.77% responded "Yes" or "Somewhat yes" to the statement, "Goodwill amortization expense and the carrying amount of goodwill after amortization are not useful for financial statement users." This does not indicate that most respondents favor "Impairment-only" because they view amortization-related information as useless.

Table 5.29 Reasons for support of "impairment-only (non-amortization)"

	1	2	3	4	5	Total
Panel A: It is difficult to estimate the useful life and amortization pattern of the carrying amount of goodwill.						
Number of responses	9	14	0	3	0	26
Percentage (%)	34.62	53.85	0.00	11.54	0.00	100.00
Panel B: The value of goodwill is maintained by firm efforts after it is acquired.						
Number of responses	10	13	0	1	2	26
Percentage (%)	38.46	50.00	0.00	3.85	7.69	100.00
Panel C: Goodwill amortization expense and the carrying amount of goodwill after amortization are not useful for financial statement users.						
Number of responses	6	2	8	8	2	26
Percentage (%)	23.08	7.69	30.77	30.77	7.69	100.00
Panel D: If an appropriate impairment test is conducted, systematic amortization of goodwill is not needed.						
Number of responses	18	7	1	0	0	26
Percentage (%)	69.23	26.92	3.85	0.00	0.00	100.00
Panel E: It reduces comparability with firms that are not required to amortize goodwill.						
Number of responses	13	9	2	2	0	26
Percentage (%)	50.00	34.62	7.69	7.69	0.00	100.00
Panel F: Amortizing goodwill weakens the signaling effect of goodwill impairment.						
Number of responses	3	7	7	5	4	26
Percentage (%)	11.54	26.92	26.92	19.23	15.38	100.00

- In Panel D, 96.15% responded "Yes" or "Somewhat yes" to the statement, "If an appropriate impairment test is conducted, systematic amortization of goodwill is not needed." This suggests strong support for impairment testing as a substitute for amortization.
- In Panel E, 84.62% responded "Yes" or "Somewhat yes" to the statement, "It reduces comparability with firms that are not required to amortize goodwill." This reflects concern about comparability across firms, particularly given that non-amortization is the international norm. Many respondents may prefer alignment with this standard.
- In Panel F, only 38.46% responded "Yes" or "Somewhat yes" to that "Amortizing goodwill weakens the signaling effect of goodwill impairment."[75] Notably, 15.38% selected "Unsure," indicating some uncertainty regarding this rationale.

Respondents were also asked to provide other reasons for preferring "Impairment-only."

(Q1-2) If you have any reasons why you think the "Impairment-only (non-amortization)" is more desirable, other those mentioned in Q1-1, please describe them below.

Three notable responses were received[76]:

- One respondent noted that "the determination of goodwill impairment indicates the success or failure of the M&A, and uniform amortization is meaningless." This aligns with the view that impairment testing better reflects the outcome of acquisitions.
- Another emphasized that "periodic accounting earnings should be closer to cash flow." This reflects the perspective that reducing accrual components enhances the quality of reported earnings, though this view is not universally held.
- A third response highlighted that "the proportion of the portion recorded as goodwill in the B/S differs depending on the type of industry." Specifically, service industries often report higher goodwill than manufacturing firms, making acquisitions appear more expensive under an amortization approach.

[75] Although the IASB argues, citing, for example, Chalmers et al. (2011), that allowing systematic amortization would dilute the signaling effect of impairment losses, responses in this survey varied. They did not support factor "6. Amortizing goodwill weakens the signaling effect of goodwill impairment" to the extent the IASB considers it important.

[76] In presenting the open-ended responses, statements such as "none/not particularly" should be excluded in advance.

5.3.3.2.3 Additional Question for Respondents Who Indicated in Q1 That "Systematic Amortization with Impairment" Is More Desirable

Respondents who indicated in Q1 that "Systematic amortization with impairment" was more desirable were subsequently asked about their reasons for this preference. The reasons listed mirrored those provided in the preparer survey.

(Q1-3) To what extent do you agree with the following reasons that "Systematic amortization with impairment" is more desirable? (Options: 1 = "Yes," 2 = "Somewhat yes," 3 = "Somewhat no," 4 = "No," 5 = "Unsure").

1. Excess earnings power represented by goodwill gradually decreases due to market competition.
2. The carrying amount of goodwill should be allocated to appropriate periods to match revenues and expenses.
3. It is impossible to distinguish between the diminished and maintained components of goodwill value.
4. It is consistent with the accounting treatment of other depreciable assets.
5. Amortization cannot be replaced by impairment.
6. It leads to prudent M&A decisions.
7. It reduces the cost of the goodwill impairment test.

Table 5.30 shows the following key findings:

- In Panel A, 80.25% of respondents agreed ("Yes" or "Somewhat yes") that excess earnings power represented by goodwill gradually diminishes due to market competition.
- In Panel B, 87.65% of respondents agreed that the carrying amount of goodwill should be allocated to appropriate periods to match revenues and expenses. This high level of agreement across Panels A and B suggests that the rationale for "Systematic amortization with impairment" lies in its alignment with the economic consumption of goodwill. These results are consistent with those observed in the preparer sample.
- In Panel C, 75.31% of respondents agreed that it is impossible to distinguish between the diminished and maintained components of goodwill. In Panel D, 87.65% of respondents agreed that this approach is consistent with the accounting treatment of other depreciable assets. Compared to preparers, users showed stronger support for "Systematic amortization with impairment," as reflected in lower percentages for "Somewhat no" and "No."
- In addition, responses to Panel D suggest that users view goodwill as an amortizable asset, similar to other depreciable assets. Responses in Panel B further indicate that users favor aligning the amortization of goodwill with the matching principle for evaluating business performance and return on investment.

Table 5.30 Reasons why "Systematic amortization with impairment" is more desirable

	1	2	3	4	5	Total
Panel A: Excess earnings power represented by goodwill gradually decreases due to market competition.						
Number of responses	31	34	7	6	3	81
Percentage (%)	38.27	41.98	8.64	7.41	3.70	100.00
Panel B: The carrying amount of goodwill should be allocated to appropriate periods to match revenues and expenses.						
Number of responses	42	29	6	3	1	81
Percentage (%)	51.85	35.8	7.41	3.70	1.23	100.00
Panel C: It is impossible to distinguish between the diminished and maintained components of goodwill value.						
Number of responses	21	40	12	5	3	81
Percentage (%)	25.93	49.38	14.81	6.17	3.70	100.00
Panel D: It is consistent with the accounting treatment of other depreciable assets.						
Number of responses	33	38	4	5	1	81
Percentage (%)	40.74	46.91	4.94	6.17	1.23	100.00
Panel E: Amortization cannot be replaced by impairment.						
Number of responses	27	28	15	8	3	81
Percentage (%)	33.33	34.57	18.52	9.88	3.70	100.00
Panel F: It leads to prudent M&A decisions.						
Number of responses	27	21	11	17	5	81
Percentage (%)	33.33	25.93	13.58	20.99	6.17	100.00
Panel G: It reduces the cost of the goodwill impairment test.						
Number of responses	12	21	20	23	5	81
Percentage (%)	14.81	25.93	24.69	28.40	6.17	100.00

- In Panel E, 67.90% agreed that amortization cannot be replaced by impairment, a view supported by a majority of preparers as well.
- In Panel F, 59.26% agreed that amortization leads to more prudent M&A decisions. While this percentage does not differ significantly from preparers' responses, two interpretations are possible: (a) amortization may not directly encourage more prudent M&A behavior, and (b) "Systematic amortization with impairment" is not viewed as a primary factor when evaluating the desirability of M&A transactions.
- Finally, in Panel G, only 40.74% agreed that it reduces the cost of goodwill impairment testing. While some respondents acknowledged cost reduction as a benefit, most did not consider it a compelling reason to prefer this method. Since users do not incur the costs of preparing financial statements, many may not view cost considerations as relevant. Additionally, some respondents may believe that listed firms should bear the cost of impairment testing as part of their financial reporting responsibilities.

Following this, respondents were invited to provide open-ended responses identifying additional reasons beyond those in Q1-3 for preferring "Systematic amortization with impairment."

(Q1-4) If you have any reasons you think "Systematic amortization with impairment" is more desirable, other than those mentioned in Q1-3, please describe them below.

We received 19 responses, summarized as follows.

- Concerns over managerial discretion in impairment-only models[77]
- Risk of incentivizing accounting irregularities and earnings management
- Doubts regarding the nature of goodwill as an asset (e.g., not excess earnings power but a residual from acquisition pricing)
- Desire for consistency with the treatment of internally generated goodwill
- Reduction of volatility in reported performance and stock prices
- Enhancing management awareness of return on invested capital and cost of capital
- Promotion of more appropriate pricing in M&A markets
- Elimination of discretion in the classification of non-amortizable goodwill and amortizable intangibles during purchase price allocation (PPA)
- Improved comparability through amortization
- Amortization period as an indicator of management's estimate of the goodwill's payback period
- Difficulty for external users in detecting impairment signals

Several responses emphasized concerns about discretion in impairment testing. From a comparability standpoint, respondents presented two conflicting views: that "Impairment-only" improves comparability, and conversely, that amortization preserves it. Further research is warranted.

5.3.3.2.4 Factors Considered Important in Determining the Amortization Period of Goodwill

Respondents who preferred "Systematic amortization with impairment" in Q1 were also asked which factors they deemed important in setting the amortization period.

---

[77] A significant portion of firms' goodwill has been impaired over the past decade, supporting the argument that systematic amortization would reduce managerial discretion. This aligns with the findings of Li and Sloan (2017).

(Q1-5) To what extent do you think the following factors are important when preparers estimate the goodwill amortization period? For each factor, please choose one of the following options (Options: 1 = "Yes," 2 = "Somewhat yes," 3 = "Somewhat no," 4 = "No," 5 = "Unsure").

1. The investment-return period based on management's business plan
2. The period over which synergies are expected to be maintained
3. Periods over which an acquirer, on a stand-alone basis, is expected to maintain higher future cash flows
4. Useful lives of related tangible assets
5. Useful lives of related other intangible assets

The key findings in Table 5.31 are summarized as follows:

- In Panel A, 76.54% agreed ("Yes" or "Somewhat yes") that the investment-return period based on management's business plan was important. While over 50% of preparers (both overall and those recognizing goodwill) agreed, only 33% of users selected "Yes," indicating a potential perception gap regarding what factors are important to preparers.
- In Panel B, only 55.46% agreed that the expected duration of synergies is an important determinant. This is lower than the percentage observed among preparers, suggesting users place less emphasis on this factor.
- In Panel C, 48.15% agreed that the period during which an acquirer, on a stand-alone basis, is expected to maintain elevated future cash flows is important. Again, this is lower than for preparers, further reflecting a divergence in perspective.

Table 5.31 Important factors in determining amortization period

	1	2	3	4	5	Total
Panel A: The investment-return period based on management's business plan						
Number of responses	27	35	11	6	2	81
Percentage (%)	33.33	43.21	13.58	7.41	2.47	100.00
Panel B: The period over which synergies are expected to be maintained						
Number of responses	11	34	23	11	2	81
Percentage (%)	13.58	41.98	28.40	13.58	2.47	100.00
Panel C: Periods over which an acquirer, on a stand-alone basis, is expected to maintain higher future cash flows						
Number of responses	15	24	33	6	3	81
Percentage (%)	18.52	29.63	40.74	7.41	3.70	100.00
Panel D: Useful lives of related tangible assets						
Number of responses	12	33	20	14	2	81
Percentage (%)	14.81	40.74	24.69	17.28	2.47	100.00
Panel E: Useful lives of related other intangible assets						
Number of responses	12	34	20	11	4	81
Percentage (%)	14.81	41.98	24.69	13.58	4.94	100.00

- In Panels D and E, 55.56% and 56.79%, respectively, agreed that the useful lives of related tangible and other intangible assets are relevant. These percentages were notably higher than those for preparers.

These findings suggest perceptual differences between preparers and users regarding the key determinants of the amortization period. While information asymmetry between these groups has long been a challenge in goodwill accounting, it is essential to promote constructive dialogue. This would help address user concerns and reduce the information gap, particularly in critical decisions such as M&A.

Respondents were also asked to identify any additional factors not listed in Q1-5 that they considered important in estimating the amortization period of goodwill.

> (Q1-6) If there are any important factors when companies estimate the goodwill amortization period, other than those listed in Q1-5, please describe them below.

Eight responses were received,[78] summarized as follows:

- Impact on profit/loss (income) for the period[79]
- Achievement of management objectives
- Duration of brand value
- Examples of other firms and past processes.

The most frequent responses indicated that firms consider the impact on income, alignment with managerial targets, and reference to numerical indicators when determining the amortization period. One respondent noted, "I honestly do not know, because there is too little disclosure on goodwill," while another observed, "It appears that there is no clear logic from corporate behavior."

5.3.3.2.5 How Should the Provisions Regarding the Amortization Period of Goodwill Be Addressed?

Furthermore, respondents who indicated in Q1 that "Systematic amortization with impairment" was the most desirable accounting treatment were subsequently asked

[78] Although ten responses were received, only two addressed amortization. One respondent stated, "It should be standardized depending on business characteristics," while another suggested that "immediate write-offs should be made." Some noted that if systematic amortization is considered to reduce the burden of impairment testing, then selecting the amortization period becomes a policy decision, not a theoretical one.

[79] One respondent, drawing on professional experience advising on M&A transactions, noted that management often sets the amortization period based on the level of earnings after amortization, regardless of the underlying economics of the transaction. The same respondent noted that more expensive acquisitions tend to be amortized over longer periods.

to evaluate three options concerning the preferred method for stipulating the amortization period.

(Q1-7) Given that the "Systematic amortization with impairment" is more desirable in accounting for goodwill, how do you think a requirement to determine the goodwill amortization period should be prescribed? Please choose an option that you think is the most desirable for you.

(Options)
1. An upper limit should be set for the amortization period (e.g., the rule should be prescribed in the form "Be amortized within ... years").
2. A uniform amortization period should be set (e.g., the rule should be prescribed in the form "Be amortized in just ... years").
3. No provision about the amortization period should be set.

The results reported in Table 5.32 are summarized as follows:

- The results show that a significant majority (81.48%) selected "1. An upper limit should be set for the amortization period." In comparison, 9.88% selected "2. A uniform amortization period should be set," and 8.64% selected "3. No provision about the amortization period should be set."
- As reflected in the free responses to Q1-4, users value information conveyed through management's choice of amortization period, as it often reflects the expected payback period of the investment. However, the low percentage (8.64%) choosing Option 3 suggests that while most respondents accept a degree of preparer discretion, they also favor the imposition of certain constraints.

The following question was then posed to respondents who selected Option 1 in Q1-7:

(Q1-8) How many years do you think should be chosen as the upper limit of the goodwill amortization period? Please choose one of the following options. If you choose "Other," please fill in the blank with any specific number of years.

Table 5.32 Provision about the amortization period

	Number of responses	Percentage (%)
1. There should be a cap on the amortization period.	66	81.48
2. A uniform amortization period should be established.	8	9.88
3. There should be no provision for amortization periods	7	8.64
Total	81	100.00

Table 5.33 Upper limit of the goodwill amortization period

	Number of responses	Percentage (%)
20 years	21	31.82
15 years	8	12.12
10 years	32	48.48
5 years	4	6.06
Other	1	1.52
Total	66	100.00

Note: Only one respondent chose "Other" and answered "1 year" in the blank

Table 5.34 Uniform amortization period

	Number of responses	Percentage (%)
20 years	0	0.00
15 years	0	0.00
10 years	4	50.00
5 years	3	37.50
Other	1*	12.50
Total	8	100.00

Note: One "other" response was listed as "3 years"

- Table 5.33 shows that, among preparers, the most frequently cited upper limit was 20 years, followed by 10 years. Among users, 10 years was the most common (48.48%), followed by 20 years (31.82%). This difference may be interpreted in two ways: users may believe that goodwill value diminishes over approximately 10 years due to market competition, or they may view a 20-year limit as allowing excessive managerial discretion.

  Respondents who selected Option 2 were also asked the following question:

> (Q1-9) How many years do you think a uniform amortization period should be? If you choose "Other," please fill in the blank with any specific number of years.

- In response to Q1-7, eight respondents (9.88%) selected Option 2. Table 5.34 reports that half of these respondents preferred a uniform period of 10 years, while the reminder proposed either 5 or 3 years.

Finally, respondents who selected either Option 1 or Option 2 for Q1-7 were asked whether exceptions to the amortization period should be permitted.

> (Q1-10) Do you think the rebuttable presumption of an amortization period for goodwill should be made? (Options: 1 = "Should be made" 2 = "Should not be made")

Table 5.35 Should the rebuttable presumption be made?

	Number of responses	Percentage (%)
1. Should be made	27	36.49
2. Should not be made	47	63.51
Total	74	100.00

- Table 5.35 shows that, among users, 63.51% answered "Should not be made," a higher proportion than among preparers. This result aligns with expectations, as users generally oppose exceptions that could increase preparer discretion.

5.3.3.3 Characterization of Goodwill as an Asset

As with preparers, users were asked about the nature of goodwill as an asset.

5.3.3.3.1 Is There a Semi-permanent, Non-amortizable Portion of Goodwill?

(Q2) Do you think there is a part of goodwill that preserves its value semi-permanently? Please select one answer from the options below.

(Options)
1. All or the majority of the value is preserved semi-permanently.
2. There is both a part that preserves its value semi-permanently and a part that does not.
3. There is no part that preserves its value semi-permanently.
4. Unsure.

- Table 5.36 reports that approximately 90% of user responses selected either "2. There is both a part that preserves its value semi-permanently and a part that does not" or "3. There is no part that preserves its value semi-permanently." However, a more detailed breakdown shows that 57.69% of users selected option 2, while 33.08% selected option 3. In contrast, among preparers, the corresponding figures were 42.92% and 46.74%, respectively.

Table 5.36 Goodwill as an asset

	Number of responses	Percentage (%)
1. All or the majority of the value is preserved semi-permanently	3	2.31
2. There is both a part that preserves its value semi-permanently and a part that does not	75	57.69
3. There is no part that preserves its value semi-permanently	43	33.08
4. Unsure	9	6.92
Total	130	100.00

5.3.3.3.2 Components of Goodwill

Additional questions were posed to respondents who selected either "1. All or the majority of the value is preserved semi-permanently" or "2. There is both a part that preserves its value semi-permanently and a part that does not" in response to Q2.

(Q2-1) The following is a list of items that are considered components of goodwill. Please select one that applies to each of the following items. (Select one for each of the following, 1 = "Amortized," 2 = "Amortized to some extent," 3 = "Not amortized much," 4 = "Not amortized," 5 = "Unsure," 6 = "It is not a component of goodwill")

(Components addressed in this survey)
1. Brand
2. Sales know-how
3. Proprietary technology
4. Business model
5. Human resources
6. Site-specific conditions

The key findings in Table 5.37 are summarized as follows:

Table 5.37 Components of goodwill

	1	2	3	4	5	6	Total
Panel A: Brand							
Number of responses	13	15	35	9	4	2	78
Percentage (%)	16.67	19.23	44.87	11.54	5.13	2.56	100.00
Panel B: Sales know-how							
Number of responses	19	27	22	3	4	3	78
Percentage (%)	24.36	34.62	28.21	3.85	5.13	3.85	100.00
Panel C: Proprietary technology							
Number of responses	19	37	14	2	4	2	78
Percentage (%)	24.36	47.44	17.95	2.56	5.13	2.56	100.00
Panel D: Business model							
Number of responses	18	33	14	3	5	5	78
Percentage (%)	23.08	42.31	17.95	3.85	6.41	6.41	100.00
Panel E: Human resources							
Number of responses	14	38	15	1	8	2	78
Percentage (%)	17.95	48.72	19.23	1.28	10.26	2.56	100.00
Panel F: Site-specific conditions							
Number of responses	10	20	27	4	7	10	78
Percentage (%)	12.82	25.64	34.62	5.13	8.97	12.82	100.00

- “Brand” (Panel A) was the only category where the percentage of respondents selecting “3. Not amortized much” or “4. Not amortized” significantly exceeded those selecting “1. Amortized” or “2. Amortized to some extent.” Except for “Site-specific conditions” (Panel F), the opposite pattern was observed in categories such as “Sales know-how” (Panel B), “Proprietary technology” (Panel C), “Business model” (Panel D), and “Human resources” (Panel E). Notably, a high proportion of both users and preparers considered “Brand” (Panel A) to be only minimally or not at all amortized.

Respondents were also asked to suggest other components of goodwill not listed in Q2-1.

(Q2-2) If there are any components considered to constitute goodwill, other than those listed in Q2-1, please write them below.

Eight responses were received[80]:

- Acquired from data (e.g., mutual use of sales and purchase price data)
- Patent, marketing, and commercial rights
- Relative advantages in regulation and taxation
- Excessive premium
- Management competence[81]

One respondent remarked, “excess earning power is difficult to reduce to individual elements; rather, it boils down to whether the business as a whole has a competitive advantage.” The most frequently mentioned components were rights-related elements such as patent and commercial rights. The inclusion of “excessive premium” in purchased goodwill was not highlighted by preparers, but it is a relevant consideration, especially given the prevalence of overpricing in M&A transactions, which often leads to impairment. This suggests that both users and preparers may consider “excessive premium” a significant component of goodwill.

5.3.3.4 Treatment of Goodwill Amount and Amortization of Goodwill in Securities Analysis

This section explores how users treat goodwill and its amortization in securities analysis.

---

[80] Although nine responses were received, one served only to supplement the answer to Q2.

[81] While “human resources” was included under the management team category, it was retained here because it was explicitly mentioned in a free response.

5.3.3.4.1 Is the Goodwill Amount Deducted from Net Assets?

The first question asked whether analysts deduct goodwill from net asset value in their analysis when a firm holds a large amount of goodwill, particularly in cases where there is doubt about the capitalization of goodwill and concerns that it may be potentially impaired.

(Q3) When conducting a securities analysis and using information on net assets, do you deduct the amount of goodwill from net assets? Please choose only one answer from the options below.

(Options)
1. It is deducted.
2. It is not deducted.
3. The treatment is not necessarily consistent.
4. Unsure.

Table 5.38 shows the following key findings:

- The most common response was "3. The treatment is not necessarily consistent" (51.54%), followed by "2. It is not deducted" (42.31%). These two responses accounted for over 90% of the total. This indicates that while some analysts deduct non-cash goodwill from net assets, others do so only in certain situations.
- International discussions have noted that users, including equity investors, often disregard the goodwill amount recorded on the balance sheet. Instead, they prefer performance indicators such as return on capital employed and return on invested capital, without adjusting for goodwill.[82] This view aligns with the findings of this study.

Table 5.38 Whether goodwill amounts are deducted from net assets

	Number of responses	Percentage (%)
1. It is deducted	7	5.38
2. It is not deducted	55	42.31
3. The treatment is not necessarily consistent	67	51.54
4. Unsure	1	0.77
Total	130	100.00

[82] See Craig et al. (2018, Slide 33).

5.3.3.4.2 Is Goodwill Amortization Expense Added Back?

The next question addressed whether goodwill amortization is added back in financial analysis.

(Q4-1) When conducting securities analysis, is goodwill amortization expense added back to earnings, considering the differences in accounting standards and amortization policies adopted by the firm that is analyzed? (Other than the cases in which amortization expense is deliberately added back, cases in which EBITDA is used as a profitability indicator are also included.) Please choose only one answer from the options below.

(Options)
1. Amortization expense is added back.
2. Amortization expense is not added back.
3. The treatment is not necessarily consistent.
4. Unsure.

The key findings in Table 5.39 can be summarized as follows:

- Approximately 40% of respondents answered "1. Amortization expense is added back." It is often asserted that many analysts and investors add back goodwill amortization when analyzing earnings.[83] However, the survey results do not fully support this claim.[84]
- Two respondent types selected "(1) Amortization expense is added back": those who do so deliberately and those who add it back implicitly through the EBITDA calculation. Although both groups selected the same option, the underlying rationale differed.
- A substantial portion (45.38%) selected "(3) The treatment is not necessarily consistent," suggesting that some analysts either use reported earnings figures as they are or add back amortization depending on the specific context. However, this variation makes interpretation challenging.

[83] For example, at the ASAF meeting held on December 6–7, 2018, a member of the Group of Latin America Standards Setters (GLASS) cited a survey of Brazilian financial institutions indicating that all analysts added back goodwill amortization (https://www.ifrs.org/-/media/feature/meetings/2018/december/asaf/asaf-meeting-summary-dec-2018.pdf, Accessed: February 18, 2026). Mr. Hans Hoogervorst, former chairman of the IASB, also stated: "We [...] know that many investors will ignore amorti[z]ation and will immediately add it back in their projections" (https://www.ifrs.org/news-and-events/2018/08/chairmans-speech-japan-and-ifrs-standards/, Accessed: February 18, 2026).

[84] It is important to note that even if amortization expenses are routinely added back, this practice does not imply that goodwill amortization is unnecessary. A comparable situation exists with EBITDA, where depreciation is added back, yet depreciation of tangible fixed assets remains standard accounting practice.

Table 5.39 Is goodwill amortization expense added back?

	Number of responses	Percentage (%)
1. Amortization expense is added back	53	40.77
2. Amortization expense is not added back	18	13.85
3. The treatment is not necessarily consistent	59	45.38
4. Unsure	0	0.00
Total	130	100.00

Table 5.40 Is there any information value in the amount of goodwill after amortization?

	Number of responses	Percentage (%)
1. Contains very useful information	19	14.62
2. Contains some useful information	83	63.85
3. Contains no useful information	18	13.85
4. Unsure	10	7.69
Total	130	100.00

5.3.3.4.3 Usefulness of the Goodwill Amount After Amortization

Finally, users were asked whether the amortized goodwill balance provides useful information for securities analysis.

(Q4-2) Do you think the amount of goodwill after deducting systematic amortization contains useful information for estimating corporate value (stock price)? Please choose only one from the following options.

(Options)
1. Contains very useful information
2. Contains some useful information
3. Contains no useful information
4. Unsure

Table 5.40 shows the following key findings:

- A combined 78.46% responded that the amortized goodwill balance "1. Contains very useful information" or "2. Contains some useful information," indicating that most users recognize its informational value. Only 13.85% selected "3. Contains no useful information," showing that while a minority finds the amortized balance unhelpful, it retains perceived analytical relevance for the majority.

5.3.3.5 Alternative Accounting Treatment of Goodwill (Part 1)

The preceding sections examined the historically adopted accounting treatments of goodwill and how users, primarily analysts, interpret goodwill-related information. This section evaluates alternative accounting treatments beyond the current methods of "Impairment-only" and "Systematic amortization with impairment," and assesses which treatments respondents found preferable.

(Q5) The following methods could be considered accounting treatments after goodwill is acquired, instead of only recognizing either "Impairment-only (non-amortization)" or "Systematic amortization with impairment."

- A method that recognizes discretionary selection of "Impairment-only (non-amortization)" or "Systematic amortization with impairment"
- A method in which goodwill that meets certain conditions (e.g., it can be proved that goodwill does not amortize semi-permanently, etc.) for each acquisition deal is not amortized, and for any other conditions, it is amortized systematically.

Taking into account the above methods, please choose one accounting treatment option that is best suited for you from the viewpoint of a financial statement user.

(Options)

1. Impairment-only (non-amortization)
2. Systematic amortization with impairment
3. Discretionary selection of "Impairment-only (non-amortization)" or "Systematic amortization with impairment"
4. Goodwill that meets certain conditions for each acquisition deal is not amortized, and anything else is amortized systematically

Table 5.41 shows the following results:

- Among the four alternatives, 55.38% of respondents identified "Systematic amortization with impairment" as the most desirable approach. This finding is consistent with the results for Q1. The next most common choice was "Impairment-only (non-amortization)," selected by 18.46% of respondents. Unlike Q1, this item did not include the "Either" option, limiting direct comparison; however, the share of respondents preferring either of the two primary options appears to have declined slightly.
- Additionally, 9.23% selected "Discretionary selection of 'Impairment-only (non-amortization)' or 'Systematic amortization with impairment,'" and 16.92% favored an approach where goodwill that meets specific criteria for each acquisition is not amortized, while all other goodwill is amortized systematically.

Table 5.41 Preferable accounting treatment methods when other possibilities are considered

	Number of responses	Percentage (%)
1. Impairment-only (non-amortization)	24	18.46
2. Systematic amortization with impairment	72	55.38
3. Discretionary selection of "Impairment-only (non-amortization)" or "Systematic amortization with impairment"	12	9.23
4. Goodwill that meets certain conditions for each acquisition deal is not amortized, and anything else is amortized systematically	22	16.92
Total	130	100.00

5.3.3.6 Alternative Accounting Treatment of Goodwill (Part 2)

Respondents were subsequently asked to evaluate the desirability of various accounting treatments, either historically implemented or conceptually possible, relative to the two currently recognized methods ("Impairment-only" and "Systematic amortization with impairment").

(Q6) There are several accounting methods other than "Impairment-only (non-amortization)" and "Systematic amortization with impairment" that could theoretically be considered after acquisition of goodwill. Please share your opinion on the following accounting treatment methods for acquired goodwill. (Options: 1 = "Desirable," 2 = "Somewhat desirable," 3 = "Somewhat undesirable," 4 = "Undesirable," and 5 = "Unsure")

1. No amortization and no impairment (acquisition cost as is)
2. Systematic amortization without impairment
3. Continual revaluation based on fair value (the difference in value is included in the profit and loss calculation)
4. Immediate charge to earnings
5. Immediate charge to equity

The results presented in Table 5.42 are summarized as follows:

- The percentages of respondents selecting "(1) Desirable" or "(2) Somewhat desirable" were as follows: Panel A (No amortization or impairment; acquisition cost unchanged) received 12.31%, Panel B (Systematic amortization without impairment) 19.23%, Panel C (Continual revaluation based on fair value (the difference in value is included in the profit and loss calculation)) 39.23%, Panel D (Immediate charge to earnings) 33.85%, and Panel E (Immediate charge to equity) 24.62%.[85]

[85] Most respondents selected "Unsure" in response to the item "Immediate charge to equity." This trend was also observed among preparers.

Table 5.42 Accounting treatments currently being discussed compared to potential alternatives

	1	2	3	4	5	Total
Panel A No amortization and no impairment (acquisition cost as is)						
Number of responses	13	3	26	86	2	130
Percentage (%)	10.00	2.31	20.00	66.15	1.54	100.00
Panel B Systematic amortization without impairment						
Number of responses	7	18	49	52	4	130
Percentage (%)	5.38	13.85	37.69	40.00	3.08	100.00
Panel C Continual revaluation based on fair value (the difference in value is included in the profit and loss calculation)						
Number of responses	13	38	32	39	8	130
Percentage (%)	10.00	29.23	24.62	30.00	6.15	100.00
Panel D Immediate charge to earnings						
Number of responses	12	32	31	47	8	130
Percentage (%)	9.23	24.62	23.85	36.15	6.15	100.00
Panel E Immediate charge to equity						
Number of responses	5	27	33	43	22	130
Percentage (%)	3.85	20.77	25.38	33.08	16.92	100.00

- None of the alternative methods were rated as more desirable than the two current approaches.
- Over 30% of respondents rated Panels C and D as "Desirable" or "Somewhat desirable." The result for Panel D, in particular, indicates that some analysts supported views expressed in previous free-response comments, namely that goodwill should be immediately expensed, reflecting its nature as a non-permanent asset.
- Panels A and B were rated "Desirable" or "Somewhat desirable" by fewer than 20% of respondents, suggesting a broad consensus on the importance of impairment in goodwill accounting for both users and preparers.
- For Panel E (Immediate charge to equity), while over 20% considered it "Desirable" or "Somewhat desirable," a notable proportion selected "Unsure," indicating a more diverse range of opinions compared to the other alternatives.

5.3.3.7 Impact of Disclosure and Accounting Treatment Related to Goodwill on Corporate Activities

As in the preparer-focused survey, users were asked whether goodwill disclosures, specifically, net asset value excluding goodwill, affect the recognition of impairment losses and influence corporate behavior, particularly in M&A decisions.

5.3.3.7.1 Impact of Disclosure of Net Asset Amount After Deducting Goodwill

(Q7) Currently, there are concerns that goodwill impairment losses are not being recorded at the appropriate time.

Therefore, so that the recording of goodwill impairment losses is timelier, an idea has been proposed to request disclosure of the net asset amount after deducting goodwill (= net asset amount-goodwill balance). Do you think asking for disclosure of net assets after deducting goodwill will encourage more timely recording of goodwill impairment losses? Choose one answer that applies from the options below. (Options: 1 = "It will encourage more timely recording of impairment loss," 2 = "If anything, it would encourage more timely recording of impairment loss," 3 = "If anything, it would not encourage more timely recording of impairment loss," 4 = "It will not encourage more timely recording of impairment loss," 5 = "Unsure")

The key findings in Table 5.43 are summarized as follows:

- While 16.15% of respondents selected "(5) Unsure," 46.15% indicated that disclosure would either "(1) It will encourage more timely recording of impairment loss", or "(2) If anything, it would encourage more timely recording of impairment loss."
- In contrast, approximately 25% of preparers responded that disclosing net asset value excluding goodwill would lead to more timely impairment recognition.
- This discrepancy may reflect differing incentives, with preparers less inclined to disclose negative information and users viewing such information as essential.

Table 5.43 Does disclosure of net assets after deducting goodwill impact the timing of impairment loss recognition?

	Number of responses	Percentage (%)
1. It will encourage more timely recording of impairment loss	25	19.23
2. If anything, it would encourage more timely recording of impairment loss	35	26.92
3. If anything, it would not encourage more timely recording of impairment loss	13	10.00
4. It will not encourage more timely recording of impairment loss	36	27.69
5. Unsure	21	16.15
Total	130	100.00

5.3.3.7.2 Impact of Goodwill Accounting on Mergers and Acquisitions

As previously noted, whether goodwill accounting influences M&A activity is a significant concern when assessing the broader impact of accounting standards on corporate behavior. Accordingly, users were asked whether post-acquisition goodwill accounting affects M&A decision-making.

> (Q8) Do you think that the choice between systematic amortization and non-amortization of goodwill has an impact on companies' decisions regarding mergers and acquisitions (M&A)? Choose one answer that applies from the options below.
>
> (Options)
> 1. It is highly likely to have an impact.
> 2. It is somewhat likely to have an impact.
> 3. It is somewhat unlikely to have an impact.
> 4. It is highly likely to have an impact.
> 5. Unsure.

The key findings are summarized as follows:

- Regarding whether the accounting treatment of goodwill (whether it is amortized) influences a firm's M&A decision-making, 83.85% of the respondents chose "1. It is highly likely to have an impact" and "2. It is somewhat likely to have an impact." Notably, 42.31% of the respondents selected Option 1.
- As shown in Table 5.44, the combined percentage of those selecting Options 1 and 2 surpassed those selecting "3. It is somewhat unlikely to have an impact" and "4. It is highly unlikely to have an impact."
- These findings suggest that users are more likely than preparers to believe that goodwill amortization influences a firm's M&A decisions.[86]

Table 5.44 Impact of accounting treatment of goodwill on M&A decisions

	Number of responses	Percentage (%)
1. It is highly likely to have an impact	55	42.31
2. It is somewhat likely to have an impact	54	41.54
3. It is somewhat unlikely to have an impact	12	9.23
4. It is highly likely to have an impact	6	4.62
5. Unsure	3	2.31
Total	130	100

[86] This finding aligns with the view that amortization period determinations are influenced by post-amortization earnings levels and the achievement of target metrics.

5.3.4 *Responses from Auditors*

5.3.4.1 Characteristics of Respondents

Before presenting the results, this section outlines the characteristics of the auditor respondents. Similar to the surveys conducted with preparers and users, the questionnaire collected information on the respondents' basic attributes. Specifically, the survey inquired about (1) years of experience as a CPA, (2) audit firm size,[87] (3) primary job responsibilities, (4) accounting standards used by client firms, and (5) the industries to which client firms belonged. Tables 5.45, 5.46, 5.47, 5.48, and 5.49 summarize these findings.

The average professional experience among respondents was 23.2 years, with a median of 22.8 years. As shown in Table 5.45, 56.31% had 20–30 years of experience, and 15.05% had more than 30 years. Only 1.0% had fewer than 10 years of experience, while 27.67% had between 10 and 20 years.

Table 5.45 Years of experience as a CPA

	Number of responses	Percentage (%)
More than 0 years but less than 10 years	6	0.97
More than 10 years but less than 20 years	171	27.67
More than 20 years but less than 30 years	348	56.31
More than 30 years	93	15.05
Total	618	100.00

Notes: Although the total number of responses used for the analysis in this paper is 620, in preparing this table, we used 618 responses, excluding 2 responses that indicated less than 1 year as the number of years of experience. The reason for this is that the number of years of experience as a CPA was very short (this survey was conducted for partners), and it was judged that there was a high possibility of incorrect entries, such as those that indicated the length of tenure at their current firms

Table 5.46 Distribution of respondents by audit firm size

	Number of responses	Percentage (%)
Big 4 audit firms	433	69.84
Second-tier audit firms	187	30.16
Total	620	100.00

[87] Respondents were also asked to identify their audit firms.

Table 5.47 Distribution of respondents by type of work in which they are engaged (multiple responses)

	Number of responses	Percentage (%)
Audit and assurance services	606	66.30
Introduction of IFRS	91	9.96
IPO support	126	13.79
General advisory services	62	6.78
AI audits	9	0.98
M&A support	9	0.98
Tax support	3	0.33
Other	8	0.88
Total	914	100.00

Table 5.48 Accounting standards adopted by firms audited by respondents

	Number of responses	Percentage (%)
J-GAAP	607	62.00
U.S. GAAP	82	8.38
IFRS	290	29.62
Total	979	100.00

Table 5.49 Distribution of the industries to which the respondents' firms belong

	Number of responses	**Percentage (%)**	18. Precision Instruments	89	3.54
1. Fishery, Agriculture & Forestry	16	0.64	19. Other Products	103	4.09
2. Mining	9	0.36	20. Electric Power and Gas	38	1.51
3. Construction	127	5.05	21. Land Transportation	50	1.99
4. Foods	107	4.25	22. Marine Transportation	19	0.76
5. Transportation & Equipment	28	1.11	23. Air Transportation	7	0.28
6. Pulp and Paper	16	0.64	24. Warehousing & Harbor Transportation	41	1.63
7. Chemical	100	3.97	25. Information & Communication	210	8.35
8. Pharmaceutical	77	3.06	26. Wholesale Trade	169	6.72
9. Oil and Coal Products	18	0.72	27. Retail Trade	190	7.55
10. Rubber Products	16	0.64	28. Banks	84	3.34
11. Glass and Ceramics Products	12	0.48	29. Securities and Commodities Futures	41	1.63
12. Iron and Steel	25	0.99	30. Insurance	28	1.11
13. Nonferrous Metals	29	1.15	31. Other Financing Business	61	2.42
14. Metal Products	43	1.71	32. Real Estate	132	5.25
15. Machinery	120	4.77	33. Services	297	11.80
16. Electric Appliances	99	3.93	34. Unclassified	29	1.15
17. Transportation Equipment	86	3.42	Total	2516	100.00

Table 5.46 categorizes respondents by audit firm size. Of the total, 433 (69.84%) were affiliated with Big 4 audit firms, and 187 (30.16%) with second-tier audit firms.

Regarding job responsibilities (multiple responses allowed), Table 5.47 reports 914 responses. Of these, 606 (66.30%) indicated engagement in audit and assurance services, suggesting that most respondents were directly involved in such work. The next most common area was IPO support, reported by 126 (13.79%) respondents, followed by IFRS implementation (91 responses, 9.96%). Only nine respondents (0.98%) identified M&A support as their primary responsibility.

Table 5.48 presents the accounting standards adopted by respondents' client firms (multiple responses allowed). Of the 979 total responses, 607 (62.00%) cited J-GAAP, 290 (29.62%) IFRS, and 82 (8.38%) U.S. GAAP. Given that there were 620 respondents, 97.90% (607/620) were responsible for firms adopting J-GAAP. Additionally, 46.77% (290/620) were responsible for firms adopting IFRS, and 13.23% (82/620) for firms adopting U.S. GAAP.

Although not displayed in the table, 49.03% (304/620) of the respondents oversaw firms that had adopted either U.S. GAAP or IFRS alongside the "Impairment-only" approach.

Finally, we asked respondents to indicate the industry of the client company under their supervision, based on the same 33 industry categories used in prior surveys (multiple responses allowed). Table 5.49 reveals a broad distribution across industries, with many respondents overseeing firms in multiple sectors. Notably, 29 respondents selected "Not limited to a specific industry" (Unclassified).

5.3.4.2 Questions Regarding Accounting for Acquisition Goodwill

"Impairment-only (non-amortization)" and "Systematic amortization with impairment."

The first question asked auditors to indicate their preferred accounting treatment of goodwill: "Impairment-only (non-amortization)" or "Systematic amortization with impairment." As in previous surveys, an "Either" option was included.

> (Q1) When a unified approach to the accounting treatment of acquired goodwill is required, which approach do you think would be better for yourself, "Impairment-only (non-amortization)" or "Systematic amortization with impairment"? (Options: "Impairment-only (non-amortization)," "Systematic amortization with impairment," and "Either")

The findings in Table 5.50 are summarized as follows. A majority of auditors (89.52%, or 555 respondents) selected "Systematic amortization with impairment" as the preferred accounting treatment, while only 6.61% (41 respondents) favored "Impairment-only (non-amortization)." This response pattern remained consistent across audit firm sizes. Specifically, among respondents from Big 4 audit firms,

Table 5.50 Desirability of "Impairment-only" versus "Systematic amortization with impairment"

	Entire		Big 4 Audit firms		Second-tier Audit firms	
	N	%	N	%	N	%
Impairment-only (non-amortization)	41	6.61	29	6.70	12	6.42
Systematic amortization with impairment	555	89.52	389	89.84	166	88.77
Either	24	3.87	15	3.46	9	4.81
Total	620	100.00	433	100.00	187	100.00

Table 5.51 Only respondents who audit both J-GAAP and IFRS firms

	Number of responses	Percentage (%)
Impairment-only (non-amortization)	26	8.93
Systematic amortization with impairment	253	86.94
Either	12	4.12
Total	291	100.00

89.84% (389) supported "Systematic amortization with impairment," and 88.77% (166) of those from second-tier audit firms expressed the same preference. These results indicate broad support among Japanese auditors for this treatment of goodwill.

Table 5.51 presents the results of the Q1 survey, focusing on auditors responsible for firms that had adopted both J-GAAP and other accounting standards. This subsample was selected to reflect more informed judgment based on practical experience with multiple standards.[88] Among these respondents, 86.94% (253 of 291) preferred "Systematic amortization with impairment," while 8.93% (26 of 291) favored "Impairment-only (non-amortization)." These findings confirm a response trend similar to that observed in Table 5.50.[89]

5.3.4.2.1 Additional Question for Respondents Who Indicated in Q1 That "Impairment-Only (Non-amortization)" Was More Desirable

An additional question was posed to those who selected "Impairment-only" in Q1, asking why they preferred this approach.

[88] Among the 13 respondents managing firms that had adopted either IFRS or U.S. GAAP, one selected "Impairment-only," 11 selected "Systematic amortization with impairment," and one selected "Either."

[89] However, it remains unclear to what extent respondents responsible for both Japanese and other standards were involved in work related to each set of standards. This ambiguity should be considered when interpreting the results.

(Q1-1) To what extent do you agree with the following reasons that "Impairment-only (non-amortization)" is more desirable? (Options: 1 = "Yes," 2 = "Somewhat yes," 3 = "Somewhat no," 4 = "No," 5 = "Unsure").

1. It is difficult to estimate the useful life and amortization pattern of the carrying amount of goodwill.
2. The value of goodwill is maintained by firm efforts after it is acquired.
3. Goodwill amortization expense and the carrying amount of goodwill after amortization are not useful for financial statement users.
4. If an appropriate impairment test is conducted, systematic amortization of goodwill is not needed.
5. Firms are negative about the fact that the goodwill amortization expense amount decreases accounting earnings.
6. It reduces comparability with firms that are not required to amortize goodwill
7. Amortizing goodwill weakens the signaling effect of goodwill impairment.

The results in Table 5.52 indicate that the most frequently cited reason for selecting "Impairment-only" (i.e., responding "Yes" or "Somewhat yes") was "1. It is difficult to estimate the useful life and amortization pattern of the carrying amount of goodwill." This reason was cited by 36 of the 41 respondents (87.80%). The second most common justification was "4. If an appropriate impairment test is conducted, systematic amortization of goodwill is not needed," with 35 respondents (85.37%) indicating agreement.

Notably, 70.73% (29 of 41) explicitly responded "Yes" to Option 1, suggesting strong support for the argument that the unpredictability of goodwill's useful life and amortization pattern underlies the preference for the impairment-only approach. Additionally, 73.17% (30 of 41) responded "Yes" or "Somewhat yes" to "2. The value of goodwill is maintained by firm efforts after it is acquired."

The next most frequently selected reason was "3. Goodwill amortization expense and the carrying amount of goodwill after amortization are not useful for financial statement users," cited by 58.54% (24 of 41). Furthermore, 56.10% (23 of 41) agreed with "6. It reduces comparability with firms that are not required to amortize goodwill." Overall, Table 5.52 shows that for the remaining reasons, fewer than half of the respondents answered "Yes" or "Somewhat yes."

The survey also included the following open-ended question regarding the preference for the "Impairment-only" approach:

(Q1-2) If you have any reasons other than those listed in Q1-1 why you prefer "Impairment-only (non-amortization)," please indicate them in the space provided below.

Table 5.52 Reasons why "impairment-only (non-amortization)" is more desirable (upper row: number of responses, lower row: percentage [%])

	(1)	(2)	**(1) + (2)**	(3)	(4)	**(3) + (4)**	(6)	Total
Reason (1)	29	7	**(36)**	1	2	**(3)**	2	41
	70.73	17.07	**(87.80)**	2.44	4.88	**(7.32)**	4.88	100.00
Reason (2)	17	13	**(30)**	4	6	**(10)**	1	41
	41.46	31.71	**(73.17)**	9.76	14.63	**(24.39)**	2.44	100.00
Reason (3)	13	11	**(24)**	6	9	**(15)**	2	41
	31.71	26.83	**(58.54)**	14.63	21.95	**(36.59)**	4.88	100.00
Reasons (4)	22	13	**(35)**	1	4	**(5)**	1	41
	53.65	31.71	**(85.37)**	2.44	9.76	**(12.20)**	2.44	100.00
Reason (5)	3	5	**(8)**	9	22	**(31)**	2	41
	7.32	12.20	**(19.51)**	21.95	53.66	**(75.61)**	4.88	100.00
Reason (6)	15	8	**(23)**	6	11	**(17)**	1	41
	36.59	19.51	**(56.10)**	14.63	26.83	**(41.46)**	2.44	100.00
Reasons (7)	9	10	**(19)**	11	9	**(20)**	2	41
	21.95	24.39	**(46.34)**	26.83	21.95	**(48.78)**	4.88	100.00

There were eight responses (excluding responses such as "Nothing"),[90] including the following: "Many acquired businesses are assumed to be going concerns, and even if an amortization period is set, the effective period does not stop at that point," and "Reason (1) in Q1-1 is the most significant. If a rational explanation could be provided, I would not be opposed to amortization, but unfortunately, there is no reason to be convinced, including in the ASBJ's research report." One respondent noted that "The current J-GAAP approach, which requires amortization and impairment by comparison with the plan at the time of acquisition, is rather complicated, and it is difficult to believe that a comparison with the plan at the time of acquisition, which is not necessarily reasonable retrospectively, would be useful in practice." Another respondent cited several reasons for their position, including that "The assumption that goodwill is amortized over time does not apply," as well as concerns regarding "consistency with IFRS and U.S. GAAP" and the "international comparison perspective."

Some respondents suggested that "It would be better to strengthen the recognition of identifiable intangible assets than at present and to perform the impairment test by recognizing as goodwill only those assets that are unexplainable from a strategic perspective in the very long term, such as premiums."

[90] In presenting the open-ended responses, certain entries were omitted, and others were revised for typographical or stylistic reasons. These revisions were limited to maintaining the original intent. Similar adjustments were made for the following questions.

5.3.4.2.2 Additional Question for Respondents Who Indicated in Q1 That "Systematic Amortization with Impairment" Is More Desirable

Reasons Why "Systematic Amortization with Impairment" Is More Desirable

This section presents additional questions posed to respondents who preferred "Systematic amortization with impairment" in Q1. Similar to those who preferred "Impairment-only," respondents were asked to explain the reasons for their preference.

(Q1-3) To what extent do you agree with the following reasons that "Systematic amortization with impairment" is more desirable? (Options: 1 = "Yes," 2 = "Somewhat yes," 3 = "Somewhat no," 4 = "No," 5 = "Unsure")

1. Excess earnings power represented by goodwill gradually decreases due to market competition.
2. The carrying amount of goodwill should be allocated to the appropriate periods to match revenues and expenses.
3. It is impossible to distinguish between the diminished and maintained components of goodwill value.
4. It is consistent with the accounting treatment of other depreciable assets.
5. Amortization cannot be replaced by impairment.
6. It leads to prudent M&A decisions.
7. It reduces the cost of the goodwill impairment test.

Table 5.53 summarizes the results. The most frequent response (89.37%, 496/555) supporting "Systematic amortization with impairment" was that "1. Excess earnings power represented by goodwill gradually decreases due to market competition" (the combined total of "Yes" and "Somewhat yes" responses). The second most common reason was that "3. It is impossible to distinguish between the diminished and maintained components of goodwill value" (79.10%, 439/555). These findings suggest that many respondents favor "Systematic amortization with impairment" based on the nature of goodwill (i.e., goodwill as an amortizable asset).

The third most cited reason was "2. The carrying amount of goodwill should be allocated to the appropriate periods to match revenues and expenses," with 421 responses (75.86%, 421/555). Notably, this response was over 10% lower than the top reason.

Additionally, 352 respondents (63.42%, 352/555) selected "5. Amortization cannot be replaced by impairment," while 314 (56.58%, 314/555) indicated "4. It is consistent with the accounting treatment of other depreciable assets."

The remaining reasons, "6. It leads to prudent M&A decisions" and "7. It reduces the cost of the goodwill impairment test," were chosen by 38.02% (211/555) and 42.88% (238/555) of respondents, respectively. Interestingly, most supporters of "Systematic amortization with impairment" did not find the reduction in

Table 5.53 Reasons why "Systematic amortization with impairment" is more desirable (upper row: number of responses, lower row: percentage [%])

	(1)	(2)	**(1) + (2)**	(2)	(3)	**(3) + (4)**	(6)	Total
Reason (1)	348	148	**(496)**	26	23	**(49)**	10	555
	62.70	26.67	**(89.37)**	4.68	4.14	**(8.83)**	1.80	100.00
Reason (2)	222	199	**(421)**	50	81	**(131)**	3	555
	40.00	35.86	**(75.86)**	9.01	14.59	**(23.60)**	0.54	100.00
Reason (3)	238	201	**(439)**	59	42	**(101)**	15	555
	42.88	36.22	**(79.10)**	10.63	7.57	**(18.20)**	2.70	100.00
Reasons (4)	144	170	**(314)**	115	111	**(226)**	15	555
	25.95	30.63	**(56.58)**	20.72	20.00	**(40.72)**	2.70	100.00
Reason (5)	157	195	**(352)**	88	95	**(183)**	20	555
	28.29	35.14	**(63.42)**	15.86	17.12	**(32.97)**	3.60	100.00
Reasons (6)	83	128	**(211)**	127	182	**(309)**	35	555
	14.95	23.06	**(38.02)**	22.88	32.79	**(55.68)**	6.31	100.00
Reasons (7)	100	138	**(238)**	116	184	**(300)**	17	555
	18.02	24.86	**(42.88)**	20.90	33.15	**(54.05)**	3.06	100.00

impairment test costs a compelling reason, despite its frequent mention as a rationale for reintroducing amortization.

Respondents who supported "Systematic amortization with impairment" were also asked the following open-ended question:

> (Q1-4) If you have any other reasons why you think "Systematic amortization with impairment" is more desirable, other than those mentioned in Q1-3, please describe them below.

Excluding "None in particular," there were 110 responses. The main themes are summarized as follows.

5.3.4.2.3 Nature of Goodwill and Non-recognition of Internally Generated Goodwill

Many respondents noted that acquired goodwill is amortized and replaced by internally generated goodwill, supporting the preference for "Systematic amortization with impairment." Illustrative comments include: "Initial goodwill is considered to amortize, and if goodwill is maintained, it is maintained at its own cost and is equivalent to internally generated goodwill"; "Impairment-only would permit recognition of internally generated goodwill until impairment is recognized, which contradicts current accounting standards"; and "The value created by the company after an acquisition has no direct relationship with goodwill at the time of acquisition."

5.3.4.2.4 Reducing Impairment Risk and Financial Soundness

Some respondents expressed concern that "Impairment-only" allows for sudden, unexpected impairment losses. For example: "If goodwill is only impaired, a surprise due to a large impairment may occur when an impairment event arises"; and "It is healthier to amortize goodwill from the perspective of investor protection to avoid large, abrupt impairments."

Others emphasized that balance sheets with large goodwill amounts risk impairment because goodwill is inherently amortizable. One comment stated: "Business gradually becomes obsolete, and as times change, sources of competitiveness, technology, and sales will deteriorate. A balance sheet with substantial goodwill may conceal the risk of impairment."

From a financial soundness perspective, respondents favored writing off goodwill through systematic amortization: "[Goodwill] cannot be determined as excess earning power, and it is problematic to record such an item as an asset. Its nature is multifaceted, and the continued presence of goodwill on the balance sheet lacks positive significance. This is not sound accounting from either an asset or profit-and-loss perspective."

5.3.4.2.5 Elimination of Discretion

A common view was that "Systematic amortization with impairment" reduces discretion and estimation compared to "Impairment-only." Comments include: "Goodwill valuation is prone to discretion, and impairment is often avoided"; "There is less room for discretion with systematic amortization"; and "Estimating the recoverable amount is highly uncertain and subjective, especially in a rapidly changing environment, which increases discretion." Relatedly, some believed systematic amortization enhances financial statement comparability: "Systematic amortization increases comparability among companies."

5.3.4.2.6 Dealing with the "Too Little, Too Late" Issue

Respondents noted that impairment alone leads to delayed recognition of goodwill decline: "There is a 'too little, too late' problem with impairment alone, which cannot be resolved without amortization"; and "Impairment alone risks that declines will not be recognized timely, raising concerns about reporting timeliness."

5.3.4.2.7 Reduction of Auditors' Responsibility and Practical Burden

Some respondents favored "Systematic amortization with impairment" for reducing practical burdens. For example: "In companies with many M&As, goodwill balances become very large, and systematic amortization is less burdensome when performance deteriorates." Another commented: "Properly assessing excess earnings capacity amortization is practically difficult, and impairment alone places excessive responsibility and burden on auditors." Several respondents expressed concern that "Impairment-only" imposes disproportionate demands on auditors.

5.3.4.2.8 Other Responses

Additional comments included: "Some IPO companies seeking IFRS listing may choose IFRS to avoid the Japanese standard of systematic amortization"; "Costs should be allocated proportionately over the period during which benefits are realized. If a company expects effects to extend over a long period, it should amortize accordingly, provided stakeholders accept the longer amortization period"; "Companies typically make investment decisions based on an assumed investment-return period. It is prudent to bear costs during the payback period, matching revenues from excess earning capacity, and subsequently recognize synergies and profits in the [profit and loss statement]"; and "This method is conservative and aligns well with the business practices of Japanese companies."

5.3.4.2.9 Factors that the Preparer Considers Important in Determining the Amortization Period of Goodwill

Respondents who preferred "Systematic amortization with impairment" were asked additional questions concerning the factors relevant to determining the amortization period of goodwill.

(Q1-5) How important do you think the factors listed below are in determining the amortization period of goodwill? Please select one answer for each factor. (Options: 1 = "Yes," 2 = "Somewhat yes," 3 = "Somewhat no," 4 = "No," 5 = "Unsure")

(Options)
1. The investment-return period based on management's business plan.
2. The period over which synergies are expected to be maintained.
3. Periods over which an acquirer, on a stand-alone basis, is expected to maintain higher future cash flows.
4. Useful lives of related tangible assets.
5. Useful lives of related other intangible assets.

Table 5.54 summarizes responses to Q1-5. Respondents who selected either "(1) Yes" or "(2) Somewhat yes" were grouped together, indicating that they considered the factor important.

Table 5.54 Important factors in determining amortization period (upper row: number of responses, lower row: percentage [%])

	(1)	(2)	**(1) + (2)**	(3)	(4)	**(3) + (4)**	(6)	Total
Factor (1)	330	183	**(513)**	21	21	**(42)**	0	555
	59.46	32.97	**(92.43)**	3.78	3.78	**(7.57)**	0.00	100.00
Factor (2)	245	227	**(472)**	48	23	**(71)**	12	555
	44.14	40.90	**(85.05)**	8.65	4.14	**(12.79)**	2.16	100.00
Factor (3)	162	234	**(396)**	103	46	**(149)**	10	555
	29.19	42.16	**(71.35)**	18.56	8.29	**(26.85)**	1.80	100.00
Factor (4)	27	111	**(138)**	211	187	**(398)**	19	555
	4.86	20.00	**(24.86)**	38.02	33.69	**(71.71)**	3.42	100.00
Factor (5)	35	144	**(179)**	198	161	**(359)**	17	555
	6.31	25.95	**(32.25)**	35.68	29.01	**(64.68)**	3.06	100.00

The most frequently cited factor was "1. The investment-return period based on management's business plan," selected by 92.43% of respondents (513/555). The second most cited factor was "2. The period over which synergies are expected to be maintained," selected by 85.05% (472/555), followed by "3. Periods over which an acquirer, on a stand-alone basis, is expected to maintain higher future cash flows," cited by 71.35% (396/555). In contrast, fewer than half of respondents identified "4. Useful lives of related tangible assets" (24.86%, 138/555) and "5. Useful lives of related other intangible assets" (32.25%, 179/555) as important.

In addition, respondents provided open-ended comments on other factors considered important in estimating the goodwill amortization period.

(Q1-6) If there are any important factors when companies estimate the goodwill amortization period, other than those listed in Q1-5, please describe them below.

After excluding responses such as "None" or "Nothing in particular," 46 responses remained. Similar responses were consolidated.[91] The key factors mentioned include:

- Duration of excess earning power
- Provisions under J-GAAP (e.g., maximum amortization period)
- Speed of the product/service lifecycle and technological obsolescence
- Market changes, including overseas expansion

[91] Some of the 51 responses included insightful perspectives on the amortization period but were excluded to focus on factors deemed important by preparers. In addition to those discussed in the main text, several respondents stated: "I think it is the period during which excess earning power continues, but it is different from synergy"; "management's intention at the time of acquisition"; and "it depends on what was purchased."

- Managerial resources and employee tenure
- Time to evaluate investment performance and managerial change
- Periodic earnings levels
- Use of practical limits (e.g., five or 10 years)
- Medium- to long-term business planning
- Business continuity period based on objective data

> (Q1-7) Given that "Systematic amortization with impairment" is more desirable as the accounting approach for goodwill, how do you think a requirement determining the goodwill amortization period should be prescribed? Please choose an option you think is the most desirable for you.
>
> (Options)
> 1. An upper limit should be set for the amortization period (e.g., the rule should be prescribed in the form "Be amortized within … years").
> 2. A uniform amortization period should be set (e.g., the rule should be prescribed in the form "Be amortized in just … years").
> 3. No provision about the amortization period should be set.

5.3.4.2.10 How Should the Provisions Regarding the Amortization Period of Goodwill Be Addressed?

Respondents who chose "Systematic amortization with impairment" in Q1 were also asked how the amortization period should be specified.

As shown in Table 5.55, 74.23% (412/555) supported "1. An upper limit should be set for the amortization period." Only 8.11% (45/555) supported "2. A uniform amortization period should be set," while 17.66% (98/555) supported "3. No provision about the amortization period should be set." Notably, more respondents favored no provision over a uniform period.

Next, we examine the responses to Q1-10 regarding the advantages and disadvantages of setting exceptions, although the order of presentation differs from the original questionnaire. This question was posed only to respondents who selected

Table 5.55 Amortization period regulations

	Number of responses	Percentage (%)
1. An upper limit should be set for the amortization period.	412	74.23
2. A uniform amortization period should be set.	45	8.11
3. No provision about the amortization period should be set.	98	17.66
Total	555	100.00

Table 5.56 Should the rebuttable presumption be made?

	Number of responses	Percentage (%)
1. Should be made	144	31.51
2. Should not be made	313	68.49
Total	457	100.00

either "1. An upper limit should be set for the amortization period" or "2. A uniform amortization period should be set" in Q1-7.

(Q1-10) Do you think the rebuttable presumption of a goodwill amortization period should be made? (Options: 1= "Should be made," 2 = "Should not be made")

As shown in Table 5.56, 313 of the 457 respondents (68.49%) selected "2. Should not be made," while 144 (31.51%) chose "1. Should be made." Consistent with the preparer and user surveys, a larger proportion of respondents opposed establishing a rebuttable presumption. Specifically, 58.56% of preparers and 63.51% of users selected "Should not be made," and the percentage was slightly higher among auditors. This finding is noteworthy, as it highlights auditors' relatively stronger opposition to a rebuttable presumption.

This section concludes with the results concerning either the maximum amortization period or the preferred uniform amortization period. First, respondents who selected "1. An upper limit should be set for the amortization period" were asked the following:

(Q1-8) How many years do you think should be chosen as the upper limit of the goodwill amortization period? Please choose one of the following options. If you choose "Other," please fill in the blank with any specific number of years.

As shown in Table 5.57, the most common response was 10 years, selected by 48.79% (201/412) of respondents. The next most frequent response was 20 years, chosen by 36.89% (152/412). These results suggest that auditors tend to favor a more conservative amortization period than preparers, who most commonly selected 20 years, followed by 10 years.

These preferences may reflect the belief that a firm's excess earning capacity typically diminishes within 10 years, as supported by academic research (see ASBJ 2015c). Accordingly, auditors may be attempting to align goodwill amortization with its underlying economic reality. Notably, 7.77% (32/412) of respondents

Table 5.57 Upper limit of the goodwill amortization period

	Number of responses	Percentage (%)
20 years	152	36.89
15 years	32	7.77
10 years	201	48.79
5 years	25	6.07
Other	2	0.49
Total	412	100.00

Table 5.58 Uniform amortization period

	Number of responses	Percentage (%)
20 years	4	8.89
15 years	2	4.44
10 years	24	53.33
5 years	13	28.89
Other	2	4.44
Total	45	100.00

selected 15 years, and 6.07% (25/412) selected 5 years. Two respondents chose "Other," both specifying 30 years as the preferred upper limit.

Respondents who selected "2. A uniform amortization period should be set" were then asked:

(Q1-9) How many years do you think a uniform amortization period should be? If you choose "Other," please fill in the blank with any specific number of years.

Among this group, the most frequently selected option was 10 years, chosen by 53.33% (24/45) of respondents, as shown in Table 5.58. The next most common response was 5 years, selected by 28.89% (13/45).[92] Only 13.3% of respondents selected either 15 years (4.44%) or 20 years (8.89%). The remaining two responses (4.44%) indicated 1 year and 7 years, respectively. Overall, the majority favored a uniform amortization period of either five or 10 years.

[92] According to a survey by the ASBJ (2015c) of JPX400 firms using consolidated J-GAAP financial statements as of March 31, 2014, the most common amortization period was 5 years (54.81%), excluding responses given in ranges. This was followed by 20 years (14.07%) and 10 years (9.63%) (par. 13). Ishii (2017) also reported 5 years as the most common period (46.02%), followed by 10 years (20.68%), based on 1760 Japanese firm-year observations from FY2007 to FY2016 (p. 30). In the present survey, 10 years was the most frequently selected period, followed by 5 years. While the results differ slightly, it is possible that respondents selected five or 10 years based on their actual practices.

5.3.4.3 Characteristics of Goodwill as an Asset

This section outlines the questions posed regarding the nature of goodwill.

5.3.4.4 Is There a Semi-Permanent, Non-amortizable Portion of Goodwill?

(Q2) Do you think there is a part of goodwill that preserves its value semi-permanently? Please select one answer from the options below.

(Options)
1. All or the majority of the value is preserved semi-permanently.
2. There is both a part that preserves its value semi-permanently and a part that does not.
3. There is no part that preserves its value semi-permanently.
4. Unsure.

As shown in Table 5.59, the most common response was "3. There is no part that preserves its value semi-permanently," selected by 54.68% of respondents (339/620). The second most common response was "2. There is both a part that preserves its value semi-permanently and a part that does not," selected by 39.68% (246/620). Together, these responses accounted for 94.36% of the total responses.

Table 5.59 Characteristics of goodwill as an asset

	Entire		Impairment-only (non-amortization)		Systematic amortization with impairment		Either	
	N	%	N	%	N	%	N	%
1. All or the majority of the value is preserved semi-permanently	7	1.13	5	12.20	2	0.36	0	0.00
2. There is both a part that preserves its value semi-permanently and a part that does not	246	39.68	25	60.98	207	37.30	14	58.33
3. There is no part that preserves its value semi-permanently	339	54.68	8	19.51	322	58.02	9	37.50
4. Unsure	28	4.52	3	7.32	24	4.32	1	4.17
Total	620	100.00	41	100.00	555	100.00	24	100.00

However, a different trend emerges when responses to Q1 are categorized into "1. Impairment-only (non-amortization)," "2. Systematic amortization with impairment," and "3. Either." Table 5.59 presents the results of Q2 responses according to these categories. In both the "Impairment-only" and "Either" groups, a greater percentage of respondents selected "2. There is both a part that preserves its value semi-permanently and a part that does not" than "3. There is no part that preserves its value semi-permanently." Conversely, in the "Systematic amortization with impairment" group, the majority selected "3. There is no part that preserves its value semi-permanently."

While further analysis is required to establish how perceptions of goodwill influence the choice of accounting treatment, the results suggest a relationship between the two.

5.3.4.5 Components of Goodwill

To explore the composition of goodwill, a follow-up question was asked, similar to previous surveys of preparers and users. This question was only directed at respondents who selected either "2. There is both a part that preserves its value semi-permanently and a part that does not" or "3. There is no part that preserves its value semi-permanently" in Q2.

(Q2-1) The following is a list of items that are considered components of goodwill. Please select one that applies to each of the following items. (Select one for each of the following, 1 = Amortized, 2 = Amortized to some extent, 3 = Not amortized much, 4 = Not amortized, 5 = Unsure, 6 = It is not a component of goodwill)

(Components addressed in this survey)
1. Brand
2. Sales know-how
3. Proprietary technology
4. Business model
5. Human resources
6. Site-specific conditions

Table 5.60 summarizes the results. Regarding the "1. Brand" component, 47.04% of respondents (119 out of 253) believed it would be amortized, based on the sum of responses to "(1) Amortized" and "(2) Amortized to some extent." For other components, 80.63% (204/253) indicated "2. Sales know-how" would be amortized; 77.08% (195/253) selected "3. Proprietary technology;" 84.19% (213/253) believed "4. Business model" would be amortized; and 74.31% (188/253) selected "5. Human resources." Regarding "6. Site-specific conditions," 39.53% (100/253) believed this component would be amortized.

Table 5.60 Components of goodwill (upper row: number of responses, lower row: percentage [%])

	(1)	(2)	**(1) + (2)**	(3)	(4)	**(3) + (4)**	(5)	(6)	Total
Element (1)	25	94	**(119)**	79	22	**(101)**	11	22	253
	9.88	37.15	**(47.04)**	31.23	8.70	**(39.92)**	4.35	8.70	100.00
Element (2)	65	139	**(204)**	15	14	**(29)**	10	10	253
	25.69	54.94	**(80.63)**	5.93	5.53	**(11.46)**	3.95	3.95	100.00
Element (3)	66	129	**(195)**	33	6	**(39)**	6	13	253
	26.09	50.99	**(77.08)**	13.04	2.37	**(15.42)**	2.37	5.14	100.00
Element (4)	75	138	**(213)**	15	5	**(20)**	12	8	253
	29.64	54.55	**(84.19**	5.93	1.98	**(7.91)**	4.74	3.16	100.00
Element (5)	69	119	**(188)**	27	9	**(36)**	18	11	253
	27.27	47.04	**(74.31)**	10.67	3.56	**(14.23)**	7.11	4.35	100.00
Element (6)	29	71	**(100)**	72	18	**(90)**	33	30	253
	11.46	28.06	**(39.53)**	28.46	7.11	**(35.57)**	13.04	11.86	100.00

An open-ended follow-up question was also asked:

(Q2-2) If there are any components considered to constitute goodwill, other than those listed in Q2-1, please write them below.

Excluding responses such as "None in particular" and "Others," 26 responses were analyzed. While it is generally assumed that goodwill (after applying PPA and identifying all identifiable intangible assets) consists of excess earning power and synergies, both of which were mentioned, respondents also identified the following components (grouped by similarity)[93]:

- Customer relationships (e.g., customer base, contract terms), network, and market share
- Industry position, barriers to entry, and alignment with megatrends
- Know-how (e.g., human resource development, manufacturing expertise), management strategies, R&D capabilities, and supply chains
- Trademarks and trade names forming the basis of the business

[93]Additional comments beyond those included in the main text were also received. For instance, regarding location, one respondent noted, "Regarding the location condition, it is thought that the location in front of a train station would depreciate, but in some cases, such as a site in a national park, which is highly unique, it is thought that there are cases where it does not amortize." The same respondent also remarked: "Goodwill components are divided into those due to [...] synergies and accounting goodwill due to temporary differences arising from mark-to-market valuations. The latter should be amortized in line with the amortization period of the related assets"; and "Goodwill should be considered as an unexplainable difference, not excess earning power. It does not indicate value. Premiums, etc. are unexplainable differences. If the appropriateness of the acquisition price can be explained by a business plan or discounted cash flows (DCF), some kind of identifiable asset should be considered to exist." Another respondent noted the general lack of transparency, stating, "The answer depends on the content."

- Corporate culture
- Control premium, price adjustments due to bidding competition, overpayment, and, in the case of share exchanges, overpayment arising from fair value measurement of shares used as consideration
- Relationships with shareholders

Although not included in prior surveys, this study also posed the following question.

(Q2-3) It is sometimes pointed out that the amount of goodwill may include an overvaluation of the merged or acquired company. Do you think that the amount of goodwill includes an overvaluation of the merged or acquired company? Please choose one from the following options.

(Options)
1. Included quite a lot
2. Somewhat included
3. Slightly included
4. Not included
5. Unsure

As shown in Table 5.61, 140 respondents (22.58%) selected "Included quite a lot," and 406 respondents (65.48%) selected "Somewhat included" in response to whether goodwill may contain an overvalued portion. These two categories together accounted for 88.06% of total responses. Most respondents believed that goodwill includes an overvalued portion. This was attributed not only to perceptions that the acquiring firm overpaid at acquisition (a view also reflected in open-ended responses to Q3-1) but also to the belief that goodwill includes under-amortized portions recognized after acquisition (see Q3-2). Some respondents further suggested that overvaluation stems from delayed impairment recognition or insufficient amortization. Overall, auditors appear to consider goodwill as likely to include, to varying extents, an overvalued portion of the acquired firm.

Table 5.61 Overvalued portion included in goodwill

	Number of responses	Percentage (%)
1. Included quite a lot	140	22.58
2. Somewhat included	406	65.48
3. Slightly included	31	5.00
4. Not included	16	2.58
5. Unsure	27	4.35
Total	620	100.00

5.3.4.6 Goodwill and Audit Quality

5.3.4.6.1 Difficulties in Auditing Goodwill

This section presents findings from a survey of auditors, focusing on challenges related to auditing goodwill and its implications for audit quality. The first question asked about difficulties in auditing goodwill.

(Q3) In conducting an audit of goodwill, how much more difficult is it, in general, to audit the valuation of goodwill compared to other assets? Please select only one from the following options.

(Options)
1. More difficult than the valuation of other assets
2. No different from the valuation of other assets
3. Other assets are more difficult to value
4. Unsure

Table 5.62 shows that 89.19% (553 out of 620) of respondents believe that goodwill is "1. More difficult than the valuation of other assets." In contrast, only 8.87% (55 out of 620) selected "2. No different from the valuation of other assets," and 0.48% (3 out of 620) selected "3. Other assets are more difficult to value." These results indicate that most auditors perceive goodwill as a more complex asset to audit relative to others.

When responses were analyzed by audit firm size, the trend remained consistent. Among respondents from Big 4 audit firms, 90.30% (391 out of 433) selected "1. More difficult," while 86.63% (162 out of 187) of respondents from second-tier audit firms selected the same option.

Respondents who selected "1. More difficult than the valuation of other assets" were then asked an open-ended follow-up question:

Table 5.62 Difficulties in auditing goodwill

	Entire		Big 4 audit firms		Second-tier audit firms	
	N	%	N	%	N	%
1. More difficult than the valuation of other assets	553	89.19	391	90.30	162	86.63
2. No different from the valuation of other assets	55	8.87	36	8.31	19	10.16
3. Other assets are more difficult to value	3	0.48	1	0.23	2	1.07
4. Unsure	9	1.45	5	1.15	4	2.14
Total	620	100.00	433	100.00	187	100.00

(Q3-1) In what ways is the valuation of goodwill in an audit more difficult than the valuation of other assets? Please explain the specific factors in the space provided below.

A total of 490 responses were received. Given the volume, only a summary of the major themes is presented below.

5.3.4.6.2 Difficulty in Verifying the Reasonableness and Appropriateness of Business Plans

Many respondents noted the challenges in evaluating the reasonableness and appropriateness of clients' business plans. For example, some stated: "It is necessary to evaluate business plans over a long period of time for the entire business related to goodwill, and the element of uncertainty in estimates of important assumptions is very large, while there are often few elements that clearly negate management's view"; "Confirmation of the appropriateness of the business plan of the acquired firm cannot be confirmed without knowing various factors such as the business of the acquired firm, past performance, and future prospects"[94]; "It is impossible to eliminate management's discretion, and it is difficult to evaluate the reasonableness and appropriateness of the business plan of the acquired company"; and "Since it is impossible for an external auditor to independently obtain sufficient information to judge the feasibility of the plan, the auditor must rely heavily on the company's provision of materials and explanations."

Several respondents also pointed to the difficulty of evaluating goodwill when the original business plan is revised, particularly during business restructuring. For example: "It is difficult when several years have passed since the original business plan when the goodwill was initially recognized, and the business plan is revised due to reorganization, etc."; and "There are often various divisions and business restructuring after acquisition, and in most cases it is impossible to permanently manage information on whether excess profitability continues."

[94] Related responses included: "I feel that the verification of company's assumptions, especially in the case of a new business model or a different business domain such as overseas, is an area that involves difficulties"; "When the source of goodwill is an innovative technology or business model, it is difficult to judge whether it has been amortized or been impaired"; and "When M&A is used to challenge a new field, and there are cases where future synergies are expected, it is often more difficult than the usual evaluation of future plans."

5.3.4.6.3 Difficulty in Valuing Goodwill due to the Existence of Many Estimates and Subjective Factors

Many respondents highlighted that goodwill valuation involves numerous estimation factors and requires objective evaluation. For instance: "The valuation of goodwill often includes many elements of estimation over a long period of time, so it is difficult to judge its appropriateness." Some respondents further noted that goodwill valuation essentially represents a valuation of the business itself: "The valuation of goodwill is a valuation of the business itself, and like stock prices in the stock market, it is affected by various factors and is highly variable."

Moreover, many respondents emphasized the difficulty in objectively evaluating factors that drive goodwill value, such as excess earnings and synergies. Examples include: "The range of the value evaluation is wider than other assets depending on the thinking strategy of the acquiring company [...] There are parts that are calculated based on management's acquisition objectives, synergies, and management strategy, which are more subjective and uncertain than other asset evaluations"; "Subjectivity and uncertainty are greater than other asset valuations, because there are parts that are calculated based on management's objectives, synergies, and management strategies"; "It is difficult to verify assumptions such as future profit growth and synergies with objective support"; and "There are many uncertainties in auditing estimates of future business plans, especially when synergies are considered, which are almost all uncertain points. In particular, when synergies are considered, there are almost always uncertainties."

Additionally, several respondents cited the "individuality (uniqueness)" of goodwill as a reason for valuation difficulty: "Most of it is an estimation factor, and it is highly individual" and "It is not possible to compare it with other goodwill." This likely reflects the limited availability of comparable examples, complicating audits. Unlike other assets, goodwill is ambiguous, which further complicates valuation: "The identity of goodwill itself is difficult to identify and its value is difficult to evaluate"; "Since the content of goodwill is unidentifiable, what should be used for valuation is different for each acquisition and is therefore difficult to verify"; "It is difficult to identify the identity of goodwill itself, making it difficult to value it"; and "Since the contents of goodwill are unidentifiable, it is difficult to verify what to value each acquisition."

5.3.4.6.4 Nature of Goodwill as an Asset

Several respondents described goodwill as an asset measured as a residual difference, making its origin and direct valuation difficult to analyze. For example, one stated, "Goodwill is the residual of the purchase price allocated to other assets and cannot be valued directly." Others emphasized that goodwill results from the allocation of identifiable assets and liabilities and involves a complex set of factors, noting, "Goodwill is a residual after the allocation of identifiable assets and liabilities and a differential concept that involves a complex set of factors. It is difficult to measure the ability to generate future cash flows compared to other assets whose purpose, use, and utility are specified, because they are residual after the allocation of identifiable assets and liabilities and is a difference concept involving a complex range of factors." Some respondents highlighted that goodwill represents the difference between the net asset equity and the purchase price, which is not directly measurable: "In the end, the amount equivalent to net asset equity and the amount equivalent to the company's equity in the net assets and the amount equivalent to the company's equity in the net assets of the company are not directly measurable. In the end, it is only the difference between the amount equivalent to the equity interest in the net assets and the value at which the company decided to acquire the asset based on various considerations."

Additionally, some noted that goodwill is simply the difference between the acquisition price and the net assets of the acquired company. In some cases, this difference may include overpricing or an unreasonable acquisition price, making a rational explanation difficult. Comments included: "For goodwill that is only a difference (residual), there are two sides of the same coin"; "The issue of the appropriateness of the acquisition price is inextricably linked to the goodwill, which is only a difference (residual)"; "It is difficult to calculate the valuation taking into account the economic reality where the components of goodwill (synergy, control premium, overpayment, etc.) cannot be separated"; and "Although it is typical in the case of bidding, it is difficult to explain why the amount determined at a competitive price is reasonable."

5.3.4.6.5 Difficulty in the Allocation of Purchase Price Allocation and Goodwill

Several respondents identified the allocation of goodwill to PPA and cash-generating units (CGUs) as a key challenge in goodwill valuation. For instance, one respondent explained, "Valuation of goodwill of business acquisition is determined based on the corporate value evaluation between the parties (including negotiation of acquisition price)." Others stated, "The valuation of goodwill of corporate acquisitions is determined based on the corporate value assessment between the parties (including negotiation of acquisition price) and is recognized as the difference with PPA, and there are many estimation factors, making objective valuation difficult, which makes audit difficult." Furthermore, some noted that evolving business plans post-acquisition complicate the identification of CGUs: "The business plan at the time of purchase makes it difficult to grasp the cash-generating unit because the business form changes in practice." Respondents also expressed difficulty in assessing whether the CGU to which goodwill is allocated genuinely has synergies, observing, "Goodwill is sometimes allocated to CGUs other than the acquired company or business to which synergies are allocated, but the judgment as to whether synergies are really generated (whether the allocation is appropriate) is extremely discretionary. It is difficult to determine whether it is appropriate for audit purposes."

5.3.4.6.6 Difficulty in Estimating the Amortization Period

Some respondents highlighted the challenge of determining an appropriate amortization period for goodwill due to a lack of clear rules. Examples included: "There are no clear rules for calculating the amortization period of goodwill, so it is difficult to judge its appropriateness"; "The calculation of the amortization period of goodwill is difficult and there is room for arbitrariness on the part of management"; and "The rationality of the impairment test given amortization is questionable, given that the amortization period of goodwill itself is considered to lack rational support." Some respondents also cited the typically long recovery period of goodwill: "The recovery period is long."

5.3.4.6.7 Cost of Impairment Testing and Need for Specialized Expertise

Several respondents emphasized that annual impairment testing under IFRS imposes significant costs on preparers and auditors. One respondent explained, "IFRS requires annual testing even if there is no indication of impairment, which is costly on the part of the entity and its auditors. This is costly on the part of the entity and the auditor." Others noted that goodwill valuation often requires specialized external expertise and sophisticated judgment, increasing its complexity relative to other assets. Comments included: "The valuation of goodwill varies depending on the cause of the goodwill and it is necessary to obtain opinions from various experts when judging its appropriateness"; and "It is often necessary for companies to use outside experts to calculate WACC, but sometimes companies lack such understanding."

5.3.4.6.8 Valuation of Goodwill and Management Responsibility Issues

Some respondents believed that recording impairment losses on goodwill raises management responsibility concerns, which, combined with the difficulty of valuing goodwill, complicates the audit process. For example: "Impairment of goodwill is only an accounting treatment in accordance with the standards, but in practice, it is easily linked to the blame of the management who made the acquisition decision." Others observed, "Unless there is governance that does not take into account the intentions of top management, there is always a lack of analysis and documentation of management decisions and results, which always results in a delay in recognizing impairment." Additionally, "When non-amortized goodwill is impaired, the amount tends to be huge and highly associated with the failure of the business, which often makes it difficult to coordinate the timing of impairment recognition and the amount of impairment measurement with the client."

5.3.4.6.9 Goodwill Audits and Litigation Risk

Respondents who selected "1. more difficult than the valuation of other assets" in Q3 were asked about their perception of litigation risk.

(Q3-2) Do you think the risk of litigation from shareholders and other users of financial statements has increased as a result of goodwill being subject to audit? Please select only one from the following options.

(Options)
1. Considerably increased
2. Somewhat increased
3. Not changing
4. Somewhat decreased
5. Considerably decreased
6. Unsure

Table 5.63 shows that the majority of respondents (combining "1. Considerably increased" and "2. Somewhat increased") acknowledged that the risk of lawsuits from users has increased due to goodwill audits overall. Specifically, 62.93% (348/553) reported that litigation risk had increased to some extent. However, 32.19% (178/553) indicated that litigation risk does not change when goodwill is audited, reflecting divergent views on the relationship between goodwill and litigation risk. This pattern remained consistent across different audit firm sizes.

Table 5.63 Goodwill audits and litigation risk

	Entire		Big 4 audit firms		Second-tier audit firms	
	N	%	N	%	N	%
1. Considerably increased	86	15.55	58	14.83	28	17.28
2. Somewhat increased	262	47.38	187	47.83	75	46.30
(Sum of 1 and 2)	**(348)**	**(62.93)**	**(245)**	**(62.66)**	**(103)**	**(63.58)**
3. Not changing	178	32.19	128	32.74	50	30.86
4. Somewhat decreased	0	0.00	0	0.00	0	0.00
5. Considerably decreased	1	0.18	1	0.26	0	0.00
6. Unsure	26	4.70	17	4.35	9	5.56
Total	553	100.00	391	100.00	162	100.00

5.3.4.6.10 Goodwill Audits and Quality Control Reviews

In addition to litigation risk, the same respondents were queried about the relationship between goodwill audits and the likelihood of receiving findings from the JICPA quality control review or monitoring by the CPAAOB.

(Q3-3) Do you think that the possibility of being pointed out in a quality control review by JICPA or in monitoring by CPAAOB has increased due to goodwill being included in the scope of audit? Please choose only one from the following options.

(Options)
1. Considerably increased
2. Somewhat increased
3. Not changing
4. Somewhat decreased
5. Considerably decreased
6. Unsure

As shown in Table 5.64, most respondents acknowledged an increased likelihood of being flagged by the JICPA's quality control review and the CPAAOB monitoring. Specifically, 88.43% (489/553) of all respondents, 86.70% (339/391) of those at Big 4 audit firms, and 92.59% (150/162) at second-tier audit firms selected either "1. Considerably increased" or "2. Somewhat increased."

5.3.4.6.11 Determination of Goodwill Impairment Recognition

Auditors were also asked about their judgments regarding the recognition of goodwill impairment, focusing on the "too little, too late" concern, where impairment losses may be understated or recognized belatedly, under two frameworks: "Systematic amortization with impairment (J-GAAP)" and "Impairment-only (U.S. GAAP/IFRS)."

Table 5.64 Goodwill audits and quality control reviews (JICPA) and monitoring (CPAAOB)

	Entire		Big 4 audit firms		Second-tier audit firms	
	N	%	N	%	N	%
1. Considerably increased	285	51.54	190	48.59	95	58.64
2. Somewhat increased	204	36.89	149	38.11	55	33.95
(Sum of 1 and 2)	**(489)**	**(88.43)**	**(339)**	**(86.70)**	**(150)**	**(92.59)**
3. Not changing	58	10.49	47	12.02	11	6.79
4. Somewhat decreased	0	0.00	0	0.00	0	0.00
5. Considerably decreased	0	0.00	0	0.00	0	0.00
6. Unsure	6	1.08	5	1.28	1	0.62
Total	553	100.00	391	100.00	162	100.00

5.3.4.6.12 Timeliness of Goodwill Impairment Recognition

The first question addressed the timeliness of impairment recognition.

(Q4-1) From the perspective of a CPA responsible for auditing, in general, what is your impression of when an entity should recognize goodwill impairment? Please select only one option from the following for "Systematic amortization with impairment (J-GAAP)" and "Impairment-only (U.S. GAAP/IFRS)." Please assume normal circumstances other than the COVID-19 pandemic.

(Options)
1. Impairment losses tend to be recognized late compared to the sign of impairment.
2. Impairment losses tend to be recognized timely compared to the sign of impairment.
3. Impairment losses tend to be recognized early compared to the sign of impairment.
4. Unsure.

Table 5.65 reveals that most respondents chose either "1. Impairment losses tend to be recognized late compared to the sign of impairment" or "2. Impairment losses tend to be recognized timely compared to the sign of impairment."[95] Notably, responses varied by accounting framework. Under "Systematic amortization with impairment (J-GAAP)," 33.06% (205/620) believed impairments tend to be recognized late, while 51.45% (319/620) considered impairments timely.

Conversely, under "Impairment-only (U.S. GAAP/IFRS)," 43.06% (267/620) reported late recognition, and 32.42% (201/620) reported timely recognition.

To analyze these results in greater detail, we categorized responses according to the accounting standards adopted by the firms audited by the respondents. Table 5.66 summarizes these findings, including responses from those responsible for both J-GAAP and non-J-GAAP firms.[96] Across all respondents, a higher proportion selected "2. Impairment losses tend to be recognized timely compared to the sign of impairment" under "Systematic amortization with impairment (J-GAAP)" than "1. Impairment losses tend to be recognized late compared to the sign of impairment." The reverse pattern emerged for "Impairment-only (U.S. GAAP/IFRS)."

---

[95] Of the respondents addressing the "Impairment-only" approach (U.S. GAAP or IFRS), 20.65% (128/620) selected "4. Unsure." This may relate to the accounting standards adopted by the firms for which these respondents were responsible. See the additional tabulation results, which report findings by the accounting standards used by the firms in question.

[96] The rationale for this analysis is the same as that provided in the supplementary analysis for Q1 (Table 5.51). Refer to that explanation for further details.

Table 5.65 Timeliness of goodwill impairment recognition

	Systematic amortization with impairment (J-GAAP)		Impairment-only (U.S. GAAP/IFRS)	
	N	%	N	%
1. Impairment losses tend to be recognized late compared to the sign of impairment	205	33.06	267	43.06
2. Impairment losses tend to be recognized timely compared to the sign of impairment	319	51.45	201	32.42
3. Impairment losses tend to be recognized early compared to the sign of impairment	34	5.48	24	3.87
4. Unsure	62	10.00	128	20.65
Total	620	100.00	620	100.00

Table 5.66 Timeliness of goodwill impairment recognition (by accounting standards)

	J-GAAP		U.S. GAAP		IFRS		J-GAAP and non-J-GAAP (U.S. GAAP or IFRS)	
	N	%	N	%	N	%	N	%
Panel A Systematic amortization with impairment (J-GAAP)								
1. Impairment losses tend to be recognized late compared to the sign of impairment	201	33.11	30	36.59	111	38.28	112	38.49
2. Impairment losses tend to be recognized timely compared to the sign of impairment	315	51.89	32	39.02	129	44.48	133	45.70
3. Impairment losses tend to be recognized early compared to the sign of impairment	33	5.44	10	12.20	19	6.55	18	6.19
4. Unsure	58	9.56	10	12.20	31	10.69	28	9.62
Total	607	100.00	82	100.00	290	100.00	291	100.00
Panel B Impairment-only (U.S. GAAP and IFRS)								
1. Impairment losses tend to be recognized late compared to the sign of impairment	261	43.00	45	54.88	139	47.93	142	48.80
2. Impairment losses tend to be recognized timely compared to the sign of impairment	195	32.13	27	32.93	116	40.00	112	38.49
3. Impairment losses tend to be recognized early compared to the sign of impairment	24	3.95	2	2.44	8	2.76	9	3.09
4. Unsure	127	20.92	8	9.76	27	9.31	28	9.62
Total	607	100.00	82	100.00	290	100.00	291	100.00

Examining the J-GAAP and non-J-GAAP (U.S. GAAP or IFRS) columns in Panels A and B of Table 5.66 reveals that 38.49% (112/291) of respondents responsible for both frameworks indicated that impairments tend to be recognized late under J-GAAP, while 48.80% (142/291) selected late recognition under the impairment-only approach. Conversely, 45.70% (133/291) reported timely recognition for J-GAAP, compared to 38.49% (112/291) for the impairment-only approach. These results confirm the patterns observed in Table 5.65, even when focusing on respondents managing firms under both accounting standards.

We asked respondents who selected "1. Impairment losses tend to be recognized late compared to the sign of impairment" to answer the following open-ended question:

> (Q4-2) Please specify in the response box below any factors that prevent the recognition of goodwill impairment at the appropriate time, e.g., inadequate accounting standards, inadequate accounting and auditing, weak governance, etc.

There were 308 responses, including examples provided within the questions. Due to the volume, we summarize the main points.

5.3.4.6.13 Inadequacies in Accounting Standards

Many respondents cited inadequacies in accounting standards as a factor,[97] specifying aspects common to both J-GAAP and U.S. GAAP/IFRS, such as the discretion in impairment recognition and the difficulty in estimating impairments. Some respondents also noted differences between J-GAAP and U.S. GAAP/IFRS.

Regarding J-GAAP, many respondents pointed out the difficulty in triggering impairment recognition because goodwill's carrying amount is amortized. Comments included: "Because amortization is in progress, the over-invested portion of goodwill is amortized over time"; "Because the carrying amount of goodwill declines systematically the degree of precision in determining impairment is low and recognition of impairment may be delayed"; "Because the carrying amount of goodwill declines regularly, the recognition of impairment tends to be slower than in the case of no amortization"; "Since the book value is systematically decreasing, the degree of precision of the impairment assessment is low and there is a possibility of delayed recognition"; and "Since the book value is decreasing due to systematic amortization, there is a tendency for recognition to be delayed compared to the case where there is no amortization."[98]

---

[97] Regarding this issue, one respondent noted, "because the subjectivity of management cannot be eliminated. In other words, we do not believe that this is a problem that can be addressed by changing accounting rules regarding the application of impairment accounting."

[98] Respondents highlighted several factors that delayed the recognition of impairment losses under J-GAAP. These included the absence of mandatory impairment testing at each reporting period,

With respect to U.S. GAAP and IFRS, some respondents stated that the larger impairment losses recorded due to the lack of systematic amortization do not prevent impairment recognition. For example: "In general, the balance is relatively smaller under J-GAAP due to amortization, and the impact of impairment tends to be larger under IFRS than under U.S. GAAP."

In addition to inadequacies in accounting standards, many respondents attributed delays in recording impairment losses to audit limitations. For example: "It is difficult to clearly reject the management plan developed by the audited company, because it is easy to be subjective about future excess earning capacity and the audited company has more information than the audited firm." Even if auditors do not make incorrect judgments, they "generally seem to be slower" and "auditors have less knowledge of the clients they are involved with and the industries to which they belong."

5.3.4.6.14 Difficulty in Estimation and Future Forecasting

As seen in Q3-1, which addressed the difficulty of valuing goodwill, many respondents identified the heavy reliance on estimates and the challenge of verifying future forecasts as causes of delayed impairment recognition. For example: "It is difficult to judge the credibility of numerical values on which auditors base their judgments, such as the management's future forecasts"; and "Since the evaluation of goodwill itself is highly subjective and has to be based on a wide range, it is inevitable that the recognition of impairment losses is delayed unless clear evidence is provided."[99,100]

5.3.4.6.15 Weak Governance and Management (Team) Issues

Many respondents associated delay with management psychology and bias, noting a tendency to avoid recognizing goodwill impairment due to fear that it reveals M&A failure, as managers wish to avoid negative internal or external evaluations. For example: "Impairment of goodwill gives the impression that the M&A has failed, and this, coupled with the management's desire to avoid impairment of goodwill as much as possible, has led to a delay in recognizing impairment. In addition,

---

the use of a two-step impairment test based on undiscounted future cash flows, and the broad interpretation of application guidelines. For example, one respondent stated, "Because of the amortization rules, we believe that this is sufficient. There is no need to make an assessment once a year at a certain timing as in IFRS, and the criteria for impairment loss are vague and open to wide interpretation."

[99] Prior research suggests that preparers may manipulate the growth rate of future cash flows and the discount rate to avoid recognizing goodwill impairment or to minimize the reported amount (Avallone and Quagli 2015). Some responses echoed this concern: "With regard to estimates (cash flows, growth rates, discount rates, etc.), while it is difficult to ensure sufficient reliability, they tend to be discretionary estimates, partly because of their monetary importance."

[100] One respondent observed, "even if there are indications, the estimation of future cash flows may result in no impairment."

in the case of non-amortized goodwill, the impact of goodwill impairment is large, so I have the impression that this tendency is becoming stronger"; "I get the impression that many firms are reluctant to take impairment losses because of the impact on stock prices, M&A failure, and the denial of management who decided to acquire in the past"; "Many managers consider goodwill impairment a management failure, so they are reluctant to take goodwill impairment losses"; and "Many companies consider goodwill impairment losses to be a management failure, and most of them are concerned about preventing impairment."

Some respondents noted management's optimistic outlook affects goodwill valuation. Examples include: "The future prospects of managers who carry out the acquisition are biased"; "Because they themselves have made acquisitions, they often have excessive expectations about the future and their ability to generate cash flows"; and "Subjective inputs tend to be optimistic, and internal controls may be weak." Additionally, some linked this tendency to auditing limitations: "Management wants to postpone impairment as much as possible, and it is practically quite difficult for auditors to deny the uncertainty of the management's estimate and make the company record impairment against the company's intention."

5.3.4.6.16 Others

A small number of respondents identified accounting literacy issues among the audited entities, citing, for example, the "low ability of the audited entity to evaluate [goodwill]" and "low accounting literacy of management."

5.3.4.6.17 Appropriateness of the Estimated Amount of Goodwill Impairment

The next question asked respondents to assess the appropriateness of the recognized goodwill impairment amount under two scenarios: "Systematic amortization with impairment (J-GAAP)" and "Impairment-only (U.S. GAAP/IFRS)."

(Q4-3) In general, what is your impression of the amount of goodwill impairment estimated by an entity from the perspective of a CPA responsible for the audit? Please select only one answer from the following options for "Systematic amortization with impairment (J-GAAP)" and "Impairment-only (U.S. GAAP/IFRS)" (assuming that the Covid-19 pandemic is not the case).

(Options)
1. The estimated impairment is generally appropriate.
2. The estimated impairment is generally overstated.
3. The estimated impairment is generally understated.
4. Unsure.

Table 5.67 Appropriateness of estimated goodwill impairment

	Systematic amortization with impairment (J-GAAP)		Impairment-only (U.S. GAAP/IFRS)	
	N	%	N	%
1. The estimated impairment is generally appropriate	377	60.81	256	41.29
2. The estimated impairment is generally overstated	54	8.71	74	11.94
3. The estimated impairment is generally understated	83	13.39	94	15.16
4. Unsure	106	17.10	196	31.61
Total	620	100.00	620	100.00

Table 5.67 shows that 60.81% (377/620) of respondents selected "1. The estimated impairment is generally appropriate" for "Systematic amortization with impairment (J-GAAP)," while 41.29% (256/620) selected this option for "Impairment-only (U.S. GAAP/IFRS)." Overall, the majority believed the impairment amount was appropriately estimated under the J-GAAP approach. Fewer respondents considered the impairment amount appropriate under U.S. GAAP/IFRS, with less than half affirming its adequacy.

Regarding "2. The estimated impairment is generally overstated" and "3. The estimated impairment is generally understated," the percentage of respondents who considered impairment understated exceeded those who considered it overstated for both approaches. For J-GAAP, 8.71% (54/620) selected "overstated," and 13.39% (83/620) selected "understated." For U.S. GAAP/IFRS, 11.94% (74/620) selected "overstated," and 15.16% (94/620) selected "understated." Notably, although many respondents indicated that impairment recognition was delayed, fewer believed the impairment amount was significantly misstated.

However, a considerable proportion of respondents were uncertain, with 31.61% (196/620) selecting "4. Unsure" for U.S. GAAP/IFRS and 17.10% (106/620) for J-GAAP.

To explore these results further, responses were recounted based on the accounting standards adopted by the firms audited by the respondents.

Panel A in Table 5.68 summarizes results for "Systematic amortization with impairment (J-GAAP)," focusing on the "J-GAAP and non-J-GAAP (U.S. GAAP or IFRS)" column. Here, 59.45% (173/291) selected "1. The estimated impairment is generally appropriate," 9.97% (29/291) chose "2. The estimated impairment is generally overstated," and 14.78% (43/291) selected "3. The estimated impairment is generally understated." These findings align with the overall results above.

Panel B in Table 5.68 presents results for "Impairment-only (U.S. GAAP/IFRS)." Focusing on J-GAAP and non-J-GAAP firms, 53.26% (155/291) considered the impairment amount generally appropriate, 10.31% (30/291) regarded it as overstated, 19.59% (57/291) considered it understated, and 16.84% (49/291) were unsure.

Respondents who selected either "2. The estimated impairment is generally overstated" or "3. The estimated impairment is generally understated" for at least

Table 5.68 Appropriateness of estimated goodwill impairment (by accounting standard adopted)

	J-GAAP		U.S. GAAP		IFRS		J-GAAP and non-J-GAAP (U.S. GAAP or IFRS)	
	N	%	N	%	N	%	N	%
Panel A: Systematic amortization with impairment (J-GAAP)								
1. The estimated impairment is generally appropriate	369	60.79	43	52.44	173	59.66	173	59.45
2. The estimated impairment is generally overstated	53	8.73	6	7.32	29	10.00	29	9.97
3. The estimated impairment is generally understated	83	13.67	17	20.73	39	13.45	43	14.78
4. Unsure	102	16.80	16	19.51	49	16.90	46	15.81
Total	607	100.00	82	100.00	290	100.00	291	100.00
Panel B: Impairment-only (U.S. GAAP and IFRS)								
1. The estimated impairment is generally appropriate	249	41.02	44	53.66	156	53.79	155	53.26
2. The estimated impairment is generally overstated	73	12.03	8	9.76	30	10.34	30	10.31
3. The estimated impairment is generally understated	92	15.16	15	18.29	56	19.31	57	19.59
4. Unsure	193	31.80	15	18.29	48	16.55	49	16.84
Total	607	100.00	82	100.00	290	100.00	291	100.00

one of the following ("Systematic amortization with impairment (J-GAAP)" or "Impairment-only (U.S. GAAP/IFRS)" in Q4-3) were subsequently asked to answer the following question:

(Q4-4) Please specify in the response box below any factors that hinder the proper estimation of goodwill impairment charges, e.g., inadequate accounting standards, inadequate accounting and auditing, weak governance, etc.

A total of 179 responses were received, excluding "not sure" and "others."[101] These responses were summarized by grouping respondents according to their Q4-3 selections.

[101] Some responses were consistent with those in Q4–2.

Respondents who selected "2. The estimated impairment is generally overstated" for both "Systematic amortization with impairment (J-GAAP)" and "Impairment-only (U.S. GAAP/IFRS)" (26 responses)

Some respondents pointed to inadequacies of accounting standards, for example, "No specific estimation criteria or estimation methods exist." Many noted weak governance and management incentives for "big bath" (excessive conservatism), such as "Goodwill impairment is a high hurdle for management to recognize impairment, but once the goodwill impairment is recognized, there seems to be an incentive to reduce the risk of subsequent cost burdens by impairing the goodwill as much as possible at once." Others observed, "Because it is practically difficult to evaluate the market value of goodwill, there are two choices: either no impairment or impairment of the entire amount," and "When the decision to impair the goodwill, the management judgment is to take a loss at once, and the losses generally tend to be large." Additionally, some respondents highlighted problems related to estimation, for instance, "The company has a strong desire and tends to make optimistic estimates."

Respondents who chose "2. The estimated impairment is generally overstated" for "Systematic amortization with impairment (J-GAAP)" and either "1. The estimated impairment is generally appropriate" or "4. Unsure" for "Impairment-only (U.S. GAAP/IFRS)" (16 responses).[102]

This group also cited inadequate accounting standards, weak governance, and "big bath" incentives. One respondent identified a problem specific to Japanese standards: "[On the one hand], there is no opportunity to recognize impairment losses mechanically through impairment tests at each period, there is a risk that impairment losses will be recognized late, on the other hand (since amortization is also in progress), there seems to be a tendency to impair the entire amount of remaining goodwill." Regarding the Japanese preparers' mindset, one stated, "In Japan, there is a sense that if impairment is going to be recognized anyway, the full amount should be written off."

Respondents who chose "2. The estimated impairment is generally overstated" for "Impairment-only (U.S. GAAP/IFRS)" and either "1. The estimated impairment is generally appropriate" or "4. Unsure" for "Systematic amortization with impairment (J-GAAP)" (26 responses).[103]

Many respondents identified inadequacies in accounting standards and weaknesses in governance. Concerning "Impairment-only" under U.S. GAAP/IFRS, comments included "In IFRS, the aged portion is considered to be included in impairment," "It takes time to measure subjective and discretionary factors, which delays timely judgment, which may result in many excessive cases," and "In the case of impairment-only, there is an incentive to record as much loss as possible when the need for impairment arises."

---

[102] Of the 16 cases, 10 respondents selected "4. Unsure" for "Impairment-only (U.S. GAAP/IFRS)."

[103] For "Systematic amortization with impairment (J-GAAP)," most respondents selected "1. The estimated amount of impairment is generally appropriate" (23 cases).

Respondents who selected "3. The estimated impairment is generally understated" for both "Systematic amortization with impairment (J-GAAP)" and "Impairment-only (U.S. GAAP/IFRS)" (42 responses)

Many cited inadequate accounting standards, auditing limitations, and weak governance. Regarding accounting standards, some pointed to the lack of systematic amortization under U.S. GAAP and IFRS and the shielding effects involved.[104,105,106] Some respondents attributed under-impairment to management optimism and bias, stating, "Management is trying to make it successful, so the business plan is set high, resulting in under-impairment,"[107] and "Management's budgeting is based on the assumption that the measures will be effective, but it is difficult to make an estimate that the measures will not be effective." Others emphasized application issues rather than standards,[108] such as management's "strong negative impression of impairment losses and a tendency to think that impairment losses should be recorded as little as possible" and "pressure to achieve performance" that leads to underestimating impairment losses.

Respondents who chose "3. The estimated impairment is generally understated" for "Systematic amortization with impairment (J-GAAP)" and either "1. The estimated impairment is generally appropriate" or "4. Unsure" for "Impairment-only (U.S. GAAP/IFRS)" (23 responses)

Some respondents specifically identified deficiencies in J-GAAP, for example, "The degree of precision of measurement may be low because book value is reduced by amortization."

---

[104] According to the IASB (2020), the shielding effect refers to the phenomenon whereby goodwill, although impaired, is protected from recognition of impairment losses due to the headroom in the cash-generating unit (CGU) to which it is allocated (IASB 2020, p. 56, para. 3.20, p. 58, para. 3.31, and p. 59, paras. 3.35–3.36). Headroom is defined as "the amount by which its recoverable amount exceeds the carrying amount of its recognized net assets—including goodwill" (IASB, 2020, p. 58, para. 3.31) and represents an unrecognized item on the balance sheet (IASB 2020, para. 3.33). This headroom comprises both pre-existing elements on the acquirer's side and those that emerge post-acquisition (IASB 2020, p. 58, para. 3.33).

[105] Some respondents argued that "there is room for discretion in the measured value if a method other than amortization is used, but on the other hand, it cannot be assumed that systematic amortization is correct, and the fact that each case is different makes it difficult to judge."

[106] Other respondents noted, "neither companies nor auditors are able to take action on impairment of goodwill because the criteria are abstract, and goodwill impairment is often a large amount."

[107] As previously discussed, respondents disagreed on whether impairment amounts were properly estimated, with views differing both across and within individual respondents depending on the assumed criteria. These discrepancies may reflect variations in respondents' practical experience. For instance, Zang (2008) finds that in the U.S., firms with higher debt ratios tend to understate impairment losses to avoid violating debt covenants, while new managers often record impairment losses as a "big bath" during transitions. This suggests that preparers may have incentives to overstate or understate goodwill impairment depending on context.

[108] Some respondents identified limitations in auditing, stating that "no matter how much access to information there is, there is a gap in information between the those involved in management and the accounting auditor." Others highlighted challenges in the standards themselves, noting that "neither companies nor auditors can easily take action on impairment of goodwill, because the standards [are] abstract, and goodwill impairment is often a large amount of money."

Respondents who chose "3. The estimated impairment is generally understated" for "Impairment-only (U.S. GAAP/IFRS)" and either "1. The estimated impairment is generally appropriate" or "4. Unsure" for "Systematic amortization with impairment (J-GAAP)" (38 responses)

Many respondents cited inadequacies in accounting standards, auditing limitations, and weak governance. For example, "It is difficult for auditors to make valid arguments against the company's estimates due to a lack of industry knowledge." Management bias toward optimistic estimates and a negative perception of impairment losses were also mentioned as causes of underestimation. One comment illustrated this: "Amortization is not evaluated as an error in investment judgment by management, but impairment may be evaluated as an error in investment judgment by management. In a situation where there is no amortization of goodwill, the company would only be judged as impaired under accounting standards, but the company tends to develop more forward-looking business plans as it depends on future excess earning power." Regarding the nature of goodwill, some respondents highlighted its ambiguity, for instance, "It is inherently unclear what really constitutes goodwill."

Respondents who chose "2. The estimated impairment is generally overstated" for either "Systematic amortization with impairment (J-GAAP)" or "Impairment-only (U.S. GAAP/IFRS)" and "3. The estimated impairment is generally understated" for "Other" (8 responses)

In addition to pointing out inadequacies in accounting standards and auditing limitations (including lack of knowledge and skepticism), some respondents cited corporate culture and management willingness as influencing factors.[109]

5.3.4.6.18 Information on Net Asset Value, Less Goodwill, and the Timeliness of Impairment Recognition

Finally, respondents were asked to comment on the idea that disclosing net asset value less goodwill might encourage timely recognition of impairment.

(Q4-5) Considering that goodwill impairment losses may not be recorded at the appropriate time, the IASB has also suggested the idea of requiring disclosure of net asset value less goodwill (= net asset value - goodwill balance) in order to make the recording of goodwill impairment losses timelier. The idea is also presented. Do you think that requiring disclosure of net asset value less goodwill would encourage more timely recognition of goodwill impairment losses? Please select one of the following options that applies to you.

[109] Additional concerns included that "the reflection of risk factors is often too lax" and "the DCF model is too specialized," indicating issues in the practical application of accounting standards.

(Options)
1. It will encourage more timely recognition of impairment losses.
2. If anything, it would encourage more timely recognition of impairment losses.
3. If anything, it would not encourage more timely recognition of impairment losses.
4. It will not encourage more timely recognition of impairment losses.
5. Unsure.

Table 5.69 shows that the most common response was "4. It will not encourage more timely recognition of impairment losses" (46.29%, 287/620). Combined with the third most common response, "3. If anything, it would not encourage more timely recognition of impairment losses" (15.81%, 98/620), these accounted for 62.1% of responses. The second most common response was "2. If anything, it would encourage more timely recognition of impairment losses" (21.13%, 131/620). When combined with respondents who selected "1. It will encourage more timely recognition of impairment losses" (5.97%, 37/620), the total reached only 27.10%. These results indicate that most respondents did not believe net asset information promotes more timely recognition of impairment losses.

5.3.4.7 Alternative Accounting Treatment of Goodwill (Part 1)

Auditors were asked which accounting treatment they preferred, considering possible alternatives beyond the current standards' "Impairment-only" and "Systematic amortization with impairment" approaches (see question options below).

Table 5.69 Does disclosure of net asset value less goodwill affect the timing of recognition of impairment losses?

	Number of responses	Percentage (%)
1. It will encourages more timely recognition of impairment losses	37	5.97
2. If anything, it would encourage more timely recognition of impairment losses	131	21.13
(Sum of 1 and 2)	**(168)**	**(27.10)**
3. If anything, it would not encourage more timely recognition of impairment losses	98	15.81
4. It will not encourage more timely recognition of impairment losses	287	46.29
(Sum of 3 and 4)	**(385)**	**(62.10)**
5. Unsure	67	10.81
Total	620	100.00

(Q5) The following methods could be considered accounting treatments after goodwill is acquired, instead of only recognizing either "Impairment-only (non-amortization)" or "Systematic amortization with impairment."

- A method that recognizes discretionary selection of "Impairment-only (non-amortization)" or "Systematic amortization with impairment"
- A method in which goodwill that meets certain conditions (e.g., it can be proved that goodwill does not amortize semi-permanently, etc.) for each acquisition deal is not amortized, and for any other conditions, it is amortized systematically.

Taking into account the above methods, please choose one accounting treatment option that is best suited for you from the viewpoint of a financial statement user.

(Options)
1. Impairment-only (non-amortization)
2. Systematic amortization with impairment
3. Discretionary selection of "Impairment-only (non-amortization)" or "Systematic amortization with impairment"
4. Goodwill that meets certain conditions for each acquisition deal is not amortized, and anything else is amortized systematically

Table 5.70 indicates that "2. Systematic amortization with impairment" was the most preferred option, receiving 494 responses (79.68%, 494/620). The next most common preference was "4. Goodwill that meets certain conditions for each acquisition deal is not amortized, and anything else is amortized systematically," chosen by 11.61% (72/620) of respondents. Additionally, 6.29% (39/620) favored "1. Impairment-only (non-amortization)," and 2.42% (15/620) preferred "3. Discretionary selection of 'Impairment-only' or 'Systematic amortization with impairment.'"

Table 5.70 More desirable accounting methods if options other than the current system are considered

	Number of responses	Percentage (%)
1. Impairment-only (non-amortization)	39	6.29
2. Systematic amortization with impairment	494	79.68
3. Discretionary selection of "Impairment-only (non-amortization)" or "Systematic amortization with impairment"	15	2.42
4. Goodwill that meets certain conditions for each acquisition deal is not amortized, and anything else is amortized systematically	72	11.61
Total	620	100.00

Table 5.71 More desirable accounting method if options outside the current system are considered (by Q1 Response)

	Impairment-only (non-amortization)		Systematic amortization with Impairment		Either	
	N	%	N	%	N	%
1. Impairment-only (non-amortization)	**36**	**87.80**	0	0.00	3	12.50
2. Systematic amortization with impairment	0	0.00	**481**	**86.67**	13	54.17
3. Discretionary selection of "Impairment-only (non-amortization)" or "Systematic amortization with impairment"	1	2.44	12	2.16	2	8.33
4. Goodwill that meets certain conditions for each acquisition deal is not amortized, and anything else is amortized systematically	4	9.76	62	11.17	6	25.00
Total	41	100.00	555	100.00	24	100.00

Table 5.71 presents Q5 responses broken down by Q1 answers ("Impairment-only (non-amortization)," "Systematic amortization with impairment," and "Either"). Most respondents who chose "Impairment-only (non-amortization)" or "Systematic amortization with impairment" in Q1 maintained their preference in Q5.[110] However, when offered the option between "3. Discretionary selection of 'Impairment-only' or 'Systematic amortization with impairment'" and "4. Goodwill that meets certain conditions for each acquisition deal is not amortized, and anything else is amortized systematically" (excluding the "Either" option), some respondents shifted their preference from their initial Q1 choice. Notably, 54.17% (13/24) of respondents who selected "Either" in Q1 chose "Systematic amortization with impairment" in Q5, while 25.00% (6/24) preferred option 4 as a more desirable treatment.

5.3.4.8 Alternative Accounting Treatment of Goodwill (Part 2)

We next solicited respondents' views on historical accounting treatments and other plausible alternatives.

[110] This analysis excludes responses that selected "Systematic amortization with impairment" in Q1 and "Impairment-only" in Q5. Although there were two such responses, including them does not alter the findings, except for minor numerical differences.

(Q6) There are several accounting methods other than "Impairment-only (non-amortization)" and "Systematic amortization with impairment" that could theoretically be considered after acquisition of goodwill. Please share your opinion on the following accounting treatment methods for acquired goodwill. (Options: 1 = "Desirable," 2 = "Somewhat desirable," 3 = "Somewhat undesirable," 4 = "Undesirable," and 5 = "Unsure")

1. No amortization and no impairment (acquisition cost as is)
2. Systematic amortization without impairment
3. Continual revaluation based on fair value (the difference in value is included in the profit and loss calculation)
4. Immediate charge to earnings
5. Immediate charge to equity

Table 5.72 shows that none of the alternative accounting methods in this question were considered "Desirable" or "Somewhat desirable" by a majority of respondents, compared to "Impairment-only" or "Systematic amortization with impairment." The two options receiving the highest combined "Desirable" and "Somewhat desirable" responses—"2. Systematic amortization with impairment" and "3. Continual revaluation based on fair value (the difference in value is included in the profit and loss calculation)"—each garnered only 104 responses (16.77%). Most respondents rated all options as either "Somewhat undesirable" or "Undesirable," with the lowest percentage of negative responses (77.10%) for "5. Immediate charge to equity" and the highest (95.16%) for "1. No amortization and no impairment (acquisition cost as is)."

Table 5.72 Comparison of currently discussed accounting treatments with other alternative possibilities (upper row: number of responses, lower row: percentage [%])

Options	(1)	(2)	(1) + (2)	(3)	(4)	(3) + (4)	(5)	Total
1. No amortization and no impairment (acquisition cost as is)	9	12	**(21)**	59	531	**(590)**	9	620
	1.45	1.94	**(3.39)**	9.52	85.65	**(95.16)**	1.45	100.00
2. Systematic amortization without impairment	23	81	**(104)**	144	367	**(511)**	5	620
	3.71	13.06	**(16.77)**	23.23	59.19	**(82.42)**	0.81	100.00
3. Continual revaluation based on fair value (the difference in value is included in the profit and loss calculation)	20	84	**(104)**	174	315	**(489)**	27	620
	3.23	13.55	**(16.77)**	28.06	50.81	**(78.87)**	4.35	100.00
4. Immediate charge to earnings	26	75	**(101)**	158	348	**(506)**	13	620
	4.19	12.10	**(16.29)**	25.48	56.13	**(81.61)**	2.10	100.00
5. Immediate charge to equity	17	77	**(94)**	121	357	**(478)**	48	620
	2.74	12.42	**(15.16)**	19.52	57.58	**(77.10)**	7.74	100.00

5.3.4.9 Impact of Accounting Treatment on Goodwill on the Behavior of the Preparer

As a final question on goodwill accounting, respondents were asked whether accounting treatment influences preparers' substantive actions, specifically M&A decisions.

(Q7) Do you think that the choice between systematic amortization and non-amortization of goodwill has an impact on companies' decisions regarding mergers and acquisitions (M&A)? Choose one answer that applies from the options below.

(Options)
1. It is highly likely to have an impact.
2. It is somewhat likely to have an impact.
3. It is somewhat unlikely to have an impact.
4. It is highly likely to have an impact.
5. Unsure.

Table 5.73 reveals that 89.19% (553/620) of respondents believed goodwill accounting may impact preparers' M&A behavior (sum of options 1 and 2). This trend persisted across audit firm size groups: 87.99% (381/433) of Big 4 respondents and 91.98% (172/187) of second-tier respondents indicated a "possibility of influence." This pattern was consistent among other groups as well. These results suggest that most auditors believe goodwill accounting affects corporate M&A decisions. Notably, a higher percentage of Big 4 respondents (60.05%) than second-tier respondents (52.41%) selected "1. It is highly likely to have an impact." Conversely, more second-tier respondents (39.57%) than Big 4 respondents (27.94%) selected "2. It is somewhat likely to have an impact." Despite this variation, the majority in both groups agreed that accounting treatment likely influences preparers' M&A behavior.

Table 5.73 Does the way goodwill is accounted for affect M&A decisions?

	Entire		Big 4 audit firms		Second-tier audit firms	
	N	%	N	%	N	%
1. It is highly likely to have an impact	358	57.74	260	60.05	98	52.41
2. It is somewhat likely to have an impact	195	31.45	121	27.94	74	39.57
(Sum of Options 1 and 2)	**(553)**	**(89.19)**	**(381)**	**(87.99)**	**(172)**	**(91.98)**
3. It is somewhat unlikely to have an impact	35	5.65	29	6.70	6	3.21
4. It is highly unlikely to have an impact	17	2.74	12	2.77	5	2.67
(Sum of Options 3 and 4)	**(52)**	**(8.39)**	**(41)**	**(9.47)**	**(11)**	**(5.88)**
5. Unsure	15	2.42	11	2.54	4	2.14
Total	620	100.00	433	100.00	187	100.00

5.4 Additional Analyses

5.4.1 The Goal of This Section

In the previous section, we explained the results of the survey research for preparers, users, and auditors separately. However, some of the questions asked in our survey include questions common to all three stakeholder groups. The following topics common to all of them were examined in the survey research.

1. Regarding the accounting treatment of goodwill, which is more desirable—the "Impairment-only" or "Systematic amortization with impairment" approach? Or, is "Either" fine? Why?
2. When using "Systematic amortization with impairment," how should the amortization period be prescribed?
3. What is the nature of goodwill?
4. How do you evaluate the possible ways of accounting for goodwill, apart from the current accounting treatments (i.e. "Impairment-only" or "Systematic amortization with impairment")?
5. Does the mandatory disclosure of additional information related to goodwill (e.g., net worth after deduction of goodwill) increase the timeliness of recognizing goodwill impairment losses?
6. Does the subsequent accounting treatment of goodwill affect acquisition behaviors?

In this section, we focus on the first and third topics listed above, which we consider particularly important in this study, and present the results of comparing the survey responses of preparers, users, and auditors. These topics have been frequently discussed in the standard setting debate regarding the subsequent accounting for goodwill. Furthermore, we refer to the results of our follow-up interviews (semi-structured interviews) to deepen our understanding of the background of the results obtained by the comparison.[111] Therefore, we believe that comparing the responses of them on the topics can be insightful for a deeper understanding of the issue.

[111] The results of the follow-up interviews are partially provided in Chap. 6. In this section, we refer to the results of the interviews and an additional interview conducted after this survey research from November 10 to December 1, 2020, and from March 12 to March 23, 2021. We interviewed four firms as preparers, two equity analysts, one credit analyst, and two user-side associations as users, four big audit firms, 2 second-tier audit firms, and one auditor-side association as auditors (Tokuga et al. 2021; Chap. 6). We summarize the detail of information on interviews in Appendix. When discussing the survey results obtained from preparers, users, and auditors, we mention to the results obtained through the follow-up interviews as necessary.

Table 5.74 "Impairment-only" versus "Systematic amortization with impairment"

	Preparers		Users	Auditors
	Entire	Nonzero goodwill balance		
1. Impairment-only	71	37	26	41
	(15.88)	(14.80)	(20.00)	(6.61)
2. Systematic amortization with impairment	328	193	81	555
	(73.38)	(77.20)	(62.31)	(89.52)
3. Either	48	20	23	24
	(10.74)	(8.00)	(17.69)	(3.87)
Total	447	250	130	620
	(100.00)	(100.00)	(100.00)	(100.00)

Note: The numbers of responses and percentages (in parentheses) are shown in the upper and lower rows, respectively

5.4.2 *Results*

5.4.2.1 Comparison of Responses Regarding the "Impairment-Only" Approach Versus the "Systematic Amortization with Impairment" Approach Among the Three Groups

First, we asked the respondents which approach to subsequent accounting treatment of goodwill was more desirable: "Impairment-only," "Systematic amortization with impairment," or "Either." Table 5.74 summarizes the responses of the three groups. The percentage of respondents who supported "Systematic amortization with impairment" was the highest: 73.38% of preparers (77.20% if the goodwill balance was not zero), 62.31% of users, and 89.52% of auditors. The results also show that there were differences in opinions among the three groups. Auditors tend to most strongly support goodwill amortization compared to preparers and users. Although more than half of the users supported "Systematic amortization with impairment," the percentage (62.31%) was approximately 26% less than that of the auditors surveyed.

However, the percentage of respondents who supported "Impairment-only" was lower than that of those who supported "Systematic amortization with impairment". For preparers, only 15.88% (14.80% for the non-zero goodwill balance sample) of the respondents chose "Impairment-only." Moreover, 20.00% of users and 6.61% of auditors supported "Impairment-only." The percentage of respondents who chose "Either" was 10.74% for preparers (8.00% for the non-zero goodwill balance sample), 17.69% for users, and 3.87% for auditors. Since it is generally believed that users are more concerned about cash flow information than other stakeholders, it is no surprise that the percentage of respondents who did not care was higher for users than for preparers and auditors.

In summary, the results of the first question suggest that "Systematic amortization with impairment" is considered a more desirable accounting treatment of goodwill by all three major stakeholders in Japan. Notably, more than 60% of the respondents, including users, supported the amortization of goodwill. This is quite interesting, considering that users are generally said to be more likely to be in favor of "Impairment-only."

5.4.2.2 Comparing the Results of Reasons Supporting "Impairment-Only" or "Systematic Amortization with Impairment"

Regarding the first question of this survey, we asked the respondents that chose "Impairment-only" or "Systematic amortization with impairment" to answer why their preferred accounting treatment was desirable. For this question, we presented multiple reasons shown in Table 5.75 and asked the respondents to rate how close the reasons were to their opinions.[112] For simplicity, we calculated the percentage of respondents who chose "Yes" or "Somewhat yes" for each reason and ranked the reasons according to the aggregated percentages.

5.4.2.2.1 Reasons for Supporting "Impairment-Only"

Table 5.75 shows that the respondents of all three groups strongly supported the following reasons: "It is difficult to predict the useful life and amortization pattern of acquired goodwill" (Reason (1)), "The value of acquired goodwill is maintained by corporate efforts in subsequent periods" (Reason (2)), and "If impairment test is properly conducted, systematic amortization of goodwill is not necessary" (Reason (4)).

The most supported reason for all groups was Reason (4). Interestingly, 96.15% of users supported this reason, implying that they believed that, even if the amortization of goodwill was abolished in J-GAAP, a rigorous impairment test would take its place for actionable information. Moreover, they might believe that impairment testing is more appropriate than systematic amortization for determining the actual goodwill value. This is consistent with the opinions of users introduced by the IASB (IASB 2004, para. BC142). However, we cannot overlook the possibility that they ignored the shielding effect caused by internally generated goodwill.[113]

Under "Systematic amortization with impairment," the amount of goodwill that cannot be recovered due to the decline in profitability may be misclassified and recorded as an amortization expense instead of an impairment loss, even if only partially. This explains why security analysts who do not want to mix the two elements of goodwill with different properties support non-amortization procedures.

---

[112] As we mentioned in the previous sections, if they had reasons other than those presented, we asked them to provide them in a free-text field.

[113] The shielding effect refers to the effect that the existence of headroom in a cash-generating unit (CGU) to which goodwill is allocated, i.e., the excess of the recoverable amount over the carrying amount of the recognized net assets including goodwill, which is off-balanced from the balance-sheet, makes it difficult to recognize impairment losses despite the impairment of goodwill (IASB 2020, p.56, par.3.20, p.58, para. 3.31, and p. 59, paras. 3.35–3.36).

Table 5.75 The reasons for supporting "Impairment-only"

	Preparers		Users	Auditors
Reason	Entire (N = 70)	Nonzero goodwill balance (N = 36)	(N = 26)	(N = 21)
1. It is difficult to predict the useful life and amortization pattern of the carrying amount of goodwill.	**2nd (85.72)**	**3rd (86.12)**	**2nd (88.47)**	**1st (87.80)**
2. The value of acquired goodwill is maintained by firm efforts after it is acquired.	**3rd (82.86)**	**1st (88.89)**	**3rd (88.46)**	**3rd (73.17)**
3. Goodwill amortization expenses and the carrying amount of goodwill after amortization are not useful for financial statement users.	6th (48.57)	7th (47.22)	6th (30.77)	4th (54.54)
4. If an appropriate impairment test is conducted, systematic amortization of goodwill is not needed	**1st (88.57)**	**1st (88.89)**	**1st (96.15)**	**2nd (85.37)**
5. (Option for preparers) The goodwill amortization expense amount decreases accounting earnings (Option for auditors) Firms are negative about the fact that the goodwill amortization expense amount decreases accounting earnings	4th (57.97)	4th (55.56)	n.a.	7th (19.52)
6. Amortization of goodwill can be a competitive disadvantage with rival firms that need not amortize the carrying amount of goodwill	5th (54.29)	5th (52.78)	n.a.	n.a.
7. It reduces comparability with firms that are not required to amortize goodwill	n.a.	n.a.	4th (84.62)	5th (56.10)
8. Amortizing goodwill weakens the signaling effect of goodwill impairment	6th (48.57)	5th (52.78)	5th (38.46)	6th (46.34)

Notes: We ranked each reason for supporting "Impairment-only" based on the percentage of respondents who selected "Yes" or "Somewhat yes" for the reason. The percentages are shown in parentheses

Reason (1) was also often cited in standard-setting accounting debates as to why the impairment-only approach is preferable to systematic amortization and is strongly supported by the respondents of all three groups. Notably, the percentage of respondents who chose "Yes" for this reason for "Impairment-only" was higher for auditors than for preparers and users (untabulated). These findings indicate that practical difficulties in determining amortization periods and/or patterns are problematic for all three groups; however, these difficulties can be more problematic for auditors.[114]

A significant number of respondents across all groups selected Reason (2) regarding their preference for "Impairment-only" over "Systematic amortization with impairment". Consequently, we did not find a significant difference in the percentage between preparers and users. However, we found a large difference in the

[114] In this regard, it can be pointed out that preparers and auditors are more likely to experience practical difficulties than users because uses never bear the cost of preparing financial statements themselves but can free ride on preparers and auditors.

percentage between auditors and the other groups. The percentage of auditors was 9.69% (15.29%) lower than that of preparers (users). This suggests that auditors supporting the impairment-only approach were more skeptical than preparers and users about firms' ability to maintain the value of goodwill through subsequent efforts.

The rationale for Reason (2) is that preparers, users, and auditors are aware of the differences between acquired and internally generated goodwill; however, it is impossible to distinguish between these two elements. For example, in our interview, a preparer from a major Japanese manufacturing firm said, "Synergies are a significant reflection of the firm's efforts to integrate the acquired firm after the acquisition (e.g., by investing additional resources to increase the competitiveness of the acquired firm or realize cost synergies). Therefore, it is difficult to distinguish the extent to which synergies are internally generated." (P-1)[115] The same respondent stated, "The purchase price is calculated based on the assumption of synergies that will arise from the integration after the acquisition, so the amount equivalent to the goodwill internally generated by the subsequent efforts is included in the initial purchase price." (P-1) In addition, another preparer from a bank in Japan stated, "Companies do unconsciously incur investment expenditures to maintain the value of goodwill. Rather, this value is naturally maintained through normal business behavior. Such additional investments are not deliberately classified as the costs of maintaining the value of goodwill." (P-2).

Another analyst we interviewed said, "It is difficult to distinguish between internally generated goodwill and acquired goodwill, and it is not clear whether analysts value this distinction." (U-4) In addition, a bond analyst explained, "Analysts have not employed any practice of separating and analyzing purchased goodwill and internally generated goodwill. I figure out that the two are theoretically different, but it is difficult for people outside a firm to judge the separation between them." (U-1) This analyst also said, "In some cases, the value of internally generated goodwill of an acquired firm can increase by using not only the resources of the acquiring firm, but also the resources of the entire corporate group." (U-1) This implies that the value of (acquired) goodwill during the post-acquisition period can change depending on the various activities of the acquiring firm, and it may be difficult to grasp the changes by tracing only a few specific operating activities.

Furthermore, preparers and users may be aware that it is challenging to distinguish between purchased and internally generated goodwill; however, they may believe that the unintentional recording of internally generated goodwill is nonproblematic. For example, an analyst from a mutual fund company said, "In future cash flow forecasts and corporate valuation by analysts, it is important to estimate 'enterprise values' that integrate acquired and internally generated goodwill. Therefore, it is not necessarily important from which the values come." (U-4) Another analyst, an officer of a Japanese security analyst association, stated, "It can be said that analysts are more tolerant than accounting professions in the recording

[115] Descriptions of the identification codes (in parentheses) used throughout this section are provided in the Appendix.

of internally generated goodwill because the appropriate evaluation of internally generated goodwill is one of the roles that analysts are required to play." (U-4) Furthermore, because the survey results differed between auditors and other stakeholders, preparers and users may have been less aware that internally generated goodwill could be recorded on a balance sheet if goodwill was not amortized. For example, one interviewee from a major financial institution in Japan said, "Additional investments are not classified as costs of maintaining goodwill. We do not consider the value of goodwill to be replaced by such investments." (P-2)

In our survey, we presented further reasons supporting "Impairment-only" (Reasons (5), (6), and (7)). For Reason (7), which refers to the "comparability" issue, we asked only users and auditors how close the given reason matched their true opinion. Table 5.75 shows that 84.62% of the users supporting the impairment-only approach thought that Reason (7) closely matched their opinion. For auditors, only 56.10% supported this. From these results, users valued "comparability" more than auditors. Considering that the analysts that we surveyed actively engaged in security analyses and advisements for investors, it is not surprising that their answers differed significantly from those of auditors who valued Reasons (1) and (4) more.

Finally, we checked the results of Reason (8). Under "Systematic amortization with impairment," the book value of goodwill decreases faster than its actual value because of goodwill amortization. In this case, even if goodwill impairment occurs, it is never recognized because the actual value is larger than the book value. Even if the recognition of goodwill impairment is triggered, there is concern that the amount of impairment loss recorded will be lower than the actual economic impairment loss. Thus, information on the amount of impairment loss will be lost. Therefore, we expected users to value Reason (8) as the reason for their strong support. Notably, the results in Table 5.75 are inconsistent with the prediction. Only 38.46% of users supported this reason, which was lower than that of preparers and auditors. Moreover, the results indicate that users were less likely to value this reason than other reasons. There are several possible interpretations of this result; however, we consider two main interpretations. First, many respondents believed that even if systematic amortization was performed, the signaling effect of impairment losses would not be largely reduced. The second interpretation is as follows: systematically amortizing goodwill reduces the opportunity to record impairment losses in the future; hence, it reduces the impact of the signaling effect. However, capital market participants do not attach much importance to impairment losses as a source of information in the first place because the accounting treatment of goodwill impairment rely heavily on management's subjective judgments. Therefore, users may question the timing and amount of goodwill impairment.

5.4.2.2.2 Reasons for Supporting "Systematic Amortization with Impairment"

We next compared the survey results to determine why some respondents preferred "Systematic amortization with impairment" to "Impairment-only." In the survey, we presented multiple reasons shown in Table 5.76 and asked the respondents to rate how close the reasons were to their opinions, as in the above analysis. Table 5.75 shows that the most supported reason for preparers and users was Reason (2). This indicates that a considerable number of respondents considered the approach desirable from the perspective of revenue and expense matching. Both preparers and users were more likely to support "Systematic amortization with impairment" based on this "matching" reason. However, for auditors, the highest proportion of respondents supported Reason (1), indicating that auditors placed more importance on properly depicting goodwill amortization. That is, auditors valued the amortizable nature of goodwill more than preparers and users did.

As shown in Table 5.76, auditors placed their most importance on Reason (3). This is supported by 79.10% of the auditor respondents. This percentage was more than 10% higher than that of preparers and users. This result indicates auditors' *conservative* attitudes, as well as their tendency to seek objective evidence.

For users, Table 5.76 shows that they placed the most importance on Reason (4) and Reason (2) (87.65% for both). Interestingly, users valued Reason (4) more than preparers and auditors, as the percentage of users who supported this reason was more than 10% higher than that of preparers and auditors. In addition, Table 5.76 shows that Reason (1) was the third most popular reason among users (80.25%), while it was the (second) most popular reason among auditors (preparers). These

Table 5.76 The reasons for supporting "systematic amortization with impairment"

	Preparers		Users	Auditors
Reason	Entire (N = 327)	Nonzero goodwill balance (N = 192)	(N = 81)	(N = 468)
1. Excess earnings power represented by goodwill gradually decreases due to market competition	**2nd (76.75)**	**2nd (78.65)**	**3rd (80.25)**	**1st (88.37)**
2. The carrying amount of goodwill should be allocated to the appropriate periods to match revenues and expenses	**1st (88.99)**	**1st (92.71)**	**1st (87.65)**	**3rd (75.86)**
3. It is impossible to distinguish between the diminished and maintained components of goodwill value	4th (63.30)	4th (63.02)	4th (67.90)	**2nd (79.10)**
4. It is consistent with the accounting treatment of other depreciable assets	**3rd (70.46)**	**3rd (73.30)**	**1st (87.65)**	5th (56.58)
5. Amortization cannot be replaced by impairment	5th (57.80)	5th (61.46)	5th (67.90)	4th (63.43)
6. It leads to prudent M&A decisions	6th (53.37)	6th (60.73)	6th (59.26)	7th (38.01)
7. It reduces the cost of the goodwill impairment test	7th (51.23)	7th (50.78)	7th (40.74)	6th (42.88)

Notes: We ranked each reason for supporting "Systematic amortization with impairment" based on the percentage of respondents who selected "Yes" or "Somewhat yes" for the reason. The percentages are shown in parentheses

results indicate that both preparers and users supported "Systematic amortization with impairment" from the perspective of the 'matching' principle, as well as the characteristics of goodwill as an amortizable asset and its consistency with the treatment of other amortizable intangible assets. With respect to the latter reason, Table 5.76 shows that many preparers and users did not believe that they should treat goodwill differently from other amortizable assets in terms of accounting treatment. Therefore, as long as goodwill and other tangible and intangible assets occur from investments that gradually erode over time and through use, it may be considered appropriate to amortize goodwill as well as other depreciable tangible and intangible assets on a regular basis.

As Table 5.76 shows, the percentage of respondents who supported Reason (5) was only 57.80% (61.46%) for preparers (preparers with a non-zero goodwill balance), 67.90% for users, and 63.43% for auditors. Among the seven reasons shown in Table 5.76, this reason was ranked fifth for both preparers and users, and fourth for auditors. These results show that a significant number of respondents in all three groups did not necessarily view "Systematic amortization with impairment" as irreplaceable, which contrasts with the result for Reason (4) in Table 5.75.

Finally, we check whether the cost of impairment tests (Reason (7)) is a crucial reason for supporting "Systematic amortization with impairment." As seen in the discussions of the FASB and IASB, the viewpoint of the costs (more precisely, the costs and benefits) of "Impairment-only" is of great significance in the discussion on the reintroduction of goodwill amortization. Surprisingly, the results in Table 5.76 show that the proportion of respondents supporting Reason (7) was the lowest for preparers and users and the second lowest for auditors. In particular, the proportion of respondents supporting Reason (7) for users and auditors was less than 50% (40.74 and 42.88%, respectively). Interviewees from two major financial institutions and one major manufacturing company in Japan stated that "regardless of whether they used "Impairment-only" or "Systematic amortization with impairment," the cost burden required for impairment testing was high in terms of time and expense." (P-2, P-4, and P-3) This could be due to the tightening of audit procedures for impairment testing. Moreover, another interpretation may indicate that the reduction in the cost of impairment testing through systematic amortization of goodwill is not as important to preparers, users, and auditors as it is for other reasons. If so, the results are interesting because reducing the costs of goodwill impairment testing has been a major issue in the subsequent accounting of goodwill.

5.4.2.3 Comparison of Responses Regarding the Nature of Goodwill

In this subsection, we compare the responses regarding how preparers, users, and auditors perceive goodwill as an intangible asset. To do so, we asked all respondents to select from the following options the one that best matched their view of the nature of goodwill: "All or the majority of the value of goodwill is preserved semi-permanently" (Option 1), "There is both a part that preserves its value

Table 5.77 The nature of goodwill

Option	Preparers: Entire	Preparers: Nonzero goodwill balance	Users	Auditors
1. All or the majority of the value is preserved semi-permanently	5	4	3	7
	(1.13)	(1.61)	(2.31)	(1.10)
2. There is both a part that preserves its value semi-permanently and a part that does not	190	111	75	246
	(42.89)	(44.58)	(57.69)	(39.70)
3. There is no part that preserves its value semi-permanently	207	117	43	339
	(46.73)	(46.99)	(33.08)	(54.70)
4. Unsure	41	17	9	28
	(9.26)	(6.83)	(6.92)	(4.50)
Total	443	249	130	620
	(100.00)	(100.00)	(100.00)	(100.00)

Note: The numbers of responses and percentages (in parentheses) are shown in the upper and lower rows, respectively

semi-permanently and a part that does not" (Option 2), "There is no part that preserves its value semi-permanently" (Option 3), and "Unsure" (Option 4).

Table 5.77 shows that some respondents from all three groups selected Options (1) or (4). For preparers, the proportion of respondents who selected Options (2) or (3) was approximately the same, although slightly higher for the latter (42.89% [44.58%] versus 46.73% [46.99%], the results for the non-zero goodwill balance sample presented in square blankets). Next, for users, 57.69% of the respondents selected Option (2) and 33.08% selected Option (3), with the former being 24.61% higher. On the contrary, for auditors, the proportion of respondents who selected Option (2) was 39.70%, and that of respondents who selected Option (3) was 54.70%. The latter exceeded the former by 15.00%. A comparison of these results shows that the respondents who considered the character of goodwill to be Option (2) or (3) were divided by their opinions. This also indicates that the response tendencies differed among the three groups. Furthermore, the comparison indicates that auditors were more skeptical about the view that the value of goodwill would be maintained semi-permanently (or permanently) in the future, even if only partially, compared to preparers and users.

To examine the results of this comparison in more depth, we analyzed the relationship between the responses to the two questions about the nature of goodwill and the more desirable accounting treatment of goodwill. Panels A–D of Table 5.78 show the results for preparers (entire sample), preparers (only non-zero goodwill balance sample), users, and auditors, respectively.

First, for preparers (both the entire and non-zero goodwill balance samples) and auditors, the results in Panels A, B, and D show that more respondents who supported "Impairment-only" considered that, although the value of goodwill could not be completely maintained semi-permanently, it could at least be partially maintained. Conversely, more respondents who supported "Systematic amortization" believed that no goodwill value could be maintained. Second, for users, Panel C indicates that both respondents who supported "Impairment-only" and "Systematic amortization with impairment" regarded goodwill, some of which could be maintained semi-permanently, whereas others could not. However, among the respondents who supported "Systematic amortization with impairment", the proportion of respondents who believed that only a part of the value of goodwill could be maintained semi-permanently was 6.18% higher than that of respondents who believed that all or almost all of the value of goodwill could be maintained semi-permanently. Overall, the results in Table 5.78 show that the responses to the two questions were related in some way, suggesting that we must consider the views on the nature of goodwill behind the individual arguments when discussing which is a more desirable subsequent accounting treatment of goodwill: "Impairment-only" or "Systematic amortization with impairment."

Table 5.78 Relationship between goodwill characteristics and desirable subsequent accounting treatment of goodwill

Option	Impairment-only	Systematic amortization with impairment	Either	Total
Panel A: Preparers (Entire Sample)				
1. All or the majority of the value is preserved semi-permanently	5	0	0	5
	(7.14)	(0.00)	(0.00)	(1.13)
2. There is both a part that preserves its value semi-permanently and a part that does not	45	125	20	190
	(64.29)	(38.46)	(41.67)	(42.89)
3. There is no part that preserves its value semi-permanently	14	176	17	207
	(20.00)	(54.15)	(35.42)	(46.73)
4. Unsure	6	24	11	41
	(8.57)	(7.38)	(22.92)	(9.26)
Total	70	325	48	443
	(100.00)	(100.00)	(100.00)	(100.00)
Panel B: Prepares (Non-zero Goodwill-balance Sample)				
1. All or the majority of the value is preserved semi-permanently	4	0	0	4
	(10.81)	(0.00)	(0.00)	(1.61)
2. There is both a part that preserves its value semi-permanently and a part that does not	26	72	13	111
	(70.27)	(37.50)	(65.00)	(44.58)
3. There is no part that preserves its value semi-permanently	6	105	6	117
	(16.22)	(54.69)	(30.00)	(46.99)
4. Unsure	1	15	1	17
	(2.70)	(7.81)	(5.00)	(6.83)
Total	37	192	20	249
	(100.00)	(100.00)	(100.00)	(100.00)

(continued)

Table 5.78 (continued)

Option	Impairment-only	Systematic amortization with impairment	Either	Total
Panel C: Users				
1. All or the majority of the value is preserved semi-permanently	3	0	0	3
	(11.54)	(0.00)	(0.00)	(2.31)
2. There is both a part that preserves its value semi-permanently and a part that does not	19	41	15	75
	(73.08)	(50.62)	(65.22)	(57.69)
3. There is no part that preserves its value semi-permanently	1	36	6	43
	(3.85)	(44.44)	(26.09)	(33.08)
4. Unsure	3	4	2	9
	(11.54)	(4.94)	(8.70)	(6.92)
Total	26	81	23	130
	(100.00)	(100.00)	(100.00)	(100.00)
Panel D: Auditors				
1. All or the majority of the value is preserved semi-permanently	5	2	0	7
	(12.20)	(0.36)	(0.00)	(1.13)
2. There is both a part that preserves its value semi-permanently and a part that does not	25	207	14	246
	(60.98)	(37.30)	(58.33)	(39.68)
3. There is no part that preserves its value semi-permanently	8	322	9	339
	(19.51)	(58.02)	(37.50)	(54.68)
4. Unsure	3	24	1	28
	(7.32)	(4.32)	(4.17)	(4.52)
Total	41	555	24	620
	(100.00)	(100.00)	(100.00)	(100.00)

Note: The numbers of responses and percentages (in parentheses) are shown in the upper and lower rows, respectively

5.4.3 Section Summary

In this section, we compared and analyzed survey responses to questions from preparers, users, and auditors in Japan (447 responses from preparers, 130 responses from users, and 620 responses from auditors). First, which of the following is desirable as a subsequent accounting treatment of goodwill: "Impairment-only" or "Systematic amortization with impairment"? Second, why do you think so? Third, what is the nature of goodwill?

The main findings are as follows: First, we found that more than 60% of respondents across preparers, users, and auditors supported "Systematic amortization with impairment"; however, the proportions varied across all groups. Surprisingly, more than 60% of the respondents in all three groups preferred "Systematic amortization with impairment" to "Impairment-only." Second, we found that the reasons why respondents favored "Impairment-only" were mostly the same across all three groups. This is also true for respondents who favored "Systematic amortization with impairment." Notably, the respondents believed that the approach was more desirable because of the appropriate matching of revenues and expenses and the declining nature of (acquired) goodwill due to market competition, whereas the respondents who supported "Impairment-only" believed that impairment testing could be replaced with systematic amortization when properly curried out. Finally, we found that different stakeholder groups had different views on the nature of goodwill. For instance, the user group had a higher percentage of respondents who believed that goodwill consisted of those whose value can be maintained semi-permanently and those whose value will never be done. For the auditor group, the percentage of respondents who believed that the value of goodwill is never maintained semi-permanently was the highest.

The results of this section provide new evidence on the differences and similarities of stakeholders' perceptions of the subsequent accounting treatments of goodwill and its nature. However, we must note that, as the analysis in the previous section, the analysis of this section have several limitations. For example, our sample consisted of only Japanese stakeholders. Thus, it is unclear whether our results can be generalized to other nations. Future research should address this issue to better comprehend the controversy that has not yet been resolved.

5.5 Summary and Remaining Issues

This study aims to contribute to the ongoing debate about whether acquired goodwill should be subject to the systematic amortization-with-impairment approach ("Systematic amortization with impairment"), or the impairment-only approach ("Impairment-only"). The study is based on a questionnaire survey of preparers, users (primarily analysts), and auditors. As described in Sect. 5.2, previous surveys, such as the Keidanren Survey and the ASBJ Surveys, have explored stakeholders' attitudes toward the accounting treatment of acquired goodwill. However, these earlier surveys were limited in scope, targeting only a small number of preparers and users, and did not include auditors.

In this study, we expanded upon these prior efforts by adding new questions and options to the survey and increasing its scope. The survey was distributed to 1379 Keidanren-affiliated firms (263 responses; 19.07% response rate) and 1339 listed firms not affiliated with Keidanren (184 responses; 13.07% response rate). Additionally, we surveyed 673 users (130 responses; 19.32% response rate). To include auditors, who were not surveyed in previous studies, we also conducted a questionnaire survey targeting 1961 partners (620 responses; 31.62% response rate) from the Big 4 audit firms and six second-tier audit firms.

The survey results revealed that approximately 70% of preparers preferred "Systematic amortization with impairment" over "Impairment-only." This trend was consistent across subsamples of Keidanren-affiliated versus non-affiliated firms and manufacturing versus non-manufacturing firms. Similarly, approximately 60% of users preferred "Systematic amortization with impairment." Notably, around 90% of auditors favored the same treatment. These findings suggest that "Systematic amortization with impairment" is generally preferred over "Impairment-only" by preparers, users, and auditors in Japan.

Regarding the reasons behind these preferences, preparers and users who supported "Impairment-only" cited the view that if an appropriate impairment test is conducted, systematic amortization of goodwill is unnecessary. For auditors, the most compelling reason for supporting "Impairment-only" was the difficulty of estimating the useful life and amortization pattern of goodwill, though they also acknowledged the argument that appropriate impairment testing could negate the need for amortization. In contrast, preparers and users who favored "Systematic amortization with impairment" emphasized that goodwill should be allocated to appropriate periods to match revenues and expenses. Users also noted that this approach aligns with the accounting treatments of other depreciable assets. Auditors, however, most commonly cited the gradual diminishment of excess earning capacity due to market competition as their rationale.

The survey also addressed various additional topics, including the desirability of regulating the amortization period for goodwill, preferred amortization periods, the choice between "Impairment-only" and "Systematic amortization with impairment," alternative accounting methods, the asset nature of goodwill, and the relationship between goodwill accounting and M&A decision-making. For users, additional questions explored whether goodwill amounts are deducted from net assets and whether goodwill amortization expense is added back in securities analysis. Auditors were asked about issues such as goodwill and audit quality, the timeliness of goodwill impairment recognition, and the appropriateness of impairment estimates. Some responses aligned with findings from prior studies, while others provided new insights that differed from previous research.

Although our survey research reveals insightful findings, several limitations remain. For instance, since this study focuses on preparers, users, and auditors in Japan, further research targeting other jurisdictions is necessary to enhance the generalizability of our insights. Furthermore, in the future, the results of this survey may change. Therefore, to clarify how stakeholders' perceptions of goodwill accounting treatment evolve, follow-up surveys will need to be conducted.

Appendix 2

See Table 5.79.

Table 5.79 The detail of the follow-up interviews

Category	Site	Interviewees	Date	Visitors
Preparers	(P-1) Leading Manufacturer (IFRS)	4 treasurers (Online)	2020/11/10 16:30–17:30	Tokuga, Miyauchi, Yamashita
	(P-2) Major Financial Institution [Bank] (IFRS)	1 officer, 3 persons in charge of the finance and accounting department	2020/11/30 14:00–15:05	Asami, Tokuga, Yoneyama
	(P-3) Leading Manufacturing Company (IFRS)	1 officer	2020/12/1 14:00–15:05	Asami, Tokuga, Yoneyama
	(P-4) Major Financial Institution [Insurance Industry] (J-GAAP)	1 officer, 3 persons responsible for the finance and accounting department	2020/12/1 15:30–16:35	Asami, Tokuga
	(P-5) Major General Trading Company (IFRS)	2 persons responsible for the finance and accounting department, 1 person in charge of the same department	2021/3/10 13:00–14:05	Asami, Tokuga, Yoneyama
	(P-6) Major Telecommunications Company [Telecommunications Industry] (IFRS)	3 treasurers (Online)	2021/3/18 13:00–14:00	Asami, Tokuga, Yoneyama
Users	(U-1) Bond Rating Agency	1 officer	2020/11/17 10:30–12:00	Asami, Tokuga, Yoneyama
	(U-2) Mutual Fund Company	1 officer	2020/11/17 13:30–14:35	Asami, Tokuga, Yoneyama
	(U-3) Major Securities Company	1 officer	2020/11/17 15:30–16:35	Asami, Tokuga, Yoneyama
	(U-4) Securities Analyst Industry Association	2 officers	2020/11/30 16:00–17:05	Asami, Tokuga, Yoneyama
	(U-5) IR Industry Association	1 officer	2020/12/1 12:00–13:05	Asami, Tokuga, Yoneyama

(continued)

Table 5.79 (continued)

Category	Site	Interviewees	Date	Visitors
Auditors	(A-1) Big 4 Audit Firm	1 officer, 2 partners 2 officers, 2 partners	2020/12/1 10:00–11:05	Asami, Tokuga, Yoneyama
			2021/3/19 11:00–12:00	Asami, Tokuga, Yoneyama
	(A-2) Certified Public Accountants Industry Association	1 officer	2021/3/12 11:00–12:00	Asami, Tokuga, Yoneyama
	(A-3) Big 4 Audit Firm	1 officer	2021/3/17 14:30–15:30	Asami, Tokuga, Yoneyama
	(A-4) Big 4 Audit Firm	1 officer, 1 partner	2021/3/18 11:00–12:00	Asami, Tokuga, Yoneyama
	(A-5) Big 4 Audit Firm	1 officer, 2 partners	2021/3/19 13:0014:00	Asami, Tokuga, Yoneyama
	(A-6) Second-tier Audit Firm	1 officer, 1 partner	2021/3/19 16:15–17:15	Asami, Tokuga, Yoneyama
	(A-7) Second-tier Audit Firm	1 partner	2021/3/23 11:15–12:00	Asami, Tokuga, Yamashita, Yoneyama

Appendix 3-Between-Group Similarity and Within-Group Homogeneity of Responses among Preparers, Users, and Auditors[116]

Yoshihiro Tokuga

Abstract

This appendix provides an exploratory analysis of survey responses on goodwill accounting, complementing the results reported in this chapter. It examines the similarity of response distributions across financial statement preparers, users, and auditors, as well as the degree of response concentration within each group. Using distribution-based measures, we find that differences in views across stakeholder groups follow a stable and consistent pattern: preparers and auditors are more closely aligned, whereas users' views are more distant from those of auditors. Moreover, within-group response concentration is broadly similar across groups, indicating that observed differences are not driven by internal fragmentation or random variation in opinions.

[116] The author gratefully acknowledges the valuable guidance of Takunori Ishihara (Associate Professor, KUAS) on the theoretical interpretation of the Wasserstein distance. The author also thanks Sajid Nisar (Associate Professor, KUAS) for assistance with the measurement of the Wasserstein distance and Wu Qi (Professor, KUAS) for support in conducting the ANOVA tests. Any remaining errors are the author's sole responsibility.

Taken together, these findings suggest that disagreements over goodwill accounting reflect structurally stable, role-based positions rather than heterogeneous or weakly formed views within stakeholder groups. This evidence provides important insights into how accounting standard setters should interpret consultation outcomes and how policies aimed at balancing stakeholder interests may be designed and evaluated.

Introduction

This appendix provides an exploratory empirical analysis of the questionnaire survey on goodwill accounting reported in this chapter, focusing on (i) similarity of responses across financial statement preparers, users, and auditors, and (ii) within-group homogeneity of responses.

Prior empirical studies on goodwill accounting have extensively examined preparers' and users' views on impairment versus amortization and market reactions to goodwill-related disclosures. However, empirical evidence comparing the distributional structure of responses among preparers, users, and auditors remains limited. In particular, to our knowledge, no prior studies jointly examine between-group similarity and within-group homogeneity using distribution-based measures. This appendix complements the broader survey of goodwill-related empirical literature presented in this chapter by focusing on the structural properties of stakeholder responses rather than on directional preferences alone.This appendix contributes to the literature in three respects. First, rather than presuming stakeholder conflicts among preparers, users, and auditors, it empirically examines whether such differences reflect fragmented views or consistently held group-level positions. Second, methodologically, it introduces the combined use of the first-order Wasserstein distance (WD1) and the Herfindahl–Hirschman Index (HHI) to survey-based accounting research, allowing for a joint assessment of between-group distributional similarity and within-group response homogeneity. Third, by focusing on the structure of opinion distributions rather than mean differences alone, this analysis provides a complementary perspective to existing empirical studies on goodwill accounting.

Analysis Method

Similarity of Responses

Recent methodological studies have emphasized the usefulness of Wasserstein-based metrics for comparing ordinal rating distributions, as these metrics capture differences in location, dispersion, and distributional shape rather than relying solely on mean differences (Seufert 2021). In applied settings, Wasserstein distance has been used to compare response distributions on a question-by-question basis and to aggregate such distances across survey items (Zhao et al. 2024). Similar distribution-based approaches have also been adopted in recent survey research to compare response patterns across groups (Kim et al. 2024). Consistent with this literature, we employ the first-order Wasserstein distance (WD1) to assess between-group similarity in survey responses.

We compared the similarity of responses among three groups: 1) preparer vs. user, 2) preparer vs. auditor, and 3) user vs. auditor. Using Python programming, we measured the first-order Wasserstein Distance (WD1) for 1, 2, and 3, and compared the three. We also examined the deviation between the mean and median for 1, 2, and 3 to determine the robustness of the results. Finally, the Friedman test[117] was employed to examine the significance level of the differences in distance between 1 and 2, 2 and 3, and 3 and 1.

Homogeneity of Responses (Concentration)

Measures of response concentration based on the HHI have been widely used to assess the degree of agreement or disagreement in survey-based expectations and attitudes. For example, the HHI has been applied to household survey data to evaluate the concentration of inflation expectations (Nishiguchi et al. 2014) and to construct index-based measures of attitudinal convergence using Likert-scale responses (Liberati et al. 2021). Following this literature, we interpret higher HHI values as indicating stronger within-group homogeneity of responses.

A higher HHI indicates a stronger convergence of opinions within a group, whereas a lower HHI suggests greater heterogeneity in views among respondents. As in the similarity analysis, we examined the concentration (i.e., degree of response concentration across categories) of responses for preparers, users, and auditors using the five options for the 32 questions. The HHI, which indicates the "concentration" of each response, was calculated, and the average concentration for each group was computed.

Given the moderate sample sizes, we focused on variance homogeneity and complemented the analysis of variance (ANOVA) with a nonparametric test. After checking the normality of the mean differences among the three groups (using Levene's test), an ANOVA was performed to measure the significance level of differences among the three groups. We confirmed that the results were qualitatively unchanged using the nonparametric Kruskal–Wallis test.

[117] As a robustness check, we also conducted pairwise Wilcoxon signed-rank tests with Holm correction, which did not alter the qualitative conclusions.

Data

Of the 38 survey questions, 32 required responses on a 5-point scale[118] (Table 5.80). Using these data, we compared the similarity and concentration of the responses among the three groups. The 32 questions are summarized in Table 5.80.

Table 5.80 Question content

Question	Question text
1	It is difficult to estimate the useful life and amortization pattern of the carrying amount of goodwill.
2	The value of goodwill is maintained by firm efforts after it is acquired.
3	Goodwill amortization expense and the carrying amount of goodwill after amortization are not useful for financial statement users.
4	If an appropriate impairment test is conducted, systematic amortization of goodwill is not needed.
5	Amortizing goodwill weakens the signaling effect of goodwill impairment.
6	Excess earnings power represented by goodwill gradually decreases due to market competition.
7	The carrying amount of goodwill should be allocated to the appropriate periods to match revenues and expenses.
8	It is impossible to distinguish between the diminished and maintained components of goodwill value.
9	It is consistent with accounting treatments for other depreciable assets.
10	Amortization cannot be replaced by impairment.
11	It leads to prudent M&A decisions.
12	It reduces the cost of the goodwill impairment test.
13	The investment-return period based on management's business plan.
14	The period over which synergies are expected to be maintained.
15	Periods over which an acquirer, on a stand-alone basis, is expected to maintain higher future cash flows.
16	Useful lives of related tangible assets.
17	Useful lives of related other intangible assets.
18	How many years do you think should be chosen as the upper limit of the goodwill amortization period? Please choose one of the following options. If you choose "Other," please fill in the blank with any specific number of years.
19	How many years do you think a uniform amortization period should be? If you choose "Other", please fill in the blank with any specific number of years.
20	Brand
21	Sales know-how
22	Proprietary technology

(continued)

[118] The remaining six questions were answered on either a three-point scale or were open-ended; thus, they were excluded from this analysis.

Table 5.80 (continued)

Question	Question text
23	Business model
24	Human resources
25	Site-specific conditions
26	No amortization and no impairment (acquisition cost as is)
27	Systematic amortization without impairment
28	Continual revaluation based on fair value (the difference in value is included in the profit and loss calculation)
29	Immediate charge to earnings
30	Immediate charge to equity
31	Do you think asking for disclosure of net assets after deducting goodwill will encourage more timely recording of goodwill impairment losses? Choose one answer that applies from the options below.
32	Do you think systematic amortization or non-amortization of goodwill has an impact on your company's (or companies') decisions regarding mergers and acquisitions (M&A)? Choose one answer that applies from the options below.

The selection rates for each of the five options (1–5) for each question are presented in Table 5.81.

Comparative Analysis of Views Among the Three Groups

The First-Order Wasserstein Distance and Implementation in Python

For ordinal survey data, the WD1[119] is naturally interpreted as the minimum amount of response mass that must be moved across scale categories to transform one group's distribution into another's. WD1 is a measure of the minimum effort required to match two distribution shapes. Unlike simple mean difference tests that measure positional differences, these tests reflect all aspects of position, spread, and skewness. For ordinal survey data, the WD1 measures the minimum amount of response mass that must be moved across scale categories to transform one group's distribution into that of another.[120]

[119] In mathematics, the Wasserstein distance (also known as the Kantorovich–Rubinstein metric) is a distance function defined between probability distributions on a given metric space, named after Leonid Vaseršteĭn.

[120] For group g and question q, the HHI was calculated as

$$\mathrm{HHI}\_\{gq\} = \Sigma\_\{k = 1\}^{\{K\}}\, \mathrm{p}\_\{gqk\}^{2},$$

where p_{gqk} denotes the proportion of respondents in group g selecting response category k for question q, and K = 5.

Table 5.81 Selection rates for each question by group

		Q1	Q2	Q3	Q4	Q5	Q6	Q7	Q8
Preparers	1. Yes	51.43%	38.57%	17.14%	52.86%	11.43%	29.66%	52.29%	15.29%
	2. Somewhat yes	34.29%	44.29%	31.43%	35.71%	37.14%	47.09%	36.70%	48.01%
	3. Somewhat no	5.71%	8.57%	17.14%	4.29%	22.86%	11.01%	5.50%	16.51%
	4. No	7.14%	7.14%	24.29%	5.71%	20.00%	7.95%	4.28%	14.98%
	5. Unsure	1.43%	1.43%	10.00%	1.43%	8.57%	4.28%	1.22%	5.20%
Users	1. Yes	34.62%	38.46%	23.08%	69.23%	11.54%	38.27%	51.85%	25.93%
	2. Somewhat yes	53.85%	50.00%	7.69%	26.92%	26.92%	41.98%	35.80%	49.38%
	3. Somewhat no	0.00%	0.00%	30.77%	3.85%	26.92%	8.64%	7.41%	14.81%
	4. No	11.54%	3.85%	30.77%	0.00%	19.23%	7.41%	3.70%	6.17%
	5. Unsure	0.00%	7.69%	7.69%	0.00%	15.38%	3.70%	1.23%	3.70%
Auditors	1. Yes	70.73%	41.46%	31.71%	53.66%	21.95%	62.70%	40.00%	42.88%
	2. Somewhat yes	17.07%	31.71%	26.83%	31.71%	24.39%	26.67%	35.86%	36.22%
	3. Somewhat no	2.44%	9.76%	14.63%	2.44%	26.83%	4.68%	9.01%	10.63%
	4. No	4.88%	14.63%	21.95%	9.76%	21.95%	4.14%	14.59%	7.57%
	5. Unsure	4.88%	2.44%	4.88%	2.44%	4.88%	1.80%	0.54%	2.70%
		Q9	**Q10**	**Q11**	**Q12**	**Q13**	**Q14**	**Q15**	**Q16**
Preparers	1. Yes	21.23%	16.21%	18.71%	17.79%	50.76%	30.89%	15.29%	4.28%
	2. Somewhat yes	49.23%	41.59%	34.66%	33.44%	39.45%	48.32%	44.34%	19.57%
	3. Somewhat no	17.23%	20.18%	22.39%	25.46%	6.73%	12.84%	25.99%	41.28%
	4. No	9.85%	11.93%	16.56%	20.55%	2.45%	5.20%	10.09%	29.05%
	5. Unsure	2.46%	10.09%	7.67%	2.76%	0.61%	2.75%	4.28%	5.81%
Users	1. Yes	40.74%	33.33%	33.33%	14.81%	33.33%	13.58%	18.52%	14.81%
	2. Somewhat yes	46.91%	34.57%	25.93%	25.93%	43.21%	41.98%	29.63%	40.74%
	3. Somewhat no	4.94%	18.52%	13.58%	24.69%	13.58%	28.40%	40.74%	24.69%
	4. No	6.17%	9.88%	20.99%	28.40%	7.41%	13.58%	7.41%	17.28%
	5. Unsure	1.23%	3.70%	6.17%	6.17%	2.47%	2.47%	3.70%	2.47%

Auditors	1. Yes	25.95%	28.29%	14.95%	18.02%	59.46%	44.14%	29.19%	4.86%
	2. Somewhat yes	30.63%	35.14%	23.06%	24.86%	32.97%	40.90%	42.16%	20.00%
	3. Somewhat no	20.72%	15.86%	22.88%	20.90%	3.78%	8.65%	18.56%	38.02%
	4. No	20.00%	17.12%	32.79%	33.15%	3.78%	4.14%	8.29%	33.69%
	5. Unsure	2.70%	3.60%	6.31%	3.06%	0.00%	2.16%	1.80%	3.42%
		Q17	**Q18**	**Q19**	**Q20**	**Q21**	**Q22**	**Q23**	**Q24**
Preparers	1. Yes	5.20%	56.96%	13.89%	4.10%	13.33%	16.92%	17.95%	17.44%
	2. Somewhat yes	27.52%	7.39%	2.78%	30.77%	50.26%	52.82%	52.82%	36.92%
	3. Somewhat no	37.61%	30.00%	41.67%	43.08%	24.10%	19.49%	16.92%	20.51%
	4. No	24.77%	3.91%	38.89%	14.36%	7.18%	6.15%	5.13%	8.21%
	5. Unsure	4.89%	1.74%	2.78%	4.62%	1.03%	2.56%	3.08%	9.23%
Users	1. Yes	14.81%	31.82%	0.00%	16.67%	24.36%	24.36%	23.08%	17.95%
	2. Somewhat yes	41.98%	12.12%	0.00%	19.23%	34.62%	47.44%	42.31%	48.72%
	3. Somewhat no	24.69%	48.48%	50.00%	44.87%	28.21%	17.95%	17.95%	19.23%
	4. No	13.58%	6.06%	37.50%	11.54%	3.85%	2.56%	3.85%	1.28%
	5. Unsure	4.94%	1.52%	12.50%	5.13%	5.13%	5.13%	6.41%	10.26%
Auditors	1. Yes	6.31%	36.89%	8.89%	9.88%	25.69%	26.09%	29.64%	27.27%
	2. Somewhat yes	25.95%	7.77%	4.44%	37.15%	54.94%	50.99%	54.55%	47.04%
	3. Somewhat no	35.68%	48.79%	53.33%	31.23%	5.93%	13.04%	5.93%	10.67%
	4. No	29.01%	6.07%	28.89%	8.70%	5.53%	2.37%	1.98%	3.56%
	5. Unsure	3.06%	0.49%	4.44%	4.35%	3.95%	2.37%	4.74%	7.11%

(continued)

Table 5.81 (continued)

		Q25	Q26	Q27	Q28	Q29	Q30	Q31	Q32
Preparers	1. Yes	5.13%	5.43%	8.14%	3.17%	2.49%	3.17%	3.82%	19.78%
	2. Somewhat yes	23.59%	4.75%	26.92%	15.84%	9.95%	15.16%	21.12%	36.40%
	3. Somewhat no	34.87%	27.83%	33.71%	32.81%	29.19%	25.57%	24.04%	26.74%
	4. No	8.72%	57.69%	26.92%	40.27%	52.71%	37.78%	35.28%	13.26%
	5. Unsure	10.77%	4.30%	4.30%	7.92%	5.66%	18.33%	15.73%	3.82%
Users	1. Yes	12.82%	10.00%	5.38%	10.00%	9.23%	3.85%	19.23%	42.31%
	2. Somewhat yes	25.64%	2.31%	13.85%	29.23%	24.62%	20.77%	26.92%	41.54%
	3. Somewhat no	34.62%	20.00%	37.69%	24.62%	23.85%	25.38%	10.00%	9.23%
	4. No	5.13%	66.15%	40.00%	30.00%	36.15%	33.08%	27.69%	4.62%
	5. Unsure	8.97%	1.54%	3.08%	6.15%	6.15%	16.92%	16.15%	2.31%
Auditors	1. Yes	10.67%	1.45%	3.71%	3.23%	4.19%	2.74%	5.97%	57.74%
	2. Somewhat yes	28.06%	1.94%	13.06%	13.55%	12.10%	12.42%	21.13%	31.45%
	3. Somewhat no	28.46%	9.52%	23.23%	28.06%	25.48%	19.52%	15.81%	5.65%
	4. No	7.11%	85.65%	59.19%	50.81%	56.13%	57.58%	46.29%	2.74%
	5. Unsure	13.04%	1.45%	0.81%	4.35%	2.10%	7.74%	10.81%	2.42%

Because there is no meaningful metric structure across survey items, we treated each question as an independent one-dimensional ordinal distribution, computed WD1 distances question-by-question, and then aggregated them across items. Thus, for each question, we computed the WD1 distance between the response distributions of each pair of groups (preparers vs. users, preparers vs. auditors, and users vs. auditors). We then compared the average distances across the 32 items to assess the overall similarity between groups. We implemented the analysis using Python and the Python Optimal Transport library.

Analysis Results

This interpretation is based on treating the five-point Likert scale as an ordinal scale with equal unit distances between adjacent response categories. Whether using the average or median value, the distance between preparers and auditors was the closest, and the distance between auditors and users was the furthest (see Table 5.82 and Fig. 5.1 for more details).

Table 5.82 WD1 for each question

Question	W1 (preparers, users)	W1 (users, auditors)	W1 (auditors, preparers)
1	0.489449	0.65904	0.510175
2	0.386588	0.633641	0.470006
3	0.549725	0.726088	0.609163
4	0.647904	0.791014	0.340629
5	0.480384	0.604858	0.426476
6	0.371422	0.644838	0.759076
7	0.153489	0.633404	0.663278
8	0.586884	0.470554	0.746981
9	0.654446	0.912962	0.540706
10	0.648495	0.409432	0.50489
11	0.499299	0.718969	0.594485
12	0.530377	0.317859	0.466652
13	0.632133	0.742935	0.350009
14	0.702406	0.850249	0.461869
15	0.430726	0.606604	0.56903
16	0.779015	0.767847	0.249737
17	0.669887	0.696241	0.241151
18	0.858654	0.280141	0.815466
19	0.874007	0.804501	0.440959
20	0.40876	0.492713	0.523613
21	0.463114	0.50788	0.590354
22	0.372205	0.403113	0.492815
23	0.398977	0.538535	0.532395

(continued)

Table 5.82 (continued)

Question	W1 (preparers, users)	W1 (users, auditors)	W1 (auditors, preparers)
24	0.419203	0.480933	0.622209
25	0.529452	0.377537	0.426256
26	0.389338	0.708422	0.654298
27	0.562798	0.48296	0.741615
28	0.639216	0.70737	0.358102
29	0.668625	0.652443	0.304242
30	0.380521	0.592132	0.48361
31	0.6649	0.757756	0.391279
32	0.798226	0.475974	0.999837

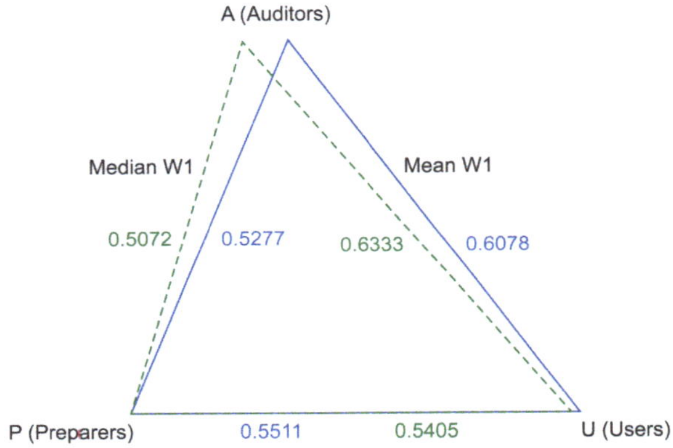

Fig. 5.1 Mean and median WD1 between group pairs

These results are consistent across mean- and median-based aggregations, suggesting that outliers in particular items do not drive ordering.

Statistical Significance and Robustness Check

Because we could not expect normality in the WD1 distribution, we used Friedman's Q test to examine whether the observed differences in WD1 across the three group pairs were statistically distinguishable across the three pairwise comparisons.

While the descriptive statistics for each test result indicate that the difference between the user and auditor responses is larger than that in the other two-way comparison figures, this difference is not statistically significant at the 5% level (see Table 5.83). Furthermore, to assess the stability of the data structure, we performed a mean versus median stability check. Pearson's second skewness coefficient (Sk_2) was used to determine whether the differences were problematic. The skewness coefficient is defined in NIST/ITL, *Engineering Statistics Handbook*, "Measures of Skewness and Kurtosis" as:

Table 5.83 Friedman's Q test

Friedman Q (tie-corected)	df	p_value	tie_correction	n_blocks	k_groups	sum_ranks_P-U	sum_ranks_U-A	sum_ranks_A-P
4.1875	2	0.120748	1	32	3	57	73	62

Comparison	Direction	n_pairs	w_plus	z	p_two_sided	p_holm	effect_size_r
P-U vs U-A	P-U < U-A	32	161	−1.916641	0.055284	0.165851	0.338818
P-U vs A-P	P-U > A-P	32	282	0.327231	0.743493	0743493	0.057847
UA vs A-P	U-A > A-P	32	352	1.636157	0.101807	0.203613	0.289234

$$\left(Sk_2 = \frac{3(\bar{x} - \tilde{x})}{s} \right)$$

Therefore, we flagged a concern if |Mean − Median| ≥ (SD/3) (≈ 0.33 × SD), or |Mean − Median| ≥ 0.30 × IQR, or if Pearson's second skewness Sk_2 = 3(Mean − Median)/SD had a large magnitude (≈ 1 or greater). We observed the following across 32 items:

$\mathrm{P-U: gap} = 0.011;\quad |\mathrm{gap}| / SD = 0.069(\mathrm{tiny}),|\quad \mathrm{gap}| / IQR = 0.047(\mathrm{tiny}),$
$\mathrm{skew} \approx +0.21.$
$\mathrm{U-A: gap} = -0.026;\ |\mathrm{gap}| / SD = 0.163(\mathrm{mild}),|\quad \mathrm{gap}| // IQR = 0.108(\mathrm{moderate}),$
$\mathrm{skew} \approx -0.49.$
$\mathrm{A-P: gap} = 0.020;\quad |\mathrm{gap}| / SD = 0.119(\mathrm{mild}),|\quad \mathrm{gap}| // IQR = 0.108(\mathrm{moderate}),$
$\mathrm{skew} \approx +0.36.$

None of the three series approaches the "problematic" thresholds. The mean–median differences were very small to moderate, indicating no red-flag skew or outlier influence.

Although the Friedman test does not indicate statistical significance at the conventional 5% level, the analysis remains informative in an exploratory sense because it reveals a stable ordinal pattern of relative distances across groups. These results suggest that auditors occupy an intermediate yet asymmetric position closer to preparers than to users. This pattern may reflect auditors' institutional proximity to preparers throughout the audit process, combined with a weaker alignment with users' informational perspectives.

Question-Type Analysis (WD1)

The questions were grouped according to their nature. Q1–Q12 addressed amortization vs. impairment treatment only. Q13–Q19 covered amortization periods when amortization is chosen, Q20–Q25 dealt with the concept of goodwill, Q26–Q30 addressed alternative accounting treatments to replace current standards, and Q31–Q32 covered other matters. The WD1 for each question type is presented in Table 5.84. The findings reveal the following. (1) Regarding the amortization period, the variation in opinions among the three parties was the greatest. (2) In every group except "Other," the responses from preparers and auditors were similar, while the responses from users and auditors differed the most. This ranking remained consistent across all groups.

We further decomposed the WD1 analysis by using the conceptual domains of the survey questions. Across all domains—goodwill amortization versus impairment, amortization period, conceptual definition of goodwill, and alternative

Table 5.84 Descriptive statistics for WD1 by question type

Comparison	Mean	Median	SD
Type 1: Amortization vs. Impairment (Q1–Q12)			
Preparers—Users	0.500	0.515	0.144
Users—Auditors	0.627	0.639	0.164
Auditors—Preparers	0.553	0.525	0.127
Friedman $\chi^2 = 2.67$, $p = 0.264$			
Type 2: Amortization Period (Q13–Q19)			
Preparers—Users	0.707	0.702	0.152
Users—Auditors	0.678	0.743	0.192
Auditors—Preparers	0.592	0.556	0.133
Friedman $\chi^2 = 1.71$, $p = 0.425$.			
Type 3: Concept of Goodwill (Q20–Q25)			
Preparers—Users	0.548	0.558	0.164
Users—Auditors	0.647	0.652	0.094
Auditors—Preparers	0.508	0.484	0.187
Friedman $\chi^2 = 1.20$, $p = 0.549$.			
Type 4: Alternative Accounting Treatments (Q26–Q30)			
Preparers—Users	0.678	0.676	0.174
Users—Auditors	0.723	0.720	0.189
Auditors—Preparers	0.635	0.623	0.146
Friedman $\chi^2 = 0.40$, $p = 0.819$.			

accounting treatments—the ordering of distances remained stable. The distance between users and auditors was consistently the largest, whereas the distance between preparers and auditors was comparatively smaller. Although the Friedman tests did not indicate statistically significant differences within each domain, the consistency of the distance structure across heterogeneous question types suggested a robust pattern in the relative alignment of views among the three parties.

Concentration of Responses Within Groups (Herfindahl–Hirschman Index)

Herfindahl–Hirschman Index

We measured within-group response concentrations using the HHI, which was calculated for each question and group.[121] We conducted a test for the differences in the average values of the three parties to determine whether significant differences existed in their response concentrations (Table 5.85).

[121] HHI was used as a concentration index for categorical response distributions. For each group g and item q, we computed HHI_{gq} = Σ_{k = 1}^{5} p_{gqk}^2, where p_{gqk} was the share of

Table 5.85 Herfindahl–Hirschman Index of responses within each group

	Q1	**Q2**	**Q3**	**Q4**	**Q5**	**Q6**	**Q7**	**Q8**	**Q9**	**Q10**
Preparers	39.06%	35.76%	22.65%	41.22%	25.06%	33.01%	41.31%	30.63%	32.74%	26.44%
Users	42.31%	40.53%	25.44%	55.33%	21.89%	33.70%	40.41%	33.82%	39.25%	27.60%
Auditors	53.48%	30.40%	24.45%	39.92%	23.02%	46.85%	31.80%	33.28%	24.48%	25.92%
	Q11	**Q12**	**Q13**	**Q14**	**Q15**	**Q16**	**Q17**	**Q18**	**Q19**	**Q20**
Preparers	23.86%	25.13%	41.85%	34.88%	29.96%	29.84%	28.37%	42.17%	34.57%	30.47%
Users	24.46%	23.46%	32.24%	29.43%	29.49%	27.94%	28.00%	35.49%	40.63%	28.21%
Auditors	23.94%	24.88%	46.51%	37.18%	30.46%	30.16%	28.37%	38.39%	37.98%	25.48%
	Q21	**Q22**	**Q23**	**Q24**	**Q25**	**Q26**	**Q27**	**Q28**	**Q29**	**Q30**
Preparers	33.37%	35.01%	34.34%	22.41%	19.91%	41.73%	26.71%	30.22%	37.68%	26.57%
Users	26.28%	31.99%	27.01%	31.72%	21.27%	48.84%	32.51%	24.98%	26.05%	24.71%
Auditors	37.60%	34.62%	39.16%	31.33%	19.32%	74.34%	42.28%	35.82%	39.68%	39.18%
	Q31	Q32	Average							
Preparers	25.31%	26.22%	31.51%							
Users	22.22%	36.27%	31.67%							
Auditors	29.91%	43.69%	35.12%							

Table 5.86 The results of Levene's test

		LEVENE statistics	Degree of freedom 1	Degree of freedom 2	P Value (Significance Probability)
Herfindahl–Hirschman Index	Mean	1.696	2	93	0.189
	Median	1.571	2	93	0.213
	Median and Adjusted degrees of freedom	1.571	2	73.337	0.215
	Trimmed mean	1.617	2	93	0.204

Levene's Test and Analysis of Variance Using SPSS

We examined the homogeneity of variances across the three groups using Levene's test.[122] The results are as follows.

The Levene statistic was 1.696, and the p-value was 0.189 (based on means). Since $p > 0.05$, the assumption of equal variances was satisfied. The test did not reject the null hypothesis of equal variances ($p = 0.189$; Table 5.86). Accordingly, one-way ANOVA was applied.

As shown in Table 5.87, the one-way ANOVA did not indicate a statistically significant difference in the mean HHI across preparers, users, and auditors ($F = 1.807$, $p = 0.170$ [>0.05; no statistically significant difference]). Although descriptive differences were found, there was no significant difference in the mean HHI scores among preparers, users, or auditors (group codes 1/2/3). We report ω^2 for the fixed-effects one-way ANOVA as the primary effect size measure (Table 5.88). The associated effect sizes were small ($\eta^2 = 0.037$; $\omega^2 = 0.017$), indicating limited

responses choosing category k. For each group g and survey question q, the HHI was calculated as

$$\mathrm{HHI}_{gq} = \sum_{k=1}^{K} p_{gqk}^{2},$$

where p_{gqk} denoted the proportion of respondents in group g who selected response category k for question q. $K = 5$ was the number of response categories. By construction, $\sum_{k=1}^{K} p_{gqk} = 1$. If responses were evenly distributed across the five categories, the HHI equaled $5 \times (0.2)^2 = 0.20$; larger values indicated a greater concentration of responses within a group.

[122] Levene's test is an inferential statistic used to assess the equality of variances for a variable calculated for two or more groups. This test is used because some common statistical procedures assume that variances of the populations from which different samples are drawn are equal. Levene's test assesses this assumption by testing the null hypothesis that the population variances are equal (called homogeneity of variance or homoscedasticity). If the resulting p-value of Levene's test is less than some significance level (typically 0.05), the obtained differences in sample variances are unlikely to have occurred based on random sampling from a population with equal variances (Levene 1960)

Table 5.87 Results of one-way ANOVA on mean Herfindahl–Hirschman Index across groups

		Sum of Squares	Degrees of Freedom	Mean Square	F Value	P Value (Significance Probability)
Herfindahl–Hirschman Index	Between groups	0.027	2	0.013	1.807	0.17
	Within groups	0.684	93	0.007		
	Total	0.711	95			

Table 5.88 Effect size measures for ANOVA (η^2, ε^2, ω^2 with 95% confidence intervals)

		Point estimation	Lower bound	Upper bound
Herfindahl–Hirschman index	η^2	0.037	0	0.124
	ε^2	0.017	0.022	0.105
	ω^2 (fixed effects)	0.017	0.021	0.104
	ω^2 (random effects)	0.008	0.011	0.055

substantive differences among groups.[123] These results indicate that the differences in response concentrations across groups are not substantively meaningful. Analysis of variance calculates the ratio of variation between groups (between-group variation) to variation within groups (within-group variation) and uses this to determine whether the difference in means is statistically significant.

HHI (Average) by Question Type

Grouping questions by conceptual focus allowed us to assess whether within-group response concentrations vary systematically across the different dimensions of the goodwill accounting debate. Table 5.89 reports the average HHI scores by question type for preparers, users, and auditors.

Before turning to the question-type analysis, we must clarify how the WD1 and HHI measures should be interpreted jointly. While WD1 captures the overall distance between response distributions across groups, it does not indicate whether such differences arise from internal disagreement within groups or from stable, internally consistent positions. The HHI complements this analysis by measuring the degree of response concentration within each group. When differences across groups are accompanied by similar or high levels of within-group concentration,

[123] Effect size measures quantify the magnitude of group differences independent of sample size.In this study, η^2 (eta squared) represented the proportion of total variance in HHI explained by group membership, while ω^2 (omega squared) provided a less biased estimate of the explained variance in the population. The small values of these indices indicated that group differences accounted for only a limited share of overall variation.

Table 5.89 Herfindahl–Hirschman Index (average) by question type

Type of Question	Question	Preparers	Users	Auditors
Type 1	Q1–Q12 Amortization vs. Impairment	31.41	34.02	31.87
Type 2	Q13–Q19 Method for Determining Depreciation Period	34.52	31.89	35.58
Type 3	Q20–Q25 Definition of Goodwill	29.25	27.75	31.25
Type 4	Q26–Q30 Alternative Method	32.58	31.42	46.26
Type 5	Q31–Q32 Others (For Reference)	25.77	29.25	36.80

such differences can be interpreted as reflecting consistently held group-level positions rather than fragmented or noisy opinions.

The results show that the response concentration was broadly similar across groups for questions related to amortization versus impairment (Type 1) and the conceptual definition of goodwill (Type 3). By contrast, for questions concerning alternative accounting treatments (Type 4), auditors exhibited substantially higher concentrations than preparers and users, indicating a more homogeneous stance within the auditor group. Overall, consistent with the interpretive framework described above, combining the HHI results with the WD1 analysis suggests that the observed differences across groups primarily reflect differences in consistently held positions rather than differences in the degree of internal disagreement within each group.

Interpreting HHI values in conjunction with WD1 yielded the following:

Type 1 (Amortization vs. Impairment)

Since the HHI was in the low 30% range for all three groups, opinions were relatively unified within each group. However, WD1 showed distance between groups, supporting the interpretation that there is internal agreement, but positions differ externally.

Type 2 (Amortization Period)

The overall HHI was somewhat higher, and WD1 was large, although the direction was not aligned between the groups. This may be because these questions involve both discretionary and technical issues.

Type 3 (Concept of Goodwill)

The HHI was low (below 30%) for all three groups. This indicates that questions about the concept of goodwill were highly abstract and that no consensus could be reached within the groups.

Type 4 (Alternative Accounting Treatment)

The auditors' HHI was exceptionally high (46.3%, compared with approximately 30% for preparers and users), indicating homogeneity in auditors' opinions regarding accounting treatment. This aligns with the high concentration of responses supporting auditors' amortization-with-impairment treatment of goodwill at 89.5% (see Table 5.50).

Type 5 (Q31–32)

Only two questions were asked; therefore, this was treated as reference information.

By combining WD1 (between) and HHI (within), we can conclude that the "discrepancy" in opinions stems not from divided views within each group, but from differences in the consistent positions formed by each group. While WD1 captures differences in the overall distribution of opinions across groups, the HHI complements this analysis by indicating whether such differences arise from internal disagreements within groups or from consistently held group-level positions.

WD1 and HHI play complementary roles in interpreting the survey results. While WD1 captures how far apart the overall distributions of responses are across groups, it does not indicate whether such differences arise from internal disagreement or from cohesive group-level positions. The HHI addresses this limitation by measuring the degree of response concentration within each group. When WD1 is large and HHI is also high, differences across groups can be interpreted as reflecting stable and internally consistent positions rather than fragmented or noisy opinions. Conversely, large WD1 combined with low HHI would suggest that observed differences are driven by heterogeneous views within groups. The joint use of WD1 and HHI thus enables a more nuanced interpretation of stakeholder differences in survey responses.

Concluding Remarks

This study examined differences in opinions regarding the accounting treatment of goodwill between and within three stakeholder groups. WD1 analyzed how far apart the distribution of opinions was across stakeholder groups. It measured the overall distance of the distribution, including the position, dispersion, and skewness of responses, rather than simply the average difference. WD1 examined whether structural differences in opinion existed among the three parties.

The WD1 measurement revealed a consistent hierarchical structure across all question types. The WD1 between preparers and auditors was relatively small, while the WD1 between users and auditors was relatively large. This suggests that the relative positional relationships are stable. The HHI measurement captured how concentrated opinions are within each group. The results reveal that the degree of opinion convergence within each group was generally similar.

Based on the WD1 and HHI results, the opinions of the three groups regarding goodwill accounting can be described as internally consistent. However, differing positions have formed within each group. This suggests that the debate surrounding goodwill accounting does not arise from mere knowledge gaps, misunderstandings, or random variations among respondents, but rather that each stakeholder has formed consistent views based on their institutional position and role. For example, the WD1 result showing a relatively close alignment between auditors and preparers, while a gap exists between auditors and users, is consistent with: 1) the institutional proximity to preparers through the audit process, and 2) the institutional arrangement in which auditors do not share the direct information generation process with users. This appendix provides supplementary yet important evidence demonstrating that differences in opinions regarding goodwill accounting are structural and not incidental.

These findings have several implications. From an academic perspective, the results suggest that differences in views on goodwill accounting are not primarily driven by random variation or internal disagreement within stakeholder groups, but rather by stable and institutionally grounded positions. This challenges interpretations that emphasize stakeholder conflict as arising from heterogeneous or poorly formed opinions. From a methodological perspective, the combined use of WD1 and HHI illustrates the value of distribution-based approaches for analyzing ordinal survey data in accounting research. From a standard-setting perspective, while this appendix does not draw normative conclusions, the observed structural similarity and homogeneity of responses suggest that debates surrounding goodwill accounting may reflect enduring role-based perspectives rather than transient misunderstandings or informational gaps.

From a methodological perspective, this appendix demonstrates the usefulness of distribution-based approaches for analyzing ordinal survey data in accounting research. By combining WD1, which captures distributional differences beyond mean responses (Seufert 2021), with the HHI as a measure of within-group homogeneity (Liberati et al. 2021), we provide a framework for distinguishing structural differences in stakeholder positions from mere random variation or internal disagreement. This approach complements existing empirical studies on goodwill accounting and offers a transferable methodology for future survey-based research in accounting.

Statement on AI Usage: During the preparation of this manuscript, the authors used AI-assisted tools such as DeepL, ChatGPT, and Gmini to improve the English expression and clarity of the manuscript. The authors thoroughly reviewed and approved the final version and take full responsibility for the content.

References

In English

Accounting Standards Board of Japan (ASBJ). 2015a. *Foreword to "Japan's modified international standards (JMIS): Accounting standards comprising IFRSs and the ASBJ modifications."* Tokyo, Japan: ASBJ.

Accounting Standards Board of Japan (ASBJ). 2015b. *ASBJ modification accounting standard No. 1 accounting for goodwill*. Tokyo, Japan: ASBJ.

Accounting Standards Board of Japan (ASBJ). 2015c. *Research on amortization of goodwill*. Research Paper No. 1. Tokyo, Japan: ASBJ.

Accounting Standards Board of Japan (ASBJ). 2016. *Quantitative study on goodwill and impairment*. Research Paper No. 2. Tokyo, Japan: ASBJ.

Accounting Standards Board of Japan (ASBJ). 2017. *Analyst views on financial information regarding goodwill*. Research Paper No. 3. Tokyo, Japan: ASBJ.

Accounting Standards Board of Japan (ASBJ), European Financial Reporting Advisory Group (EFRAG) and Organismo Italiano di Contabilità (OIC). 2014. *Should goodwill still be amortised? Accounting and disclosure for goodwill*. Tokyo, Japan: ASBJ, Brussels, Belgium: EFRAG, and Roma, Italy: OIC.

Amano, Y. 2020. "Real effects of intangibles capitalization-empirical evidence from voluntary IFRS adoption in Japan," *Journal of International Accounting Research*, 19(3):19–36.
Avallone, F., and A. Quagli. 2015. "Insight into the variables used to manage the goodwill impairment test under IAS 36," *Advances in Accounting*, 31(1): 107–114.
Ayres, D. R., T. L. Neal, L. Reid, and J. E. Shipman. 2019. "Auditing goodwill in the post-amortization era: Challenges for auditors," *Contemporary Accounting Research*, 36(1): 82–107.
Nishiguchi, S., J. Nakajima, and K. Imakubo. 2014. Disagreement in households' inflation expectations and its effects on inflation dynamics. Bank of Japan Review Series, No. 14-E-1. https://www.boj.or.jp/en/research/wps_rev/rev_2014/data/rev14e01.pdf
Biddle, G. C., and G. Hilary. 2006. "Accounting quality and firm-level capital investment," *The Accounting Review*, 81: 963–982.
Biddle, G. C., G. Hilary, and R. S. Verdi. 2009. "How does financial reporting quality relate to investment efficiency?" *Journal of Accounting and Economics*, 48: 112–131.
Bloomfield, R., M. W. Nelson, and E. Soltes. 2016. "Gathering data for archival, field, survey, and experimental accounting research.," *Journal of Accounting Research*, 54: 341–395.
Carcello, J. V., T. L. Neal, L. C. Reid, and J. E. Shipman. 2020. "Auditor independence and fair value accounting: An examination of nonaudit fees and goodwill impairments," *Contemporary Accounting Research*, 37(1): 189–217.
Cedergren, M.C., B. Lev, and P. Zarowin. 2015. "SFAS 142, conditional conservatism, and acquisition profitability and risk," *Working Paper*, Available at SSRN: https://ssrn.com/abstract=2695055.
Chalmers, K., J. M. Godfrey, and J. Wester. 2011. "Does a goodwill impairment regime reflect better underlying economic attributes of goodwill?" *Accounting & Finance*, 51:634–660.
Craig, T., W. H. Lee, and D. Fang. 2018. *Goodwill and impairment*. IFRS® Foundation. CMAC meeting, 01 November 2018, Agenda Paper 5A.
Dickinson, V., and G. A. Sommers. 2012. "Which competitive efforts lead to future abnormal economic rents? Using accounting ratios to assess competitive advantage," *Journal of Business Finance & Accounting*, 39: 360–398.
Financial Accounting Standards Board (FASB). 2011. *Testing goodwill for impairment. Accounting Standards Update (ASU) No. 2011-08*. Norwalk, CT: FASB.
Financial Accounting Standards Board (FASB). 2017. *Simplifying the test for goodwill impairment. Accounting Standards Update (ASU) No. 2017-04*. Norwalk, CT: FASB.
Financial Accounting Standards Board (FASB). 2019. *Invitation to comment on identifiable intangible assets and subsequent accounting for goodwill.* Norwalk, CT: FASB.
Francis, J., J. D. Hanna, and L. Vincent. 1996. Causes and effects of discretionary asset write-offs. *Journal of Accounting Research*, 34: 117–134.
Francis, J. R., and X. Martin. 2010. "Acquisition profitability and timely loss recognition," *Journal of Accounting and Economics*, 49: 161–178.
Gao, R., and X. Yu. 2020. "How to measure capital investment efficiency: A literature synthesis," *Accounting & Finance*, 60(1): 299–334.
Garcia Lara, J. M., B. Garcia Osma, and F. Penalva. 2016. "Accounting conservatism and firm investment efficiency," *Journal of Accounting and Economics*, 61: 221–238.
International Organization of Securities Commissions (IOSCO). 2023a. *Consultation on goodwill.* Madrid, Spain: IOSCO.
International Organization of Securities Commissions (IOSCO). 2023b. *Recommendations on accounting for goodwill.* Madrid, Spain: IOSCO.
International Accounting Standards Board (IASB). 2004. *IFRS 3: Business Combinations.* London, U.K.: IASB.
International Accounting Standards Board (IASB). 2020. *Discussion paper: Business combinations—Disclosures, goodwill and impairment*. London, U.K.: IASB.
International Accounting Standards Board (IASB). 2024a. *Exposure draft business combinations—Disclosures, goodwill and impairment*. London, U.K.: IASB.
International Accounting Standards Board (IASB). 2024b. *Basis for conclusions on exposure draft business combinations—Disclosures, goodwill and impairment*. London, U.K.: IASB.

Kim, S., Lee, J., and Park, Y. 2024. "LLM-Mirror: A generated-persona approach for survey response simulation and comparison," *Working Paper*, Avilable at: https://arxiv.org/abs/2412.03162.
Kravet, T. 2014. "Accounting conservatism and managerial risk-taking: corporate acquisitions," *Journal of Accounting and Economics*, 57: 218–240.
Kothari, S. P., Ramanna, K., and Skinner, D. J. 2010. "Implications for GAAP from an analysis of positive research in accounting," *Journal of Accounting and Economics*, 50(2–3), 246–286.
Levene, H. 1960. "Robust tests for equality of variances." In I. Olkin, H. Hotelling, et al. (Eds.), *Contributions to probability and statistics: Essays in honor of Harold Hotelling* (pp. 278–292). Stanford, CA: Stanford University Press.
Li, Z., P. K. Shroff, R. Venkataraman, and I. X. Zhang. 2011. "Causes and consequences of goodwill impairment losses," *Review of Accounting Studies*, 16: 745–778.
Li, K. K., and R. G. Sloan. 2017. "Has goodwill accounting gone bad?" *Review of Accounting Studies*, 22: 964–1003.
Liberati, C., Camussi, S., and Ranci, C. 2021. "Measuring tolerant behavior: An index-based approach using survey data," *Journal of Business Cycle Research*, 17(1): 1–25. https://doi.org/10.1515/jbnst-2019-0030
Roychowdhury, S., N. Shroff, and R. S. Verdi. 2019. "The effects of financial reporting and disclosure on corporate investment: A review," *Journal of Accounting and Economics*, 68(2–3): 101246.
Peters, S. J. 2021. Goodwill: Investor perspectives improve disclosures, rather than revert to amortization. CFA Institute. https://rpc.cfainstitute.org/sites/default/files/-/media/documents/survey/cfa-goodwill-survey-without-appendices-2021.pdf (Accessed 2025-11-19)
Riedl, E. J. 2004. "An examination of long-lived asset impairments," *The Accounting Review*, 79(3): 823- 852.
Seufert, M. 2021. "Statistical methods and models based on quality of experience distributions," *Quality and User Experience*, 6(1): 1–24. https://doi.org/10.1007/s41233-020-00044-z
Shakespeare, C. 2020. "Reporting matters: The real effects of financial reporting on investing and financing decisions," *Accounting and Business Research*, 50(5): 425–442.
Shroff, N. 2017. "Corporate investment and changes in GAAP," *Review of Accounting Studies*, 22: 1–63.
Staff of the Accounting Standards Board of Japan (ASBJ staff) and staff of the Hong Kong Institute of Certified Public Accountants (HKICPA stuff). 2020. *Goodwill: Improvements to subsequent accounting and an update of the quantitative study.* Tokyo, Japan: ASBJ, and Wanchai, Hong Kong: HKICPA.
Zhao, W., Zhang, Y., and Li, H. 2024. "Distributional comparison of survey responses using Wasserstein distance." In *Proceedings of the 2024 Language Resources and Evaluation Conference (LREC)*, pp. 1–9. https://aclanthology.org/2024.lrec-main.1539
Zang, Y. 2008. "Discretionary behavior with respect to the adoption of SFAS No. 142 and the behavior of security prices," *Review of Accounting and Finance*, 7(1): 38–68.

In Japanese

Accounting Standards Borad of Japan (ASBJ). 2024. *Kigyo kaikei kijun tekiyo shishin dai 10-go: kigyo ketsugo kaikei kijun oyobi jigyo bunri-to kaikei kij un ni kansuru tekiyo shishin (ASBJ Guidance No. 10: Guidance on accounting standard for business combinations and accounting standard for business divestitures).* Tokyo, Japan: ASBJ.
Daigo, S. 2007. "Jizokuteki kyōsō yūi no keiei senryaku to noren no shōkyaku genson ronsō no tenbō (Prospects for business strategies for sustainable competitive advantage and the debate over goodwill amortization and impairment)," *Kaikei* (*Accounting*), 171(4): 508–521.
Ishii, T. 2017. "Noren no shōkyaku kikan no settei ni okeru shōrai gyōseki yosoku no eikyō (The impact of future performance forecasts on the setting of goodwill amortization periods)," *Saga Daigaku Keizai Ronsyu* (*Saga University Economic Review*), 50(3): 23–38.

Jin, M. 2016. *Teiseiteki data bunseki* (*Qualitative data analysis*), Tokyo, Japan: Kyoritsu Shuppan Co, LTD.

Keidanren (Japan Business Federation). 2017. *Noren no kaikei shori ni kansuru ankēto kekka no seiri (Organizing the results of a questionnaire on the accounting treatment of goodwill).* Nippon Keizai Dantai Rengōkai Kin'yū Shihon Shijō Iinkai Kigyō Kaikei Bukai (Japan Business Federation, Committee on Financial and Capital Markets), Tokyo, Japan: Keidanren.

Keizai Doyukai (Japan Association of Corporate Executive). 2023. *Noren no kisokuteki shōkyaku ni kansuru ankēto chōsa kekka (Survey results on the systematic amortization of goodwill).* Regulatory and Competition Policy Committee, chaired by Naoaki Mashita, Tokyo, Japan: Keizai Doyukai. https://www.doyukai.or.jp/policyproposals/2023/230706.html. (Accessed 2026-02-20)

Nakano, M., F. Ohtsubo, and Y. Takasu. 2015. "Kaikeijō no hoshushugi ga kigyō no tōshi suijun risuku teiku kabunushi kachi ni oyobosu eikyō (The effect of accounting conservatism on corporate investment levels, risk taking, and shareholder value)," Kin'yū Kenkyū (*Monetary and Economic Studies*), 34(1): 99–145.

Obinata, T. 2013. Riekiritsu no jizokusei to heikin kaiki (*Profitability persistence and mean Reversion*). Tokyo, Japan: Chuokeizai-sha.

Suda, K., T. Sasaki, M. Nakajima, and S. Okuda. 2011a. "Naibu tōsei to gabanansu ni kansuru nichibei hikaku (I)–Sābei chōsa no kekka (A Japan-U.S. comparison on internal control and governance I– Results of Survey Research) ," *Kaikei* (*Accounting*), 179(6): 906–922.

Suda, K., T. Sasaki, M. Nakajima, and S. Okuda. 2011b. "Naibu tōsei to gabanansu ni kansuru nichibei hikaku (II Kan)–Sābei chōsa no kekka (A Japan-U.S. comparison on internal control and governance II– Results of Survey Research)," *Kaikei* (*Accounting*), 180(1): 115–129.

Suzuki, J. 2016. *Shitsumonshi dezain no gihō [Dai 2-han]* (*Questionnaire design techniques 2nd ed*)., Kyoto, Japan: Nakanishiya Shuppan Co, LTD.

Tokuga, Y., T. Miyauchi, and T. Yamashita. 2020. *Noren no Kaikei shori ni kansuru chosa (Suervey on the Accounting Treatment of Goodwill).* Kyoto University, Faculty of Economics, Discussion Paper Series No. J-18-004.

Tokuga, Y., T. Miyauchi, T. Yamashita, M. Yoneyama, and Y. Asami. 2021. Noren no kaikei shori ni kansuru chosa to sono bunseki: Sakuseisha, riyosha, kansanin no kaito no tokucho to hikaku (*Suervey on the Acoonting Treatment of Goodwill: Characteristics and Comparison of Responses from Preparers, Users, and Auditors).* Kyoto University, Faculty of Economics, Discussion Paper Series No. J-21-002.

Yamashita, T., T. Miyauchi, and Y. Tokuga. 2021. *Noren no kaikei shori ni kansuru chosa: Kansanin no kaito to sono bunseki (Survey on the Accounting Treatment of Goodwill: Auditors' responses and analysis).* Kyoto University, Faculty of Economics, Discussion Paper Series No. J-20-007.

Chapter 6
Perception of Preparers, Users, and Auditors–Follow-Up Interviews

Masaki Yoneyama, Yoshihiro Tokuga, Yuko Asami, Toshitake Miyauchi, and Tomoaki Yamashita

6.1 Purpose and Organization of This Chapter

As elucidated in Chap. 5, the questionnaire survey administered by our research team disclosed an unexpected finding: statistically significant variations were observed in the level of support for systematic amortization with impairment approach (hereafter, "systematic amortization with impairment") among users, preparers, and auditors of financial statements. Nonetheless, notable similarities were also identified across these groups concerning the rationales provided for endorsing either systematic amortization with impairment or the impairment-only approach (hereafter, "impairment-only").

This chapter originates from the integration and substantial revision of Yoneyama et al. (2021) and Yoneyama et al. (2025).

M. Yoneyama (✉)
Graduate School of Economics, The University of Tokyo, Tokyo, Japan
e-mail: yoneyama@e.u-tokyo.ac.jp

Y. Tokuga
Department of Business Administration, Faculty of Economics and Business Administration, Kyoto University of Advanced Science, Kyoto, Japan

Y. Asami
Graduate School of Economics, Nagoya University, Aichi, Japan

T. Miyauchi
Faculty of Management, Otemon Gakuin University, Osaka, Japan

T. Yamashita
Department of Business Administration, Faculty of Economics, Fukui Prefectural University, Fukui, Japan

Y. Tokuga, M. Yoneyama (eds.), *Controversies Over Accounting for Goodwill*,
Contributions to Finance and Accounting,
https://doi.org/10.1007/978-981-92-0156-3_6

Even among auditors—who strongly favored systematic amortization with impairment —and among users—who showed some support for the impairment-only approach—the reasons for supporting systematic amortization with impairment focused on a few key options, most notably "to achieve a proper matching of revenues and expenses over time."

While these empirical patterns have been identified, the factors driving intergroup differences and those explaining the "commonalities beyond group boundaries" in their reasoning are still unclear. Additionally, questions have arisen about whether researchers and practitioners interpret the abstract concepts used to justify each stance in the same way.

This chapter supplements the questionnaire findings by conducting two sets of interviews. The first involved users, preparers, and auditors, focusing on elucidating the determinants of the similarities and differences among their responses. The second targeted only users to identify the factors that give rise to diverse opinions within the user group.

6.2 Interviews Regarding Accounting for Goodwill-Exploring the Background on the Results of the Questionnaire Survey

6.2.1 Purpose of This Section

This section summarizes the interview survey results that explore the background of the responses provided in the questionnaire survey by Yoshihiro Tokuga, Toshitake Miyauchi, and Tomoaki Yamashita, "A Survey on the Accounting Treatment of Goodwill" (Kyoto University Graduate School of Economics Discussion Paper Series No. J-18-004), April 5, 2019 (2nd edition) (hereinafter Tokuga et al. (2019)).

The results of the questionnaire survey were compiled and summarized by Tokuga et al. (2019). The survey asked financial statement preparers and users (a) if they preferred systematic amortization with impairment or impairment-only and (b) the reasons for favoring one over the other. While the details are left to the original source, it is important to note that (1) the preparers of financial statements as well as their users supported systematic amortization; (2) users' support for systematic amortization is not as homogeneous as that of preparers, with a non-negligible percentage of "either will do" responses; (3) preparers' support for systematic amortization is homogeneous regardless of whether the company is a member of Keidanren or not, and whether it is a manufacturing or non-manufacturing company.

In addition, (4) there was strong support for a method that sets a maximum amortization period of 10 years for purchased goodwill while enabling the management to exercise discretion in determining the specific period.

However, the findings of the questionnaire survey raised some questions.

- Why do preparers as well as users in Japan support systematic amortization? In the hearing conducted by the Financial Accounting Standards Board of the U.S., most users supported the non-amortization (impairment-only) approach. What causes the difference between two jurisdictions?
- Why do respondents uniformly support systematic amortization, although the patterns for expensing goodwill have different impacts on income depending on whether the firm is a manufacturer or non-manufacturer, a member or non-member of Keidanren, and so on?
- Why was the method of setting a maximum amortization period, while enabling management to exercise discretion in determining a specific period, widely supported?
- Respondents who oppose systematic amortization implicitly assume that the value of goodwill should be maintained and/or enhanced by additional investments after M&A. What do the Japanese market participants think of this argument? (Do Japanese preparers and users understand and accept that the value of purchased goodwill appears to be maintained but it declines because of the collection of invested money and/or competition among companies? The value appears to be stable, because new internally generated goodwill compensates for the decline in the value of the purchased goodwill.)
- According to the opponents of systematic amortization, it would result in double counting of expenses if expenses based on systematic amortization and those based on maintaining and enhancing goodwill are reported. What do Japanese market participants think of this argument? (Do they think that it does not constitute double counting of expenses in the first place, or do they regard the argument as plausible but not significant?)
- The IASB is currently reviewing the accounting for goodwill because expensing goodwill is said to be "too little, too late."[1] Is it commonly believed in Japan that the Japanese market is free from the "too little, too late" problem because it requires systematic amortization?

Although various research methods explore these issues in detail, this study addresses this issue using a method called elite interviews. "Elites" (i.e., individuals in positions of influence within their organizations) are assumed to maintain a broad overview of their organizations and are likely to aggregate the "average opinion of their members."[2] This study is based on the results of a questionnaire survey conducted by Tokuga, Miyauchi, and Yamashita (2019). It helps ascertain whether the

[1] At the IASB, the discussion has been framed not as a "too little, too late" issue but rather as a "too late" issue. The debate has been limited to the impairment of goodwill.

[2] This approach has drawbacks as well as strengths. A typical limitation is the possibility that the experts may not be able to fully capture the views of organizational members or may aggregate only biased perspectives. However, the extent of bias among the present respondents can be assessed by comparing their responses with the average results from the survey. Moreover, even if the respondents' views are not fully representative of their organizations, their contributions to this study would still be valuable, provided that the information they offer is rich and insightful.

interpretations made by Tokuga, Miyauchi, and Yamashita (with Asami and Yoneyama joining them) are arbitrary.

The remainder of this chapter is organized as follows. Sect. 6.2.2 outlines the interview survey. Sect. 6.2.3 summarizes the insights obtained from the interviews. Building on these steps, Sect. 6.2.4 discusses the issues that have been clarified and those that remain unresolved.

6.2.2 Outline of Interview Survey

Interviews with the experts were conducted between November 10, 2020, and March 23, 2021. The attributes of the subjects are as follows.[3]

- Preparers: Six preparers (two working for manufacturers, one for a major general trading company, one for a major telecommunications company, and the other two for financial institutions)
- Users: Six users (two equity analysts, one credit analyst, one belonging to an investor relations association, and two to a professional user association)
- Certified Public Accountants: Seven CPAs (four belonging to major audit firms, two to mid-tier audit firms, and one to a professional association; all were representatives or board members.)

The interviewers were Yoshihiro Tokuga, Masaki Yoneyama, and Yuko Asami.[4] Although interviews were conducted during the COVID-19 pandemic, most were face-to-face.[5]

Before the interviews were conducted, we sent the participants a summary of the questionnaire survey results compiled by Tokuga et al. (2019), along with the specific items to which we sought their responses.[6] On the day of the interviews, we followed the list of questions that had been distributed in advance to the respondents. However, responding to every item was not mandatory because the interviews were conducted using a "semi-structured" approach. In this approach, while a standardized set of questions is prepared for all prospective respondents, the interviewer is allowed to adjust the emphasis placed on each issue depending on the context of the conversation. This may involve probing topics more deeply, while

---

[3] On August 3, 2021, our research group interviewed individuals other than users, preparers, and auditors—specifically, Mr. Toshitake Inoue, then Director of the Corporate Disclosure Division at the Financial Services Agency, and Mr. Atsushi Kogasaka, Chairperson of the Accounting Standards Board of Japan (ASBJ).

[4] Tokuga was present in all interviews. In a few interviews where both Asami and Yoneyama could not be present, Toshitake Miyauchi and Tomoaki Yamashita assisted Tokuga.

[5] Interviews with one company (a major pharmaceutical company) were conducted online by Tokuga, Miyauchi, and Yamashita.

[6] See the materials sent in advance on which the interview survey was based at the end of this article.

skipping others. We chose this method because, in exploring the background of the issues identified through the questionnaire survey, the semi-structured approach would be the most effective in eliciting rich and meaningful information. Acknowledging the limitations of our prior understanding, we deliberately captured insights that might emerge from unanticipated turns in the conversation.

Since all interview participants were busy professionals, the interviews were scheduled for 1 hour initially. Respondents were also informed beforehand that they did not need to answer every question, which aimed to promote more open and honest responses. We believed this approach would most effectively gather their specialized knowledge and experience. Consequently, each respondent typically focused on three or four main issues in their answers.

Based on the above overview of the interview process, Subsect. 6.2.3. summarizes and organizes the new perspectives that emerged during the interviews.

6.2.3 Summary and Analysis of Results

6.2.3.1 Differences Between the Parties Regarding the Reasons in Favor of Systematic Amortization

6.2.3.1.1 Why Do the Preparers Support Systematic Amortization?

We first summarize the preparers' responses regarding why they generally support systematic amortization. While some expressed personal or company-level support for a non-amortization approach (impairment-only), the same questions were posed to them and their responses were collected. The preparers' views can be summarized as follows.

- The observed: "familiarity," "indoctrination," and the "educational effect"
  - In the early stages of accounting education, the rationale for systematic amortization, namely, the importance of matching costs with revenues over time to appropriately determine periodic income, is widely disseminated through textbooks.
  - The ongoing promotion of systematic amortization by organizations such as the ASBJ and Keidanren reinforces this rationale, effectively embedding it into practice.
  - Preparers have become accustomed to the current standards and are generally satisfied with its application, leading to limited support for considering the cost of a standard change.
- Management stability is highly valued, and there is a widespread desire to avoid drastic fluctuations in financial performance.
  - Managers are held accountable when impairment losses cause significant volatility in income. By systematically amortizing goodwill, it becomes

possible to avoid or mitigate shocks to income that might otherwise be perceived as surprises.

- Recognizing a large amount of goodwill implies substantial future amortization expenses, which may negatively affect performance. This encourages a more cautious evaluation of future earnings and imposes discipline on M&A activities.

As noted in the summarized responses above, some answers were not fully anticipated beforehand. Frequent references to "familiarity" and "the influence of accounting education" were unexpected, as they imply potentially significant—and possibly underestimated—costs related to deviating from established rules and establishing a new consensus. Additionally, the unexpectedly high number of respondents who preferred to avoid situations where impairment losses increase earnings volatility and are seen by users as a negative surprise suggests that the costs of maintaining accountability to users regarding the recognition of such losses may be higher than initially thought.

Users' responses regarding why preparers generally support systematic amortization can be summarized as follows.

- Most managers consider investments in goodwill as natural extensions of investments in tangible capital assets. The notion that funds invested in goodwill must be expensed in association with the revenues generated— that is, matched with revenue as they are recovered—is widely supported.
- Additionally, firms' beliefs that they must achieve a profit level set as a benchmark are deeply ingrained. Consequently, systematic amortization, which contributes to earnings smoothing, is preferred.

When comparing preparers' own responses with users' perceptions of how preparers think, it is noteworthy that users' references to the "incentive to meet benchmark earnings" can be seen as accurately identifying preparers' underlying motive of "avoiding volatility in financial performance."

Furthermore, the notion—endorsed by users—that investments in goodwill constitute an extension of investments in tangible capital assets reflects a prevalent interpretation commonly presented in Japanese standard accounting textbooks within Japan. Such instructional content, through repeated exposure during educational processes, may become deeply ingrained and influence individuals' fundamental perspectives on accounting. From this standpoint, it can be asserted that users generally possess a well-founded understanding of the rationale behind why preparers advocate for systematic amortization.

6.2.3.1.2 Why Do Users Support Systematic Amortization?

Next, we summarize the findings from interviews with the users. The key points from users' responses regarding the reasons for supporting systematic amortization are as follows.

- Users have become accustomed to analyzing financial information based on systematic amortization, as required under Japanese GAAP, reflecting an acceptance of the status quo.
  - However, the sense of "familiarity" depends on the type of information upon which users predominantly rely when performing corporate valuation. For example, sell-side analysts typically customize their valuation methods to meet client requirements, whereas buy-side analysts are frequently obliged to adopt investment approaches that align with their employer's internal systems.
  - The number of users conducting valuations based on cash flows, either in addition to or instead of accounting-based information, has increased over time. The kind of information a user finds familiar depends on factors such as when and where they studied analytical methods (e.g., in the U.S. or Japan) and when they began working as analysts.
- Some analysts were "overly cautious," fearing blame if their forecasts were inaccurate—particularly when they fail to anticipate impairment losses.
  - However, certain impairment losses are difficult to predict. Application of systematic amortization decreases the likelihood of recognizing impairment losses, thereby reducing the risk of being held accountable for inaccurate forecasting.

The summary above suggests that users' stances toward accounting information differ; specifically, their approaches to using accounting data in corporate valuations vary.[7] Despite having different perspectives among users, their overall support for systematic amortization is not as clear as that of preparers. In fact, some users expressed a more passive acceptance of the status quo; since there was no evidence that the benefits of changing the accounting treatment would outweigh the costs, they saw no reason to push for reform. From the authors' standpoint, responses emphasizing "familiarity" were somewhat unexpected. The authors had anticipated answers along the lines of "Compared with earnings figures under an impairment-only approach, the earnings calculated under systematic amortization are smoother. When forecasting future cash flows based on accounting earnings, smoother figures are easier to work with." Instead, many respondents referred to their habitual use of systematic amortization, indicating that it may be a matter of custom rather than a deliberate preference.

---

[7] Users can be divided into two groups. One group evaluates corporate value based on accounting earnings, supplementing this information as needed with cash flow data. The other group relies on cash flow information to assess corporate value. The former group is expected to support systematic amortization; however, since they also consider cash flow information, their support may not be particularly strong. In some cases, their support may reflect little more than a passive acceptance of the status quo, rather than a strong conviction that the current approach should be maintained.

By contrast, the latter group opposes systematic amortization, much like users in Europe or in the United States. While the current findings indicate that the former group still represents the majority of users, the field is undergoing transition, and the latter group may eventually come to predominate.

This finding suggests that, even more than the prior questionnaire survey (Tokuga et al. 2019), support for systematic amortization varies between preparers and users. Moreover, support among users is not uniform. This can be considered a "new finding" unique to the present interview study.[8]

The original question posed to respondents was "Why do Japanese users generally support systematic amortization with impairment?" However, some interviewees expressed a preference for non-amortization (impairment-only). These respondents pointed out that in jurisdictions where goodwill is not amortized, such as the United States, managers involved in M&A must engage in annual discussions with auditors regarding whether an impairment should be recognized. They also face regular questioning from analysts, such as "Why hasn't impairment been recorded?" From this perspective, constant pressure to justify the absence of impairment is considered a form of discipline in managerial behavior. Thus, these users viewed the impairment-only model as desirable because it helps enforce accountability and constrains managerial discretion.[9]

6.2.3.2 Why Do Users Have Different Views on Whether Systematic Amortization Is Necessary or Not?

During the preparation stage, all interviewees were initially supposed to share their personal views on systematic amortization. However, during the actual interviews, users spent more time discussing why their opinions varied about the need for systematic amortization rather than expressing their own positions. Therefore, the next section will specifically explore the reasons behind the differing perspectives among users on this topic.

This topic closely relates to the question explored earlier—why users show weaker support for systematic amortization compared to preparers. As a result, some overlap in analyzing the interview results was unavoidable. Nonetheless, this section continues its discussion without avoiding such duplication.

Several interviewees highlighted that users employ diverse investment strategies, and their need for accounting information varies accordingly. In this context, the essential information can be generally divided into two categories: (a) earnings data that are effectively smoothed to aid in predicting future stable cash flows, and (b)

[8] Among the additional responses obtained from preparers, some echoed those of users, particularly with respect to their "familiarity with the information disclosed under the current standards." One respondent also pointed out that "users are likely to add back systematically recorded amortization expenses when evaluating corporate value, and if that is the case, whether or not systematic amortization is applied may not be a significant issue."

[9] Regardless of whether systematic amortization with impairment or a non-amortization (impairment-only) approach is adopted, some respondents noted that users require information on the accumulated amortization balance. This is because when combined with the current book value, such information enables users to determine the original acquisition cost—that is, the initial investment amount. With this information, users can calculate useful indicators such as pre-amortization ROI and compare them with industry averages.

information reflecting exogenous shocks, such as unexpected events or surprises, which could impact future performance.

A key insight from the interviews was that many users assess corporate value mainly through earnings-based models. For these users, smoothed earnings—which reflect a proper matching of revenues and expenses—are preferred. Assuming that purchased goodwill is gradually consumed over time via market competition, earnings that incorporate systematic amortization tend to be more stable than those calculated using an impairment-only approach. Consequently, these users are more inclined to favor systematic amortization.

In contrast, users who see impairment losses as management's formal acknowledgment of unexpected performance decline tend to oppose systematic amortization. They believe impairment losses would happen less often with systematic amortization. These users, focused on improving future forecast accuracy, aim to extract internal information about unforeseen performance drops. However, managers often hesitate to disclose poor results voluntarily, fearing damage to their reputation and evaluations. When impairment losses are recognized, managers are responsible for explaining their causes, providing users with valuable insider insights. Since goodwill is not amortized under the impairment-only approach—which keeps it on the books at its original value—this method is perceived as increasing the likelihood of impairment triggers. Consequently, users favor the impairment-only model.

Certainly, users who favor "smoothed earnings" likely also regard the internal information disclosed during impairment loss recognition as significant, including detailed explanations of the circumstances contributing to performance decline. Nonetheless, there is a tension between the two frameworks: one that enables prompt impairment recognition and another that promotes the generation of smoothed earnings. Users who prefer systematic amortization seem to prioritize the provision of smoothed earnings information.

This raises the remaining question: on what basis do users who support the impairment-only approach— in which impairment is more readily triggered—evaluate corporate value? Although the interviews did not find answers to this question and the following remains speculative, many interviewees seemed to frame users' investment approaches as a binary distinction: those primarily reliant on earnings and those primarily reliant on cash flows.[10] From this perspective, it can be inferred that users who support the impairment-only approach evaluate corporate value based primarily on cash flow information, with accounting data (including impairment-related disclosures) playing only a supplementary or secondary role.

As outlined earlier, the interview results indicate that users fall into two main groups: those who primarily evaluate corporate value using "smoothed earnings" data, and those who depend mainly on cash flows, considering accounting details like impairment losses as secondary. Additionally, the position each user takes is not

[10] While this type of user also uses cash flow information, some users who primarily rely on cash flows do not use earnings information at all. In other words, the dichotomy is asymmetric.

necessarily based on personal beliefs, educational background, or a consistent value system. Instead, these stances can change flexibly depending on client expectations or the institutional environment. This flexibility likely explains why users differ in their opinions on the importance of systematic amortization.

The conclusions from the interview survey are summarized above. However, they raise an important new question: if user support for systematic amortization varies, what criteria should determine the choice between systematic amortization with impairment and non-amortization (impairment-only)? If support for one method were heavily skewed, similar to that among preparers, it might be reasonable to decide based on the majority preference. But the interviews show that, although systematic amortization with impairment has broader support among users, this support is not overwhelming. Therefore, relying solely on a simple majority to reflect the "voice of the market" seems inappropriate.

Possible criteria for evaluating the "superiority" of systematic amortization with impairment versus non-amortization (impairment-only) include not only "the degree of stakeholder support" but also "compatibility with widely accepted models of corporate valuation." However, both earnings-and cash flow-based investment approaches are widely practiced. Moreover, both types of models depend on input data estimates such as earnings or cash flows, and the cost of producing such estimates remains unclear. Hence, it is difficult to determine the superiority of either approach based on alignment with corporate valuation models alone.[11]

In the debate over whether to adopt systematic amortization with impairment or non-amortization (impairment only), there is no need for systematic amortization with impairment since analysts add back goodwill amortization expenses. This perspective is based on users who rely primarily on cash flow for investment decisions. When estimating cash flows from earnings, such users add back expense items rooted in past cash outflows, such as goodwill amortization, as a typical example.[12] From their perspective, this adjustment is unnecessary or redundant as it would not have been needed had amortization not been applied in the first place.

If this were the sole and most significant concern for users, then, in a context where user preferences vary, systematic amortization would probably be the best option. This is because for users trying to predict stable future cash flows based on permanent income, systematic amortization is a crucial method for smoothing earnings.

[11] Furthermore, even if there are differences between systematic amortization with impairment and non-amortization (impairment-only) in terms of their compatibility with "standard corporate valuation models," it does not necessarily mean that only the information required by the more compatible and widely accepted model should be provided. This is because, at least in the short term, investment performance based on widely accepted models may underperform. Therefore, it is difficult to make a definitive judgment about whether the information needs of users who adopt such non-standard investment styles should be accommodated.

[12] Furthermore, as long as EBITDA (Earnings Before Interest, Taxes, Depreciation, and Amortization) is used as a performance metric, goodwill impairment losses as well as depreciation expenses on tangible fixed assets are added back.

In contrast, for users who rely on cash flows, the systematic amortization of goodwill is a redundant procedure. However, the need to adjust expense items rooted in past or future outflows applies to many items, including those subject to accrual or deferral accounting. In this sense, cash-flow-oriented users are already accustomed to making such "add-backs," and even if amortization is redundant, they can perform necessary adjustments without incurring significant cost. Moreover, even if the systematic amortization of goodwill were eliminated, adjustments for other deferred or accrued items would still be required. Hence, systematic amortization appears to be a reasonable approach. It enables the provision of information aligned with the needs of earnings-oriented users without placing an undue burden on those who rely primarily on cash flows.[13]

The current interview study indicates that the differing views among users on systematic amortization with impairment versus non-amortization (impairment-only) are not necessarily due to a wish to avoid the "redundant" task of reconciling amortization expenses. Instead, the main disagreement revolves around whether a volatile earnings environment—where impairment losses are more frequently recognized—is preferable because it allows users to hold management accountable and access more internal information, or whether a stable earnings environment with fewer fluctuations is better. As previously mentioned, this is a mutually exclusive choice; only one of these conditions can be achieved.

Ultimately, in a setting in which user preferences are not uniform, the choice between systematic amortization with impairment and non-amortization (impairment-only) leads to the unavoidable and difficult question of which standard or criterion should guide the decision.

6.2.3.3 The Effect of Firm Attributes on the Support for Systematic Amortization

The earlier questionnaire survey, conducted before the interviews, showed that companies using Japanese GAAP were more supportive of systematic amortization compared to those following international standards like IFRS or US GAAP. It also became evident that even companies adopting international standards generally preferred systematic amortization with impairment over an impairment-only approach. The first finding can be reasonably explained by considering that companies with large amounts of purchased goodwill, facing difficulties in meeting investor-expected earnings due to amortization costs, may have chosen IFRS to avoid such expenses. Conversely, the second finding was less predictable, and it was challenging to forecast what kind of explanations would emerge from the subsequent interviews conducted under these ambiguous circumstances.

First, regarding why Japanese GAAP adopters support systematic amortization more strongly than international standard adopters, several respondents suggested

[13] In the present interviews, one respondent with a user background expressed a similar view.

that some companies adopted IFRS to avoid the amortization burden associated with purchased goodwill.

Second, when focusing on companies applying international standards, the responses explaining their relatively strong support for systematic amortization were qualitatively like those of respondents from Japanese companies. Specifically:

- There was a clear desire to avoid situations in which they would be held accountable for providing detailed explanations as to "why an impairment occurred."
  - By systematically amortizing purchased goodwill, companies can reduce the likelihood of triggering impairment recognition, thereby avoiding situations in which the management would face scrutiny of their performance and be required to justify the basis for impairment amounts and related decisions.
- Impairment tests are costly not only in terms of the difficulty in the judgment required to determine whether an impairment is necessary but also in terms of the difficulty in the actual execution of the impairment process. In addition to the decision-making costs associated with impairment testing, systematic amortization of goodwill helps companies avoid these additional costs.[14]

The above observation suggests that, to varying degrees, both Japanese GAAP and IFRS adopters perceive the current impairment process, including its procedural burden and explanatory requirements, to be cumbersome. This perception contributes to their support for the systematic amortization of goodwill regardless of the accounting standards they apply. Recognizing this possibility is a key finding of this study.

6.2.3.4 Amortization Period in the Case of Systematic Amortization

In the survey conducted before the interviews, one question asked how to determine the amortization period if systematic amortization were to be used. Most respondents did not support applying a uniform amortization period across all cases. Instead, many favored setting an upper limit of around 20 years for preparers and 10 years for users as general guidelines. However, it also appeared that certain "exceptional cases," likely involving large-scale M&A transactions, might require a longer recovery period for invested capital or the dissipation of additional earnings from the acquisition. As a result, there was also significant support for setting the maximum amortization period as the "longest reasonably foreseeable period," which is defined as 20 years.

[14] As a key insight gained from the present interview study, the "cost burden associated with impairment losses" is perceived as a serious concern by the parties involved. However, the interviews did not clarify which aspect of the impairment process gives rise to this burden—for example, whether the high cost stems from the effort required to identify indications of impairment, or from the time and resources needed to estimate the loss amount. Further investigation into this area is warranted.

In addition, the pre-interview questionnaire listed "investment recovery period" and "the period over which goodwill contributes to excess returns (i.e., the period until excess profits disappear)" as potential reference points for determining the amortization period. However, through informal discussions with survey respondents and readers of the discussion paper summarizing the results, doubts emerged if there might have been discrepancies in interpretation between our research group and the respondents regarding what exactly was meant by "investment recovery period" or "the period over which goodwill contributes to excess returns."[15]

Considering this, the interview included following questions:

(a) Why did a method that sets an upper limit on the amortization period while allowing managers to exercise discretion within that limit receive support?
(b) Why was a method that permits an amortization period exceeding the set upper limit in principle—provided that sufficient justification can be offered—supported?
(c) Why was the 10-year upper limit strongly favored as a rule?
(d) What specific period did respondents envision when referring to the "investment recovery period" or "the duration over which (purchased) goodwill continues to generate excess returns?"

Rather than enforcing a uniform amortization timeframe regardless of the M&A transaction type, most stakeholders, including preparers and users, favored giving managers the discretion to set the period within a predetermined maximum. This period indicates the manager's view on either the investment recovery timeline or how long the purchased goodwill will generate excess profits. Such perspectives offer vital internal insights that can only be revealed with managerial discretion. Imposing a fixed amortization schedule would hide this key information. Therefore, users generally opposed a one-size-fits-all approach and instead supported allowing managers to determine the amortization period within defined parameters.[16]

Thus, it is unnecessary to impose an upper limit on the amortization period. Nevertheless, support was not for "complete managerial discretion," but rather for "discretion within a specified upper limit." This suggests that beyond the concern about accessing internal information, support likely reflects a shared recognition that, except in a very small number of exceptional cases, companies have rarely encountered M&A transactions in which a recovery period exceeding 20 years could be reasonably assumed.

---

[15] Furthermore, there might also be differences in understanding among the members of the research group.

[16] The inherent difficulty of estimating an appropriate amortization period can explain why the non-amortization (impairment-only) approach was supported. In fact, some respondents (users) who favored the impairment-only model expressed concern that, under a system in which managerial discretion is allowed within a specified upper limit, managers might routinely select the maximum allowable period—regardless of their actual expectations—simply to avoid providing a detailed explanation of how they view future recovery of the investment.

Preparers also supported a method that allows for managerial discretion within a fixed upper limit. For instance, an interviewee from the life insurance industry explained that some M&A transactions in this sector involve very long-term investment recoveries due to the nature of the business model. Nonetheless, the same respondent noted that, from a conservative perspective, an upper limit such as 10 years would still be acceptable. Similarly, a respondent from manufacturing acknowledged that some projects might have extended recovery periods but stressed the importance of setting a cap on the amortization period to ensure financial stability.

Next, we turn to the analysis of responses regarding how the terms "investment recovery period" and "duration of goodwill's (synergistic) effect" were interpreted. As responses focused on the concept of "investment recovery," the following discussion focuses on that aspect.

The most definitive perspective on this matter was provided by a respondent affiliated with a user. This respondent observed that certain preparers interpret the "investment recovery period" as the duration required for the cumulative undiscounted cash inflows to equate to the initial investment, without accounting for the requisite return on capital (i.e., without calculating the discounted present value). Since the required return is not incorporated, it is conceivable that even if the invested capital appears to be "recovered" within the designated amortization period, the net present value of the investment may still be less than the original amount, indicating a negative return. Given the existence of such varied interpretations concerning the meaning of "investment recovery," it is reasonable to infer that different respondents may hold differing understandings of what the term signifies. Several respondents also expressed concerns regarding the multiplicity of interpretations, including the individual previously mentioned.

After confirming that the term "investment recovery period" has multiple meanings, we analyze the similarities and differences between this measure of amortization and the "the period over which goodwill contributes to excess returns (synergy)." The analysis focuses on two questions: (a) whether these two concepts are essentially equivalent and (b) if they are not, which one should determine the amortization period.

Most respondents recognized that the "investment recovery period" and the "period over which goodwill contributes to excess returns" are different. They also believed that estimating how long goodwill impacts excess returns is more challenging than determining the investment recovery period. According to them, management's investment recovery plans, which explicitly specify the expected recovery timeframe, can serve as objective evidence to justify the proposed amortization period. In contrast, objectively substantiating how long synergies will last proves much more difficult. Many respondents highlighted this difference in the availability of objective evidence as a key factor in distinguishing between the two.

The results from the interview study on amortization periods are summarized above. An unexpected finding for the authors was the widespread support for a method that, in principle, relies on managerial judgment to determine the amortization period. In the United States, where discussions about reinstating goodwill amortization have recently restarted, efforts have been focused on reaching a consensus on a standard 10-year amortization period. The reasons behind this international difference still need to be explored in future research.

The authors were surprised to find that the "investment recovery period" garnered wider support than the "period over which goodwill contributes to excess returns" as the preferred method for setting amortization periods. The former often comes with objective evidence, such as business plans from management, while the latter is harder to substantiate. Essentially, the availability of objective evidence seems to be the critical factor influencing support for one approach over the other. This was unexpected, as the authors had generally believed that both business planning and estimating goodwill's useful life rely on forecasts of future cash flows, making them conceptually similar. The divergence in understanding between respondents and the authors on this issue remains an important topic for future research.

Another noteworthy and unforeseen discovery from the interviews was the variety of interpretations regarding the concept of "investment recovery".[17] The interpretation of the "investment recovery period" delineates the duration necessary for the total undiscounted cash flows generated by an investment project to equal the initial investment amount, which diverges significantly from methodologies based on discounted present value. Whether this approach—calculating recovery without discounting future cash flows—should be regarded merely as a "simplified approach" suitable solely for short-term investments, or whether it is indeed employed in long-term, large-scale investment decisions, remains an open question for subsequent research.

6.2.3.5 The Existence and Severity of the "too little, too late" Problem

In this interview study, we sought expert opinions on the criticism that the impairment accounting standard is not functioning effectively; specifically, the claim that the recognition of goodwill-related expenses, comprising both amortization and impairment losses, is delayed and understated, often referred to as the "too little, too late" problem.[18] This line of questioning was motivated by the concern that easy-to-understand slogans like "too little, too late" may reflect divergent interpretations and could cause significant misunderstandings.

We first summarize the preparers' views. Given that the companies interviewed were generally high-performing, the dominant view was that, in the sense that the standard is being applied as written, the "too little, too late" issue does not arise.

---

[17] When referring to "investment recovery," interpretations were divided over whether the discounted present value method should be used. Furthermore, there were differing views on whether to consider additional expenditures incurred after the initial investment—so-called revenue expenditures.

[18] Here, the "too little, too late" issue is interpreted in accordance with the Accounting Standards Board of Japan (2020).

However, preparers did not rule out the possibility that, within the bounds of compliance with accounting standards, impairment losses could be delayed or understated. For example, one respondent described the "shielding effect": a scenario where internally generated goodwill by the acquiring company adds positive value and is combined with purchased goodwill from the acquired company during impairment testing. In such cases, a decline in the acquired goodwill's value might be hidden by the ongoing value of the internally generated goodwill, reducing the likelihood of recognizing impairment.

Moreover, if the decline in the value of purchased goodwill exceeds the shielding effect, impairment recognition is required. In such cases, it is necessary to objectively demonstrate that the decline in value is irreversible. This entails not only financial costs but also time-related costs, specifically, the procedural requirements involved in the due process. When due process is followed, impairment decisions take time, resulting in delayed recognition of impairment losses.[19] The respondents also acknowledged this reality.

As previously outlined, the criterion employed by preparers to evaluate the existence of a "too little, too late" issue is whether the judgment has been rendered in accordance with applicable accounting standards. Even if impairment losses are recognized subsequently or in lesser amounts than users might anticipate—due to the shielding effect or the necessity for a cautious assessment of whether an irreversible decline in value has occurred—such recognition is not considered indicative of a "too little, too late" problem, provided the decision complies with GAAP. This implicit assumption was clearly reflected in the responses.

Next, we examine users' perspectives. Several users expressed that regarding the "too little, too late" issue, those who invest considerable effort and resources in financial statement analysis already anticipate declining performance and future impairments even before they are officially recognized in accounting records. They see it as a given that the market expects poor performance in advance. These users view impairment losses based on accounting as a retrospective confirmation of whether the actual loss aligns with their prior expectations. Under this view, when a performance decline can be reasonably predicted using other information, accounting-based impairment acts as a way to validate these expectations after the fact. In this context, the impairment system works as intended, and the "too little, too late" problem either does not occur or does not cause significant issues.

However, several users mentioned the existence of "unforeseen impairment losses." For users whose profession involves information intermediation, such unforeseen impairments may face blame or reputational damage. Consequently, they strive to detect early signs of impairment using a variety of indicators. Nevertheless, it is not always possible to anticipate every impairment in advance and "unanticipated impairment losses" are sometimes recognized. These types of

[19] In addition, some respondents noted that delays in impairment recognition may also result from the time required to persuade management—since impairment effectively represents an admission of investment failure—and from the need to avoid reputational damage related to the company's acquisition strategy.

impairments end up being "too little, too late." The implication of user responses seems to be that such outcomes are, to some extent, unavoidable.[20]

In summary, interview results indicate that stakeholders do not share a common understanding of the "too little, too late" problem or what needs to be addressed. Specifically, preparers see the issue as related to whether impairment standards are applied correctly, while users focus on whether adequate information is provided to evaluate the performance of acquired businesses, i.e., the sources of goodwill. Even if an impairment assessment complies with GAAP, a sudden or unexpected loss may still be perceived as "too little, too late." Analysts and other users often try to predict impairments by spotting early warning signs and setting expectations ahead of time. However, impairments caused by external factors are generally harder to anticipate. Therefore, preparers and users approach the "too little, too late" issue from fundamentally different viewpoints.

In discussions on the accounting treatment of goodwill, it is common for the "too little, too late" issue to be invoked without a clearly shared definition. The findings of this study suggest that debates that ostensibly take place on common ground may in fact be talking past one another. This was one of the key insights revealed through the interviews.[21]

6.2.3.6 Nature of Purchased Goodwill

In academic debates on whether purchased goodwill should be systematically amortized, attention has traditionally been centered on its nature of purchased goodwill. The question of whether goodwill depreciates over time has attracted considerable interest. In the present interviews, we gathered expert opinions on this issue.

While the question "Does goodwill depreciate?" addresses purchased goodwill—separate from internally generated goodwill—it remains unclear how market participants perceive two related issues: (a) whether it is possible to reliably distinguish purchased goodwill from internally generated goodwill, and (b) if such a distinction is meaningful. Therefore, in addition to exploring whether goodwill depreciates, we also aimed to gather opinions on the feasibility of differentiating

[20] One user stated: both managers who recognize impairment losses and information intermediaries (such as analysts) who fail to anticipate such losses in advance are held accountable. However, the nature of performance deterioration differs depending on whether it results from factors beyond management's control or from controllable factors. The respondent suggested that a distinction should be made between the two. One could argue that responses to the "too little, too late" problem should also vary depending on the underlying cause of the impairment.

[21] This study assumes that the problems surrounding the expense recognition of goodwill amortization manifest in the form of the "too little, too late" issue. However, in a questionnaire survey conducted by the authors' research group targeting certified public accountants between December 2020 and January 2021, some responses suggested that impairment losses are also being used to engage in "big bath" accounting. The big bath phenomenon implies that the recognized impairment loss is "too much." Whether the problems inherent in the current accounting standards can be adequately characterized as "too little, too late" is a topic for future research.

between internally generated goodwill, arising from post-acquisition investments or expenses, and purchased goodwill.

The responses received were as follows: Some users mentioned that "some goodwill does depreciate, while other goodwill retains its value semi-permanently." The view that "goodwill should be classified into depreciating and non-depreciating types" was the second most supported opinion, after the belief that "all goodwill depreciates." Since the question did not explicitly define "goodwill" as "purchased goodwill," respondents might have interpreted it as referring to the combined value of both purchased and internally generated goodwill resulting from subsequent investments—meaning the total value—which could decrease over time.

Interviewees were subsequently asked to evaluate scenarios in which an acquisition proved successful and the value of goodwill was maintained or even increased. Specifically, they were questioned on whether they accepted the premise that, although the value of purchased goodwill tends to decline over time alongside the recovery of the initial investment, additional value can be generated through subsequent investments in the form of internally created goodwill—thus maintaining or increasing the overall goodwill value. This inquiry was conducted considering a commonly observed argument within international accounting discussions: that "a rational manager should endeavor to preserve or enhance the value of goodwill resulting from an acquisition, and therefore, systematic amortization—which presumes a gradual diminution of goodwill value regardless of such efforts—is inconsistent with managerial behavior." Unsurprisingly, this perspective supports the non-amortization (impairment-only) methodology.

Consistent with this line of argument, proponents of systematic amortization often offer the following counterpoint: "What rational managers strive to maintain or enhance is the total value of goodwill, including internally generated goodwill created through post-acquisition business activities—not the value of purchased goodwill alone. The fact that the total value of goodwill is preserved or increased can coexist with the depreciation of purchased goodwill."

Given the results of the prior questionnaire survey, which provided support for systematic amortization regardless of whether respondents were preparers or users, it was expected that interviewees would similarly express the view that "while purchased goodwill depreciates, it is offset by the creation of internally generated goodwill."

The interview results confirmed this expectation. All respondents agreed with the notion that "the preservation of total goodwill value is the result of internally generated goodwill compensating for the decline in purchased goodwill."[22] These findings suggest that the perspective— "the value of purchased goodwill itself gradually declines as the expected cash flows are realized, but if internally generated goodwill created through post-acquisition activities not only compensates for that loss but exceeds it, then the total goodwill value is preserved or even enhanced"—is not only

[22] However, one respondent (a user) noted that not all analysts accept that "the apparent preservation of total goodwill value is due to the gradual replacement of purchased goodwill by internally generated goodwill."

understood within the academic community but is also widely accepted among market participants, including practitioners.

However, several responses suggested that practitioners do not necessarily share insights commonly shared within the academic community. This discrepancy becomes evident in discussing the question: "In what kinds of cases does purchased goodwill persist (without depreciating) over a reasonably foreseeable period?" One interviewee cited as an example of an "effectively perpetual" case the situation in which purchased goodwill is primarily composed of brand image, which is the source of excess earnings.[23]

Indeed, a brand image that is difficult for competitors to replicate can be a long-term source of excess profitability. However, in most cases, the value of the brand image is maintained or enhanced through additional investment after acquisition. In the case under discussion, purchased goodwill reflects expectations about future cash flows derived from the brand image. Once those cash flows are realized, the purchased goodwill is replaced by tangible or other assets, thereby losing its value. From this perspective, what the interviewee regarded as "persisting over a reasonably foreseeable period" was not the purchased goodwill but rather the total goodwill—including internally generated goodwill created after the acquisition.[24]

As previously discussed, in scenarios where purchased goodwill predominantly comprises brand image that yields substantial cash flows, the intrinsic value of the acquired goodwill should not be considered enduring over the long term. Instead, it is expected to diminish relatively early as these cash flows are generated. The attribution of such brand-related goodwill as an example of "effectively perpetual" purchased goodwill indicates a notable disparity in perspectives between academic scholars and market practitioners concerning the nature and definition of the amortization of purchased goodwill.

This situation probably stems from a lack of sufficient explanation—particularly the kind expected by the academic community—regarding what exactly is being preserved in cases of brand-based goodwill and why such a view is warranted. The series of interviews conducted in this study highlighted areas in which the academic

[23] The respondent was likely referring to brands that are difficult to treat as separable intangible assets—specifically, those for which it is difficult to make definitive statements regarding transferability.

[24] In the main text, we introduced only the academic view that the purchased goodwill exemplified—goodwill primarily composed of brand value—gradually loses its value. However, in reality, some scholars agree that brand-related goodwill can be treated similarly to a replacement asset under the replacement cost approach, thereby justifying the maintenance of its book value. This perspective regards such goodwill as an asset that provides a constant stream of services, maintained through ongoing expenditures. The central issue in this debate is whether there is an analogy between "maintaining a certain level of transport service by replacing rails and sleepers" and "preserving brand value through additional expenditures." For prior studies discussing whether purchased goodwill can be viewed as a replacement-type asset, see Yamauchi (2010), Obinata (2012), and Saito (2017).

community's "accountability" in terms of explanatory clarity has not yet been fully achieved.[25]

The interview study also found that some respondents (users) who did not support systematic amortization emphasized that the key factor in corporate valuation is the "total value of goodwill," whether it arises from purchased goodwill or internally generated goodwill through investments. For those who primarily assess corporate value based on cash flow data and view accounting information as supplementary, the fact that accounting earnings reflect "realized outcomes that turn expectations into facts"—and thus exclude internally generated goodwill, which remains within expectations—may not be particularly significant. This group of users was among the most intriguing findings of the interviews.

6.2.4 Conclusion: Summary and Prospects

This study extends the work of Tokuga et al. (2019), who surveyed both financial statement preparers and users about their preferred accounting treatment—whether systematic amortization with impairment or non-amortization (impairment-only)—for purchased goodwill, along with their reasons. The current research summarizes the follow-up interviews conducted to understand the background behind the responses and offers interpretations of the results. The key insights from these interviews are as follows:

1. Support for systematic amortization among users was generally more passive than that among preparers. Moreover, the valuation methods employed by users, particularly analysts, were not determined by individual beliefs or convictions, but instead were flexibly shaped by factors such as the analytical models used within their organizations or the preferences of their clients. This suggests that the support for systematic amortization among users may not be as robust as the questionnaire results suggest.
2. In certain international contexts, some argue that "the periodic amortization expense for goodwill is added back when valuing firms, and therefore such information has no real value." In Japan, whether or not one supports systematic amortization, interest in this matter seems to be relatively limited.
3. The motivation to avoid systematic amortization has been cited—both in prior academic research and by several interview respondents—as a major reason for the voluntary adoption of IFRS. However, this interview study revealed that the

[25] Past discussions surrounding accounting standards have generally assumed users who primarily rely on accounting information as their main input. However, some users who evaluate corporate value primarily based on cash flow information, viewing accounting information as supplementary or secondary. How to engage with such users—specifically, to what extent their interests should be considered—emerged through the interview study as an "unresolved issue" that warrants further consideration.

substantial monetary and time costs associated with impairment testing may lead even IFRS adopters to prefer systematic amortization if allowed.[26]

4. Users showed greater interest in whether management should decide the amortization period than in how to set its upper limit. This indicates that many users see the management's choice as a useful source of internal information. Meanwhile, preparers did not want total freedom, but preferred to have some flexibility within a set framework, allowing them to justify their decisions.
5. Terms like "the period over which the investment in purchased goodwill is expected to be recovered" or "the period over which goodwill is expected to generate excess returns" have been used with various interpretations, leading to concerns about possible misunderstandings. Unlike estimating the useful lives of tangible assets, many practitioners find it much more challenging to determine the amortization periods for purchased goodwill, especially when they can be supported by objective evidence.
6. The expression "too little, too late" is often used without a precise definition and can be interpreted differently. Both preparers and users have different understandings of what qualifies as a "too little, too late" situation. Furthermore, even among users, the interpretation of the term varies depending on the context in which it was used.
7. There was broad agreement on two key points: first, goodwill depreciates over time; and second, distinguishing between purchased goodwill and internally generated goodwill, especially goodwill created through additional post-acquisition investments, is difficult. However, it remained unclear whether references to "the depreciation of goodwill" referred to purchased goodwill, to the overall value of goodwill including internally generated components, or whether the very notion of disaggregating goodwill into separate components was commonly accepted. Furthermore, noticeable differences in perspective (differences in emphasis/degree of concern/level of interest) between academic scholars and market participants (both preparers and users) were observed for "why the distinction between purchased and internally generated goodwill matters" and "how such a distinction should be made, at least conceptually, if not operationally." These gaps may hinder the possibility of conducting common ground discussions.

Although the interviews were originally conducted as a follow-up to the previous questionnaire survey, the insights obtained went beyond a mere follow-up and offered suggestions for significant issues previously addressed by the academic community.

For example, in these interviews, both preparers and users indicated that applying impairment accounting to goodwill restrains M&A when profitability prospects are uncertain. This may be referred to as a "preemptive disciplining effect" on M&A (the first effect). Similarly, both preparers and users responded that the application of impairment accounting to goodwill creates incentives—relative to scenarios in

[26] See Financial Services Agency (2015) and Nakano (2020) for related literature.

which such accounting is not applied—to clarify the locus of responsibility within organizations regarding the success or failure of M&A transactions. This may be termed the "organizational accountability effect" in M&A (the second effect).

Additionally, a commonly noted effect is the "signaling effect to the market." When an external negative shock impacts a target company, market participants try to gauge the extent of its profit decline. Although disclosures of impairment losses on goodwill and long-lived assets generally happen after market expectations are set, companies use these disclosures to indicate how significantly the shock has affected them. Investors then update their expectations based on the implicit information conveyed through the impairment losses. The importance of impairment information in this context has been widely acknowledged by both preparers and users.

What expectations are placed on goodwill impairment information and what roles it plays are topics of ongoing debate within the academic community. Although interview-based research is subject to certain inherent limitations, the fact that useful insights related to such debates were obtained is a key contribution of this study. Moving forward, we intend to explore how the findings of these interviews can be leveraged to inform academic discourse and how best to do so.[27]

---

[27] Before conducting this interview survey, our research group shared the following set of research questions: (1) Why do many preparers support the systematic amortization with impairment, even though the nature of goodwill differs depending on firm characteristics? (2) Why do more than 60% of Japanese analysts—unlike their counterparts overseas—support the systematic amortization with impairment? (3) Why did preparers, analysts, and auditors all show greater support for "the management's investment recovery plan" than for "the duration of synergies" when determining the amortization period? (4) How do preparers and analysts conceptualize the distinction between internally generated goodwill and acquired goodwill? (5) How do they evaluate cases in which the recognition of impairment losses is effectively avoided through the implementation of systematic amortization?

As described in the main text, we obtained at least partial answers to several of these research questions. For (1), respondents pointed out that (a) arguments justifying systematic amortization have become widely disseminated through accounting education, (b) stable financial performance is desirable for managers, and (c) systematic amortization functions as a disciplining mechanism to deter unprofitable mergers and acquisitions. Regarding (2), most respondents did not perceive the current requirement for systematic amortization as problematic. As for (3), many interviewees remarked that estimating the duration of synergies is inherently more difficult than estimating the period of investment recovery. For (4), although many respondents agreed that acquired goodwill is gradually replaced by internally generated goodwill, it remained uncertain whether their reasoning was based on definitions and assumptions consistent with those adopted by the research group. In other words, the findings suggest that, with regard to (4), there may have been a "dialogue of the deaf," in which interviewers and interviewees used the same terms but understood them differently. Finally, concerning (5), the interviews reported in Sect. 6.2 did not elicit sufficient responses. The examination of this issue, along with research question (4), was therefore deferred to the interviews described in Sect. 6.3.

6.3 Exploring the Differences in Perceptions Surrounding the Accounting Treatment of Goodwill: What Is Creating the Perception Gap Between Analysts and Academics?

6.3.1 Purpose of This Section

This section summarizes the results of an interview survey conducted between September and December 2022 with analysts who are knowledgeable about accounting practices (for details, refer to the appendix).[28] The research group to which the author belongs has long been trying to identify the causes of disagreements among securities market participants regarding the appropriate accounting for goodwill. As part of this research, the group has previously revealed through questionnaire surveys and follow-up interviews that among Japanese market participants, there is broad support for the systematic amortization of goodwill (amortization with impairment test). When asked about the reasons for supporting systematic amortization, many responses were grounded in accounting perspectives widely accepted in Japan, such as the matching principle and income as a surplus of invested capital (a close linkage between accounting income and cash flow).[29]

These findings can be reasonably interpreted. However, closer examination of the responses raises questions about whether the key definitions of some technical terms, implicitly assumed by the research team (as the questioner), were adequately communicated to the respondents. For example, one justification for systematic amortization was: "Even if goodwill remains total, the portion corresponding to purchased goodwill should be decreasing. The maintenance of the total amount is due to the replacement of purchased goodwill with internally generated "new" goodwill." Scholars often note that the effect on income differs between purchased goodwill and newly generated goodwill through post-acquisition efforts. Nevertheless, practitioners tend to highlight the practical challenges in distinguishing between these two types of goodwill, even when discussing the same issues.

As shown in the example, when designing questionnaires or interview surveys aimed at practitioners, it's essential to ensure that both the surveyor and respondents have a shared understanding of the terminology used. The research group, aware of this issue, has worked to reduce perception gaps during surveys. However, in practice, some responses that were hard to interpret occurred, often relying on the surveyor's assumptions or resulting in ambiguity.

---

[28] The interviews were conducted by the five authors of this paper who have been working on this research topic. Their employers and positions at the time of the interviews are as follows. Yoshihiro Tokuga (Professor, Kyoto University of Advanced Sciences), Masaki Yoneyama (Professor, Graduate School of Economics, University of Tokyo), Yuko Asami (Professor, Faculty of Economics, Gakushuin University), Toshitake Miyauchi (Associate Professor, Otemon Gakuin University), and Tomoaki Yamashita (Associate Professor, Fukui Prefectural University)

[29] See Tokuga et al. (2018, 2021), Asami et al. (2021), Yoneyama et al. (2021), and Asami et al. (2022).

Considering this experience, the research group decided to launch a spin-off project based on its main research theme: investigating the sources of international conflict over accounting for goodwill. Specifically, the group explored the

(a) Where do the perception gaps between practitioners and academic researchers manifest?
(b) Why do these gaps arise?
(c) How do these gaps hinder mutual understanding?

The group conducted an additional series of interviews with analysts, a group in which perception gaps seemed particularly pronounced, and endeavored to investigate the causes and effects of these gaps. This paper presents the results of this investigation.

The remainder of this paper is organized as follows. In Sect. 6.3.2, the purpose of the survey is briefly restated and the specific questions posed to achieve the research objectives are described. Details concerning the timing and format of the interviews as well as the selection method for interviewees are also explained. Section 6.3.3 summarizes the interview results and discusses their implications for this research topic. Common themes emerging from the interviews are identified, and where answers diverged, efforts are made to attribute the divergence to respondent characteristics. Based on these examinations, Sect. 6.3.4 provides a summary.

6.3.2 Outline of the Interview Survey and Purpose of the Questionnaires

6.3.2.1 Selection of Interviewees and Outline of the Interview Process

As noted in Sect. 6.2, the results of past questionnaires (e.g., free-response columns) and interviews suggested that the gap in perception seemed to be the most serious among the users of financial statements and academics who conducted the surveys. Therefore, the research group decided to conduct additional interviews with users of their financial statements. They were elected from members of the Business Accounting Research Group of the Securities Analysis Association of Japan (the SAAJ). They are particularly knowledgeable about accounting practices in Japan.[30]

Five members of the Business Accounting Research Group agreed to conduct interviews, which were held from September to December 2022 (see Table 6.1 in 6.5.4 for details).

To gain a better understanding of the purpose of the interviews, our research group distributed a questionnaire to the interviewees in advance. Since many

[30] For more information on the Business Accounting Research Group, see https://www.saa.or.jp/apps/list/com_meibo_57.html. The current membership is different from when the interviews were conducted.

Table 6.1 Basic interviewee data

Interviewees	Relationship with the author	Form of interview	Reference materials	Written reply	Effective date
A	Member of Corporate Accounting Study Group, Securities Analysts Association of Japan	Online interview	Yes	Yes	September 26, 2022 from 12:00 p.m. to 2:00 p.m.
B	Member of Corporate Accounting Study Group, Securities Analysts Association of Japan	Face-to-face interview	No	No	September 29, 2022 from 11:00 a.m. to 1:00 p.m.
C	Member of Corporate Accounting Study Group, Securities Analysts Association of Japan	Online interview	No	Yes	October 6, 2022 from 4:30 p.m. to 6:30 p.m.
D	Member of Corporate Accounting Study Group, Securities Analysts Association of Japan	CARF seminar	N/A	N/A	October 20, 2022 from 6:00 p.m. to 8:00 p.m.
E	Member of Corporate Accounting Study Group, Securities Analysts Association of Japan	Online interview	Yes	No	October 21, 2022 from 10:00 a.m. to 12:00 p.m.
F	Member of Corporate Accounting Study Group, Securities Analysts Association of Japan	Online interview	No	Yes	December 5, 2022 from 4:00 p.m. to 6:00 p.m.
G	Member of Corporate Accounting Study Group, Securities Analysts Association of Japan	Hybrid interview	No	Yes	December 26, 2022 from 2:00 p.m. to 4:00 p.m.

interviewees answered the questionnaire in advance, we conducted interviews to delve deeper into their answers.

6.3.2.2 Summary of Questions

Next, we outline the questions that are central to the interviews. As shown in the question themes can be divided into three categories.

1. The perception gap between financial statement users and academics
2. Preference for accounting for the purchased goodwill
3. Educational background of the interviewees

Of these, Question 1 directly reflects the objective of the interview. Question 2 applies Question No.1 to the context of a conflict over accounting for goodwill. Question 3 is somewhat different from the former questions. Below is the reason we have added Question 3. During the first round of interviews conducted with the three types of stakeholders, users of financial statements had a more mixed preference for desired accounting for goodwill than preparers or auditors of financial statements. Users showed some support for the option of non-amortization (impairment-only) compared with auditors and preparers, who overwhelmingly favored systematic amortization with impairment.

When financial statement users were asked for this reason in the first round of interviews, they indicated that their preferences depended on the analysis tools employed by their company. In other words, their preferences were influenced by their working environment. If their company adopted an income-based analysis, they would become accustomed to an income-oriented approach and vice versa. Although this scenario was possible, the limited number of interviews made it difficult to generalize the results. Given this, we decided to ask the current group of interviewees the same question to see if we could obtain the same level of confidence as in the past.

6.3.2.3 Specific Questions and Their Objectives

6.3.2.3.1 Questions Regarding the Perception Gap Between Financial Statement Users and Academics

Some of the explanations that provide a reasonable interpretation of the systematic amortization of goodwill are not simple arguments but a series of inferences based on certain assumptions that conclude that regular amortization of goodwill is desirable. When academics discuss arguments supporting the systematic amortization of goodwill, the presumption is that they share a common understanding of the premises of the argument and method of reasoning. On the other hand, it is an empirical proposition that arguments in academia involving certain "barriers to entry" are supported by the same shared perceptions in dialogue with practitioners as they are in dialogue among academics.[31] While elaborating on academic findings, common sense in academia may diverge from common sense in practice. Our Question 1: "Please tell us if there exists any gap that may persist between scholarly insights and the practical intuition for professionals." is the most direct reflection of this central research concern.

Question 1, which was the most general, was followed by Questions 2–4. They were prepared to assist interviewees who might have found it difficult to respond to the overly abstract nature of Question 1. These questions contextualize the content of Question 1 by applying it to more specific cases.

Question 2 is: "Academics often divide the financial statement users into two categories: one is those who evaluate corporate value based mainly on cash flow

[31] We do not intend to make a "patronizing" argument that common sense in academia should be equally accepted outside of academia, although we dare to use a poor expression. This survey is rooted in the concern that academics, including the authors, may be relying on jargon and neglecting efforts toward mutual understanding with practitioners.

information and the other is those mainly on accounting information. The latter category is further divided into two subcategories: one emphasizing income statement information and the other emphasizing balance sheet information. How do you think of the distinction? In other words, can you specify one source of information that is most valuable for your business in securities evaluation?"

This question examines the appropriateness of the academic framework for analyzing sounds for practitioners. It is a foundational principle of academia to endeavor to understand accounting phenomena by deconstructing them into simpler components. However, if the majority of practitioners use both accounting information (such as income statements and balance sheets) and cash flow data concurrently, they may find it challenging to comprehend why academics endeavor to specify the most valuable data source. Given that several respondents in the initial round of interviews indicated that they employ both cash flows and accounting information without distinction, we sought to verify whether they share a reductionist perspective.

Question 3 is: "It is a widely accepted finding among academics that the competitiveness surrounding companies is generally severe, and that superior knowledge and/or know-how once possessed by a specific company will disappear in approximately five to seven years, unless they are protected by the government. Does this align with your experience? Also, do you agree with the argument that so long as purchased goodwill, which reflects the competitive superiority, depreciates over time, systematic amortization is the most desirable way of accounting?"

This question aims to assess how well-known the concept of mean reversion in profit margins is among practitioners and whether both academics and practitioners share a common understanding of this phenomenon. It also inquires whether, assuming shared understanding, the regression of profit margins to the industry average justifies systematic amortization of goodwill. Since profit margins tend to revert to the industry mean, this implies that not only purchased goodwill but also internally generated goodwill will diminish over time. Providing a consistent interpretation for non-amortization that maintains purchased goodwill at book value unless impairment occurs is challenging. Instead, the evidence suggests that systematic amortization is more plausible. We seek to determine if this explanation aligns with practitioners' experiences and whether both academics and practitioners see mean reversion as a basis for systematic amortization.[32]

Question 4 asks: "It is sometimes said that standards must be developed with the "average investor" in mind. On the other hand, investors use accounting information in a great variety of ways, and it is impossible to aggregate opinions about the "average investor". In light of your own experience, do you think that financial statement users' views on accounting standards are so varied that they are impossible to aggregate? Or can you find some sort of "broadest shared understanding or common

[32] For mean reversion of profit margins, see Lundholm, and Sloan (2019), Palepu et al. (2013), Penman (2013), and Obinata (2013), among others. See Fukui and Takahashi (2022) for an interpretation of the phenomenon of mean reversion of profit margins in relation to the decay of goodwill.

ground"? Please let us know if there are any cases in which users' views differ greatly from each other in the accounting standards setting process."

Question 6 is: "We wonder if there is any sharp conflict among financial statement users regarding a specific accounting treatment (e.g., systematic amortization with impairment vs. impairment-only). If this happens, in what case? If a conflict occurs, which organization attempts to resolve it and in which way?" As discussed below, Questions 4 and 6 share many similarities. Hence, we address both questions together.

Questions 4 and 6 ask the interviewees in what cases conflicts regarding the "preferred method of accounting measurement and disclosure" among users of financial statements are likely to arise or have arisen, and how they converge. (if any).

In establishing accounting standards, there is an implicit assumption of an "average investor," and the aim is to create standards aligned with their decision-making process. However, our initial survey showed that support for systematically amortizing goodwill and for not amortizing it was fairly evenly divided, particularly among analysts. While the former option was more popular, the support for the latter was still significant.

These two methods are in dualistic conflict in the sense that if one is adopted, the other cannot be adopted. In such case, it is difficult to assume the image of "average investors" because there is no room left for the adoption of the other if one is adopted. If this is the case, standard setting based on "average investors" will not work.[33] Questions 4 and 6 asked whether such dysfunction is avoided because there is no notable conflict in the first place (in other words, because analysts' views are generally homogeneous, except the conflict regarding accounting for goodwill) or because there are practices, organizations, and institutions that contribute to mitigating the conflict. The following section determines whether this is the case.

Question 5 asks the interviewees: "By what criteria are accounting standards evaluated in terms of their quality or effectiveness for financial statement users?" This question is virtually unanswered by academics pursuing academic rigor.[34] On the other hand, practitioners who use accounting information in their daily work are likely to have specific requests and suggestions for improvement rooted in problems (e.g., lack of usability) with the accounting information that the current standards create. Such requests should provide clues for understanding the specific content of "decision-useful information" about which academics are not fully informed. This question was prepared based on these expectations.

---

[33] Standards development based on the "average investor profile" implicitly assumes the existence of accounting and disclosure practices favored by most investors.

[34] A forced response will be subject to an extremely large number of restrictions and reservations.

6.3.2.3.2 Questions Related to Accounting for Goodwill

This section contains questions that help ascertain the cases in which there is a gap between practitioners' and academics' perceptions in the debate over preferred accounting for goodwill, and how this gap affects the dialogue between them. Among these questions, Question 1 states, "We academics consider the immediate write-off of purchased goodwill (charged to capital surplus) to be one of the conceivable options. Would this also be conceivable (or reasonably anticipated) for financial statement users?"[35]

Many researchers studying goodwill accounting widely recognize that, in some jurisdictions, charging purchased goodwill to capital surplus was a common practice in the past. However, it remains unclear whether practitioners are aware of this option, as their interests often differ from academic perspectives. These differing perceptions of available options influence judgments about the most appropriate accounting treatment for goodwill. We initially suspected that practitioners would generally not favor immediate write-offs, particularly those charged to capital surplus.

Question 2 is: "The difference between value-in-use based on the cash flow subjectively estimated by the management and a certain value supported by any objective evidence is called internally generated (subjective) goodwill. But there are different views on what constitutes internally generated goodwill. Is the difference from market value called internally generated goodwill? Or is internally generated goodwill the difference with book value? Or are these issues not of interest in the first place?"

Under current accounting standards, during a business combination, the target company's assets and liabilities are reassessed at market value. The difference between these revalued net assets (also known as net asset market value) and the consideration paid for the business is recognized as goodwill (or negative goodwill). Essentially, the standard is based on the idea that the difference between value-in-use and market value constitutes goodwill or negative goodwill.

If the present value of expected future cash flows from a business project equals the invested amount (or the market value of the business assets tied to the project), the project is expected to generate only a normal return, equal to the cost of capital. If purchased goodwill is considered part of the consideration for a business combination that reflects expectations of excess returns, it should be measured as the excess of market value. This rigorous academic argument assumes that the net assets valuation method determines the characteristics of accounting income. It is unclear whether this complex logic has been widely accepted among practitioners. Therefore, we aimed to determine if a recognition gap has developed between practitioners and academics.

Question 3 is: "There is an argument that useful information can be expected in a situation where impairment test relating to purchased goodwill are more likely to

[35] See Saito and Fukui (2022a, b) for a new discussion of this issue.

be triggered. On the other hand, there is an argument that if the easy but precise estimation of permanent income is the ultimate goal, impairment test should not be easily triggered, as impairment test causes unnecessary fluctuations in net income. Which view described above do you think is more widely supported?" This finding is controversial among academics.

Suppose the goal is to provide decision-useful information to investors. A question then arises: Which type of information related to impairment losses is most important for this objective? Some argue that the information on impairment losses itself is the most crucial. Others believe that the projected stream of future earnings after the impairment test holds even greater significance. The latter group also contends that the impairment test should be the best method for estimating the ongoing stream of future earnings.

The first approach highlights that information about investment failures is only partially disclosed. It suggests that inside information spillovers are expected regarding the extent and causes of performance decline when analyzing impairment losses. Conversely, the second approach focuses on impairment losses as a tool for predicting a steady stream of future earnings. Here, the emphasis is not on the impairment loss itself but on how future earnings after impairment tests better represent permanent income. We developed Question 3 to determine which perspective is more widely endorsed by practitioners.

Question 4 further asks: "An argument is widely known that expenses based on systematic amortization of goodwill is added back to earnings in the valuation of corporate value. Do most of financial statements users add back goodwill to earnings? If so, what kind of model do they use to evaluate corporate value? And what is your personal opinion on this point?" This argument is one that the IASB often mentions as the view of stakeholders in favor of the non-amortization (impairment-only) of goodwill. Users of financial statements add back the expense based on the systematic amortization of goodwill because they view it as something that "need not be deducted" when assessing the performance of an entity. If this is the case, the scenario envisioned seems to be that it is better not to amortize goodwill from the outset. However, this cannot be reduced to simple explanations. There are a variety of explanations for why adding goodwill to earnings is appropriate. Some reasons may lead to non-amortization (impairment-only) of goodwill, which is widely observed; however, others may be consistent with the systematic amortization of goodwill. Further investigation is required to confirm the context of the argument regarding the pros and cons of systematic amortization.

For instance, consider the rationale for reinstating goodwill, which posits that "cash flow constitutes the primary input within the decision-making model. The addition of expenses devoid of cash outflows, such as amortization expenses, is essential for estimating cash flows based on earnings data." In this context, the *comparison is performed between cash flow information and earnings data, rather than among various types of earnings data. Should* this scenario be applicable, the common practice of adding back expenses merely indicates that a subset of decision-makers relies predominantly on cash flow as their primary input. Consequently, this should not influence the determination regarding whether goodwill should be systematically amortized.

However, it would be a different situation if users, for whom earnings information is the primary factor in their decision-making, demanded the reintroduction of amortization expenses into earnings. Such behavior indicates that these users believe systematic amortization expenses do not accurately reflect the company's performance. In this case, a comparison between systematic amortization with impairment and non-amortization (impairment-only) of goodwill would be necessary, especially regarding the measurement of preferred income and its disclosure. Question 4 was prepared because the authors lacked sufficient knowledge of the decision-making models assumed by these users.

Finally, Question 5 is: Is it common for analysts to revise their earnings forecasts based on publicly disclosed information regarding goodwill impairment losses? Thus, how are impairment losses used to revise expectations?

Some argue that much of the information about impairment losses is already widely known before it is officially disclosed. From this perspective, the effect of announcing an impairment loss only comes from elements that were not expected beforehand. Although many academic studies have examined how much information about impairments is integrated before disclosure, practitioners may be unaware of these researches. Additionally, perceptions of how much information is prepriced may vary: practitioners often draw deep insights from a small number of cases, while academics analyze large samples to identify broader trends. In this context, we decided to address this question.

6.3.2.3.3 Questions Related to Accounting Education and Other Education Received in the Past and How Accounting Information Is Used

The final section contains questions about the interviewees' prior educational background. The reason for including these questions is to address the research question: What distinguishes analysts who prioritize cash flow information from those who emphasize earnings information?

During our first round of interviews, one interviewee stated that his analytical methods as an individual analyst depended on the company's database and analytical tools. This implies that if they operate in an environment focused on cash flow (earnings), they tend to develop a style emphasizing cash flow (earnings), and the same applies in reverse. Question 3 was designed to see if other analysts share this view. It asks: "In a previous interview, an analyst mentioned that decision-making models are based on his employer's systems and databases rather than personal beliefs. Do you agree?"

However, the authors hypothesized an alternative scenario regarding users' analytical styles. In this scenario, we hypothesize that accounting education received before college or recurrent education after employment may have a greater impact on analytical style. In my experience, what I first learned in accounting and financial accounting courses is ingrained in my memory, whether good or bad, and it is difficult to erase it. While we acknowledge the influence of environmental factors provided by the companies where they work, we also consider the possibility that the content of their initial learning (for those who do not have a degree in commerce, business administration, or economics, the training provided by the company may be equivalent) may have influenced their decision-making styles. Questions 1 and 2 were prepared to examine the impact of educational background.

The specific questions are as follows. Question 1: "Please tell us about your education and training history as an analyst. In particular, what is your training history on how financial accounting works and how to use financial information in investment decisions, or how to account for purchased goodwill?" Question 2: "Accounting standards are constantly being updated. Sometimes changes occur in the dimensions of fairly fundamental ideas that underpin the system of accounting standards. What recurrent education opportunities regarding accounting do financial statement users take advantage of?"

The following describes the questions asked in the interview survey and their purpose. In the next section, we discuss the survey results and analyze the findings.

6.3.3 *Overall Results of Interviews and Discussion on the Results*

6.3.3.1 Responses Regarding the Perception Gap Between Financial Statement Users and Academics

In response to a general question about the perception gap between users and academics analyzing the practice from a broad perspective, it was noted that, in helping investors make decisions, academics might not distinguish between analysis aimed at identifying short-term mispricings and that focused on assessing long-term fundamental value (Interviewee A).

In empirical research, we find that some focus on short-term changes in stock prices relative to published financial information, whereas others focus on long-term impacts. However, how differences in the scope of analysis (short-versus long-term) affect the accounting information required has rarely been discussed in academic research on accounting standards and/or conceptual frameworks. Interviewee A suggests that unless the scope of analysts is specified, no implications could be obtained regarding the usefulness of accounting information.

Interviewee C pointed out that if several academics are primarily (almost exclusively) interested in financial information and not in non-financial information, especially information pertaining to sustainability, this may create a gap for practitioners who typically integrate both financial and non-financial information to assess the value of a company.[36] Academics reserve their judgment on the

[36]At the time of this writing, at the end of 2024, the importance of sustainability information and integrated reports is widely known among market participants; however, this interview was conducted in the fall of 2022, and the interviewee is justified in his assessment that he had foresight.

usefulness of newly disclosed information until objective evidence support it unless it is considered self-evident considering widely accepted hypotheses. This response is inevitable because it involves a "lifeline" for academics, but it may be perceived as indecision or inaction in response to a changing environment by practitioners, who are required to make quick judgments.

Another interviewee (Interviewee F) noted that most analysts rarely interact with academic research results. They suggested that if goodwill is viewed as a reflection of expectations for excess returns, and academics discuss the decline in purchased goodwill value as a standard part of transforming those expectations into actual cash flow, this assumption might itself be a source of discrepancy. F also reminded us that all interviewed analysts are highly skilled in accounting. Essentially, Interviewee F emphasized that their responses do not always represent the average or consensus among analysts. This highlights the importance of clarifying what is meant by "average".

Another respondent highlighted that in relation to Question 2—"When analyzing as a financial statements user, which is more important: cash flow or earnings?"—academic discussions typically begin with forecasting a company's permanent income based on sustainable future cash flows. The second stage involves estimating corporate value from this projected permanent income. In practice, however, value-added generated by a company is measured in a way that is neither cash flow nor permanent income, and the company's value is assessed directly using this measure. Sometimes, the company's value is directly evaluated based on value-added generated over a specific period, without relying on sustainable cash flows or permanent income (Interviewee G).

The analytical approaches mentioned by the interviewees are implicitly rooted in projections of sustainable cash flow and permanent income. This is because one cannot assume a value-added that is not supported by these factors. To understand the causal relationships involved in accounting phenomena, academics try to decompose and reduce observed facts into simple elements. The emphasis on sustainable cash flows and permanent income was derived from this focus. The results of the analyses by academics acknowledge that reduced elements are combined and used in practice as a more complex model. Nevertheless, the interviewee's point is important because it made us realize that the idea of "elemental reductionism" may hinder communication with practitioners.

As discussed, Question 2 asked about the primary sources of information (cash flow, income, or both). One interviewee stated that analysts interested in short-term stock price fluctuations base their analysis on income, whereas those interested in long-term corporate value base their analysis on cash flow.[37] (Interviewee A).

Another respondent pointed out that although the comparative superiority between cash flow and income varies from entity to entity, in any case, a

[37] In conjunction with this, financial institutions and credit analysts who review credit also place a high priority on cash flow.

multifaceted analysis is dominant, using both as inputs for decision-making, depending on the objective and phase of the analysis (Interviewee F).

This respondent also emphasized that (a) income information is vital for assessing business performance, with net income at the bottom line regarded as the primary metric in evaluations; (b) the indirect estimation of future cash flows derived from net income is deemed to be more predominant than direct estimation based on actual cash flows; (c) even if there are differences between foreign securities companies and Japanese firms regarding the balance of cash flows and income, these differences are relative rather than absolute; and (d) for credit rating analysts, Japanese companies predominantly focus on safety indicators related to income statements and balance sheets, whereas foreign companies consider not only safety indicators based on accounting figures but also those derived from cash flow information.

This respondent further commented on the determinants of users' analytical style. The person pointed out that the affiliation of securities companies may not be a key factor. Rather, the sector and team to which each analyst belongs has more influence. The person also commented that analysts consider the multifaceted impact of goodwill impairment. Analysts consider both the impairment loss itself and the future income stream after impairment. These responses are closely related to our research questions, which we found to be useful.

The other respondent (Interviewee G) stated that few analysts base their investment decisions solely on income data. Instead, many evaluate corporate value by estimating future cash flows derived from income-related information. This respondent also highlighted the difference between performance measurements based on changes in equity securities and those based on accounting income. Changes in equity securities fluctuate in the expectation dimension, with immediate gains or losses resulting from these fluctuations. In contrast, accounting income is recognized only when supported by actual cash flows. The respondents noted that many analysts struggle with how to effectively connect these two approaches.

We next analyze the responses to Question 3, in which we ask if the respondents accept the argument that both purchased and internally generated goodwill depreciate through competition among firms and that accounting income reverts to the industry average after a certain period. All respondents (A, C, F, and G) agreed. In addition, one respondent pointed out (Interviewee G) that while it is true from practical experience that mean reversion generally occurs, some firms have generated excess profits for a long period of time, albeit as an exception. This phenomenon has also been observed in prior academic research and the responses described above suggest that the practical experiences and results of academic research, including exceptional cases, are consistent.

Another respondent (Interviewee F) commented that while the respondent could personally accept this view, the argument of academics that goodwill reflects an expectation of future excess returns may not necessarily be accepted by many analysts. This respondent stated that, for many analysts, it may be easier to understand the argument based on the premise that purchased goodwill constitutes a portion of invested capital. In other words, because accounting income is calculated as the surplus of the invested amount of money, it would be easier for many analysts to appropriately understand the argument in the context of matching costs and revenues. This respondent further stated that, based on practical experience, not all purchased goodwill reflects a superior source of excess return and that it may include an amount equivalent to an overpayment resulting from an optimistic valuation.

We then analyze the responses to Question 4, which asked about "the average investors." One respondent (Interviewee A) answered that most investors accept published accounting standards as a given and few analysts are interested in how differences in accounting standards affect their work as analysts. According to this respondent, analysts' views on the superiority or inferiority of alternative accounting standards generally vary because of the lack of interest described above. The respondent further added that some analysts made judgments based on their self-interest (not the public interest). For example, some payoffs are closely linked to the success or failure of M&A. They may prefer accounting standards that encourage (or discourage) M&As, in which accounting information is more beneficial to their own business. Their presence may have contributed to this variation.

Another respondent (Interviewee C) noted that traditionally, sell-side analysts tend to focus on short-term goals, whereas buy-side analysts usually adopt a long-term perspective. He mentioned that there could be differing opinions on suitable accounting practices, depending on their scopes. However, sell-side analysts have increasingly shifted toward a long-term outlook in recent years. As a result, the gap between the two types of analysts may be narrowing.

Yet another respondent (Interviewee F) stated that, limited to domestic users, there are rarely conflicting views on preferred accounting for goodwill. According to this respondent's practical experience, the major conflicts were between users and other stakeholders, or between domestic and foreign users.

Another respondent pointed out that in industries that require a number of accounting procedures that differ from those of general business companies (e.g., the insurance industry), the degree of understanding of the required procedures varies widely among analysts (Interviewee G). In such cases, the person claimed that an average should not be taken to equally reflect the views of both well-versed (minority) and ill-versed (majority) analysts. In other words, the respondents' view was that it is not always best to consider accounting procedures based on average investor profiles.

On the other hand, in response to Question 6, which was combined with Question 4 in Sect. 6.3, one respondent pointed out that the Japan Securities Analysts Association and Japan Securities Dealers Association differ in their stances on the necessity of lobbying, even though both organizations represent users (Interviewee A). Another respondent related the expression "sharp conflict" to Question 6. in response to accounting for goodwill. Some analysts believe that it is more important than anything else to expend the cost of purchased goodwill in the body of financial statements, while others believe that there is no need to stick to systematic amortization if sufficient information is disclosed in the form of notes to replace systematic amortization, and the conflict between the two could be regarded as sharp (Interviewee C).

Another respondent (Interviewee F) answered that the person still remembers that the SAAJ had a different opinion on whether total equity, excluding goodwill, should be presented in the balance sheet, which is the proposal made by the IASB in 2021. However, the also answered that there were no sharp conflicts regarding an issue deeply related to the basic concepts underlying the current system of accounting standards. This respondent stated that when analysts had divergent views on desirable accounting procedures, organizations such as SAAJ tried to reflect minority opinions as much as possible, rather than just publishing the majority view as the user's view when submitting a comment externally. The person also pointed out that analysts may have divergent views on implementation issues and very few views on theoretical issues.

Another respondent (Interviewee G) noted that costly lobbying often has "poor value" for analysts who can freely process and recombine publicly available financial information with respect to their own analysis. Accounting standards that are not user-friendly for analysts are likely to be user-friendly for other stakeholders. In this case, accounting standards should be modified by another party with strong lobbying skills, even if the analyst does not take concrete action. It was the respondents' opinion that this may be why analysts have little opportunity to strongly advocate for changes in accounting standards as an organization (e.g., SAAJ).

The last question, Question 5, asked about the determinants of good or bad accounting standards in a very abstract manner. One respondent (Interviewee A) responded to a question on accounting standards that clearly distinguish between realized results supported by appropriate facts and unrealized results that remain in the expected dimension. Another respondent emphasized user-friendliness. Friendliness is multifaceted, and a wide range of factors were considered: friendliness for long-term earnings forecasts, accessibility to the aggregate market value of financial assets necessary for analyzing dividend reserves, and the duplicability of the estimation process adopted by preparers (Interviewee C).

Another interviewee (Interviewee G) noted that accounting standards that allow too much discretion for preparers in earnings management are undesirable. They also pointed out that current standards do not consistently distinguish between results from business investments—based on cash collected—and financial investments—based on market value changes. This inconsistency can make it hard to understand the true state of business activities. Another respondent (Interviewee F) mentioned that good accounting standards facilitate easy calculation of performance metrics like return on capital. In this context, it is also crucial to ensure full disclosure of market value information for financial instruments, maintain comparability over time and across sectors, provide sufficient supplemental information about the impact of different accounting procedures, and minimize the number of reconciliations needed when converting income into decision-making inputs.

6.3.3.2 Answers Regarding Accounting for Goodwill

Although some of the responses were already introduced in (1), we consolidate the responses regarding accounting for goodwill. The first question within this context asked whether the immediate write-off of goodwill was acceptable to analysts. In this question, we considered the case where goodwill is charged to capital surplus or retained earnings, rather than being expensed for the period; however, in some cases, respondents seemed to assume goodwill write-offs were charged to expenses. In the following, we consolidate only the responses obtained with write-offs charged to capital surplus or retained earnings.

One respondent was opposed to immediately amortizing goodwill charged to capital surplus, arguing that goodwill, especially purchased goodwill, holds value. Immediate write-offs would understate assets because the fair value was validated during the transaction with a third party (Interviewees C and F). Another respondent shared this perspective and added that analysts could still perform their analysis, if needed, based on hypothetical financial reports that assume goodwill is immediately charged to capital surplus, separate from GAAP income. However, not all mergers and acquisitions require adjustments assuming instant write-offs; some analyses are performed with capitalized goodwill. Consequently, one respondent believed that goodwill should not be uniformly and immediately charged to capital surplus across all companies (Interviewee G).

Next is Question 2, which asked for the definition of internally generated goodwill. For this question, only responses consistent with the interviewers' intent were summarized. Not surprisingly, this question directly reflected the perception gap between academics and practitioners. In other words, few responses were in the expected context. However, Interviewees C and F agreed that the difference between consideration and successful net asset market value based on identifiable assets and liabilities is considered goodwill. One respondent expressed doubt about using the consideration of acquisition as the basis for calculating goodwill. Based on practical experience, the person claimed that a non-negligible number of business combinations resulted in overpayment. If goodwill is positioned as a reflection of the expectation of excess returns, only the portion of the acquisition that has actual support should be considered as goodwill. (Interviewee G).

Question 3 asked whether the respondents found information value in the impairment loss itself or whether they focused on the future streams of income <u>after</u> impairment. The dominant response to this question was that although a large impairment loss may distort net income or loss in a particular year, its recognition is acceptable because the impairment loss contains information useful for the analysis (Interviewees A, C, F, and G). Although this was not necessarily the case, no responses were related to forecasting permanent income. This suggests that practitioners and academics cannot share the idea of conducting impairment assessments for ease of forecasting permanent income. In this sense, practitioners are concerned only with the value of the impairment loss.

Now, we consolidate the answers to Question 4. It asked whether the analyst adds back the expense caused by the amortization of goodwill, and if so, whether this is a reason to deny the systematic amortization of goodwill.

One respondent noted that add-backs are performed when valuing a company from a long-term perspective, since they rely on cash flow data for this analysis. Conversely, other respondents indicated that they approach valuation from a short-term perspective using income data, which they believe should include systematic goodwill amortization. Essentially, Interviewees A and C suggested that even when they do add back, it does not imply that amortization of goodwill is unnecessary.

Another respondent mentioned that expense add-backs would be performed because alternative performance measures (APM), such as the enterprise value on earnings before income tax, depreciation, and amortization multiple (EV/EBITDA), are commonly used in corporate analysis. They added that, for Japanese companies, this practice helps compare them with firms in other jurisdictions that follow IFRS (Interviewee F). This respondent explained that amortizing goodwill is essential to represent income as the excess of the invested capital, and the presence of expense add-backs does not argue against systematic goodwill amortization.

Question 5 asked if analysts factor in yet-unidentified impairments in their corporate valuations through information channels other than financial statements before the release of impairment loss. If this is true, the impairment loss information is not surprising for users. One respondent (Interviewee G) indicated that, in many cases, the prospect of poor performance has already been incorporated into evaluation without waiting for accounting impairment. However, the fact that impairment loss is fairly expected in advance does not suggest that impairment losses lack information value. Impairment losses not factored into the prior analysis may cause a decline in stock prices.

Another respondent characterized impairment as a process through which a company's management formally recognizes the failure of its investment (Interviewee A). Before the realization of impairment, the company's management does not communicate any indications of poor performance to analysts, even if such poor performance over a certain period is widely acknowledged among analysts. Conversely, once an impairment test is conducted, both the preparer and user share the presumption that the investment has failed, thereby enabling them to pose pertinent questions to the company. Considering these effects, the respondent argued that, regardless of whether poor performance was previously apparent, the announcement of impairment facilitates access to necessary information. Another respondent (Interviewee C) remarked that impairment is often linked to modifications in management plans, which may lead to revisions in long-term earnings forecasts based on the new information derived from these revised plans coupled with impairment. The two respondents highlighted herein agree on the value of the ancillary effects associated with impairment.

Another respondent (Interviewee F) responded that a large decline in income in the year in which an impairment loss is reported is not a problem and the impairment loss is incorporated into the earnings revisions for the current and subsequent years. This response was expected for Question 3. The respondent who answered that "the impairment loss itself is not the most important piece of information provided in relation to the impairment test, but it is used to revise the estimate for the stream of sustainable future incomes" did not answer Question 3 to the same effect. This may suggest that the specifications in Question 3 did not match the intent of the question.

6.3.3.3 Responses Regarding Accounting Education Received in the Past and How Accounting Information Is Used

Finally, we inquired about how accounting education has affected the interviewees' analytical styles. We combined the responses to Questions 1 and 2, as both focus on respondents' educational histories, including any additional education they received after joining the company. In contrast, Question 3 addresses the impact of their working environment on their decision-making style. Therefore, we summarized the responses to Question 3 separately from those to Questions 1 and 2.

In response to questions about their educational background, one respondent explained that they gained knowledge of accounting standards through their work, which was closely related to these standards, and they kept it updated regularly (Interviewee A). Another respondent is in a similar situation but specifically referenced the Financial Accounting Standards Foundation's Accounting Personnel Development Support Program as a training opportunity (Interviewee C). A third respondent also mentioned the same training opportunities as the first two. Besides internal ongoing training programs, this respondent also referenced support seminars organized by audit firms and the Japanese Institute of Certified Public Accountants, especially when major accounting standards are released (Interviewee F). Yet another respondent indicated that, apart from these channels, the individual might also receive support from their current company (Interviewee G).

The next question concerned the impact of working environment on analytical style. All the respondents answered that they were affected by the surrounding environment. The most interesting response was that the firms in which they worked encouraged their analysts to use a common database and analytical tools to ensure the uniformity of analyst reports (i.e., to provide reports with a certain level of quality assurance) (Interviewee C). On the other hand, some respondents (Interviewee G) pointed out that the tools provided by their employers are general purpose and not necessarily easy to use when analyzing financial institutions. In such cases, the respondents (Interviewees. G) responded that they developed their own analysis tools that considered the differences in the environment faced by individual companies and conducted their work based on these tools.

6.3.4 *Summary and Future Issues*

6.3.4.1 Findings from the Responses: Regarding the Perception Gap Between Financial Statement Users and Academics

As previously described, several useful findings were obtained during the second round of interviews. Finally, we summarize the most important findings regarding the gaps between practitioners.

Initially, when asked about the inputs to the decision-making model as an analyst, most respondents noted that the importance varies between income and cash flow information depending on whether the forecast is short-term or long-term. Some respondents also mentioned that a mix of both income and cash flow data is used for analyses in both timeframes.

In the discourse among standard setters concerning the systematic amortization with impairment or non-amortization (impairment-only) of goodwill, it is sometimes emphasized that either income or cash flows, but not both, serve as the primary input. A typical illustration is the assertion that "systematic amortization of goodwill is not beneficial because it is reintegrated in the user's analysis. Consequently, there should be no systematic amortization." Furthermore, second-round interviews revealed that analysts conducted analyses based on both income and cash flows. The observation that "there are instances when amortization expenses are added back, yet there are also situations requiring performance measures not based on adding back" was an exceedingly significant finding. This nuance helps contextualize the arguments presented by accounting standard setters.

Second, another important finding is that within a certain period, a company's profit margin (with some exceptions) reverts to the mean. This reversion is based on the argument for all goodwill, including internally generated goodwill. As long as this phenomenon is given, non-amortization (impairment-only) is unacceptable because it assumes that the value of goodwill is not impaired in principle. The question remains: why there is a certain support for the treatment of non-amortization (impairment-only), which would be inconsistent with the return to the mean. The return was consistent not only with academic research but also with the intuitive understanding of analysts involved in practice.

The next question: is whether the analytical tools and databases possessed by the industry in which analysts work affect their decision-making models. At this point, the dominant response was "yes," as predicted. The suggestion that firms are luring analysts toward homogenous analytical methods (perhaps to homogenize analyst expectations) was unexpected but also consistent with prior predictions.

Furthermore, regarding analysts' fundamental interest in the status of accounting standards, they appear indifferent to new releases, modifications, or eliminations of standards. In other words, they are tolerant of any accounting standards, exhibiting a "passive stance" toward standards setting. This attitude aligns with their overall response that there is no significant disagreement among analysts about the current state of accounting standards.

6.3.4.2 Findings from the Responses: Regarding Accounting for Goodwill

Comments on the addition of expenses regarding the amortization of goodwill have been discussed in the previous section. This section consolidates the responses to the other questions.

First, generally, technical questions about accounting for goodwill were not answered, aligning with the interviewers' intention, when compared to broader questions about the perception gap between academics and practitioners. Although this issue is important for aligning the accounting standards system with underlying concepts, analysts showed less interest in issues lacking direct practical benefits or those they have not encountered in practice. This aligns with common sense, and it will be crucial to foster mutual understanding through careful explanations beforehand when engaging with practitioners, especially on topics like alternative procedures such as immediate charge to capital surplus, to ensure well-aligned discussions and shared premises.

A similar issue arose in the question of whether impairment losses per se are important to the analysis, or whether they are important as a tool for making net income a better proxy for permanent income. The former perspective allows for frequent reports of impairment losses, whereas the latter aims to avoid distorting net income. Systematic amortization is considered a tool for avoiding unnecessary fluctuations in net income.

This issue is closely related to practitioner analyses. Therefore, this topic is of significant interest. Nevertheless, responses were skewed toward the usefulness of impairment loss, and advocates for enhancing the predictability of permanent income were scarce. This is probably because in actual stock value and corporate valuation, analysis is conducted based on models that indirectly reflect permanent income, rather than explicitly predicting permanent income. As mentioned in the previous sections, academics reduce the process of forecasting corporate value based on individual elements. If the reduced results are consistent with the thinking style of practitioners, no problem would arise. However, if there is a discrepancy, the discussion falls into the "irreconcilable differences" that the author faced in this study. It is one of the causes of the perception gap between academics and practitioners.

Finally, we summarize the responses regarding the extent to which analysts incorporate performance deterioration into their forecasts before impairment announcements. This question aligns with the issue of the timeliness of impairment losses. Several respondents noted that they see value in the indirect effects of reporting impairment losses. For instance, when management formally recognizes poor performance, it becomes easier for analysts to ask questions during briefings, based on the shared assumption of poor performance. Academics who are not involved in practice tend to overlook these causal paths. This may also contribute to the perception gap between practitioners and academics.

We obtained findings through second-round interviews, which were supported by objective evidence regarding the perception gap between practitioners and academics. However, the facts obtained remain unclear. It remains a challenge to collect further empirical evidence by mentioning the findings obtained from the interviews.

6.4 Summary and Remaining Issues

As mentioned earlier, the interview surveys discussed in this chapter were conducted to supplement the questionnaire survey described in Chap. 5. The main goal was to gain insights into why Japanese stakeholders—including users, preparers, and auditors—generally support the systematic amortization of goodwill, despite their different professional roles. Since the interviews used a semi-structured format, several new and unexpected findings emerged in areas beyond the original scope, although not all responses directly addressed the initial research question. The chapter concludes with a summary of the key findings of this study.

6.4.1 Findings from the Interviews Reported in Sect. 6.2

The interviews summarized in Sect. 6.2 yielded the following observations:

1. **Users' limited support for systematic amortization.**
   Overall, users, particularly financial analysts, expressed relatively little support for systematic amortization. This may be attributed to the flexibility with which analysts modify their valuation approaches, depending on the analytical models used within their organizations and the preferences of their clients.
2. **Absence of a well-known international argument.**
   The interviews did not reveal the argument often cited in international discussions: "regular amortization of purchased goodwill is added back in firm valuation and therefore has no informational value."
3. **Awareness of the cost implications of IFRS adoption.**
   Although IFRS adoption is motivated by the desire to avoid goodwill amortization, preparers recognized that IFRS adoption entails strict impairment testing requirements, which would impose additional costs.
4. **Preferences regarding discretion in determining the amortization period.**
   Under a systematic amortization regime, users preferred that management be granted discretion when setting the amortization period to gain access to internal information. In contrast, preparers favored methods to help justify the amortization period they had chosen.
5. **Ambiguity in the interpretation of abstract concepts.**
   Abstract notions frequently invoked in the goodwill debate—such as the "investment recovery period," the phrase *"too little, too late,"* and the "distinction between purchased and internally generated goodwill"—were used in

multiple senses. Market participants were unaware of the extent of the semantic ambiguity.

Among these, point (5) is particularly significant for this study. Although the interviews were conducted solely in Japan, where the respondents operate in a broadly similar institutional environment, the interpretations of the abstract concepts underlying both systematic amortization with impairment and impairment-only approach substantially varied. This suggests that in international discussions involving participants from diverse jurisdictions, the range of interpretations applied to such abstract concepts is likely to be even wider.

6.4.2 Findings from the Analyst-Focused Interviews Reported in Sect. 6.3

The interviews described in Sect. 6.3, which were limited to analysts, yielded the following findings.

1. **Use of both cash flows and earnings in valuation.**
   None of the respondents relied exclusively on cash flows or earnings as inputs for firm valuation; most referred to both. However, it remains unclear whether earnings are used directly as inputs in valuation models or indirectly as tools for forecasting cash flows.
2. **Mean reversion not linked to support for amortization.**
   Although most respondents agreed that firms' profitability reverts to the mean, this recognition does not necessarily translate into support for systematic amortization. Hence, there may be insufficient consensus between practitioners and academics concerning the interpretation of the abstract concept of "mean reversion in profitability."
3. **Limited focus on the predictive role of impairment.**
   When discussing the "enhancement of the usefulness of accounting information through impairment recognition," many respondents focused on the informational value of impairment losses, while very few referred to their potential contribution to forecasting *permanent income.*

These findings, similar to those in Sect. 6.2, suggest that the abstract concepts invoked to justify or oppose systematic amortization are subject to multiple interpretations. The questionnaire survey results reported in Chap. 5 imply the existence of such interpretive diversity; however, the interviews conducted in this chapter provide more concrete evidence that these concepts are understood in divergent ways. This is the principal contribution of this study.

6.4.3 Remaining Issues

Simultaneously, the inquiry into why Japanese market participants—including users, preparers, and auditors—continue to prefer systematic amortization remains unresolved, despite the two rounds of interviews conducted thus far. One plausible explanation is that these groups have all been exposed to a relatively homogeneous accounting education system. However, this hypothesis has yet to be empirically substantiated. A more detailed examination of this matter will be provided in Chap. 8.

Appendix 4

Questionnaire Used in the Interviews (Sect. 6.2)

On Accounting for Goodwill

Question 1

It has been suggested that, unlike surveys in European countries or the United States, a greater proportion of preparers in Japan support the systematic amortization of goodwill along with impairment testing. Why do you think this difference exists?

Question 2

The proportion of preparers supporting systematic amortization together with the impairment test (73.4%) appears to be more than 10% higher than that of analysts (62.3%). What factors may account for this discrepancy?

Question 3

What do you think accounts for the differences in responses between companies that use Japanese GAAP and those that follow other accounting standards? Conversely, why do many preparers who use US GAAP or IFRS continue to favor systematic amortization alongside impairment tests, even though these standards forbid systematic amortization?

Question 4

Although no statistically significant differences were identified, there were slight variations in responses between manufacturing and non-manufacturing firms as well as between companies that are members of Keidanren and those that are not. How would you interpret these differences? Alternatively, why do you think that these differences are minimal?

Question 5

Responses regarding the rationale for supporting systematic amortization together with impairment tests and for supporting impairment-only approaches were similar between preparers and users. Why do you think this is true? Is it reasonable to interpret this as users placing importance on matching and allocation?

Question 6

If you were to respond by yourself, which approach would you support: systematic amortization combined with an impairment test or an impairment-only approach? Please explain your reasoning in this regard.

On the Method and Duration of Goodwill Amortization

Question 7

When comparing the approach of setting an upper limit on the amortization period to applying a uniform amortization period, why do you think that the latter tends to result in shorter periods? Do you believe that responses based on uniform amortization periods reflect the actual practice more accurately?

Question 8

Among those who support setting an upper limit on the amortization period, the majority of preparers chose "within 20 years," whereas the majority of users chose "within 10 years." What could explain this discrepancy?

Question 9

Regarding the impairment test of goodwill, some argue that it is "too little, too late." What are your views of this critique?

Question 10

Some claim that while purchased goodwill appears not to be amortized, in reality, it is replaced over time by internally generated goodwill, thus effectively being consumed. What is your perspective of this perspective? In practice, it is difficult to distinguish between purchased and internally generated goodwill.

Question 11

In mergers and acquisitions, goodwill is recorded in correspondence with deferred tax liabilities (DTLs) that do not reflect true excess earnings capacity because of the recognition of identifiable intangible assets. In certain cases, this leads to an impaired charge. What are your opinions of this issue?

Finally, we would appreciate it if you could share any thoughts or observations regarding goodwill based on your experiences and day-to-day practice.

Questionnaire Used in the Interview Survey (Sect. 6.3)

The Perception Gap Between Financial Statement Users and Academics

1. Please let us know if there is anything in the discussions of academics that you feel is out of touch with the real world from the point of view of market participants.
2. For example, in academic circles, it is common to divide financial statement users into two categories: those who evaluate corporate value based on cash

flows and those who evaluate corporate value based on accounting information (this position is further divided into two categories: those who emphasize flow profit/loss information and those who emphasize stock information). (This position is further divided into one that emphasizes the flow of profit-and-loss information and one that emphasizes stock information.) What are your thoughts about this distinction? (How do you use accounting information to evaluate corporate value?).

3. Academics agree that "the competitive environment in which companies operate is generally harsh, and the superior knowledge and know-how possessed by certain companies alone will disappear in approximately five to seven years unless they are protected or restricted by the government or other entities." Does this view apply in practice? Also, do you think that from this fact we can conclude that "since purchased goodwill depreciates over time, regular amortization is desirable?"
4. It is sometimes said that standards must be developed with the "average investor" in mind. On the other hand, investors use accounting information in several ways, and it is impossible to aggregate opinions about the "average investor." Considering your experience, do you think that financial statement users' views on accounting standards vary so much that they are impossible to aggregate? Or is there some sort of "greatest common denominator" that emerges? Please let us know if there are any cases in which the users' views differ significantly.
5. At the risk of sounding very abstract, what is the measure of "good or bad accounting standards" for financial statement users?
6. Is financial statement users sharply opposed to accounting treatment (regular amortization vs. non-amortization, which may not be a good example)? If this happened in the past, and in what cases? If there is certain support for both positions, what form of lobbying would a user group like the Analysts' Society use?

Accounting for Goodwill

1. We consider immediate amortization of goodwill (surplus charge) as an conceivable option. Is this method feasible for financial statement users?
2. The difference between the use (utilization) value based on cash flows subjectively expected by corporate management and the value supported by some form of objective fact is called subjective goodwill. Different views exist on what constitutes subjective goodwill. Is this difference from the market value called subjective goodwill? Or is subjective goodwill different from book value? Are these issues not of primary interest in the first place?
3. There is an argument that "useful information can be expected in situations where impairment tests related to purchased goodwill are more likely to be triggered." On the other hand, there is an argument that "if the estimation of permanent income is the ultimate goal, it is better not to have impairment tests that cause year-to-year variations in income." Which view do you think is the most widely supported?

4. There has been some discussion in the field of standards development regarding the inclusion of amortization of goodwill in assessing corporate value. Are most of them adding goodwill? If so, what types of models do they use to evaluate corporate value? What is your opinion on this point?
5. Is it common for analysts to revise their earnings forecasts and corporate value estimates based on publicly disclosed goodwill impairment losses (information)? Thus, how are impairment losses used to revise expectations?

Accounting Education Received in the Past

1. What is your education/training history as an analyst? Particularly, please tell us about your training in financial accounting and how to use financial information to make investment decisions or account for purchased goodwill.
2. Accounting standards are constantly being updated. Sometimes, changes occur in the dimensions of the fundamental ideas that underpin the body of accounting standards. What recurrent educational opportunities related to accounting are available to financial statement users?
3. In a previous interview, you mentioned that the investment decision-making methods used by analysts are dependent on the systems and databases possessed by the companies they work for, and not on their personal beliefs. Do the analytical tools and databases of the company greatly constrain decision-making models followed by analysts and others?

Summary of the Interview Surveys Not Fully Reflected in the Main Text

Summary of the Interview Survey of Interviewee B

1. Career as an Analyst

   Interviewee B began working as an analyst in 1984 and is a seasoned professional with extensive experience. His early analysis work was primarily manual, with few databases or calculation software, and he used homemade programs to improve efficiency. He also noted that the creation of a database by hand and the improvement in operational efficiency resulted in the faster production of reports and improved accuracy.
2. Analytical Methods and Data Use

   Interviewee B followed a style of thorough fundamental and meticulous analysis of changes in financial statements. For example, he examined the impact of changes in accounting standards and earnings forecasts on a specific company through comparisons with other companies and industry averages. Inspired by the experience of making mistakes by relying too much on the information provided by the company under analysis, Interviewee B improved the reliability of his analysis results by utilizing data provided by the company, as well as statistics and industry interviews.

3. The Evolution of the Analyst Industry
   According to Interviewee B, in the early days, data collection and analysis were dominated by manual work; however, database development progressed only after the 1990s. He added to this prior analysis an approach that emphasized the speed and use of diverse information sources due to the influence of foreign securities firms.
4. Changes in Investor Relations (IR)
   Early in Interviewee B's career, companies did not provide information to analysts. Gradually, IR departments were developed and the information that analysts needed was provided. Despite this, Interviewee B continued to improve his methods of collecting information through direct communication with the top management.
5. Challenges Facing the Analyst's Industry and Its Future
   Interviewee B was worried that some analysts tend to accept companies' information at face value. He has emphasized the importance of independent analysis by examining data from companies and highlighted the significance of raw data. He also pointed out the need to find insights that cannot be gained from processed information alone.

Summary of the Interview Survey of Interviewee E

1. Goodwill valuation and analysis methods
   Interviewee E explained that goodwill is evaluated from two perspectives:
   (a) Safety on the Balance Sheet: The respondent stated that he would consider the impact of any impairment in goodwill, as the financial balance could deteriorate.
   (b) Estimation of cash flows: The respondents answered that goodwill impairment is also used as information that affects the profitability and future cash flows of related businesses.
2. Difference in perspective between equity analyst and credit analyst
   Interviewee E stated that credit analysts focus more on financial security and the ability to repay principal than equity analysts. He also noted that they often have a greater understanding of accounting than equity analysts in terms of reconciling a company's financial information in detail.
3. Opinion on the pros and cons of goodwill amortization
   Interviewee E stated that it is important to review the capitalization of goodwill from time to time because of the need to focus on balance sheet safety.
4. Influence of education and background
   Interviewee E stated that an analyst's educational background and professional experience impact their interpretation of accounting information and their analytical approach. Additionally, Interviewee E observed that credit analysts generally provide more accurate analyses compared to equity analysts, owing to greater access to internal corporate data and detailed information.

5. Use of information on goodwill
   Interviewee E responded that impairment loss information rarely comes as a surprise, and, in most cases, he anticipates a situation in advance in which performance deteriorates. However, he also stated that if the amount of impairment is unexpected, the impairment loss information could affect the rating.

Basic Interviewee Data (Table 6.1)

Statement on AI Usage During the preparation of this manuscript, the authors used AI-assisted tools such as DeepL and ChatGPT to improve the English expression and clarity of the manuscript. The authors thoroughly reviewed and approved the final version and take full responsibility for the content.

References

Accounting Standards Board of Japan (ASBJ). (2020). Comments on the IASB Discussion Paper "Business Combinations—Disclosures, Goodwill and Impairment." December 28. Retrieved from https://www.asb.or.jp/jp/wp-content/uploads/20201228.pdf, ASBJ

Asami, Yuko, Toshitake Miyauchi, Tomoaki Yamashita, and Masaki Yoneyama (2021). "A Comprehensive Study on Accounting for Goodwill," Gakushuin University Research Institute for Economics and Management (GEM) Discussion Paper Series 21-1, 2021 (https://www.gakushuin.ac.jp/univ/eco/gem/works/research/discuss/No21_1.pdf)

Asami, Yuko, Toshitake Miyauchi, Tomoaki Yamashita, and Masaki Yoneyama (2022). "Accounting for Goodwill in Business Combinations – Empirical Analysis and Questionnaire Survey," Gakushuin University Research Institute for Economics and Management (GEM) Discussion Paper Series 22-1, 2022 (https://www.gakushuin.ac.jp/univ/eco/gem/works/research/discuss/No22_1.pdf)

Financial Services Agency of Japan (FSA). (2015). IFRS Adoption Report. April. Retrieved from https://www.fsa.go.jp/singi/singi_kigyou/siryou/kaikei/20150415/01.pdf, FSA

Fukui, Yoshitaka and Mioko Takahashi (2022). "Mean reversion: Statistical inevitability without economic substance," Journal of Business Accounting, 75 (1), 97-103.

Lundholm, Russell and Richard Sloan. 2019. *Equity Valuation and Analysis with e-Val,* Fifth Edition. Seattle, WA, USA, Kindle Direct Publishing.

Nakano, Takayuki (Ed.). (2020). Insights into IFRS Adoption: Analysis of Mandatory and Voluntary Adoption in Major Countries and Japan, Tokyo, Japan, Dobunkan Publishing.

Obinata, Takashi. (2012). Consistency analysis and empirical research. In T. Obinata (Ed.), Foundations of Accounting Standards Research (Ch. 20), Tokyo, Japan, Chuo Keizai-sha.

Obinata, Takashi (2013). Profitability Persistence and Mean-Reversion, Tokyo, Japan, Chuo Keizai-sha, Inc.

Palepu, Krishna G., et al. (2013). Business *Analysis and Valuation,* Fifth Edition, International Edition, Mason, OH, USA, South-Western.

Penman, Stephen H. (2013). Financial *Statement Analysis and Security Valuation,* Fifth Edition. New York City, NY, USA, McGraw-Hill.

Saito, Shizuki (2017). Amortization and impairment of goodwill: The confusion of business combination accounting standards. Kaikei (Accounting), 69(1), 13–20.

Saito, Shizuki and Yoshitaka Fukui (2022a). "Accounting Recognition and Economic Analysis of Goodwill (1)", Kaikei, 201 (3), 2022–03.

Saito, Shizuki and Yoshitaka Fukui (2022b). "Accounting Recognition and Economic Analysis of Goodwill (2)", Kaikei, 201 (4), 2022–04.

Tokuga, Yoshihiro, Toshitake Miyauchi, and Tomoaki Yamashita. (2018). "Survey on Accounting for Goodwill," Discussion Paper Series No. J-18-004, Graduate School of Economics, Kyoto University, 2018 (https://www.econ.kyoto-u.ac.jp/~tokuga/wp-content/uploads/2019/05/No.J-18-004.pdf)

Tokuga, Yoshihiro, Toshitake Miyauchi, Tomoaki Yamashita. (2019). Survey on the Accounting Treatment of Goodwill (Kyoto University Graduate School of Economics Discussion Paper Series No. J-18-004, 2nd edition). April 5.

Tokuga, Yoshihiro, Toshitake Miyauchi, Tomoaki Yamashita, Masaki Yoneyama, Yuko Asami. (2021). "A Survey on Accounting for Goodwill and Its Analysis – Characteristics and Comparison of Responses of Preparers, Users and Auditors," Graduate School of Economics, Kyoto University, Discussion Paper Series No. J-21-002, 2021 (https://www.econ.kyoto-u.ac.jp/dp/papers/j-21-002.pdf)

Yamauchi, Aki (2010). *Accounting for Goodwill.* Tokyo, Japan, Chuo Keizai-sha.

Yoneyama, Masaki, Yoshihiro Tokuga, and Yuko Asami. (2021). "Interviews on Accounting for Goodwill – Exploring the Background to the Results of Questionnaire Survey Responses-," Gakushuin University, Research Institute for Economics and Management (GEM) Discussion Paper Series 20-1, 2021 (https://www.gakushuin.ac.jp/univ/eco/gem/works/research/discuss/No20_1_20210811.pdf)

Yoneyama, Masaki, Yoshihiro Tokuga, Yuko Asami, Toshitake Miyauchi, Tomoaki Yamashita (2025). "Exploring Differences in Perceptions on Accounting for Goodwill — What Creates the Perception Gap Between Analysts and Academics?-," Gakushuin University, Research Institute for Economics and Management (GEM) Discussion Paper Series 24-2, 2025 (https://www.gakushuin.ac.jp/univ/eco/gem/works/research/discuss/20250105_02.pdf)

Chapter 7
Empirical Studies on the 'Too Little, Too Late' Issue

Toshitake Miyauchi and Tomoaki Yamashita

7.1 Purpose and Organization of this Chapter

When standard setters establish, revise, or abolish accounting standards, they usually gather market participants' opinions through the publication of discussion papers, exposure drafts, or draft accounting standards. However, their methods are not necessarily based on systematic academic approaches. We conducted a questionnaire survey and interviews with preparers, users, and auditors to address standard-setting issues related to subsequent accounting for acquired goodwill from an academic perspective. From a bird's-eye view, we identified the perceptions of major market participants—preparers, users, and auditors—that could influence accounting standard setting.

On the one hand, the "too little, too late" issue (i.e., the impairment of goodwill is not recognized in a timely manner, or even if recognized, the amount of impairment loss recognized is too small) has been identified with respect to subsequent accounting for acquired goodwill. This issue has also been noted previously. However, according to the results obtained from our interviews (Chap. 6), some

This chapter is based on the discussion paper by Miyauchi and Yamashita (Miyauchi and Yamashita 2022). We would like to thank Masayoshi Suzuki (Gakushuin University at that time), Chihiro Kato (Gakushuin University at that time), Hidetoshi Kyogoku (Gakushuin University at that time), and Takuto Kawakami (Gakushuin University) for their great cooperation in collecting the data used in this study.

T. Miyauchi (✉)
Faculty of Management, Otemon Gakuin University, Osaka, Japan
e-mail: tomiyauc@otemon.ac.jp

T. Yamashita
Department of Business Administration, Faculty of Economics, Fukui Prefectural University, Fukui, Japan

Y. Tokuga, M. Yoneyama (eds.), *Controversies Over Accounting for Goodwill*, Contributions to Finance and Accounting,
https://doi.org/10.1007/978-981-92-0156-3_7

preparers suggested that they had applied impairment accounting in accordance with their accounting standards and recognized impairment losses in a timely manner. That is, the "too little, too late" issue has not occurred in their opinion.[1]

On the other hand, according to the interview data, one financial analyst believed that users who made at least a certain effort to analyze financial statements were aware of the symptoms of deteriorating performance, that is, the prospect that an impairment loss will eventually be recognized prior to the actual recognition of impairment losses. In other words, the results of the user interviews suggest that users may have some insight into the occurrence of impairment losses before a firm announce goodwill impairment. If this view is correct, the potential impairment of goodwill is factored into the stock price, and the announcement of a goodwill impairment loss provides only confirmatory information.

Based on the above conflicting views of preparers and users, we examine whether the "too little, too late" issue is actually occurring, seeking to answer the following question: What are the empirical facts of this issue? Specifically, we adopt a fact-finding perspective and conduct several event studies on goodwill impairment announcements in this chapter. The importance of comparing the empirical facts obtained from event studies based on the perceptions of major stakeholders in the standard-setting process, namely preparers, users, and auditors, must be clarified. Through this examination, it is possible to clarify "whether the perceptions of these stakeholders are consistent with the empirical facts, whether they are not based on empirical facts, or whether some of the perceptions are consistent with the empirical facts but others are inconsistent," thereby revealing part of the reason why the issue related to subsequent accounting for goodwill has become more complex.

The remainder of this chapter is organized as follows. In Sect. 7.2, we present details of a short-term event study conducted to test whether the goodwill impairment losses announced by firms contain information content previously unknown to market participants. In Sect. 7.3, we describe a long-term event study conducted to examine the likelihood of goodwill impairment losses being priced into stock prices. In Sect. 7.4, we present an analysis performed using the stock trading volume in response to the announcement of goodwill impairment loss to test whether there is information content that cannot be detected simply by examining the stock price reaction when the stock price does not move or when the price movement is small. Finally, we conclude the chapter in Sect. 7.5.

Notably, previous studies have reported that impairment losses that are recognized and announced late after the impairment of goodwill do not contain information useful for investment decision-making and have undetectable/weak stock price explanatory power (Zang 2008; Li et al. 2011; Bens et al. 2011; Li and Sloan 2017). In this sense, the event studies described in Sects. 7.2 and 7.4, which analyze

[1] Strictly speaking, this view assumes timeliness "to the extent permitted by accounting standards" and does not deny the possibility that the recognition of impairment may be delayed beyond the timing expected by users due to the existence of shielding effects or the time required to determine whether the decline in value is irreversible in the recognition of impairment. The Board's opinion assumes timeliness "to the extent permitted by accounting standards."

short-term stock price and volume reactions, test the appropriateness of the perception of "timely impairment losses" on the part of preparers, assuming the semi-strong market efficiency. Meanwhile, the event study analyzing long-term stock price reactions, described in Sect. 7.3, tests the appropriateness of users' perceptions with regard to their awareness that impairment losses will eventually be recognized prior to the recognition of goodwill impairment losses (Bartov et al. 1998; Hirschey and Richardson 2002, 2003).

7.2 Event Study of Short-term Returns

7.2.1 Introduction

In this section, we present a short-window event study of goodwill impairment loss pronouncements. The findings of the event study conducted on a sample of firms in countries and jurisdictions that have adopted U.S. GAAP or IFRS are as follows: (1) The amount of goodwill impairment losses after the transition to impairment-only accounting standards is not detected to be significantly correlated with stock returns (Jarva 2014), and (2) In the analysis, the amount of goodwill impairment loss is distinguished between the portion that has already been factored into the stock price (expected impairment loss) and the portion that has not been factored in the stock price (unexpected impairment loss), it was reported that the unexpected impairment loss of goodwill in the period of systematic amortization has significant negative explanatory power for abnormal returns, but that the unexpected impairment loss of goodwill in the period after the transition to the impairment-only approach does not generate abnormal returns around the event date, or has no or weak explanatory power for abnormal returns (Zang 2008; Li et al. 2011; Bens et al. 2011).[2]

Shimada (2010) conducted a short-term event study of goodwill impairment with Japanese firms, using data reported in Nikkei Telecom and other online news databases from April 2005 to the end of August 2009, and found that the CAR[−1, +1] on the event date was significantly negative. Kimura (2017) also conducted an event study on intangible asset impairment losses (including goodwill impairment losses) on financial closing dates from 2007 to 2016 and found a negative stock price effect for intangible asset impairment losses (including goodwill impairment losses).

However, in terms of an event study that uses a sample of Japanese firms, there is no analysis of the period from after April 2005 to the end of August 2009, which is the period covered by Shimada (2010). There is also no study that compares the information content of impairment losses between the "systematic amortization with impairment" approach (Japanese GAAP) and the "impairment-only (non-amortization)" approach (U.S. GAAP or IFRS).

---

[2] For a review of empirical findings from other countries rather than Japan, please refer to Chap. 4

7.2.2 Research Design

In this section, we address a Ball and Brown (1968)-type short-window event study to analyze the information content of goodwill impairment losses for firms applying Japanese GAAP that require systematic amortization with impairment approach and firms applying IFRS that require the impairment-only approach. Abnormal returns are calculated using the following methodology:

$$AR_{i,t} = \{(P_{i,t} - P_{i,t-1}) / P_{i,t-1}\} - \{(M_t - M_{t-1}) / M_{t-1}\} \quad (7.1)$$

where,

$AR_{i,t}$: Abnormal return of firm i at time t
$P_{i,t}$: Daily closing price of firm i's stock at time t
M_t: Theoretical stock price at time t estimated from the market model
t: from −10 to +10

Abnormal return is obtained by subtracting the normal return corresponding to the period from the actual return of firm i at time t. The theoretical stock price (M_t) used to calculate the normal return follows Li et al. (2011), who demonstrate the announcement effect of goodwill impairment losses, and Landsman et al. (2012), who analyzed the announcement effect of mandatory IFRS adoption. We constructed a model (market model) to estimate actual returns using TOPIX returns, using return data for the period from −20 to −150 days, excluding the event period, from the perspective of the event date; we added $t = -10$ to $t = +10$, and estimated by substituting the actual TOPIX returns from $t = -10$ to $t = +10$ into the estimation model.

$$AR_t = \frac{1}{N} \times \sum_{i=1}^{N} AR_{i,t} \quad (7.2)$$

$$CAR_t[t, t+1] = \sum_{t=t}^{t+1} AR_t \quad (7.3)$$

The abnormal return at time t in the sample (AR_t) is obtained as the average of the total abnormal returns of the firms comprising the sample at time t divided by the number of sample firms, as shown in eq. (7.2), where N is the number of firms in the sample. *CAR* is obtained as the cumulative value of AR_t, which is also obtained in eq. (7.2), for 2 days at time t and $t + 1$. To calculate the abnormal returns described in this section, firms' stock prices and TOPIX data were obtained from the Toyo Keizai Stock Price CD-ROM, 2014 and 2021 editions.

To analyze the information content included in the goodwill impairment losses announced by the sample using Japanese GAAP (hereafter, the J-GAAP sample) and the sample using IFRS (hereafter, the IFRS sample) from a fact-finding perspective, we set the following null hypothesis. We determine whether the null hypothesis can be rejected by analyzing whether a statistically significant negative AR and CAR[0, +1] are observed on the event date.

H_0: At the time of the goodwill impairment announcement, there is no difference between the actual return on the firm's stock and the normal return based on the theoretical stock price.

In the event study, a mean test (t-test) is performed on the abnormal stock return, which is the difference between the actual stock return and the theoretical stock return. Owing to the small sample size, a Wilcoxon signed-rank test is also conducted as a nonparametric test that does not assume that the distribution follows a normal distribution.

7.2.3 Sample Selection Procedures and Data

In conducting the event study in this report, the sample for the analysis is the one in which goodwill impairment losses were reported in the Nihon Keizai Shimbun, rather than using the goodwill impairment loss data in the archival data,[3] in order to analyze the information content of goodwill impairment losses only.

The sample used in this study was obtained as follows (see Table 7.1). First, using Nikkei NEEDS, we selected Japanese listed firms with an impairment loss-to-sales ratio of more than 0.5% for the period from the fiscal year ending March 2007 to the fiscal year ending March 2019.[4] The reason for selecting this period was to cover the period when the accounting standard for the impairment of fixed assets was implemented in Japan and to exclude the impact of the pandemic caused by the new coronavirus (COVID-19).[5] Since information on impairment losses on goodwill alone is not available from the database, we use the total amount of impairment losses, including goodwill, to calculate the ratio of impairment losses to sales. We also include firms with an impairment loss-to-sales ratio greater than 0.5% in our analysis. As in previous studies, this is done to reduce the time and effort required

Table 7.1 Sample selection

Sample selection conditions	Number of observations (cases)
Goodwill is recorded as an asset	23,375
Of the above, goodwill is recognized as an asset and impairment losses are recognized	14,252
Of the above, the amount of impairment losses is more than 0.5% of net sales	2379
Of the above, goodwill impairment is reported in a Nikkei newspaper article	64

[3] Nikkei NEEDS does not provide data concerning the amount of impairment losses solely related to goodwill.

[4] In this study, we require that firms be listed at the time the data are obtained to calculate this ratio.

[5] However, to mitigate the impact of the year in which the mandatory application of the standard began (fiscal year ended March 31, 2006), we set 2007 as the starting year of the sample period.

to collect the data manually by excluding impairments that are too insignificant in advance.

Then, for the firms extracted by the method described above, we conducted a newspaper article search using Nikkei Telecom (search words: firm name and "impairment") and identified articles excluding commentary articles on specific firms or industries that mentioned goodwill impairment losses including one-time amortization of goodwill.[6] In cases where there were multiple articles, those with the earliest coverage were used. In cases where it was difficult to determine whether to include the article in the sample, we obtained timely disclosure materials from Kaiji Net (an online database of Japanese firms' annual reports and other disclosure documents), and checked their contents.

From the newspaper articles collected in this manner, we collected the date of publication of the article and the amount of goodwill impairment loss. In this study, the publication date of the article is taken as the announcement date ($t = 0$) regarding the goodwill impairment loss. However, if the publication date of the article was not a transaction date, the announcement date was taken immediately following the transaction date. In many cases, newspaper articles do not mention the amount of goodwill impairment loss. Therefore, if the amount can be collected from a newspaper article, we collect that amount. If the amount is not available from the newspaper article, we collect information on the amount of goodwill impairment loss from notes in the annual securities report for the relevant year. The sample size obtained using this procedure is 64.[7] Of these, 59 are firms applying Japanese GAAP that required a systematic amortization with impairment approach and 5 are firms applying IFRS that required the impairment-only approach.

7.2.4 Analysis Results

Figures 7.1 and 7.2 show the AR and CAR[0, +1] calculated for the entire sample. The charts show that on the event date ($t = 0$), the AR was approximately −1.6% and the CAR[0, +1] was approximately −2.9%, indicating negative abnormal returns.

Tables 7.2 and 7.3 present the results of the significance tests for the AR and CAR[0, +1] at each time point. Figure 7.3 shows that a negative response

[6] This lump-sum amortization of goodwill is related to para. 32 in the "Practical Guidelines for Capital Consolidation Procedures in Consolidated Financial Statements" (*Renketsu Zaimu Shōhyō ni okeru Shihon Renketsu Tetsuzuki ni kansuru Jitsumu Shishin*). According to this provision, when an entity writes down the shares of a subsidiary in its parent-only financial statements, it is required to additionally amortize the goodwill in its consolidated financial statements.

[7] However, the sample size considered for the analysis described in Sect. 7.2 was 63 (58 firms applying Japanese GAAP and 5 firms applying IFRS). This is because there was one sample for which stock prices over a long period of time could not be collected from Toyo Keizai Stock Price CD-ROM used by the author in collecting stock price data. In the analyses described from Sect. 7.3 onward, the Nikkei daily stock return data were used instead of the Toyo Keizai Stock Price CD-ROM mentioned above.

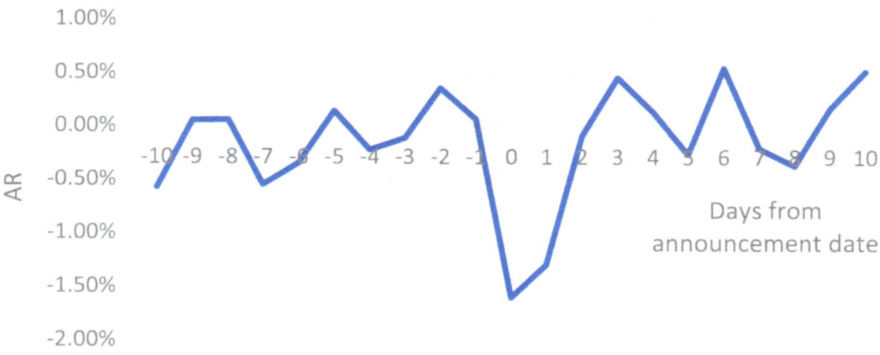

Fig. 7.1 Trends in abnormal return (entire sample)

Fig. 7.2 Cumulative abnormal return (entire sample)

(significant at the 1% level) was detected for the difference between the mean and median of AR at $t = 0$ when the goodwill impairment loss was announced and at $t = +1$ the day after the goodwill impairment loss was announced, respectively.

Table 7.4 reveals that there were statistically significant negative responses at the $t = -1$ time point, the $t = 0$ time point, and the $t = +1$ time point for the 2-day cumulative abnormal return CAR[0, +1]. In particular, the response at the $t = 0$ time point was −2.903% (mean) and −2.382% (median), which is stronger than at the previous and following time points.[8]

[8] Since timely disclosure information may disclose information on the recording of goodwill impairment losses the day before the newspaper report, we also conducted an analysis on CAR[−1, +1]. As a result, for the t-test, a significant negative CAAR is detected at −2.842% (1% level) at day 0 and −2.999% (1% level) at day +1 from the event date. As for the Wilcoxon signed-rank test, a significant negative CMAR was found at −0.879% (5% level) at day −1, −1.677% (1% level) at day 0, −1.938% (1% level) at day +1, and −1.349% (5% level) at day +2 from the event date. These

Table 7.2 Significance of abnormal return (entire sample)

Time	AAR (%)	t-value	p-value	MAR (%)	Wilcoxon-Z	p-value
−10	−0.577	−1.223	0.226	0.267	0.062	0.951
−9	0.050	0.175	0.861	−0.006	−0.288	0.774
−8	0.055	0.210	0.835	0.192	0.897	0.370
−7	−0.551	−1.487	0.142	−0.127	−0.787	0.431
−6	−0.345	−1.001	0.321	0.200	−0.267	0.789
−5	0.141	0.435	0.665	0.018	0.116	0.907
−4	−0.225	−0.574	0.568	−0.128	−1.212	0.226
−3	−0.114	−0.411	0.683	−0.196	−1.164	0.244
−2	0.353	0.722	0.473	−0.108	−0.466	0.642
−1	0.061	0.146	0.884	−0.252	−0.075	0.940
0	−1.603**	−2.913	0.005	−0.961**	−2.595	0.009
+1	−1.300**	−2.990	0.004	−0.721**	−3.019	0.003
+2	−0.096	−0.297	0.768	0.041	−0.205	0.837
+3	0.456	1.031	0.306	−0.102	−0.438	0.661
+4	0.134	0.311	0.757	−0.215	−0.329	0.742
+5	−0.262	−1.239	0.220	−0.151	−1.547	0.122
+6	0.548	1.665	0.101	0.069	0.746	0.456
+7	−0.206	−0.813	0.419	−0.263	−0.883	0.377
+8	−0.368	−1.666	0.101	−0.378**	−1.972	0.049
+9	0.164	0.431	0.668	−0.096	0.021	0.984
+10	0.519*	1.700	0.094	0.178	1.308	0.191

Notes: Time represents the number of days before and after the event, with the event date as 0. AAR represents the average abnormal return at each time point, and MAR represents the median abnormal return at each time point. t-value and Wilcoxon-Z represent the test statistics for the t-test and Wilcoxon signed-rank test, respectively. p-value means the significant probability for t-test or Wilcoxon signed-rank test. ***, **, and * indicate significance levels of 1%, 5%, and 10%, respectively (two-tailed test)

Figures 7.3 and 7.4 show the AR and CAR[0, +1] calculated for the J-GAAP sample. The figures show that on the event date ($t = 0$), AR and CAR[0, +1] indicate abnormal returns of approximately −1.4% and −2.7%, respectively.

Tables 7.4 and 7.5 present the results of the significance tests for the AR and CAR[0, +1] for the J-GAAP sample at each time point. Table 7.4 shows the results for the mean and median AR at $t = 0$ when the goodwill impairment loss was announced and at $t = +1$ the day after the goodwill impairment loss was announced, respectively, with a negative response (significant at the 5% level) detected.

Table 7.5 shows that there were statistically significant negative responses at the $t = -1$, $t = 0$, and $t = +1$ time points for the 2-day cumulative abnormal return CAR[0, +1] for the sample applying Japanese GAAP. In particular, the response at

are similar to the results for CAR[0, +1], indicating a significant negative stock price reaction around the event date.

Table 7.3 Significance of cumulative abnormal return [0, +1] (entire sample)

Time	CAAR (%)	t-value	p-value	CMAR (%)	Wilcoxon-Z	p-value
−10	−0.527	−0.907	0.368	0.135	0.096	0.924
−9	0.105	0.336	0.738	0.068	0.459	0.646
−8	−0.496	−0.974	0.334	0.162	0.418	0.676
−7	−0.897	−1.609	0.113	0.033	−0.555	0.579
−6	−0.204	−0.500	0.619	−0.063	−0.589	0.556
−5	−0.084	−0.152	0.879	−0.431	−1.492	0.136
−4	−0.339	−0.571	0.570	−0.402**	−2.074	0.038
−3	0.238	0.352	0.726	−0.304	−1.171	0.242
−2	0.414	0.844	0.402	−0.127	0.555	0.579
−1	−1.542**	−2.349	0.022	−0.997**	−2.697	0.007
0	−2.903***	−4.204	0.000	−2.382***	−3.943	0.000
+1	−1.396**	−2.224	0.030	−0.952**	−2.615	0.009
+2	0.360	0.622	0.536	−0.232	−0.644	0.520
+3	0.590	0.806	0.423	−0.566	−0.685	0.494
+4	−0.128	−0.310	0.758	−0.341	−0.698	0.485
+5	0.287	0.695	0.490	0.175	0.199	0.843
+6	0.343	0.749	0.457	−0.302	−0.363	0.717
+7	−0.573	−1.567	0.122	−0.196	−1.349	0.177
+8	−0.203	−0.444	0.659	−0.086	−0.767	0.443
+9	0.684	1.211	0.230	0.147	0.719	0.472
+10	0.874	1.549	0.126	0.352	1.335	0.182

Notes: Time represents the number of days before and after the event, with the event date as 0. CAAR represents the cumulative average abnormal return at two time points, t and t + 1, and CMAR represents the median of the cumulative average abnormal return. t-value and Wilcoxon-Z represent the test statistics for the t-test and Wilcoxon signed-rank test, respectively. p-value means the significant probability for t-test or Wilcoxon signed-rank test. ***, **, and * indicate significance levels of 1%, 5%, and 10%, respectively (two-tailed test)

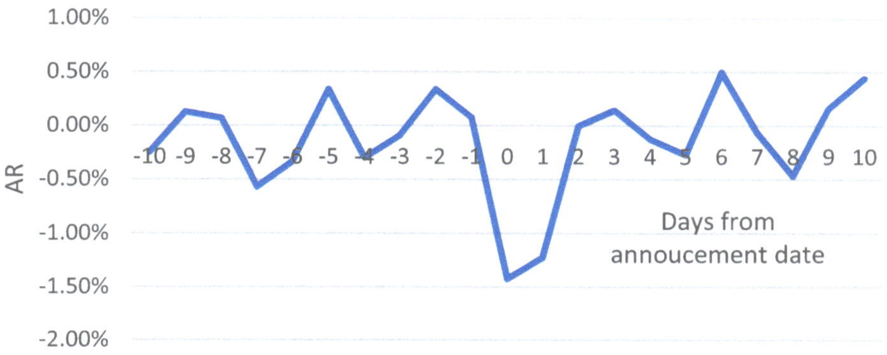

Fig. 7.3 Trends in abnormal return (J-GAAP sample)

Table 7.4 Significance of abnormal return (J-GAAP sample)

Time	AAR (%)	t-value	p-value	MAR (%)	Wilcoxon-Z	p-value
–10	–0.251	–0.639	0.525	0.297	0.499	0.618
–9	0.126	0.418	0.678	0.003	–0.027	0.978
–8	0.067	0.237	0.813	0.176	0.894	0.371
–7	–0.574	–1.430	0.158	–0.059	–0.685	0.493
–6	–0.335	–0.904	0.370	0.262	–0.182	0.856
–5	0.340	1.045	0.300	0.083	0.670	0.503
–4	–0.301	–0.714	0.478	–0.152	–1.490	0.136
–3	–0.096	–0.344	0.732	–0.215	–1.421	0.155
–2	0.339	0.650	0.518	–0.104	–0.376	0.707
–1	0.075	0.165	0.869	–0.141	0.012	0.991
0	–1.427**	–2.470	0.017	–0.754**	–2.125	0.034
+1	–1.227**	–2.621	0.011	–0.681**	–2.536	0.011
+2	–0.004	–0.013	0.990	0.070	0.135	0.892
+3	0.145	0.429	0.669	–0.186	–0.708	0.479
+4	–0.126	–0.321	0.749	–0.243	–0.639	0.523
+5	–0.273	–1.233	0.223	–0.188*	–1.684	0.092
+6	0.501	1.440	0.155	0.057	0.538	0.591
+7	–0.067	–0.259	0.797	–0.215	–0.329	0.742
+8	–0.470**	–2.029	0.047	–0.456**	–2.396	0.017
+9	0.158	0.382	0.704	–0.151	–0.081	0.935
+10	0.443	1.371	0.176	0.142	0.956	0.339

Notes: Time represents the number of days before and after the event, with the event date as 0. AAR represents the average abnormal return at each time point, and MAR represents the median abnormal return at each time point. t-value and Wilcoxon-Z represent the test statistics for the t-test and Wilcoxon signed-rank test, respectively. p-value means the significant probability for t-test or Wilcoxon signed-rank test. ***, **, and * indicate significance levels of 1%, 5%, and 10%, respectively (two-tailed test)

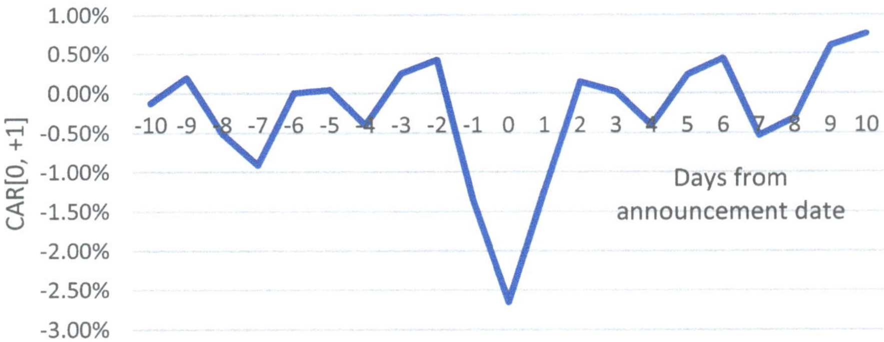

Fig. 7.4 Cumulative abnormal return (J-GAAP sample)

Table 7.5 Significance of cumulative abnormal return [0, +1] (J-GAAP sample)

Time	CAAR (%)	t-value	p-value	CMAR (%)	Wilcoxon-Z	p-value
−10	−0.125	−0.252	0.802	0.237	0.523	0.601
−9	0.193	0.582	0.563	0.106	0.770	0.441
−8	−0.507	−0.920	0.362	0.173	0.561	0.575
−7	−0.909	−1.502	0.139	0.152	−0.314	0.754
−6	0.004	0.011	0.991	0.037	−0.174	0.862
−5	0.038	0.065	0.949	−0.427	−1.188	0.235
−4	−0.397	−0.619	0.538	−0.558**	−2.381	0.017
−3	0.243	0.331	0.742	−0.267	−1.227	0.220
−2	0.414	0.788	0.434	−0.054	0.561	0.575
−1	−1.352*	−1.948	0.056	−0.95**	−2.234	0.026
0	−2.654***	−3.642	0.001	−1.624***	−3.426	0.001
+1	−1.231*	−1.827	0.073	−0.814**	−2.032	0.042
+2	0.140	0.261	0.795	−0.253	−0.639	0.523
+3	0.019	0.036	0.971	−0.720	−0.987	0.324
+4	−0.399	−1.027	0.309	−0.479	−1.150	0.250
+5	0.227	0.512	0.611	0.093	−0.159	0.874
+6	0.434	0.881	0.382	−0.330	−0.112	0.911
+7	−0.537	−1.360	0.179	−0.180	−1.065	0.287
+8	−0.312	−0.631	0.531	−0.292	−1.165	0.244
+9	0.601	0.988	0.328	−0.056	0.275	0.783
+10	0.753	1.248	0.217	0.253	0.879	0.380

Notes: Time represents the number of days before and after the event, with the event date as 0. CAAR represents the cumulative average abnormal return at two time points, t and t + 1, and CMAR represents the median of the cumulative average abnormal return. t-value and Wilcoxon-Z represent the test statistics for the t-test and Wilcoxon signed-rank test, respectively. p-value means the significant probability for t-test or Wilcoxon signed-rank test. ***, **, and * indicate significance levels of 1%, 5%, and 10%, respectively (two-tailed test)

the $t = 0$ time point has a value of −2.654% (mean) and −1.624% (median) at the 1% significance level.[9]

The result (rejecting the null hypothesis) that goodwill impairment losses under Japanese GAAP (systematic amortization with impairment) generate negative abnormal returns is consistent with the findings of Shimada (2010), Li et al. (2011), and Bens et al. (2011), which show that even after amortizing acquired goodwill, the goodwill impairment losses have informational value. The results also support the factual perception of users that the announcement of goodwill impairment losses contains only confirmatory information.

[9] Similar to the entire sample, the analysis of CAR[−1, +1] for the J-GAAP sample shows that for the t-test, a significant negative CAAR of −2.579% (1% level) at day 0 and day −2.659% (1% level) at day +1 from the event date is detected. For the Wilcoxon signed-rank test, a significant negative CMAR was found at −0.844% (10% level) at day −1, −1.591% (1% level) at day 0, −1.763% (1% level) at day +1, and −1.763% (1% level) at day +1, −1.160% (5% level) at day +2 from the event date. These are consistent with the results for CAR[0, +1].

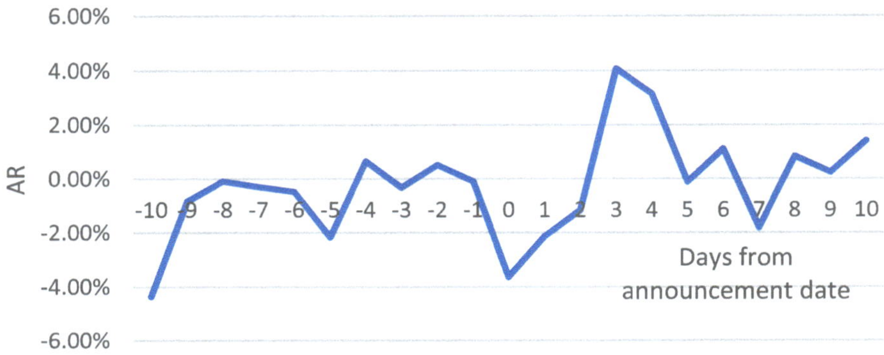

Fig. 7.5 Abnormal return (IFRS sample)

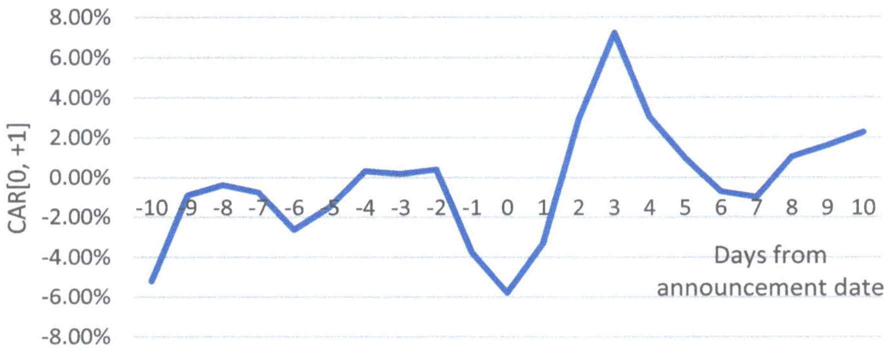

Fig. 7.6 Cumulative abnormal return (IFRS sample)

Figures 7.5 and 7.6 show the evolution of AR and CAR[0, +1] for the IFRS sample. These figures show the occurrence of negative abnormal returns around the event date for the IFRS sample. Table 7.6 presents the results of the significance tests at each time point for the ARs in the IFRS sample. At $t = 0$ when goodwill impairment losses are announced, the mean and median of the ARs are −3.649% and −1.868%, respectively, all of which are observed to be statistically significant at the 10% and 5% levels. The mean and median of the ARs are −2.142% and −2.102%, respectively, at $t = +1$ and are significant at the 5% level.

Table 7.7 presents the results of the significance tests at each time point for the CAR[0, +1] of the IFRS sample. At $t = 0$, the mean and median of the cumulative abnormal returns are −5.791% and −5.200%, respectively, and are significant at the 5% level. At $t = +1$, the cumulative abnormal returns are −3.299% and −3.149%, respectively, and are significant at the 5% level.[10]

[10] Since timely disclosures may disclose information on the recording of goodwill impairment losses the day before the newspaper report, we also analyze the CAR [−1, +1] for the IFRS sample.

Table 7.6 Significance of abnormal return (IFRS sample)

Time	AAR (%)	t-value	p-value	MAR (%)	Wilcoxon-Z	p-value
−10	−4.355	−1.160	0.311	−1.834	−1.214	0.225
−9	−0.834	−1.086	0.339	−0.433	−0.944	0.345
−8	−0.086	−0.196	0.854	0.363	−0.135	0.893
−7	−0.287	−0.711	0.516	−0.593	−0.674	0.500
−6	−0.464	−0.642	0.556	−0.059	−0.405	0.686
−5	−2.163	−1.681	0.168	−1.427*	−1.753	0.080
−4	0.661	1.044	0.356	0.500	0.944	0.345
−3	−0.327	−0.219	0.837	0.642	0.135	0.893
−2	0.513	0.406	0.706	−0.912	−0.405	0.686
−1	−0.098	−0.197	0.853	−0.410	−0.674	0.500
0	−3.649*	−2.174	0.095	−1.868**	−2.023	0.043
+1	−2.142**	−3.055	0.038	−2.102**	−2.023	0.043
+2	−1.157	−1.447	0.222	−0.791	−1.214	0.225
+3	4.070	1.021	0.365	0.318	0.944	0.345
+4	3.149	1.075	0.343	0.628	1.214	0.225
+5	−0.124	−0.165	0.877	0.248	0.135	0.893
+6	1.100	1.045	0.355	0.762	0.674	0.500
+7	−1.818	−2.014	0.114	−1.362**	−2.023	0.043
+8	0.823	1.635	0.177	.253**	2.023	0.043
+9	0.234	1.376	0.241	0.402	1.214	0.225
+10	1.405	1.614	0.182	1.311	1.214	0.225

Notes: Time represents the number of days before and after the event, with the event date as 0. AAR represents the average abnormal return at each time point, and MAR represents the median abnormal return at each time point. t-value and Wilcoxon-Z represent the test statistics for the t-test and Wilcoxon signed-rank test, respectively. p-value means the significant probability for t-test or Wilcoxon signed-rank test. ***, **, and * indicate significance levels of 1%, 5%, and 10%, respectively (two-tailed test)

Large abnormal returns occur in the CAR[0, +1] of the IFRS sample, which are not required to amortize goodwill. This result differs from those of Jarva (2014), Li et al. (2011), and Bens et al. (2011). These results are consistent with the statement in the interview that preparers recognized goodwill impairment losses in a timely manner. Although the number of the IFRS-applied firms is small and we must be cautious in generalizing the results, the analysis presented in this section shows that both J-GAAP- and IFRS samples support the idea that the announcement of goodwill impairments has informational value.

As a result, a significant negative CAAR is detected for the t-test, with −5.889% (5% level) at day 0 and −6.948% (1% level) at day +1 from the event date. For Wilcoxon's signed rank test, a significant negative CMAR is detected at −6.514% (5% level) at the event date and −6.560% (5% level) at day +1. These are similar to the results for CAR[0, +1], which indicate significant negative stock price responses around the event date.

Table 7.7 Significance of cumulative abnormal return [0, +1] (IFRS sample)

Time	CAAR (%)	t-value	p-value	CMAR (%)	Wilcoxon-Z	p-value
−10	−5.189	−1.180	0.303	−0.688	−1.214	0.225
−9	−0.920	−1.248	0.280	−0.355	−0.944	0.345
−8	−0.372	−0.565	0.602	−0.443	−0.405	0.686
−7	−0.751*	−2.221	0.091	−0.652*	−1.753	0.080
−6	−2.627	−1.393	0.236	−0.815	−1.483	0.138
−5	−1.503	−1.588	0.187	−1.711	−1.214	0.225
−4	0.334	0.384	0.720	1.142	0.674	0.500
−3	0.186	0.441	0.682	−0.304	0.405	0.686
−2	0.414	0.358	0.738	−0.938	0.405	0.686
−1	−3.747	−2.098	0.104	−2.316*	−1.753	0.080
0	−5.791**	−3.323	0.029	−5.200**	−2.023	0.043
+1	−3.299**	−3.687	0.021	−3.149**	−2.023	0.043
+2	2.913	0.722	0.510	−0.177	−0.405	0.686
+3	7.219	1.044	0.355	1.155	1.214	0.225
+4	3.024	1.303	0.262	0.876	1.483	0.138
+5	0.976	1.367	0.243	1.683	1.483	0.138
+6	−0.718	−1.098	0.334	−0.122	−0.944	0.345
+7	−0.995	−1.723	0.160	−1.109	−1.214	0.225
+8	1.057**	2.842	0.047	0.697**	2.023	0.043
+9	1.639	2.004	0.116	1.815	1.483	0.138
+10	2.278	1.918	0.128	2.986	1.214	0.225

Notes: Time represents the number of days before and after the event, with the event date as 0. CAAR represents the cumulative average abnormal return at two time points, t and t + 1, and CMAR represents the median of the cumulative average abnormal return. t-value and Wilcoxon-Z represent the test statistics for the t-test and Wilcoxon signed-rank test, respectively. p-value means the significant probability for t-test or Wilcoxon signed-rank test. ***, **, and * indicate significance levels of 1%, 5%, and 10%, respectively (two-tailed test)

7.2.5 *Summary*

In this section, we describe a short-window event study focusing on the announcement of goodwill impairment losses as one of several analyses undertaken to test the empirical facts in an exploratory manner against market participants' perception of facts about the subsequent accounting treatment of goodwill.

For the entire sample, significant negative ARs and CARs are observed around the event date. In the J-GAAP sample, a significant negative AR was detected at $t = 0, +1$, and the CAR shows the strongest significant negative response at $t = 0$. In addition, for the IFRS sample, a significant negative AR is observed at $t = 0, +1$ and a strongly significant negative response is observed in the CAR at $t = 0$. similar to the results for the J-GAAP sample. It should be noted, however, that the mean AR at the $t = 0$ time point is significant at the 10% level, which is statistically weak.

To identify the impact of goodwill impairment announcements, this study focuses only on cases in which goodwill impairments were reported in newspaper articles.

However, the sample size is smaller than originally expected because of the large number of goodwill impairment cases that were not reported in newspaper articles. This is one limitation of the present study. In particular, the sample includes only five IFRS samples; thus, we advise caution when generalizing the results.

The analysis presented in this section has several other limitations. First, we do not incorporate into our analysis the presence or absence of "signs of impairments" such as deterioration in operating income or operating cash flows. In addition, although there is a problem with the limitation of obtaining quarterly financial data, we recognize the need to perform an analysis that considers these data. Third, earnings announcements may be made simultaneously with goodwill impairment announcements. In this case, the reactions to goodwill impairment loss and earnings surprises are intermingled. These issues need to be addressed in future studies.

7.3 Event Study of Long-term Returns

7.3.1 Introduction

In the previous section, we use the short-term stock returns to analyze market reactions to goodwill impairment announcements. Most previous studies, including the analysis presented in the previous section, have focused on stock returns over a short window around the announcement date to examine the market reaction to the announcement of goodwill impairment losses (Francis et al. 1996; Hirschey and Richardson 2002, 2003; Bens et al. 2011; Li et al. 2011; Knauer and Wöhrmann 2016; Shimada 2010; Kimura 2017). However, relatively few studies have focused on the evolution of stock returns over time for announcements of goodwill impairment losses (Hirschey and Richardson 2002, 2003. Shimada 2011). As these studies show, by analyzing long-term stock returns before and after announcements of goodwill impairment losses, it is possible to examine whether the market anticipates the occurrence of such losses and incorporates them into stock prices even before announcements of goodwill impairment are made.[11] In this section, we examine the market reaction to announcements of goodwill impairment losses by focusing on cumulative abnormal returns (CARs) over a long period before and after the announcements.

7.3.2 Related Studies and Issues for Consideration

The movement of long-term stock returns before and after announcements of asset write-offs, not limited to goodwill, has been of interest from the viewpoint of

[11] However, the longer the window of analysis considered, the more likely it is that the effects of events other than the focal event may be included, which presents a limitation of this study.

whether asset write-offs are timely or if market participants perceive that asset profitability is declining even before the announcements are made (Alciatore et al. 1998, pp. 31–32). Bartov et al. (1998), using a U.S. sample, report a downward trend in cumulative abnormal returns well before asset write-off announcements are made, and find that market participants are aware that an asset's value has been impaired long before the announcement (Alciatore et al. 1998, pp. 31–32), indicating that the market anticipates that asset write-offs will occur. In addition, Bartov et al. (1998, p. 329) report that the average cumulative abnormal return continues to decline over time after an asset write-off, indicating that, while the market participant anticipates that an asset is impaired to some extent even before it is announced, the information content of the announcement is not fully incorporated into stock prices.

In their U.S.-based study, Hirschey and Richardson (2002, 2003) focus on the announcement of goodwill impairment losses and examine the market reaction in the long term in addition to the market reaction in the short term.[12] In their analysis, they report negative cumulative abnormal returns in the period prior to goodwill impairment announcements (from −250 to −10 days). This result suggests that market participants have some foresight regarding the impairment incurred on goodwill even before the announcement. However, they also report that, in some subsamples, cumulative abnormal returns are negative in the post-announcement period. Based on this result, they suggest that market participants may not fully understand the information on goodwill impairment losses and may exhibit a underreaction (Hirschey and Richardson 2003, p. 83). These results are consistent with those reported by Bartov et al. (1998).

Finally, following Hirschey and Richardson (2003), Shimada (2011) examines long-term market reactions to goodwill impairment announcements using data from Japanese listed firms that announced goodwill impairment losses during the period from April 2005 to August 2009 (event window: $t = -250$ to $t = +250$). Shimada (2011) observes negative cumulative abnormal returns even before the announcement for samples of firms that did not announce any news other than goodwill impairments and firms in the manufacturing industry. However, Shimada (2011) points out that the cumulative abnormal returns start to fall not so early, but around 20 days before the announcement. Shimada (2011) also shows that for the period after the announcement date, the cumulative abnormal return increases from approximately +50 days and eventually takes a positive value. These results differ from those of Hirschey and Richardson (2003).

The results of prior studies generally indicate that market participants predict that goodwill is impaired even before the goodwill impairment announcement, and that this is reflected in the stock price. In addition, the Accounting Standards Board of Japan [ASBJ] (2017) and Chap. 6 present the view that market participants expect an impairment in goodwill even before it is announced, and in this sense, the

[12] Hirschey and Richardson (2002, 2003) analyze the period from 1992 to 1996, when goodwill was amortized in the U.S. Therefore, the results of their studies are comparable to those of this study, which uses a sample of firms that employ Japanese GAAP.

recognition of goodwill impairment is not timely.[13] The empirical results of previous studies are consistent with the interview results. However, the market reactions before and after goodwill impairment announcements have not been verified using recent data. Therefore, in this section, we revisit the market reaction over a long period before and after the announcement using relatively recent data collected over the period from the fiscal year ending March 31, 2007 to the fiscal year ending March 31, 2019, used in the analysis presented in the previous section.

7.3.3 Research Design

7.3.3.1 Measuring Variables

In this section, to examine the changes in stock returns over a long window before and after the announcement of goodwill impairment losses, we calculate the cumulative abnormal returns for the 250 trading days before and after the announcement date ($t = 0$), following Bartov et al. (1998), Hirschey and Richardson (2003), and Shimada (2011). The cumulative abnormal return (CAR) for the analysis period is calculated as follows. First, the abnormal return ($AR_{i,t}$) for each firm is calculated by the difference between individual stock returns ($RET_{i,t}$) and market returns ($RET_{m,t}$) for the same period.[14]

$$AR_{i,t} = RET_{i,t} - RET_{m,t} \tag{7.4}$$

Then, the cumulative abnormal return over $t = t_1$ to $t = t_2$ is calculated for each firm by summing the $AR_{i,t}$ from $t = t_1$ (the start of accumulation) to $t = t_2$ ($t = -250, -249, \ldots, 249, 250$).

$$CAR_{i,(t_1,t_2)} = \sum_{t=t_1}^{t_2} AR_{i,t} \tag{7.5}$$

In addition, this study calculates the average cumulative abnormal return for the entire sample and each subsample to determine how it evolves over the event window. The average CAR is calculated as follows (where N is the sample size):

$$CAR_{(t_1,t_2)} = \frac{1}{N}\left(\sum_{i=1}^{N} CAR_{i,(t_1,t_2)}\right) \tag{7.6}$$

---

[13] However, as mentioned in Chap. 6, some of the impairments incurred on goodwill may not be foreseeable to analysts.

[14] Therefore, the method of measuring abnormal returns differs from that presented in the previous section, which used a market model.

7.3.3.2 Data

In this section, as in the previous section, we use the 64 announcements of goodwill impairment losses. For the analysis presented in this section, we obtain financial data from Nikkei NEEDS and stock data from the Nikkei NEEDS daily stock return data. Market returns are required to calculate the abnormal returns. In this section, we calculate the value-weighted and equally-weighted returns as market returns using the return data for individual stocks from the Nikkei NEEDS daily stock return data.

7.3.4 Analysis Results

7.3.4.1 Abnormal Returns

First, we review the average abnormal returns for the entire sample, as Fig. 7.7 shows. Panels A and B in Fig. 7.7 show the results when value-weighted and equally-weighted average returns are used as market returns, respectively.

As Fig. 7.7 indicates, a decline in cumulative abnormal returns is observed well before the announcement date. This finding suggests that impairments to goodwill are expected by market participants at a relatively early stage, similar to the U.S. results of Hirschey and Richardson (2002, 2003). In addition, this result is consistent with the results of interview surveys indicating that goodwill impairment losses are, to some extent, anticipated by analysts before they are recognized in accounting or the fact that impairment is announced (ASBJ 2017; Chap. 6). However, for the period after the announcement date, we do *not* observe a continuous decline in cumulative abnormal returns over a long period of time, as shown in Fig. 2 of Hirschey and Richardson (2003). Unlike the results of Bartov et al. (1998) and Hirschey and Richardson (2003), this result does not support the argument that stock prices cannot fully incorporate the information content of impairment losses by announcement date and underreact to the announcements.

In addition, Row (1) of Table 7.8 shows that for [−250, −10] and [−1, +1], both the mean and median of the cumulative abnormal returns are negative and statistically significant (at the 1% level), while for post-announcement [+10, +250], the mean and median are negative and statistically insignificant. These results suggest that the information content regarding goodwill impairment losses may have been incorporated into stock prices to a significant degree before and on the day after the announcement date.[15] However, in the period after the announcement date, we find no evidence of underreaction to the announcement of goodwill impairment losses.

[15] The above results differ from those presented by Shimada (2011), although we cannot strictly compare our results with that of Shimada (2011). Specifically, the analysis described in this section shows that cumulative abnormal returns began to decline earlier than the results presented by Shimada (2011), and that there is no significant increase in cumulative abnormal returns after the

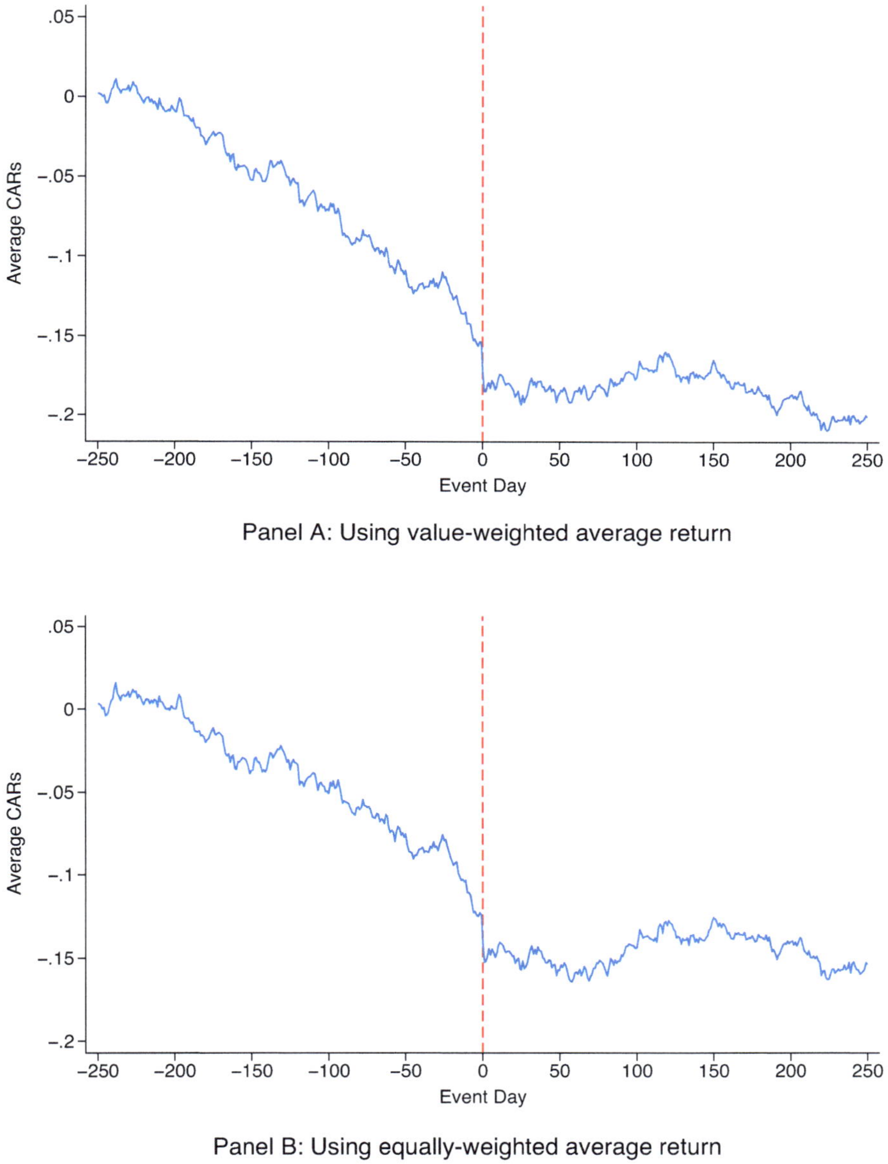

Fig. 7.7 Trends in average cumulative abnormal returns. (Panel A) Using value-weighted average return. (Panel B) Using equally-weighted average return

7.3.4.2 Separate Analysis of Japanese GAAP Adopters and IFRS Adopters

To examine these results in more detail, we review the results of our analysis using a subsample. The sample used in this study includes a sample of firms that have adopted IFRS (N = 5), although the number is quite small. Therefore, we check the results for the sample of only firms adopting Japanese GAAP (N = 59), excluding these firms, from Row (2) of Table 7.8. The results show that the results for the sample of firms adopting Japanese standards are generally similar to those for the entire sample. Although the number of observations is small and care must be taken in interpreting the results, the results for the sample of firms adopting IFRS (Row (3) in Table 7.8) show that, unlike the sample of firms adopting Japanese GAAP only, only the cumulative abnormal returns of [−1, +1] are negative and statistically significant at the 5% level.[16] For the results for [−250, −10], both the mean and median cumulative abnormal returns are negative, but not statistically significant. Furthermore, for the results of [+10, +250], the mean and median are negative and positive, respectively, but are not statistically significant.

The following possibilities can be considered to explain these results. First, it is possible that firms applying IFRS make more timely announcements of goodwill impairment than firms applying Japanese GAAP due to differences in the frequency of impairment testing. It is also possible that the difference in attributes between the two makes it difficult for market participants to detect impairments on the goodwill of firms applying IFRS. Other possibilities should be considered in the interpretation of the results. Nevertheless, further research is required to understand the mechanisms underlying these results.

7.3.4.3 Excluding Cases Where the Goodwill Impairment Announcement Date Is Close to the Earnings Announcement Date

Our sample includes cases in which the goodwill impairment announcement (or newspaper report) date is close to the earnings announcement date (1 day before or after the announcement date).[17] As earnings announcements make much more information available to market participants than goodwill impairment loss

announcement date, which Shimada (2011) finds. The reasons for this difference may be due to differences in the sample and the method used to calculate cumulative abnormal returns.

[16] This result is consistent with the results of the previous section.

[17] The earnings announcement date included in Nikkei NEEDS is "the date when an earnings report (*Kessan tanshin*) is filed with the stock exchange or the Securities Dealers Association" (the data definitions of Nikkei NEEDS, December 17, 2018 edition, the information in parentheses added by the authors), which more precisely means the announcement of earnings report (*Kessan tanshin*). However, for cases in which the difference between the annual earnings announcement date and the newspaper report date exceeds 90 days, we also examine whether the gap between the quarterly earnings announcement date and the newspaper report date is one day.

Table 7.8 Mean and median cumulative abnormal returns

			[−250, −10]				[−1, +1].				[+10, +250]			
			Mean	Median	t-value	z-value	Mean	Median	t-value	z-value	Mean	Median	t-value	z-value
(1)	Entire Sample (N = 64)	[VW]	−0.132	−0.069	−3.225***	−3.150***	−0.031	−0.022	−3.734***	−3.879***	−0.010	−0.006	−0.284	−0.321
		[EW]	−0.110	−0.096	−2.822***	−2.708***	−0.030	−0.020	−3.856***	−4.253***	−0.007	−0.057	−0.177	−0.415
(2)	J-GAAP sample (N = 59)	[VW]	−0.141	−0.070	−3.201***	−3.140***	−0.028	−0.022	−3.236***	−3.374***	−0.003	−0.014	−0.093	−0.302
		[EW]	−0.117	−0.099	−2.790***	−2.710***	−0.027	−0.019	−3.345***	−3.804***	−0.002	−0.057	−0.052	−0.491
(3)	IFRS sample (N = 5)	[VW]	−0.027	−0.004	−0.479	−0.405	−0.060	−0.066	−3.047**	−2.023**	−0.087	0.061	−0.470	−0.135
		[EW]	−0.030	−0.093	−0.439	−0.674	−0.061	−0.058	−2.824**	−2.023**	−0.062	0.076	−0.304	0.135
(4)	Firms excluding those with almost the same announcement dates (N = 46)	[VW]	−0.120	−0.069	−2.450**	−2.660***	−0.027	−0.018	−3.968***	−3.458***	−0.037	−0.041	−0.924	−0.901
		[EW]	−0.122	−0.102	−2.675**	−2.704***	−0.028	−0.021	−4.688***	−4.070***	−0.048	−0.061	−1.112	−1.185
(5)	Non-repeat firms (N = 49)	[VW]	−0.161	−0.086	−3.148***	−3.099***	−0.026	−0.022	−2.623**	−2.850***	−0.002	−0.014	−0.047	−0.065
		[EW]	−0.143	−0.110	−2.982***	−2.910***	−0.025	−0.019	−2.672**	−3.208***	0.010	−0.056	0.219	−0.015
(6)	Low (N = 22)	[VW]	−0.116	−0.113	−2.851***	−2.451**	−0.019	−0.018	−2.899***	−2.678***	−0.065	−0.110	−1.517	−1.607
		[EW]	−0.100	−0.104	−2.726**	−2.386**	−0.021	−0.017	−3.475***	−3.133***	−0.072	−0.100	−1.531	−1.867*
(7)	Mid (N = 21)	[VW]	−0.157	−0.059	−1.693	−1.929*	−0.028	−0.018	−2.376**	−1.964**	0.011	0.061	0.181	0.052
		[EW]	−0.131	−0.076	−1.449	−1.442	−0.029	−0.023	−2.835**	−2.346**	0.031	0.031	0.496	0.434
(8)	High (N = 21)	[VW]	−0.126	−0.068	−1.658	−1.547	−0.047	−0.034	−2.192**	−2.416**	0.028	0.069	0.374	0.713
		[EW]	−0.100	−0.068	−1.423	−1.373	−0.041	−0.032	−1.963*	−2.242**	0.024	0.023	0.294	0.295

Notes: VW indicates the value-weighted average return, and EW indicates the equally-weighted return. Mean represents the mean of the cumulative abnormal returns, and Median represents the median. t-value and z-value represent the results of t-test and Wilcoxon signed-rank test (two-tailed test), respectively. ***, **, and * represent statistically significant at the 1%, 5%, and 10% levels, respectively

announcements, market participants are more likely to react to other information rather than goodwill impairment losses. Therefore, we repeat the above analyses when we exclude from our sample the cases where the goodwill impairment announcement date is almost the same as the earnings announcement date (N = 46). The results in Row (4) of Table 7.8 show a trend similar to that for the entire sample.

7.3.4.4 Results Excluding Cases Where Announcements Are Made Multiple Times During the Same Period

The sample also includes some firms that have made goodwill impairment announcements more than once during the analysis period (hereafter, repeat firms). We therefore re-conduct the analysis after excluding these repeat firms from the sample (leaving a subsample of non-repeat firms). The results in Row (5) of Table 7.8 indicate that our findings remain unchanged.

7.3.4.5 Results by the Size of Goodwill Impairment Losses

Finally, we reexamine the results of the analysis when the sample is split by the size of goodwill impairment losses.[18] The reason for this is to account for the possibility that the size of the impairment loss could result in different market reactions on the announcement date and in periods before and after the announcement date. For example, the larger the size of the impairment, the more negative the market reaction to the announcement is expected to be. In addition, as we have already seen, the market may anticipate the occurrence of goodwill even before the announcement. Therefore, the larger the size of the impairment, the larger the reduction in cumulative abnormal returns over time prior to the announcement date may be. Of course, the size of the goodwill impairment depends on factors such as the extent of previous amortization (under systematic amortization with impairment approach) and the management's discretionary actions, which may lead to different results from those expected above.[19]

Based on the above, in this section, we examine the cumulative abnormal returns by subsample based on goodwill impairment loss divided by sales (the ratio of goodwill impairment to sales). We divide the sample into three groups: Low (N = 22), Mid (N = 21), and High (N = 21). Figure 7.8 summarizes the average cumulative abnormal returns for the three groups: Low, Mid, and High. Panel A

---

[18] In this study, we collect the amount of goodwill impairment from newspaper articles if available, and otherwise from notes in annual reports. Note that this analysis assumes that market participants are informed of the amount of goodwill impairment that would be reported in the annual report (or at least an amount close to it) on the announcement date. It may be possible to supplement the amount of goodwill impairment not from the annual report, but from the timely disclosure materials closer to the announcement date. The assumption is too strong and future research should improve this point.

[19] Further, different results from previous analyses may be observed for long-term cumulative abnormal returns after the announcement date.

Fig. 7.8 Trends in average cumulative abnormal returns by impairment size. (Panel A) Using value-weighted average return. (Panel B) Using equally-weighted average return

shows the graph when value-weighted average returns are used as market returns, and Panel B shows the graph when equally-weighted average returns are used. Rows (6) through (8) in Table 7.8, as in the previous sections, show the mean and median of [−250, −10], [−1, +1], and [+10, +250] for each group when the value-weighted average returns are used and equally-weighted average returns, respectively.

As Panels A and B in Fig. 7.8 show, the cumulative abnormal returns for Low, Mid, and High decrease over the long-term window even before the announcement date.

In particular, the results of the Low group shows a gradual decline in cumulative abnormal returns over the long window than the Mid and High groups, while the Mid and High groups show a large decline in cumulative abnormal returns closer to the announcement date. Rows (6) through (8) in Table 7.8 show that only Low has consistently negative and statistically significant results for cumulative abnormal returns for [−250, −10] prior to the announcement date (for Mid, statistically significant results are obtained only with the Wilcoxon signed-rank test when using the value-weighted average return). Thus, it is possible that market participants are able to anticipate impairments incurred on goodwill at a relatively early stage prior to the announcement only when the size of the impairment is relatively small.

The results, also shown in Table 7.8, confirm that for both groups, the cumulative abnormal returns are consistently negative and statistically significant for [−1, +1] announcements and for the periods before and after the announcements. This result is consistent with the trends in cumulative abnormal returns shown in Fig. 7.8. Multiple comparisons among the three groups were conducted using the t-test with Bonferroni correction and Wilcoxon-signed rank test, and no statistically significant differences are observed in any of the cases (untabulated). Thus, the results do not show that market reactions to announcements vary depending on the size of goodwill impairment announcements.

Finally, for the period [+10, +250] after the announcement date, we observe different patterns of accumulated abnormal returns between the Low groups and the Mid and High groups in both Panels A and B of Fig. 7.8. For Low, the average cumulative abnormal return is relatively flat for a while after the announcement, but it turns downward again approximately 150 days after the announcement date. Meanwhile, the average cumulative abnormal returns for Mid and High continue to show a gradual downward trend for a while after the announcement, but then show an upward trend. These results suggest that the market may overreact to the announcement for Mid and High.[20] Note that Table 7.8 shows that the mean and median cumulative abnormal returns for [+10, +250] are consistently negative for the Low group and consistently positive for the Mid and High groups. However, the results are not statistically significant in most cases, and there is no evidence that the mean and median of the cumulative abnormal returns are different from zero for the [+10, +250] period as a whole.

7.3.5 *Summary*

In this section, we investigate the long-run stock performance behavior before and after the announcement of the goodwill impairment loss. The results in this section

[20] It is also possible that there are other additional events after the announcement or that related information that can affect stock prices continue to be released.

show that cumulative abnormal returns have been declining on average since well before the announcement ($t = -250$ to $t = -10$). This result suggests that the impairment of goodwill was at least partially anticipated by market participants well before the announcement was made. This result is consistent with the empirical results of previous studies (Bartov et al. 1998; Hirschey and Richardson 2003; Shimada 2011) and interviews (ASBJ 2017; Chap. 6). However, the results of the analysis of cumulative abnormal returns since the announcement date in this section do not, as a whole, provide evidence of market underreaction since the announcement date. This result differs from that of Hirschey and Richardson (2003), who showed an underreaction to goodwill impairment losses.[21] Note that the analysis, in which the sample is divided into three groups by impairment size, provides evidence that for the group with smaller impairment size, the market expects goodwill to occur at an earlier stage. By contrast, for the larger impairment group, we observe a pattern of cumulative abnormal returns in the post-announcement period that appears to be an overreaction to the announcement. The reasons for these results are not clear from the analysis discussed in this section, and remain a topic for future research.

Note that the analyses of short-term market reaction presented in the previous section (and the results of [−1, +1] in Table 7.8) confirm the negative market reactions on and immediately after the announcement date, indicating that the goodwill impairment loss announcements contain new information for market participants. This is consistent with the results presented this section, which focus on long-term cumulative abnormal returns. In other words, the two results indicate that the information content of goodwill impairment losses is partially expected and reflected in stock prices even before the announcement. However, the market does not know all of the information content in advance, and the information content is revealed to market participants only after the announcement is made (Bartov et al. 1998; Hirschey and Richardson 2003).[22]

7.4 Event Study of Short-term Trading Volume Responses

7.4.1 Introduction

Thus far, we have used stock returns to analyze market reactions in the short and long run. In this section, we examine the market reaction to announcements of

[21] Note that while Shimada (2011) reports a significant increase in cumulative abnormal returns after announcements (p. 47, Figs. 1 and 2), a similar result is not observed in the analysis presented in this section. Because the sample and analysis methods used by Shimada (2011) in the analysis are different from those in this section, it should be noted that a simple comparison with the results in this section is not possible.

[22] However, for the larger impairment groups (Mid and High in the analysis), there may have been an overreaction to the announcements.

goodwill impairment losses from a different perspective using abnormal trading volume instead of stock returns.

Many studies examining market reactions to goodwill impairment announcements, including the analyses discussed in the previous sections, have focused on short- or long-term stock returns (Francis et al. 1996; Hirschey and Richardson 2002, 2003; Bens et al. 2011; Li et al. 2011; Knauer and Wöhrmann 2016; Laurion et al. 2023; Shimada 2010, 2011; Kimura 2017). The stock return approach is the primary method used to analyze the stock market reaction to news, and the same is true for announcements of goodwill impairment losses. The trading volume approach is also one of the leading methods for examining stock market reaction to news (e.g., Beaver 1968; Ball and Shivakumar 2008). This is because, unlike the analysis using stock returns, the analysis using trading volume is characterized by its ability to detect changes in individual stock investors' expectations (and hence trading among investors), even when no change in expectations is observed for the market as a whole (Beaver 1968, pp. 69–70; Bamber et al. 2011, p. 431).

Although previous studies have paid little attention to analyzing trading volume responses to announcements of goodwill impairment losses, as mentioned above, volume-based analysis has the advantage of detecting changes in individual investors' expectations that cannot be observed in stock returns. Regarding the economic significance of goodwill impairment losses, some argue that the recognition of goodwill impairment losses is a useful signal of merger and acquisition (M&A) failure, while others point out that goodwill impairment losses are only recognized in small amounts and the timing of their recognition is not timely (the "too little, too late" issue), and that they do not bring new information to market participants and, if they do have informational value, it is only confirmatory value (IASB 2020, para. 3.88; Accounting Standards Board of Japan 2017, paras. 20, 29, 30, and 42). If the market as a whole had anticipated in advance that goodwill would be impaired, and this information had been factored into the stock price in advance, no market reaction (change in market-wide expectations) on the announcement date would be observed in the stock return. However, even in such a case, the analysis using trading volume allows us to examine the reactions of market participants to the announcements of the goodwill impairment losses from a different angle. In this section, in light of the above, we examine stock market reactions to announcements of goodwill impairment losses by analyzing trading volume reactions.

7.4.2 *Research Design*

7.4.2.1 Variable Measurement

To examine the trading volume response to goodwill impairment announcements, this analysis requires the measurement of abnormal trading volume. In this study,

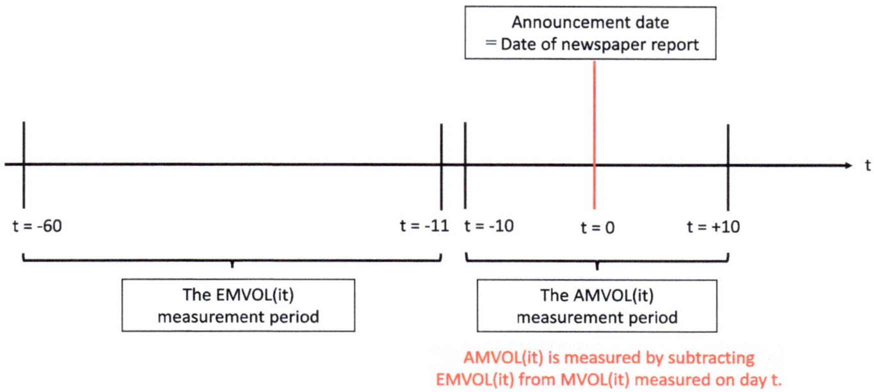

Fig. 7.9 Measurement of abnormal trading volume

abnormal trading volume is measured using a market-adjusted trading volume reaction following Watkins (2022):

$$AMVOL_{i,t} = MVOL_{i,t} - EMVOL_{i,t} \tag{7.7}$$

where $AMVOL_{i,t}$ represents the abnormal trading volume for firm i on day t ($t = -10\ldots, -1, 0, +1, \ldots, +10$). In this section, $t = 0$ represents the event date (announcement date), and $t = -10$ to $+10$ is the event period. $MVOL_{i,t}$ represents the market-adjusted trading volume for firm i on day t, which is the volume for firm i on day t minus the equally-weighted average of the trading volume for all available stocks on day t. $EMVOL_{i,t}$ represents the market-adjusted expected trading volume of firm I on day t. However, since the value cannot be observed directly, we use the average $MVOL_{i,t}$ for the 50 days prior to the event period ($t = -60, \ldots, -11$) as a proxy.[23] Figure 7.9 shows the timeline of the abnormal trading volume measurement in this study.

7.4.2.2 Data

The sample used in this section comprises 64 announcements on goodwill impairment losses, which were also used in Sects. 7.2 and 7.3 of this chapter. As in the previous section, financial data are obtained from Nikkei NEEDS and stock data are obtained from the Nikkei NEEDS daily stock return database.

[23] The results obtained when $MVOL_{i,t}$ is calculated with $t = -70, \ldots, -21$ are similar to those in this section. In addition, the results using standardized unexpected volume as the abnormal volume are generally similar to those in this section. The Appendix reports the results of the analysis using standardized unexpected volume.

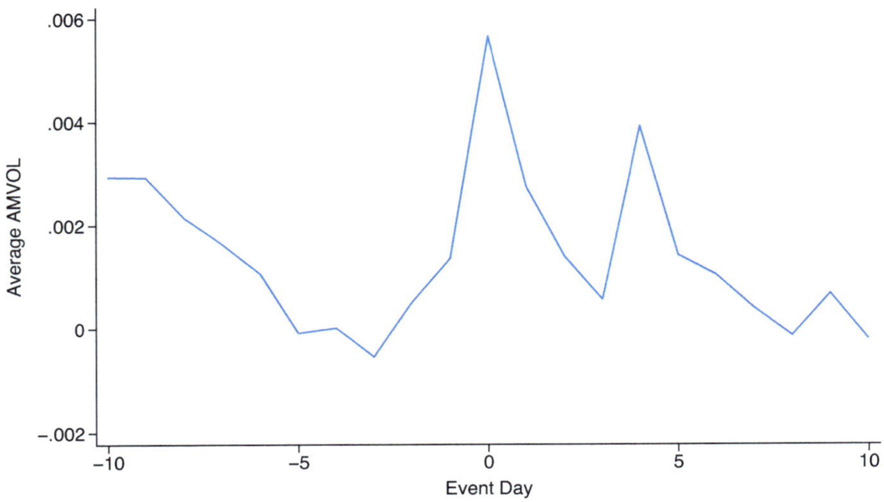

Fig. 7.10 Trend in abnormal trading volume (entire sample N = 64)

7.4.3 Analysis Results

7.4.3.1 Results for the Entire Sample

Column (1) in Table 7.9 and Fig. 7.10 show the market reaction to goodwill impairment announcements (average change in $AMVOL_{i,t}$) for the entire sample (64 cases).[24] The table and figure confirm that the abnormal trading volume is larger on the announcement date ($t = 0$), indicating that the market reacts to announcements of goodwill impairment losses. This result suggests that announcements of goodwill impairment losses have information content that changes the trading behavior of market participants. In addition, Fig. 7.10 shows that there is a large abnormal trading volume response not only on the announcement date but also in the subsequent period $t = +4$ (however, both the t-test and Wilcoxon signed-rank test are not significant). As discussed later, the movement of the abnormal trading volume at $t = +4$ is caused by a sample of firms other than those adopting Japanese GAAP (i.e., the IFRS sample).[25]

[24] Although the median abnormal volume is also shown in Table 7.9 for reference purposes, we essentially discuss the average results below.

[25] Although figures are omitted, the above results are generally similar when firms that made multiple announcements of goodwill impairment losses during the sample period are excluded from the sample. The same is true for the analysis of Japanese GAAP-adopting firms and IFRS-adopting firms that follow.

Table 7.9 Abnormal trading volume

	(1)				(2)				(3)				(4)				(5)			
	Entire sample (N = 64)				J-GAAP sample (N = 59)				IFRS sample (N = 5)				Almost the same date as earnings announcement (N = 16)				J-GAAP sample excluding firms with almost the same announcement dates (N = 43)			
Event Day	Mean	median	t-value	z-value	Mean	median	t-value	z-value	Mean	Median	t-value	z-value	Mean	median	t-value	z-value	Mean	median	t-value	z-value
−10	0.003	0.000	1.372	0.889	0.001	0.000	1.175	0.951	0.025	0.000	0.984	−0.674	0.000	0.000	−0.221	0.207	0.002	0.000	1.231	0.954
−9	0.003	0.000	1.584	0.709	0.001	0.000	1.666	0.876	0.021	−0.001	0.959	−0.674	0.002	0.000	1.130	0.362	0.001	0.000	1.210	0.797
−8	0.002	0.000	1.443	−1.017	0.001	0.000	1.084	−0.913	0.011	−0.001	0.925	−0.674	0.002	−0.001	0.575	−1.344	0.001	0.000	0.907	−0.217
−7	0.002	0.000	1.551	0.421	0.001	0.000	1.263	0.551	0.009	−0.001	0.914	−0.674	0.000	−0.001	−0.082	−1.448	0.001	0.000	1.628	1.678*
−6	0.001	0.000	0.974	−0.996	0.001	0.000	0.803	−0.921	0.003	0.000	0.715	−0.674	0.000	−0.001	−0.193	−1.551	0.001	0.000	0.917	−0.097
−5	0.000	−0.001	−0.110	−1.786*	0.000	−0.001	−0.886	−1.668*	0.005	−0.001	0.761	−0.674	0.000	−0.001	−0.036	−0.931	−0.001	−0.001	−1.130	−1.292
−4	0.000	0.000	0.028	−2.133**	−0.001	0.000	−1.718*	−2.015**	0.007	−0.001	0.849	−0.674	0.000	0.000	−0.555	−1.086	−0.001	0.000	−1.708*	−1.678*
−3	−0.001	0.000	−1.033	−1.632	−0.001	0.000	−1.901*	−1.578	0.003	−0.001	0.716	−0.405	0.000	0.000	−0.093	0.569	−0.001	0.000	−2.139**	−2.004**
−2	0.001	0.000	0.785	−1.037	0.000	0.000	0.634	−0.800	0.002	−0.001	0.536	−0.674	0.000	0.000	−0.230	0.000	0.001	0.000	0.803	−0.881
−1	0.001	0.000	1.692*	0.642	0.001	0.000	1.628	0.808	0.001	−0.001	0.464	−0.674	0.003	0.000	1.572	1.086	0.001	0.000	0.861	0.290
0	0.006	0.003	4.924***	5.845***	0.006	0.003	4.644***	5.487***	0.004	0.004	3.556**	2.023**	0.010	0.005	2.793**	2.792***	0.004	0.003	4.287***	4.842***
1	0.003	0.001	3.512***	3.879***	0.003	0.001	3.291***	3.615***	0.003	0.000	1.561	2.023**	0.007	0.003	2.562**	2.482**	0.001	0.001	2.807***	2.632***
2	0.001	0.000	2.515**	2.287**	0.001	0.000	2.186**	2.008**	0.004	0.002	1.219	1.214	0.003	0.001	2.239**	1.862*	0.000	0.000	0.922	1.063
3	0.001	0.000	1.086	0.642	0.001	0.000	1.375	1.004	−0.002	0.000	−1.245	−1.214	0.003	0.001	1.603	1.344	0.000	0.000	0.182	0.193
4	0.004	0.000	1.082	0.675	0.000	0.000	0.951	0.845	0.045	−0.001	0.970	−0.405	0.002	0.001	1.336	1.189	0.000	0.000	−0.204	0.254
5	0.001	0.000	1.203	0.876	0.000	0.000	1.070	0.989	0.014	0.000	0.957	−0.405	0.001	0.000	1.006	0.724	0.000	0.000	0.554	0.652
6	0.001	0.000	1.246	0.642	0.000	0.000	0.886	0.694	0.009	−0.001	0.911	−0.405	0.001	0.000	0.793	0.362	0.000	0.001	0.428	0.543
7	0.000	0.000	0.787	0.321	0.000	0.000	0.513	0.528	0.002	−0.002	0.586	−0.405	0.000	0.000	0.345	0.259	0.000	0.000	0.378	0.447
8	0.000	0.000	−0.278	−0.990	0.000	0.000	−0.963	−0.913	0.003	−0.001	0.708	−0.405	0.000	0.000	0.460	0.621	−0.001	0.000	−1.372	−1.437
9	0.001	0.000	1.205	0.729	0.001	0.000	1.189	0.981	0.000	−0.002	0.188	−0.405	0.001	0.000	0.765	0.827	0.001	0.000	0.932	0.604
10	0.000	0.000	−0.389	−0.809	0.000	0.000	−0.932	−0.747	0.003	−0.001	0.763	−0.674	0.000	0.000	−0.791	−0.776	0.000	0.000	−0.730	−0.423

(*Continued*)

Table 7.9 (continued)

	(6) Low (N = 20)				(7) Mid (N = 20)				(8) High (N = 19)			
Event Day	Mean	median	t-value	z-value	Mean	median	t-value	z-value	Mean	median	t-value	z-value
−10	0.001	0.000	1.544	1.157	0.003	0.000	1.121	0.933	0.000	0.000	−0.809	−0.402
−9	0.001	0.000	1.690	1.269	0.004	0.000	1.549	1.269	0.000	−0.001	−0.276	−0.885
−8	0.000	−0.001	−0.764	−1.083	0.005	0.000	1.434	1.344	−0.001	−0.001	−2.293**	−1.811*
−7	0.001	0.000	1.662	1.195	0.003	0.001	1.647	1.829*	−0.001	−0.001	−1.564	−1.811*
−6	0.000	0.000	−2.038*	−1.456	0.004	0.001	1.254	1.120	−0.001	−0.001	−1.715	−1.610
−5	0.000	0.000	−0.787	−0.747	0.000	0.000	0.027	0.112	−0.001	−0.002	−1.874*	−2.133**
−4	−0.001	−0.001	−2.035*	−1.941*	0.000	0.000	−0.335	0.411	−0.001	−0.001	−1.492	−1.891*
−3	0.000	0.000	−1.472	−2.016**	−0.001	0.001	−1.022	0.187	−0.001	0.000	−1.644	−1.368
−2	0.000	0.000	−0.025	−0.411	0.002	0.000	1.355	0.933	−0.001	−0.001	−2.045*	−2.012**
−1	0.000	0.000	0.177	0.261	0.003	0.001	1.273	0.933	0.002	0.000	0.990	0.322
0	0.002	0.002	3.966***	3.285***	0.006	0.003	3.133***	3.248***	0.009	0.003	2.830**	3.139***
1	0.001	0.001	2.168**	1.829*	0.002	0.001	1.790* (1.790*)	1.456	0.006	0.003	2.567**	2.897***
2	0.000	0.000	0.839	0.709	0.002	0.001	1.527	1.531	0.002	0.000	1.360	1.207
3	0.000	0.000	0.247	−0.149	0.001	0.001	1.098	1.269	0.001	0.000	0.922	0.402
4	0.000	0.000	0.021	−0.037	0.000	0.001	0.690	0.747	0.001	0.000	0.745	0.402
5	0.000	0.000	1.280	0.933	0.000	0.001	0.608	0.821	0.000	0.000	0.236	0.040
6	0.000	0.000	0.194	0.037	0.000	0.000	−0.358	−0.149	0.001	0.001	1.394	1.207
7	0.000	0.000	0.822	0.635	−0.001	0.000	−1.104	−0.821	0.001	0.000	1.583	0.885
8	0.000	0.000	−0.430	−0.896	−0.001	0.000	−0.639	−0.149	0.000	0.000	−0.606	−0.926
9	0.001	0.001	1.802* (1.802*)	1.605	0.001	0.000	0.689	0.523	0.000	0.000	0.089	−0.483
10	0.000	0.000	1.374	1.120	−0.001	0.000	−0.774	−0.747	−0.001	−0.001	−1.530	−1.408

Notes: Mean indicates the mean value of abnormal trading volumes. Median indicates the median value of abnormal trading volumes. t-value indicates the result of a t-test. z-value indicates the result of a Wilcoxon signed-rank test (two-tailed test). ***, ** and * indicate statistical significance at the 1%, 5%, and 10% levels, respectively. The results from (4) to (8) are obtained using only the J-GAAP sample

7.4.3.2 Separate Analysis of the J-GAAP and IFRS Samples

Column (2) in Table 7.9 and Panel A in Fig. 7.11 show the trends in average $AMVOL_{i,t}$ for the J-GAAP sample (N = 59). Although the IFRS sample is small (N = 5), and comparisons are difficult, Column (3) in Table 7.9 and Panel B in

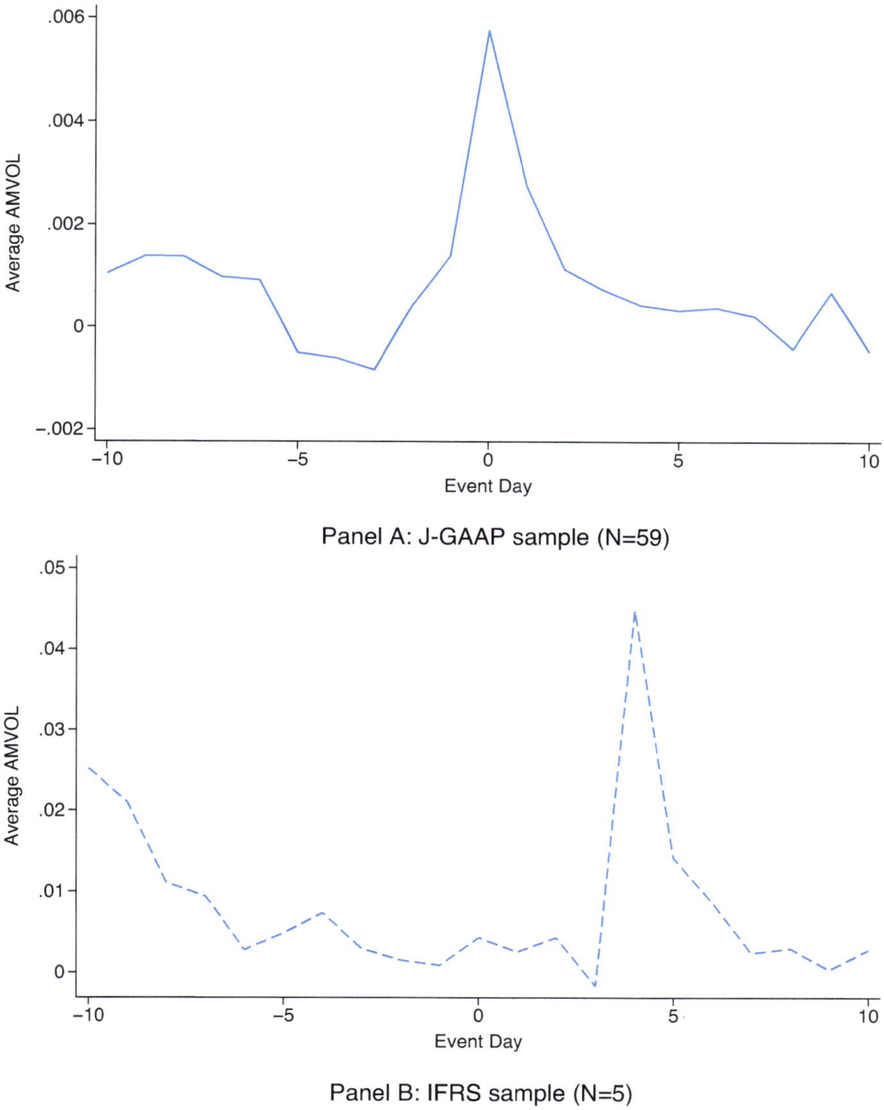

Fig. 7.11 Trends in abnormal trading volume (by accounting standards). (Panel A) J-GAAP sample (N = 59). (Panel B) IFRS sample (N = 5)

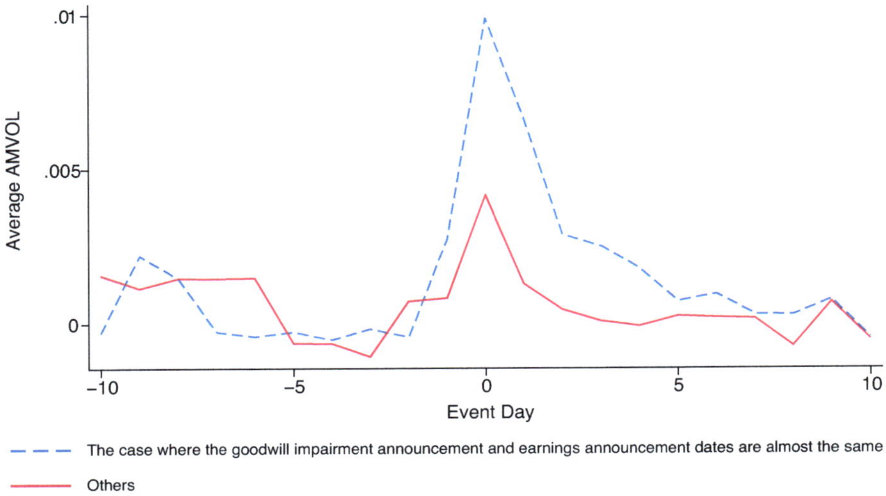

Fig. 7.12 Trends in abnormal trading volume (results after taking into account the gap with the date of the earnings announcement, N = 59)

Fig. 7.11 show the trends in abnormal volume as a reference. These results show the positive response of abnormal trading volume to the announcement date for both firms applying Japanese GAAP and IFRS. This result is consistent with the results of the analysis of abnormal returns in Sect. 7.2. From Panels A and B in Fig. 7.11, we can also confirm that the abnormal trading volume reaction at $t = +4$, which is indicated in the results for the total sample, is not observed for the sample of firms adopting Japanese GAAP but occurs for the sample of firms adopting IFRS (although, as Column (3) in Table 7.9 shows, the abnormal volume reaction at $t = +4$ is not statistically significant).

7.4.3.3 Excluding a Sample Whose Earnings Announcement Date Is Almost the Same as the Goodwill Impairment Announcement Date

As seen in the analysis presented in the previous section, our sample includes cases in which the goodwill impairment announcement and earnings announcement dates are quite close (N = 16). Therefore, we also check the results when such cases are excluded from the J-GAAP sample (N = 43).[26] The results are shown in Columns (4) and (5) of Table 7.9 and Fig. 7.12. In the subsequent analyses, we exclude firms applying IFRS from the entire sample.

[26] As in the previous section, we also exclude from our analysis some samples for which the gap between the date of the announcement of quarterly results and the date of the newspaper report is only one day.

As the table and figure show, both samples with a gap of 1 day between the goodwill impairment announcement and the earnings announcement dates (both are almost the same) and those without such a gap show large abnormal trading volume responses on the goodwill impairment announcement date ($t = 0$). In Fig. 7.12, it appears that the sample with the same goodwill impairment announcement date as the earnings announcement date has a larger trading volume reaction on the goodwill impairment announcement date than other samples. However, we found no evidence of a statistically significant difference between the two (untabulated).[27]

7.4.3.4 Results by Size of Impairment Loss

Up to this point, the analysis has been conducted without considering the amount of goodwill impairment. However, as in the previous section, this section also presents an analysis based on the possibility that the reaction to abnormal trading volume differs depending on the size of the impairment losses. For example, a simple approach would be to assume that the larger the goodwill impairment (i.e., the greater the damage to goodwill value), the greater the impact on corporate performance, the greater the impact on market participants, and the greater the reaction of abnormal trading volume. However, in reality, as discussed in the previous section, the size of goodwill impairment depends on factors such as whether the goodwill is amortized (and, if so, to what extent) and discretionary actions by management.[28] Therefore, it is possible that the prediction above does not hold true.[29] In light of the above discussion, we examine abnormal trading volume reactions when the size of goodwill impairment is considered.

Specifically, as in the analysis in the previous section, we calculate the ratio of goodwill impairment divided by sales (at the end of the previous period) and divide the sample into three groups according to the size of the ratio. Again, the group with the highest value of the ratio is called High (N = 19), the group in the middle is called Mid (N = 20), and the group at the bottom is called Low (N = 20). Columns (6) and (7) in Table 7.9 and Fig. 7.13 show the results, which confirm that the abnormal trading volume response is particularly large on the announcement date ($t = 0$) for the High, Mid, and Low groups, as in the previous results. In addition, Fig. 7.13 shows that the volume reaction on the announcement day appears to be larger for

[27] Comparing the mean and median for these two subsamples, the results of the t-test and Wilcoxon rank-sum test were t-value = 1.602 (p-value = 0.127) and z-value = 1.023 (p-value = 0.306), respectively.

[28] Some analysts are of the view that amortization of goodwill reduces the amount of the impairment loss and thus undermines its informational content (e.g., ASBJ 2017).

[29] For example, if management has previously avoided recognizing goodwill impairment and losses have accumulated, resulting in a large goodwill impairment, the fact that goodwill is impaired may have been anticipated to a significant degree in advance by market participants. In this case, there may not be enough new information in the announcement of the goodwill impairment losses to change the behavior of market participants, and no abnormal volume reaction may be observed.

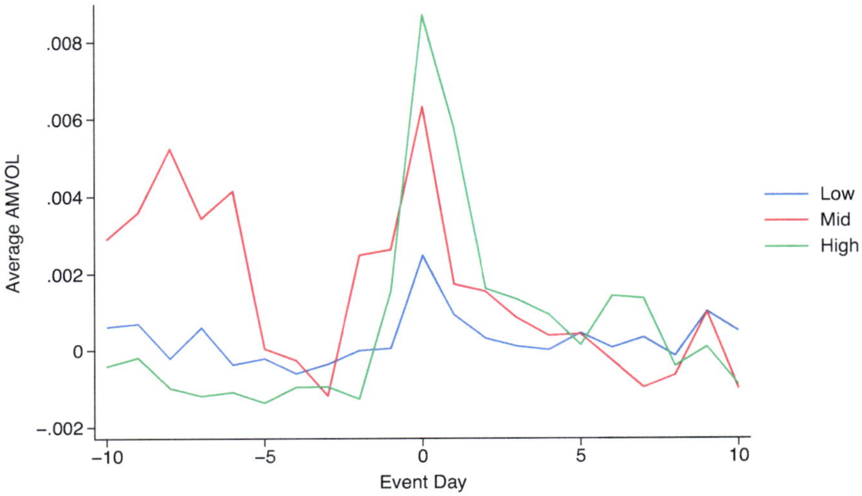

Fig. 7.13 Trends in abnormal trading volume (by size of impairment losses, N = 59)

the Low, Mid, and High groups, in that order. The results in Table 7.9 show that the average abnormal trading volume for High is 0.009, which is larger than 0.007 for Mid and 0.002 for Low (for the median, the values are 0.002 for Low, 0.003 for Mid, and 0.003 for High). However, the results of multiple comparisons of the mean and median of abnormal trading volume for these three groups with the t-test and Wilcoxon rank-sum test with Bonferroni correction do not show statistically significant differences in any case, indicating that there are no differences in the response of abnormal trading volume on the announcement dates between the groups.[30]

To examine the impact of the size of the goodwill impairment on abnormal trading volume in more detail, we estimate the following regression model:

$$\begin{aligned} AMVOL[0,+1]_i \left(AMVOL[-1,+1]_i\right) = \alpha_i &+ \beta_1 GWIMP_i + \beta_2 SIZE_i + \beta_3 EA_i \\ &+ \beta_4 OTHERIMP_i + \beta_5 REPEAT_i \\ &+ \beta_6 YEAR2010 + \beta_7 MANUFACTURE_i \\ &+ \varepsilon_i \end{aligned} \tag{7.8}$$

where $AMVOL[0,+1]_i$ ($AMVOL[-1,+1]_i$) is the sum of the market-adjusted abnormal trading volume from $t = 0$ to $t = +1$ (or $t = -1$ to $+1$). The explanatory variable

[30] However, multiple comparisons of the mean and median abnormal trading volumes immediately before and after the announcement date ($t = -1$ and $+ 1$) using the same method reveal a statistically significant difference at the 10% level only for the mean values of High and Low immediately after the announcement date (p-value = 0.055). This result indicates that the group with the largest impairment (High) has a higher level of abnormal trading volume immediately after the announcement date than the group with the smallest impairment (Low). It should be noted, however, that the Wilcoxon rank-sum test does not detect statistically significant differences even at the 10% level.

of interest is $GWIMP_i$, which is the amount of goodwill impairment loss divided by sales at the end of the previous period. Based on the aforementioned discussion, the larger the size of the goodwill impairment, the greater the impact on the market; then, the coefficient of the variable is expected to be positive. However, if a large amount of goodwill impairment is the result of avoiding the recognition of impairment in the past and information regarding the recognition of impairment is well known among market participants, it is possible that the response of abnormal trading volume is smaller as the size of the impairment increases. In this case, the coefficient is expected to be negative. However, as we confirm in the abovementioned abnormal trading volume trend, the size of goodwill impairment may not significantly affect the market response. In this case, the value of the coefficient is not expected to differ from zero.

Moreover, firm size ($SIZE_i$) is included in the model to control for the firm *i*'s information environment; we use the natural logarithm of total assets at the beginning of the period as $SIZE_i$. In addition to goodwill, if the firm records other impairment losses or extraordinary losses related to other fixed assets, this may have affected the abnormal volume response. $OTHERIMP_i$ is included in the model as a dummy variable that takes one when other impairment losses or extraordinary losses are announced in the same newspaper article, and zero otherwise. $REPEAT_i$ is a dummy variable that takes one if the firm has announced goodwill impairment losses in the past during the analysis period and zero otherwise. In our sample, announcements of goodwill impairment losses are concentrated in 2010. This is likely due to the impact of the global financial crisis and other factors. Therefore, we include a dummy variable ($YERR2010_i$) in the model to indicate that it is the year 2010. In addition, since previous studies using stock returns have shown that the market reaction differs between the manufacturing and non-manufacturing sectors, this study also includes a dummy variable ($MANUFACTURE_i$) in the model that takes one for the manufacturing sector and zero for the non-manufacturing sector. The basic statistics and correlation coefficients for these variables are summarized in Tables 7.10 and 7.11. As with the sample used in the regression analysis, we use only the J-GAAP sample. In the analysis, standard errors are computed using robust standard errors.

Table 7.10 Summary statistics for variables used in regression analysis

		N	Mean	SD	Min	P25	P50	P75	Max
(1)	*AMVOL[0, +1]*	59	0.009	0.015	−0.011	0	0.004	0.010	0.084
(2)	*AMVOL[−1, +1]*	59	0.01	0.018	−0.016	0	0.005	0.011	0.093
(3)	*GWIMP*	59	0.028	0.036	0	0.006	0.013	0.034	0.146
(4)	*SIZE*	59	12.466	1.713	7.571	11.412	12.728	13.712	15.51
(5)	*EA*	59	0.136	0.345	0	0	0	0	1
(6)	*OTHERIMP*	59	0.542	0.502	0	0	1	1	1
(7)	*REPEAT*	59	0.119	0.326	0	0	0	0	1
(8)	*YEAR2010*	59	0.051	0.222	0	0	0	0	1
(9)	*MANUFACTURE*	59	0.542	0.502	0	0	1	1	1

Table 7.11 Correlation matrix between the variables used in regression analysis

	(1)	(2)	(3)	(4)	(5)	(6)	(7)	(8)	(9)
(1)		0.9403*	0.1864	−0.1737	0.1163	−0.1059	−0.1262	−0.2039	−0.1658
(2)	0.9337*		0.2303	−0.1619	0.1221	−0.1139	−0.1631	−0.1858	−0.1279
(3)	0.3828*	0.3555*		−0.1999	0.3053*	−0.0899	−0.0862	−0.2356	−0.016
(4)	−0.1003	−0.1333	−0.4031*		−0.1192	0.2877*	0.3447*	0.2718*	0.3536*
(5)	0.1599	0.2254	0.3448*	−0.1484		−0.1331	−0.1453	−0.0917	0.0657
(6)	−0.0344	−0.008	−0.1096	0.2458	−0.1331		0.2318	0.2126	−0.0243
(7)	−0.1352	−0.1561	−0.1002	0.3186*	−0.1453	0.2318		−0.0849	0.0214
(8)	−0.127	−0.1222	−0.1527	0.2537	−0.0917	0.2126	−0.0849		−0.0971
(9)	−0.2129	−0.2123	−0.1208	0.3527*	0.0657	−0.0243	0.0214	−0.0971	

Notes: The lower left of this table shows Pearson's correlation coefficients, and the upper right shows that Spearman's rank correlation coefficients. The variables correspond to those in Table 7.10, which are numbered the same as in that table. Note that * indicates statistically significant at the 5% level

As shown in Table 7.12, the sign of the coefficient of $GWIMP_i$ is positive, indicating a relationship in which the larger the size of the goodwill impairment, the larger the abnormal volume reaction on and around the announcement date. However, this result is not statistically significant. Therefore, the results of the regression analysis presented in Table 7.12 do not provide evidence that the size of the goodwill impairment affects the abnormal trading volume reaction to the announcement of the goodwill impairment. The coefficients of $REPEAT_i$ and $MANUFACTURE_i$ are negative and statistically significant at the 10% level. The coefficient of $YEAR2010_i$ is also negative and statistically significant at the 5% level. As confirmed by the results for the entire sample, these results show that while the market responded to announcements about goodwill impairment losses, there is no evidence that the size of the impairment loss has affected this response. Rather than the size of impairment losses, the regression results indicate that market participants react differently depending on factors such as whether announcements regarding goodwill impairment losses made in previous years, the sector (manufacturing or non-manufacturing), and the timing of the announcements.

7.4.4 Summary

In contrast to the analysis and previous studies discussed in the previous section of this chapter, this section presents the results of the analyses of trading volumes. The analyses reveal a significant abnormal trading volume response to announcements of goodwill impairment losses, especially on the day of the announcement, which suggests that market participants react to goodwill impairment announcements and change their behavior. However, our analyses do not provide evidence that the reactions varies with the size of the impairment. Further studies are needed to determine

Table 7.12 Results of regression analysis using trading volume

	(1)	(2)
Dependent Variable =	AMVOL[0, +1].	AMVOL[−1, +1].
	Coef. (t-value)	Coef. (t-value)
GWIMP	0.166	0.160
	(1.47)	(1.22)
SIZE	0.002	0.002
	(1.58)	(1.22)
EA	0.002	0.007
	(0.22)	(0.67)
OTHERIMP	0.001	0.003
	(0.19)	(0.52)
REPEAT	−0.009*	−0.011*
	(−1.77)	(−1.86)
YEAR2010	−0.012**	−0.013**
	(−2.35)	(−2.35)
MANUFACTURE	−0.008*	−0.009*
	(−1.89)	(−1.86)
Const.	−0.019	−0.015
	(−1.12)	(−0.72)
N	59	59
Adjusted R^2	0.133	0.115

Notes: ***, **, and * denote statistical significance at the 1%, 5%, and 10% level, respectively (two-tailed test). Standard errors are calculated using robust standard errors

when there are differences in market reaction to goodwill impairment loss announcements.

7.5 Summary and Remaining Issues

Based on the results of the previous surveys and interviews, this chapter presents an empirical analysis of the "too little, too late" issue as perceived by stakeholders, especially users. Specifically, we analyze short- and long-term stock price reactions (Sects. 7.2 and 7.3) to announcements of goodwill impairment losses (from March 2007 to March 2019), focusing on abnormal stock returns and trading volume reactions (Sect. 7.4). The results confirm that stock prices and trading volumes react to announcements of goodwill impairment losses and that announcements contain new information content. In addition, when the sample is split into the J-GAAP and IFRS samples, negative abnormal returns and cumulative abnormal returns are observed on the announcement date ($t = 0$) for both sub-samples. Furthermore, positive and statistically significant abnormal trading volume responses are observed on the announcement date for both sub-samples, suggesting that the market reacts to goodwill impairment loss announcements. Overall, these results suggest that announcements of goodwill impairment losses are likely to provide new information to market participants. Nevertheless, the size of the IFRS sample is small, and the results should be interpreted with caution.

This study focuses not only on short-term but also on long-term cumulative abnormal returns. The results also reveal that the cumulative abnormal returns have declined even before the announcement of goodwill impairment losses. This result suggests that market participants may be aware of impairments in goodwill from an early stage, which is consistent with the results of interview surveys, such as ASBJ (2017) and Chap. 6. Similar to the short-term analysis, the results of splitting the sample into the J-GAAP and IFRS samples confirm a decreasing trend in cumulative abnormal returns over a long period before the announcement date for the J-GAAP sample; however, no reliable results show a similar trend for the IFRS sample. Whether this result can be interpreted as a result of firms applying IFRS (the impairment-only approach) recognizing impairment losses in a more timely manner than those applying Japanese GAAP (the systematic amortization with impairment approach) or whether there are some other possibilities requires further studies.[31]

Looking at the long-term cumulative abnormal stock returns by the size of goodwill impairment losses, the results show that the cumulative abnormal stock returns before and after the announcement date are negative regardless of the size of goodwill impairment losses, but a decreasing trend in cumulative abnormal returns over the long term from before the announcement date is observed only for the small amount of goodwill impairment losses. Based on the above interpretation, market participants could expect some impairment of goodwill for the smaller impairment group but not enough for the larger impairment group. The validity of this interpretation and the reasons for the above results are the subject for future discussion.

Appendix 5

In Sect. 7.4 of this chapter, we use *market-adjusted* abnormal trading volume as the abnormal trading volume. However, other methods of estimating abnormal volume are possible, such as estimating abnormal returns using a market model, which uses the model's estimation results to estimate abnormal trading volume (see, for example, Garfinkel and Sokobin 2006. Watkins 2022.). Therefore, in this appendix, we confirm the expected volume estimation results using the model with reference to Garfinkel and Sokobin (2006) and Watkins (2022). In this case, the abnormal trading volume is measured using the following equation:

[31] For example, it may be difficult to detect that goodwill is impaired for the IFRS sample. It is also possible that the sample size is simply too small to obtain significant results.

$$SAVOL_{i,t} = \left[LVOL_{i,t} - E\left(LVOL_{i,t}\right)\right] / S_{i,[-70,-21]} \tag{7.9}$$

Here, $SAVOL_{i,t}$ represents the standardized abnormal trading volume for firm i on day t ($t = -10, \ldots, +10$). $LVOL_{i,t}$ is the natural logarithm of the volume on day t for firm i. Further, $E(LVOL_{i,t})$ represents the expected trading volume on day t for firm i. Furthermore, $S_{i,[-70,-21]}$ is the standard deviation of the residuals calculated by the following model from −70 to −21 days prior to the event period. However, because $E(LVOL_{i,t})$ cannot be observed in practice, it is measured using parameters obtained by estimating the following model with −70 to −21 days of data.

$$LVOL_{i,t} = \alpha_i + \beta_i \mathrm{Re}t_{i,t} + \varepsilon_{i,t} \tag{7.10}$$

Here, $Ret_{i,t}$ represents daily stock returns (daily) and $LVOL_{i,t}$ is the same as that defined earlier. Note that Garfinkel and Sokobin (2006) and Watkins (2022) estimate models that allow for different coefficient values depending on whether the sign of $Ret_{i,t}$ is positive or negative, but in this Appendix, we use a simplified model that does not consider the sign difference of $Ret_{i,t}$. Using the parameters obtained by estimating eq. (7.10), we calculate $E(LVOL_{i,t})$ from −10 to +10 days as follows (where the estimate of α_i *is* a_i and the estimate of β_i *is* b_i):

$$E\left(LVOL_{i,t}\right) = a_i + b_i Ret_{i,t} \tag{7.11}$$

We also estimate a regression model to test the effect of goodwill impairment magnitude on abnormal trading volume, and we estimate the next regression model, described here in the Appendix.

$$\begin{aligned} SAVOL\left[0,+1\right]_i \left(SAVOL\left[-1,+1\right]_i\right) = {} & \gamma_i + \delta_1 GWIMP_i + \delta_2 SIZE_i + \delta_3 EA_i \\ & + \delta_4 OTHERIMP_i + \delta_5 REPEAT_i \\ & + \delta_6 YEAR2010 + \delta_7 MANUFACTURE_i \\ & + \varepsilon_i \end{aligned} \tag{7.12}$$

The definitions of the variables are the same as those used in the main analysis, except for the dependent variable. The dependent variable $SAVOL[0, +1]_i$ ($SAVOL[-1, +1]_i$) is the sum of the standardized abnormal volume at $t = 0$ and $t = +1$ ($t = -1$ to $+1$).

The following series of figures and tables present the results of the regression analysis and the results for $SAVOL_{i,t}$ (mean values) estimated using the methods described above (Tables 7.13 and 7.14; Figs. 7.14, 7.15, 7.16, and 7.17). Although the main conclusions are generally the same as those in the main analyses, some differences can be observed in the analysis results. The main differences are summarized as follows:

- The abnormal increase in trading volume at $t = +4$ for IFRS adopters shown in this study is not observed (instead, a large drop is observed at $t = -3$, which is

Table 7.13 Abnormal trading volume

	(1)				(2)				(3)				(4)				(5)			
	Total sample (N = 64)				J-GAAP sample (N = 59)				IFRS sample (N = 5)				Almost the same date as earnings announcement (N = 16)				J-GAAP sample excluding firms with almost the same announcement dates (N = 43)			
Event Day	Mean	median	t-value	z-value	Mean	median	t-value	z-value	Mean	median	t-value	z-value	Mean	median	t-value	z-value	Mean	median	t-value	z-value
−10	0.343	0.147	1.675* (1.675*)	1.538	0.220	0.218	1.571	1.593	1.785	−0.206	0.841	−0.405	0.229	0.607	0.881	1.241	0.217	0.127	1.291	1.051
−9	0.207	0.000	1.031	0.247	0.129	0.080	0.844	0.536	1.124	−0.526	0.570	−0.674	0.336	−0.056	1.161	0.259	0.052	0.125	0.287	0.302
−8	0.069	−0.166	0.379	−0.575	−0.003	−0.079	−0.020	−0.528	0.916	−0.635	0.626	−0.405	−0.057	−0.309	−0.151	−1.138	0.017	0.059	0.098	0.000
−7	0.342	0.077	1.735*	1.070	0.311	0.112	1.703*	1.268	0.701	−0.668	0.488	−0.674	0.085	−0.225	0.228	0.000	0.396	0.177	1.880* (1.880*)	1.546
−6	−0.009	−0.106	−0.054	−0.555	−0.025	−0.103	−0.165	−0.400	0.184	−0.437	0.163	−0.405	−0.211	−0.378	−0.739	−0.879	0.044	0.120	0.249	0.169
−5	−0.002	−0.125	−0.008	−0.381	−0.015	−0.124	−0.087	−0.189	0.156	−1.072	0.111	−0.405	0.336	0.304	0.967	0.879	−0.145	−0.183	−0.750	−0.785
−4	−0.182	−0.389	−1.056	−2.044**	−0.225	−0.372	−1.512	−1.847*	0.312	−0.880	0.221	−0.674	−0.242	−0.407	−0.687	−1.136	−0.219	−0.184	−1.359	−1.569
−3	−0.156	−0.300	−0.939	−1.629	−0.195	−0.293	−1.271	−1.506	0.304	−0.635	0.257	−0.405	−0.017	−0.077	−0.051	−0.227	−0.257	−0.300	−1.501	−1.690*
−2	−0.055	−0.229	−0.353	−0.689	−0.070	−0.227	−0.449	−0.566	0.120	−0.535	0.135	−0.674	−0.084	−0.160	−0.214	−0.259	−0.065	−0.269	−0.406	−0.604
−1	0.403	0.303	2.578**	2.307**	0.405	0.396	2.541**	2.355**	0.371	0.228	0.494	0.135	0.776	0.720	2.224**	1.913*	0.267	0.188	1.535	1.497
0	1.544	1.261	8.393***	6.086***	1.511	1.191	7.872***	5.767***	1.938	1.572	2.800***.	2.023**	2.070	2.442	4.817***	3.103***	1.303	1.150	6.399***	4.902***
1	0.750	0.540	4.826***	4.220***	0.718	0.542	4.504***	3.955***	1.135	0.348	1.625	1.483	1.080	0.812	2.797**	2.430**	0.583	0.526	3.567***	3.127***
2	0.513	0.362	3.276***	2.989***	0.444	0.323	2.916***	2.687***	1.329	0.921	1.485	1.483	1.070	1.134	4.012***	2.792***	0.211	0.300	1.223	1.099
3	0.178	0.339	1.049	1.371	0.297	0.438	1.797*	1.879*	−1.216	−0.429	−1.522	−1.753*	0.915	1.027	2.893**	2.534**	0.066	0.289	0.362	0.543
4	0.261	0.067	1.147	0.341	0.184	0.097	1.079	0.596	1.176	−0.992	0.513	−0.405	0.230	0.092	0.661	0.569	0.166	0.097	0.845	0.302
5	0.224	0.156	1.156	0.869	0.160	0.219	1.012	1.087	0.980	−0.572	0.553	−0.405	0.194	0.170	0.572	0.776	0.148	0.219	0.823	0.761
6	0.287	0.226	1.591	1.376	0.230	0.230	1.456	1.490	0.944	−0.482	0.651	−0.405	0.328	0.107	0.959	0.909	0.196	0.234	1.095	1.183
7	0.280	0.305	1.667	1.670*	0.303	0.341	1.923*	1.986**	0.016	−0.872	0.013	−0.405	0.210	0.378	0.650	1.136	0.336	0.248	1.840*	1.823*
8	0.000	−0.027	0.000	−0.709	−0.025	−0.017	−0.165	−0.619	0.293	−0.467	0.272	−0.405	0.438	0.205	1.577	1.862*	−0.197	−0.369	−1.139	−1.606
9	0.210	0.070	1.309	0.582	0.239	0.088	1.483	0.863	−0.130	−0.663	−0.156	−0.405	0.355	0.225	1.516	1.193	0.199	−0.202	0.980	0.435
10	0.025	0.058	0.151	0.308	0.008	0.195	0.050	0.445	0.226	−0.249	0.239	−0.405	0.047	0.256	0.172	−0.052	−0.006	0.095	−0.030	0.374

−10	0.237	0.374	0.885	0.635	0.330	0.065	1.606	1.456	0.088	0.127	0.336	0.563
−9	0.329	0.204	1.176	0.896	0.021	0.065	0.086	0.261	0.032	−0.048	0.116	−0.161
−8	0.065	0.001	0.260	0.224	0.320	0.088	0.932	0.597	−0.415	−0.541	−2.253**	−1.972**
−7	0.426	0.411	1.318	1.195	0.665	0.430	1.896*	1.717*	−0.181	−0.272	−0.738	−0.845
−6	−0.191	−0.310	−1.232	−1.344	0.196	0.321	0.592	0.635	−0.083	0.099	−0.308	−0.402
−5	0.064	0.024	0.249	0.187	0.020	−0.171	0.058	0.299	−0.134	−0.477	−0.441	−0.563
−4	−0.223	−0.386	−0.822	−1.157	0.049	0.030	0.198	−0.080	−0.517	−0.463	−2.104*	−2.112**
−3	0.010	−0.282	0.032	−0.485	−0.235	−0.183	−0.943	−0.896	−0.378	−0.384	−1.515	−1.285
−2	0.117	−0.069	0.493	0.000	−0.027	−0.295	−0.087	−0.187	−0.313	−0.227	−1.178	−0.926
−1	−0.005	−0.117	−0.023	−0.224	0.438	0.565	1.286	1.232	0.803	0.923	3.701***	2.897***
0	1.296	0.826	3.403***	3.061***	1.245	1.101	4.339***	3.173***	2.016	2.057	6.546***	3.702***
1	0.478	0.530	1.950* (1.950*)	1.755* (1.755*)	0.275	0.382	1.116	1.344	1.435	1.351	5.199***	3.541***
2	0.084	−0.149	0.273	−0.037	0.449	0.254	1.845*	1.829*	0.817	0.496	3.812***	3.179***
3	−0.145	−0.325	−0.461	−0.597	0.534	0.491	1.977*	1.904*	0.512	0.682	2.019*	2.133**
4	−0.023	−0.344	−0.069	−0.597	0.246	0.132	1.073	0.933	0.335	0.339	1.035	0.926
5	−0.091	−0.344	−0.321	−0.560	0.167	0.307	0.663	1.008	0.418	0.414	1.442	1.449
6	−0.098	0.089	−0.375	−0.112	0.168	0.129	0.599	0.597	0.663	0.725	2.541**	2.069**
7	0.157	−0.012	0.544	0.373	−0.052	0.084	−0.194	−0.075	0.860	0.744	3.832***	3.027***
8	−0.242	−0.338	−1.011	−1.381	−0.052	−0.342	−0.169	−0.187	0.232	0.146	1.028	0.885
9	0.492	0.054	1.421	0.523	−0.035	−0.047	−0.147	0.000	0.264	0.251	1.160	0.893
10	0.444	0.361	1.731*	1.643	−0.411	−0.106	−1.195	−0.859	−0.009	−0.037	−0.041	0.000

Notes: Mean indicates the mean value of abnormal trading volumes. Median indicates the median value of abnormal trading volumes. t-value indicates the result of a t-test. z-value indicates the result of a Wilcoxon signed-rank test (two-tailed test). ***, ** and * indicate statistical significance at the 1%, 5%, and 10% levels, respectively. The results from (4) to (8) are obtained using only the J-GAAP sample

Table 7.14 Regression analysis results using trading volumes

	(1)	(2)
Dependent Variable =	SVOL[0, +1]	SVOL[−1, +1]
	Coef. (t-value)	Coef. (t-value)
GWIMP	5.300	5.008
	(0.46)	(0.34)
SIZE	−0.191	−0.298
	(−0.68)	(−0.82)
EA	0.800	1.904
	(0.82)	(1.46)
OTHERIMP	0.035	0.715
	(0.05)	(0.83)
REPEAT	0.393	0.720
	(0.35)	(0.52)
YEAR2010	−1.822**	−2.418**
	(−2.19)	(−2.11)
MANUFACTURE	−0.212	0.210
	(−0.28)	(0.22)
Const.	4.495	5.487
	(1.43)	(1.38)
N	59	59
Adjusted R-sq	−0.020	0.024

Notes: ***, **, and * denote statistical significance at the 1%, 5%, and 10% level, respectively (two-tailed test). Standard errors are calculated using robust standard errors

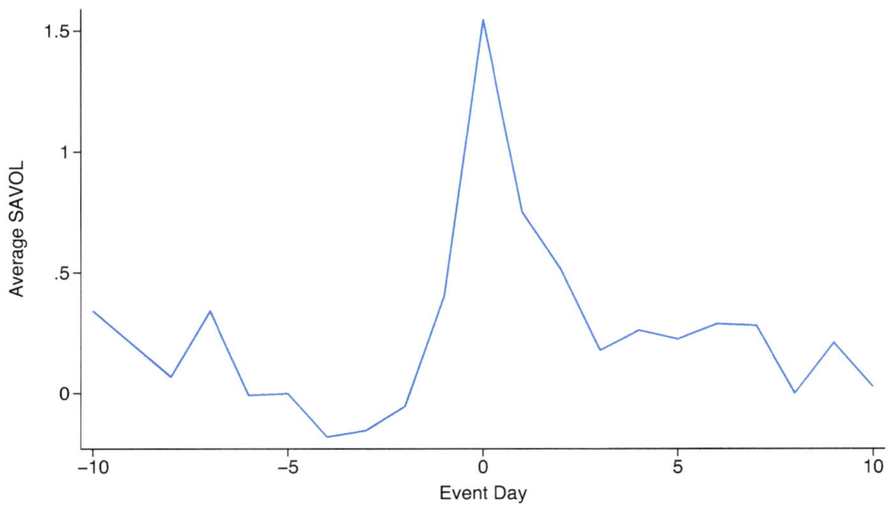

Fig. 7.14 Trend in abnormal trading volume (entire sample, N = 64)

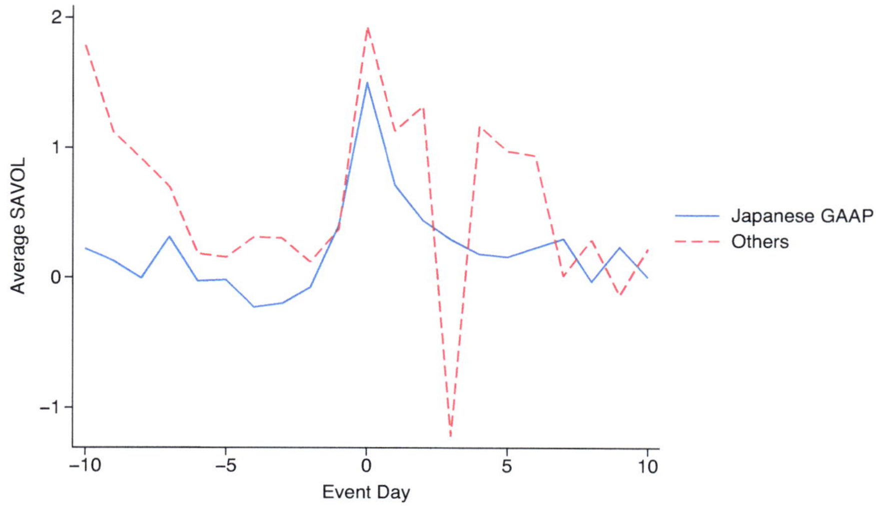

Fig. 7.15 Trends in abnormal trading volume (by accounting standards, N = 64)

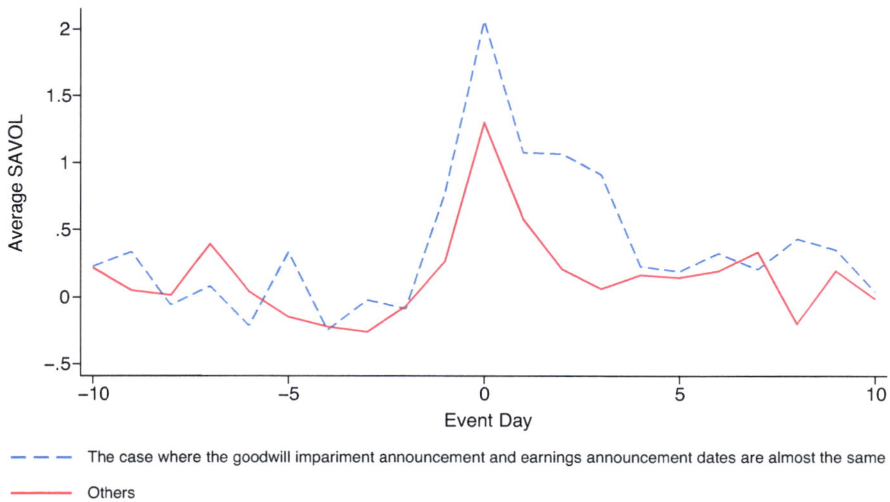

Fig. 7.16 Trends in abnormal trading volume (results after taking into account the gap with the earnings announcements date, N = 59)

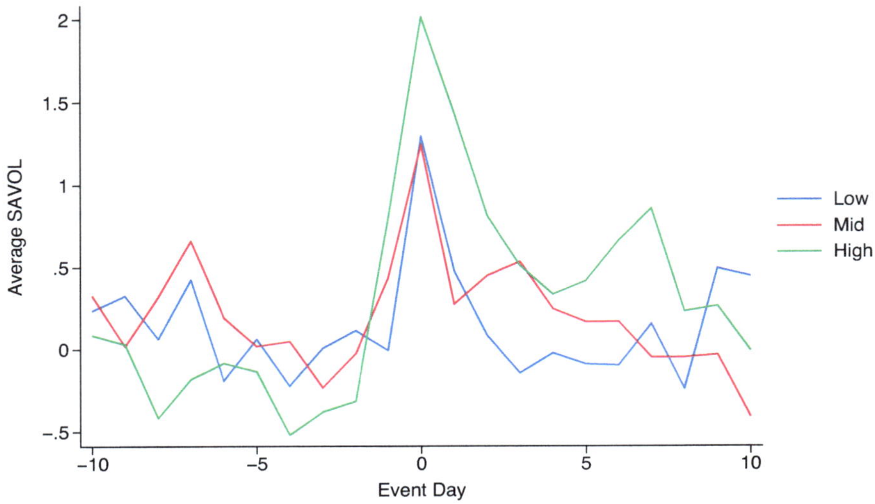

Fig. 7.17 Abnormal trading volume (by the size of impairment losses, N = 59)

statistically significant at the 10% level, although only with the Wilcoxon signed-rank test).

- In contrast to the main results, a statistically significant difference is found in the response to abnormal trading volume on the announcement date when the sample is divided between those where the goodwill impairment announcement and the earnings announcement dates are within ± 1 day and others (but only for the results of the Wilcoxon rank-sum test [z-value = 1.722, p-value = 0.085], and no significant difference is detected by the t-test).
- When the sample is divided into three groups (Low, Mid, and High) based on the size of impairment losses, statistically significant positive abnormal trading volume responses are confirmed for Mid and High, even after the announcement date ($t = +2$ and + 3), whereas, for Low, statistically significant positive responses are confirmed at the 10% level only for the average abnormal trading volume on +10 days. Furthermore, for High, statistically significant positive abnormal trading volume responses are confirmed from $t = -1$ to $t = +3$, and on +6 and +7 days.
- In this Appendix, as in the main analyses, we describe multiple comparisons of means and medians among the three groups divided by the size of goodwill impairment losses, performed using t-tests and Wilcoxon rank-sum tests with Bonferroni correction, respectively (multiple comparisons were performed from $t = -1$ to $t = +1$). The results (untabulated) show no statistically significant differences in the announcement date in any case. However, statistically significant differences are detected at the 5% level (p-value = 0.032) for the medians of High and Low on the day before the announcement, and for the means and medians of High and Low and High and Mid on the day after the announcement (1% level for the difference between the means of High and

Mid (the difference between the High and Mid means is at the 1% level [p-value = 0.007], the difference between the medians is at the 5% level [p-value = 0.021], the difference between the High and Low means is at the 5% level [p-value = 0.033], and the difference between the medians is at the 10% level [p-value = 0.098]).

- The results of the regression analysis (Table 7.14) show no statistically significant results, except for the coefficients of *YEAR2010* (*GWIMP is* not significant, similar to the main results). The fit of the model (adjusted R^2) is much lower than the estimation results in the main study, and the adjusted R^2 in Column (1) is negative (using *AMVOL[0, +1]*).

Statement on AI Usage: During the preparation of this manuscript, the authors used AI-assisted tools such as DeepL and Gemini to improve the English expression and clarity of the manuscript. The authors thoroughly reviewed and approved the final version and take full responsibility for the content.

References

In English

Accounting Standards Board of Japan (ASBJ). (2017). *Analyst Views on Financial Information Regarding Goodwill.* Research Paper No. 3. Tokyo, Japan: ASBJ.

Alciatore, M., Dee, C. C., Easton, P., & Spear, N. (1998). "Asset write-downs: A decade of research", *Journal of Accounting Literature*, 17:1–39.

Ball, R. and P. Brown (1968). "An empirical evaluation of accounting income numbers", *Journal of Accounting Research*, 6(2):159–178.

Ball, R., & Shivakumar, L. (2008). "How much new information is there in earnings?", *Journal of Accounting Research*, 46(5):975–1016.

Bamber, L. S., Barron, O. E., & Stevens, D. E. (2011). "Trading volume around earnings announcements and other financial reports: Theory, research design, empirical evidence, and directions for future research", *Contemporary Accounting Research*, 28(2):431–471.

Bartov, E., Lindahl, F. W., & Ricks, W. E. (1998). "Stock price behavior around announcements of write-offs", *Review of Accounting Studies*, 3(4):327–346.

Beaver, W. H. (1968). "The information content of annual earnings announcements", *Journal of Accounting Research*, 6(Supplement):67–92.

Bens, D. A., Heltzer, W., & Segal, B. (2011). "The information content of goodwill impairments and SFAS 142", *Journal of Accounting, Auditing & Finance*, 26(3):527–555.

Francis, J., Hanna, J. D., & Vincent, L. (1996). "Causes and effects of discretionary asset write-offs", *Journal of Accounting Research*, 34:117–134.

Garfinkel, J. A., & Sokobin, J. (2006). "Volume, opinion divergence, and returns: A study of post-earnings announcement drift", *Journal of Accounting Research*, 44(1):85–112.

Jarva, H. (2014). "Economic consequences of SFAS 142 goodwill write-offs", *Accounting and Finance,* 54(1):211–235.

Landsman, W. R., E. L. Maydew, and J. R. Thornock (2012). "The information content of annual Earnings announcements and mandatory adoption of IFRS", *Journal of Accounting and Economics*, 53(1):34–54.

Laurion, H., Robinson, S., & Tice, F. M. (2023). "*Credibility of Managers' Fair Value Assessments: Evidence from Smaller-than-Expected Goodwill Impairments*", Available at SSRN 3817765.

Hirschey, M., & Richardson, V. J. (2002). "Information content of accounting goodwill numbers", *Journal of Accounting and Public Policy*, 21(3):173–191.
Hirschey, M., & Richardson, V. J. (2003). "Investor underreaction to goodwill write-offs", *Financial Analysts Journal*, 59(6):75–84.
International Accounting Standards Board (IASB). (2020) *Discussion Paper: Business Combinations-Disclosures, Goodwill and Impairment*. IASB.
Knauer, T., & Wöhrmann, A. (2016). "Market reaction to goodwill impairments", *European Accounting Review*, 25(3):421–449.
Li, Z., Shroff, P. K., Venkataraman, R., & Zhang, I. X. (2011). "Causes and consequences of goodwill impairment losses", *Review of Accounting Studies*, 16(4):745–778.
Li, K. K., & Sloan, R. G. (2017). "Has goodwill accounting gone bad?", *Review of Accounting Studies*, 22(2):964–1003.
Watkins, J. (2022). "Consequences of prescribed disclosure timeliness: Evidence from acceleration of the Form 8-K filing deadline", *The Accounting Review*, 97(7):429–463.
Zang, Y. (2008). "Discretionary behavior with respect to the adoption of SFAS No. 142 and the behavior of security prices", *Review of Accounting and Finance*, 7(1):38–68.

In Japanese

Kimura, A. (2017). "Jisshō bunseki: genson sonshitsu ni taisuru tōshika no hannō to hyōka (Empirical analysis: Investors' reaction to and evaluation of impairment losses)," *Shōken anarisuto jānaru (Securities Analysts Journal)*, 55(11):24–32.
Shimada, N. (2010). "Noren no kaikei jōhō no yūyōsei (The usefulness of accounting information of goodwill)," *Nempō keiei bunseki kenkyū* (*Annual Review of Business Analysis)*, 26:74–82.
Shimada, N. (2011). "Noren no genson jōhō ni taisuru shōken shijō no hannō (Securities Market Reaction to Goodwill Impairment Information)," *Gendai shakai to kaikei (Modern Society and Accounting)*, 5:37–49.
Miyauchi, T., & Yamashita, T. (2022). "Noren no Genson Sonshitsu no Jōhō Naiyō ni Kansuru Jisshō Bunseki (An empirical analysis of the information content of goodwill impairment losses)", Otemon Gakuiun University Discussion Paper No. 2022-2.

Chapter 8
Accounting Perspective and Accounting Education

Toshitake Miyauchi, Yuko Asami, Yoshihiro Tokuga, Masaki Yoneyama, and Yamashita Tomoaki

8.1 Purpose and Organization of This Chapter

As discussed in Chap. 5, whether goodwill should be amortized (or, in line with recent international discussions, whether amortization should be reintroduced to goodwill) is an issue that has long been debated in international accounting standard-setting. Currently, the limitations (problems) of the approach that requires only impairment of goodwill (hereinafter referred to as "impairment-only"), including the so-called "too little, too late" issue, are being increasingly recognized (e.g., ASBJ, EFRAG, and OCI 2014; IASB 2020; ASBJ staff and HKICPA staff 2020).

This chapter is based on the discussion paper (Miyauchi et al. 2022).

T. Miyauchi (✉)
Faculty of Management, Otemon Gakuin University, Osaka, Japan
e-mail: tomiyauc@otemon.ac.jp

Y. Asami
Graduate School of Economics, Nagoya University, Aichi, Japan

Y. Tokuga
Department of Business Administration, Faculty of Economics and Business Administration, Kyoto University of Advanced Science, Kyoto, Japan

M. Yoneyama
Graduate School of Economics, The University of Tokyo, Tokyo, Japan

Y. Tomoaki
Department of Business Administration, Faculty of Economics, Fukui Prefectural University, Fukui, Japan

Y. Tokuga, M. Yoneyama (eds.), *Controversies Over Accounting for Goodwill*, Contributions to Finance and Accounting,
https://doi.org/10.1007/978-981-92-0156-3_8

Therefore, we conducted a questionnaire survey of financial statement preparers, financial statement users, and auditors regarding issues related to the subsequent accounting treatment of goodwill in 2019–2021. Based on the analysis of the results, we have conducted feedback-type visit interviews with preparers, users, and auditors. The results are presented in Chaps. 5 and 6.

The purpose of the above surveys was to investigate the perception of facts attitudes of major capital market participants in terms of stakeholders who may influence accounting standard setting. Through the analyses of Chaps. 5 and 6, several characteristics regarding response trends as well as factors that may have influenced response trends were identified. Specifically, the following response trends were noted.

1. Japanese preparers, users, and auditors all support "systematic amortization with impairment" as the accounting treatment for goodwill.
2. If goodwill is to be amortized, most of the three respondent groups support the view that "a maximum amortization period should be set;" however, preparers support a maximum amortization period of 20 years, while users and auditors support a maximum amortization period of 10 years.
3. Behind the uneven responses of users (analysts) are analysts who studied accounting at Japanese universities and gained practical experience at Japanese securities firms as well as analysts who studied accounting at U.S. universities or gained experience at foreign securities firms. The former uses the balance sheet, income statement, and all cash flows to make investment decisions, whereas the latter uses only cash flows, which may have affected their answers.
4. Of the three, auditors showed the highest support for "systematic amortization with impairment," in that they seek to avoid the possibility of recording internally generated goodwill and support a conservative 10-year amortization period limit for goodwill.

These trends in responses and the factors that may affect them raise the possibility that, in addition to "habituation" to Japanese accounting standards and "imprinting" by the Keidanren and other Japanese accounting standard setters, accounting education at Japanese universities and other institutions of higher education and education through the CPA examination may strongly influence the responses.

Therefore, this study investigates what educators at universities, professional schools, and other educational institutions emphasize and what type of thinking and education they provide concerning the perception of facts common to Japanese stakeholders (theories and concepts that differ from those of their Western counterparts). Accordingly, we aim to analyze the possibility that accounting education at institutions such as universities and professional education, including preparation for the Japanese CPA and tax accountant examinations, influence how stakeholders think about accounting for goodwill, and, moreover, indirectly influence accounting standard setting.

8.2 Survey Design and Results

In this section, we present the survey results and the content of the questions asked. First, an overview of the survey methodology of this chapter is presented. The survey was conducted from March 1–31, 2022, targeting 1698 members (excluding graduate student members) of the Japanese Accounting Research Association. A letter requesting cooperation was sent to the members, which included the URL for the online survey and a QR code that could be used to access it. Responses were provided via an online form,[1] In total, 279 responses were received (response rate: 16.4%).

The survey collected information on respondents' basic characteristics; therefore, this section describes their characteristics before the survey results are discussed below. Specifically, we asked questions regarding (1) the regional section to which the respondent belonged in the Japanese Accounting Research Association, (2) the attributes of the organization for which the respondent worked (e.g., university or audit firm), (3) age range, (4) length of teaching experience, (5) main research methods employed by respondents, and (6) lecture courses for which the respondent has been responsible. Tables 8.1, 8.2, 8.3, 8.4,8.5 and 8.6 summarize the results of the responses to these questions.

Table 8.1 shows the aggregate results of the Japanese Accounting Research Association by regional branch to which the respondents belonged. Of the 279 total respondents, 111 (39.8%) belonged to the Kanto Branch, which had the largest number of members, followed by 90 respondents (32.3%) who were members of the Kansai Branch.[2]

Table 8.2 shows the attributes of the respondents' employers. Of the total respondents, 197 (70.6%) were university faculty members affiliated with "private universities," followed by 40 (14.3%) with "national universities" and 19 (6.8%) with "public universities[15]". The ten "others" included three public organizations such as

Table 8.1 Regional branch in the Japanese Accounting Research Association

Regional branch	Number of responses	Percentage (%)
Hokkaido branch	7	2.5
Tohoku branch	8	2.9
Kanto branch	111	39.8
Chubu branch	23	8.2
Kansai branch	90	32.3
Kyushu branch	39	14.0
Others	1	0.4
Total	279	100.0

[1] In considering the wording and structure of the survey questions, two pilot tests were conducted with university faculty in the accounting department.

[2] One respondent stated that he had recently moved and did not belong to any Branch.

Table 8.2 Employer attributes

Workplaces	Number of responses	Percentage (%)
National University	40	14.3
Public University	19	6.8
Private University	197	70.6
Technical Colleges	1	0.4
Commercial High School	0	0.0
Private Accounting School	0	0.0
Private Company	8	2.9
Vocational School	0	0.0
Auditing firm	4	1.4
Certified Public Tax Accountant	0	0.0
Others	10	3.6
Total	279	100.0

Table 8.3 Age groups

Age	Number of responses	Percentage (%)
35 and under	35	12.5
36–45 years old	70	25.1
46–55 years old	85	30.5
56 years and up	89	31.9
Total	279	100.0

national public officers, three retired professors, one visiting professor and outside director at a private university, one certified tax accountant firm, one Japanese Institute of Certified Public Accountants, and one self-employed.

Table 8.3 shows the age groups to which the respondents belong. The "56 years and older" group had the most people, accounting for 89 (31.9%) of the respondents. Among the others, 85 (30.5%) were in the "46–55" age group and 70 (25.1%) were in the "36–45" age group. Age groups were divided into 10-year age increments.

Table 8.4 shows the aggregate results for the respondents' length of teaching experience. A total of 101 respondents (36.2%) indicated that they had an teaching experience of "20 years or more." The other categories are in 5-year increments, making it impossible to make a simple comparison; however, this group had the largest number of responses. The other length of teaching experience groups had approximately 40 to 50 responses. The "within 4 years" category includes respondents with no teaching experience since the question asked respondents to choose this answer if they did not have a teaching experience.

Table 8.5 shows the results of the research methods primarily employed by respondents (multiple responses allowed). The 279 respondents provided a total of 414 responses, and "Percentage A (%)" shows the percentage of the total number of

Table 8.4 Length of teaching experience

Teaching experience	Number of responses	Percentage (%)
4 years and less	49	17.6
5–9 years	47	16.8
10–14 years	43	15.4
15–19 years	39	14.0
20 years or more	101	36.2
Total	279	100.0

Table 8.5 Main research methods

Research Methods	Number of responses	Percentage A (%)	Percentage B (%)
Normative studies	155	55.6	37.4
Empirical studies using archival data	96	34.4	23.2
Other empirical studies	53	19.0	12.8
Experimental studies	14	5.0	3.4
Mathematical research using analytic models	16	5.7	3.9
Historical research	65	23.3	15.7
Other	15	5.4	3.6
Number of responses	279 (414)		100.0

[a]The questions were multiple-choice/allowed responses; thus, Percentage A represents the number of responses to each option as a percentage of the total number of respondents (279), and Percentage B represents the number of responses to each option as a percentage of the total number of responses (414)

responses for each research method to the 279 respondents (the total percentage does not add up to 100%). "Percentage B (%)" shows the breakdown of the total number of responses (414) by the 279 respondents.

The most frequently adopted method was "normative research," which 155 of the 279 respondents (Percentage A: 55.6%). The next most common was "empirical research using archival data," which 96 respondents selected (Percentage A: 34.4%). The third most common choice was "historical research," selected by 65 respondents (Percentage A: 23.3%). Of the 15 who responded with "other," 12 performed qualitative research (interviews, fieldwork, case studies, action research).

Table 8.6 Lecture courses taught

Lecture	Number of responses	Percentage A (%)	Percentage B (%)
Bookkeeping	162	58.1	26.1
Financial statement theory	116	41.6	18.7
Accounting (principles of accounting)	127	45.5	20.4
Management accounting (including cost accounting)	74	26.5	11.9
Auditing	27	9.7	4.3
International accounting (including IFRS explanations)	42	15.1	6.8
Tax accounting	19	6.8	3.1
Others	34	12.2	5.5
Not teaching accounting-related courses	20	7.2	3.2
Number of responses	279 (621)		100.0

[a]Since the responses to the multiple-choice questions were accepted, Percentage A represents the number of responses to each option as a percentage of the total number of 279 respondents, and Percentage B represents the number of responses to each option as a percentage of the total number of 621 responses. However, the option "I do not teach accounting-related courses" was not included as a multiple-choice option

When "empirical research using archival data" is added to "other empirical research" and "experimental research," the total of 163 (Percentage A: 58.4%, Percentage B: 39.4%) exceeds the number for "normative research," suggesting that researchers in the accounting field have experienced recent a shift in the research methods they use most commonly.

Table 8.6 shows the results regarding the lectures (multiple responses allowed) the respondents conducted, with a total of 621 responses received from 279 respondents. Percentage A shows the number of responses for each subject as a percentage of the 279 total respondents (the total does not add up to 100%), and percentage B shows the number of responses for each subject as a percentage of the 621 total responses.

The most frequently taught subject was "Bookkeeping," with 162 cases (Percentage A: 58.1%, Percentage B: 26.1%), followed by "Accounting (Principles of Accounting)," with 127 (Percentage A: 45.5%, Percentage B: 20.4%). This was followed by "Theory of Financial Statements" with 116 (Percentage A: 41.6%, Percentage B: 18.7%), "Management Accounting (including Cost Accounting)" with 74 (Percentage A: 26.5%, Percentage B: 11.9%), and "International Accounting (including explanation of IFRS [International Financial Reporting Standards])" with 42 (Percentage A: 15.1%, Percentage B: 6.8%). The 34 "other" courses included business analysis (financial statement analysis, corporate valuation) in 17 cases, finance (financial management, corporate governance, securities investment)[3] in 6 cases, environmental accounting in 3 cases, public accounting in 3 cases, accounting history in 2 cases, and other subjects. Twenty respondents indicated that they did not teach accounting-related courses.[4]

8.3 Influences of Accounting Education

This section provides an overview of the results of the survey on the emphasis placed on corporate accounting laws and regulations, accounting standards and basic conceptual document, and concepts and ideas in lectures on accounting-related subjects at universities and other institutions of higher education. Of the 279 total survey respondents, 259 are included in the tabulated results in this section, excluding the 20 respondents who indicated that they "do not teach courses on accounting-related subjects." Table 8.6 shows the courses that respondents teach.

Q7. How much emphasis do you place on the following business accounting laws and regulations in your lectures (options: 1 "much emphasis," 2 " somewhat emphasis," 3 "neutral," 4 "not much emphasis," 5 "little emphasis").

(Corporate accounting laws and regulations)

1. Company Law
2. Financial Instruments and Exchange Law
3. Corporate Tax Law

Table 8.7 illustrates the results for the responses to Q7, which asked how much importance respondents placed on various corporate accounting laws and regulations in lectures on accounting-related subjects. "Financial Instruments and Exchange Law" was the most emphasized, with 50.6% (131/259) of the respondents 1 placing importance on it, which increased to 80.7% (209/259) when combining those respondents with those who answered 2, indicating that it is somewhat

[3]Although finance itself is not an accounting-related subject, respondents who note teaching finance in the "other" category are understood to be teaching bookkeeping, financial statement theory, management accounting, or other subjects in addition to finance. Respondents who only teach finance are included in the "Not teaching accounting-related subjects" category.

[4]Respondents who selected this option were not included in the answers to questions Q.7–Q.12, which are referenced in Sect. 8.4.

Table 8.7 Emphasis on business accounting laws and regulations in lectures

Corporate accounting laws and regulations	1 Much emphasis	2 Somewhat emphasis	3 Neutral	4 Not much emphasis	5 Little emphasis	Total Percentage (%)
Company law	81	110	31	26	11	259
	31.3	42.5	12.0	10.0	4.2	100.0
Financial instruments and exchange law	131	78	19	21	10	259
	50.6	30.1	7.3	8.1	3.9	100.0
Corporate tax law	23	62	63	73	38	259
	8.9	23.9	24.3	28.2	14.7	100.0

emphasized. The results are likely related to the positioning of the purpose of accounting as providing information useful for investors when making decisions, and that the Financial Instruments and Exchange Law[5] has become increasingly important.

Q8. How much emphasis do you place on the following accounting standards and basic conceptual documents in your lectures (options: 1 "much emphasis," 2 " somewhat emphasis," 3 "neutral," 4 "not much emphasis," 5 "little emphasis").

(Accounting standards and basic conceptual documents)
1. Corporate Accounting Principles
2. Regulations for Financial Statements
3. Current Japanese Accounting standards (Accounting standards issued by the Accounting Standards Board of Japan [ASBJ])
4. IFRS (International Financial Reporting Standards)
5. Conceptual Framework of the ASBJ
6. Conceptual Framework of the International Accounting Standards Board

Next in importance was the Company Law, with 31.3% (81/259) of the respondents answering 1, and 73.7% (191/259) represented the combined ratio of those who answered either 1 or 2.

Table 8.8 shows the results for the responses to Q8, which asked how much importance the respondents gave to various accounting standards and basic conceptual documents in lectures on accounting-related subjects. The most emphasized was "current Japanese accounting standards (accounting standards issued by the ASBJ)," with a combined total of 83.0% (215/259) answering either 1 or 2. This may reflect that the latest accounting standards are taught in courses such as bookkeeping. The next most emphasized topic was "Corporate Accounting Principles,"

[5]The Financial Instruments and Exchange Law was enacted in June 2006, and the Company Law came into effect in May 2006.

Table 8.8 Emphasis on accounting standards and basic conceptual documents in lectures

Accounting standards and basic conceptual documents	1 Much emphasis	2 Somewhat emphasis	3 Neutral	4 Not much emphasis	5 Little emphasis	Total Percentage (%)
Corporate accounting principles	80	102	41	25	11	259
	30.9	39.4	15.8	9.7	4.2	100.0
Regulations for financial statements	63	85	66	27	18	259
	24.3	32.8	25.5	10.4	6.9	100.0
Current Japanese accounting standards (accounting standards issued by the accounting standards Board of Japan [ASBJ])	142	73	28	10	6	259
	54.8	28.2	10.8	3.9	2.3	100.0
IFRS (international financial reporting standards)	77	97	47	25	13	259
	29.7	37.5	18.1	9.7	5.0	100.0
Conceptual framework of the ASBJ	70	72	57	36	24	259
	27.0	27.8	22.0	13.9	9.3	100.0
Conceptual framework of the IASB	56	67	64	45	27	259
	21.6	25.9	24.7	17.4	10.4	100.0

with 70.3% (182/259) of respondents rating the importance as either 1 or 2. Answers of 5 and 4 were provided by 13.9% (36/259) of the respondents, possibly indicating that only a small number of faculty members do not place much importance on "Corporate Accounting Principles."

"IFRS (International Financial Reporting Standards)" was ranked as the next highest for importance, with 67.2% (174/259) of the respondents answering either 1 or 2. Regarding the "Conceptual Framework of the ASBJ" and the "Conceptual Framework of the IASB," 54.8% (142/259) and 47.5% (123/259) of the respondents, respectively, rated these as either 1 or 2. Based on these responses, "Conceptual Framework" was clearly given more importance than we had previously assumed. However, the totals for 5 and 4 were relatively higher for Conceptual Framework than for the other options, indicating that a reasonable number of respondents did not place much importance on Conceptual Framework.

Table 8.9 shows the results for the responses to Q9. The most important principle was " matching revenues and expenses" with a total of 92.7% (240/259) of the respondents answering either 1 or 2. Only 1.5% (4/259) responded with either 4 or 5, indicating that very few faculty members did not consider " matching revenues and expenses" to be important. The next most emphasized principle was the "distinction between equity and profit," with a total of 83.8% (217/259) responding with either 1 or 2. The third most important concept was "acquisition cost (transaction price)," with 81.9% (212/259) of respondents selecting either 1 or 2.

"Fair value (market value)" and "discounted present value (value in use)" were also highly emphasized, with 75.7% (196/259) and 76.8% (199/259) of

Table 8.9 Emphasis on accounting concepts and principles in lectures

Accounting concepts and principles	1 Much emphasis	2 Somewhat emphasis	3 Neutral	4 Not much emphasis	5 Little emphasis	Total Percentage (%)
Matching revenues and expenses	161	79	15	2	2	259
	62.2	30.5	5.8	0.8	0.8	100.0
Distinction between equity and profit	137	80	30	7	5	259
	52.9	30.9	11.6	2.7	1.9	100.0
Fact of transaction	88	90	55	18	8	259
	34.0	34.7	21.2	6.9	3.1	100.0
Book value of net assets	52	82	86	27	12	259
	20.1	31.7	33.2	10.4	4.6	100.0
Economic value of the entity	66	100	61	23	9	259
	25.5	38.6	23.6	8.9	3.5	100.0
Acquisition cost (transaction price)	122	90	33	11	3	259
	47.1	34.7	12.7	4.2	1.2	100.0
Fair value (market value)	83	113	43	14	6	259
	32.0	43.6	16.6	5.4	2.3	100.0
Discounted present value (value in use)	88	111	46	10	4	259
	34.0	42.9	17.8	3.9	1.5	100.0

respondents, respectively, providing an answer of either 1 or 2. For the other concepts, the totals for 1 and 2 also exceeded 50%, indicating that the respondents emphasized all the concepts listed in this question.

Q9. How much emphasis do you place on the following accounting concepts and principles in your lectures (options: 1 "much emphasis," 2 " somewhat emphasis," 3 "neutral," 4 "not much emphasis," 5 "little emphasis").

(Accounting concepts and principles)

1. Matching revenues and expenses
2. Distinction between equity and profit
3. Fact of transaction
4. Book value of net assets
5. Economic value of the entity
6. Acquisition cost (transaction price)
7. Fair value (market value)
8. Discounted present value (value in use)

Table 8.10 Emphasis on accounting concepts in lectures (1)

	1	2	3	4	5	Total
Accounting concepts	Much emphasis	Somewhat emphasis	Neutral	Not much emphasis	Little emphasis	Percentage (%)
Actual disclosure	108	89	42	11	9	259
	41.7	34.4	16.2	4.2	3.5	100.0
Appropriate periodic profit/loss calculation	157	79	16	4	3	259
	60.6	30.5	6.2	1.5	1.2	100.0
Comparability	84	107	43	19	6	259
	32.4	41.3	16.6	7.3	2.3	100.0
Conservatism	45	95	77	30	12	259
	17.4	36.7	29.7	11.6	4.6	100.0

Next, Q10 and Q11 addressed how much emphasis respondents placed on "accounting concepts" in their lectures.

Q10 How much emphasis do you place on the accounting concepts in your lectures (options: 1 "much emphasis," 2 " somewhat emphasis," 3 "neutral," 4 "not much emphasis," 5 "little emphasis").

(Accounting approach)

1. Actual disclosure
2. Appropriate periodic profit/loss calculation
3. Comparability
4. Conservatism

Table 8.10 shows the results for the responses to Q10. The most emphasized accounting concept was "appropriate periodic profit and loss accounting," with 91.1% (236/259) of respondents providing a score of either 1 or 2. The combined total of 1 and 2 exceeded 50% for all accounting concepts listed here, indicating that all generations emphasized them. However, the percentage of respondents who answered 3 was higher for "conservatism" than for the other three accounting concepts, indicating that the importance of this concept is relatively low.

Table 8.11 shows the results for the responses to Q11. The accounting concept most emphasized was "recording past transaction facts," with a combined percentage of 85.7% (222/259) for responses of 1 or 2. This has been influenced by the content of bookkeeping lectures. In terms of items respondents scored as 1 or 2, the second most important was "to understand the Japanese accounting system and the

Table 8.11 Emphasis on accounting concepts in lectures (2)

Accounting Concepts	1 much emphasis	2 somewhat emphasis	3 neutral	4 not much emphasis	5 little emphasis	Total Percentage (%)
To record the facts of past transactions	127	95	23	11	3	259
	49.0	36.7	8.9	4.2	1.2	100.0
To show profit figures close to permanent profits	23	62	100	53	21	259
	8.9	23.9	38.6	20.5	8.1	100.0
To use financial figures as they are to evaluate the economic value of a firm	22	67	86	53	31	259
	8.5	25.9	33.2	20.5	12.0	100.0
To bring the book value of net assets closer to the corporate value	10	41	102	58	48	259
	3.9	15.8	39.4	22.4	18.5	100.0
To understand the Japanese accounting system and the theories that support it as faithfully as possible	89	100	42	20	8	259
	34.4	38.6	16.2	7.7	3.1	100.0
To understand the Japanese accounting system relative to the IFRS, etc.	62	95	57	26	19	259
	23.9	36.7	22.0	10.0	7.3	100.0

theories that support it as faithfully as possible," with 73.0% (189/259); the third most important was "to understand the Japanese accounting system relative to IFRS and other accounting systems," with a combined ratio of 60.6% (157/259).

Q11. How much emphasis do you place on the accounting concepts and principles in your lectures (options: 1 "much emphasis," 2 " somewhat emphasis," 3 "neutral," 4 "not much emphasis," 5 "little emphasis").

(Accounting concepts and ideas)

1. To record the facts of past transactions.
2. To show profit figures close to permanent profits.
3. To use financial figures as they are to evaluate the economic value of a firm.
4. To bring the book value of net assets closer to the corporate value.
5. To understand the Japanese accounting system and the theories that support it as faithfully as possible.
6. To understand the Japanese accounting system relative to the IFRS, etc.

Table 8.12 Changes in lecture content in the last 10 years

changes in lecture content	Number of responses	Percentage A (%)	Percentage B (%)
Almost no change	48	18.5	13.3
Changed in response to changes in current Japanese accounting standards	172	66.4	47.6
Changed to a hybrid between 'revenue and expense approach' and 'asset and liability approach'	92	35.5	25.5
Changed to 'asset and liability approach' to reflect international trends	35	13.5	9.7
Others	14	5.4	3.9
Total	259 (361)		100.0

[a]The questions were multiple-choice/allowed responses; Percentage A represents the number of responses to each option as a percentage of the 259 respondents, and Percentage B represents the number of responses to each option as a percentage of the 361 respondents

However, the percentages of respondents who gave a score of 3, which was "neutral," or of 4 or 5 were higher for items related to accounting views and norms, such as "to show profit figures close to permanent profits" (to show highly persistence of profits through income smoothing by management's cost allocation, etc.), "to allow financial figures to be used directly for evaluation of the economic value of the firm" and "to make the net asset book value closer to corporate value" (to show corporate value as net asset book value on the balance sheet as what management thinks it should be).

This may initially appear to contradict the finding of the strong emphasis placed on "understanding the Japanese accounting system relative to IFRS and other accounting systems;" however, it may indicate that only rules are taught without touching on accounting views and other norms.[6]

For Q12, respondents were asked about changes in their lecture content over the last 10 years, and the results are summarized in Table 8.12 (multiple responses allowed). A total of 361 responses were received from 259 respondents. Percentage A shows the number of responses for each subject as a percentage of the 259 respondents (the total does not add up to 100%), and percentage B shows the number of responses for each subject as a percentage of the 361 total responses.

[6] In Q12, which asked whether the content of lectures had been changed, one of the free description answers under "Other" was "We have changed to lectures that do not bring the accounting view to the forefront since 10 years ago," which may have been related to this.

Q12. In the last 10 years, have you changed the content of your lectures (multiple choice)?

If your teaching experience is less than 10 years, please answer within the range of your own teaching experience.

1. Almost no change
2. Changed in response to changes in current Japanese accounting standards
3. Changed to a hybrid between 'revenue and expense approach' and 'asset and liability approach'
4. Changed to 'asset and liability approach' to reflect international trends
5. Others (   )

The number of responses for "little or no change" was 48 (Percentage A: 18.5% and B: 13.3%). Of those 48 respondents, 21 oversaw lectures on "managerial accounting (including cost accounting)." In addition, 12 respondents who taught courses other than managerial accounting (including cost accounting) had been teaching for 9 years or less. These findings indicate that many of the respondents who have been teaching courses on bookkeeping, financial accounting, international accounting, auditing, and tax accounting for over 10 years have changed the content of their lectures in the last 10 years.

The most common response was "change to reflect changes in current Japanese accounting standards" with 172 responses (Percentage A: 66.4% and B: 47.6%). "Change to a hybrid between 'revenue and expense approach' and 'asset and liability approach'" and "change to the asset-liability approach to reflect international trends" received 92 (Percentage A 35.5% and B 25.5%) 35 (Percentage A 13.5% and B 9.7%) responses, respectively.

Fourteen "other" open-ended responses were obtained. Among them, regarding the accounting perspectives of 'revenue and expense approach' and 'asset and liability approach', responses included "I try to convey that different approaches lead to different interpretations of the same event," and conversely, "I changed my lectures 10 years ago to one in which the accounting perspective is not emphasized." In addition to these responses, the following statements were obtained:

- Changes in response to the demands of corporate management and the business environment (e.g., Sustainable Development Goals)
- Changes in accordance with revisions to tax laws and other rules and systems
- Change from an explanation of accounting standards to lectures from the perspective of using accounting figures
- Changes in response to the deepening of the lecturer's own thinking and awareness

8.4 Findings of Accounting for Goodwill

This section provides an overview of the results of the survey conducted to examine the perceptions of the academic community regarding the accounting treatment of goodwill. First, in Q13, respondents were asked which accounting treatment for goodwill was closest to their own views. Then, in Q14 and subsequent questions, they were asked to provide the reasons for their choice.

Q13. From the perspective of disclosure of the actual situation in the Japanese market environment, which accounting method is closest to your opinion regarding the accounting treatment of goodwill?

(Accounting method options)

1. Fair value measurement at each period
2. Impairment-only
3. Systematic amortization with impairment
4. Systematic amortization-only
5. Diminishing amortization
6. Increasing amortization
7. Immediate write off (equity)
8. Immediate write off (expense)
9. None of the above ((1) through (8))
10. Other treatment method (   )

Table 8.13 shows the results for the responses to Q13. Notably, these survey results only capture the opinions of respondents, and are not intended to state that either "the majority is correct" or "the minority is incorrect."

Table 8.13 Accounting treatment of goodwill that is close to own view

Accounting method options	Number of responses	Percentage (%)
Fair value measurement at each period	25	9.0
Impairment-only	18	6.5
Systematic amortization with impairment	192	68.8
Systematic amortization-only	25	9.0
Diminishing amortization	2	0.7
Increasing amortization	0	0.0
Immediate write off (equity)	5	1.8
Immediate write off (expense)	3	1.1
None of the above ((1) through (8))	9	3.1
Other treatment method	0	0.0
Total	279	100.0

Table 8.14 Reasons for selecting "fair value measurement every period" or "impairment-only"

Reasons for choice	1 Close	2 Somewhat close	3 Neither close nor far	4 Not very close	5 Not close	Total Percentage (%)
Because they are trying to capture the value of goodwill	20	17	5	0	1	43
	46.5	39.5	11.6	0.0	2.3	100.0
Because the useful life and cost pattern of goodwill is difficult to predict	16	16	8	2	1	43
	37.2	37.2	18.6	4.7	2.3	100.0
Because the amortization cost of goodwill and the balance after amortization contain little information content related to investment decisions	10	15	13	3	2	43
	23.3	34.9	30.2	7.0	4.7	100.0
Because differences in the impact on performance due to differences in the frequency of mergers and acquisitions, as in the case of amortization, are small	5	13	16	7	2	43
	11.6	30.2	37.2	16.3	4.7	100.0

The most frequent response was "systematic amortization with impairment" at 68.8% (192/279). When the number of responses to the three accounting treatments with a systematic amortization component, "systematic amortization-only," "diminishing amortization," and "increasing amortization," were added to the "systematic amortization with impairment" category, the total number of responses was 78.5% (219/279).

However, 6.5% (18/279) of respondents chose "impairment-only." In addition, 9.0% (25/279) of the respondents selected "fair value measurement at each period," which is more than the "impairment-only" accounting treatment. When these two respondents are combined, the total is 15.4% (43/279).

Next, 1.8% (= 5/279) of the respondents chose " immediate write off (equity)" and 1.1% (= 3/279) chose "immediate write off (expense)". Nine respondents selected "none of the above" (cannot be narrowed down to one treatment).

The next questions, Q14–Q18, ask about the reasons for selecting the accounting method selected in Q13.

Table 8.14 shows the results of the responses to Q14. The reason chosen as the closest reason for selecting "fair value measurement at every period" or "impairment-only" as the accounting treatment for goodwill was "because they are trying to capture the value of goodwill," and the combined percentage of 1 and 2 was 86.0% (37/43). The next closest reason selected was "because the useful life and cost pattern of goodwill is difficult to predict," with 74.4% (32/43) endorsing this option. "Because the amortization cost and amortized balance of goodwill contain little information content regarding investment decisions" was also selected by 58.1% (25/43) of respondents in terms of the total percentage of 1 and 2. These indicate that goodwill amortization patterns are difficult to predict and goodwill after amortization expense deduction and amortization expense are considered to have no informational value. The responses endorsing "fair value measurement at each period" and "impairment-only" also included reasons for the negative evaluation of systematic amortization of goodwill. No responses for the "other descriptive responses" category suggested that the reasons provided as question items were their primary ones.

Q14. If you chose (1) " fair value measurement at each period" or (2) "impairment-only" in 13, please indicate the reasons for your choice. How close are reasons (1) to (4) below to your opinion? (Answer: 1 "Close," 2 "Somewhat close," 3 "Neither close nor far," 4 "Not very close," 5 "Not close").

(Reasons covered in this survey)

1. Because they are trying to capture the value of goodwill.
2. Because the useful life and cost pattern of goodwill is difficult to predict.
3. Because the amortization cost of goodwill and the balance after amortization contain little information content related to investment decisions.
4. Because differences in the impact on performance due to differences in the frequency of mergers and acquisitions, as in the case of amortization, are small.
5. If you have any other comments, please provide them in the space provided.

Next, Q15. asks about the reasons for selecting accounting methods that involve the concept of systematic amortization. Table 8.15 shows the results for the responses to Q15. The reason considered closest to that for which respondents chose

Table 8.15 Reasons for selecting "systematic amortization with impairment," "systematic amortization-only," "diminishing depreciation," or "increasing depreciation"

Reasons for choice	1 Close	2 Somewhat close	3 Neither close nor far	4 Not very close	5 Not close	Total Percentage (%)
Because they are pursuing appropriate periodic accounting	76	113	22	5	3	219
	34.7	51.6	10.0	2.3	1.4	100.0
Because it is difficult to record appropriate amounts of impairment losses in a timely manner given the interests of the preparers	47	89	58	18	7	219
	21.5	40.6	26.5	8.2	3.2	100.0
Because it is difficult to record appropriate amounts of impairment losses in a timely manner due to the shielding effect of internally generated goodwill	37	62	88	24	8	219
	16.9	28.3	40.2	11.0	3.7	100.0
Because financial soundness can be maintained	50	85	50	24	10	219
	22.8	38.8	22.8	11.0	4.6	100.0

accounting treatment including " systematic amortization with impairment" was "because they are pursuing appropriate periodic profit/loss accounting," with the total of 1 and 2 accounting for 86.3% (189/219) of the responses. The next closest reason in terms of the sum of 1 and 2 was "it is difficult to record appropriate amounts of impairment losses in a timely manner, given the interest of the preparer," with 62.1% (136/219). The third most common reason was "to maintain financial soundness," with 61.6% (135/219), indicating that conservatism supports amortization treatment.

Q15. If you chose (3) "Systematic amortization with impairment", (4) "Systematic depreciation only," (5) "Decreasing amortization," or (6) "Increasing amortization" in 13, please tell us the reason for your choice. How close are the reasons (1) to (4) below to your opinion? (Answer: 1 "Close," 2 "Somewhat close," 3 "Neither close nor far," 4 "Not very close," 5 "Not close").

(Note the difference in the meaning of impairment in (2) "impairment-only" and (3) " systematic amortization with impairment" ※1).

(Reasons for inclusion in this survey)

1. Because they are pursuing appropriate periodic accounting.
2. Because it is difficult to record appropriate amounts of impairment losses in a timely manner given the interests of the preparers.
3. Because it is difficult to record appropriate amounts of impairment losses in a timely manner due to the shielding effect of internally generated goodwill ※2
4. Because financial soundness can be maintained.
5. If you have any other comments, please provide them in the space provided.

   ※1 Impairment in the case of "impairment-only" means a direct value adjustment of goodwill, while impairment in the case of "systematic amortization with impairment" means an adjustment of the cost to be amortized.

   ※2 The shielding effect refers to "the effect that the fact that the purchased goodwill recorded at the time of M&A depreciates is hidden by the internally generated goodwill in the acquiring firm before the M&A or the internally generated goodwill in the combined firm after the M&A."

The reason "it is difficult to record impairment losses in a timely and appropriate manner due to the shielding effect of internally generated goodwill," which is identified as a problem with the "impairment-only" accounting standard, was selected by 45.2% (99/219), which is below the majority. The large number of respondents who selected 3" neither close nor far" (40.2%, 88/219) indicates that the public may not generally recognize the shielding effect of internally generated goodwill, including the concept of it.

Seven respondents selected "other descriptive responses," with the main reasons, including some that provided additional explanations for the reasons given in Q15, being as follows:

- As long as there is no agreement on the nature of goodwill, systematic amortization is preferable because it has the least impact on profit and loss.
- The value of goodwill decreases with time. It should be included in the recovery calculation at some point in time, and the only way to determine the amortization period is to use a deemed calculation. The significance of continuing to initially report goodwill in the B/S as a result of denying amortization is unclear.
- The systematic amortization of goodwill is desirable because it allows the annual cost to be determined, and it is desirable to combine it with impairment in order to disclose whether the M&A was successful or unsuccessful.
- The calculation of the acquisition price, which is the basis for the initial measurement of goodwill, leaves some room for managerial discretion on the part of the measurer. In light of the fact that arbitrariness can intervene in the measurement in the first place, we believe that reducing goodwill by amortization will ultimately lead to the elimination of discretion.
- Consistency with the overall accounting system is important in the accounting treatment of goodwill. Since the Japanese accounting system can be said to be based on an revenue and expense approach, we believe that "systematic amortization with impairment" is appropriate.

Table 8.16 summarizes the responses to Q16. The two most common reasons for choosing "immediate write off (equity)" or "immediate write off (expense)," in terms of the total percentage of 1 and 2, were "because excess earnings will be reflected in future profit/loss calculations even if they are not recorded on the balance sheet" and "because we should not record assets with no value," both of which were supported by 75.0% (6/8). This was followed by "because assets with no clear value should not be recorded," which was considered a close second by 62.5% (5/8) of the respondents.

Table 8.16 Reasons for selecting "Immediate write off (equity) " or "Immediate write off (expense)"

Reasons	1 Close	2 Somewhat close	3 Neither close nor far	4 Not very close	5 Not close	Total Percentage (%)
Because assets with no value should not be recorded	1	5	1	0	1	8
	12.5	62.5	12.5	0.0	12.5	100.0
Because assets whose value is not clear should not be recorded	2	3	0	0	3	8
	25.0	37.5	0.0	0.0	37.5	100.0
To maintain consistency with the non-recording of internally generated goodwill	0	3	1	2	2	8
	0.0	37.5	12.5	25.0	25.0	100.0
Because excess earnings will be reflected in future profit/loss calculations even if they are not recognized on the balance sheet	3	3	1	0	1	8
	37.5	37.5	12.5	0.0	12.5	100.0

Q16. If you selected (7) "Immediate write off (equity)" or (8) "Immediate write off (expense)" for Q13, we would like to ask you why. How close do the reasons (1) to (4) below come to your opinion? (Answer: 1 "Close," 2 "Somewhat close," 3 "Neither close nor far," 4 "Not very close," 5 "Not close").

(Reasons addressed in this survey)

1. Because assets with no value should not be recorded.
2. Because assets whose value is not clear should not be recorded.
3. To maintain consistency with the non-recording of internally generated goodwill.
4. Because excess earnings will be reflected in future profit/loss calculations even if they are not recognized on the balance sheet.
5. If you have any other comments, please provide them in the space provided.

One "other descriptive response" was received, stating that the respondent's reason for favoring of derecognition of goodwill as an asset is not the presence or absence of value, but rather the issue of identifiability.

Next, we asked the reason respondents selected "none of the above" (i.e., cannot be narrowed down to one treatment) as the accounting treatment for goodwill as a descriptive answer in Q17.

Q.17 If you chose "none of the above" in Q13., please explain why.

Nine responses were received in response. The main content of the responses were as follows:

- I am unable to make a judgment because I have no knowledge of the consequences of each
- of the accounting alternatives presented.
- I am unable to determine whether goodwill decreases through competition because there is limited reliable academic knowledge on the subject. On the one hand, if goodwill is considered part of the cost of investment and goodwill generally diminishes within a reasonable period, the combination of systematic amortization with impairment treatment could be supported. On the other hand, if it is not necessary to consider goodwill part of the cost of investment, immediate write off (equity) may be a viable option.
- As long as there is accounting discretion in assessing goodwill impairment, either systematic amortization or immediate write off (expense) should not be used. If a large loss is to be recorded in a given year, economic activity will be affected.

Q18. If you selected "other processing method (   )" in Q13, please explain why and describe your opinion.

No respondents selected "other processing method (descriptive answer) for Q13;" thus, no descriptive answers were provided for Q18.

Table 8.17 shows the results of the responses for Q19. First, 11 respondents selected "the value of all or most of the purchased goodwill is maintained semi-permanently by subsequent replenishment of the value with internally generated goodwill". Six respondents selected "the value of the purchased goodwill does not depreciate independently of the subsequent replenishment of the value by the internally generated goodwill." A total of 6.1% (17/279) of the respondents selected "the value of purchased goodwill does not diminish regardless of the subsequent replenishment of value by internally generated goodwill."

Table 8.17 Economic nature of purchased goodwill

Economic nature of goodwill	Number of responses	Percentage (%)
The value of all or most of the purchased goodwill is maintained semi-permanently by subsequent replenishment of the value of the purchased goodwill with internally generated goodwill	11	3.9
The value of purchased goodwill does not decrease independent of the subsequent replenishment of the value by the internally generated goodwill	6	2.2
The value of purchased goodwill is both maintained semi-permanently and not maintained semi-permanently by the subsequent replenishment of the value by the internally generated goodwill	99	35.5
The value of purchased goodwill includes both the portion that is maintained semi-permanently and the portion that is not maintained, but the portion that is maintained does not decrease, irrespective of the replenishment of value by the internally generated goodwill	28	10.0
The value of purchased goodwill is not maintained semi-permanently, even if the value is subsequently replenished by the internally generated goodwill	93	33.3
The value of purchased goodwill is not replenished by the internally generated goodwill	29	10.4
Others	13	4.7
Total	279	100.0

Next, 28 respondents (10.0%) selected "the value of purchased goodwill is both semi-permanently maintained in value and not maintained, but the portion that is maintained in value does not decrease, independent of the replenishment of value by the internally generated goodwill. The portion that is maintained is considered to be semi-permanently maintained (even if not replenished by internally generated goodwill)."

The most frequent response was "the value of purchased goodwill is both semi-permanently maintained and not semi-permanently maintained by subsequent replenishment of the value with internally generated goodwill," accounting for 35.5% (99 responses) of all respondents. The next most frequent response was "the value of purchased goodwill is not maintained semi-permanently even if it is subsequently replenished by internally generated goodwill," accounting for 33.3% (93 responses) of the total number of respondents. Although both groups acknowledge that much of the initially recognized purchased goodwill itself decreases, they are divided on whether it can be maintained semi-permanently by replenishing its value with internally generated goodwill. The percentage of both combined (68.8%, 192/279), is equivalent to allowing much of the initially recognized purchased goodwill itself to diminish.

Of the respondents, 10.4% (29 responses) selected "the value of purchased goodwill (decrease) will not be replenished by the internally generated goodwill. It is judged that this group understands that ex-post internally generated goodwill may enhance off-balance sheet internally generated goodwill, but will not enhance on-balance sheet purchased goodwill (decrease in value)."

Q19. Please select the option that best describes your understanding of the economic nature of purchased goodwill.

1. The value of all or most of the purchased goodwill is maintained semi-permanently by subsequent replenishment of the value of the purchased goodwill with internally generated goodwill.
2. The value of purchased goodwill does not decrease independent of the subsequent replenishment of the value by the internally generated goodwill.
3. The value of purchased goodwill is both maintained semi-permanently and not maintained semi-permanently by the subsequent replenishment of the value by the internally generated goodwill.
4. The value of purchased goodwill includes both the portion that is maintained semi-permanently and the portion that is not maintained, but the portion that is maintained does not decrease, irrespective of the replenishment of value by the internally generated goodwill.
5. The value of purchased goodwill is not maintained semi-permanently, even if the value is subsequently replenished by the internally generated goodwill.
6. The value of purchased goodwill is not replenished by the internally generated goodwill.
7. Please provide any other comments you may have.

We obtained 13 responses for "other descriptive response." The main responses provided are as follows:

- The purchased goodwill, which is created by the premium paid to prevent other companies from buying the target firm of M&A, has no value (as an asset) at all.
- The components of goodwill are so varied that I cannot answer the question.
- It depends on the business model of the firm.
- It is a case-by-case basis.
- The goodwill purchased, which is a technical asset on the books, is neither a receivable nor an investment intended to be recovered, and has no substance or economic characteristics in the first place.

Table 8.18 reflects the cross-tabulation of the results for the responses to Q13, "accounting for goodwill that is similar to your own view," and Q19, "understanding the economic nature of goodwill."

Most respondents who endorsed "fair value measurement at each period" or "impairment-only," accounting for goodwill, which does not include a systematic amortization component, either believed that the economic nature of goodwill

Table 8.18 "Q19. Understanding of the economic nature of goodwill" and "Q13. Accounting treatment of goodwill" (cross-tabulation)

		Fair value measurement at every period	Impairment-only	Systematic amortization with impairment	Systematic amortization-only	Diminishing amortization	Increasing amortization	Immediate write off (equity)	Immediate write off (expense)	None of the above ((1) through (8))	Other treatment method	Total
Economic nature of goodwill	The value of all or most of the purchased goodwill is maintained semi-permanently by subsequent replenishment of the value of the purchased goodwill with internally generated goodwill	3	3	4	1	0	0	0	0	0	0	11
	The value of purchased goodwill does not decrease independent of the subsequent replenishment of the value by the internally generated goodwill	0	4	1	1	0	0	0	0	0	0	6
	The value of purchased goodwill is both maintained semi-permanently and not maintained semi-permanently by the subsequent replenishment of the value by the internally generated goodwill	11	3	69	11	2	0	0	2	1	0	99
	The value of purchased goodwill includes both the portion that is maintained semi-permanently and the portion that is not maintained, but the portion that is maintained does not decrease, irrespective of the replenishment of value by the internally generated goodwill	6	3	17	1	0	0	1	0	0	0	28
	The value of purchased goodwill is not maintained semi-permanently, even if the value is subsequently replenished by the internally generated goodwill	4	2	75	8	0	0	1	1	2	0	93
	The value of purchased goodwill is not replenished by the internally generated goodwill	1	3	22	2	0	0	0	0	1	0	29
	Others	0	0	4	1	0	0	3	0	5	0	13
Total		25	18	192	25	2	0	5	3	9	0	279

means that the majority of the value of purchased goodwill will be maintained (with or without value replenishment by internally generated goodwill), or that a portion of purchased goodwill will be maintained, and a substantial portion of that value will be maintained (with or without value replenishment by internally generated goodwill).

However, several respondents who supported “systematic amortization with impairment,” “systematic amortization-only,” or “diminishing amortization” as the accounting treatment for goodwill, which includes a systematic amortization-like element, had differing opinions in terms of whether the goodwill can be maintained semi-permanently by replenishing its value through internally generated goodwill, but many of them choose the option of allowing the initially recognized purchased goodwill itself to decrease. Alternatively, they appeared to understand that a decrease in purchased goodwill could not be replenished by internally generated goodwill.

For both the former and the latter, the results of the responses were generally consistent with respondents’ understanding of the economic nature of goodwill and the accounting treatment of goodwill that they support.

8.5 Summary and Remaining Issues

This chapter conducts a questionnaire survey on accounting education in higher education institutions, including universities, in order to examine whether accounting education—both at universities and in professional training programs such as preparation for the Certified Public Accountant (CPA) and tax accountant examinations—may influence stakeholders’ views on the accounting treatment of goodwill and, more broadly, may indirectly affect accounting standard setting. This questionnaire survey also investigates perspectives within the academic community regarding the accounting treatment of goodwill.

Following the results of a questionnaire and interview survey on “accounting treatment of goodwill” conducted before the present survey, which targeted financial statement preparers, users, and auditors, Chap.5 and 6 noted the possibility that, in Japan, accounting education at universities and other institutions of higher education and education such as that through JCPA examinations strongly influenced responses (e.g., accounting treatment of goodwill supported). This provides the context for the present survey.

The key findings for this chapter are as follows. First, regarding corporate accounting laws and regulations, “Financial Instruments and Exchange Law” (80.7%) and “Corporate Law” (73.7%) were emphasized in courses on accounting-related subjects. Next, regarding accounting standards and basic conceptual documents, survey respondents emphasized relatively newer accounting standards, such as “current ASBJ accounting standards” (83.0%), “IFRS” (67.2%), and “ASBJ conceptual framework” (54.8%), while also continuing to emphasize “corporate accounting principles” (70.3%).

Regarding the concepts and principles emphasized in the lectures, "matching revenues and expenses" (92.7%), "distinction between equity and profit" (83.8%), and "acquisition cost (transaction price)" (81.9%) were emphasized, and in other questions, "appropriate periodic accounting" (91.1%) was also emphasized, revealing that lectures cover ideas derived from corporate accounting principles.

Furthermore, 82.8% (299/361) of the respondents had changed the content of their lectures in the last 10 years, with the most common reasons being "change to reflect changes in current Japanese accounting standards" (47.6%), "change to a hybrid of the income cost approach and asset liability approach" (25.5%), and "change to an asset-liability approach to reflect international trends" (9.7%). Combined with the above results, this indicates that, although lecture content has changed, the concepts and ideas of " revenue and expense approach" and "appropriate periodic profit and loss accounting" continue to be emphasized.

Next, to investigate the academic community's views on accounting for goodwill, respondents were about the accounting treatment of goodwill that was closest to their own views and the reasons for those views. The results showed that the option that came closest to that of the majority of the respondents was "systematic amortization with impairment" (68.8%), and when the number of responses to the other three accounting treatments that include a systematic amortization component (systematic amortization-only, diminishing amortization, and increasing amortization) was added, this increased to 78.5%. In contrast, 15.4% of respondents supported accounting treatments that emphasize the measurement of the value of goodwill, with 6.5% and 9.0% endorsing "impairment-only" or "fair value measurement at each period," respectively.

The more applicable reason provided for supporting accounting treatment with systematic amortization was "because it pursues appropriate periodic accounting" (86.3%). However, the response provided that was closest to the reason why respondents supported accounting treatments that emphasize the measurement of the value of goodwill was "because it seeks to capture the value of goodwill" (86.0%).

Regarding trends in the responses obtained from the questionnaire survey, notably, the concepts emphasized in accounting education ("matching revenues and expenses") are consistent with the accounting treatment supported as accounting for goodwill ("systematic amortization with impairment") and the reasons for supporting it ("proper periodic profit and loss calculation").

The results obtained from this survey are only observations presented as a summary of the respondents' answers and are not intended to promote support for systematic amortization of goodwill accounting treatment. In addition, the survey did not delve into the content of accounting education for the JCPA and tax accountant examinations (as mentioned in the appendix below), and the findings are limited to the content of education at universities and other institutions of higher education.

In the analysis presented in this chapter, we focus on accounting education as one of the factors that may lead both practitioners and researchers to support the systematic amortization of goodwill. However, accounting standard setting is also likely influenced by the aggregation of stakeholders' interests and by competing accounting theories. Accordingly, the findings of this chapter suggest that accounting education constitutes one important factor, but not the sole determinant, in shaping views on goodwill accounting. In addition, whether these results generalize to other countries remains an open empirical question for future research.

Although we collected data on several questions with this survey, we did not go as far as a crosstabulation analysis (or discussion of the results) between data such as the respondents' age range, employed research methods, courses taught, emphasized accounting concepts in lectures, or supported accounting methods of goodwill. A cross-tabulation analysis of these responses will be the subject of future work.

Appendix 6[7]

Tomoaki Yamashita

T. Yamashita
Department of Business Administration, Faculty of Economics, Fukui Prefectural University, Fukui, Japan

The Goal of This Appendix

We presented the results of the survey of preparers, users, and auditors (Chap. 5), as well as the survey of accounting researchers on accounting education (this chapter). The surveys of preparers, users, and auditors showed that most respondents in each group preferred "systematic amortization with impairment" for the subsequent accounting treatment of goodwill. This preference was highest among auditors, followed by preparers, and then users. Among users who expressed the lowest preference, about 62% favored this approach, while among auditors who expressed the highest preference, about 90% favored it.

The systematic amortization and impairment approach for subsequent accounting of goodwill receives greater support among Japanese stakeholder groups than "impairment-only." Although multiple factors may contribute to this preference, making comprehensive analysis challenging, the findings of this chapter indicate that concepts related to the revenue and expense view (or the income statement approach) remain prominent in accounting education in Japanese universities. This ongoing emphasis in education suggests that accounting education may significantly influence the survey results. Both academics and practitioners in Japan may emphasize net income concepts grounded in the revenue and expense view, and

[7] I would like to thank Hidetoshi Kyogoku (Gakushuin University at that time), Takuto Kawakami (Gakushuin University), and Rina Matsumoto (Gakushuin University at that time) for their invaluable assistance with the analysis in this Appendix.

explanations of the current accounting system and its rationale based on these concepts likely still play a significant role in accounting education. The strong support for "systematic amortization with impairment" among auditor respondents indicates that understanding the principles underlying the current system is essential for passing professional accounting qualification exams, such as the CPA exam, which may have affected our survey results.

Building on the previous discussion, this appendix examines how accounting education affects stakeholders' preferences for subsequent goodwill accounting from a perspective distinct from the main analysis's survey on accounting education. Specifically, we conducted an additional analysis focusing on the Japanese CPA examination.

The Approach of This Study

In Japan, the certified public accountant qualification is awarded to individuals who pass the CPA examination administered by the Certified Public Accountants and Auditing Oversight Board (CPAAOB) and complete practical training.[8] During their specialized accounting education for the CPA examination, future auditors receive intensive instruction on the concepts underlying Japan's current accounting system.[9]

Therefore, if the concepts related to the revenue and expense view continue to be positively regarded as the underlying principle supporting Japan's current accounting system, then studying for the CPA examination is expected to influence accountants' views on the subsequent accounting for goodwill. Furthermore, this is anticipated to lead to a convergence of views among auditors regarding the subsequent accounting for goodwill.

Christensen and Demski (2002, pp. 422–423) highlight the importance of considering accounting education beyond its narrow definition, such as university lectures—the primary focus of this chapter—to include the Certified Public Accountant examination, a key qualification for the accounting profession. They emphasize auditors' role in promoting coordinated behavior in accounting practice. To illustrate how auditor-coordinated behavior efficiently spreads among firms, they identify three levels, each characterized by competition: accounting education, textbooks, and professional standards (qualification exams and exam preparation programs). It is difficult to directly apply their argument to explain the consistent

[8] See "About the Certified Public Accountant Examination." (URL: https://jicpa.or.jp/cpainfo/applicant/examination/, Accessed: November 4, 2025)

[9] The Certified Public Accountant Examination scope is summarized and published annually on the website. A review of this summary shows that, for the accounting section—specifically Financial Statement Theory—the scope includes the regulations, standards, and underlying concepts of Japan's current accounting system, although concepts from international accounting standards are also included in the scope (e.g., Summary of Examination Scope for Fiscal Year 2026).

views of auditor respondents on the subsequent accounting for goodwill found in our survey. However, they emphasize the broader role of accounting education, including qualification exams. Their discussion suggests that, when considering accounting education as a factor in our results, it is insufficient to focus solely on university-level accounting education; qualification exams and other aspects of accounting education should also be considered.

Based on the above discussion, this study examines the extent to which the revenue and expense view concepts are emphasized in the Japanese CPA examination from a positive perspective. If these concepts are positively evaluated and frequently tested in the actual CPA examination, examinees are likely to devote time and effort to learning them and to develop a favorable attitude toward these concepts.

Research Design

This study analyzes essay-type examination questions in accounting from fiscal year 2009 to fiscal year 2018. Although the Certified Public Accountant Examination includes both multiple-choice and essay-type components,[10] this study considered only the essay-type questions. This focus was chosen because essay-type questions are more likely than multiple-choice questions to assess examinees' understanding of the concepts underlying the current accounting system. As a result, the essay-type examination was deemed more appropriate for this analysis. Additionally, although the essay-type examination includes questions on bookkeeping and management accounting, this study excluded those topics from its analysis.

For this additional analysis, three coders (graduate students majoring in accounting) classified the essay-type examination questions for each academic year as either essay-type or other types (e.g., calculation problems).[11] They then categorized these questions as either related or unrelated to concepts associated with the revenue and expense view.[12] The coders further examined only those questions not classified as *unrelated* to the revenue and expense view, assessing whether these questions positively evaluated concepts related to the revenue and expense view.[13] Each coder independently classified the questions, after which all three reviewed the classifica-

[10] The Japanese CPA examination comprises two parts: a multiple-choice examination and an essay examination, which are administered on separate days. Candidates must pass both examinations.

[11] This study examines essay-type examination questions at the sub-item level, following the main question and sub-question structure, because classifying questions at the major question or sub-question level was sometimes challenging.

[12] The revenue and expense view includes concepts such as matching revenue and expenses, realization, cost allocation, and recovery of invested capital.

[13] In this study, each coder assessed whether the questions were presented from a perspective supporting the concepts related to the revenue and expense view, or whether the questions favored these concepts. Questions that critically examined the concepts or were presented from a neutral standpoint were classified as "not evaluated positively."

tions together to identify and resolve any issues. Questions with unresolved disagreements among the coders were excluded from the analysis. Of the 161 questions considered, 10 were excluded due to unresolved disagreements, resulting in 151 questions analyzed in this study.

Furthermore, following the analysis described above, this study verifies the stated intentions behind the essay-type examination questions published on the CPAAOB website. At the end of this Appendix, we present our conclusion by comparing our question classification and analysis results with the published stated intentions.

Results

Figure 8.1 presents the annual percentage changes in questions classified as unrelated to concepts associated with the revenue and expense view and those classified as not *unrelated* (blue and orange lines, respectively). Few essay-type examination questions were unrelated to the revenue and expense view. Although some year-to-year fluctuations occurred, the overall trend from fiscal year 2009 to fiscal year 2018 remained largely stable. Therefore, the importance of concepts related to the revenue and expense view did not decline in Japan's CPA examination during the analysis period.[14]

Figure 8.2 presents the annual percentage trend of questions classified as positively evaluating concepts related to the revenue and expense view among those not unrelated to these concepts (orange line). This result indicates that essay-type examination questions addressing these concepts are primarily framed from a perspective that favors them. Alternatively, there are almost no essay-type examination questions that require a critical perspective on the revenue and expense view.

Conclusion

This study demonstrates that many essay-type questions in Japan's CPA examination are related to concepts associated with the revenue and expense view. These concepts are generally presented positively in such questions. The CPAAOB has also published the rationale for essay-type examination questions on its website. A review of this content confirms that, during the analyzed period, no questions were intended to critically evaluate the concepts and principles of the current Japanese accounting system. This indicates that the revenue and expense view concepts are

[14] Including questions from fiscal years 2018 and later, which are not examined in this analysis, may reveal different trends. This limitation presents a challenge for future research.

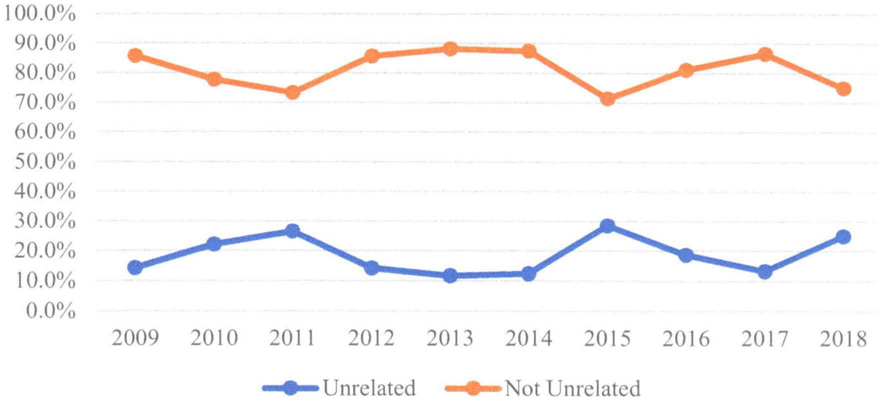

Fig. 8.1 Classification of the essay-type CPA examination questions by relation to the concepts related to the revenue and expense view

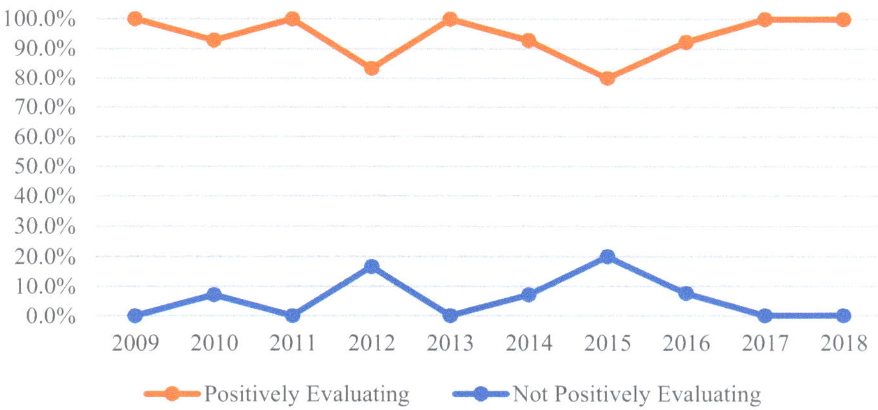

Fig. 8.2 Proportion of the essay-type CPA examination questions positively evaluating the concepts related to the revenue and expense view

not regarded critically or negatively within the CPA examination.[15] These findings indicate that preparing for the CPA examination allows auditors to become familiar with revenue and expense view concepts and to develop a positive perspective toward them. If auditors adopt this positive perspective as the standard through their CPA exam studies, it may partially explain why over 90% of auditor respondents in

[15] The primary analysis adheres to the coders' classifications and adjustments, and the discussion is based on these results. Further research is needed on the content of CPA examination questions, including the stated intentions of the essay-type questions.

the survey supported "systematic amortization with impairment" for subsequent goodwill accounting. The results support the view that broad accounting education, including qualification examinations and their preparation, is one factor underlying the survey results, specifically for auditors.

This study identified several remaining challenges. It analyzed why most auditor survey respondents supported "systematic amortization with impairment" approach as the preferred subsequent accounting treatment for goodwill, considering CPA exam content and broadly defined accounting education. However, these findings do not explain results from surveys of preparers or users. Investigating the reasons for high support for "systematic amortization with impairment" among other Japanese stakeholder groups in our survey, as discussed, from the perspective of accounting education may provide valuable insights. Analyzing survey results for preparers and users from this perspective remains an important empirical question for future research.

Statement on AI Usage: During the preparation of this manuscript, the authors used AI-assisted tools such as DeepL, ChatGPT, and Gemini to improve the English expression and clarity of the manuscript. The authors thoroughly reviewed and approved the final version and take full responsibility for the content.

References

In English

Accounting Standards Board of Japan (ASBJ), European Financial Reporting Advisory Group (EFRAG), and Organismo Italiano di Contabilità (OIC) (2014), *Should Goodwill Still Not Be Amortised? Accounting and Disclosure for Goodwill.*

Accounting Standards Board of Japan (ASBJ) and Hong Kong Institute of Certified Public Accountants (HKICPA) staff (2020) *Goodwill: Improvements to subsequent accounting and an update of the quantitative study.*

Christensen, J. A., and J. S. Demski (2002) *Accounting Theory: An Information Content Perspective.* New York, NY: McGraw-Hill/Irwin.

International Accounting Standards Board (IASB) [2020] *Discussion Paper: Business Combinations – Disclosures, Goodwill and Impairment.*

In Japanese

Miyauchi, T., Y. Tokuga, Y. Asami, M. Yoneyama, and T. Yamashita. 2022. Kaikei Kyouiku ni kansuru *Shitsumonhyō chōsa – Noren no Kaikei shori to no kankei wo chushi ni (Questionnaire survey on accounting education: Focusing on the relationship with accounting treatment of goodwill).* Kyoto University Discussion Paper No. J-22-001.

Chapter 9
Concluding Remarks and Future Issues

Masaki Yoneyama

To conclude this study, this chapter provides an overview of the findings. It then revisits the initial research theme, summarizing clarified aspects and identifying unresolved issues.

9.1 Review of the Findings of Our Research

9.1.1 Chapter 1: Introduction, Purpose, and Structure of Our Research

Chapter 1 highlights the focus of the book on consistently addressing the unresolved controversy over the accounting treatment of purchased goodwill in business combinations—specifically, whether to apply the systematic amortization with impairment approach (hereafter, "systematic amortization with impairment") or the impairment-only approach (hereafter, "impairment-only") —persisting for over 140 years without a conclusion, even at the International Accounting Standards Board (IASB).

The debate between systematic amortization with impairment and impairment-only became prominent when the U.S. Financial Accounting Standards Board (FASB) in 2001 and the IASB in 2004 prohibited the pooling-of-interests method and mandated the purchase method (acquisition method). Chapter 1 provides preparatory groundwork by confirming how the allowance for non-amortization (impairment-only) of goodwill was granted in exchange for adopting the purchase

M. Yoneyama (✉)
Graduate School of Economics, The University of Tokyo, Tokyo, Japan
e-mail: yoneyama@e.u-tokyo.ac.jp

Y. Tokuga, M. Yoneyama (eds.), *Controversies Over Accounting for Goodwill*, Contributions to Finance and Accounting,
https://doi.org/10.1007/978-981-92-0156-3_9

method, illustrating that this outcome resulted from political compromise. It briefly outlines the structure of the book to present the approach and methods employed to explain why the goodwill accounting controversy has not converged since the early 2000s.

Finally, Chapter 1 specifies the book's uniqueness: (1) it expands the analysis scope beyond IASB-published materials to include statements from jurisdictional representatives at the Accounting Standards Advisory Forum (ASAF), highlighting that the unresolved controversy partly stems from the unorganized mixing of fundamentally different issues; (2) it conducts a large-scale questionnaire survey in Japan targeting financial statement users, preparers, and auditors, revealing significant differences in values, beliefs, and perceptions that were previously assumed to be homogeneous; and (3) it utilizes Japan's institutional context, where both IFRS and Japanese GAAP are applied and recognized as "accepted practices," allowing for comparative analysis of systematic amortization with impairment and non-amortization (impairment-only) within the same market.

9.1.2 Chapter 2: Organizing the Argument Points in the Process of Accounting Standards Setting

Chapter 2 reviews the IASB/ASAF's 9-year deliberations on goodwill accounting from the post-implementation review of IFRS 3 (PiR 3) through the IASB's 2022 decision not to reintroduce amortization. It shows that the debate extended well beyond the conventional dichotomy between systematic amortization with impairment and impairment-only.

The chapter argues that the persistence of the issue cannot be explained by technical disagreements over measurement methods alone. Instead, the central difficulty lies in the unresolved tension between defining goodwill and maintaining consistency with the asset concept in the Conceptual Framework. As attempts to clarify goodwill's nature increasingly expose potential non-asset components (for example, overpayment), the IASB/ASAF ultimately abandoned the pursuit of a conceptually grounded definition and retained the operational definition embedded in IFRS 3, treating goodwill as a single asset for accounting purposes.

Chapter 2 then examines a range of allocation-based and valuation-based measurement approaches and explains why none were adopted. The analysis highlights trade-offs between conceptual refinement and practicability—greater theoretical sophistication tends to reduce operationality, increase cost and complexity, and expand reliance on management discretion. This outcome contributed to a shift from a measurement-centric to a disclosure-centric strategy within the IASB's project.

To interpret this process, the chapter organizes the IASB/ASAF discussions along three interrelated dimensions: (1) theoretical and conceptual issues, (2) practical application problems, and (3) standard-setting judgements. Building on this organization, the remainder of the book examines (a) the implicit theories behind competing positions, (b) their consistency with empirical observations, and (c) how stakeholders' values and factual perceptions vary and why.

9.1.3 Chapter 3: Theoretical Issues

Chapter 3 of this book focused on whether conceptual/theoretical analyses can provide a rational interpretation for (i) systematic amortization with impairment) and (ii) non-amortization (impairment-only), and whether a difference in the rationality of the two approaches can be identified. The conclusion was that both systematic amortization with impairment and non-amortization (impairment-only) have significant problems, and neither approach is superior to the other. Relying solely on deductive reasoning, one cannot justify either method exclusively. Therefore, to determine the superior accounting approach, value judgements concerning the relative seriousness of the issues inherent in systematic amortization with impairment and non-amortization (impairment-only) must be assessed. Examining market participants' value judgements (their views on accounting) and their factual perceptions is essential to identifying any superiority between the two accounting alternatives.

If, hypothetically, accounting standard setters in various jurisdictions have not accepted this observation and believe that "the issue ought to be settled by theory," this misunderstanding contributes to the ongoing confusion surrounding the accounting for goodwill. Conversely, if there is a consensus that the debate cannot be resolved at the theoretical level, future research must focus on environmental constraints and market participants' factual perceptions, including decision-making models and the environmental constraints they face, which are closely related to the rationality of the accounting for goodwill. As indicated here, the analysis in this chapter offers insights into the persistence of this controversy and potential avenues for resolution.

On the assumption that goodwill is recognized as an asset and that this recognition ties up capital, it is important to note that the principles distinguishing capital from profit are compromised under both systematic amortization with impairment and non-amortization (impairment-only). Systematic amortization with impairment is relatively superior to non-amortization (impairment-only), as it alleviates the issue of capital tied up in goodwill for an extended period, provided that impairment criteria are not triggered.

However, when the purchase (acquisition) method is applied, even with systematic amortization, a conflict with the principle of separating capital from profit remains. This raises the persistent question of whether a business combination must be viewed as "the acquisition or purchase of one company by another" and, if so, whether the purchase (acquisition) method is also unavoidable.

The summary presented relates the findings of Chap. 3 to the primary purpose of this book. This chapter is crucial in determining the direction of the discussion.

Furthermore, as a standalone study, it makes a significant contribution to the existing literature. For many years, accounting for goodwill has primarily centered on the distinction between capital and profit. Today, the view that goodwill should be regarded as an asset—shared by both systematic amortization with impairment and non-amortization (impairment-only)—is widely accepted. However, historically, researchers focused on the rationale for capitalizing goodwill as an asset. The question of whether goodwill should be systematically amortized or carried at cost without amortization is part of the broader issue of its accounting treatment. One of the important contributions of Chap. 3 is its clarification of the need to consider a wider range of alternatives.

Why have the "other alternatives regarding the accounting for goodwill" that once attracted researchers' interest ceased to be discussed? Chapter 3 elucidates that some business combinations involve the acquisition of one company by another, while others do not have a clear acquirer–acquiree relationship. In the latter case, shareholders of the combining entities contribute their interests, which are then pooled and restructured. In the former case, the equity of the acquiree's shareholders is liquidated through the business combination, making it acceptable if the distinction between capital and profit changes before and after. Conversely, in the latter type of business combination, there is no reason for the transaction to trigger a change in the distinction between capital and profit. If this distinction does change, it indicates a distortion in the separation between capital and profit.

The premise that "all business combinations are transactions between companies and, therefore, that an acquirer–acquiree relationship can always be identified" suggests that the recognition of goodwill as an asset is something to be taken for granted.[1] However, further examination is warranted to determine whether this premise is indeed inevitable.

9.1.4 Chapter 4: Empirical Issues

The conclusion in Chap. 3 is that rational interpretations of accounting treatments depend on the environment of market participants and governing principles. In other words, unless we clarify the empirical facts surrounding accounting for goodwill, we cannot derive implications for its accounting. These "empirical facts" are diverse and include evidence on the relevance of accounting information and stock price reactions to specific disclosures, as shown through archival studies. Chapter 4 conducts a comprehensive survey of prior empirical studies on goodwill published in top-tier academic journals to confirm findings regarding the impact of related parties' incentives on the disclosure of goodwill-related information and investors'

[1] The discussion here is by no means a proposal to revert to the former practice of "choosing between the purchase method and the pooling-of-interests method." Rather, the point is to highlight that the move toward exclusive reliance on the purchase method is rooted in very strong value judgements.

reactions to details like the balance of goodwill, amortization expense, and impairment losses.

The results of this survey are outlined in Chap. 4, with key findings summarized as follows:

(a) A review of studies analyzing the time-series behavior of firms' earnings shows that, except for a subset of highly profitable firms, abnormal earnings tend to mean-revert to a level close to the cost of capital within 5–10 years. Thus, firms' abnormal earnings, even considering ex-post efforts, do not persist indefinitely.
(b) Evidence on whether managers recognize goodwill impairment timely is mixed. However, many studies indicate that managerial incentives, such as executive compensation and financial covenants, often delay goodwill impairment recognition. This issue is influenced by firm-level attributes, including ownership structure and corporate governance strength, as well as country-level factors like institutional enforcement, auditor size, and analyst coverage.
(c) Research examining the usefulness of information on goodwill and goodwill impairment losses in contracting reveals changes in executive compensation structures and a loss of effectiveness in financial covenants in debt contracts. Although the number of studies is small, these findings highlight significant implications for compensation contracts.
(d) In relation to other research topics, prior studies indicate that information on goodwill and impairment predicts future performance; conflicts between auditors and managers can be quantified; the length of the systematic amortization period for goodwill signals future performance to the equity market; and combining systematic amortization with impairment testing incentivizes managers to recognize impairment.

Taken as a whole, prior empirical analyses have uncovered facts that provide a basis for rational interpretations of systematic amortization together with impairment testing. However, depending on the sample period, jurisdiction, and research methods, evidence also exists in favor of non-amortization (impairment-only) or solely non-amortization. If standard setters understand the implications of these empirical studies and apply these insights correctly, each jurisdiction will adopt different positions on the systematic amortization with impairment versus non-amortization (impairment-only) of goodwill, reflecting the particular empirical findings upon which they rely. Thus, the variation in empirical results does not necessarily heighten conflict; rather, it aligns with the existing confusion regarding whether goodwill should be systematically amortized.[2] The contribution of this chapter in relation to the overarching research theme of this book is as described above.

This chapter additionally contributes to existing literature by highlighting specific points. Since the early 2000s, only firms applying J-GAAP among major

[2] The dispersion in empirical results also tends to encourage cherry picking. Cherry picking, in turn, can exacerbate conflicts and give rise to even greater confusion.

jurisdictions systematically amortize goodwill. Thus, the necessary data to examine the incentives and effects of systematic amortization with impairment, compared to non-amortization (impairment-only), can now only be sourced from the Japanese market. Recent years have seen an increase in empirical studies on the Japanese market published in English; however, a substantial body of work remains in Japanese. While institutional differences across jurisdictions are often said to have narrowed, significant differences persist. This survey, informed by knowledge of the institutional features of the Japanese market and empirical studies published in Japanese, was conducted under optimal conditions for examining the subsequent accounting for goodwill.

Moreover, aside from the overarching research theme of this book, the following findings make a significant contribution to the academic discourse. Empirical analyses reveal facts that can be interpreted in relation to market participants' value judgements and the perception of facts, or to technical issues that constrain specific accounting practices. However, these facts are rarely taken into account when developing accounting standards. This oversight likely stems from the difficulty in interpreting research findings based on statistical and econometric methodologies, coupled with the belief that academic research focusing on *average* effects is not helpful for practitioners concerned with measuring and disclosing earnings at the individual firm level.

9.1.5 Chapter 5: Questionnaire Survey of Preparers, Users, and Auditors

As stated in Chap. 3, it is not possible to determine a priori—based on deductive reasoning alone—the superiority or inferiority of systematic amortization with impairment versus non-amortization (impairment-only). Evaluations of systematic amortization with impairment and non-amortization (impairment-only) will vary based on the environmental constraints and factual perceptions of market participants. To probe the confusion surrounding goodwill accounting, it is essential to ascertain market participants' views on: their perception of goodwill as an asset; the rationale for performing systematic amortization (or the argument against it); and how goodwill-related accounting information informs their decision-making. Additionally, it is necessary to examine the gaps or discrepancies between empirical facts (clarified in Chap. 4) and the perceptions of market participants.

Returning to Chap. 2, an analysis of debates among standard setters revealed differing preferences for goodwill accounting among financial statement users, preparers, auditors, and academics across various jurisdictions, indicating a universal phenomenon. This finding suggested that, contrary to the familiar anecdote regarding Japan—where "users, preparers, and auditors support systematic amortization of goodwill"—factual corroboration is needed. This chapter surveys Japanese market participants to investigate their preferred accounting for goodwill, the reasons behind it, and how perceptions of goodwill differ among users, preparers, and auditors. We also included stakeholder-specific questions regarding the uses of accounting information and auditing issues related to goodwill and surveyed perceptions relevant to those stakeholders. We chose a questionnaire survey as the method to elicit factual perceptions from market participants.

As detailed in Chap. 5, the survey revealed the following: (a) support for systematic amortization is highest among auditors, followed by preparers, then users, with statistically significant differences among these groups (Japanese market participants do not uniformly support systematic amortization); (b) factors such as Keidanren membership (indicating industry association influence), manufacturing versus non-manufacturing status (indicating growth mode), or application of J-GAAP versus IFRS do not show marked differences among preparers; (c) when we added the option "either is acceptable," a notable number of respondents (both preparers and users) selected it; (d) respondents supporting systematic amortization emphasized the importance of profit and loss information (the revenue–expense view); and (e) there was broad support for viewing goodwill as part of the investment cost and seeking consistency with accounting for other fixed assets involved in business activities.

To resolve accounting conflicts over goodwill across jurisdictions, mutual understanding is essential regarding the support for systematic amortization with impairment versus non-amortization (impairment-only), as well as the reasons behind these approaches. We must first identify, in each jurisdiction, the preferences of users, preparers, and auditors for either approach, their justifications, and the extent of their support. Even in Japan, where the notion that "systematic amortization of goodwill is supported with a single voice" has rarely been challenged, our survey findings suggest otherwise. This indicates that other jurisdictions also require comprehensive surveys of users, preparers, and auditors to facilitate a more constructive debate on the accounting for goodwill.

In the above questionnaire, we included answer choices related to the rationales for supporting systematic amortization with impairment or non-amortization (impairment-only), focusing on abstract concepts such as the replacement of acquired goodwill by internally generated goodwill and the economic useful life of goodwill. We hoped respondents would share our understanding of these concepts.

However, interpretations varied significantly. While the responses were identical in form, they reflected differing underlying ideas based on varying interpretations. Respondents may have been "sharing the same bed but dreaming different dreams." This divergence made accurately interpreting the survey results challenging. In response, our research group conducted an additional survey of individuals representing each respondent group to explore the situations leading to differences in interpretation and their effects.

Mismatches and inconsistencies in conceptual understanding can lead to miscommunication and impede the development of effective solutions. We scrutinize the differences in understanding abstract concepts between the researchers administering the survey and the practitioners responding. Similar discrepancies may arise among market participants or standard-setting bodies across jurisdictions. Our research group's focus on probing these divergences—through an additional survey to identify their causes—was driven by the expectation that such efforts could provide insights into the overarching research question of this book: "Why has the international conflict over the accounting for goodwill remained unresolved for so many years?"

9.1.6 Chapter 6: Follow-up Interviews of Preparers, Users, and Auditors

As discussed in Chap. 5, our research group's questionnaire survey revealed statistically significant differences in support for systematic amortization among users, preparers, and auditors of financial statements. However, there were also notable commonalities in the rationales provided for either systematic amortization with impairment or non-amortization (impairment-only). While auditors strongly supported systematic amortization with impairment, some users favored non-amortization (impairment-only). Despite the difference in the accounting for goodwill between them, the reasons for supporting systematic amortization centered on a few key responses for both of them, particularly the need "to achieve proper matching of income and expenses over time."

Despite identifying these patterns, the factors driving the differences among groups, as well as the commonalities in their stated reasons, remain unclear. Additionally, concerns arose regarding whether the abstract concepts justifying systematic amortization with impairment or non-amortization (impairment-only) are interpreted similarly by researchers and practitioners.

In light of these observations, Chap. 6 supplements the questionnaire results with two sets of interviews. The first set targets users, preparers, and auditors, focusing on factors contributing to similarities and differences in their responses.[3] The second set targets only users, aiming to identify elements leading to differences of opinion within the user group.

Key findings from the former set of interviews are as follows:

1. Support for systematic amortization among users was generally more passive than among preparers. Additionally, the valuation methods employed by users—particularly analysts—were shaped more by organizational analytical models and client preferences than by individual beliefs or convictions.

[3] In this section, we also examine the extent to which such a "same words, different understandings" phenomenon regarding abstract concepts gives rise to serious problems. To ensure that the survey would be comprehensive, we included an official of the Financial Services Agency, as the representative of regulatory authority, and a full-time member of Accounting Standards Board of Japan among the interviewees.

2. Arguments that "the periodic amortization expense for goodwill is added back when valuing firms, rendering such information valueless" are less common in Japan than in overseas cases.
3. The motivation to avoid systematic amortization has been noted in prior academic research and by interview respondents as a key reason for voluntary IFRS adoption. However, this study revealed that the costs of impairment testing required by IFRS may lead even adopters to prefer systematic amortization if given the choice.[4]
4. Users expressed interest in whether the determination of the amortization period should be left to managerial discretion, indicating that many view management's choice as valuable internal information. Conversely, preparers preferred bounded discretion—flexibility within a predefined framework, accompanied by the ability to justify their choices.
5. Concepts related to goodwill amortization, such as "the period over which the investment in purchased goodwill is expected to be recovered," were interpreted in various ways, raising concerns of potential misunderstandings. Many practitioners found it more challenging to determine amortization periods for purchased goodwill that could be substantiated by objective evidence compared to estimating the useful lives of tangible assets.
6. The term "too little, too late" lacks a clear definition and is open to varied interpretations. Preparers and users have differing views on what constitutes a "too little, too late" situation. Among users, the term's meaning also varies based on the context of its application.
7. There was broad agreement on two key points: first, that goodwill generally depreciates over time, and second, that distinguishing between purchased goodwill and internally generated goodwill—especially from post-acquisition investments—is difficult in practice. However, it remained unclear whether "the depreciation of goodwill" referred specifically to purchased goodwill, the overall value including internally generated components, or if disaggregating goodwill into separate components was commonly accepted. Notable differences in perspective were observed between academic scholars and market participants (preparers and users) regarding the significance of distinguishing between purchased and internally generated goodwill, as well as the conceptual or operational methods for making this distinction. These gaps may hinder discussions on common ground.

By contrast, the key findings of the other set of interviews can be summarized as follows:

1. None of the respondents indicated that they relied exclusively on either cash flows or earnings as inputs to their firm valuation models; the vast majority stated that they referred to both.

[4] See Financial Services Agency (2015) and Nakano (2020) for related literature.

2. Although many interviewees accepted the notion that firms' profitability tends to revert to the mean, this recognition did not necessarily translate into support for systematic amortization.
3. When discussing the "enhancement of the usefulness of accounting information through the application of impairment accounting," many respondents focused on informational value of impairment losses, whereas very few addressed their potential contribution to forecasting permanent income.

Taken together, the findings from the two interview surveys indicate that the abstract concepts used to justify either systematic amortization with impairment or non-amortization (impairment-only) approach are subject to multiple interpretations. The stronger evidence supporting this interpretation—originally suggested by the questionnaire results in Chap. 5—constitutes the principal contribution of this chapter.

However, the reason Japanese market participants—users, preparers, and auditors—favor systematic amortization remains unanswered, despite the two sets of interviews discussed herein. One plausible explanation is that these participants have been exposed to a homogeneous system of accounting education. This scenario, however, lacks empirical substantiation. A more detailed discussion of this issue is provided in Chap. 8.

Finally, this analysis examines whether researchers (conducting the survey) and practitioners (responding to it) share similar interpretations of the abstract concepts related to systematic amortization with impairment and non-amortization (impairment-only). While a comprehensive conclusion was not reached, results indicate discrepancies in understanding between researchers and practitioners for certain items.

For instance, maintaining the total amount of goodwill does not imply that the value of purchased goodwill is preserved. Typically, internally generated goodwill, created through post-acquisition operating efforts, compensates for the decline in purchased goodwill. Proponents of systematic amortization frequently invoke this reasoning, and many interviewees acknowledged it. However, this explanation emphasizes that the decline in purchased goodwill is primarily due to the recovery of expected cash flows. When anticipated excess returns from the business combination materialize as cash recovery, the value of purchased goodwill naturally decreases. Researchers clearly visualize this prior decline being subsequently replaced by internally generated goodwill, whereas practitioners often lack clarity on this process.

A similar pattern was observed regarding the "economic useful life" of goodwill. For researchers, this term refers to the period during which the current investment project continues to generate excess returns, or until the expected excess returns from alternative investments surpass those from the ongoing project. In contrast, some interviewees did not draw a clear distinction between this notion and the conventional "payback period," defined as the number of years required for cumulative, undiscounted cash inflows to exceed the initial investment.

Taken together, these findings suggest that the abstract concepts justifying systematic amortization with impairment or non-amortization (impairment-only) of goodwill are interpreted in various ways. Moreover, little attention has been given to these interpretive differences. Such discrepancies may arise in the development of international accounting standards, where representatives from different jurisdictions negotiate. Their impact could be significant. Highlighting the "same bed, different dreams" phenomenon may help explain the persistence of international disagreements over goodwill accounting, which is another important contribution of this book.

9.1.7 Chapter 7: Empirical Studies on the 'Too Little, Too Late' Issue

In the interviews reported in Chap. 6, many financial statement users stated they become aware of a deterioration in firm performance through non-accounting information channels before impairment losses are recognized in the financial statements. They believe these alternative channels mitigate the "too little, too late" problem. When the definitive impairment loss amount is disclosed through accounting with some delay relative to these sources, it allows users to verify their prior expectations about performance deterioration. Thus, the relationship between accounting and non-accounting channels may be viewed as a favorable division of roles, where the former provides "richer" confirmation of information initially conveyed by the latter. The interview responses suggest that respondents can obtain information about impairment through channels other than financial reporting, indicating that the "too little, too late" problem is less significant than often claimed in public debate.

However, the evidence from the interviews is based on subjective evaluations and perceptions. Whether market participants actually identify information about performance deterioration from alternative sources before impairment losses are disclosed, and incorporate that information into their valuations, is an empirical question. Analyses in Chap. 7 indicate that, to a considerable extent, the market anticipates impairment before formal announcement, consistent with interviewee statements. Nonetheless, stock price and trading volume reactions at the time of impairment announcement suggest that the disclosure continues to convey incremental information. These findings align with prior empirical research. While practitioners and market participants often dispute the informational value of impairment loss recognition, this study suggests that its informational value remains an open question.

Moreover, in choosing between (a) systematic amortization of goodwill and (b) non-amortization until an impairment trigger arises, it is crucial to consider whether the "too little, too late" problem actually exists and, if so, how severe it is. If the "too little, too late" problem is indeed serious, then—abstracting from sample selection bias—it should be more pronounced among IFRS adopters than among firms applying Japanese GAAP. From the perspective of comparing market participants' perceptions of the existence and severity of the "too little, too late" problem with the empirical evidence, this chapter examines the seriousness of the problem by comparing Japanese GAAP adopters and IFRS adopters. Although the differences are minor, results indicate that the "too little, too late" problem is more severe for IFRS adopters, suggesting that market participants have largely recognized its existence and severity.

Market participants' views on the role of financial reporting and their perceptions of the economic nature of goodwill influence judgements about the relative merits of systematic amortization with impairment versus non-amortization (impairment-only). If these views align with empirical evidence, they are likely stable over the long term. Conversely, if they contradict empirical evidence, perceptions may change more rapidly. Stability in judgements regarding the superiority or inferiority of systematic amortization may influence debates on the appropriateness of goodwill accounting. Resolving or converging opposing views is facilitated when market participants' value judgements and factual perceptions are stable. In contrast, unsupported views on financial reporting and factual perceptions may hinder the resolution of conflicts over goodwill accounting. Consistently confirming that interviewees' responses align with empirical evidence is crucial when analyzing the results of interviews.

9.1.8 Chapter 8: Accounting Perspective and Accounting Education

The motivation for Chap. 8 stems from the findings of the questionnaire survey in Chap. 5 and the interview surveys in Chap. 6. These analyses indicated that support for systematic amortization of goodwill varies among users, preparers, and auditors of financial statements, likely reflecting differences in underlying interests. However, responses advocating for either systematic amortization with impairment or non-amortization (impairment-only) demonstrated remarkable homogeneity, cutting across these basic differences. Chapters 5 and 6 suggest that this homogeneity may result from the uniformity of accounting education in Japan. Traditionally, accounting courses in Japanese higher education primarily target students aiming for professional qualifications, such as certified public accountants and licensed tax accountants. Consequently, when lectures focus on certification examinations, their content tends to become standardized in alignment with past exam trends.

However, this reasoning is speculative and lacks empirical support. To address this, we conducted a questionnaire survey targeting academics responsible for accounting education, inquiring about their main objects of instruction (e.g., accounting standards and/or their conceptual foundations) and educational policies. The results can be summarized as follows.

(a) With respect to laws and regulations related to financial accounting referred to in university accounting courses, respondents placed greatest emphasis on the *Financial Instruments and Exchange Act* (80.7%), followed by the *Companies Act* (73.7%).
(b) Regarding accounting rules covered in teaching, respondents reported emphasizing current accounting rules, specifically: "current accounting standards issued by the ASBJ" (83.0%), "IFRS" (67.2%), and the "ASBJ Conceptual Framework" (54.8%). Additionally, the traditional "*accounting principles for business enterprises (Kigyo-Kaikei-Gensoku)*" (70.3%) remain important.
(c) As for basic concepts and principles emphasized in lectures, the most frequently cited principles were "matching of revenues and expenses" (92.7%), "distinction between capital and income" (83.8%), and "historical cost (transaction-based)" (81.9%). Additionally, responses indicated that "appropriate income determination" (91.1%) is also heavily emphasized. These results suggest that traditional *accounting principles for business enterprises (Kigyo-Kaikei-Gensoku)* are still widely taught in university courses.
(d) Concerning changes in lecture content over the past 10 years, 82.8% of respondents (299 out of 361 responses, counting multiple answers) reported altering their course content. The most common reasons were "changes in response to current Japanese GAAP" (47.6%), "a hybrid content combining the revenue–expense approach and the asset–liability approach" (25.5%), and "an asset–liability approach reflecting the demand for international unification" (9.7%). These responses suggest that many lectures focus on the evolution of accounting standards in response to environmental changes, while relying on stable, fundamental concepts.
(e) When asked about their preferred accounting treatment for goodwill, the most frequent response was "systematic amortization with impairment" (68.8%). Including similar responses ("systematic amortization only," "declining balance depreciation," and "incrementing depreciation") raises the proportion to 78.5%. The primary reason for supporting systematic amortization was "because it pursues appropriate income determination" (86.3%). In contrast, support for accounting that emphasizes appropriate valuation on the balance sheet was limited to 15.4%, with this choice mainly supported by the argument that "it seeks to (and must) capture the value of goodwill" (86.0%).

These results indicate that a significant majority of academics focus their education on Japanese accounting standards, emphasizing income information. While over half of the respondents also teach IFRS, the findings suggest that IFRS and its underlying conceptual foundation are not taught systematically; rather, IFRS is used to "relativize" Japanese accounting standards, placing them in comparative perspective.

Why, then, do so many academics provide education centered on an income-oriented perspective? As members of the securities market community, academics naturally emphasize income-oriented recognition, measurement, and disclosure, which justifies a substantial portion of lecture time dedicated to explaining the rationale for such systems. However, an "optimal" system of accounting standards is not universal across time and jurisdictions. If many academics consider it their responsibility to explain how accounting standards may evolve in response to environmental shifts—the "dynamics" of standard setting—then it is inappropriate for all educational resources to be devoted solely to current accounting standards and their supporting conceptual foundations.

The questionnaire results indicate that accounting education heavily emphasizes the current Japanese accounting system. Simply asserting that "the current Japanese accounting system is taught because stakeholders support it" does not satisfactorily explain these results. An additional explanation is needed: many students in accounting courses aim to become certified public accountants (CPAs) or licensed tax accountants, prompting lecturers to focus on the current Japanese accounting system to meet these needs.

However, to claim that "demand for qualification-oriented education has produced accounting education biased toward the current Japanese accounting system," one must assume that the CPA and licensed tax accountant examinations test understanding of current accounting standards and their underlying concepts. This assumption requires empirical validation. Chapter 8 investigates the proportion of questions in the essay-type tests of the Japanese CPA examination that (a) ask for reasonable interpretations of current accounting standards versus (b) ask for discussions that are neutral or critical regarding these standards. To minimize subjectivity in classification, multiple collaborators categorized the questions, re-examining instances where differing judgments were made. The results show that an overwhelming majority of CPA examination questions require reasonable interpretations of current accounting standards.

If lectures are tailored uniformly to prepare students for these professional qualification examinations, and if early specialized education shapes lasting professional mindsets, then part of the homogeneity in values and perceptions among users, preparers, and auditors can be traced to the education received at higher institutions.

However, this conclusion is not necessarily robust. The hypothesis that "accounting perspectives cultivated during early higher education persist regardless of subsequent environmental changes" can only be accepted if similar investigations are conducted in other jurisdictions—particularly where accounting education is closely linked to professional qualification examinations, as in Japan—and if similar common perspectives among users, preparers, and auditors of financial statements are observed. This chapter's survey aims to serve as a foundation for researchers in other jurisdictions who may conduct comparable studies in the future.

9.2 Overall Conclusion: Returning to the Original Research Question

Finally, we summarize the findings and limitations of this study. The central concern throughout this book has been why the international controversy over accounting for goodwill remains unresolved despite previous efforts. The discussions in this book provide several answers to this research question.

9.2.1 The Spread of Theoretical Analyses Without Explicit Constraints

One factor contributing to the ongoing international controversy over accounting for goodwill is that neither systematic amortization with impairment nor non-amortization (impairment-only) can avoid distorting the distinction between capital and income. As long as the premise that a "proper distinction between capital and income should be maintained" is upheld, it is impossible to claim one method is superior to the other. If each jurisdiction attempts, through a priori reasoning, to support either systematic amortization with impairment or non-amortization (impairment-only), this stance hinders the resolution of the controversy.

This discussion does not imply that comparing systematic amortization with impairment and non-amortization (impairment-only) is futile. Even if both methods are flawed from the perspective of fundamental financial accounting principles, it remains possible to examine their relative superiority or inferiority from various perspectives:

- What role is financial accounting supposed to play?
- Given that goodwill is regarded as an asset, what is the basic nature of purchased goodwill as an asset?
- In what manner does goodwill decrease in value?
- How technically difficult is it to measure the value of goodwill?

However, the questionnaire and interview surveys conducted with Japanese market participants indicated a limited shared recognition of the multi-layered structure of issues surrounding goodwill accounting. Similarly, many remarks at ASAF meetings and some IASB materials tended not to make explicit the three interrelated dimensions identified in Chap. 2—conceptual/theoretical questions, practical application constraints, and standard-setting judgements. This lack of a common map of the debate may hinder progress toward resolution.

The problems from theoretical analyses lacking explicit constraints could be alleviated if parties advocating for systematic amortization with impairment or non-amortization (impairment-only) acknowledged the factual perceptions and value judgements underpinning their arguments. Efforts to communicate these premises to one another are essential. However, the survey results suggested that parties find it difficult to understand the differences in positions on systematic amortization with impairment and non-amortization (impairment-only). The fact that differences in value judgements and factual perceptions have not been consciously recognized may have exacerbated the above problems.

9.2.2 The Assumption of an Ambiguous "Average Investor" and the Use of Abstract Concepts that Permit Multiple Interpretations

Another reason the international controversy remains unresolved is that market participants do not uniformly share views on systematic amortization with impairment versus non-amortization (impairment-only). These views depend on investors' decision-making models, environmental conditions, and value judgements regarding a "desirable investment environment." Even if a consensus is reached on the objective of "providing information useful for investors' decision-making" and on enhancing comparability, this does not clarify whether systematic amortization with impairment or non-amortization (impairment-only) is superior.

Investors exhibit significant differences in (a) their distinction between and use of cash flow information and accounting information, (b) their emphasis on stock-based information from the balance sheet versus flow-based information from the income statement, and (c) their prioritization of smoothed net income versus impairment losses reflecting irregular events. The setting of accounting standards involves a social choice amidst heterogeneous investors. With limited information available, determining the superior social choice theoretically is a challenging task. Therefore, pre-specifying a judgement process based on obtainable information is essential as a second-best course of action. Insufficient attention to these issues may hinder the resolution of the controversy.[5]

9.2.3 Questioning Whether Efforts Have in Fact Been Made to Resolve the Issue

Another factor contributing to the unresolved international controversy is that debates over accounting for goodwill have not consistently been organized around resolving the issue as a primary goal. This can be observed in some discussions at ASAF meetings. Our analysis of remarks by jurisdictional representatives suggests

[5] Because accounting standards form a coherent system, judgements about whether to amortize goodwill, and about when and in what amounts to recognize impairment losses on goodwill, also affect the accounting applied in other areas. The fact that insufficient attention has been paid to this may likewise be hindering the resolution of the controversy.

that participants often framed their positions through jurisdiction-specific institutional contexts and stakeholder landscapes, repeatedly emphasizing preferred approaches (either systematic amortization with impairment or impairment-only) rather than jointly working through cross-jurisdictional trade-offs and decision criteria.

If the primary objective were truly to achieve convergence or mitigate the controversy, there would first be a shared diagnosis of the sources of disagreement across the three dimensions—conceptual/theoretical issues, practical application constraints, and standard-setting judgments—and of how these interact across jurisdictions. It would then be necessary to evaluate which differences are resolvable in the short term and what adjustments, compromises, or sequencing (including disclosure-focused steps) would be required. In reality, however, the claims presented were often position-confirming and did not foster "engaged" or "well-coordinated" dialogue. To prevent international debates on accounting for goodwill from wasting resources, more effort must be devoted to clarifying and prioritizing the sources of disagreement.

9.3 Can "New Evidence" No Longer Be Expected?

This chapter concludes by highlighting the key implications for the overarching research theme of this book. The IASB terminated its discussions on accounting for goodwill, stating no "new evidence" justified changing existing requirements. The prior decision of the U.S. FASB to cease its deliberations likely influenced this outcome. A comprehensive survey of previous studies in this book indicates that a sufficient amount of valuable information for standard-setting has already been gathered.

Nevertheless, whether this justifies freezing the development of standards is a matter of debate. Even if the likelihood of emerging empirical findings that could challenge conventional wisdom is low, and despite extensive outreach to ensure that the views of market participants have already been fully canvassed (so that in that sense it is difficult to find "new evidence"), a change in classifying, organizing, and interpreting these facts—and in reflecting them in standard-setting (that is, in the framework of thought)—would still make it possible to derive new implications from facts that have already been uncovered. The following discussion elaborates on this point.

9.3.1 The Distribution of Market Participants' Views, Which Is Not Reflected in the Volume of Comment Letters

The IASB's decision to suspend discussions on accounting for goodwill cites a lack of "new evidence." This suggests a view that opinions for and against systematic amortization with impairment versus non-amortization (impairment-only) of goodwill are evenly balanced; thus, maintaining the status quo is the only option. This implies a judgement that the "arguments are evenly matched." However, it is unclear what evidence the IASB used to conclude that the arguments are balanced. In the absence of further explanation, it is likely that this "even balance" judgement stems from the volume of comment letters received.

It is well known that comment letters are not submitted uniformly by stakeholders; rather, they are skewed toward parties with strong interests. If the IASB is surveying global securities markets to strike a balance between efficiency and fairness, then a judgement of "even balance" based solely on comment volume may misinterpret the "actual voice" of market participants.

9.3.2 New Evidence Generated by "Weighting" Comments Based on Qualitative Differences

As the discussion reveals, the reasons cited by market participants for and against systematic amortization with impairment versus non-amortization (impairment-only) are heterogeneous, encompassing both theoretical and practical arguments, value-based judgements (whose validity is difficult to assess against empirical evidence), and accounting perspectives. Among these comments, some warrant "particular deference" given the IASB's objectives, while others "need not necessarily be accorded much weight."

For instance, if the Board aims to determine and disclose smoothed earnings that predict sustainable future cash flows, comments such as "the non-amortization approach is preferable because it facilitates impairment triggering" lack significance. Similarly, if the IASB assumes investors use earnings—derived from a coherent set of accounting standards—as inputs for forecasting future cash flows, the viewpoint that some investors who prioritize cash flows simply add back goodwill amortization does not command particular respect. These examples illustrate that the IASB's conceptualization of investors as primary decision-makers—who they are and how they utilize accounting information—can distinguish comments deserving of special consideration from those that do not.

If, despite these qualitative differences, the IASB abstracts from comment quality and bases decisions solely on response volume, it risks misreading market participant consensus. Reclassifying comments based on importance and persuasiveness, relative to the IASB's objectives, can reveal whether support for systematic amortization with impairment or non-amortization (impairment-only) predominates. This approach may yield new evidence on the choice between these methods, despite the underlying empirical facts being unchanged.[6] A similar analysis can be conducted for the empirical academic research cited in standard-setting. Utilizing the framework in Chap. 4 of this book can provide additional insights from this research. The project should not be paused until these efforts are completed.

Throughout the history of accounting, public opinion has fluctuated in its support for specific accounting methods. Cost-based accounting became established after excessive reliance on fair values (continuous revaluation at market value) faced criticism. Decades later, criticisms of historical cost accounting prompted vigorous calls for fair value accounting. This book illustrates a similar pattern in the controversy over business combinations accounting, particularly regarding purchased goodwill. In response to criticisms of the purchase method—which requires the recognition of purchased goodwill—the pooling-of-interests method, which does not recognize purchased goodwill, was once advocated. Later, intense criticism of pooling-of-interests led to the adoption of the acquisition method as the global standard. These examples demonstrate oscillation and reversal in accounting thought and practice.

Such changes were not initiated by those directly involved in accounting but instead were triggered by events that negatively impacted national economies, such as the Great Depression and financial crises. Notably, accounting has often been blamed for these undesirable events. During the global financial crisis, fair value accounting and mark-to-market accounting faced intense criticism for their alleged pro-cyclical impacts on the business cycle.

While international accounting standard setters have maintained the status quo, claiming "no new evidence" has emerged, the issue of rising balances of purchased goodwill has intensified. Both proponents of systematic amortization with impairment and non-amortization (impairment-only) likely agree that the *too little, too late* problem has been exacerbated. If the status quo is defended solely based on being "too big to fail," history suggests that markets may face a major crash. To avert such an outcome, it is crucial to re-examine the potential future consequences of leaving the commitment to the status quo unchallenged.[7] The present moment may well be the last opportunity to do so.

Statement on AI Usage: During the preparation of this manuscript, the author used AI-assisted tools such as DeepL and ChatGPT to improve the English expression and clarity of the manuscript. The author thoroughly reviewed and approved the final version and takes full responsibility for the content.

[6] In doing so, careful attention must be paid to whether the abstract concepts referred to in the comments are being used in the same context as that assumed by the staff analyzing those comments.

[7] If inaction is maintained despite the prospect of a potential market crash, this may indicate that there is a problem with the due process of the accounting standard-setting body.

References

Financial Services Agency [2015]: *IFRS Adoption Report* April 15, 2015 (https://www.fsa.go.jp/en/news/2015/20151113-1/01.pdf)

Nakano [2020]: Takayuki Nakano (ed.), *Insights from IFRS Adoption: An Analysis of Mandatory and Voluntary Adoption in Major Countries and Japan,* Tokyo, Japan, Dobunkan Shuppan.